KEITH HARING THE POLITICAL LINE

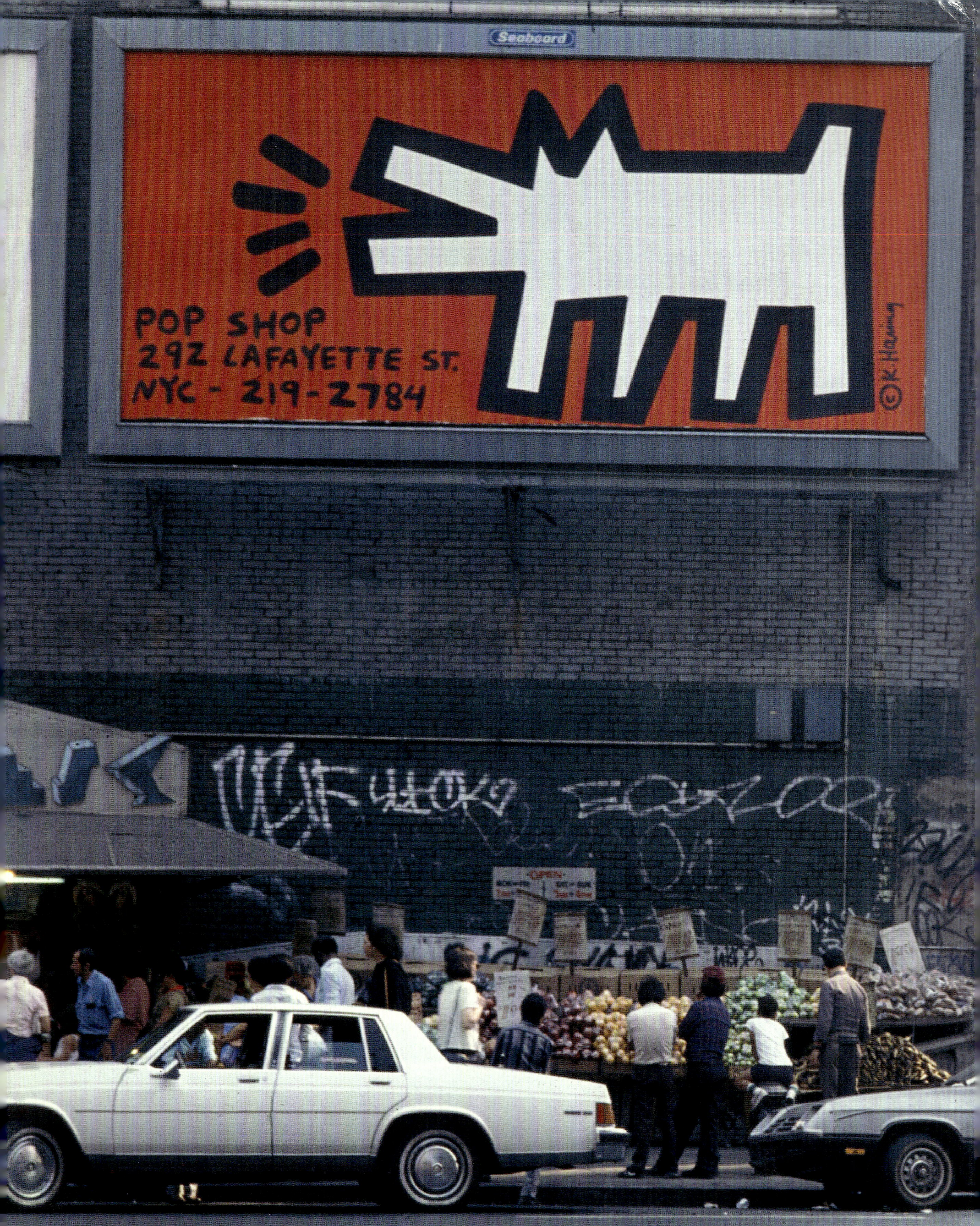
Seaboard
POP SHOP
292 LAFAYETTE ST.
NYC - 219-2784
©K.Haring
OPEN

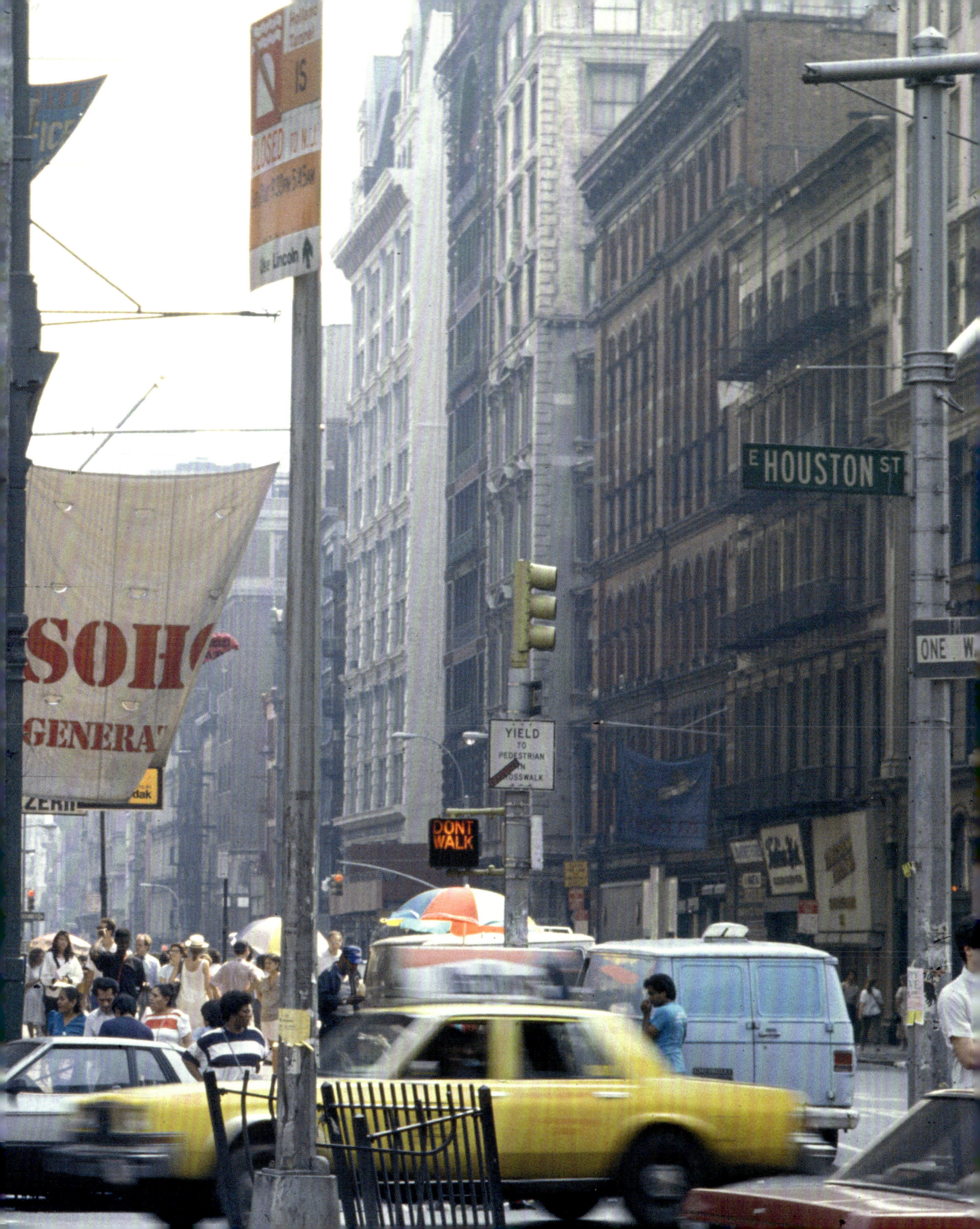

E HOUSTON ST
SOHO
DONT WALK
YIELD
TO
PEDESTRIAN
CLOSED
Lincoln

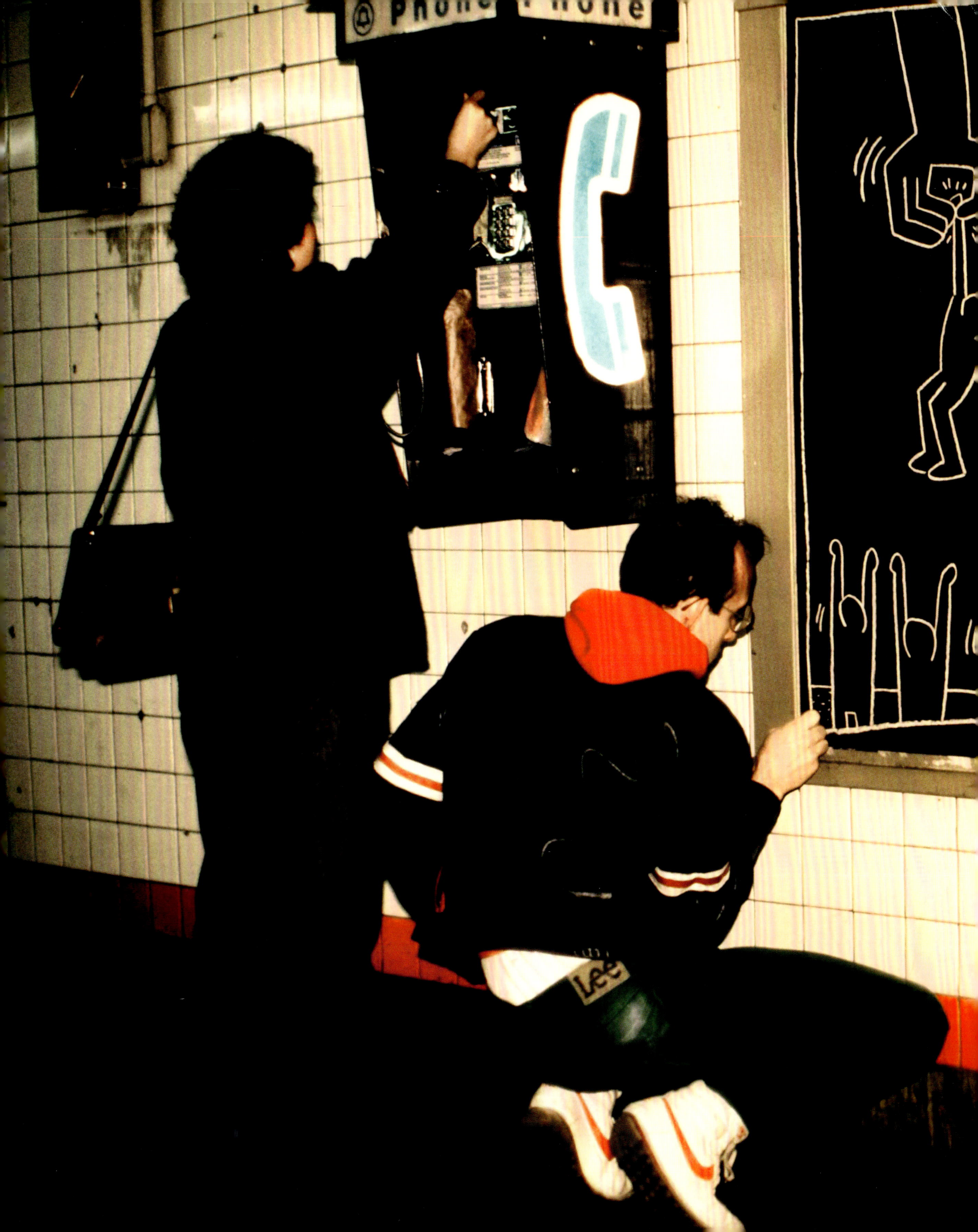
Lee

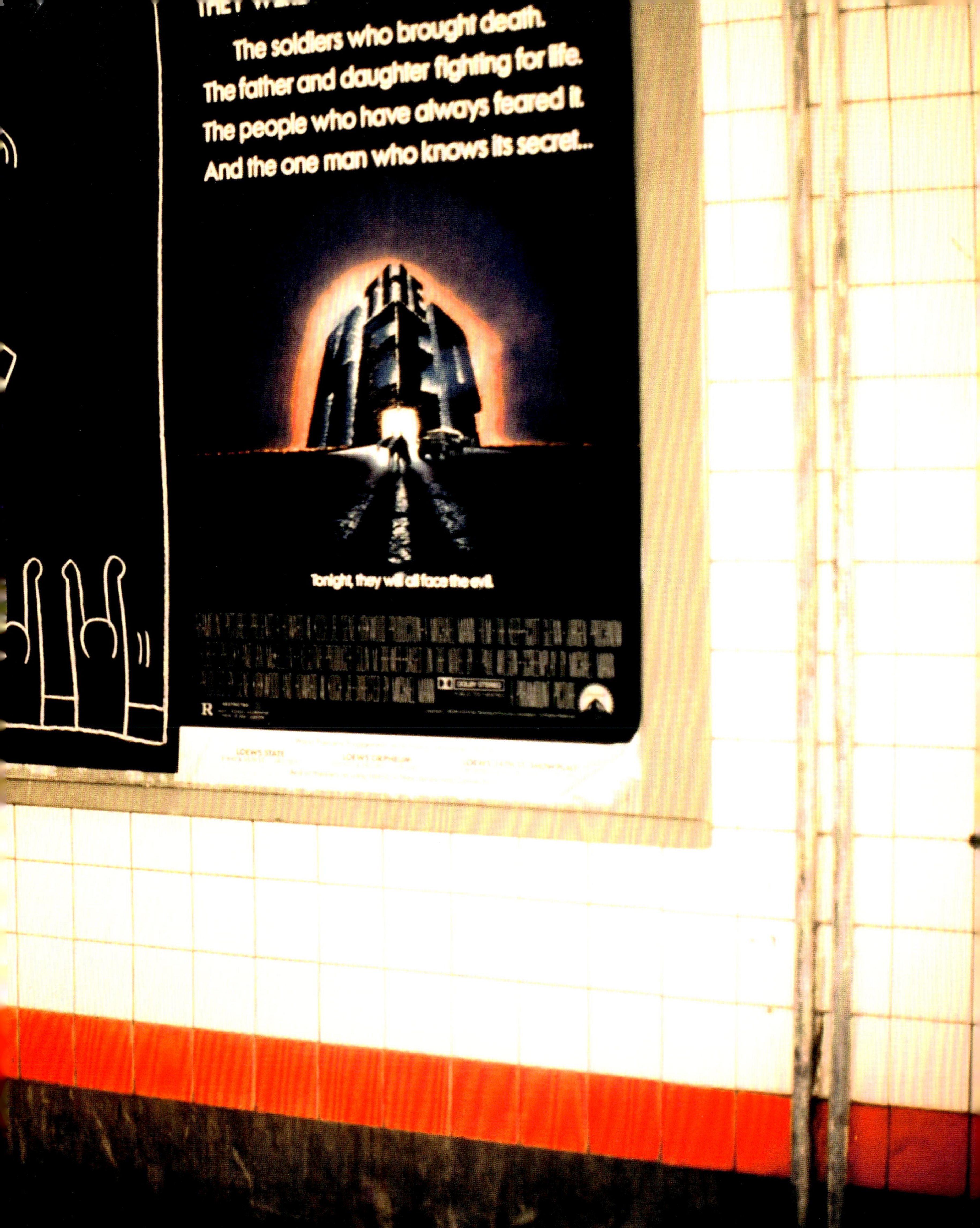
The soldiers who brought death.
The father and daughter fighting for life.
The people who have always feared it.
And the one man who knows its secret...
Tonight, they will all face the evil.
R

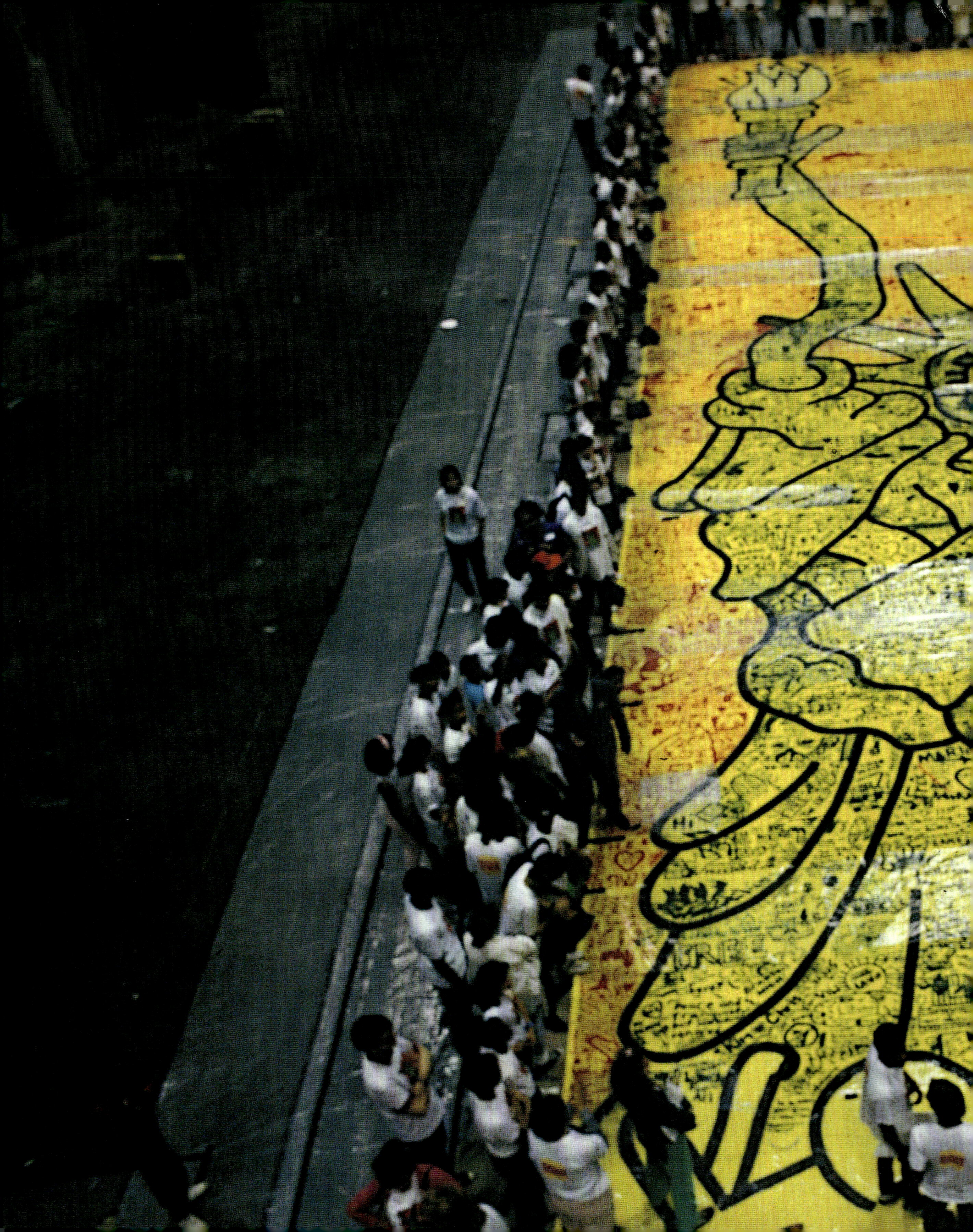

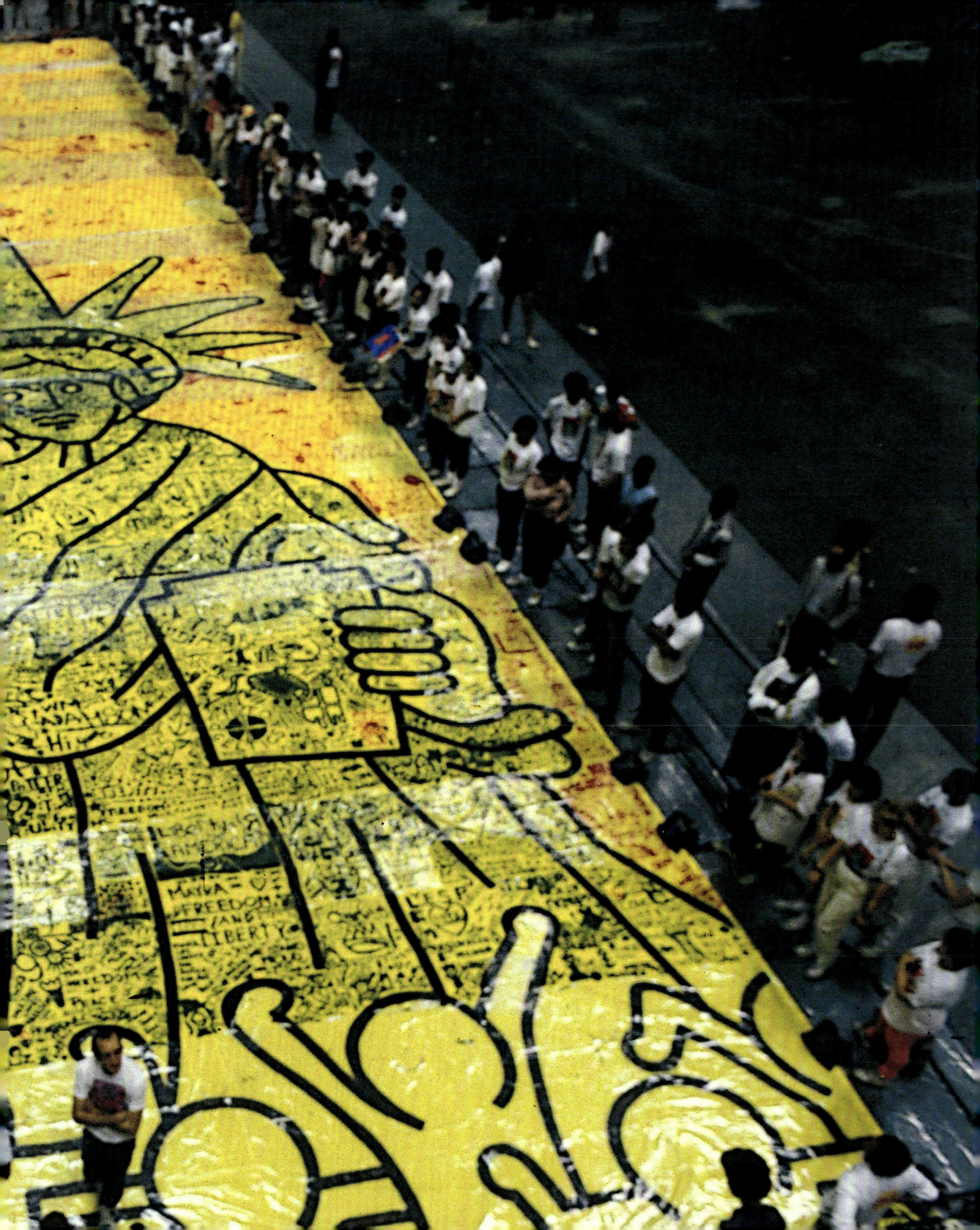

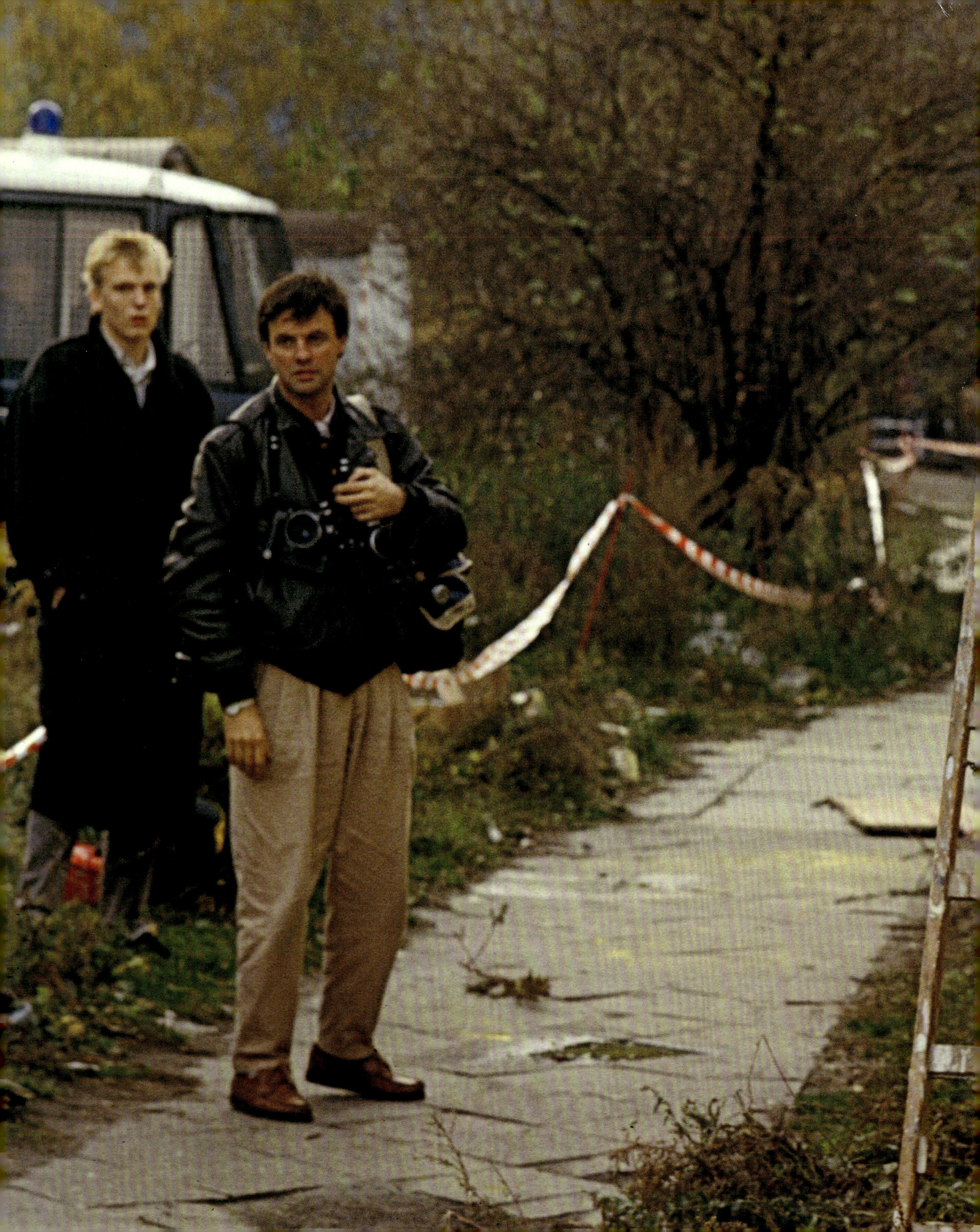

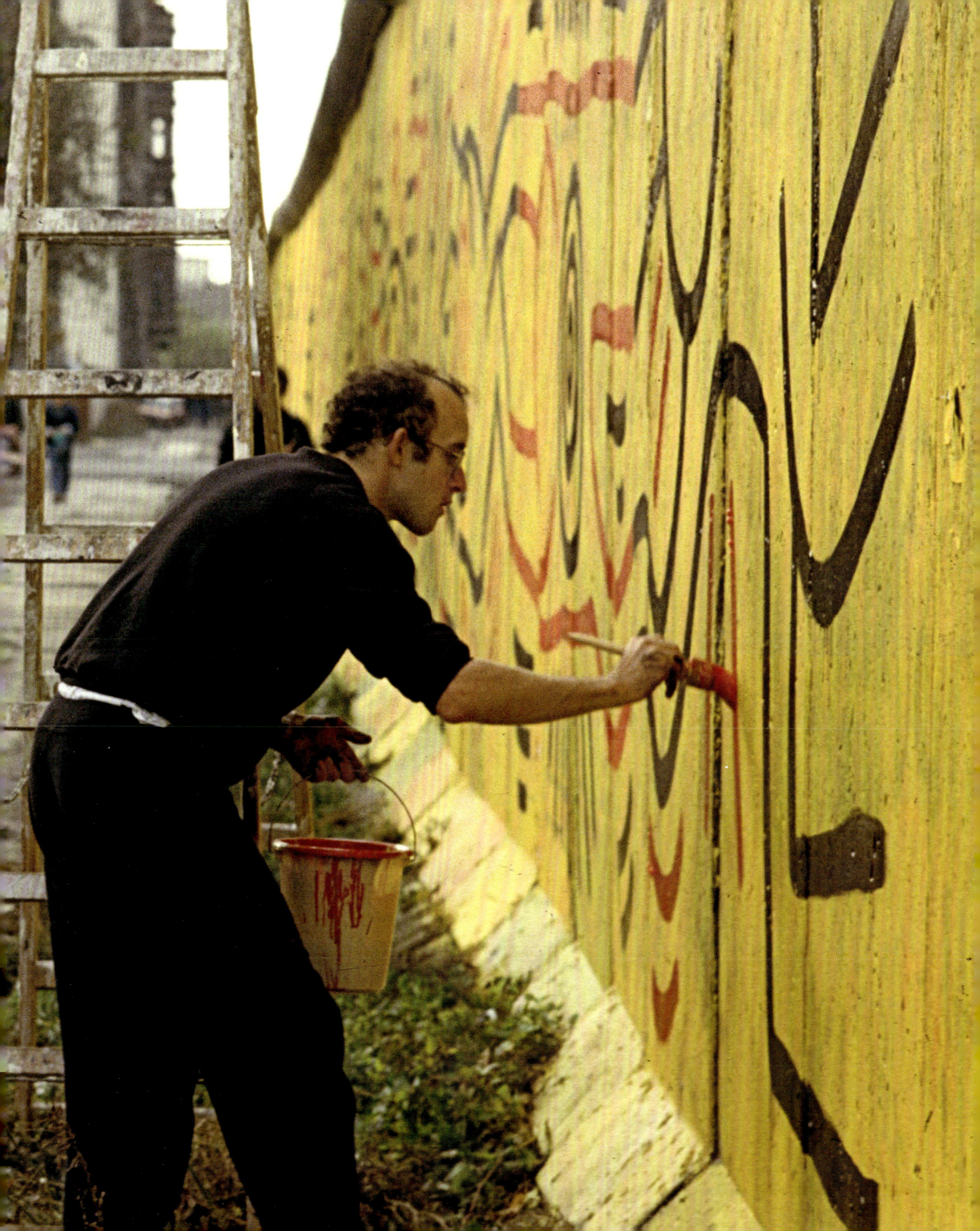

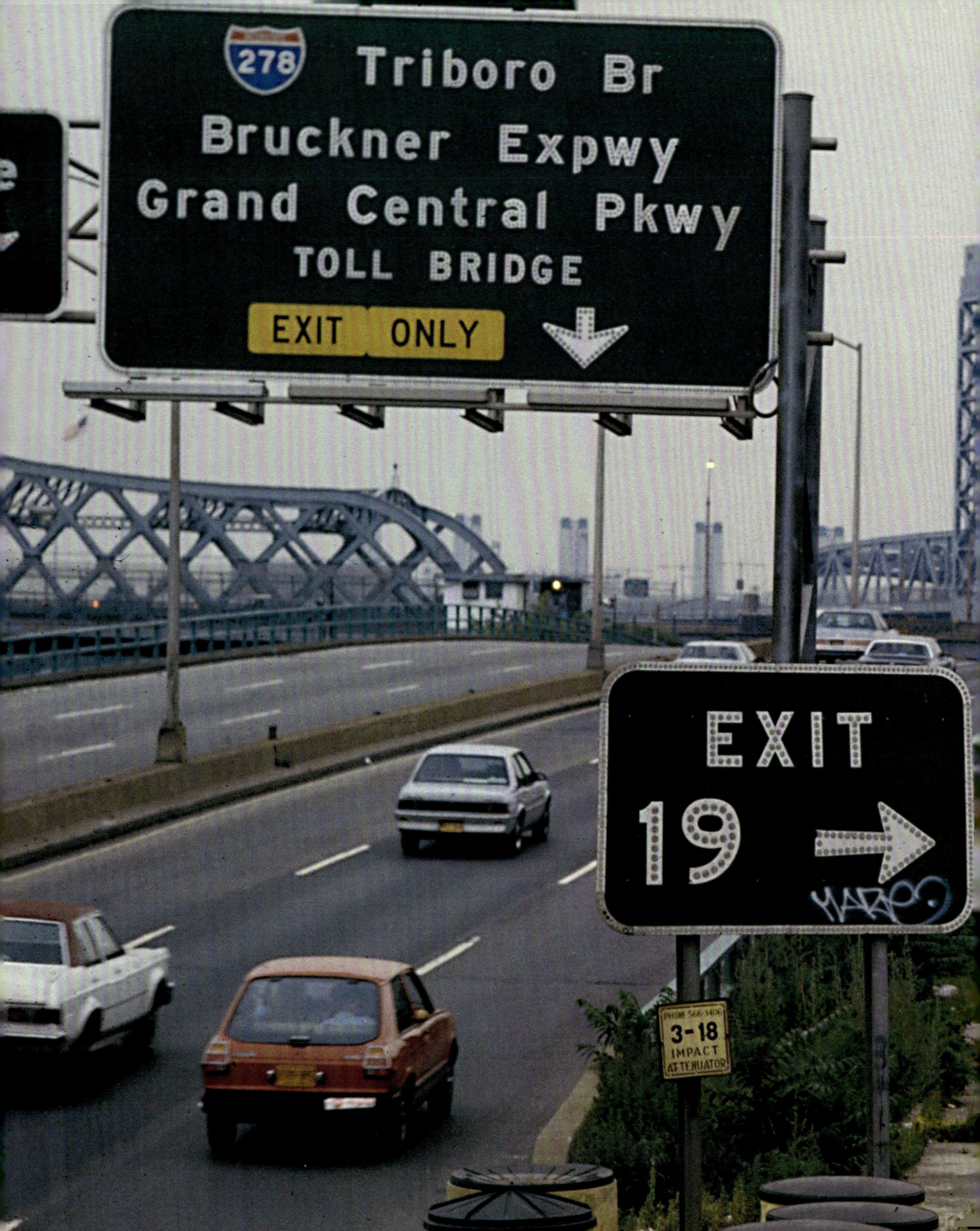
278
Triboro Br
Bruckner Expwy
Grand Central Pkwy
TOLL BRIDGE
EXIT ONLY
EXIT
19
3-18
IMPACT
ATTENUATOR

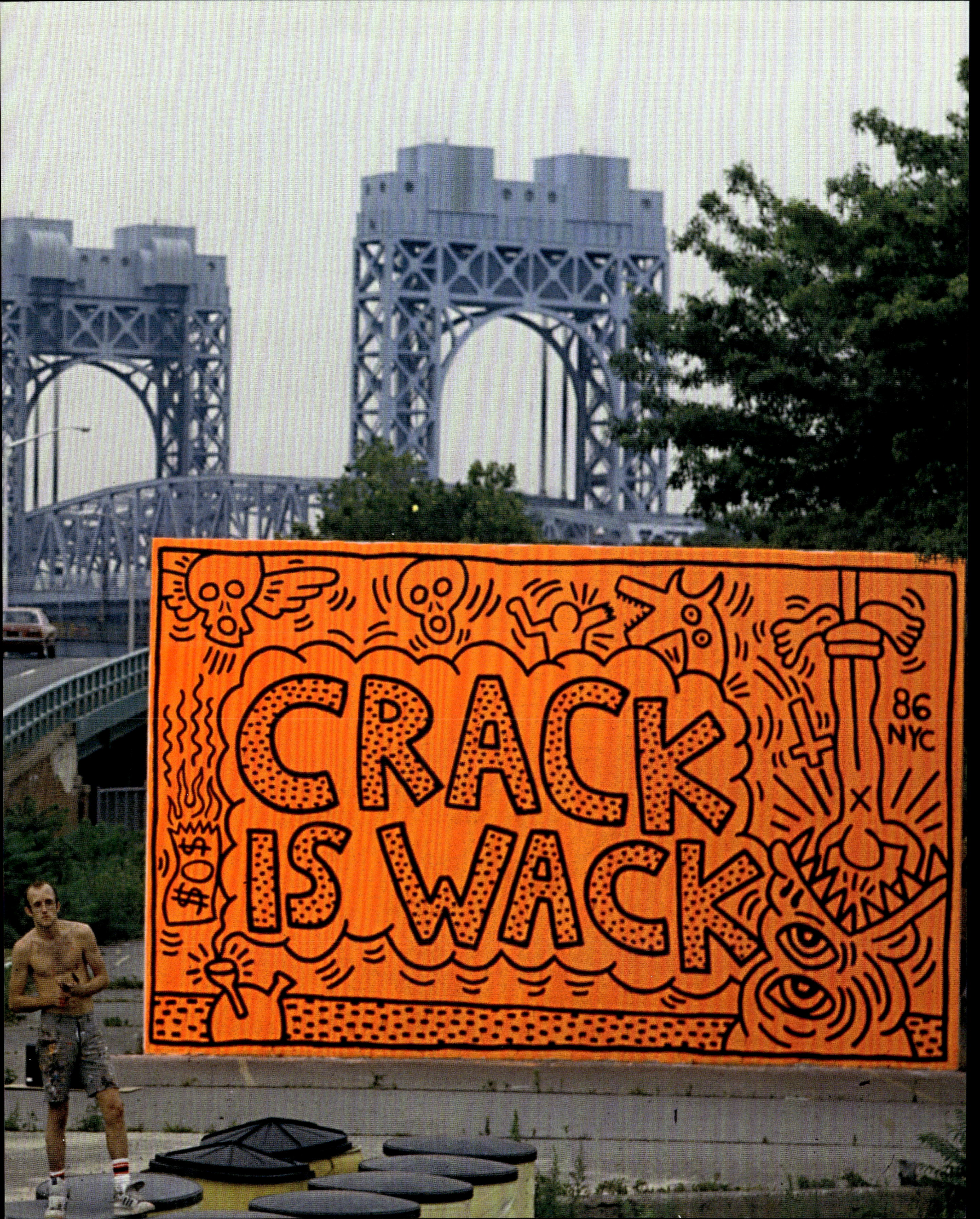
CRACK
IS WACK
86
NYC

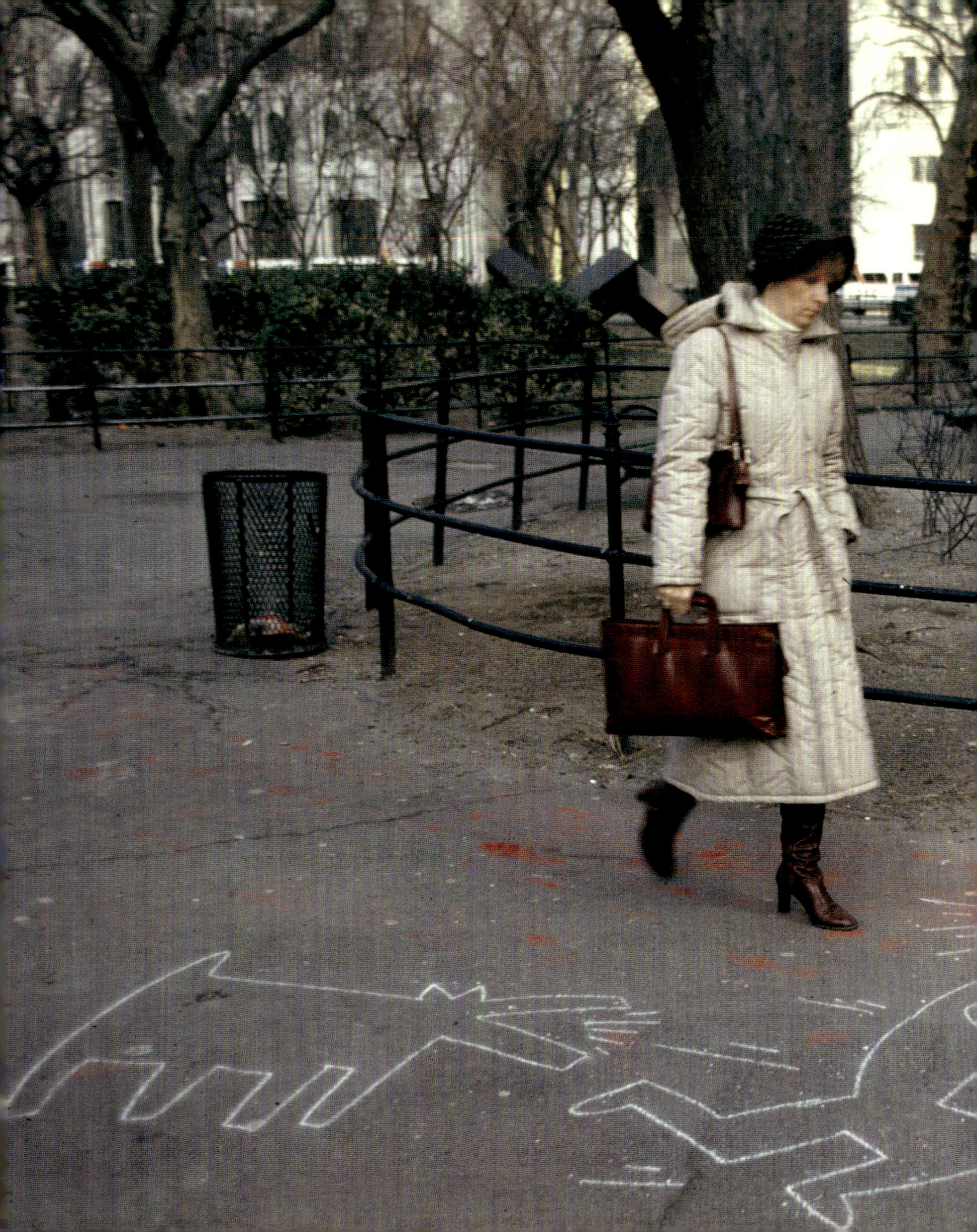

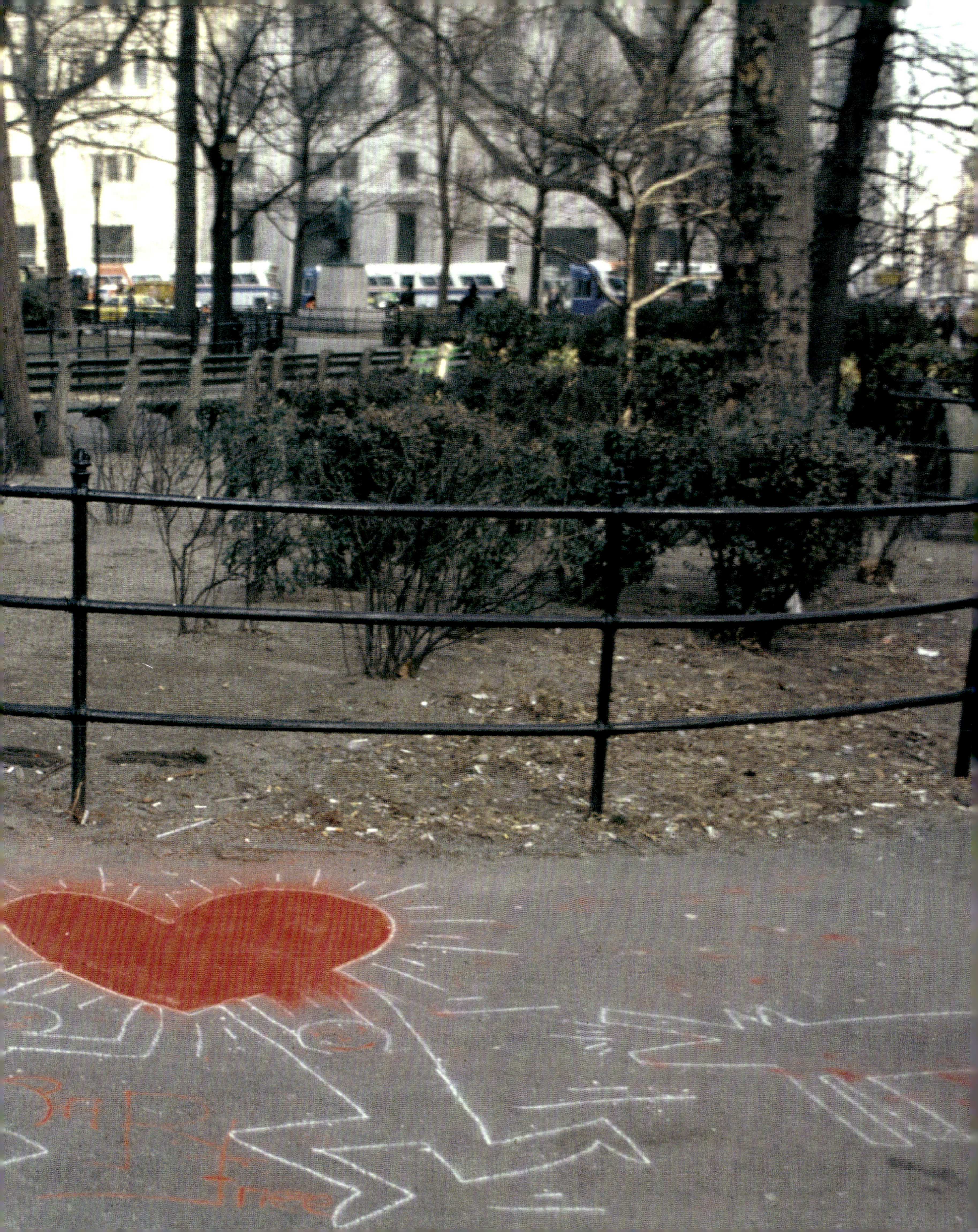

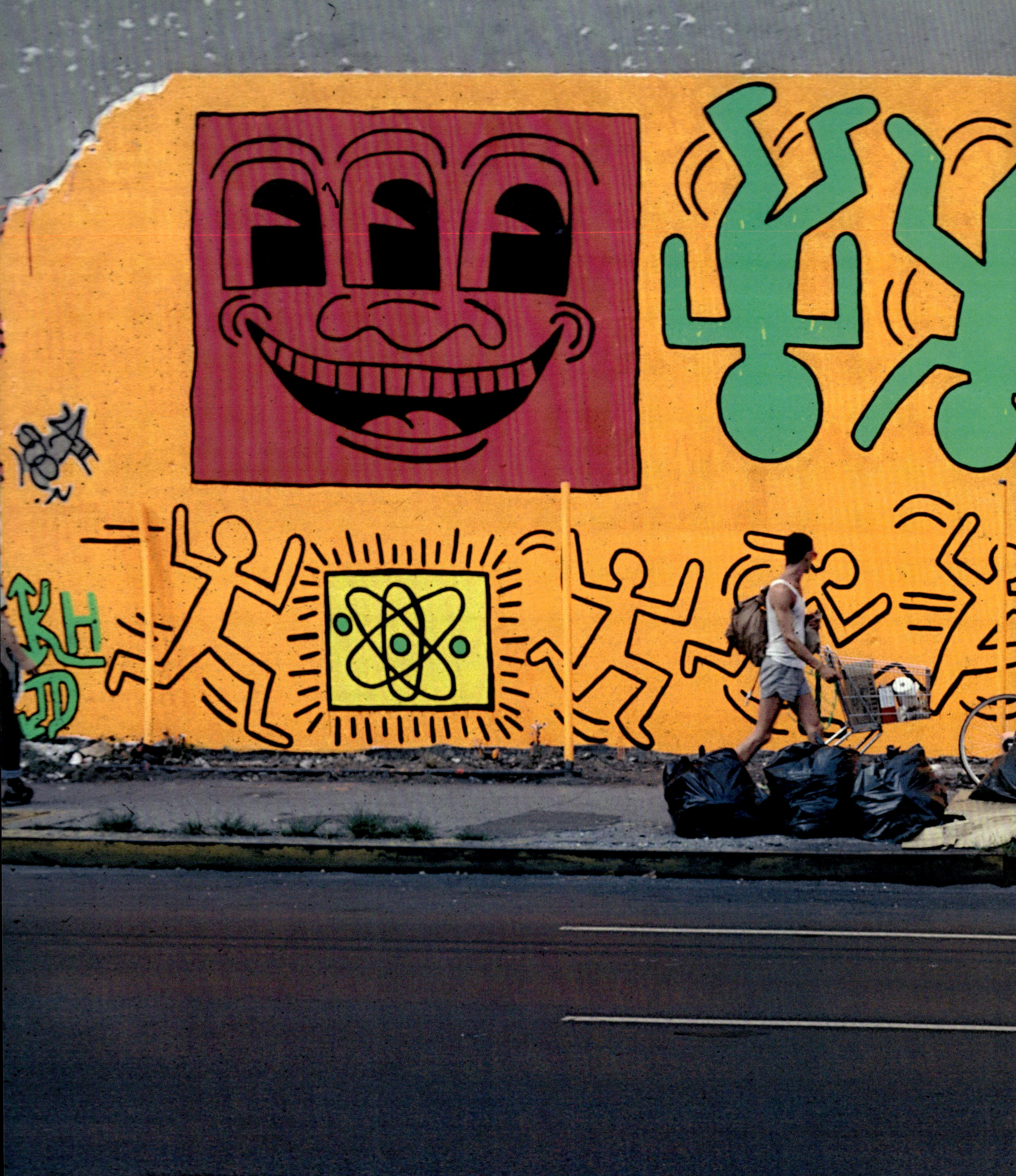

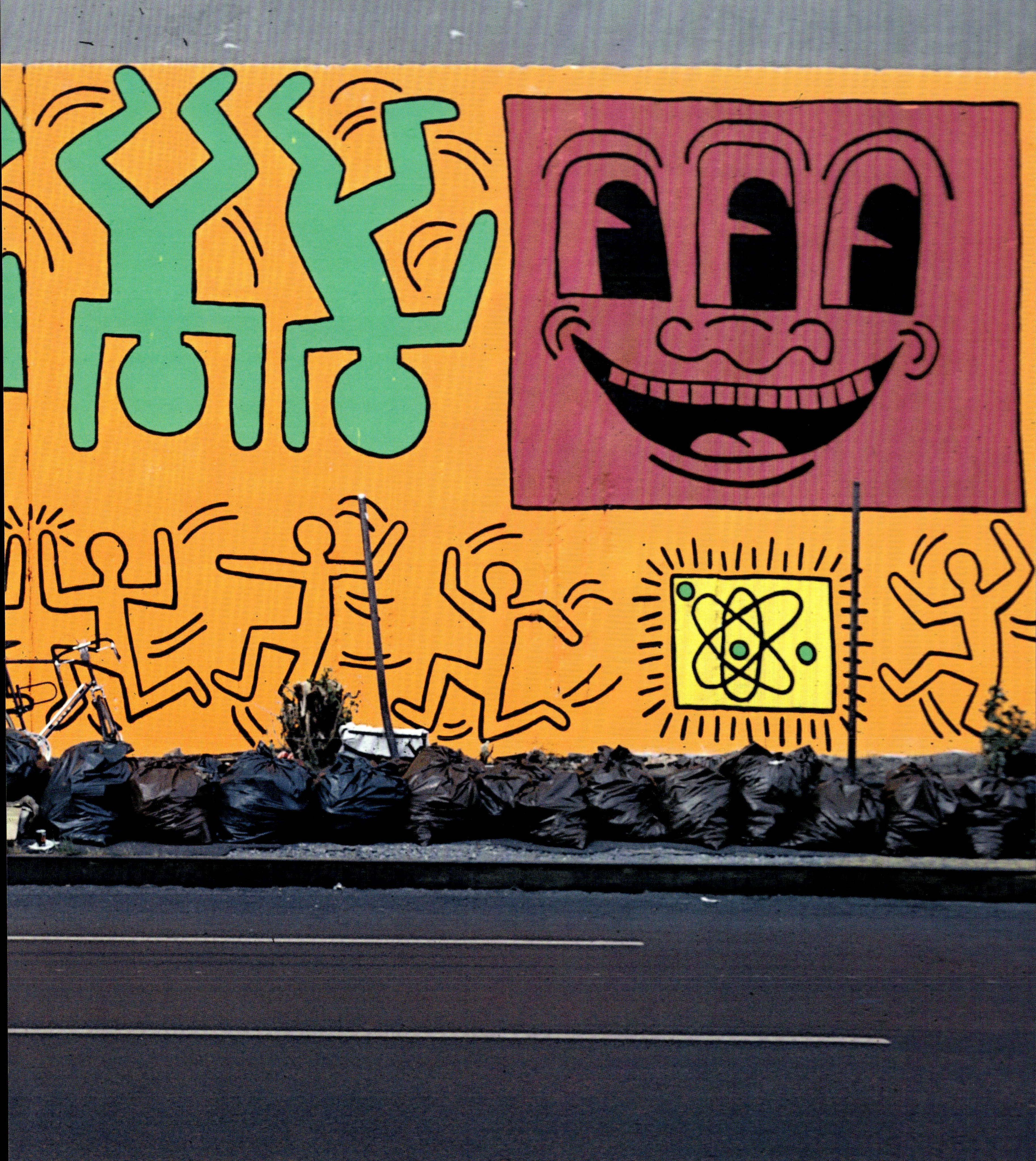

Opening photo gallery

pp. 2–3
Pop Shop billboard on Houston Street at Broadway, New York, 1987

pp. 4–5
Keith Haring drawing in a subway station, New York, 1984

pp. 6–7
Keith Haring with members of CityKids and New York public schoolchildren who collaborated with the artist on the *CityKids Speak on Liberty* banner, New York, 1986

pp. 8–9
Keith Haring painting on the Berlin Wall, 1986

pp. 10–11
Keith Haring next to the first iteration of his *Crack Is Wack* mural, Harlem River Drive at East 128th Street, New York, 1986

pp. 12–13
A chalk drawing by Keith Haring in Madison Square Park, New York, 1982

pp. 14–15
A mural by Keith Haring on Houston Street at the Bowery, New York, 1982

Photographs by Tseng Kwong Chi

KEITH HARING THE POLITICAL LINE

EDITED BY DIETER BUCHHART
WITH CONTRIBUTIONS BY JULIAN COX, JULIA GRUEN,
CARLO McCORMICK, JULIAN MYERS-SZUPINSKA, GLENN O'BRIEN,
TONY SHAFRAZI, ROBERT FARRIS THOMPSON, AND GIORGIO VERZOTTI

FINE ARTS MUSEUMS OF SAN FRANCISCO

DELMONICO BOOKS • PRESTEL
MUNICH LONDON NEW YORK

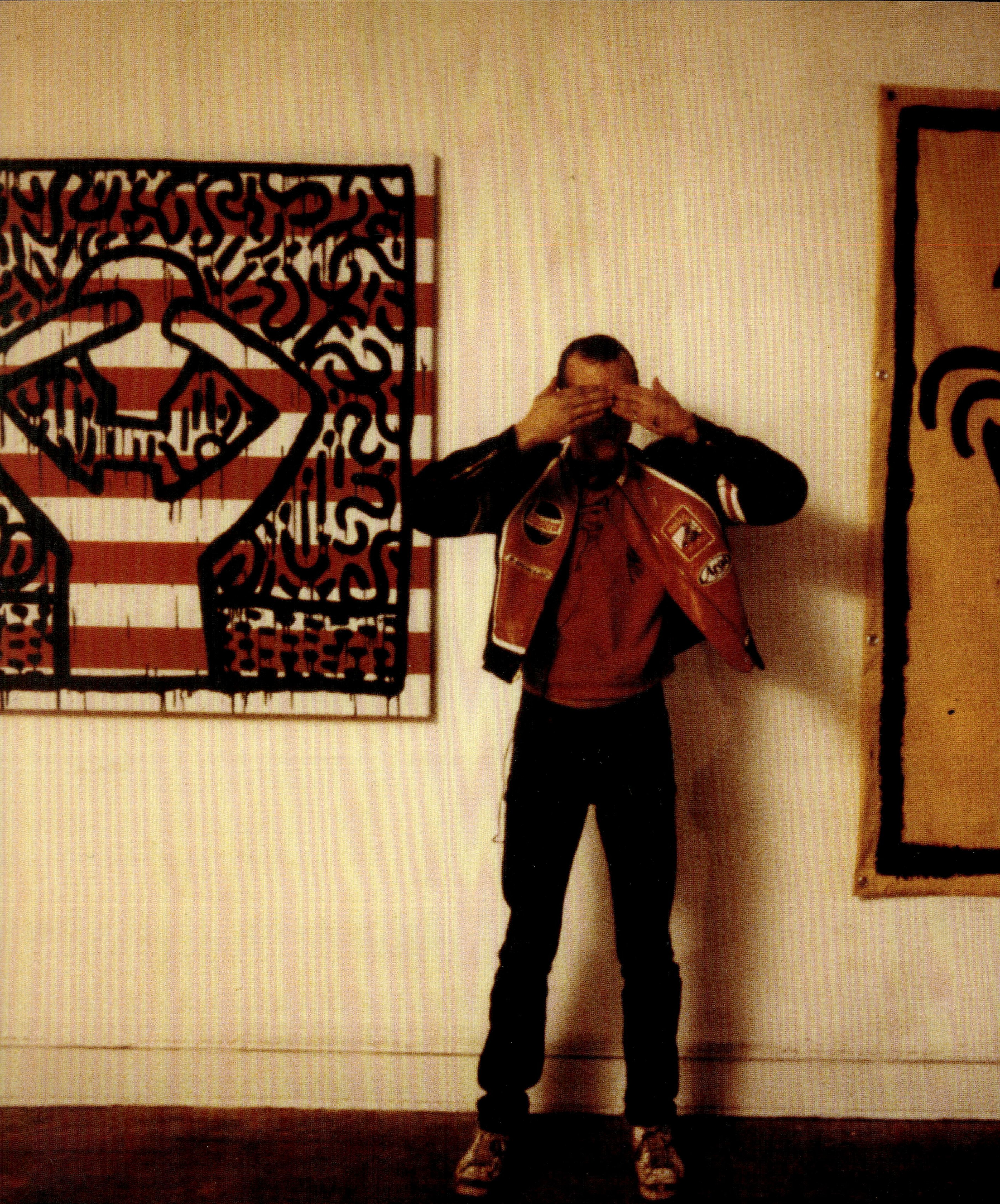

CONTENTS

Keith Haring, 1981.
Photograph by Klaus Wittmann

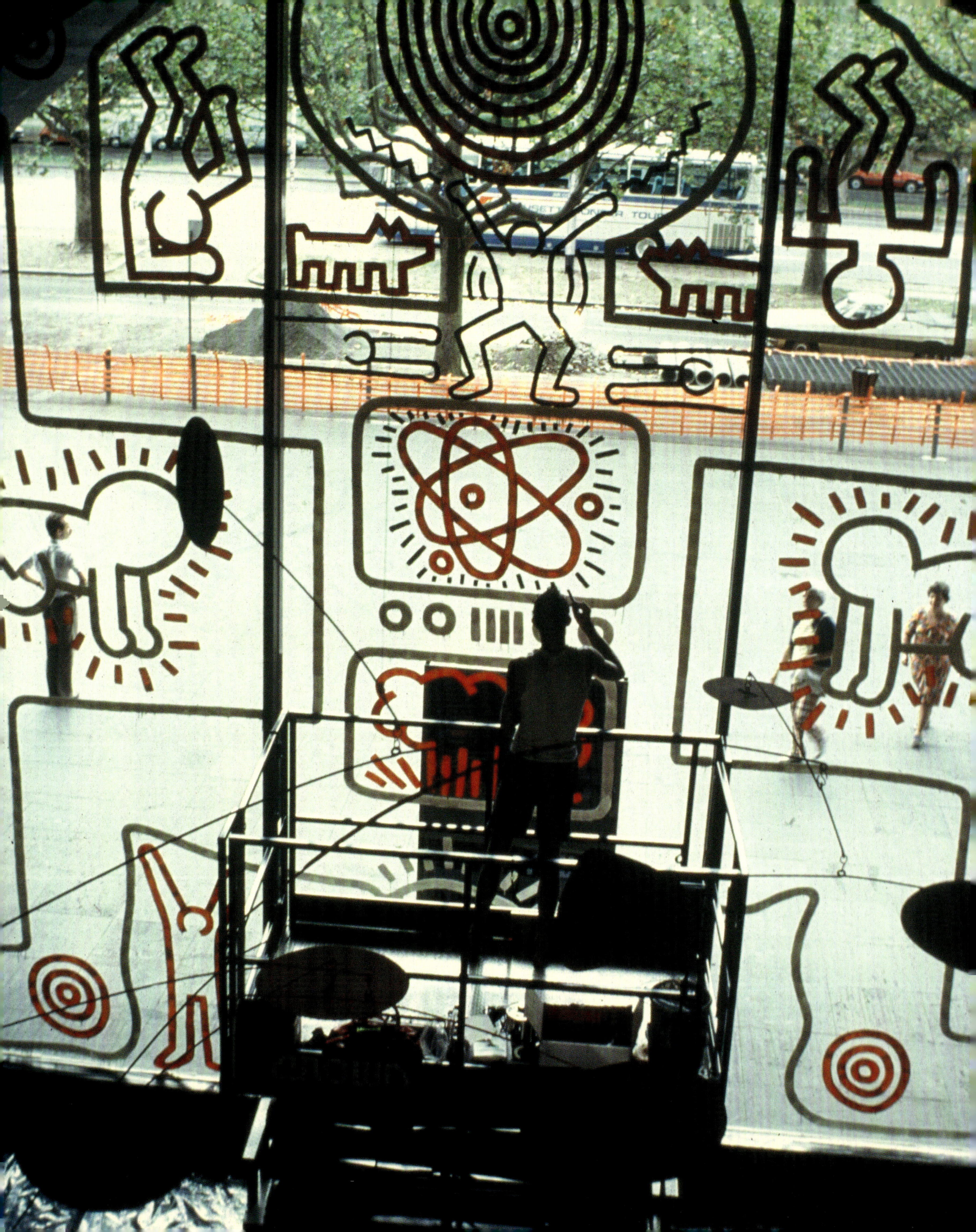

FOREWORD

We are proud to present *Keith Haring: The Political Line*, the first major exhibition to examine the political nature of Haring's art. A Pop icon of the 1980s whose bold style and prodigious output brought him global recognition, Haring is little recognized for his engagement with the social and political challenges of his time. His work in a variety of media unapologetically denounces racism, capitalism, homophobia, dictatorship, atomic war, environmental degradation, and the excesses of technology and mass media.

Haring was protean in his interests, collating ideas from various sources, weaving them into his artistic processes, and creating a style singularly his own. His art is instantly recognizable and speaks for his generation and to those that have followed. Haring hoped that his paintings, drawings, sculptures, and murals would become widely known, and we wish to further this mission by introducing his exuberant practice to our audiences.

Our donors and sponsors make it possible for the Museums to bring ambitious exhibitions to San Francisco. I am grateful to those individuals and institutions who have provided leadership support for this exhibition: Penny and James George Coulter, Sloan and Roger Barnett, the Ray and Dagmar Dolby Family Fund, the Shimmon Family, the Buena Vista Fund of the Horizons Foundation, the Keith Haring Foundation, and Richard and Peggy Greenfield. My thanks are offered further to the many lenders who have generously shared their works of art with our public, including Her Highness Sheikha Salama bint Hamdan Al Nahyan, Barbara Gladstone Gallery, the Barnetts, the Broad Art Foundation, Suzanne Geiss, Glenstone, Sandy Heller, Jane Holzer, Sir Elton John and David Furnish, Alona Kagan, David LaChapelle, Jean Lignel, Suzy Lustgarten, Martos Gallery, the Mugrabi Collection, Mike de Paola, Richard Prince, the Rubell Family Collection, Adam Sender, the Tony Shafrazi Gallery, Muna Tseng, Larry Warsh, Victor Van de Weghe, and several generous anonymous lenders. This catalogue is published with the assistance of the Andrew W. Mellon Foundation Endowment for Publications.

I thank Diane B. Wilsey, president of the Board of Trustees, and Richard Benefield, deputy director, for their support in arranging this presentation at the Museums. My heartfelt appreciation also is given to our guest curator, Dieter Buchhart, who conceived and shaped the exhibition and book, and to Julian Cox, the Museums' founding curator of photography and chief administrative curator, who collaborated on all aspects of the show and publication. I extend gratitude to the other catalogue contributors, Julia Gruen, Carlo McCormick, Julian Myers-Szupinska, Glenn O'Brien, Tony Shafrazi, Robert Farris Thompson, and Giorgio Verzotti, for their thoughtful texts on Keith Haring's life and art.

Julia Gruen, executive director of the Keith Haring Foundation, New York, further helped us at every stage of this project, with assistance from her colleagues Annelise Ream, creative director; Elen Woods, archivist; Fawn Krieger, education director; and Julie Joseph, registrar. It has been an honor and a pleasure to work with the Foundation to make Keith Haring's legacy manifest at our Museums.

Keith Haring painting on the Waterwall of the National Gallery of Victoria, Melbourne, Australia, 1984. Photograph by Tseng Kwong Chi

COLIN B. BAILEY
DIRECTOR OF MUSEUMS
FINE ARTS MUSEUMS OF SAN FRANCISCO

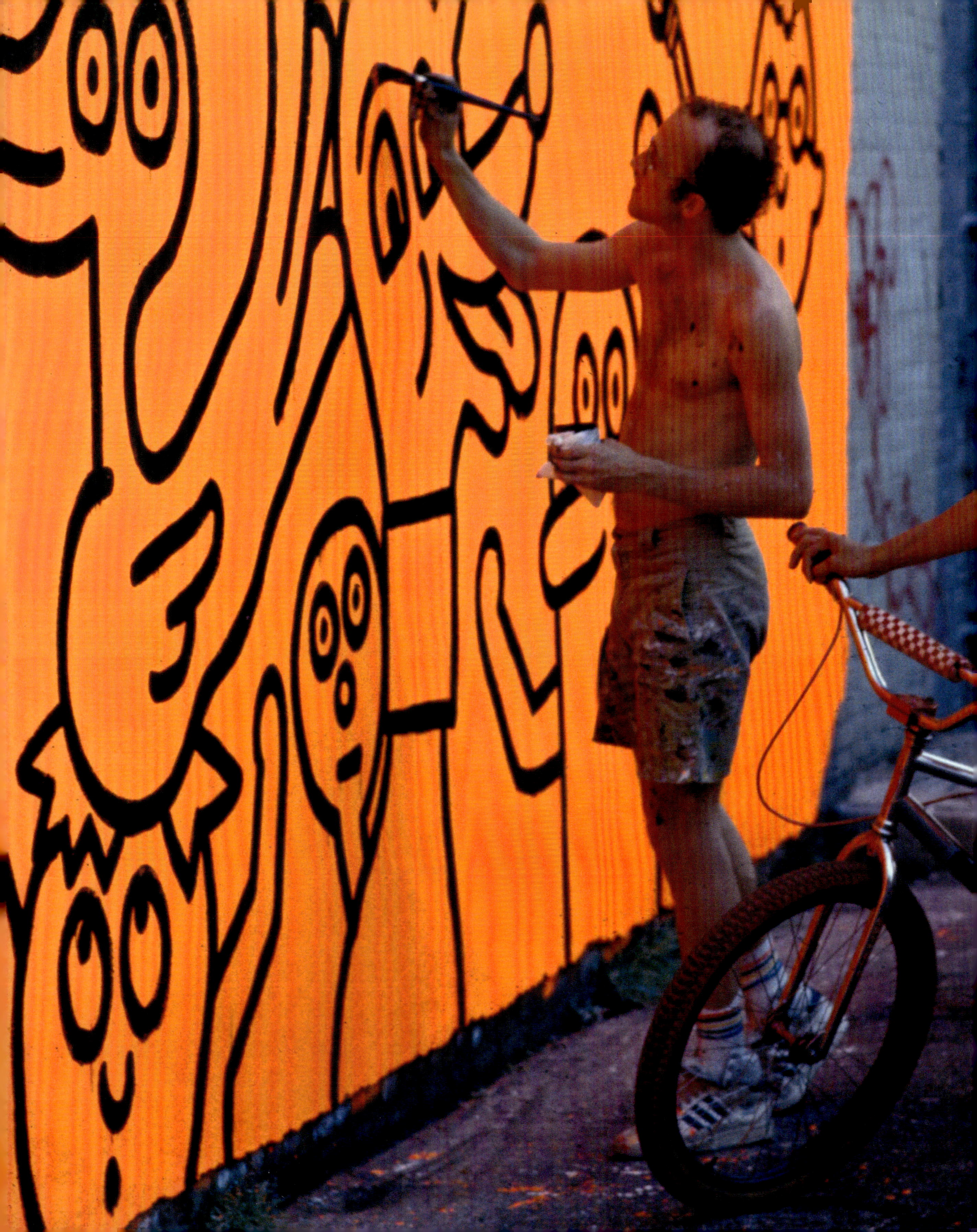

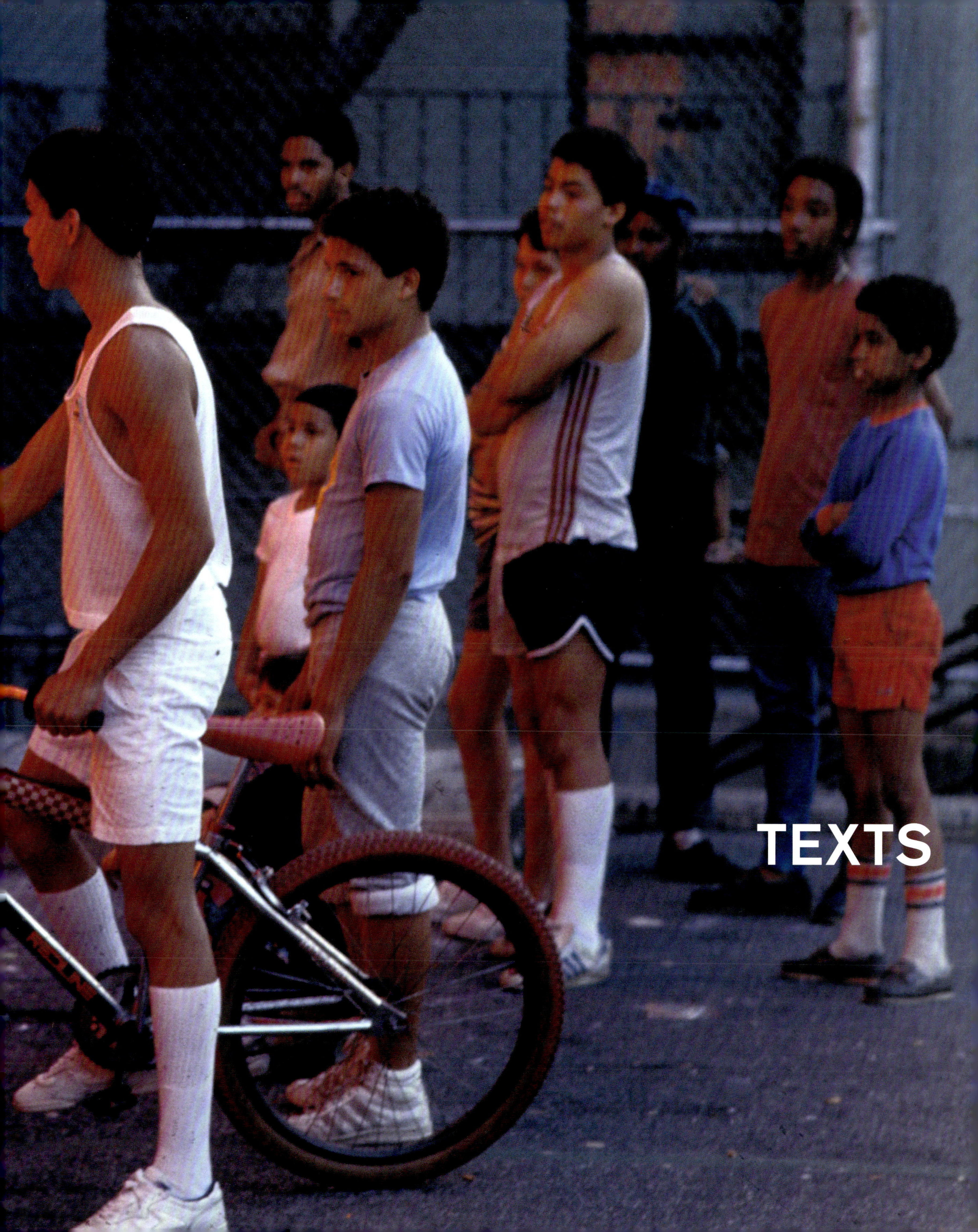

TEXTS

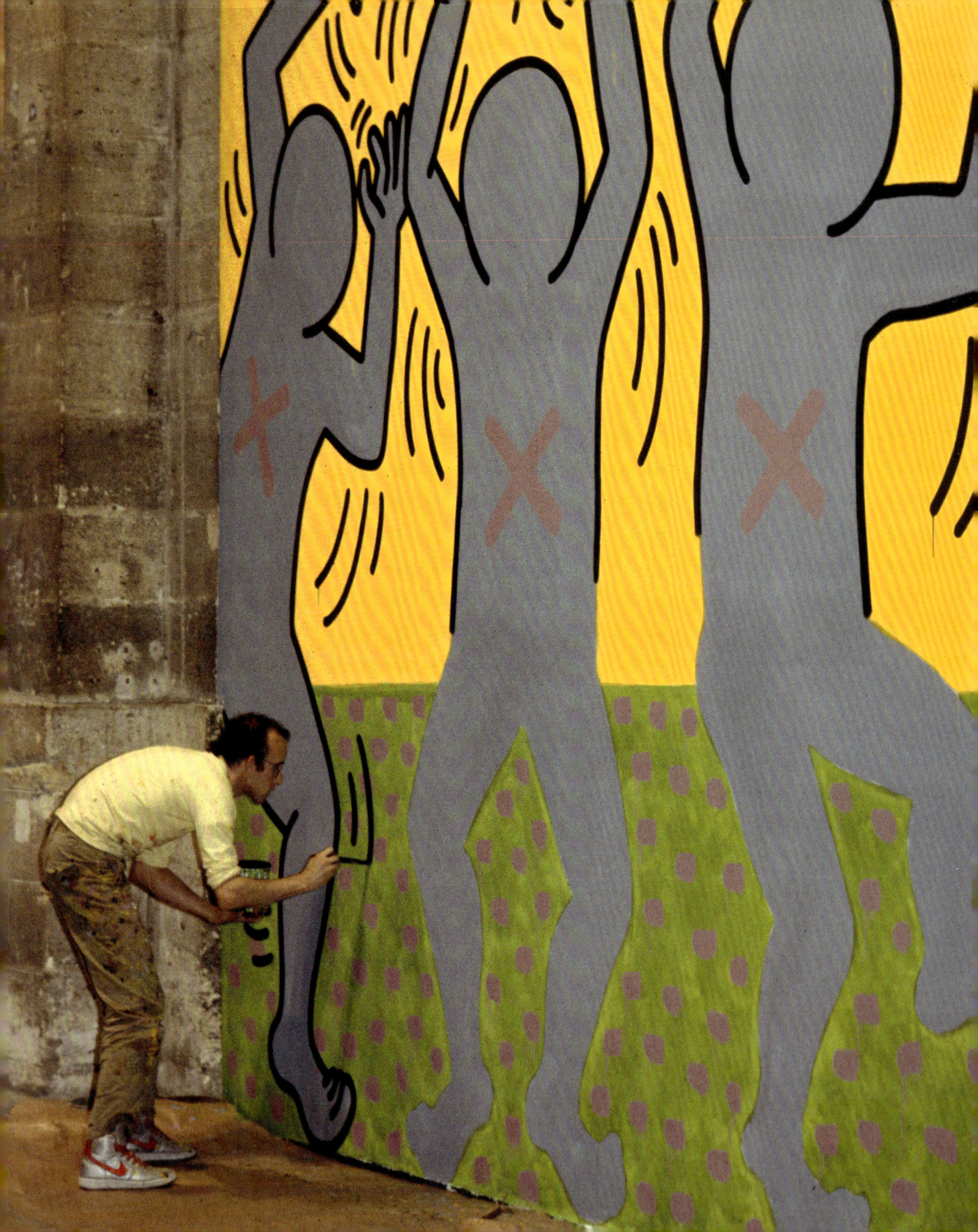

INTRODUCTION: SOCIAL JUSTICE AND PUBLIC DISPLAY

I know I am solid and sound,
To me the converging objects of the universe perpetually flow,
All are written to me, and I must get what the writing means.

—Walt Whitman, *Leaves of Grass*[1]

Keith Haring had a brief but blazing life. Although exuberant and indefatigable by nature, he succumbed to AIDS before the age of thirty-two, but in a short career that spanned little more than a decade he produced a voluminous, pulsating body of work. The act of art-making allowed Haring to formulate a visual universe that gave meaning to his emotional life. He strove to approximate the philosophical breadth and relentless, all-embracing energy of Walt Whitman's verse as well as the poet's ideas about personal freedom and the example of fully developing one's potential with an attitude of emotional openness.

Art was Haring's safety net and the place where he could articulate some of his most passionate beliefs and intimate feelings. Fluent in a variety of media, particularly drawing and painting, Haring's art was direct and often confrontational. He wanted it to be relevant to everyday life, and hewn from it. He was acutely aware of being among a new generation of Americans, and was inextricably linked to the times in which he lived. He stated, "I consider myself a perfect product of the space age not only because I was born in the year that the first man was launched into space, but also because I grew up with Walt Disney cartoons."[2] Shaped by the radical politics of the 1960s and the horrors of the Vietnam War, Haring had an uncomfortable relationship to the politics of Reagan-era America. He was inherently suspicious of organized power, religion, and political structures and perceived them as oppressors to his quest for personal freedom. He saw the role of the artist as antagonist, as provocateur, with a responsibility to speak out against inequity and injustice. Haring was absolute in his desire for his work and its message to reach as wide an audience as possible.

As a student just out of his teens and recently relocated from a short stint in Pittsburgh to New York City, Haring articulated his lofty ambitions in a journal entry written during his first semester as a student at the School of Visual Arts in fall 1978: "I am interested in making art to be experienced and explored by as many individuals as possible with as many different individual ideas about the given piece with no final meaning attached.

(pp. 22–23)
Keith Haring painting the *Life Is Fresh, Crack Is Wack* mural at P.S. 97, New York, 1986. Photograph by Tseng Kwong Chi

(opposite)
Keith Haring painting *The Ten Commandments* at CAPC Musée d'Art Contemporain de Bordeaux, France, 1985. Photograph by Tseng Kwong Chi

JULIAN COX

The viewer creates the reality, the meaning, the conception of the piece."[3] He was already obsessed with documenting and recording his artistic output and how it meshed with his personal life. Enamored of television, film, and photography, Haring understood how these media might be employed as recording systems and creative vessels for his practice. As he submerged himself within the overlapping social and artistic worlds of New York City, Haring used photography extensively to document his practice and help forge his personal and political identities. Early in Haring's career, the artist Tseng Kwong Chi photographed Haring's studio work, and later he shot his public works and events; Kwong Chi's resulting photography documents almost all of Haring's artistic output (see pp. 2–15).

Haring also seems to have relished turning the camera on himself, and between 1980 and 1988 he made many self-portraits, particularly with his Polaroid SX-70.[4] In photographic self-portraits, artists select a setting, position the camera, and decide when to trip the shutter (either remotely or with a pneumatic release). Ultimately, however, they can never quite know what the camera sees at the moment of exposure, and images of unexpected candor or metaphoric potential may emerge. In one bust-length self-portrait, Haring dons his round-rimmed glasses, a red ski mask, and a black leather jacket. His eyes and mouth are the only visible parts of his anatomy (fig. 1). This kind of self-portraiture may be understood as a form less of self-disclosure than of play-acting. As a likeness, it conceals more than it reveals. It shows not the self but self-exploration and self-presentation, yet as a personification of Haring's impish, shape-shifting identity, it hits close to the mark.

Gifted with an ability to connect with people, Haring met Andy Warhol not long after Haring's first major solo show at the Tony Shafrazi Gallery in 1982. Separated in age by three decades, the two men had in common upbringings in the heart of Pennsylvania (Warhol hailed from Pittsburgh, Haring from Kutztown, an agricultural community), a frankness about their sexualities (both were openly gay), and resolute artistic ambitions. They became good friends, and at the time of Warhol's death in 1987, Haring acknowledged his debt to the older artist: "Andy's life and work made my work possible. . . . He was the first *real* public artist. . . . He addressed the phenomena of the camera and the recorded image in a way that Duchamp only hinted at. . . . He became a teacher for a generation of artists now, and in the future, who grew up on Pop, who watched television since they were born, who 'understand' digital knowledge."[5] Warhol had been ever present at gallery openings and art-world events during the

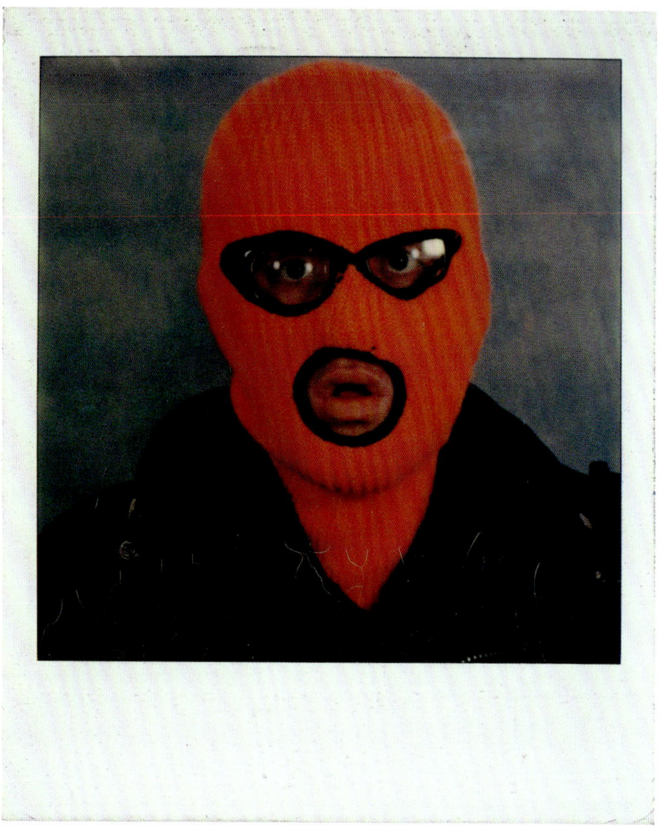

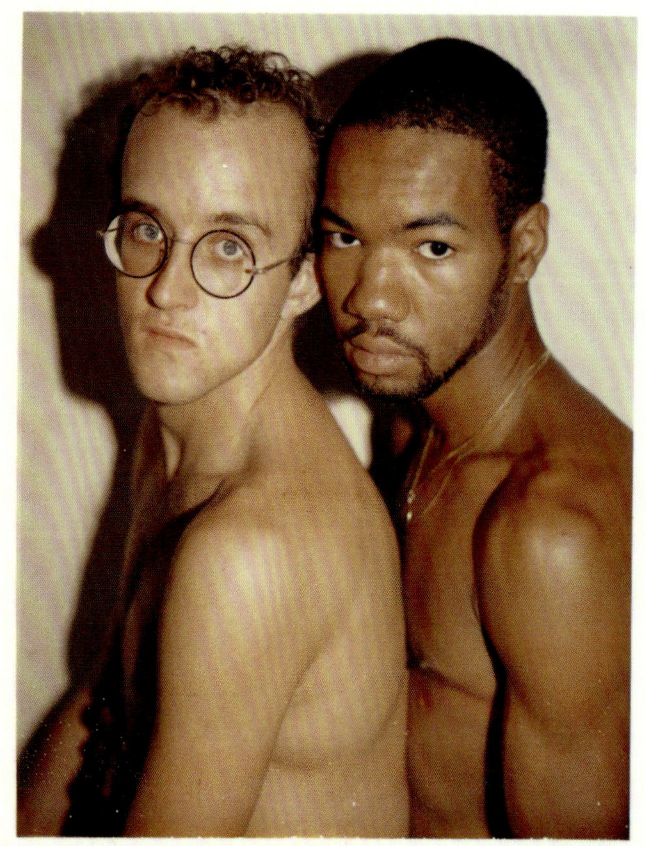

1980s, and he also used a Polaroid camera (as well as a single-lens reflex camera) to document his inner circle of friends and collaborators. His double portrait of a shirtless Keith Haring and his lover at the time, Juan Dubose (fig. 2), is emphatically candid and intimate and was made in preparation for several forty-by-forty-inch painted portraits of the couple. While Warhol helped many of his young friends cope with problems caused by their early successes, he was acutely aware of the ravaging impact of AIDS and joined with them to campaign for increased awareness of the illness and funding for cures. Warhol's activism was an important model for Haring; in 1976, Warhol made Polaroids of Jimmy Carter from which the Democratic National Committee published screenprints to help cover campaign costs; and in 1980, he created another edition of screenprints (finished with diamond dust) to support Senator Edward Kennedy's run in the Democratic presidential primary.[6]

Even before his arrival in New York, Haring had been inspired by Robert Henri's 1923 publication *The Art Spirit*, a manifesto that advocated for a life-enhancing, noncommercial, nonacademic art generated as the outward expression of a person alive to the world and the senses. Haring also discovered the writings of Jean Dubuffet, and found resonance in the French artist's skeptical view of the conception of beauty in Western culture. This reading stayed with Haring such that, when organizing an exhibition of anonymous art at Club 57 in New York in 1980, he included a Dubuffet quote in the announcement: "For myself, I aim for an art which would be in immediate connection with daily life, which could start from our daily life and which would be a very direct and very sincere expression of our real life and real moods."[7] Haring took this attitude out into the street, which was to be the laboratory for his first forays into public art with messages for large audiences. Drawn to the energy of graffiti art and the propulsive beats of hip-hop culture, Haring made tags and drawings on the surfaces of a medley of public spaces, including advertising billboards, scaffolding on construction sites, and the pavement. Some of his earliest street works were collages composed of cut-up headlines from the *New York Post* (see pls. 54–59) that were cheaply photocopied and pasted up on walls and the bases of lampposts, guerrilla-style.[8] These works, with absurdist wordings such as "Mob Flees at Pope Rally" and "Reagan's Death Cops Hunt Pope" (pl. 54), made no literal sense, but in their graphic patterning and chance reordering they provided random insights to passersby. Haring later remarked about them, "People had no idea where they were coming from, but they really made one of the first big marks in people's consciousness."[9]

Riding the subway to and from his apartment uptown, Haring noticed a more explicit opportunity in the form of expired advertising panels in subway stations that were temporarily covered with black paper, waiting for the next poster to be added. Between 1980 and 1985, despite multiple fines and an arrest for "criminal mischief" in January 1982,[10] Haring made thousands of chalk drawings on these subway "blackboards," creating inventive compositions that radiated with energy. The execution of each drawing was a performance, carried out with speed and assurance in the moments before a train arrived at or departed from the platform. The rapidity of their creation made for distinct, instantly recognizable imagery and a vocabulary of explicit forms that includes barking dogs, radiant babies, pulsing TVs, zapping spaceships, and amorphous, multi-limbed figures. Though on the surface the drawings may appear childishly simple, they were conceived for immediate audience readability. The sheer volume of the drawings distributed throughout the subway system had the power of a mass media campaign, even if individually they were ephemeral and fugitive in nature, easily erased or pasted over with an incoming advertisement. As Jeffrey Deitch has explained: "Masquerading as cartoons, they had thousands of subway riders a day studying sketches for Armageddon—drawings bubbling with unrestrained eroticism and spinning with signs of destruction."[11] A Polaroid snapshot in the collection of the Keith Haring Foundation shows the artist's puckish response to a poster advertising the 1981 film *Amin: The Rise and Fall* (fig. 57), a biopic that details the controversial actions and atrocities of the Ugandan dictator Idi Amin, whose violent overthrow in 1979 ignited the Uganda-Tanzania war. The Subway Drawings are just one of many examples of Haring's creative activation of urban public structures to address contemporary political concerns in his art. They were at once rigorous, accessible, and political.

In the 1980s, public art was encouraged and funded, enabling Haring to expand his practice and his social reach by taking on a range of endeavors. Under public auspices, he often worked closely with children, wherever possible involving them as participants and collaborators in his site-specific workshops and public art projects. On a single day in December 1985, Haring completed a monumental seventy-foot-long mural composed of twenty-four panels for the gymnasium at the South of Market Childcare Center in San Francisco (also known as the Saint Patrick's Daycare Center), a facility serving preschool children and their families. One of sixteen such public works painted at hospitals and children's centers during his lifetime, the mural

1

Keith Haring, self-portrait, c. 1980. Polaroid. Collection of the Keith Haring Foundation

2

Andy Warhol, *Keith Haring and Juan Dubose*, 1983. Polaroid Polacolor print. J. Paul Getty Museum, Los Angeles, 98.XM.168.7

is full of playful kinetic energy, with dancing two-headed figures, grinning alligators, a frog prince, and a self-portrait along the right border with Haring shown waving at the viewer, paintbrush in hand, with his patch of curly hair, rounded glasses, and trademark Nike sneakers (fig. 3).[12] The work remained in place until 2006, when the center was forced to relocate to other premises in the city. The mural was disassembled and later acquired by a private collector.[13] A similarly ambitious public project, which Haring realized the following year, was his two-sided *Crack Is Wack* mural, painted on the wall of a handball court located at East 128th Street and Harlem River Drive in New York (fig. 4). It cautions against the use of crack, the potent, highly addictive form of cocaine whose use reached epidemic proportions in the mid to late 1980s and which was in especially virulent circulation in New York City. Haring had friends who were addicts and struggled to gain access to appropriate treatment and counseling from the public health system, so this work was fueled by a sense of personal urgency as well as political intent.[14] The mural remains in situ today and is maintained by the Keith Haring Foundation under the aegis of the New York City Department of Parks and Recreation.

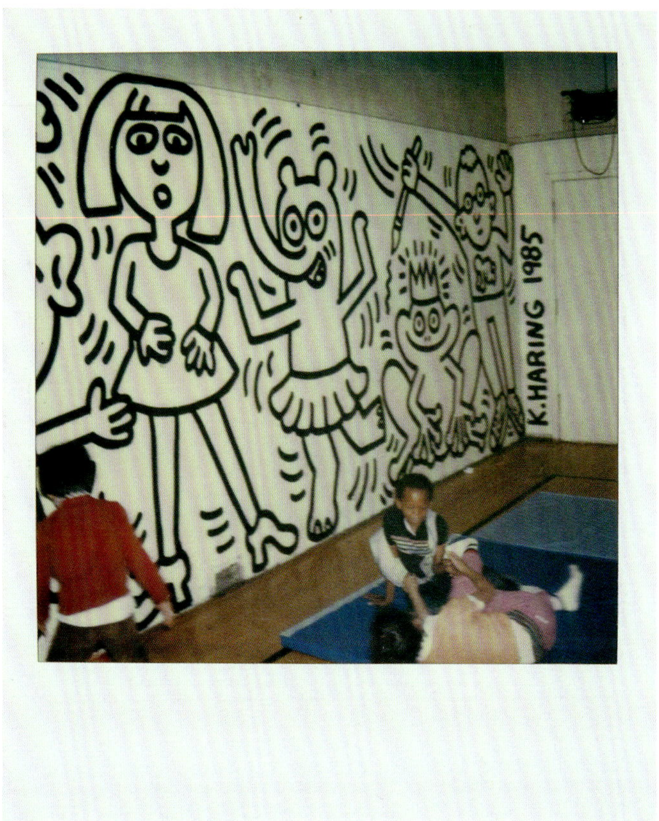

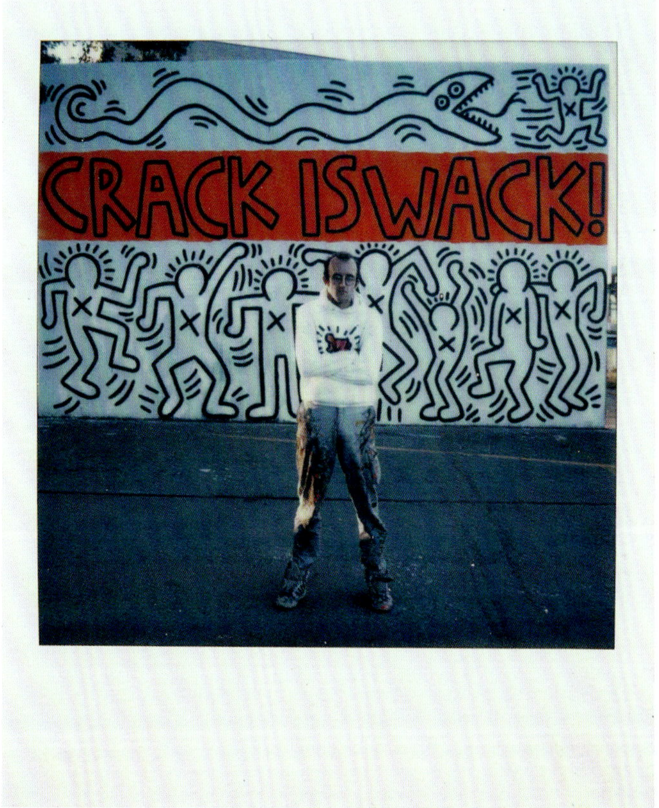

Haring's activism was directed in practical ways toward issues that he cared about. On June 12, 1982, he handed out posters of his own making at the largest antinuclear rally ever held in the United States, when more than a million people marched from the United Nations headquarters to Central Park to protest against the proliferation and deployment of nuclear weapons. He printed more than twenty thousand posters at his own expense, and, with his friends, he distributed them for free (fig. 5).[15] Six years later, when traveling in Japan, he visited the Hiroshima Peace Memorial Museum, a jolting experience that prompted a lengthy entry in his journal: "It is incredible that this destruction was caused by a bomb that was made in 1945, and that the level of sophistication and number of nuclear warheads has increased since then. . . . The frightening thing is that people debate and discuss the arms race as if they were playing with toys. . . . There was one photo of a pile of human bodies that was beyond reality. Pictures of radioactivity's aftereffects that were nothing short of science-fiction horror. Descriptions of black raindrops, photos of melted faces, etc., etc."[16] Haring's exposure to the legacy of Hiroshima increased his awareness of and concern about the dangers of nuclear proliferation and the perils of atomic contamination. The imagery in his later works, such as *The Last Rainforest*, 1989 (pl. 172), is pushed to Hieronymus Bosch–like extremes, with multitudes of squirming mythical creatures and demons scattered throughout a ravaged vision of hell in an apocalyptic, primordial forest.

The specter of celebrity and fame is never far from the surface in any consideration of Haring's art and life, and the artist's comprehension of the power of

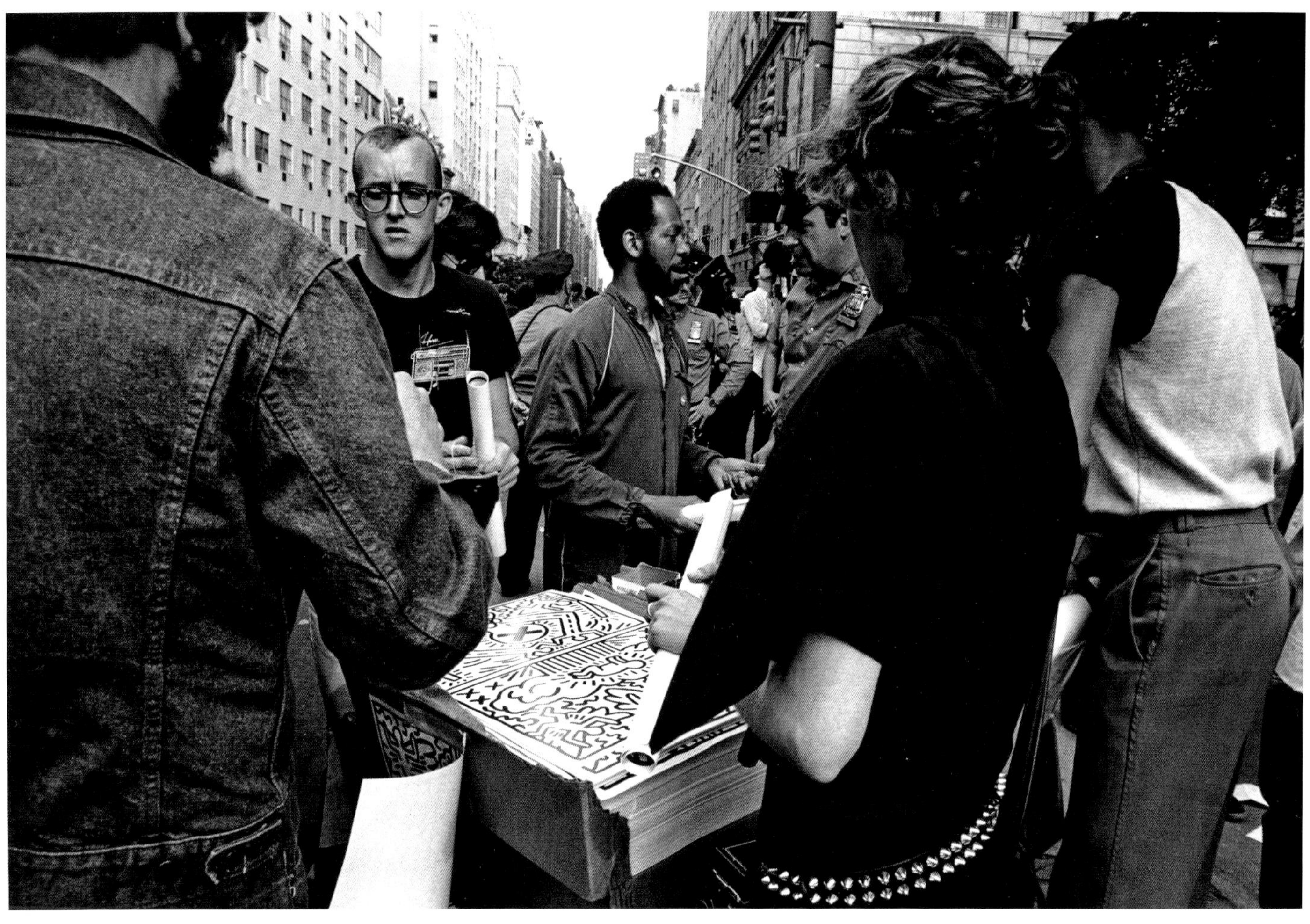

3 (opposite, top)

Unknown photographer, Saint Patrick's Daycare Center mural by Keith Haring, San Francisco, December 1985. Polaroid. Collection of the Keith Haring Foundation

4 (opposite, bottom)

Unknown photographer, Keith Haring in front of his *Crack Is Wack* mural, East 128th Street and Harlem River Drive, New York, October 6, 1986. Polaroid. Collection of the Keith Haring Foundation

5 (above)

Joseph Szkodzinski, Keith Haring with Samantha McEwen and Juan Dubose handing out free posters at antinuclear rally, New York, June 12, 1982. Gelatin silver print. Collection of the Keith Haring Foundation context and media was also pervasive. His large-scale acrylic-on-canvas painting *Untitled (Apartheid)*, of 1984 (pl. 142), was made into posters, badges, and T-shirts, and he proudly wore one of the latter on March 5, 1988, the night of the "Free South Africa" benefit concert held in New York to support the dismantling of apartheid in South Africa and the release of its most vociferous incarcerated opponent, Nelson Mandela. Haring was photographed alongside the boxer Sugar Ray Leonard (fig. 6), who donned a matching Haring-designed T-shirt. The pop-music icon Michael Jackson (fig. 7) also attended to support the cause. The immediacy of the Polaroid process provided instant gratification at a time when other photographic systems did not allow it, and Haring used the format to share his experiences directly with his friends and peers. If Haring did not make the exposure himself, the camera was handed off to a member of his entourage to document the person or the event. The fluidity of this exchange with the camera is evident in Haring's first encounter with the runway model, singer, and movie actress Grace Jones, who holds up for review a Polaroid by Haring (fig. 8) made while he was painting her body in preparation for a portrait session by photographer Robert Mapplethorpe.[17] For Haring and Jones, the meeting ignited a productive friendship, which led to an important 1985 collaboration at the Paradise Garage, recorded by photographer Tseng Kwong Chi (see fig. 22), who observed Haring consulting images of East African Masai body painting before covering Jones's body with his own designs.[18] Haring would also paint Jones's skin for the feature film *Vamp* and for her music video "I'm Not Perfect (But I'm Perfect for You)."

The verve and physicality of Haring's art-making were well matched with his desire to create work with a public purpose. He taught himself to execute ambitious compositions with tremendous focus and speed, a skill that could be equally well deployed in the studio or on the street. He reveled in the performative aspect of his practice, channeling his physical strength and imagination to produce art that met his expectations for personal liberation and a full embrace of life. Even as he confronted his failing health and the onset of his premature death at the age of thirty-one, he retained an ardent belief in the power of art to vivify and transform at a truly public level. The last entry in his journal, from September 22, 1989, describes his reaction to the Leaning Tower of Pisa: "Every time you look at it, it makes you smile."[19] The phrasing is a fitting epitaph for his own life's work.

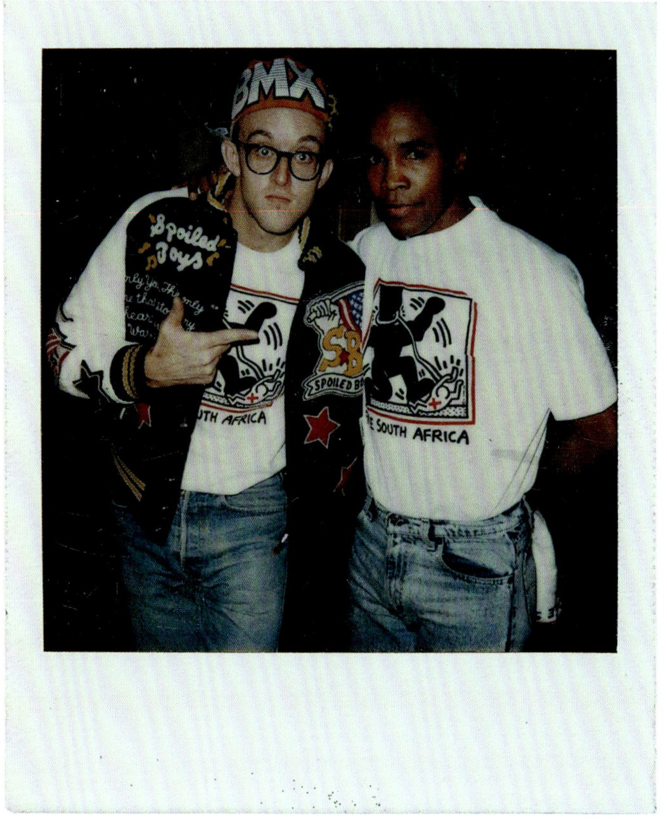

6 (above)

Unknown photographer, Keith Haring and Sugar Ray Leonard, "Free South Africa" benefit concert, New York, March 5, 1988. Polaroid. Collection of the Keith Haring Foundation

7 (opposite, top)

Unknown photographer, Keith Haring and Michael Jackson, "Free South Africa" benefit concert, New York, March 5, 1988. Polaroid. Collection of the Keith Haring Foundation

8 (opposite, bottom)

Unknown photographer, Keith Haring and Grace Jones, body painting with signature by LA ROC (Angel Ortiz), July 28, 1984. Polaroid. Collection of the Keith Haring Foundation

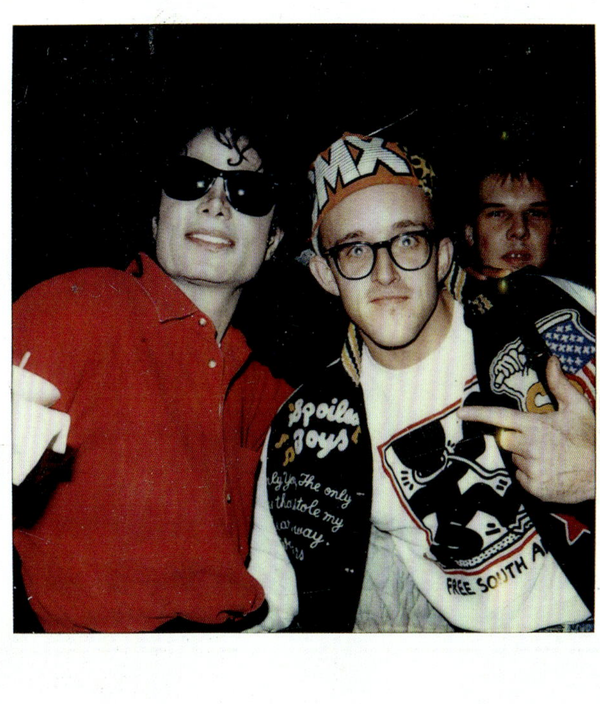

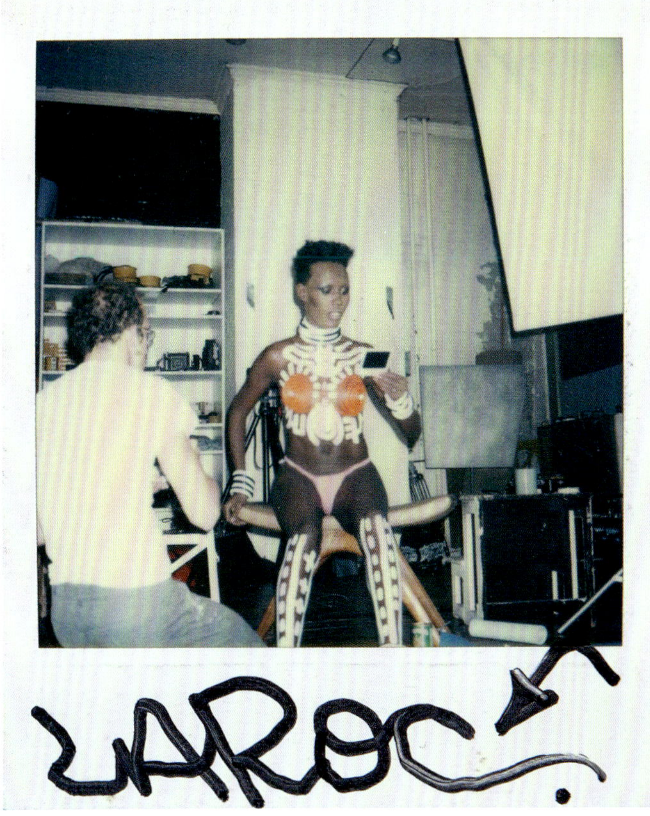

Notes

1. Whitman quoted in Keith Haring, *Keith Haring Journals* (New York: Penguin Classics deluxe ed., 2010), 75–76. Haring wrote down four verses drawn from Whitman's poetry in his journal entry for October 4, 1979, including the one quoted here.
2. Haring quoted in Germano Celant, *Keith Haring*, exh. cat. (Turin, Italy: Castello di Rivoli; Sydney: Museum of Contemporary Art, 1994), 178.
3. Haring quoted in Jeffrey Deitch et al., *Keith Haring* (New York: Rizzoli, 2008), 13.
4. For details on the Polaroid SX-70, see the essay by Peter Buse in Mary-Kay Lombino, *The Polaroid Years: Instant Photography and Experimentation* (New York: DelMonico Books/Prestel, 2013), 37–48. There are more than 1,600 Polaroids (in various formats, but predominantly SX-70) in the archives of the Keith Haring Foundation. They record his mural commissions and public works, personal travels, friends, parties, artworks, collection inventories, and special events. The archive also includes more than thirty-five Polaroid self-portraits (see figs. 51–54). Haring inscribed many of the Polaroids with locations and a year, and some are signed by the people who appear in the pictures (e-mail correspondence from Elen Woods, archivist, Keith Haring Foundation, May 22, 2014).
5. Haring, *Keith Haring Journals*, 154–155.
6. See Gordon Baldwin and Judith Keller, *Nadar/Warhol: Paris/New York* (Los Angeles: J. Paul Getty Museum, 1999), 220.
7. The exhibition was titled *Keith Haring Presents Anonymous Art*, and the Dubuffet quote was included in an announcement dated October 29, 1980. The original is in the archives of the Keith Haring Foundation. Haring mentions Dubuffet several times in his journals: see particularly *Keith Haring Journals*, 129.
8. Haring acknowledged his debt in the collages to William Burroughs and Brion Gysin as well as to Jenny Holzer. See Deitch et al., *Keith Haring*, 52–53.
9. Haring quoted in ibid., 53.
10. Haring describes his work in the subway and his arrest at length in ibid., 114–115.
11. See Jeffrey Deitch, "Why the Dogs Are Barking," originally published in Robert Pincus-Witten et al., *Keith Haring*, exh. cat. (New York: Tony Shafrazi Gallery, 1982), 17–20, reprinted in Elisabeth Sussman et al., *Keith Haring*, exh. cat., Whitney Museum of American Art, June 25–September 21, 1997 (New York: Whitney Museum of American Art; Boston: Bulfinch/Little, Brown, 1997), 84.
12. I am grateful to Jane Weil, a San Francisco resident and former board member of the Saint Patrick's Daycare Center, for sharing information about the mural and her recollection of both its creation and the circumstances surrounding its removal and sale in 2006. I am also indebted to Frank Ditto, a photographer who documented the de-installation of the mural in 2006 and who shared the photographs with me.
13. For a description of the closing of the Saint Patrick's Daycare Center and its relocation to another part of the city, see Jesse Hamlin, "Haring Mural Up for Sale," *San Francisco Chronicle*, January 9, 2006, www.sfgate.com/bayarea.article/san-francisco-Haring-mural-up-for-sale-A-2524078.php#ixzz2ChtO68NS (accessed June 18, 2014).
14. Haring's first mural at the site, in June 1986, was created without the city's permission, and he was fined and required to paint over it. He returned in October of the same year and made a new mural, this time with permission from the appropriate authority.
15. See Deitch et al., *Keith Haring*, 228–230. For more information on the June 12, 1982, protest, see also David Cortright, *Peace: A History of Movements and Ideas* (Cambridge: Cambridge University Press, 2008), 145.
16. Haring, *Keith Haring Journals*, 296.
17. Mapplethorpe's photographs of Grace Jones were published in *Interview* (October 1984). Andy Warhol was also present at Haring's first meeting with Grace Jones and made black-and-white photographs of Haring painting her body. See Baldwin and Keller, *Nadar/Warhol*, 181.
18. Andy Warhol was present this day, too, and made photographs of Haring at work on the Grace Jones body painting. The photographs are in the collection of the Andy Warhol Foundation for the Visual Arts, New York. See ibid.
19. Haring, *Keith Haring Journals*, 367.

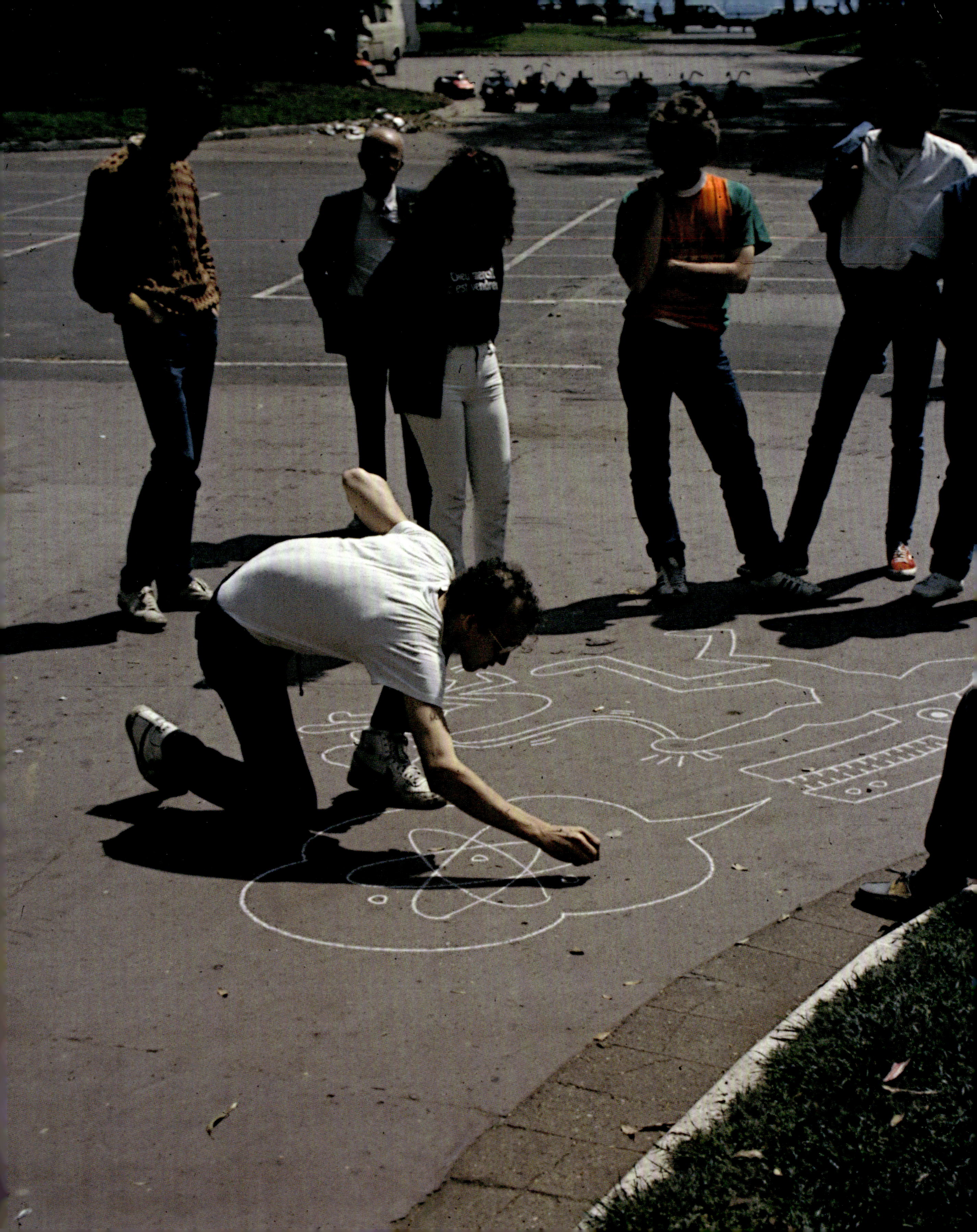

THE ENDLESS POLITICAL LINE

I think Keith is a prophet in his life, his person, and his work. In that way, he's like Paul Klee, who was probably the most influential artist of the twentieth century—certainly through his art, his writings, his teaching. Keith will influence other painters—probably profoundly. By association, Keith is part of the whole New York subway system. Just as no one can look at a sunflower without thinking of Van Gogh, so no one can be in the New York subway system without thinking of Keith Haring. And that's the truth.

—William S. Burroughs [1]

They seem to be ubiquitous: Keith Haring pins, T-shirts, watches, refrigerator magnets, and posters with radiant babies, flying angels, smiling faces, barking dogs, and people carrying glowing red hearts. From April 1986 to September 2005, Haring's merchandise could be purchased in the Pop Shop he founded in downtown Manhattan; today it can be ordered through the online version of the store.[2] Since the artist's death, in 1990, the range of merchandise featuring his images seems to have been extended and updated ad infinitum, now including even iPhone cases. It was precisely this level of commercialization that prompted numerous art critics, museum personnel, and even artists to maintain a critical distance from Haring. Elisabeth Sussman noted on the occasion of the retrospective she organized at the Whitney Museum of American Art in 1997: "There has also been widespread critical dismissal of his work, partly in response to his popularity and partly [in response] to the commercialization perceived to be behind his Pop Shop products."[3] Multiple exhibitions followed the Whitney's, although the retrospectives tended to focus on the abundance of works on show rather than on meaningful art-historical assessments,[4] whereas smaller exhibitions, such as *Heaven and Hell*[5] and *Keith Haring, 1978–1982*,[6] analyzed facets of the artist's oeuvre and initiated more serious examinations.

What is the background of this alleged commercialization (specifically, the opening of the Pop Shop)? How does it relate to Haring's predominantly political orientation, to which little attention has been paid? And was Sussman's observation fitting when she remarked, "He did work too fast, for too many shows, as if he knew or suspected that his days would be short. And his desire to please was enormous"?[7] The later work of Pablo Picasso, whose son Claude made a connection between his father's process and Haring's (see below), was also heavily criticized and rejected in his lifetime for being too fast and too accommodating. Was Picasso, as Werner Spies put it, "painting against time,"[8] in a battle against aging and death, and therefore was his later work an expression of his artistic pursuit of "immediacy"?[9] Or were his late works just "unconnected smearings, executed by a restless old man in the antechamber of death"?[10] Similarly, were Haring's energy and his obsession to work constantly merely expressions of a too-fast, too-accommodating, and too-commercial enterprise, or were they part of his artistic practice? And is his impact truly limited to "the history of his time,"[11] or can Haring still be considered relevant today?

Keith Haring drawing with chalk on pavement, Naples, Italy, 1983.
Photograph by Tseng Kwong Chi

DIETER BUCHHART

In his drawings, posters, murals, paintings, sculptures, and subway art, Keith Haring sought social justice and change. He fought against the oppression of the individual by dictatorship, racism, religion, and capitalism. He campaigned for children's welfare and against crack and AIDS and was at the forefront of the American protest against apartheid in South Africa. He spoke out against the nuclear menace during the Cold War and against increasing environmental damage in the world brought about by industrialization. Haring was not a utopian, but he had a dream: that there would never be an end, for everything could always be the origin of something new. He was one of the most political artists of his time, even though he never saw his art as the spreading of doctrines: "I don't think art is propaganda; it should be something that liberates the soul, provokes the imagination and encourages people to go further. It celebrates humanity instead of manipulating it." [12]

The Endless Political Line in Public Spaces

In his 1978 sketchbook, above a small drawing (fig. 9), Haring wrote the question "Why didn't you 'finish' it?" He responded below: "The drawing is 'finished' from the time you start with the first line. There are places you can 'stop' the drawing and call it 'finished.' But it is never *really* 'finished' until time and space itself are 'finished.' There are always infinitely more things you can do to the composition, the trouble is knowing when to stop. The beauty is knowing when to stop. I choose when to stop, but my work is never 'finished' and always 'finished.'. . ." [13] At the age of twenty, Haring was already pointing out that every individual line is already a finished drawing, that lines are interrupted only to be resumed in the very next moment, and that the line, therefore, continues perpetually. Claude Picasso, now administrator of the Picasso estate, was reminded of his father by Keith Haring's intensive work process. A door painted by Pablo Picasso motivated Claude Picasso to invite other artists to do the same, including Haring:

> In painting Jasmin's door [Jasmin is Claude Picasso's son], Keith attacked the problem head on, just as my father would have done. I mean, my father would look at a blank canvas, go up to it, then start painting without stopping. When he stepped back, the painting would be finished. And that's just how Keith approached Jasmin's door. He just stayed close, close to the door, painting it from top to bottom—bending on his knees, and never once stepping back to see how it looked. Only after he had covered the entire door did he step back, and that's when the door was finished and became a marvelous painting. [14]

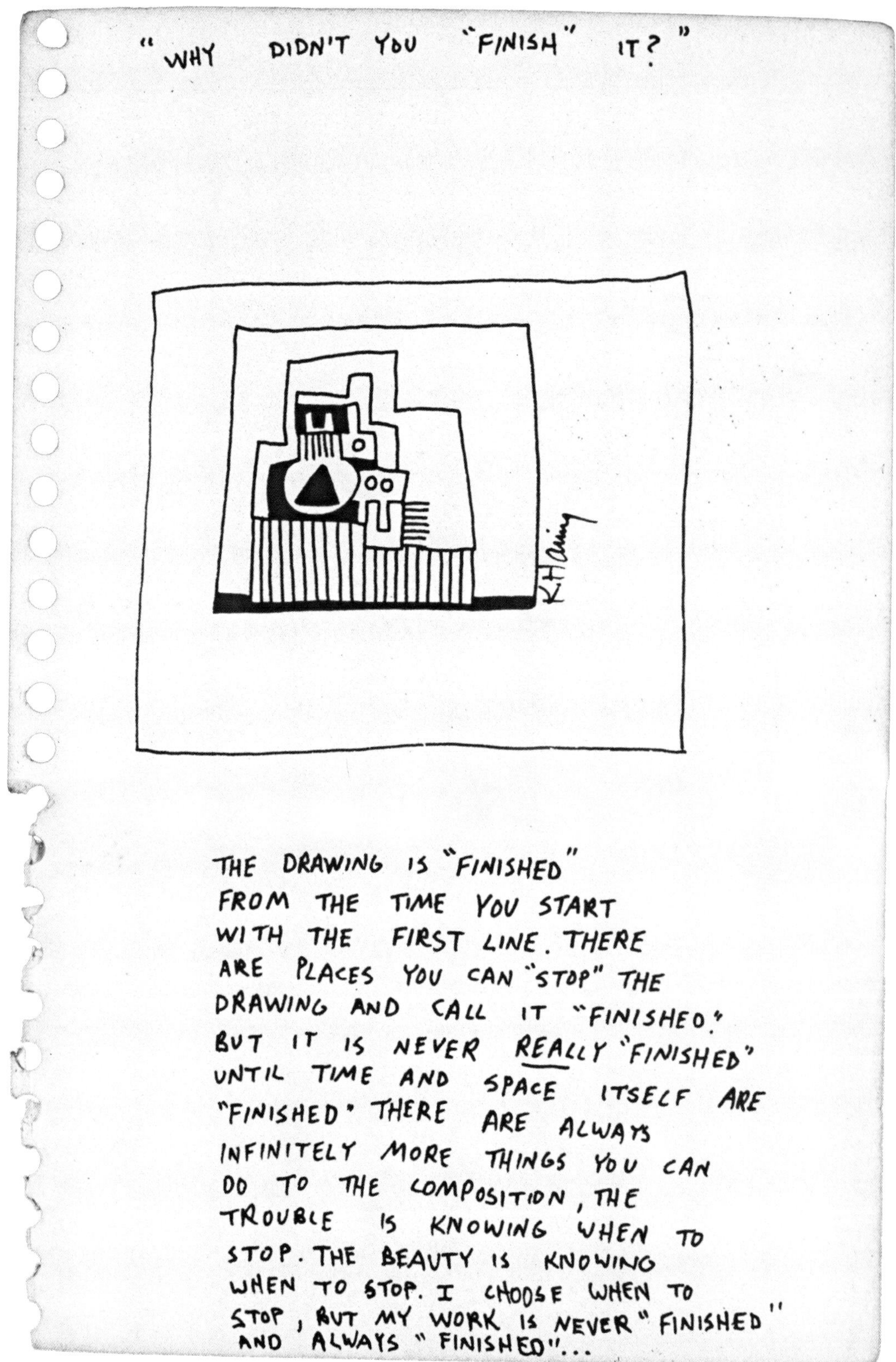

9

Keith Haring, *Untitled*, 1978. Ink and pencil on paper, 7 x 5 in. (17.8 x 12.7 cm). Collection of the Keith Haring Foundation

Like Picasso, Haring worked in one continuous session, without (unnecessary) breaks or stepping back from a work before its completion. Indeed, as demonstrated by video evidence, both artists shared a similar talent for turning a piece into a balanced composition by, without apparent previous planning, beginning with a seemingly random line and advancing without hesitations, disruptions, or corrections. Picasso's method can be seen in Henri-Georges Clouzot's 1956 documentary *Le mystère Picasso*: filmed through a glass plate, the artist is painting nonchalantly. Multiple video documents exist of Haring at work in a similar manner. Both artists were constantly trying to negotiate between *disegno* and *colore*,[15] even though line always remained the dominant element for Haring.[16]

Whether expressed in his written journals, his drawings, or his paintings, Haring's line was always the carrier of significance. This is demonstrated in the video *Painting Myself into a Corner* (see fig. 21), recorded during Haring's time at the School of Visual Arts (SVA) in New York City, in which he rapidly fills a sheet of paper with a drawing covering the entire floor, leaving just enough space in the upper right-hand corner to allow himself to sit. Sussman accurately described such works as "performance drawing,"[17] even though this term could be applied equally well to Haring's *Manhattan Penis Drawings for Ken Hicks* and his Subway Drawings.

Haring realized his Penis Drawings as performances, as radical acts against the establishment, making them in front of Tiffany's and the Museum of Modern Art in New York, among other places (see fig. 36 and pls. 37–53). These works appear to be his first performative protests against a consumer-capitalist society and prudish views of sexuality. He turned drawing into a political act whose explosive nature still can be perceived in the drawings and in the meticulous listing of the places in which he created the penis images. It is in this sense that the following statement is understood best: "The drawings which I do have very little in common with drawings in the classical sense as they developed during the Renaissance, and the drawings that imitate life or make a lifelike impression. My drawings do not try to imitate life, they try to create life, to invent life."[18] Therefore, it is not just the resulting drawing, but the entire performative act of drawing, that creates and invents life.

Haring's five thousand to ten thousand Subway Drawings, produced almost maniacally between 1980 and 1985, under constant risk of arrest, can be understood in a similar fashion.[19] These drawings were integrated naturally into his daily commutes. The artist used the extremely fragile medium of white chalk on black sheets of paper hung in subway stations within unused advertising spaces: "Drawing with chalk on this smooth black paper was a completely new experience for me. It was one continuous line; no interruptions needed to be made, as with a brush or whatever else was already dipped in the paint. It was a continuous line, an extremely strong line graphically, and it was subject to a time limit. I had to work as fast as I could. And nothing could be corrected. So mistakes could not even be allowed, as it were. I had to be careful not to get caught."[20] Haring rushed down the platforms, stopped to cover a black sheet with a drawing made at lightning speed, without interruption, then moved on to the next one. He developed his entire visual language—among other subjects, he had studied semiotic theory at SVA—from his perception that images could work like words.[21] The Subway Drawings became the essential foundation of his art: they "sort of became the perfect environment or laboratory to work out all those ideas I was discovering."[22] In the process, "the man behind the subway drawings," as Gina Belafonte labeled him, developed his own artistic vocabulary.[23]

The Subway Drawings met the artist's desire to produce art for everybody: "The public has a right to art. The public [has] been ignored by most contemporary artists. The public needs art, and it is the responsibility of a 'self-proclaimed artist' to realize [that] the public needs art, and not to make bourgeois art for the few and ignore the masses. Art is for everybody."[24] Through these works, Haring was able to direct his partially politicized messages to a wider audience: his art became a public political action aimed at the establishment and its repression of its citizens.

Haring already had begun modifying billboards in 1979. Influenced by Jenny Holzer's *Truisms*[25] and William Burroughs's "cut-up technique,"[26] he posted hundreds of photocopies of newly arranged headlines from the *New York Post* to "lampposts and newsstands" (see pls. 54–59).[27] The messages from the summer and fall of 1980, which included *Reagan Slain by Hero Cop* (pl. 57) and *Reagan's Death Cops Hunt Pope* (pl. 54), played with twisted headlines in a decidedly anti-authoritarian fashion.[28] These works lacked the element of performance, however, unlike the Subway Drawings, which were openly created by the artist in front of an audience in order to emphasize not only the act of creation, but also his political, anarchic act against the system:

> It is impossible to separate the activity and the result. The act of creation itself is very clear and pure. But this creation immediately results in a "thing" that has a "value" that must be reckoned with. Even the subway drawings, which were quite obviously about the "act," not the "thing," are now turning up, having been "rescued" from destruction by would-be collectors. Possibly only the murals on cement walls that cannot be removed and the computer drawings, which can be rearranged at will, are free from these considerations.[29]

The removal of his drawings, their "rescue" from subway stations and platforms, inherently contrasted with Haring's intentions, and he discontinued the series in 1985.

Against the Oppression of the Individual

Haring considered himself to have been socialized in the 1960s: "Most of my political concerns and social concerns came from my life experiences. Partly being born in the late '50s and growing up in the '60s and sort of being around that counterculture but not being able to participate. Definitely being very affected by that and being of the age at the time when I [was] most impressionable, like seeing the Vietnam War on TV when I was ten years old, seeing race riots on television, and reading *Life* magazine."[30] Accordingly, the rebellion against the state and against de-individualization played an important role in his iconography.

The artist employed various signs, and he changed the meanings of them depending on their contextualization with other signs. For instance, the symbol of the dog takes on various manifestations. In a 1981 painting, two dogs with open mouths attack a graffiti sprayer (pl. 102). The composition is dramatized by splashes of red that stand for the gushing blood of the sprayer and for Haring's spray paint. The scene, like many of Haring's works, is set in complete two-dimensionality, as in the novel *Flatland: A Romance of Many Dimensions*, written in 1884 by the English clergyman and scholar Edwin A. Abbott. In the first chapter, the author encourages the reader to "imagine a vast sheet of paper on which straight Lines, Triangles, Squares, Pentagons, Hexagons, and other figures, instead of remaining fixed in their places, move freely about, on or in the surface, but without the power of rising above or sinking below it, very much like shadows—only hard with luminous edges—and you will then have a pretty correct notion of my country and countrymen."[31] Haring's figures live in Flatland, reduced to their simplest silhouettes, usually without distinct features, interchangeable and easily reproducible.

They are signs, or rather icons in the sense of the philosopher and logician Charles Sanders Peirce, creating immediate relations to the object through their structural similarity.[32] But in Haring's "sign language," the relationship of the icons to one another constitutes their meanings, which the artist uses to play with identifiable social codes. For example, the silhouette of the dog with the wide-open mouth, totally devoid of meaning in itself, can represent a barking, biting, or panting dog; it is only in combination with the falling human silhouette and the spray can that the context becomes intelligible. In other works, Haring's dog is depicted as a golden calf, or

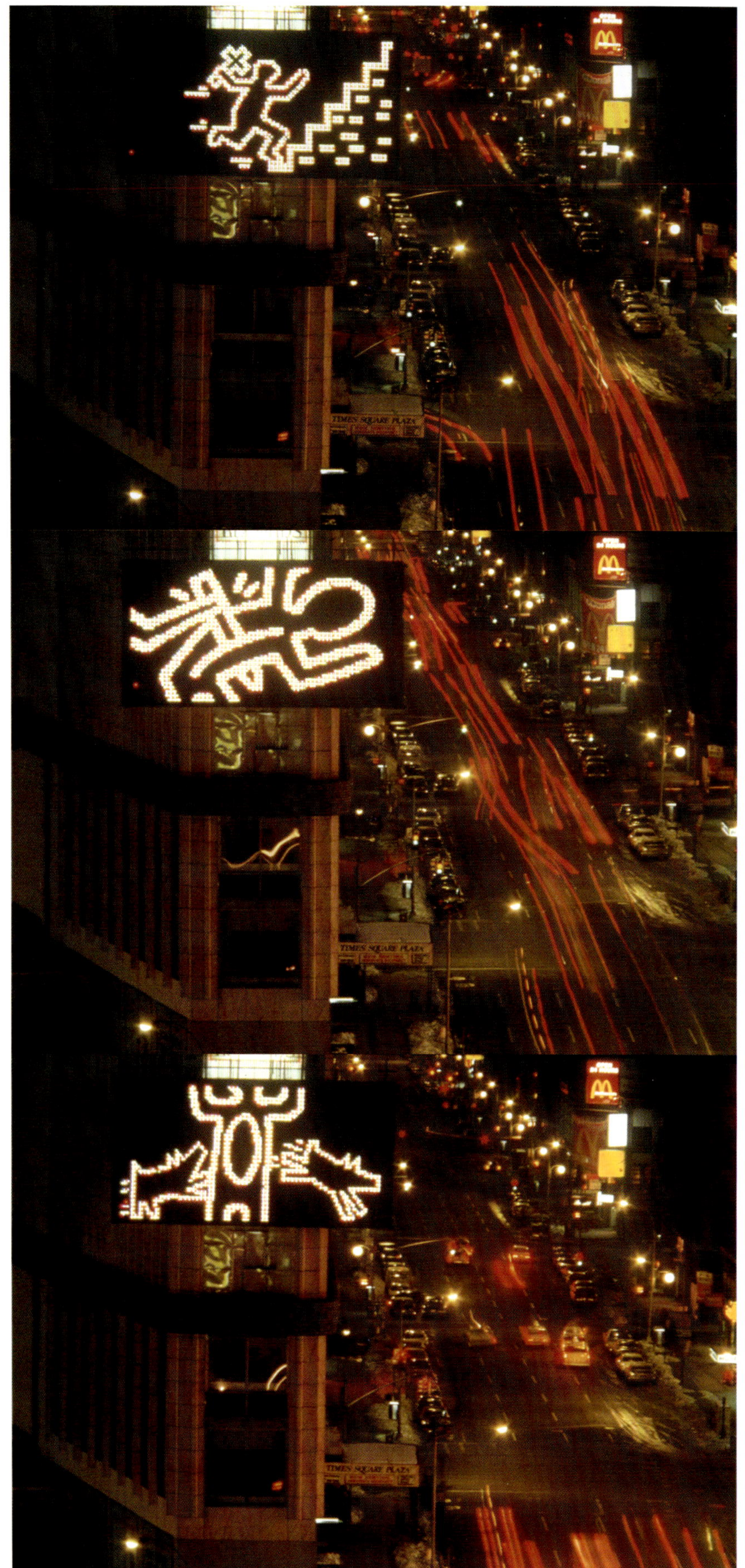

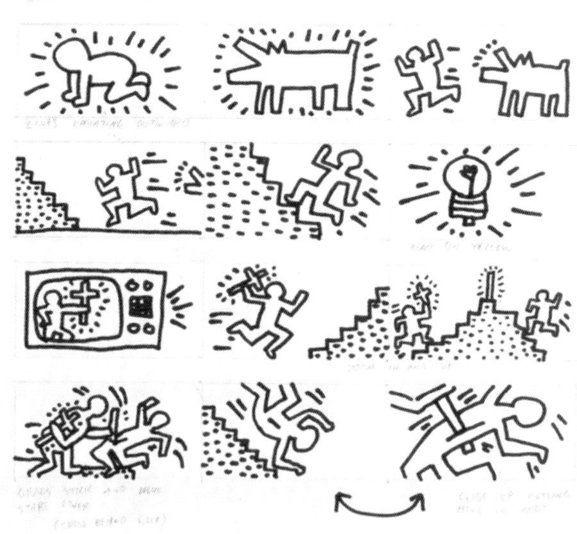

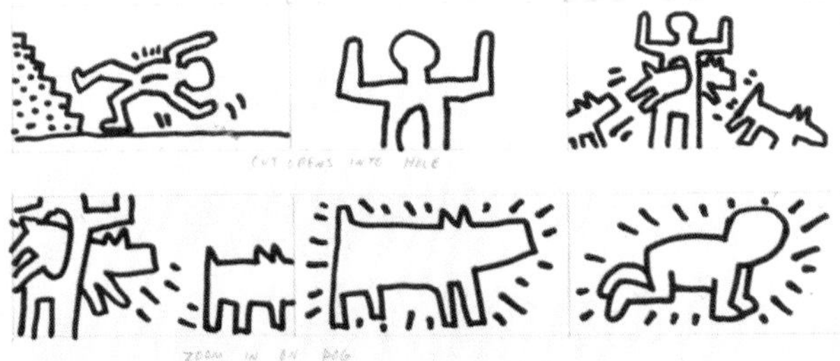

it is copulating with another dog or a human, or it is highlighted by the rays of a UFO. In one of Haring's first paintings on vinyl tarpaulins from 1982 (pl. 120), he drew a silhouette of a standing man with a large hole in his stomach, which serves as a hoop for dogs to jump through. The artist noted: "Actually, this image of the man with a hole in his stomach came after I heard of John Lennon's assassination. . . . I woke up the next morning with this image in my head . . . and I always associated that image with the death of John Lennon."[33] Haring was referring to the shooting of Lennon by Mark David Chapman in front of the Dakota building in New York City. Haring stretched the bullet hole into a gigantic opening, reminiscent of a detail in a comic strip, that can be interpreted as a ring by means of its red outline.

The theme is evident in *Times Square Spectacolor Billboard Animation* from 1982 (fig. 10; see also figs. 11–12), which begins with a radiant baby and a radiant dog followed by a barking dog chasing a man. The man tries to escape by running up a flight of stairs; a lightbulb lights up—a sudden inspiration—and a TV appears, showing a man with a cross in his hand. Another man with a cross in his hand, coming from the opposite direction, runs up the stairs. As the fleeing man and the man with the cross meet on a platform at the top of the stairs, the cross is hidden behind the one man's back and replaced by a stick that had been put on the platform. The fleeing man is stabbed with the stick and falls backward down the stairs, but he begins to float upward when he reaches the last step, as the small hole in his body expands to become the large ring-shaped hole that the dogs jump through on the artist's tarp. The animation ends with the radiant dog and baby.

The violent scene of the murder of the man running from the dog leads to the image on the tarp; the dogs that were chasing the man now jump through his body, penetrating it. The individual scenes are linked, although Haring continually gave them new meanings with subtle changes and new contexts. As with the icons, the individual scenes become signs, their meanings often revealed only in reciprocal interactions with other scenes, or they remain open to many different interpretations. The artist also depicted the scene on the tarp in another drawing, in which the dogs jump through the body of a man who holds a radiant stick in his hand, which may have been used against him or by him.

10 (opposite)

Keith Haring, *Times Square Spectacolor Billboard Animation*, 1982. Photographs by John Marchael

11–12 (above)

Keith Haring, *Times Square* storyboard, 1982. Ink on paper, each 14 x 17 in. (35.5 x 43.1 cm). Collection of the Keith Haring Foundation

In another cartoonlike series, this one on a yellow steel beam, dogs chase people (fig. 13); one of the dogs eventually transforms into a human being, who then stumbles and falls down. As in a movie, the scenes in this Flatland are connected and in motion, as are the standing, visibly amused dogs that kick, throw, and trample people as if in a danse macabre (pls. 106–107). In a 1983 painting, the dogs' heads morph into crocodile masks (pl. 115), and the dancing animals are revealed as gigantic, murderous henchmen, mercilessly crushing a group of people, mistreating ragdoll-like victims who appear to be chosen at random, evoking associations with the Holocaust and Nazis.

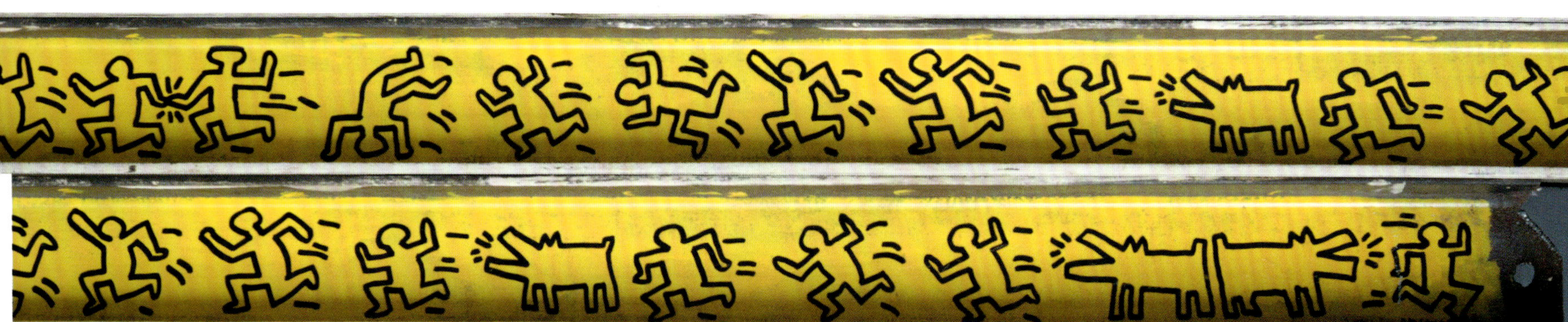

Yet it would be a mistake to believe that all these generic silhouettes of dogs and people in some way suggest the artist's pursuit of standardization: "It is important to the future existence of the human race that we understand the importance of the individual and the reality that we are all different, all individuals, all changing and all contributing to the 'whole' as individuals, *not* as groups or products of 'mass-identity,' 'anti-individual,' 'stereotyped' groups of humans with the same goals, ideas and needs."[34] Haring created easily legible icons of dogs and standing, walking, falling men to highlight our society's systematic attempts at de-individualization. His work invites the viewer, whether a random passerby or a visitor to an exhibition, to stand up against mass identities and stereotypes, to break authority's stick, as does the green-rimmed, red-silhouetted man on a tarp from 1982 (pl. 114). The stick that was used to threaten, beat, and kill people—to crush their skulls (pl. 17)—has to be broken, and the oppressors have to be confronted.

On another canvas, painted with white outlines on a black background (pl. 111), the individual is marked with a red cross, and hands from all corners of the composition pull him apart by his limbs. Haring joined the man in his scream: "I am me. I may look like you, but if you take a closer look you will realize that I am nothing like you at all. I am very different."[35] People are different and can be distinguished by their individualities. By using icons, Haring tried to provoke the power of our imagination and to encourage us to take the next step toward individuality. His art is not propaganda, but it celebrates the humanity in each of us.

The "Great White Way": Against Capitalism, Colonialism, and the Church

In his mathematical satire of the social hierarchy of Victorian culture, Edwin A. Abbott described a two-dimensional land in which life, reduced by one dimension, is lived on a flat plane. The bodies of the main characters—characters who are able to see, hear, and feel—are only contours, and so are their homes. Like the walls in our three-dimensional world, the closed contours are not penetrable, although, for the inhabitants of Flatland, homes are neither open nor closed. The question of a missing dimension arises only when the Sphere, a visitor from the three-dimensional Spaceland, causes a stir by pointing out that the Flatlanders' houses must be open because she is able to see their inside and outside at the same time. The Flatlanders' reliance on their traditions and their adherence to established social structures lead to the imprisonment of the character the Square, who tried to spread the news of his discoveries upon his return from a journey to the three-dimensional society.

The examination of uncritical, culturally imposed certainties is characteristic of Haring's work. He trod a fine line between cultures, emphasizing diversity, the inconsistencies of history, and a world filled with racism and oppression. As he noted in 1987: "Most of the evil in the world is done in the name of good (religion, false prophet, bullshit artists, politicians, *businessmen*). The whole concept of 'business' is evil. Most white men are evil. The white man has always used religion as the tool to fulfill his greed and power-hungry aggression. Business is only another name for control. Control of mind, body, and spirit. Control is evil."[36] In 1988, he created *The Great White Way* (pl. 143), a large pink canvas penis. Adorned with the symbols of the cross, the dollar, a cut diamond, and a crown, the penis "climaxes" in an orgy of oppression, deprivation of liberty, and murder.

13

Keith Haring, *Untitled* (*Beam*) (detail), 1982. Marker on metal, 7 x 240 x 6½ in. (17.8 x 609.6 x 16.5 cm). Collection of Larry Warsh

For Haring, the "evil white man" and his symbols stand for exploitation, oppression, poverty, and slavery.

In 1981, he drew a reclining African American man masturbating on a speech bubble spelling out USA; opposite, he placed a "superman" behind a wild crowd of people, surrounded by symbols of power: the dollar sign, the cross, the letters USA, and a five-pointed star inside a circle, the latter being interpreted as, among other things, a Freemason emblem, an occult symbol of protection, and the red star of Communism (if drawn without the circle). In a 1985 painting (pl. 153), the star clearly becomes that red star, on a tank functioning as the head of a muscular man with an erect penis who is burning dollar bills. On the right side, Haring labeled the painting *USA 85*, linking it to a series of drawings and paintings he named with the years of their creations, his personal "State of the Union."

Haring's artistic revenge against capitalism and consumer society was widespread and dramatic. A monster pig on a large-format canvas (pl. 159) spews a green stream of products that drown a group of people, seen only as eyes and noses. Those escaping the stream suck on the pig's teats, drinking its capitalist milk: the perfect cycle of consumption. In a 1988 tondo (pl. 158), the artist further accentuated the theme, painting a frontal view of the pig, with dollar signs on its nose, bloodshot yellow eyes, and decaying yellow teeth, devouring people. And yet, as a successful, well-paid artist, Keith Haring had an ambivalent relationship with money: "Money itself is not evil, in fact it can actually be very effective for good if it is used properly and not taken seriously. You have to be objective about money to use it fairly. It doesn't make you any better or more useful than any other person. Even if you use your money to help people . . . that doesn't make you better than somebody who has no money but is sympathetic and genuinely loving to fellow humans." [37]

A similar ambivalence is reflected in his Andy Mouse paintings, combined portraits of Mickey Mouse and Andy Warhol. On the one hand, Andy Warhol was a friend and a great artistic model for Haring: "Andy's life and work made my work possible. . . . I honestly think he was the most important artist since Picasso." [38] On the other hand, Warhol was the perfect embodiment of the artist as businessman. As Warhol stated, "Being a good businessman is the most fascinating form of art. Making money is art, working is art, and good business is the best art." [39] Warhol multiplied dollar bills in some compositions as representations of money, allowing the images to speak as objects without any illusions. He broke down all boundaries between business and art, adopting principles of industrial society and calling his studio the Factory, thereby identifying his art, created with the help of assistants, with mass production. But whether Warhol meant to glorify consumer products as icons of modernity in an affirmation of capitalism or whether he intended to transmit an ironic message about the portrayed versus the experienced world of consumption is an argument that continues to this day. Since Warhol's death in 1987, his image as a star artist is more and more understood as a mask that, like his silkscreen prints, mirrors the mechanisms of modern capitalist consumer society. Nevertheless, a likely deliberate critical ambivalence about Warhol's oeuvre remains, leaving unanswered the question of whether the artist truly wanted to criticize the system or sharpen viewers' perceptions of the consumer and media landscapes that dominate our society.

In *Andy Mouse—New Coke*, from 1985 (pl. 155), the black outline of Andy Mouse is drawn on a red background alongside sketches of Mickey Mouse's face in different stages of completion; all are superimposed over the white letters "NEW! Coke® / 354ml / 12FLOZ," with yellow dollar signs indicating the key currency of capitalism. The work can be interpreted in two ways: as a critique of capitalism, with Andy Mouse as the businessman supporting the exploitation carried out by large corporations, or as a tribute to Warhol, who, like a virus, undermined the system of the "white man." As Haring remarked about Warhol, "He challenged the whole commodity-oriented direction of the Art world by beating them at their own game." [40]

Haring, LA II, and an Attack on the Culture of the "Great White Way"

Haring's rejection of the so-called Great White Way is also revealed in his collaboration with LA II, or Little Angel II, a.k.a. Angel Ortiz. [41] The relationship began in 1981, after Haring had seen LA II's "graffiti signiture": "It stood out because it was absolutely perfect and beautiful." [42] LA II was fourteen years old at the time and by no means an established artist, "this kid whose tags Keith went crazy about." [43] Together they designed tarps and collaborated on signs (see pl. 84), murals, many three-dimensional objects, including a shelf (see pl. 99), and many fiberglass sculptures, such as *Statue of Liberty* (pl. 85). Shrunk to roughly human size, the Statue of Liberty was painted in a Pop color scheme and then covered with symbols and tags by both artists. *The* American symbol of freedom and independence was thus defiled with sharp colors and graffiti tags as a political act.

Haring and LA II also selected for their fiberglass sculptures an Egyptian sarcophagus (pl. 89); classical pillars with capitals (see pl. 100); vases (see pl. 86); the Little Mermaid, the iconic symbol of Copenhagen; Venus from Botticelli's *Birth of Venus*; and garden-gnome Smurfs. All are signs, the latter mostly ironic, of Western cultural development, in particular of the Great White Way. Haring remarked: "This irony is even more apparent in the plaster sculptures I did with L.A. 2. . . . We began combining our two styles to create an overall surface of intermingling lines. All of the work we have done is about 'surface' and usually covers and transforms an object it is applied to."[44] They transformed cultural symbols, using different materials and scales, into Pop objects of our consumer society, with no respect for their cultural and political implications. Quite the opposite: Haring's merciless settling of the score with the white man and the oppression of the individual was taken even further when it was combined with LA II's graffiti.

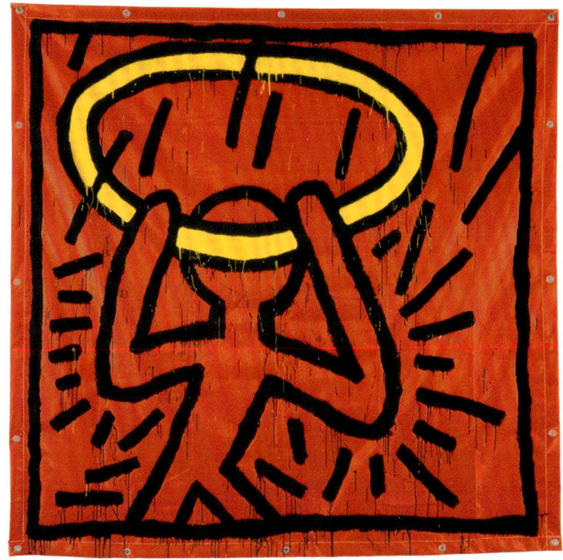

"Protect Me from What I Want"

Haring's critical argument was characterized by his rejection of fundamentalism and the role of the church in the oppression of the population, whereby he also rejected generalizing answers: "You can only help and encourage people to live for themselves. The most evil people are the people who pretend to have answers. The fundamentalist Christians, all dogmatic 'control religions,' are evil. The original ideas are good. But they are so convoluted and changed that only a skeleton of good intentions is left."[45] As early as *Times Square Spectacolor Billboard Animation*, the man with the cross had murdered the fugitive. In a drawing labeled *USA 1981* in its upper left-hand corner, two figures cut the penis off a man hanging by his feet, while two large arrows coming from the lower corners of the composition point at the savage scene (pl. 104).

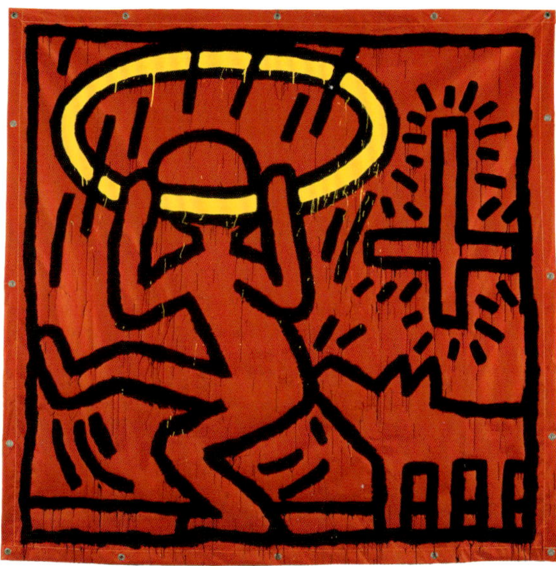

An early comic drawing on three tarps from 1982 lends insight into Haring's views of religion (figs. 14–16 and pls. 147–148). In the first composition, a figure appears to catch a glowing yellow ring, similar to a halo; in the next scene, an inverted radiant cross and a dog are added; and in the final tableau, the human figure holds the cross in its hand, activating the ring that then imprisons the figure. The dog seems to look up in front of the powerful cross and ring. In a 1983 tarp, Haring became more specific: an anthropomorphic monster appears to crush a cross-bearing person with its tongue, perhaps implying that ideology means death to the individual. This reading is supported by Haring's collaboration with Jenny Holzer on a 1986 offset poster for a public art project in Vienna. Over a drooling, slobbering mask with menacing teeth and eyes, Haring drew a cross, while Holzer added, "Protect Me from What I Want." The poster seems to be a call for help to escape religion's ideological trap. The bodies impaled on crosses in *The Great White Way* and other works speak an even clearer visual language.

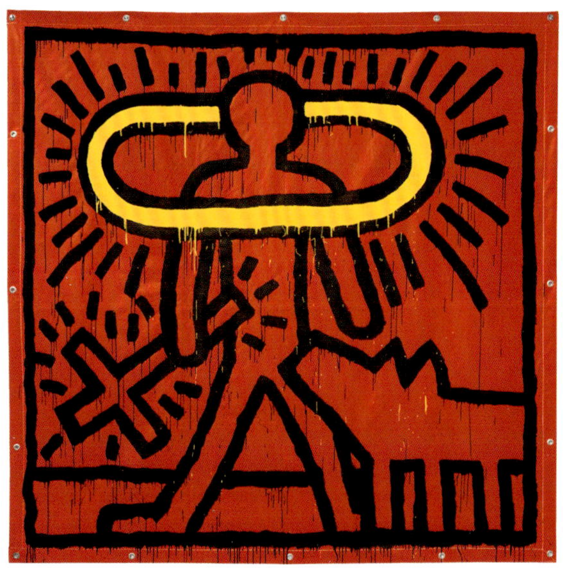

Haring elaborated on these thoughts in a 1985 canvas tarp (pl. 151) on which a humanoid pig-monster

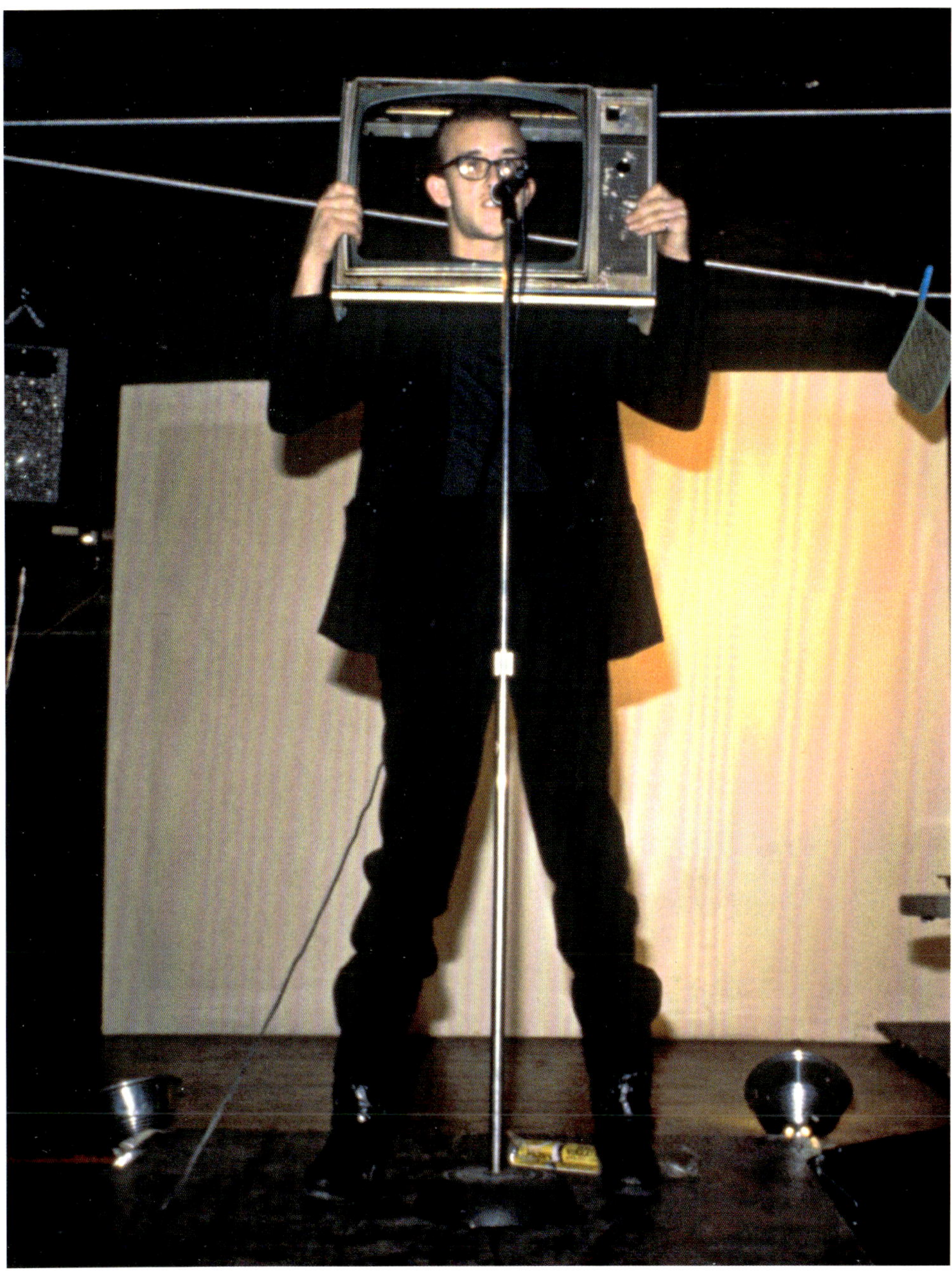

dominates the scene. Its snout is chained and, through a TV and its backside, it appears to speak with realistically drawn mouths, while it holds in its hands a burning Bible (identifiable by a cross) that births wriggling snakes like those associated with Medusa. In the lower left corner lies a brain with a cross stuck in it. Long, sharp tongues shoot out of the monster's two orifices, piercing a man throwing money and snatching the money, and cutting off his penis with a pair of scissors. Here Haring clearly referenced televangelism and the church's ambivalent relationship with money while he issued a warning of the dangers of dogmatic ideologies.

Despite his rejection of dogmatic "control religion," the artist was well aware of the importance of faith for many people: "People need this 'belief' to explain and justify their existence. The different facets (or faces) of religion are different only because people are committed to the idea of 'different' cultures and different 'nationalistic values.' The common denominator is always the same. Whether voodoo or Buddhism it all comes down to the same thing, really."[46]

Fear of Machines and Computers in an Age of Mass Communication

Haring understood the significance of mass communication. In his early works, he experimented with video. In 1978, he extolled video as "a medium capable of reaching higher levels of communication—more involved than painting / sculpture."[47] He appreciated the possibility of easily spreading his ideas through video and other media but remained wary of their manipulative qualities. When he framed his head with a television during a performance at Club 57 in June 1980 (fig. 17), he was already referencing the impending replacement of our reality by technology. His aversion toward then-emerging computer technologies was unmistakable: "The silicon computer chip has become the new life form. Eventually the only worth of man will be to service and serve the computer. Are we there? In a lot of ways we are."[48]

He understood new technologies not only as competition, but also as a threat to creativity and individuality: "The artist of this time is creating under a constant realization that he is being pursued by the computers. We are threatened. Our existence, our individuality, our creativity, our lives are threatened by this coming machine aesthetics. It is going to be up to us to establish a lasting position of the arts in our daily lives, in human existence."[49] Computers replace the heads of murderous monsters in a 1984 tarp (pl. 167), on which even a brain is depicted as an on-screen representation. In a large-format tarp from 1983 (pl. 136), the machine becomes an overwhelming menace to humanity.

14 (opposite, top)

Keith Haring, *Untitled*, 1982. Vinyl paint on vinyl tarpaulin, 84 x 84 in. (213.4 x 213.4 cm). Private collection

15 (opposite, middle)

Keith Haring, *Untitled*, 1982. Vinyl paint on vinyl tarpaulin, 84 x 84 in. (213.4 x 213.4 cm). Private collection

16 (opposite, bottom)

Keith Haring, *Untitled*, 1982. Vinyl paint on vinyl tarpaulin, 84 x 84 in. (213.4 x 213.4 cm). Private collection

17 (above)

Acts of Live Art, Club 57, New York, June 1980. Photograph by Joseph Szkodzinski

In the spirit of James Cameron's 1984 science fiction action movie *The Terminator*, in which Arnold Schwarzenegger plays a cyborg assassin sent back in time to kill a human, Haring was driven by the fear that machines could be the end of humanity, but he saw the best defense strategy in art: "This is for me the question that will decide my position in the arts. In life . . . how do we help the human race to realize its predicament? And if you do not see it as a predicament, how do you help to prepare humankind for the reality of a machine-aesthetic world? Am I a comrade to the computer or to the entire history of humanity? The history of art rests on our shoulders."[50] Not surprisingly, instead of using television to communicate, Haring favored the personal acts of creating his countless Subway Drawings, handing out posters, performing in public, and finally establishing his Pop Shop to distribute his art to a wider public. How he would have felt about the Pop Shop on the Internet remains open to debate.

Haring's Fight against Racism and Apartheid

In his fight against racism and discrimination, in his life and in his art, Haring tried to draw attention to his rejection of the "evil white man": "All stories of white men's 'expansion' and 'colonization' and 'domination' are filled with horrific details of the abuse of power and the misuse of people. / I'm sure inside I'm not white. . . . I'm glad I'm different. I'm proud to be gay. I'm proud to have friends and lovers of every color. I am ashamed of my forefathers. I am *not* like them."[51] He rejected his white heritage and opposed the history of his ancestors.

Haring was deeply shocked by the murder of the African American graffiti artist Michael Stewart by transit police, and he demanded "an eye for an eye" in retaliation.[52] Two years later, in 1985, he processed the incident in *Michael Stewart—USA for Africa* (pl. 145). The monumental canvas shows Stewart being brutally strangled by white hands, his foot crushed by a white foot, with a dollar/hand and crosses positioned menacingly nearby. In the upper right corner, the planet is broken open and an enormous stream of blood pours out, appearing to drown all the people in the world. In this work, the Apocalypse has arrived.

Haring also positioned himself against the apartheid system in South Africa (see fig. 18). In one of a series of works (pl. 142), an oversized black figure, held on a leash by a smaller white figure, steps on his oppressor, seemingly in an act of liberation. Haring used the subject for a poster he distributed in public. In other versions of the work, the leash turns into a snake and becomes a symbol of oppression that eats the white man.

In *Prophets of Rage* (pl. 144), the oppressed black figure has broken the chains, seized a crown, hung the white man by his feet, and decapitated him. Haring's deep concern about racism and violence finds its final expression in the bloody demise of the oppressor.

Apocalypse: Ecocide, the Cold War, and the End of Humanity

Inspired by the 1972 publication of *The Limits to Growth,* by Donella H. Meadows, Dennis L. Meadows, Jørgen Randers, and William W. Behrens,[53] and the growing impact of the ecological movement in the early 1980s, Haring became dedicated to the fight against new technologies and against the threat of humanity's extinction through environmental pollution and the nuclear menace of the Cold War. He unfailingly considered art to be "the way we define our existence as human beings," and he made it everyone's responsibility: "We know that 'humans' determine the future of this planet. We have the power to destroy and create. We, after all is said and done, are the perpetrators of the destruction of the Earth we inhabit."[54] His outlook was pessimistic, even though he considered humanity's impending self-destruction a choice: "The destruction of this planet, this solar system, by human beings would not be an end to life. It would go on without us. / We have a choice, whether we wish to continue evolution on this planet or not. / I vote 'yes.'"[55]

On June 12, 1982, Haring attended a large antinuclear rally,[56] where he distributed more than twenty thousand posters (fig. 5), whose production he had paid for himself, with the help of his friends. The lower half of the poster's image depicts the beginning of a war, represented by two figures with large sticks walking toward each other; the upper half is dedicated to the all-destroying explosion of a nuclear bomb. Haring also incorporated a mushroom cloud into a series of other works, including a black tarp from 1982 (pl. 131), on which he reduced the lower scene to two dogs flanking the explosion and depicted red crosses, indicating targets, all over the composition. His visit to the Hiroshima Peace Memorial Museum on July 28, 1988, brought home to him the impact of a nuclear attack: "It is incredible that this destruction was caused by a bomb that was made in 1945, and that the level of sophistication and number of nuclear warheads has increased since then. Who could ever want this to happen again? To anyone? The frightening thing is that people debate and discuss the arms race as if they were playing with toys. All of these men

18

Keith Haring distributing "Free South Africa" posters, Central Park, New York, June 1986. Photograph by Tseng Kwong Chi

19

Keith Haring, *Safe Sex*, 1985. Acrylic on canvas, 120 x 120 in. (304.8 x 304.8 cm). Collection of the Keith Haring Foundation

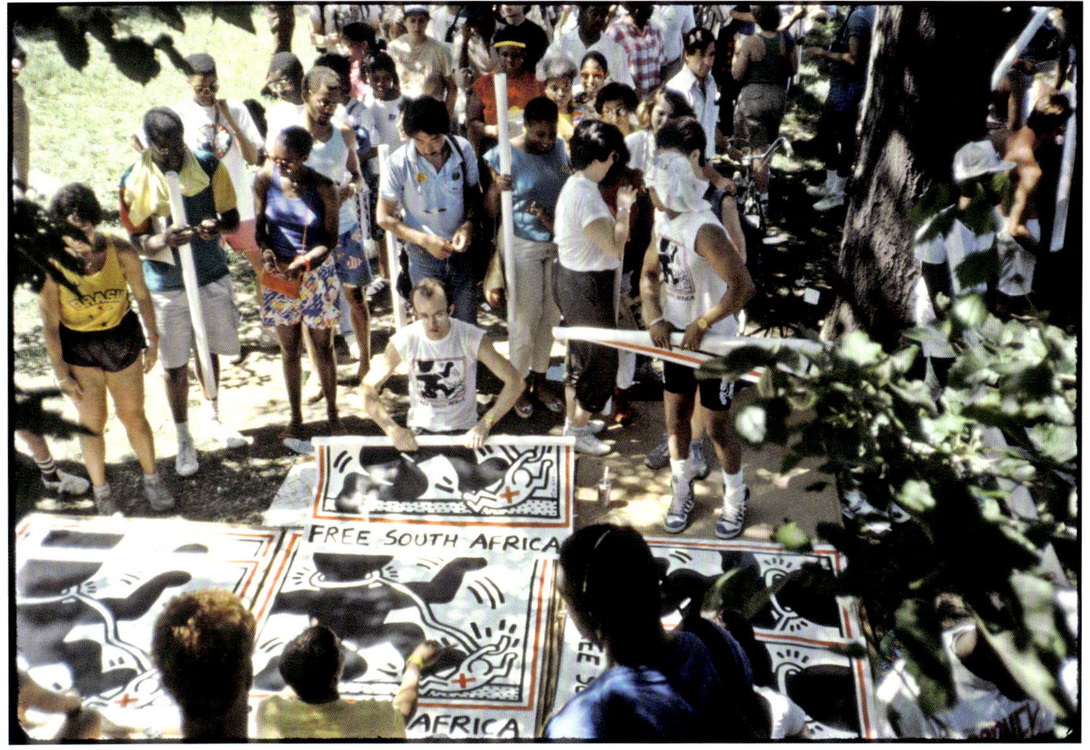

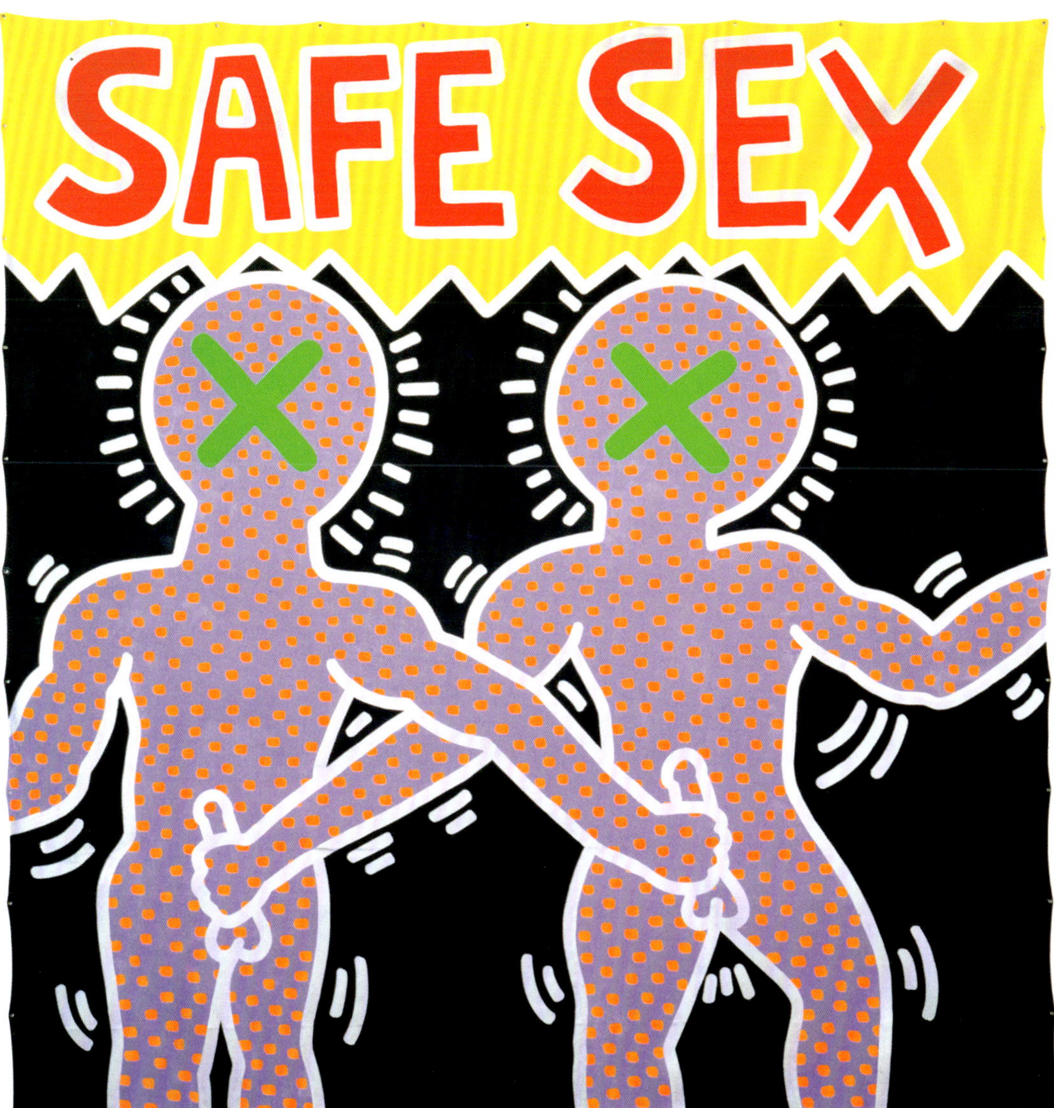

should have to come here, not to a bargaining table in some safe European country."[57]

In an untitled work from 1984, the tongue of Death, mutated into a snake, hunts its prey in front of an apocalyptic orange-red mushroom cloud towering over what appears to be an endless stream of people. In another untitled work (pl. 173), masses of people spring from a wound in a white man's foot, while planet Earth, spiked on a spear, bleeds. The masses are compressed and locked together to form an ornamental design in *Brazil* (pl. 174), and are eventually obliterated in *Unfinished Painting*. In *The Last Rainforest* (pl. 172), reminiscent of Hieronymus Bosch's work, Haring translated demons and mythical creatures into his iconography. The complex scenery leaves little hope of saving the "last" rainforest, the symbol of an untouched, primordial nature and diversity. Nevertheless, on January 27, 1990, three weeks before his death, Haring—with sumi ink on a brush—wrote about his series of drawings titled *Against All Odds* (pls. 175–194), created the previous October: "These drawings are about the Earth we inherited and the dismal task of trying to save it—against all odds."[58] He described how he had been listening to Marvin Gaye's pessimistic record *What's Going On* for two hours. Gaye's invitation in the song "Save the Children"—to "save a world that is destined to die"—resonated with Haring.

AIDS: From Sex to Death

"SAFE SEX," Haring wrote in 1985 above two monumental silhouettes holding each other's penises (fig. 19). This invitation and warning to practice safe sex was made three years before he was diagnosed with HIV. His battle against AIDS became a personal war and an artistic cause, too. Haring had suspected he was infected for some time, as he, perhaps, revealed in a 1985 self-portrait (pl. 205), in which he covered his face with red spots as a sign of contagion. Looking back, he stated: "During most of the time when the virus was being spread in the late '70s and early '80s in New York, there were all kind[s] of promiscuous activities in every corner of the city, in which I was very much a part. So after my ex-lover became sick, it became apparent that I was eventually becoming sick, and people that I had already had sex with had already died. I was living as if it was a reality."[59] In a series of works from 1985, after some of his friends had already succumbed to AIDS, he approached the subject head-on. On a yellow canvas (fig. 20), he drew a man surrounded by flying skulls and corpses, carrying a small sign with a red cross around his neck. The body of the man is portrayed in a state of disintegration, creating a picture of the disease's horror.

After his diagnosis, he personified the virus as a monstrous sperm hatching from an egg on a black background; he used a fine double contour, so that the line itself was filled with black, a symbolic representation of the deadly danger (pl. 197). On May 5, 1989, he completed the black-and-white diptych *Untitled (for James Ensor)* (pl. 198). On the canvas labeled "1," a skeleton urinates on a small patch of flowers; on the canvas "2," the skeleton reaches for the more fully grown flowers, indicating, perhaps, that life goes on without the artist, and also without humanity.

In his last painting (pl. 206), Haring depicted a jubilant crowd ready to fight against oppression, suffering, death, and downfall. For him, the battle ended on February 16, 1990. He single-handedly continued his line from his first to his last works of art. "All the drawings generate from what happens in the first drawing. I just 'let' it happen. Each drawing builds on the previous drawings and advances the 'story.'"[60]

Haring's lines remain finished and unfinished. His political line also seems to be never-ending. His battle against drugs and AIDS, his commitment to a better, fairer world, and his desire to paint in the public spaces of New York, Paris, and Tokyo—and even on the Berlin Wall—were expressed in his works and in signs that have become a part of our everyday speech. His "urban guerrilla art" remains in our collective consciousness,[61] as does the Pop Shop. Leo Castelli rightly noted about the Pop Shop: "I don't think that this is commercial at all. If he opens a store as he did, that is part of his art. The store itself is a work of art."[62] If Haring had opened his Pop Shop at the Documenta13 in 2012, nobody would have missed the political context—that is how modern Haring was in his appreciation of humanism and in his refusal to remain silent because "IGNORANCE = FEAR" and "SILENCE = DEATH."[63]

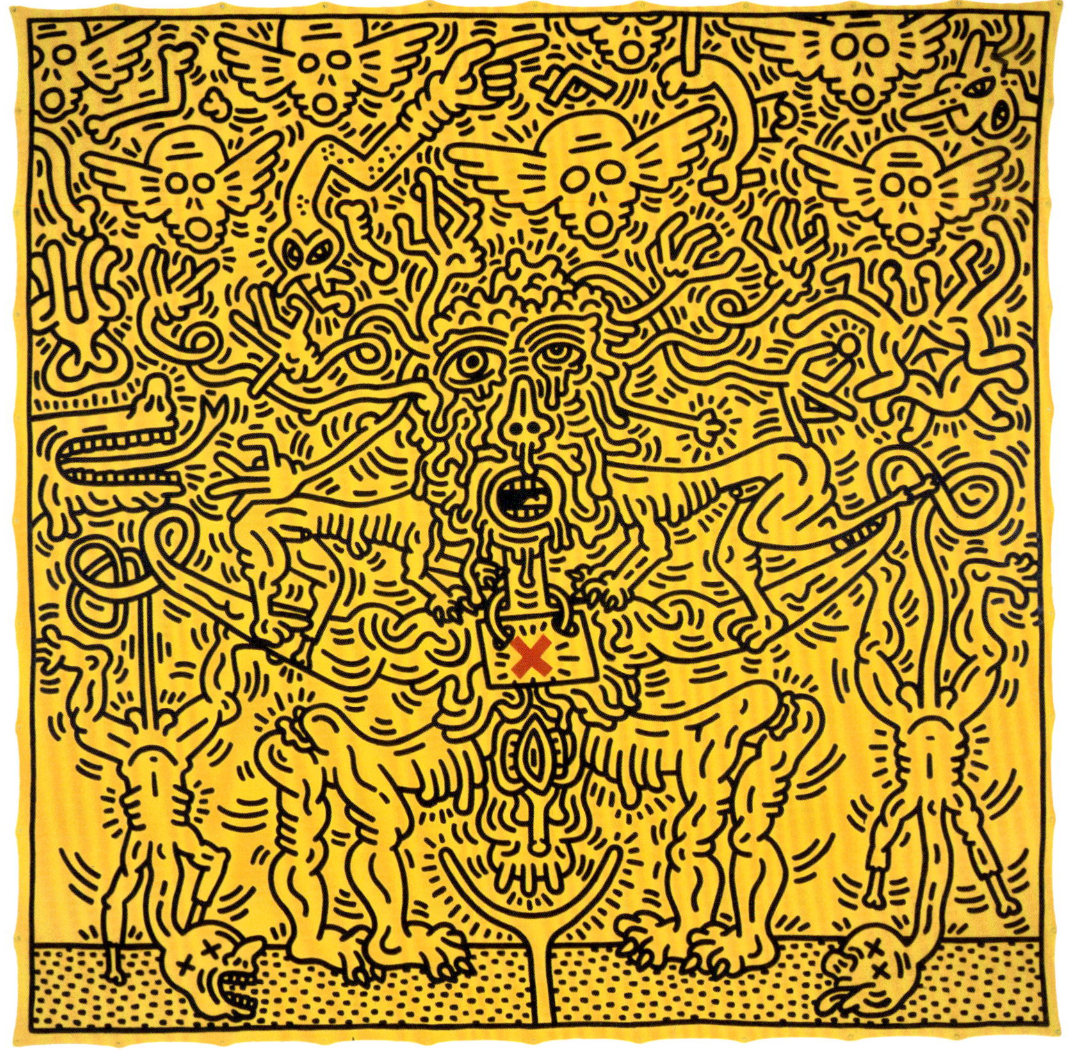

20 (previous page)

Keith Haring, *Untitled*, 1985. Acrylic and enamel on canvas, 20 x 120 in. (304.8 x 304.8 cm). Ludwig Forum für Internationale Kunst, Aachen, Germany

Notes

1. William S. Burroughs on Keith Haring in John Gruen, *Keith Haring: The Authorized Biography* (New York: Prentice Hall, 1991), 183–184.
2. The virtual Pop Shop is found at www.pop-shop.com.
3. Elisabeth Sussman, "Songs of Innocence at the Nuclear Pyre," in Elisabeth Sussman et al., *Keith Haring*, exh. cat., Whitney Museum of American Art, June 25–September 21, 1997 (New York: Whitney Museum of American Art; Boston: Bulfinch/Little, Brown, 1997), 24.
4. See Gianni Mercurio, ed., *The Keith Haring Show*, exh. cat., La Triennale di Milano, September 27, 2005–January 29, 2006 (Milan: Skira, 2005); Gianni Mercurio, ed., *Keith Haring*, exh. cat., Musée d'art contemporain de Lyon, France, February 22–June 29, 2008 (Milan: Skira, 2008); Jean-Gabriel Mitterand, *Keith Haring*, exh. cat., Dexia Banque International à Luxembourg, June 5–September 15, 2007 (Turin, Italy: Skira, 2007).
5. Götz Adriani, ed., *Keith Haring: Heaven and Hell*, exh. cat., Museum für Neue Kunst, ZKM Karlsruhe, Germany, September 23, 2001–January 6, 2002; Museum Boijmans Van Beuningen, Rotterdam, the Netherlands, May 10–July 21, 2002 (Ostfildern, Germany: Hatje Cantz Verlag, 2002).
6. Raphaela Platow, ed., *Keith Haring: 1978–1982*, 2nd ed., exh. cat., Kunsthalle Vienna, May 28–September 19, 2010; Contemporary Arts Center, Lois and Richard Rosenthal Center for Contemporary Art, Cincinnati, Ohio, February 26–September 5, 2011; Brooklyn Museum of Art, New York, March 16–July 8, 2012 (Nuremberg, Germany: Moderne Kunst Nürnberg, 2011).
7. Sussman, "Songs of Innocence at the Nuclear Pyre," 24.
8. Werner Spies, ed., *Picasso. Malen gegen die Zeit* [*Painting against Time*], exh. cat., Albertina, Vienna, September 21, 2006–January 7, 2007; K20 Kunstsammlung Nordrhein-Westfalen, Düsseldorf, Germany, February 3–May 28, 2007 (Ostfildern, Germany: Hatje Cantz Verlag, 2006).
9. Brassaï, *Gespräche mit Picasso* [*Conversations with Picasso*] (Reinbek bei Hamburg, Germany: Rowohlt Taschenbuch Verlag, 1966), 137.
10. See collector and art historian Douglas Cooper's review, after the artist's death, of Picasso's late works, *Connaissance des arts* 257 (July 1973): 23.
11. Sussman, "Songs of Innocence at the Nuclear Pyre," 24.
12. Keith Haring, *Keith Haring Journals* (New York: Penguin Classics deluxe ed., 2010), xiii.
13. The drawing is taken from a sketchbook containing drawings made in Pittsburgh and New York. I am grateful to Julia Gruen at the Keith Haring Foundation for this insightful information. The drawing is reproduced in *Keith Haring, Sketchbooks*, exh. cat., Gladstone Gallery, May 4–July 1, 2011 (New York: Gladstone Gallery, 2011).
14. For Claude Picasso on Keith Haring, see Gruen, *Keith Haring: The Authorized Biography*, 175.
15. Giorgio Vasari discussed the conflict between *disegno* and *colore* in the sixteenth century, which led to fierce disputes. See Giorgio Vasari, *The Lives of the Artists*, Oxford World Classics, trans. Julia Conway Bondanella and Peter Bondanella (Oxford and New York: Oxford University Press, 2008); Steffi Roettgen, "Venedig oder Rom—Disegno e Colore. Ein Topos der Kunstkritik und seine Folgen" ["Venice or Rome—Line or Color: A Topos of Art Criticism and Its Consequences"], *Zeitenblicke* 2, no. 3 (2003).
16. For more on Haring's conflict between painting and drawing, see Ulrike Gehring, "*Disegno e Colore*: The Reconciliation of Two Rivals in the Art of Keith Haring," in Adriani, ed., *Keith Haring: Heaven and Hell*, 134–147. For more on Picasso, see Spies, ed., *Picasso. Malen gegen die Zeit*, 37–38.
17. Sussman, "Songs of Innocence at the Nuclear Pyre," 12.
18. Haring quoted in Germano Celant, ed., *Keith Haring* (Munich: Prestel Verlag, 1992), 116.
19. It is unknown how many Subway Drawings Haring produced; the estimate of between five thousand and ten thousand appears realistic and is derived from the fifteen thousand photographs taken by Tseng Kwong Chi (some drawings appear in two or three images). I am grateful to Julia Gruen for this information.
20. Haring quoted in Jason Rubell, "Keith Haring: The Last Interview," *Arts Magazine* (September 1990): 59. Haring was arrested on multiple occasions, although the actual number of arrests is not known. I am grateful to Julia Gruen for this information.
21. Cf. Haring's statements in Elisabeth Aubert, prod. and dir., *Drawing the Line: A Portrait of Keith Haring* (West Long Branch, NJ: Kultur, 1989), documentary film, 30 min.
22. Haring's statement in ibid.
23. Ibid.; Gina Belafonte was the narrator of Aubert's documentary.
24. Haring, *Keith Haring Journals*, 17.
25. Cf. Sussman, "Songs of Innocence at the Nuclear Pyre," 12.
26. Haring quoted in "Keith Haring: Cut-Up Street Works, 1980," in Jeffrey Deitch et al., *Keith Haring* (New York: Rizzoli, 2008), 52.
27. Ibid., 53.
28. For more on public-space projects in 1980, see ibid.; and Sussman, "Songs of Innocence at the Nuclear Pyre," 12–14.
29. Haring, *Keith Haring Journals*, 210–211.
30. Haring's statement in Aubert, *Drawing the Line*.
31. Edwin A. Abbott, *Flatland: A Romance of Many Dimensions, with Illustrations by the Author, A SQUARE* (Boston: Little, Brown, 1899 [1884]), 5.
32. Charles S. Peirce, *Semiotische Schriften* [*Semiotic Writings*], vol. 1, 1865–1903, ed. Christian J. W. Kloesel and Helmut Pape (Frankfurt am Main, Germany: Suhrkamp taschenbuch wissenschaft, 2000), 205–206.
33. Haring quoted in Gruen, *Keith Haring: The Authorized Biography*, 69–70.
34. Haring, *Keith Haring Journals*, 16.
35. Ibid.
36. Ibid., 164.
37. Ibid., 134.
38. Ibid., 154–155.
39. Andy Warhol quoted in Paolo Bianchi, Christoph Doswald, and Claudio Gallio, *Andy Warhol—Joseph Beuys. Gegenspieler* [*Antagonists*] (Frankfurt am Main, Germany: Fischer Taschenbuch Verlag, 2000), 13.
40. Haring, *Keith Haring Journals*, 154–155.
41. "The Great White Way" is a nickname for the length of Broadway between 42nd and 53rd Streets in New York City, including the Broadway Theater District and Times Square. In 1880, Broadway between Union Square and Madison Square was one of the first electrically lighted streets in the United States. By the 1890s, the blocks between 23rd and 34th Streets were so brightly lit by advertising signs that the nickname was coined, and it was carried over to the Times Square area after the theater district moved uptown.
42. Haring quoted in Gruen, *Keith Haring: The Authorized Biography*, 80.
43. See Fab Five Freddy on Keith Haring in ibid., 67.
44. Haring, *Keith Haring Journals*, 115.
45. Ibid., 164.
46. Ibid., 129–130.
47. Haring quoted in Synne Genzmer, "Performing the Signal: On Keith Haring's Video Works," in Platow, ed., *Keith Haring: 1978–1982*, 123.
48. Haring, *Keith Haring Journals*, 23.
49. Ibid., 24.
50. Ibid., 26.
51. Ibid., 164–165.
52. In ibid. (165–166), Haring declared: "Today I read in the *New York Times* that all of the officers who killed Michael Stewart were again dismissed of charges. Continually dismissed, but in their minds they will never forget. They know they killed him. They will never forget his screams, his face, his blood. They must live with that forever. I hope in their next life they are tortured like they tortured him. They should be birds captured early in life, put in cages, purchased by a fat, smelly, ugly lady who keeps them in a small dirty cage up near the ceiling while all day she cooks bloody sausage and the blood splatters their cage and the frying fat burns their matted feathers and they can never escape the horrible fumes of her burnt meat. One day the cage will fall to the ground and a big fat ugly cat will kick them about, play with them like a toy, and slowly *kill* them and leave their remains to be accidentally stepped on by the big fat lady who can't see her own feet because of her huge sagging tits. An eye for an eye. . . . I'm not afraid of anything I'd ever done. Not ashamed of anything."
53. Donella H. Meadows et al., *The Limits to Growth* (Post Mills, VT: Chelsea Green Publishing Co., 1972).
54. Haring, *Keith Haring Journals*, 129.
55. Ibid., 26–27.
56. "Antinuclear Rally, 1982," in Deitch et al., *Keith Haring*, 228.
57. Haring, *Keith Haring Journals*, 295–296.
58. Keith Haring, *Against All Odds, 20 Drawings—Oct. 3, 1989* (Rotterdam, the Netherlands: Bébert Publishing House, 1990), s.p.
59. Haring quoted in "Diagnosed with HIV, 1988," in Deitch et al., *Keith Haring*, 444.
60. Haring, *Against All Odds*.
61. Sussman, "Songs of Innocence at the Nuclear Pyre," 14.
62. Castelli's statement in Aubert, *Drawing the Line*.
63. The 1989 poster *Ignorance=Fear* is illustrated in Marc Gundel, *Keith Haring: Short Message: Posters 1982–1990* (Munich: Prestel Verlag, 2002), cat. 79, pl. 57.

A Note to the Reader

The exhibition and catalogue *Keith Haring: The Political Line* is organized according to the social and political issues that Keith Haring explored in his art. The plate section of this catalogue follows the themes described in my essay:

1. Early Works and Storyboards: pls. 1–36
2. The Endless Political Line in Public Spaces: pls. 37–83
3. Haring, LA II, and an Attack on the Culture of the "Great White Way": pls. 84–86 and 89
4. Against the Oppression of the Individual: pls. 87–129
5. Fear of Machines and Computers in an Age of Mass Communication: pls. 134–140
6. Haring's Fight against Racism and Apartheid: pls. 141–145
7. "Protect Me from What I Want": pls. 146–152
8. The "Great White Way": Against Capitalism, Colonialism, and the Church: pls. 143 and 153–163
9. Apocalypse: Ecocide, the Cold War, and the End of Humanity: pls. 130–133 and 164–194
10. AIDS: From Sex to Death: pls. 195–206

—DB

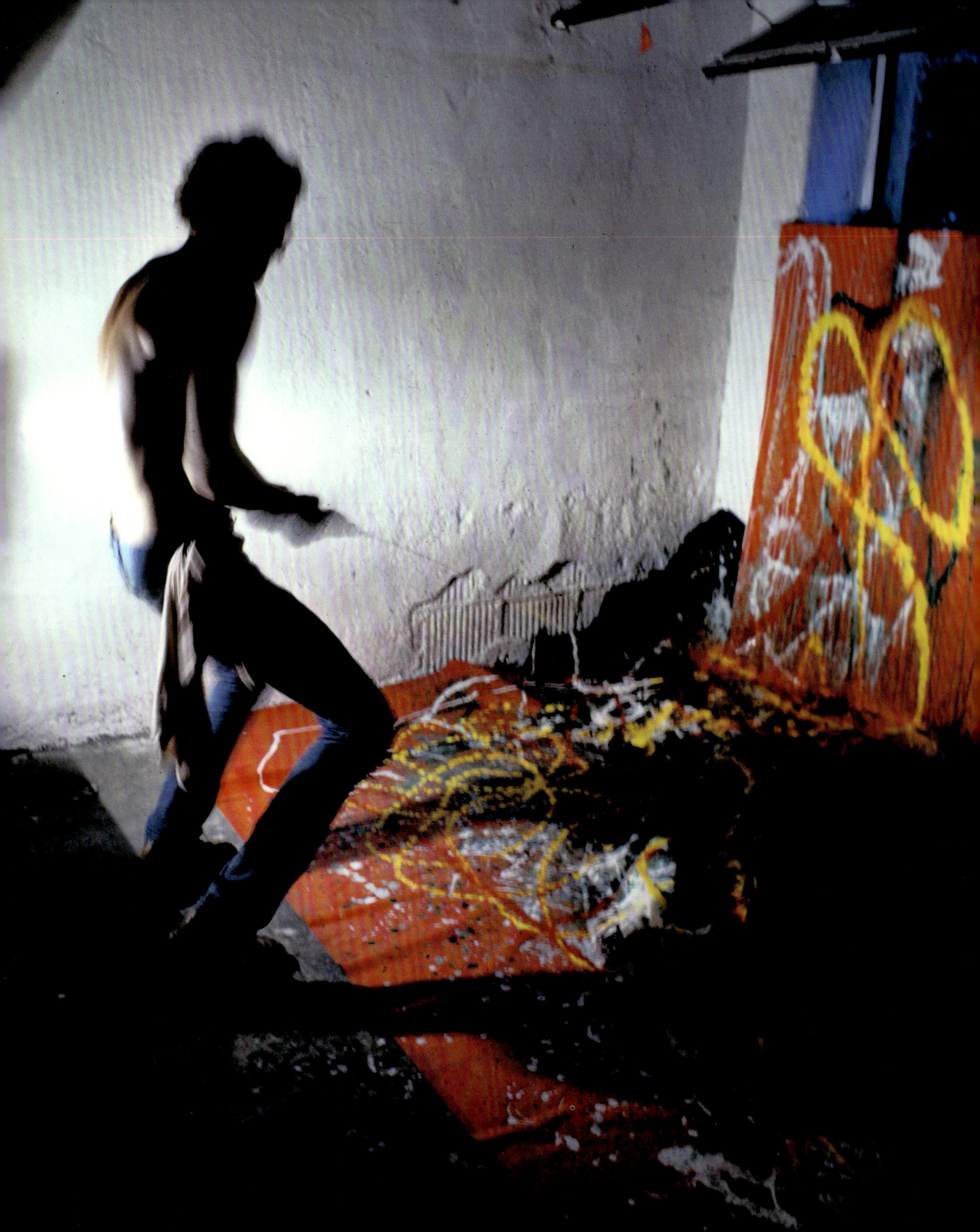

NOTES ON THE ART AND LIFE OF KEITH HARING

There is no substitute for the speed and confidence of total commitment to the moment.

—Eric Haze, New York artist, 2012

Writing is like dancing.

—Julio Cortázar, from an incomplete story about jazz and Bix Beiderbecke, n.d.

Overture

Keith Haring was born on May 4, 1958, in Reading, Pennsylvania. He grew up in nearby Kutztown. Painting and drawing attracted him from an early age. Seeking fame and artistic inspiration, he moved to New York City in 1978. There he worked at first in a more or less abstract style, sometimes on an enormous scale.

In 1979, he painted, Pollock-like, on canvases laid on the floor at the School of Visual Arts in New York. Bent over, barefoot and bare chested, he let his patterns take him where they would (see fig. 21). He worked in a tight combination of order—establishing the boundary of a painting and staying within it—and ecstasy, letting interlocking abstract patterns push, pull, and jostle one another like excited dancers on a ballroom floor. Then, in about 1980, it happened: abstract fragments morphed into recognizable figures—the crawling baby, the running dog, flying saucers, B-boys (break dancers) doing head spins, even Mickey Mouse.

Haring had his dark moments. They were very dark indeed—the ashes of a crawling baby rising in a mushroom cloud, a barking dog subjected to bestiality, copulating monsters in nightmare scenarios—possibly influenced by Picasso's grotesques of the 1930s and 1940s. But even his monsters made social commentary. Haring symbolized the AIDS virus as a short, black-horned snake breaking out of an egg, looking around for human prey (see pl. 199). He called this horror "demon sperm."[1] It was his way of reminding us of the imperative of safe sex.

Parallel to Haring's sadness, and his social conscience, ran something else: an allegiance to the dance in all its powers of transcendence. His love of dance ran at least as deep as Edgar Degas's famed preoccupation with ballerinas. Although he did not break, or spin on his head, Haring knew how to work up—and keep—a sweat, dancing for hours at the Roxy, an epicenter of hip-hop choreography, and even more frequently at the famed locus of house music, the Paradise Garage in SoHo. The Paradise Garage was so important to him, his diaries reveal,[2] that he would literally arrange his business commitments in Tokyo or Berlin—no matter how far from New York—so that he would not miss the mass euphoria of the hottest weekend nights. In the process he caught the motion of his time in his art.

Keith Haring performing action painting at the School of Visual Arts, New York, 1978. Photograph by Tseng Kwong Chi

ROBERT FARRIS THOMPSON

Getting to Know You

I first met Keith Haring in the summer of 1984. Kurt Thometz introduced us. I wandered happily around Haring's studio, then located several stories up at the corner of Broadway and Houston. I never met a more camera-ready guy. He posed. He chatted. He positioned himself within the jaws of a large sculpture of the barking dog and let himself be photographed. Everything seemed fair game for his hand—walls, paper, pyramids, floors, canopic-like urns, even a replica of the Statue of Liberty. There was a lot of humor, much of it sexual, from a man who once passed a subway advertisement selling Chardon Jeans, and—after a quick parry with his felt pen—suddenly it was selling hard-ons. You'd have to be living at the bottom of the Hudson River not to notice how much his art owed to raw sexual energy. I stumbled out of his studio dazed but determined to meet with him again, and to talk about music and dance.

We met at a Brazilian restaurant, Amazonas (now closed), on Broome Street near Broadway. Keith told me to be at the Roxy nightclub on a certain night. Afrika Bambaataa was to be the DJ. So I entered that enormous dance hall. I was accosted by a young black man who asked, "What the fuck are you, a cop?" I answered, "No, man, I'm an art historian from Yale University, and I have come to document the glories of your hip-hop choreography." Whereupon he threw me the "funk" sign—thumb and middle fingers concealed, pointer and little finger thrust out like horns. This meant, "You cool." Then Keith walked in, spotted me, and started drawing crawling babies on a page in my notebook.

Haring Takes on Body Art

Haring told me once—and I never forgot—that "primordial styles make you new."[3] This was no idle comment. It lies behind his drawings of spaceships zapping the pyramids of Egypt and ancient-looking urns blazing with modern images. Haring's primordial work before 1979 prepared him for handling the human frame. At the time he was working in terms of a tight interaction of boundary-making abstract shapes filled with animating strokes, also abstract. The latter functioned as a vitalizing bloodstream flowing within the forms. Consider the cover of the *Keith Haring Blank Book*: figuration rules, but abstract inner markings remain. The outlines of human shapes are green. Inner markings are black. Totally improvised black dashes, zigzags, and target-like forms enliven the figures they fill. As Alicia Churchill, an artist and collector of Haring drawings, remarked, "The inner designs are improvised but developed 'til they fill the space evenly. Keith had deep intuition as to where to start and where to finish."[4] So it was not that much of an existential leap to enliven anatomy with similar sparks and markings. This became evident when in

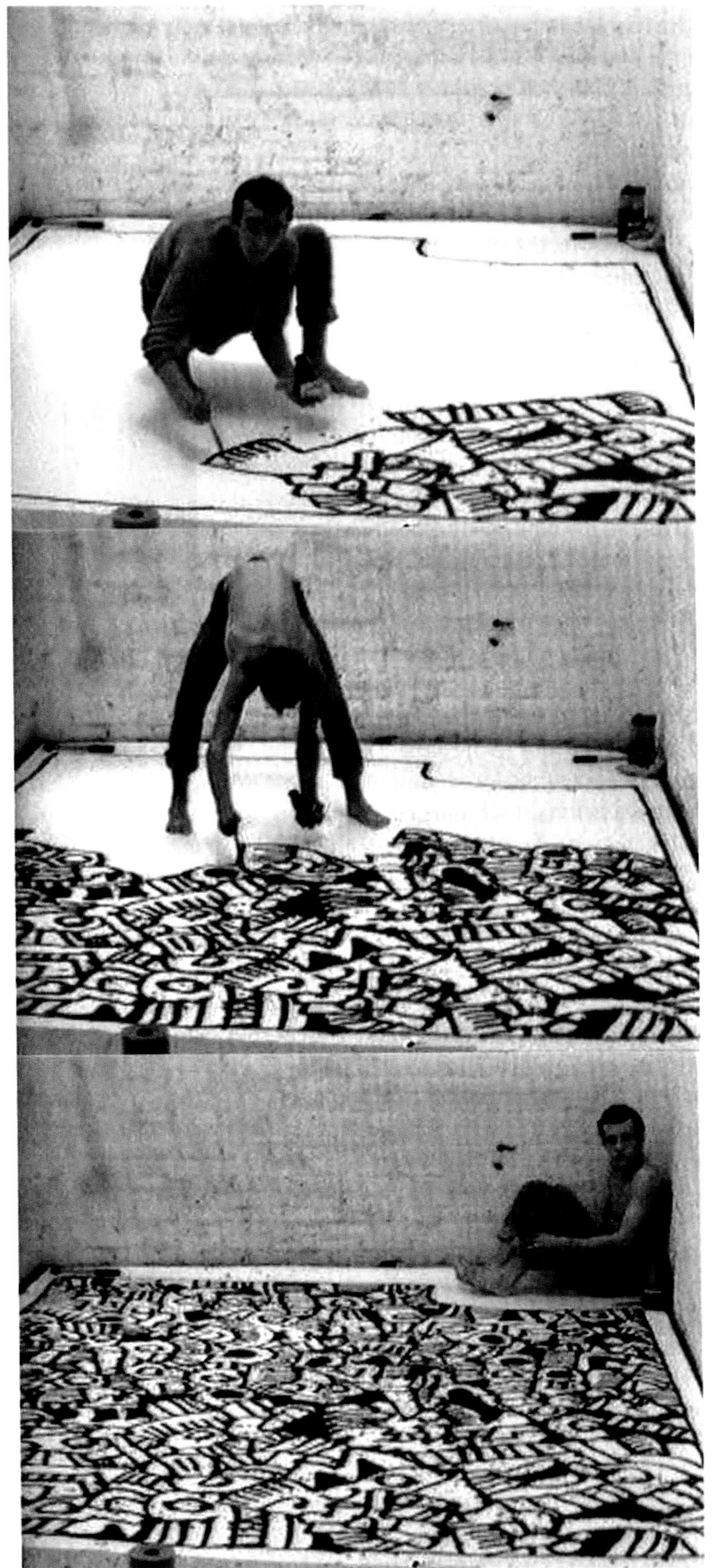

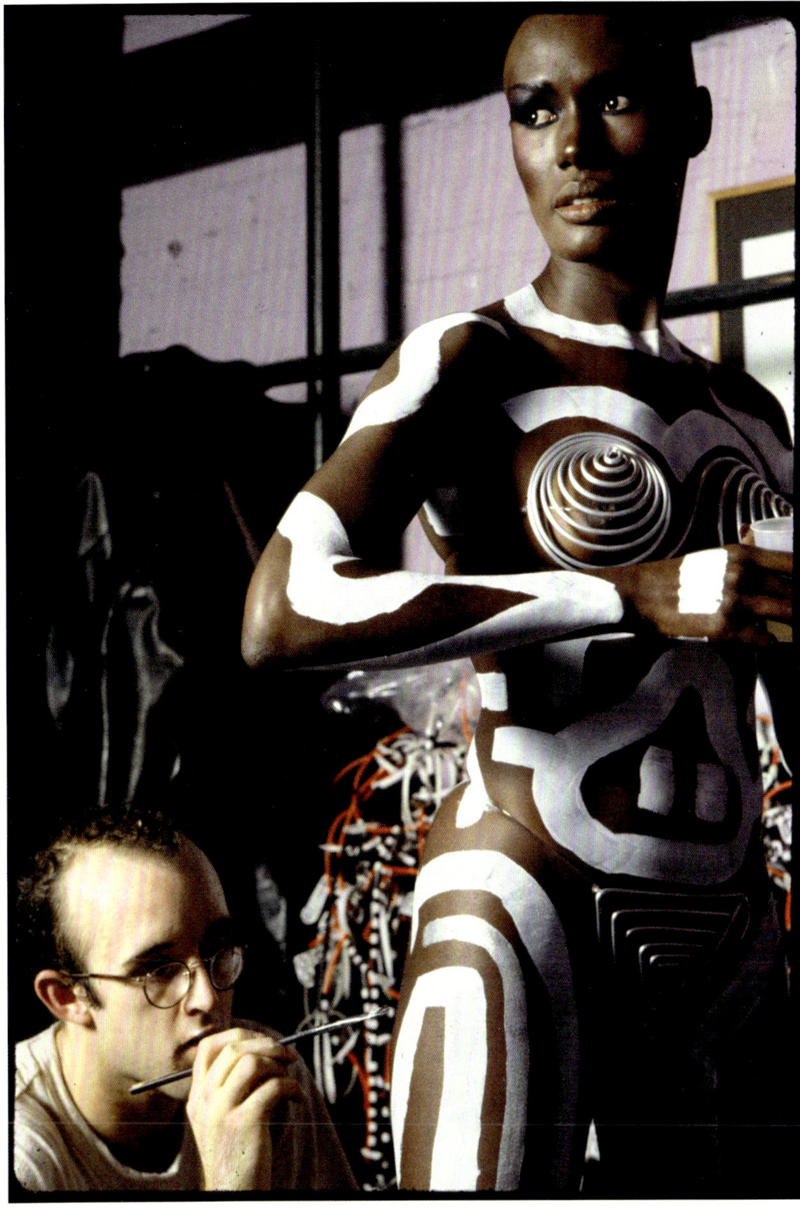

21

Keith Haring, stills from *Painting Myself into a Corner*, 1979. 33 min. Shot at the School of Visual Arts, New York

22

Keith Haring painting Grace Jones for a concert at the Paradise Garage, New York, 1985. Photograph by Tseng Kwong Chi

1983 Haring painted the body of Bill T. Jones, noted New York choreographer and dancer (see fig. 60). The primal boundaries were given: head, torso, limbs. Haring emphasized Jones's eyes with concentric lines that played off their natural roundness. Back and shoulders carried patterns that contradicted the symmetry of the body. Targets, recalling the *Blank Book*, covered Jones's rump and upper thighs. Ankles and feet read like X-rays of their bones.

There was another occasion for this form of art. One night in New York, in the fall of 1985, after I had gone to sleep, the phone rang. It was Keith. He said, "Be at the Paradise Garage at 4 a.m." "Why?" "I'm painting Grace Jones's body." Grace Jones was a reigning diva of the '80s, tall, powerful, and beautiful. I was there in a heartbeat, Nikon around my neck. Tseng Kwong Chi, the court photographer to the works of Haring, was there already, clicking away. He told me that he had seen Keith getting ready for this shoot by studying photographs of Masai men in Kenya painting white stripes on their naked black bodies in preparation for an initiation.

This study made a difference. The impact of East Africa on SoHo is reflected in lines that were broader and relatively simplified. Haring striped the right arm of Jones in Masai fashion (fig. 22). Then his own sense of design took over. A Bill Jones–like target pattern lit up her bottom. Snakelike white twisting curves lavished her legs with predictive motion. It was almost as if Haring were aware of the Kongo saying *Nyoka i sensu dya makinu* (The snake is the key emblem of the dance). When the artist came to address Grace Jones's head, a strong horizontal stroke signified her importance.

Prior to painting Grace Jones, Haring had prepared a column on the Paradise Garage dance floor with white stripes and patterns as a matrix for the diva. When Grace Jones stood against the column, she seemed to melt into its patterns. Then she stepped forward and started to sing "Take Me to the River." That's the way it went that night.

The Artist as Activist

Haring was no stranger to serious causes. His politics carried into his art over and over again. His famous cut-ups, pasting together faux headlines, not so obliquely challenged Ronald Reagan's conservatism, Vatican high-handedness, and other targets (see pls. 54–59). He was outraged at the scandal of South African apartheid and did a drawing of a huge black person chained and immobilized that needed no translation. He was a passionate AIDS activist as well, painting pink triangles emblazoned with the ACT UP motto: *Silence=Death*. The *New York Times* art critic Holland Cotter praised "the tough, contentious, often radical nature" of Haring's art.[5]

His politics involved other issues also, including the relation of his work to that of his contemporary artist colleagues Jean-Michel Basquiat, Eric Haze, John Ahearn, and Rammellzee. All were initially New York street artists who fought the patronizing attitude of *arte erudita*, the so-called mainstream. They fought to enter the museum world. They won, by dint of hard work and creative restlessness, but they did this without losing the vitality of their street art beginnings.

New York graffiti art starts with crudely scrawled signatures, which sophisticated street artists call "tags." The street artists were making consciously artistic, elaborate markings. The vision got richer until the letters became almost sculptural in their degree of visual projection. Lines and letters were caused to intersect in a manner that, at its best, resembled Celtic interlace. The street called it "wild style." It was calligraphy. Letters were art. Embodied in this development lay a challenge: Will you copy or bring in something new?

This is where Jean-Michel Basquiat made his entrance. He was not so much painting letters as he was writing witty, gnomic statements in prominent places in New York where stars of the art world might see them. Here is an example:

> THE WHOLE LIVERY LINE
>
> BOW LIKE THIS WITH
>
> THE BIG MONEY ALL
>
> CRUSHED INTO THEIR FEET[6]

When Basquiat turned to painting on canvases, statements on the wall were transferred to his new medium and morphed into symbols and magical incantations, such as naming parts of his physical frame—lungs, spleen, hand—to make his body strong. The symbols included coins to make him rich and crowns to make him king. For similar reasons, he showed off his knowledge of jazz, blues, opera, sports, cinema, and history. His was an art of assertive facts as well as names. You could sense the presence of an intellectual behind it.

Eric Haze started with street emblems—stars, parallel lines, arrows—making his presence known through sheer control and pacing. With ambitious shifts to larger scales and more prominent settings (meaning art galleries), Haze was able to bring his signature motifs to the attention of art historians as well as denizens of the street.

John Ahearn put sculpture, not writing, on the walls of the inner city. He lifted it up, way up, several stories up. High over the streets of the Bronx, he fixed plaster-body impressions of the Latino and black inhabitants of the neighborhoods, showing them at work and at play. This was light-years removed from painting a name on the wall. He loved Latinos and blacks. He respected their role as sovereigns of the street.

Haring strongly admired his colleague Rammellzee. "Rammellzee," he told me in 1984, "is a wizard."[7] Rammellzee quickly passed from graffiti to fine art. He saw letters as armored vehicles. He turned them into sculptures bristling with guns, wheels, and other assertive objects. The sight of squadrons of Rammellzee-armed letters flying in a room at a SoHo art gallery retrospective at the Suzanne Geiss Company in the spring of 2012 was beyond remarkable.

Haring's art ran parallel to the work of Basquiat, Haze, Ahearn, and Rammellzee. In 1982, like a street artist, he "graffitized" the bottom of a lamppost in New York with a perfectly centered image of the crawling baby. The street, in effect, answered, "Baby, huh, well, here's our impression"—and someone painted, a bit shakily, on an adjacent panel, an infant with a wry smile and three wisps of hair.[8] Haring entered the subways not with a spray gun, but with a gentle piece of white chalk. He drew neat, easily readable images on black paper used to cover advertisements whose time had expired. He considered the subway his laboratory. Here he worked out new patterns and new combinations, including friezes of dogs and infants. During appropriate holidays—Christmas, New Year's, Valentine's Day—he dedicated these works to the city of New York. This was one reason that he was outraged when collectors started bringing him subway drawings to sign. Around 1985, Haring discovered that someone, smart but sneaky, was pasting the black paper very, very lightly so that it could be immediately and safely removed once a drawing covered it. "How dare you?" he responded, and the underground work ended.

Haring and the Dance

Dancers and the dance ennoble the art of Keith Haring. Even his barking dog eventually stood on his hind legs and started boogying. There is an undated photograph of the artist dancing on the roof of a building in Tokyo in which Afro-Atlantic canons have taken over: Haring's legs bend deeply and his torso bends forward. His left hand moves at an angle to his forearm, echoing an idiom of the streets.

Haring's contact with hip-hop choreography goes back at least to October 1981. At that time, the photographer–graffiti expert Martha Cooper documented an early expression of the tradition at a New York art space called The Kitchen (fig. 23). Her photograph illustrates a young dancer, Doze Green, of the Rock Steady Crew. Doze is in the air. He is

23

Doze Green at The Kitchen, New York, 1981. Photograph by Martha Cooper

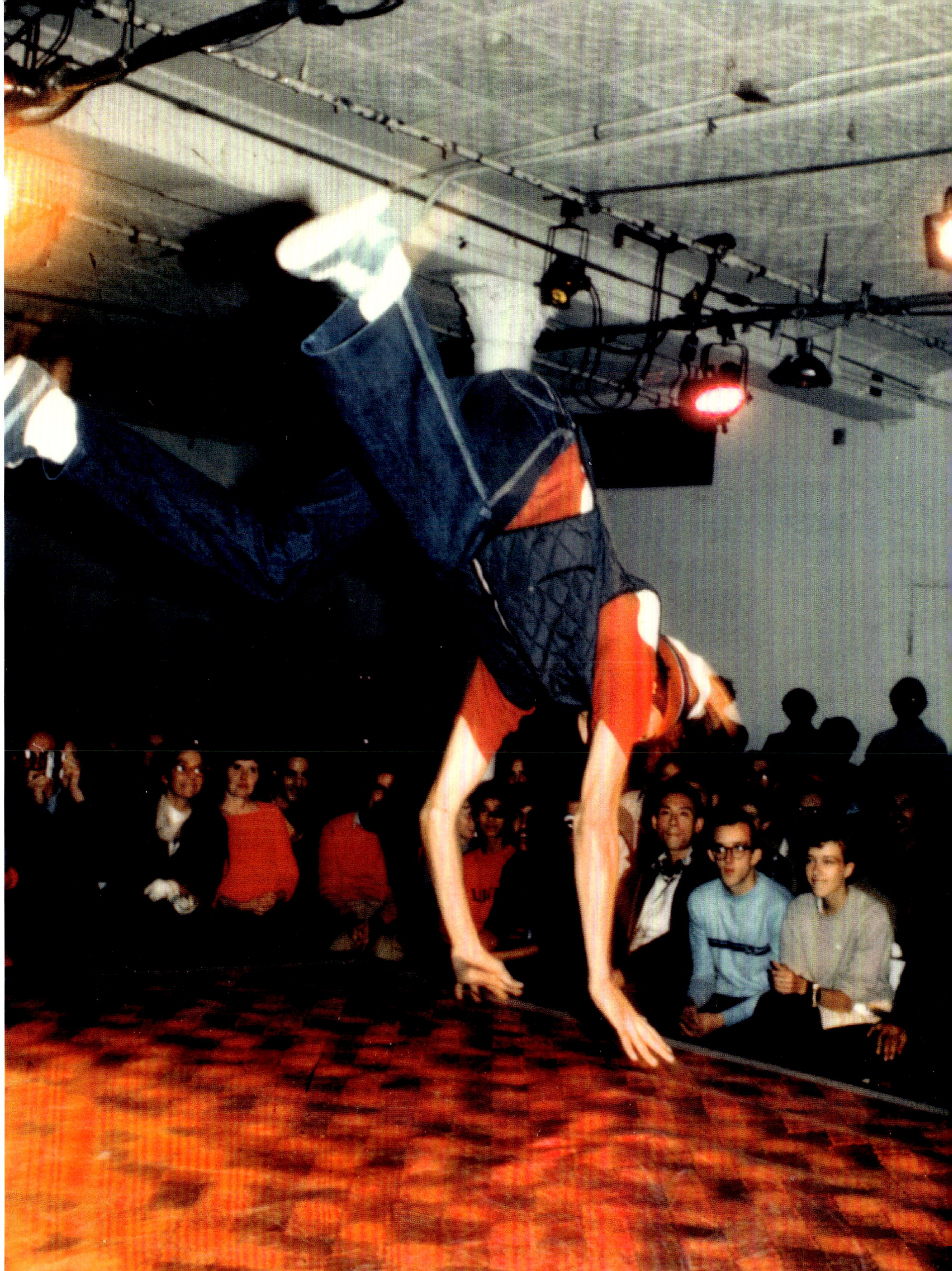

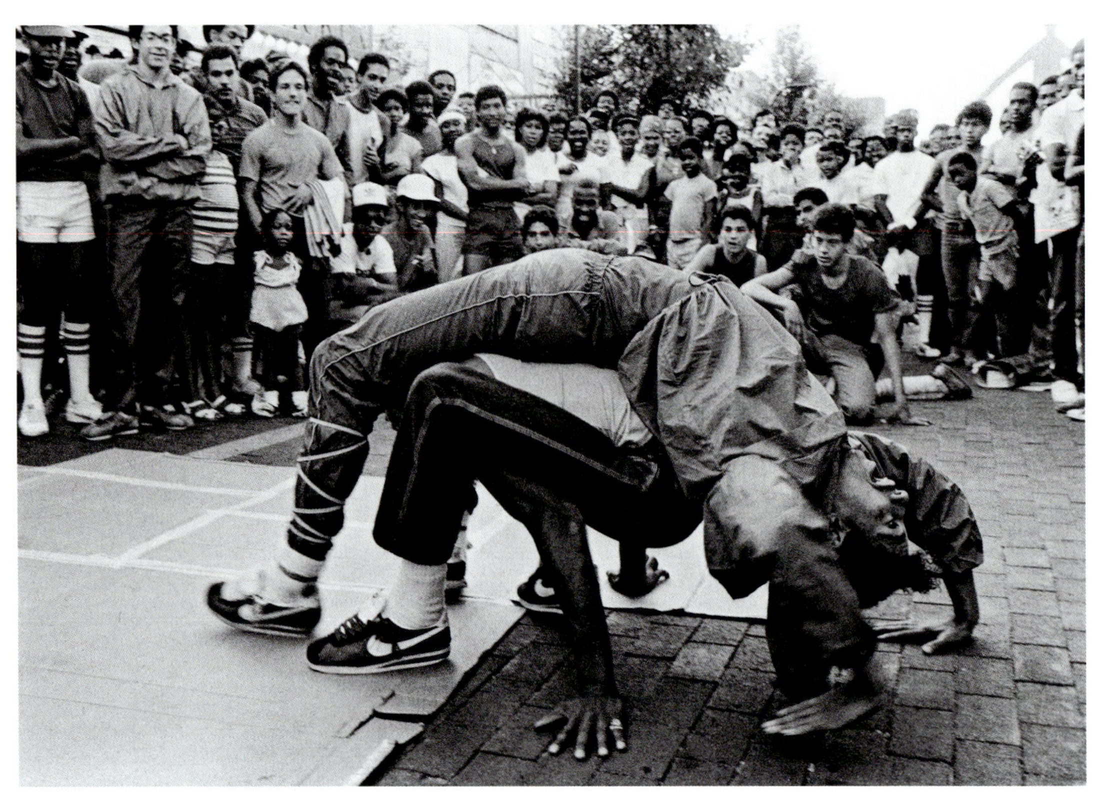

1983

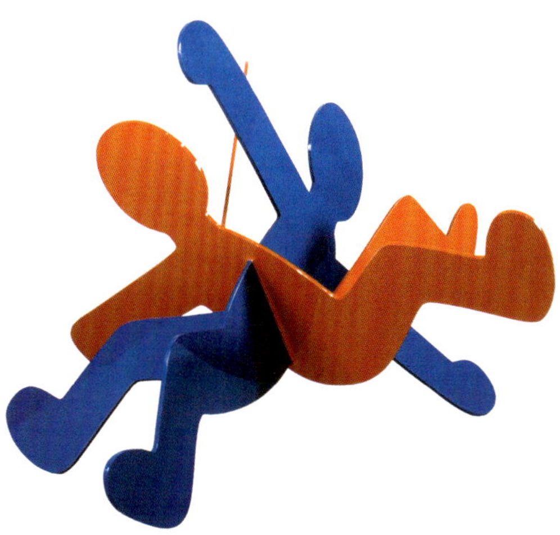

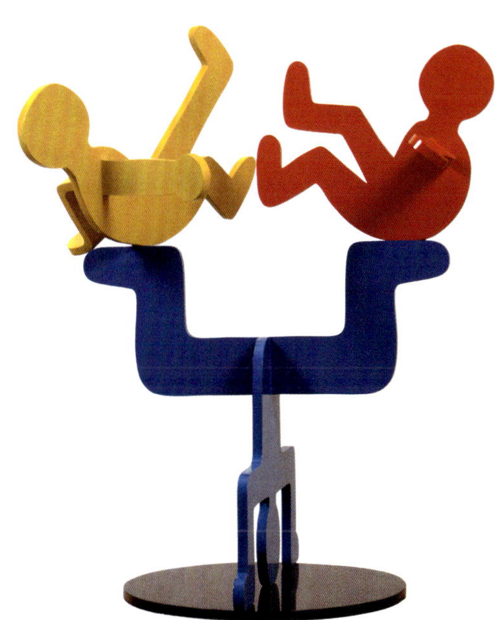

24 (opposite, top)

Hernando Molina and Steffan Clemente of the Rock Steady Crew doing the spider move, Queens, New York, 1984. Photograph by Martha Cooper

25 (opposite, bottom)

Keith Haring, *Untitled*, 1983. Woodcut, 24 x 30 in. (61 x 76.2 cm). Collection of the Keith Haring Foundation

26 (above, top)

Keith Haring, *Untitled* (*Breakers*), 1987. Painted aluminum, 45½ x 60 x 63⅛ in. (115.6 x 152.4 x 160.2 cm). Private collection

27 (above, bottom)

Keith Haring, *Untitled*, 1983. Painted aluminum, 38 x 31 x 21 in. (96.5 x 78.7 x 53.3 cm). Private collection

about to land on his hands and flaunt his ability to move athletically upside down or to gather momentum for a series of spins. Seated right in front of him, missing nothing, we find Keith Haring (in a blue shirt) and Tseng Kwong Chi (black bow tie). It was one of many such encounters. One night I saw Keith at the Roxy, where B-boys and B-girls were freestyling all over the place. The graffiti artist Fred Brathwaite (Fab Five Freddy) witnessed a similar sequence:

> One day Futura and I gave a party at my studio and the Rock Steady Crew came. And Keith came. We all clapped our hands and the Rock Steady Crew started dancing—which inspired Keith [to draw and paint] guys spinning on their heads.[9]

On January 9, 1986, on a blank page in my notebook, Keith drew—and named—the basic hip-hop dance-hall figures occurring in his work. He shows four B-boys in action as well as the DJ whose beats make them move. They are reacting to break-beat music, hence their nickname. Break-beat music DJs use double turntables, playing the same record on each turntable. When, say, a conga drum break ends on one disc, it continues immediately on the other. Pioneered by a Jamaican DJ from the South Bronx named Kool Herc, it was an ingenious solution to the demand for nonstop improvisation.

Haring's DJ is amusingly post-hominid. He's a robot. He's working one disc with his right hand while holding extra vinyl in his left. With his right hand he is making the needle move back and forth within the vinyl grooves, creating an effect called scratching. Haring's drawing shows one dancer upside down, executing a head spin; two young men horizontal on the floor with intersecting bodies; and a figure standing up gesturing with angulated arms and hands. Neatly and economically, Haring introduced me to the two sides of hip-hop choreography: *down-rocking*, or athletic spins and other actions close to the ground, and *electric boogie*, featuring stand-up mimes, with dancers sometimes even donning the white gloves of the icon of mime, Marcel Marceau. By examining both sides of the equation, we can identify the selections Haring made that went straight into his art.

Down-Rocking (Break Dancing)

Down-rocking embraces five basic moves: (1) top rock, an accelerated, fast-stepping style taken directly from the *paseo* of the Puerto Rican dance tradition known as *bomba*; (2) break, or descent to the ground, often on one's hands; (3) swipes, or acrobatic motions imparting momentum to the dancer, who then (4) spins, in counted revolutions, on his or her head, bottom, back, or shoulders; and (5) the freeze, in which the dancer comes to a complete halt, frozen in an improvised gesture.

In his drawings, Haring focused on hand spins and head spins. He also drew two-person intersections of bodies, one low and parallel to the ground, the other diving across him at a right angle to his torso. This was the spider move, so named because the limbs of the dancers roughly resembled the legs of a spider. These moves, done carelessly, could be dangerous, but the best dancers achieved beauty through bravery.

Head spins reached a visual climax in a mural that Haring and the DJ Juan Dubose executed on the north side of Houston near the Bowery in the summer of 1982 (see pp. 14–15). Framed by enormous clown faces with three eyes, four B-boys demonstrate head spins. Balancing on both hands or propelling their bodies with one hand, they spin on the tops of their heads. As they do so, their legs pretzel in a direct citation of hip-hop choreography.

Haring often drew two or more dancers in action. This is why he favored the spider move, elaborating creative versions of it. Compare the Rock Steady Crew executing a spider move in Queens in 1984 (fig. 24) with a woodcut from 1983 (fig. 25). In the woodcut, one dancer dives over the other, as in the original. Haring inserted black dashes and lightning bolts within the red contours of their bodies.

In 1987, returning to crisscrossing horizontal bodies, Haring made a sculpture called *Untitled* (*Breakers*) (fig. 26) in which two bodies intersect as a red dancer dives through a blue dancer. Their arms—wide open and welcoming—depart from the canon. We sense an enactment of principle: work with your buddy; share space in relation to time.

Haring combined head spins and butt spins in never-never compositions. He elaborated on this departure in the medium of metal sculpture. In a 1983 work, a blue dancer spins on his head and supports two other dancers, one gold, one red, who spin on the soles of the blue dancer's feet. In the process, the three bodies turn into a candelabrum of action (fig. 27).

Electric Boogie: From Shamans to Show Business

Down-rocking, as we saw, involves a horizontal sequence of acrobatic acts—break, spin, freeze, and stand up again. In contrast, electric boogie continuously looks to stand-up mimes and impressions:

> It especially mimes things that flicker, black and white films of the earliest period, Saturday morning TV, bad [i.e., jerky] animation, strobe lights in action. It mimes robots. It mimes things that tick with fragmented pulse, hydraulic this and animal that. It mimes waves of [electrical] current, rippling from body to body. It mimes the conventions of bas-relief figures from ancient Egypt.[10]

At its deepest level, electric boogie dramatizes the presence of spirit, a concept that goes far back in African American cultural history. Among the San of southern Africa, a shaman once drew what it felt like to be hit with the spirit. His legs, arms, and torso tremble with ecstatic pleasure. Lightning-like pulses run down his neck, limbs, and torso.[11] The reading of lightning (or electricity) as a metaphor for the trembling of religious ecstasy continues in Central Africa, especially in traditional Kongo culture. The nuances of the Kongo term for spirit possession, *mayembo*, make this clear:

> *Mayembo*: state of enthusiasm and ecstasy of a ritual expert [*nganga*] who has fallen under the influence of [the spirit in] his major charm [*nkisi*]; convulsive movements of the muscles; shivering; electricity.[12]

The San people compared trembling to lightning. The Bakongo, brought in great number to the United States during the slave trade, also made correlations among religious ecstasy, the coming of the spirit, and electricity. This led to a powerful metaphoric renaming of an important manifestation of Western technology. When the first telegraph lines were installed in Kongo, traditionalists, struck by the movement of the wires in the wind, sometimes accompanied by a hum, called the phenomenon *nsinga dya mayembo* (ecstasy on the wire). Ecstatic trembling of the shoulders in a state of spirit possession spread across America wherever black traditional churches were established:

> Cut to the Solomon brothers who [brought together elements] that became the electricboogie. While attending services of the First Corinthians Baptist Church in West Fresno, California, they saw women on the front row jerking and trembling with the spirit.[13]

This may or may not have been a direct inspiration for the Solomon brothers, inventors of early electric boogie in California hip-hop, who were also fascinated by robotic motions and imitated them. They improvised strong vibrations, rattling torso and limbs, and called it "poppin'," if executed at a moderate tempo, or "tickin'," if things went very fast. This was West Coast boogaloo. The East Coast took the moves, reset them for the pace of, say, James Brown's soul music, and renamed the dance electric boogie.[14] This happened in the late '70s, at about the same time Haring came up to New York from Kutztown. He watched the B-boys shimmer as if under strobe-light bombardment, watched them mime the flicker of silent films, watched them become robots. Shortly thereafter, a new figure emerged among the Haring dolphins, flying saucers, and barking dogs—a man made of electricity, jagged with lightning-like contours. One of these high-voltage figures was so powerfully charged that he was able to turn on a lightbulb simply by holding it in the palm of his hand.

Haring drew the passing of energy from dancer to dancer. Imagine, first, two members of the New York hip-hop crew The Whiz. A black dancer passes an electrical current to a bare-chested Dominican dancer. Waves of current flow from the left arm of the black man to the waiting right hand of the Latino athlete. First the latter's right arm comes alive, then his shoulders, and finally his left arm completes a train of tremors. This was a two-person wave, interpreted by Haring. Compare a green-and-red woodcut from 1983 (fig. 28). A wave curves down the right arm of one performer, who kicks out a leg for emphasis. The current reaches his hand. It passes through the hand of the other dancer and runs up the curve of his arm.

In addition to lightning-like figures and the two-man wave, Haring did studies of Team Tut electric boogie. What is Team Tut? "It's a pile-up of dancers," explained Hernando Molina, of the Rock Steady Crew of New York. "It's guys on top of one another, or one guy behind another, all of them making sharp, angled signs with their hands, which we call 'throwing hieroglyphs.'"[15] These gestures were intended to suggest the bas-relief conventions of classical Egyptian art. Tut, of course, is an abbreviation of Tutankhamun. Compare two New York B-boy stars: Molina (known as Sweepy) in a white shirt and Steffan Clemente (Mr. Wiggles) in black with a red cap (see fig. 29). They show us how the barrios absorbed, apparently via television, gestures from the land of the Nile. Clemente angles his hands with consummate sharpness. Molina thrusts out a leg so that it reads as a third arm of Clemente's. "In the Tut," stresses Molina, "you're always making signs."[16] Haring richly observed this process. There is a chalk-on-paper work, dated 1984, now in the collection of Michael

28

Keith Haring, *Untitled*, 1983. Woodcut, 24 x 30 in. (61 x 76.2 cm)
Collection of the Keith Haring Foundation

29

Hernando Molina and Steffan Clemente in a Team Tut pose, c. 1996.
Photograph by Ian Churchill

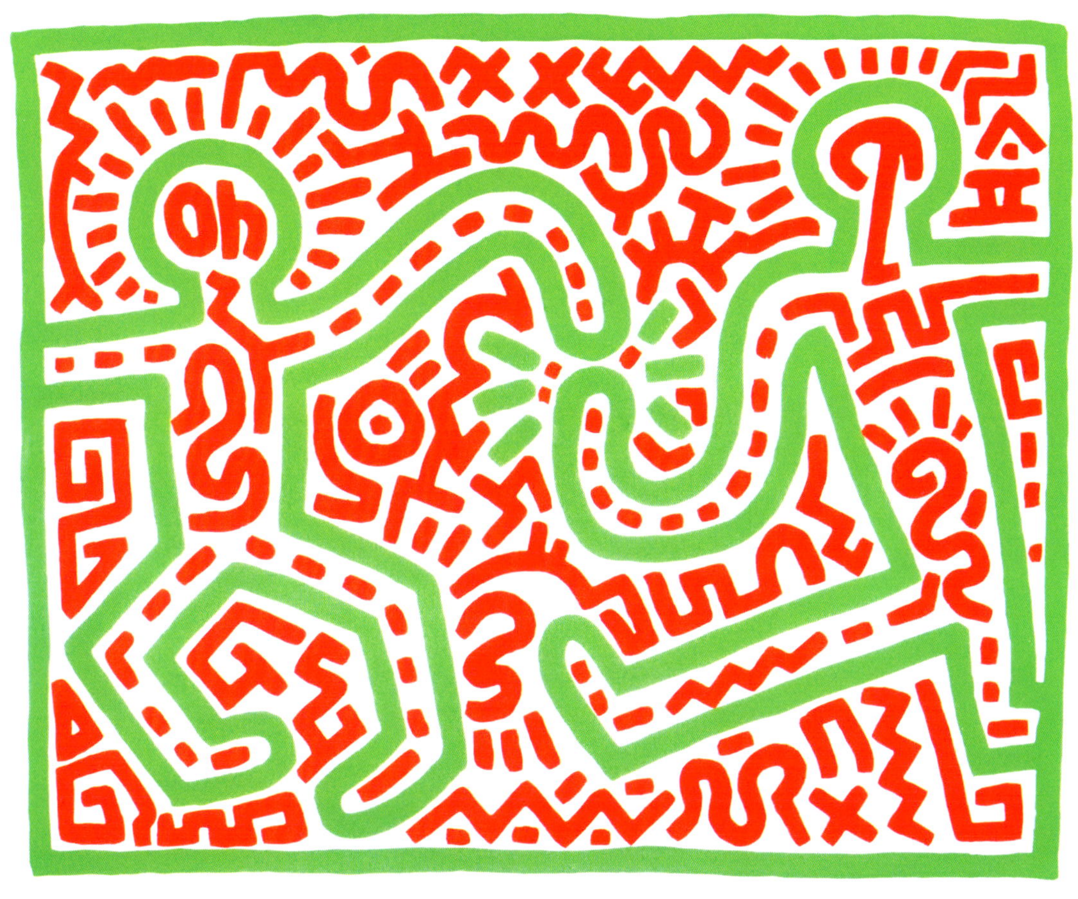

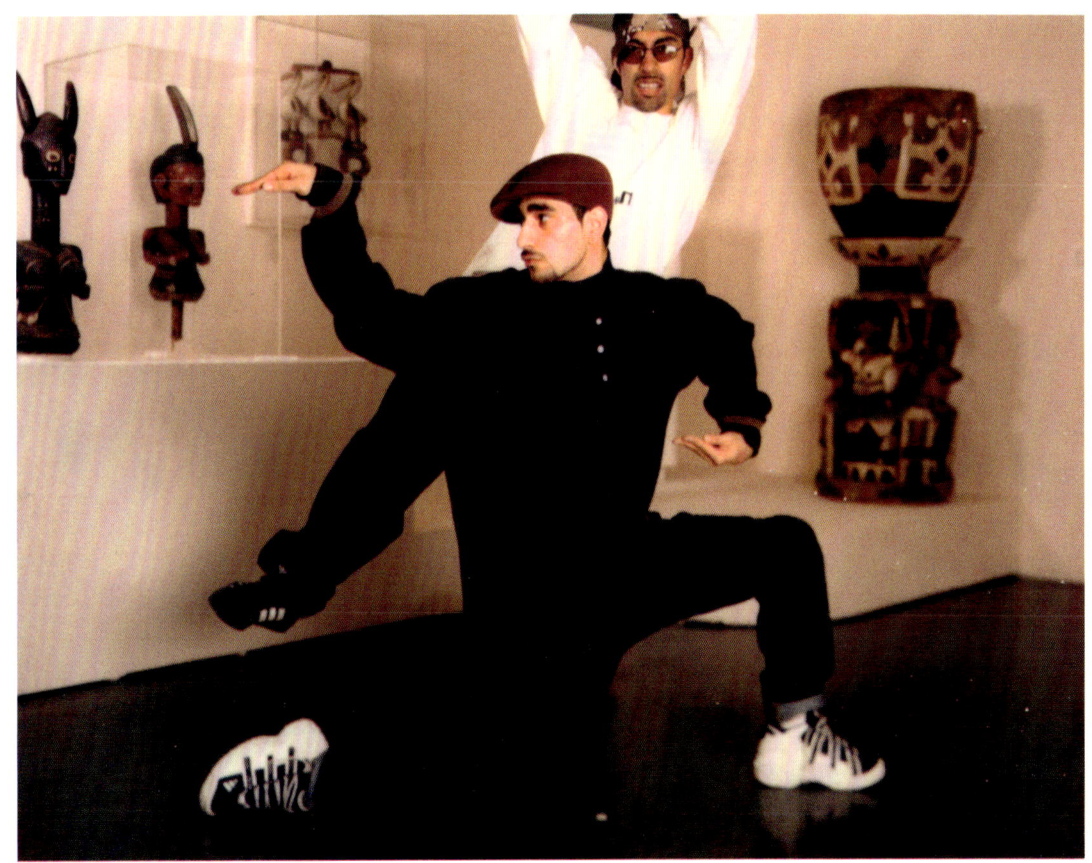

Sweeney, that makes this point (fig. 30). The angle-making dance unfolds before us. Haring augmented the number of dancers from two to seven. He also turned this intensified vision into sculpture, in which a barking dog supports four figures gesturing the sign for pile-up (fig. 31).

Envoi

Haring moved from abstraction to figuration in 1980. He started with running figures, pyramids, crawling babies, flying saucers, and dogs. The earliest dogs were blocky in shape. They were silent. Slightly later they started to bark. They were possibly based on the Haring family dog, a Weimaraner named Mumbo, who lived with Keith's family in Kutztown from around 1968 to 1985.[17]

Haring never stopped drawing. Committed to the moment, he practiced unceasingly, like John Coltrane rehearsing scales between gigs. Haring's images radiate the fluency that comes from constant enactment. He saw the boys from the barrios invent tough-bodied forms of self-expression. He was dazzled by the range of their moves—inspired by everything from mimes of helicopters to acts of human puppetry to gestures borrowed from the conventions of the longest-running style in the history of art, the art of ancient Egypt. Haring not only drew or turned into sculpture street moves and gestures, he also intuited their value: they were ideal social interactions.

We come, at the end, to an acrylic on canvas, painted in 1988 (pl. 199). Two dancers have so intricately synchronized their impulses that they become a pair of scissors. Signaling happiness with upraised hands, they restore to freedom a third dancer by cutting loose the bonds that had immobilized him. The point is liberation. The place could be the Paradise Garage.

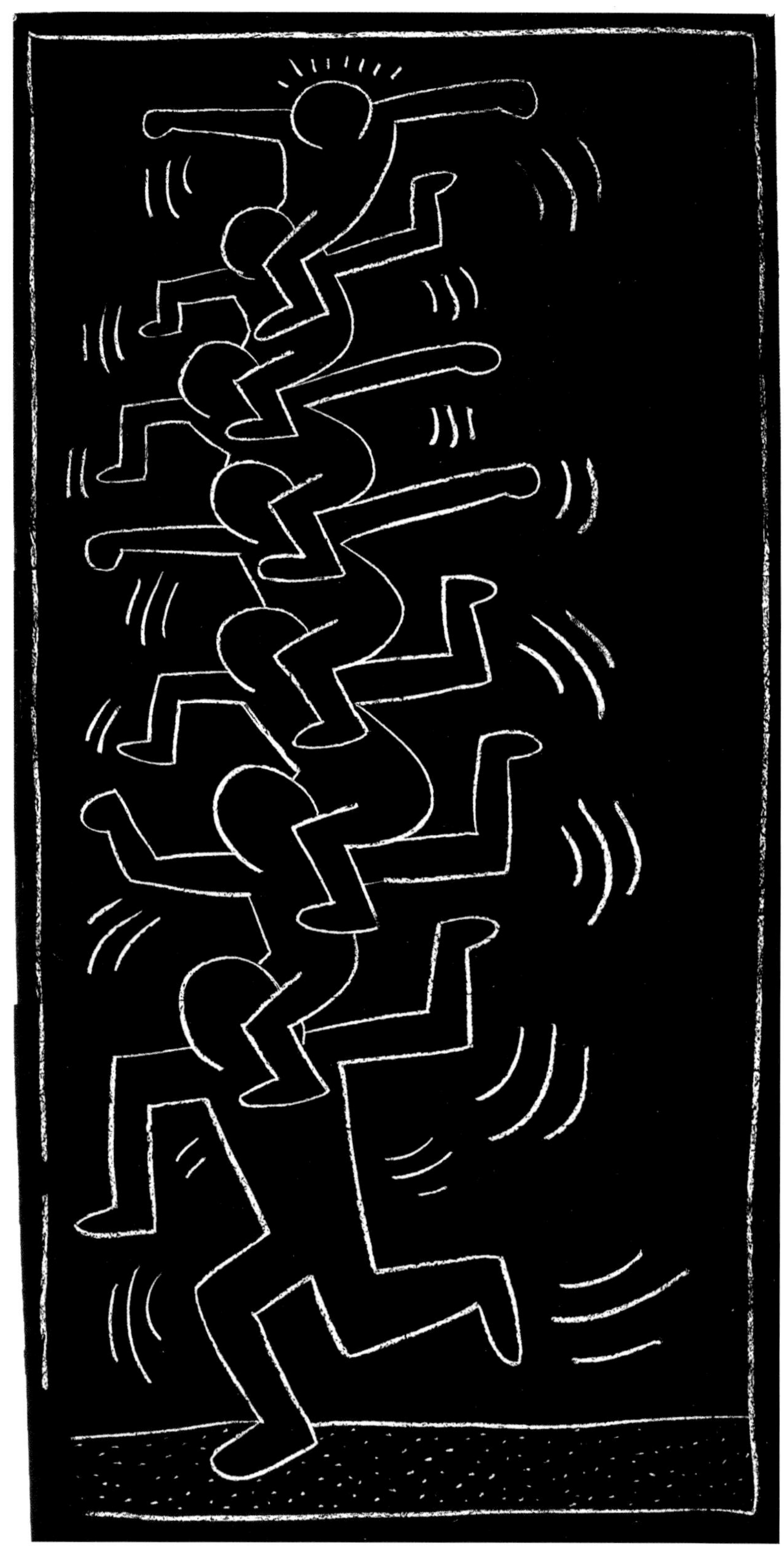

30

Keith Haring, *Untitled* (*Subway Drawing*), 1984. Chalk on paper, 82 x 42 in. (208.3 x 106.7 cm). Collection of Michael Sweeney

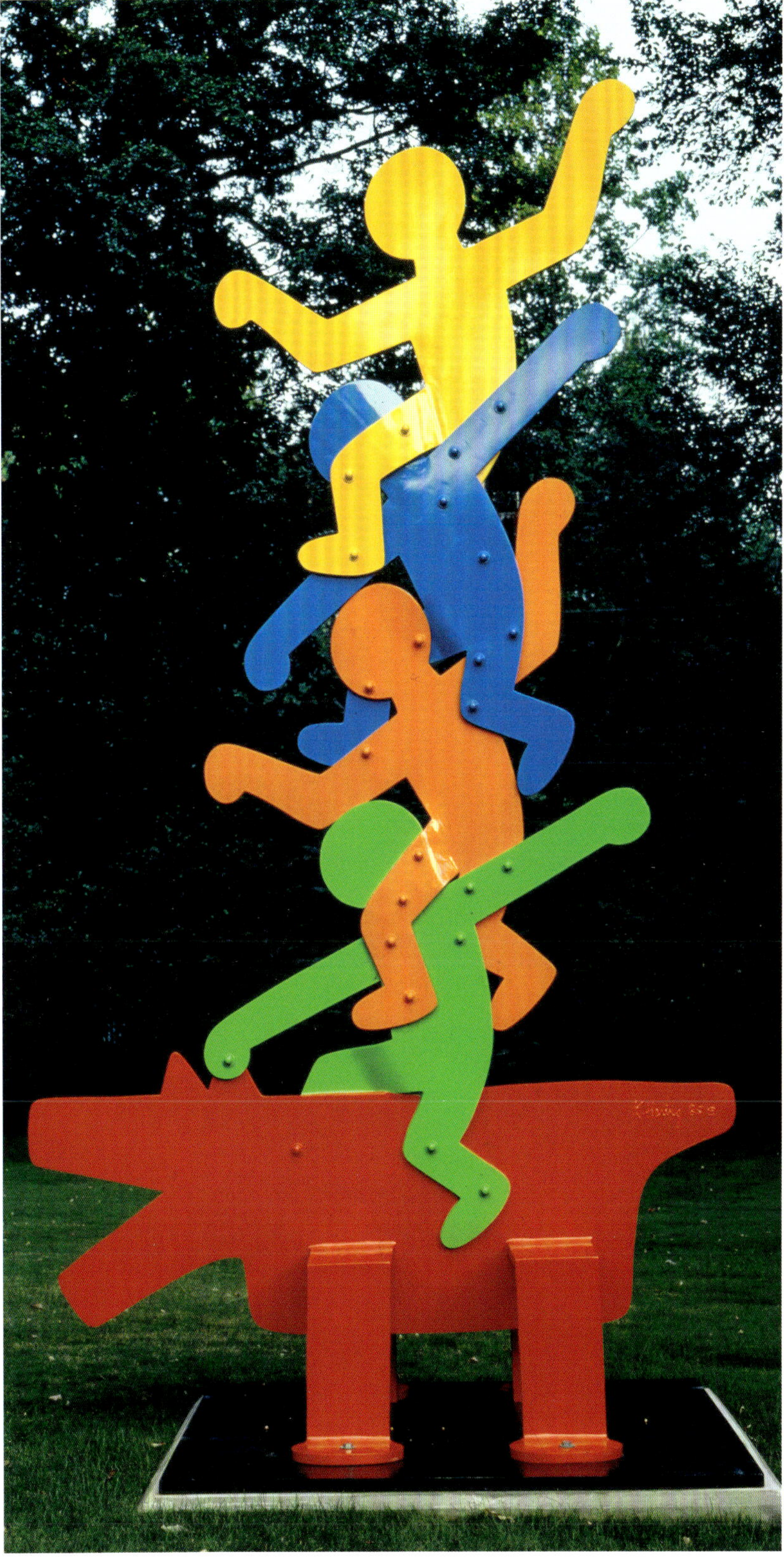

31

Keith Haring, *Untitled*, 1985. Painted aluminum, 173 x 94 x 48 in. (439.4 x 238.8 x 121.9 cm). Private collection

Notes

1. Author in conversation with Keith Haring, in his studio, summer 1988.
2. Keith Haring, *Keith Haring Journals* (New York: Viking-Penguin paperback ed., 1997).
3. Author in conversation with Keith Haring, summer 1984.
4. Author in conversation with Alicia Churchill, Lynn, Massachusetts, August 18, 2012.
5. Holland Cotter, "Dancing Again with Keith Haring," *New York Times*, June 22, 1997, C25.
6. Robert Farris Thompson, "Requiem for the Degas of the B-Boys, Keith Haring," *Artforum* (May 1990): 137.
7. Author in conversation with Keith Haring, SoHo, summer 1984.
8. Keith Haring quoted in Elisabeth Sussman et al., *Keith Haring*, exh. cat., Whitney Museum of American Art, June 25–September 21, 1997 (New York: Whitney Museum of American Art; Boston: Bulfinch/Little, Brown, 1997), 9.
9. Fred Brathwaite quoted in ibid., 154.
10. Robert Farris Thompson in ibid., 219.
11. David Lewis-Williams and Thomas Dowson, *Images of Power: Understanding Bushman Rock Art* (Johannesburg: Southern Book Publishers, 1989), 87.
12. Karl Laman, *Dictionnaire kikongo-français, M–Z* (Farnborough, UK: Gregg, 1964), 512.
13. Robert Farris Thompson, "Hip-Hop 101," *Rolling Stone* 470 (March 27, 1986): 95–100.
14. Author interview with Steffan Clemente, break dancer, New York, October 1996.
15. Author interview with Hernando Molina, break dancer, New York, October 18, 1996.
16. Ibid.
17. Author telephone interview with Joan Haring, Keith's mother, October 26, 1996.

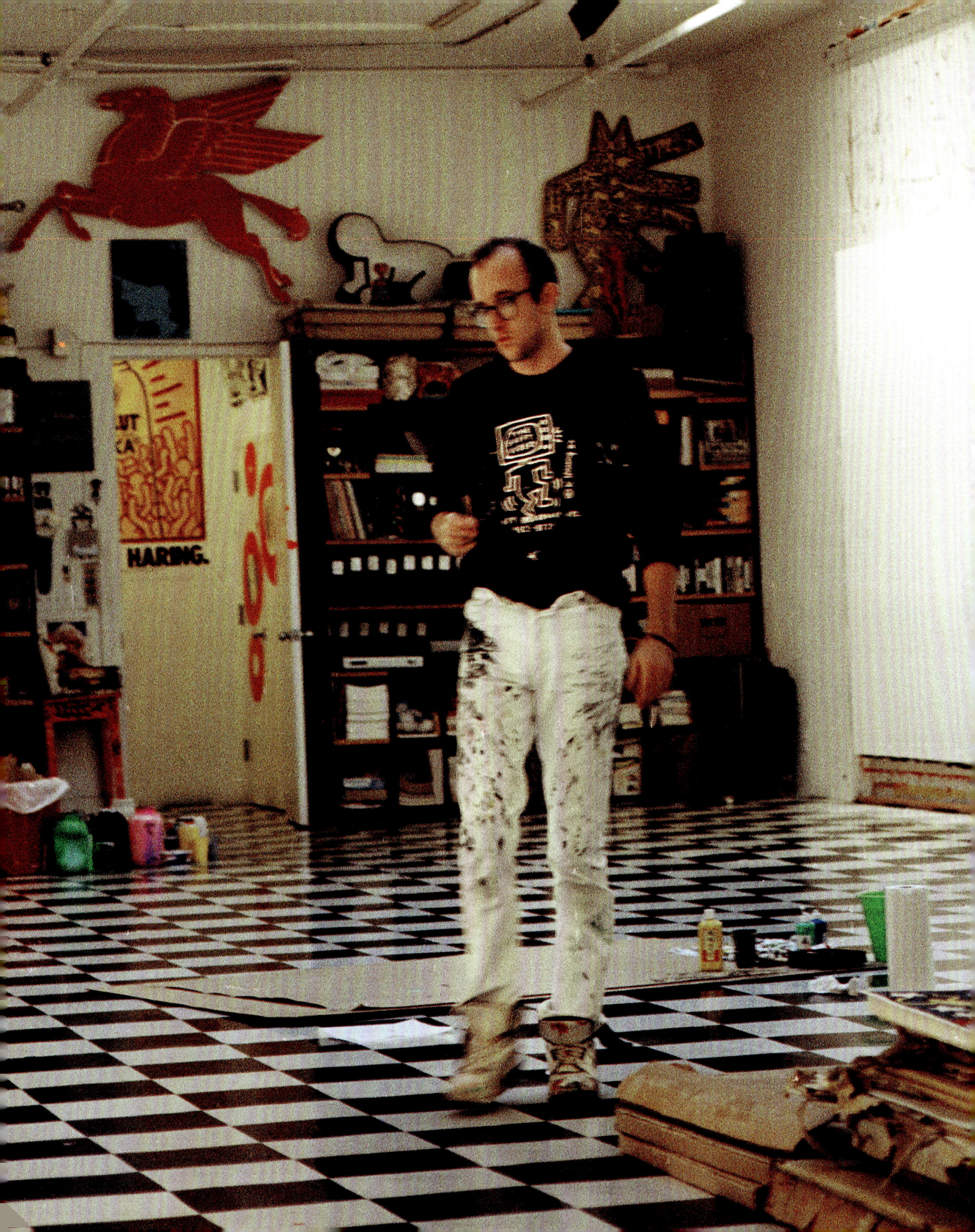
HARING.

BREAKING OUT

GLENN O'BRIEN: The first work of Keith's that I think I ever saw was some collage stuff on the street, like *Reagan Slain by Hero Cop* or *Pope Killed for Freed Hostage* [see pls. 54–59].

JULIA GRUEN: Those were the cut-up *New York Post* headlines.

GO'B: Which were really political. I remember the first time I saw one of those, I was up by 61st and Broadway.

JG: Those were very early, 1980. It's very interesting that you brought that up because those are certainly among the earliest street interventions that he did that were deliberate. These early collage works were really significant. I think that Keith was always very intrigued by the kind of cut-up method of Brion Gysin and [William] Burroughs, what Gysin and Burroughs took from the Surrealists. As a young man, even before he came to New York, Keith was really fascinated by the Surrealist movement, and then he began to discover the Beat generation, and that triggered this immense outpouring of the use of language in these different ways. As you track his visual development, moving from the written word to symbology, you can see how informed he was by the semiotics he studied in school and the meaning and value of signs, what they represent by themselves, what happens when you put them together. That speaks quite directly to this idea of taking something as straightforward as a headline but reproducing it, transforming it, and somehow subverting it, which was also very much in the spirit of the times, too.

DIETER BUCHHART: Were there many of those in public spaces? Did he do a lot of reproductions?

JG: Well, I don't know exactly how many originals he made, but he photocopied them by the hundreds and pasted them all over the city.

GO'B: It was just before he was well known, but all of the bands were doing posters.

JG: Wheat-pasted posters.

GO'B: And Jean-Michel [Basquiat] did a lot of those; the postering thing was really big then. Things would stay up for a week and then they'd get covered up by some other thing.

JG: That's a very good point, because this very typical, low-cost advertising medium for concert posters, gallery shows, nightclub performances, little events, whether pasted on construction barriers in the street, on lampposts, and so on, were, above all, ephemeral and temporary. I don't know how conscious Keith was of this, but there was a pretty direct line from doing these postings to making the Subway Drawings, which were also ephemeral.

Keith Haring in his studio, New York, 1988.
Photograph by Baptiste Lignel

A CONVERSATION BETWEEN JULIA GRUEN AND GLENN O'BRIEN
MODERATED BY DIETER BUCHHART

GO'B: And which were also in an advertising space; the city would rent these frames for a specific time, and then when their time was up, they would put up the black. It was really brilliant of him to use them.

JG: That was also 1980, and this was really his great epiphany—riding the subway every day as he did, taking note of the fact that in between these advertisements in the stations (for a movie or cosmetics or chicken or whatever it was), there would occasionally be these blank panels. Could there be a more seductive context than a framed blank surface in a subway station just begging for some kind of intervention? After all, these panels were affixed to a wall and were seen by millions of commuters from all over the city. He immediately saw the black paper that covered the expired ads; it reminded him of a blackboard, and he thought that the correct medium for that surface would be chalk. And then he just went crazy and did thousands of these drawings.

GO'B: But for every one that survived, there has to be a lot that got covered.

JG: Exactly. And it's interesting because of course the ones that did survive had been stolen from the subway stations. We were very aware that people just went down there, in the middle of the night, and cut them out of the frames. Some people even took the whole frame. With some of the drawings that still exist, you can see that they're made on top of layers and layers of posters. Keith completely objected to people taking the drawings; he wouldn't endorse the practice. He felt they were very much site-specific works. Their ephemerality was due to the fact not only that they were temporary and would be papered over, but also that he drew them with chalk. This was part of the mystery and wonder of the pieces. For those of us who were observing these things pop up all over the city, there was a startling reaction to this visual vocabulary that was able to really grab your attention, despite the millions of agitated people, the noisy, smelly, hot, disgusting environment with conventional advertisements screaming at you; somehow these anonymous, deceptively simple images had real power.

GO'B: It's funny because I remember talking to Basquiat about unauthorized graffiti as unauthorized public art. But that was a concept: "Fuck the government; I'm going to make art for the public."

JG: That was pretty much Keith's sentiment, too. But because he began that way, there is a segment of the art-viewing public, both those who were around when he was making these early works and some today, who were most comfortable having Keith defined as only a graffiti artist. It was easier to box him into a category, which confined him, but endowed him with a certain street credibility. People did call Keith a graffiti artist, which he always refuted and denied. He respected the graffiti writers and was awed by their daring and technique. He was inspired and influenced by their work. But he used chalk on a temporary surface and did these underground works at all times of the day, often with thousands of people walking by. He wasn't clandestinely leaving his tag on the trains in the middle of the night. Since his death, especially with the explosion of attention to what is now called street art, people regard Keith as a kind of godfather of this movement, if you will, from a political standpoint.

GO'B: It was really daring because you could get your head clubbed for doing that.

DB: He was also arrested, wasn't he?

JG: He was arrested several times. There's one story we should probably look up where the cops locked him in a bathroom in the subway station. He was arrested many times, but he took great pride in recalling how, after about a year or two of doing these drawings, the cops would come up to him and ask him for his autograph.

GO'B: Because he continued to do it in the subway after he was already famous, which is . . .

JG: Unusual.

GO'B: Unusual, yeah. Because Jean-Michel was so freaked out by Michael Stewart, he never did anything on the street after a certain hour.

JG: Keith was very conscious of and deeply upset by the Michael Stewart episode and made an incredible painting about it in 1985. He kept a newspaper clipping about the story on the wall of his studio. But Keith continued doing the Subway Drawings well into the mid-1980s.

DB: Why did he stop?

JG: The reason that he gave was that people just kept stealing them. "What is the point? My intent has now been corrupted. And I don't want to give people any more material to steal." But it's interesting that the Pop Shop opened in 1986, not long after he stopped drawing in the subways. Keith's ambition and goal to have his images accessible to the general public, not only the art world, were maintained throughout his career. He began as a street artist, making works for the public and for the masses, not for the elite. You can find quotes from Keith where he speaks about that very issue, how the art world is too elitist and that art should be for everybody. There was a drive in him to make that a reality through his own art. But to say that he didn't have very high ambitions to be taken seriously as a fine artist is not true. There are always people who seem unable to reconcile that Keith's ambitions encompassed not only this impulse to intervene in public daily life, which stayed with him throughout his career, but also his sincere wish to be taken seriously and respected as a gallery and museum artist. At the time, there was no precedent, and the first response of both the art world *and* the graffiti world to this concept was the same: sellout.

GO'B: No precedent for . . . ?

JG: For the Pop Shop. A single-artist boutique. Nobody had ever done anything like that. Of course, he was influenced by Andy [Warhol]'s philosophy of art as a business, as well as [Claes] Oldenburg's *Store* series [1961–1964].

GO'B: I think it was probably the example of Andy making ads; he was an example for our generation. They didn't feel confined to the gallery.

JG: Andy was a great mentor of Keith's and a great friend, too. Keith consulted him when he was thinking about doing the Pop Shop. He wanted his blessing. Andy was the first one to say about himself that he did a lot of work just for the money. He was outspoken and unashamed about that. People certainly thought that Keith was doing his Pop Shop for the money, but in fact there was only one year during his life when the shop made a profit. He was not naive; he gave the interviews, he read the press, and he was criticized right, left, and center for having opened this store and for creating this thing that was looked at as a crazy enterprise for anyone with fine-art aspirations. Keith was quite hurt by the criticism he received, because he felt that as a living artist who was very much part of his own work, and a celebrity of sorts by that time, people should understand and even embrace what he was doing, no matter how radical. He hated defending his actions. But it didn't stop him. Not for one minute.

GO'B: I think that when the first generation of Pop artists came out, some people perceived it as a new ball game, as "those rules don't apply anymore," and Andy was the prime example of doing weird things outside of the art world. I saw Keith and the kids of that generation as trying to fulfill the promise of Pop art.

JG: All the money that was made in the shop went back into producing inventory and to paying the rent and salaries of the people who worked there, so this was never a money-making venture. Keith suffered a real blow when he opened the second shop in Tokyo. In the late '80s, Tokyo was *the* city. After New York, it was Tokyo. Keith was convinced that if he were to open another branch of the shop, "the only place I would consider opening [it] is Tokyo, because they really get me!" Keith had been to Japan several times already by this point and had long been inspired by Eastern calligraphy. He really loved Japan and got a lot of positive acclaim there. Because real estate

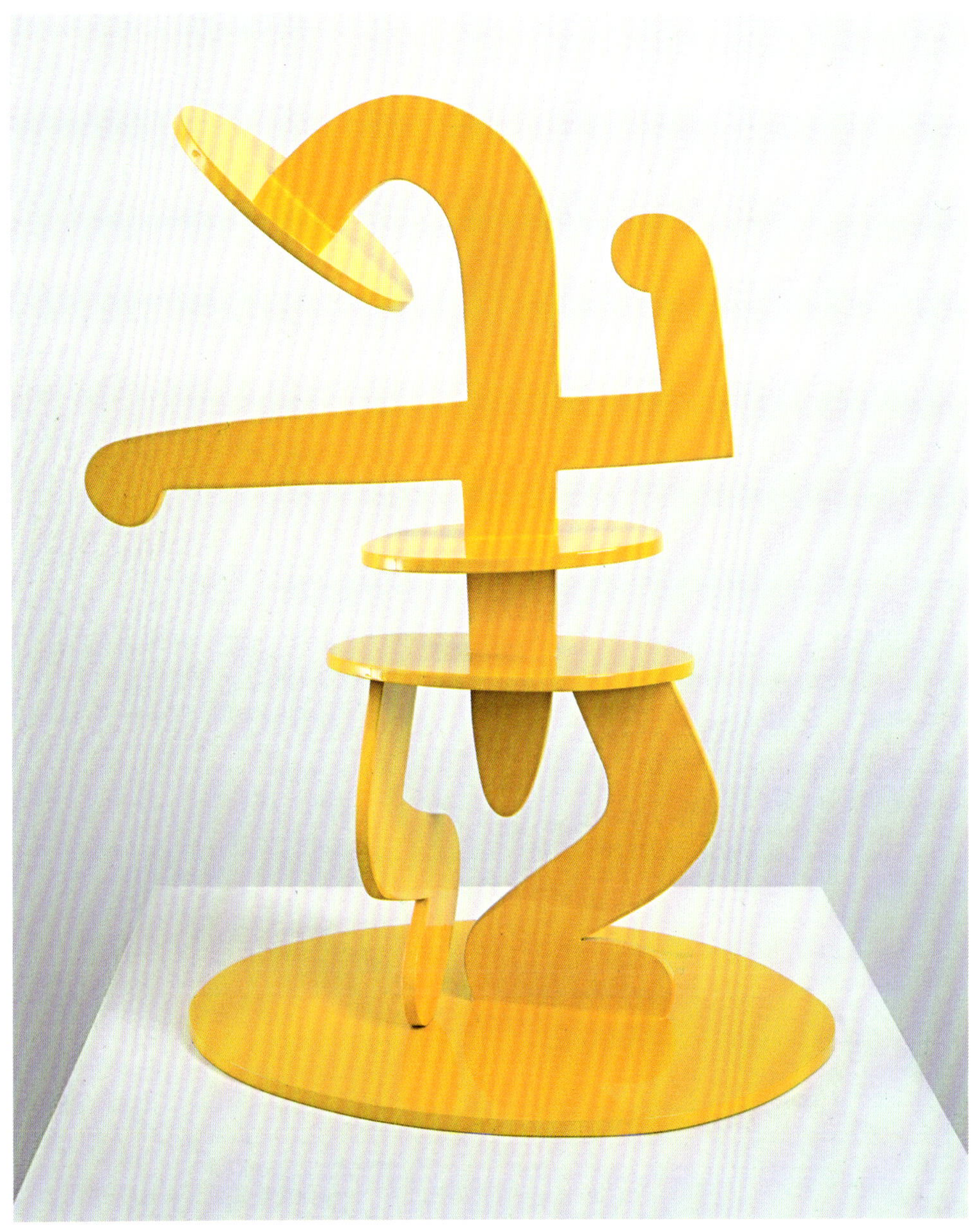

32

Keith Haring, *Julia*, 1987. Painted aluminum, 24 x 19⁵⁄₈ x 14⁵⁄₈ in. (61 x 49.8 x 37.1 cm). Private collection

in Tokyo is unspeakably expensive, the decision was made that instead of moving into an existing retail space, the shop would actually be built of two shipping containers put together in an L shape and installed on a plot of land that was in a very good neighborhood, right across the street from Brooks Brothers! As with the New York shop, Keith wanted to control all aspects of the shop, and since so much depended on the quality of reproduction, he was really involved in quality control.

His need for this control demanded that much of the merchandise for the Tokyo shop be produced in the United States. The problem was that by the time the product got to Japan, it was incredibly expensive. A T-shirt, which we would sell in the store in New York for $20, by the time it got to Japan, would be $45. Today that really doesn't sound like much, but back then it was kind of outrageous. The shop in Tokyo did not work because people wouldn't pay the high prices. His products were copied and sold from street vendors around the corner for a third of the price, so there was no way that this shop could survive. It was a real shock for him. He had this idealistic dream that this was a city and a culture that understood him and that somehow because of their love of American pop culture, and their love of him and his artwork, they would never question something like the price of the goods. Because by this point in time, Keith's fame was almost the equivalent of Andy's; it was the same level of celebrity. But to no avail—the shop opened in January of 1988 and closed that September.

DB: What about the work with LA II [Angel Ortiz], which I think was a pretty political chapter: How did you perceive that collaboration? LA was very young—fourteen years old—when they started to collaborate. Was he already doing graffiti?

JG: Yes, that's how Keith found him, because he kept seeing his tags. As Keith was starting to meet some of the graffiti writers in the late '70s and early '80s, he began asking them: "Who's making this tag? 'Cause he's got such a great line." They met in '80 or '81, when LA was just a kid, still in school. In 1982, they collaborated on some astonishing pieces that were included in Keith's first big solo show, at the Tony Shafrazi Gallery. In '83, they went together to Tokyo for a show at Galerie Watari. Keith and LA also painted the facade of a building in Tokyo. The following year, they painted the interior of the Fiorucci store in Milan. What initially drew Keith to LA II was the tag. He kept seeing these tags, "LA II" and "LA ROC," drawn in this beautiful calligraphic line. There are many people who believe it was LA II who gave Keith the inspiration for works that Keith later made on his own, works containing a few iconic figures with a lot of buzzing lines around them—not just the action lines, which Keith had always used, but those squiggles, dots, and embellishments that filled the entire background and dotted the lines.

DB: For me, it's a breaking with the cultures of the past, which is why the collaboration is very political. By taking these very well-known . . .

JG: Icons. Those objects are some of the most brilliant of the collaborations Keith and LA made. Keith was amused by the kitschy replicas of Greek urns, historic figures, and iconic artworks, such as the Little Mermaid, [portraits of] Marie-Antoinette [and] Louis XIV, Tutankhamun, the Statue of Liberty, Michelangelo's *David*, the Botticelli *Venus*, and so on. There was a great Pop element in all this, because most of the replicas they worked on in this series were actually garden statuary. Keith and LA would paint these kitschy fiberglass statuettes in fluorescent colors and then both artists would completely cover the surface in black-ink calligraphy. In retrospect, it's sort of surprising, given some of Keith's very strong antireligious sentiments, that he never decorated those ubiquitous garden statues of Jesus, Mary, and Joseph. Those could have been amazing!

GO'B: And of course Andy did all that stuff with iconic figures: money, Campbell's soup, Marilyn Monroe. . . .

JG: There was an incredible energy created between this small-town gay kid, Keith Haring, who came to New York and went to art school, coming into contact with this underground graffiti movement of young people from the city's Lower East Side housing projects and the South Bronx. The combination of Keith's and LA II's disparate influences and techniques created a kind of artistic nuclear fission. It's pretty amazing that Keith, to use a cliché, really was the zeitgeist in a way.

DB: Indeed, he commented on ecocide at the time when the movement against the destruction of nature had nearly just begun. It also started in his works. But that brings me to Haring the activist, who made those twenty thousand antiapartheid posters that he gave away. Can you tell us more about that?

GO'B: Norman Mailer wrote this book, *The Faith of Graffiti* [1974]; graffiti was incredibly impressive, but for me it was about reclaiming the city for individuals instead of corporations, making your name, your signature, into a sign and saying, "I am here." The key to the Jean-Michel Basquiat–Kenny Scharf–Keith Haring generation: "We can do what they're doing, but we can make it art, and we can have content." Keith really had content.

JG: He's a storyteller. Much of his symbolism and figures are already in our lexicon, but the simplicity of their rendering is deceptive. A great amount of his work is indeed very political—in fact, you might be able to make that argument about all of his work—because the movement that gave birth to him, that made him possible, was a political movement. Keith's

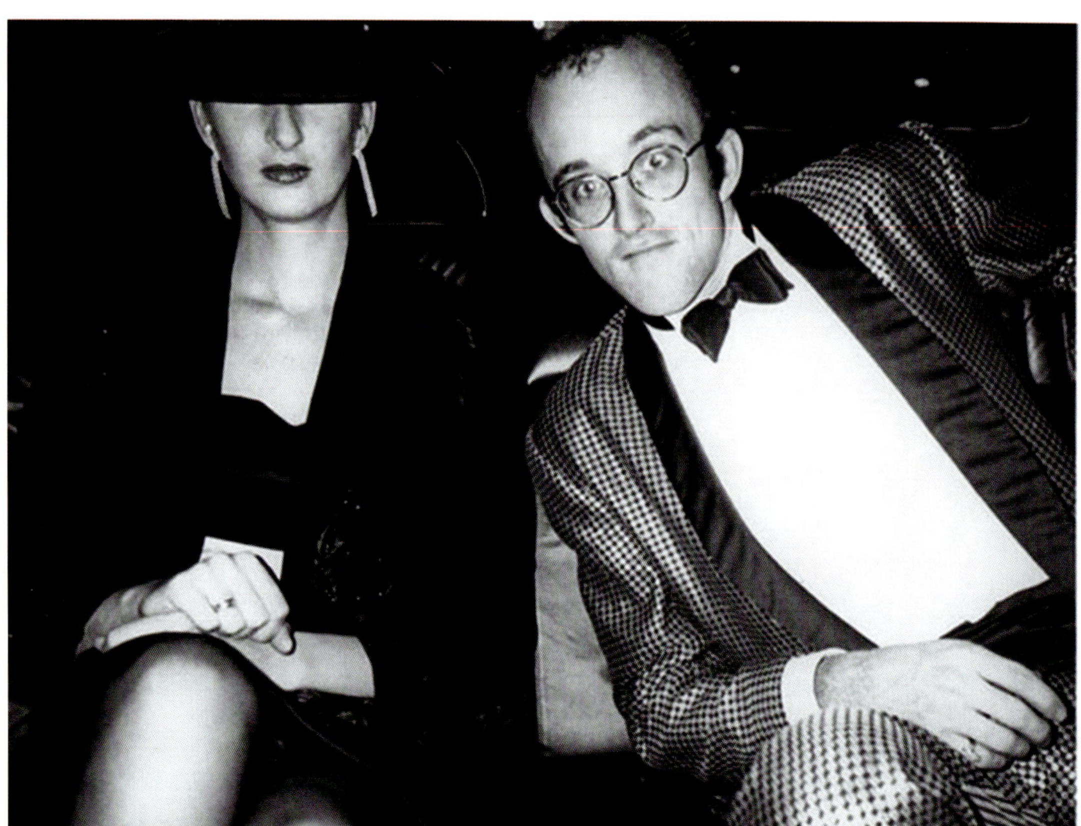

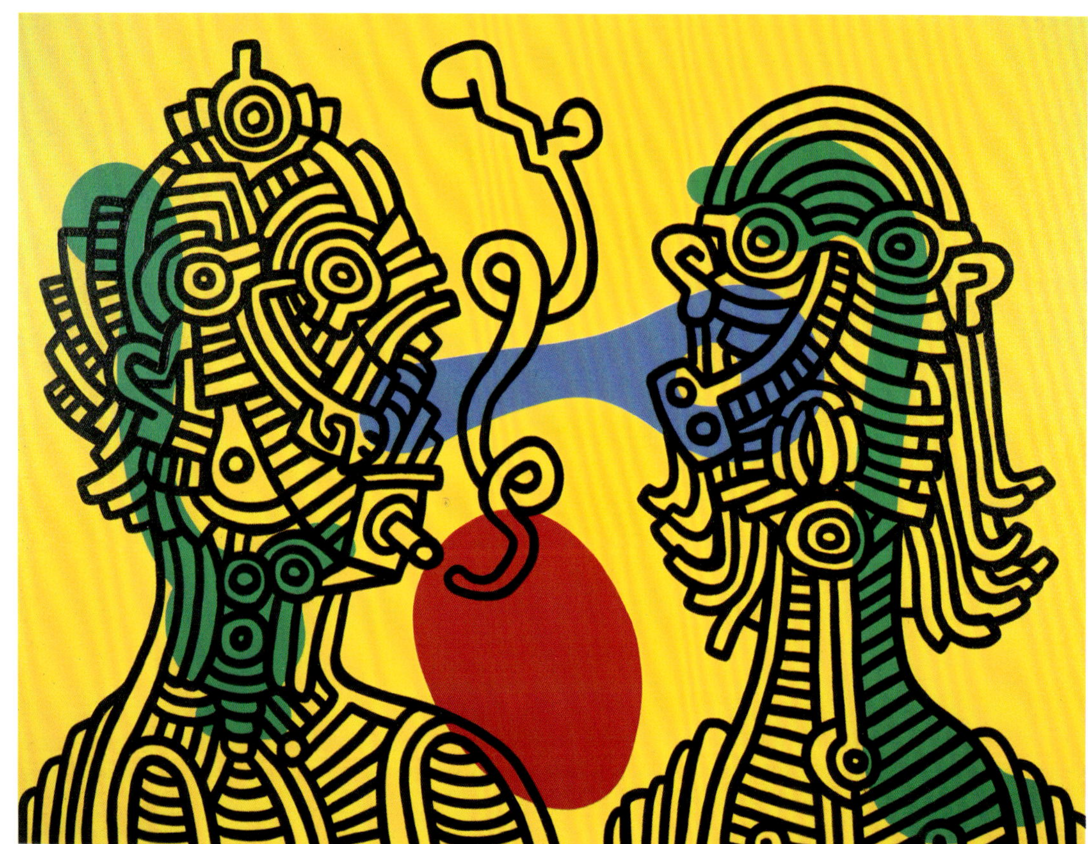

33

Julia Gruen and Keith Haring, New York, 1986. Photograph by Andy Warhol

34

Keith Haring, *Keith and Julia*, 1986. Oil and acrylic on canvas, 36 x 48 in. (91.4 x 121.9 cm). Private collection

first solo show, at the Shafrazi Gallery, was at the end of '82, and the antinuclear rally in Central Park, which was the biggest antinuclear rally that this city had ever seen, was that June. Keith the gallery artist, although he had already shown at P.S.122 and with Hal Bromm, was not yet on the main stage. Keith the underground activist artist was a man of mystery because he'd never signed his subway drawings, so nobody really knew who he was. To have printed up this wordless antinuclear poster and then enlisted his friends to join him in Central Park and sit at a table rolling up posters and handing them out to people—it was a spontaneous act of political engagement and meant a lot to Keith and to his friends. I don't know if the distribution of that poster was impactful, but it certainly was meaningful to him.

GO'B: You have to remember that Three Mile Island was huge in New York. That made everybody antinuclear, and we did a TV party about Three Mile Island. I made T-shirts with a headline from the *New York Post*. And there are pictures of me wearing this shirt. It was on everybody's mind. And it was only ten, twelve years after Stonewall. I think that the politics of Keith and the politics of Jean-Michel, they were the politics of our community. He expressed what everybody else felt.

JG: Keith's hometown is very close to Harrisburg, so he was very much thinking about that, too.

DB: And racism as well: Was it a special theme for him? Or was it just apartheid?

JG: Keith came from a middle-class family in a very small town in Pennsylvania, and he was very conscious that this was a very homogeneous, white, Christian society. Part of the excitement of exploring outside those boundaries was not only that he was, at last, able to find community—the gay community and the creative community—where he was not the outsider, where he could feel at home in himself, but [also that] he found a place of incredible diversity and color, with all the accompanying tensions, that he had never experienced before. It's always remarkable to me that the town where he grew up is only about two and a half hours from New York City, but it's a world away. He had a yearning to belong, but also to experience the other, and maybe some of that came from feeling all along that he *himself* was the other or another. But a big part of his initiation into the New York life was experiencing the intensity of the pre-AIDS gay nightlife and the enormous ethnic diversity. He had a number of long-term boyfriends, several of whom were either African American or Latino. He was drawn to these different cultures, and very curious about them.

DB: Was it really a statement? Because he speaks in his diaries about this "white man" as a very negative, capitalistic, at that time Christian, right-wing corporation guy from colonialism up to his time.

JG: Absolutely. He has written about being ashamed of being white. He has said that on the inside he felt black. We cannot take those words away from him.

GO'B: I had a lot of conversations like that. It's part of the tradition. Norman Mailer wrote "The White Negro" in 1959 [*sic*, 1957], and it was about how hipsters were people who felt black, who were rebelling against white culture or the lack of culture in white people.

JG: Later in his career, a great deal of his time and energy was consumed by his quest to delay his death from AIDS, and the imagery of disease and death, which had been present from the earliest years, really began to dominate his work. These later works perhaps don't elicit quite as much analysis as some of the earlier political statements and social-issue concerns that are sometimes less obvious.

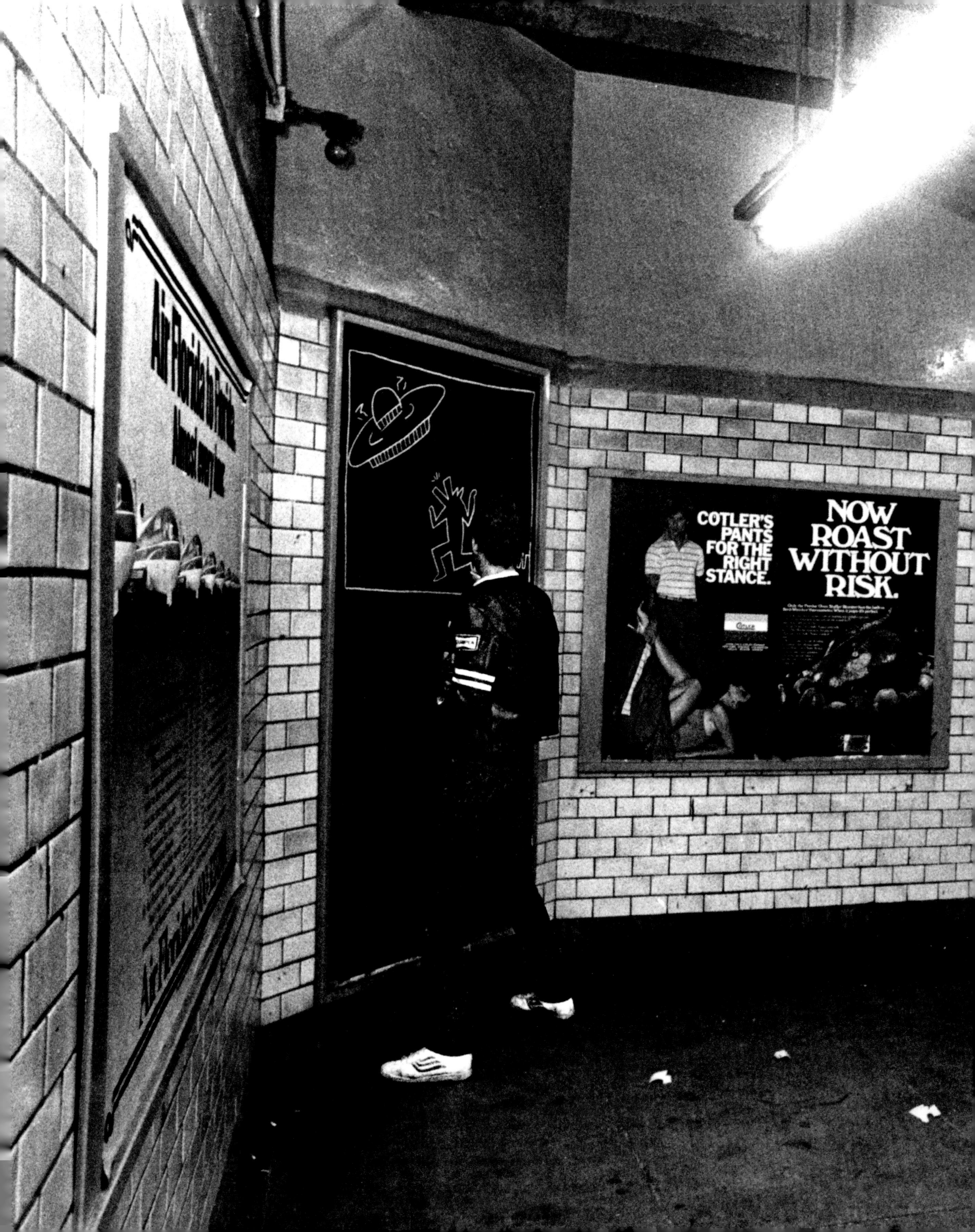
COTLER'S PANTS FOR THE RIGHT STANCE.
NOW ROAST WITHOUT RISK.

URBAN FRAGMENTS

When our entire environment is a manufactured one, we cannot pretend that the "artificial" activity of the artist can and should remain restricted to the private domestic sphere, as in periods when privacy was synonymous with "culture" and environment with "nature."

—Xavier Rubert de Ventós, *Heresies of Modern Art* (1979)

Subway Drawing

A photograph exposes a bare passageway (see opposite). Fluorescent light glares on ceramic bricks above a cement floor stained with the accumulated residue of a thousand spills and a hundred drunks' late-night pissings. This is no place one would stay for long, but rather one to hurry past on the way to somewhere else. But someone *has* paused in this spot: framed off-center between stairwell and photographer is a man in racing jacket and white sneakers, his crouched pose evincing a body in a suspension of fluid motion. His figure is framed on either side by advertisements. To the left, waiting airplanes offer us a trip to Florida, helpfully exposing the fleet that might rescue us from this catacomb, should we have the fare; and on the right, notices promote Cotler's pants ("For the Right Stance") and "risk-free" roast turkey—an effective summary of advertising's reliance on giddy slogans of comfort, convenience, and escape to reach passing consumers.

The man's attention focuses on the rectangle of black paper that frames him, an absence where another ad may soon appear. Just visible is the chalk with which he has begun to draw a schematic picture against its void: a quick frame delimits a flying saucer while an agitated werewolf chases off the foreign invader. If we read the ensemble, as the photograph prompts us to do, we would discover consonances within its imagery, now restaged as a battle. The ads themselves, or even the decrepit "future" of the surrounding architecture, are written as "alien" forms dedicated to kidnapping the frantic hybrid below; and the scrappy figure (the surrogate of the artist himself) as a resistant animal force, truly alive among the false plenitudes, the death-life of pants, fowl, and Florida. The active elaboration of the drawing itself in time—and this, after all, is what the photograph aims to show us—is the fulcrum by which these images are brought into comparison, and by which *resistance* is made more than the theme of the drawing.

Keith Haring drawing in a subway station, New York, 1980.
Photograph by Ivan Dalla Tana

JULIAN MYERS-SZUPINSKA

The reader will already have gathered, from the Pop-ubiquity of these particular renderings of dog-man and UFO, if not from this essay's presence in a catalogue of his work, that the photograph's subject is Keith Haring. In turn, this assignment of identity conveniently locates us in New York's subway system in the early 1980s, during which time (1980–1985) Haring often produced drawings in just this way. (The photograph was taken by the Milanese art photographer Ivan Dalla Tana, who worked during this period for several of New York's prominent galleries.)[1] These drawings take their place in an extended discourse on the city in Haring's early work, which finds articulation both in his subject matter and in his practice: the former most explicitly in his notebooks and drawings from 1978–1979, including his *Manhattan Penis Drawings for Ken Hicks* (1978), in the current exhibition; and the latter in the abstract painting fragments, flyers, and Xerox collages Haring posted in public spaces in 1980, along with the Subway Drawings themselves. Articulating that this activity was part of a certain sort of *political* program—or at least a reimagining of the relation between art and urban space—will be the job of the next pages.

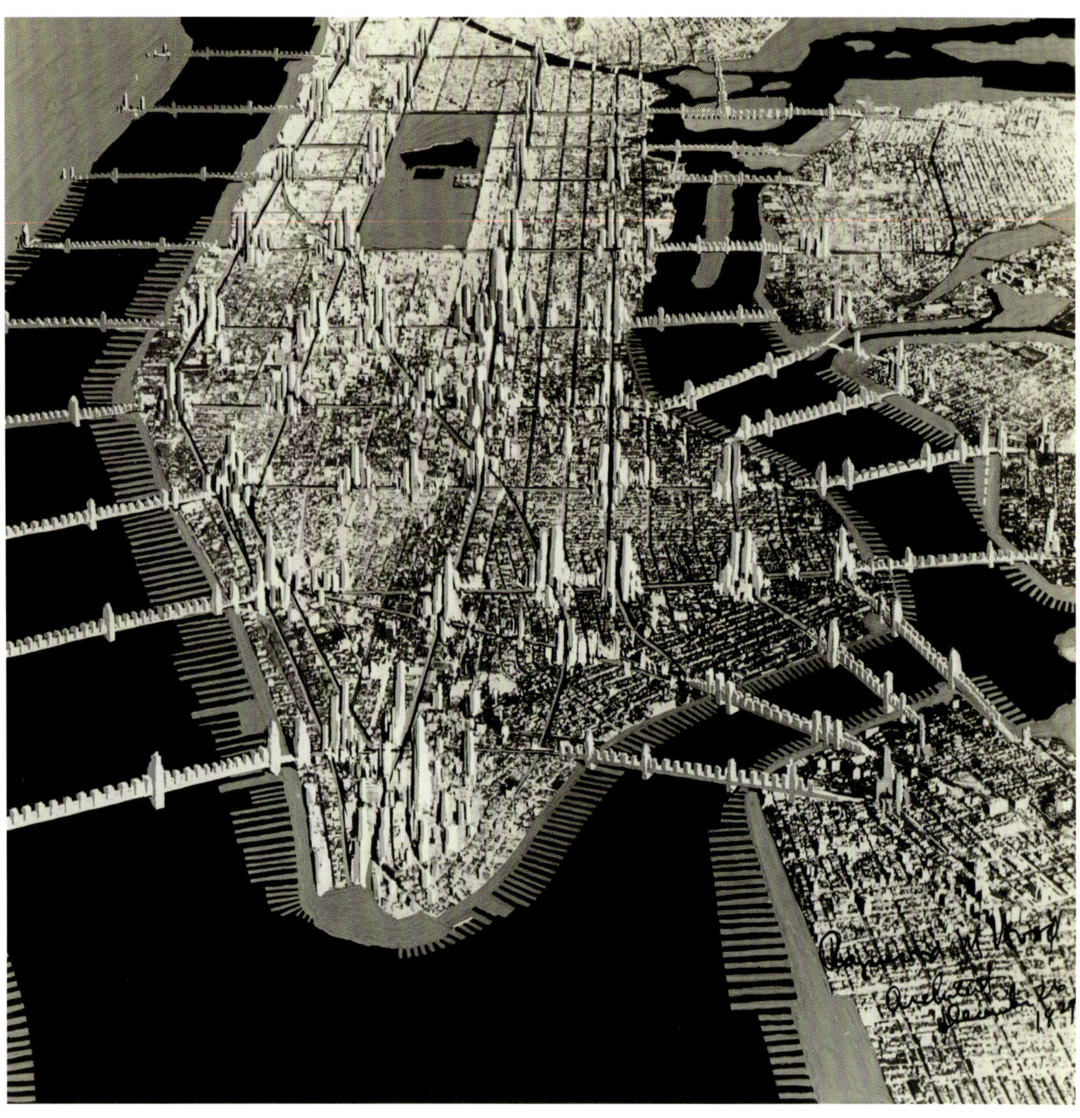

35

Raymond Hood (1881–1934), proposal for *Manhattan 1950*, 1929. Montage of aerial photograph and drawing, 8 x 8 in. (20.3 x 20.3 cm). Collection of the New-York Historical Society, The Raymond Hood Photograph Collection, 1911–1933

36

Keith Haring, *#12* from the series *Manhattan Penis Drawings for Ken Hicks*, 1978. Graphite on paper, 8½ x 5½ in. (21.6 x 14 cm). Collection of the Keith Haring Foundation

Abstracted Force Components

Accounts of Haring's encounter with New York City in the late 1970s understandably focus on the artist's personal experiences—his enrollment in the School of Visual Arts (SVA) in 1978 and his enthusiastic embrace of street art, dance music, and gay subculture—each of which formed his artistic practice in powerful ways. In no small way did the city seem to the teenager from provincial Kutztown, Pennsylvania, to be the most amazing and vibrant place on earth.[2] Yet this impression of his new urban life would have been held in tension with others, perhaps more encompassing in nature, of the city as machine, as dream, and as gritty urban reality. Let me set out what I take those other impressions to be.

In 1978, Dutch architect Rem Koolhaas wrote that, in the early twentieth century, "a new culture (the Machine Age?) [had] selected Manhattan as a laboratory: a mythical island where the invention and testing of a metropolitan lifestyle and its attendant architecture could be pursued as a collective experiment in which the entire city became the factory of man-made experience, where the real and the natural ceased to exist"[3] (see fig. 35). Publishing in the same moment, French sociologist Jean Baudrillard argued that by the 1970s this "invention and testing" had achieved a definitive, disconcerting result. "The city is no longer the politico-industrial zone that it was in the nineteenth century," he claimed; "it is the zone of signs, the media and the code."[4]

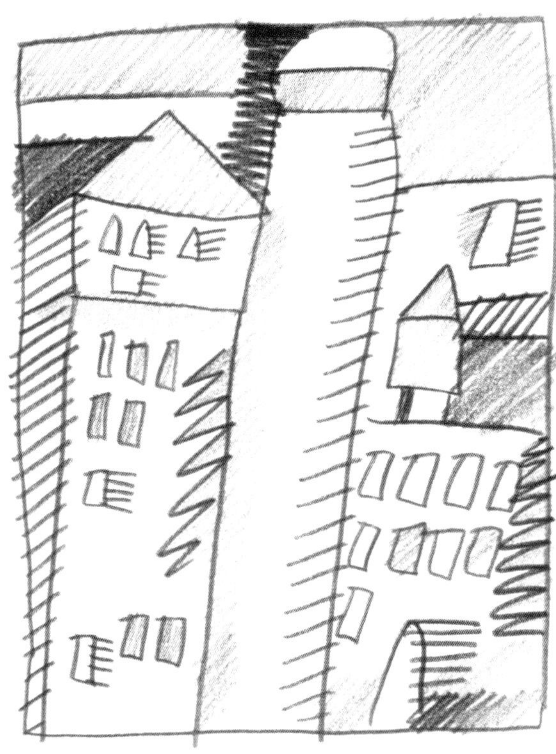

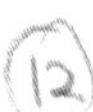

In these radical descriptions, the delirious machine dream of New York City imagined in the 1920s by architects such as Raymond Hood and Harvey Wiley Corbett had redoubled and mutated (these were the conditions that made possible Koolhaas's historical glance backward); the new city was a "space-time of the terrorist power of the media,"[5] of surfaces, signs, and flows of capital. As manufacturing (and therefore the collective space of the factory and of labor) deserted New York, "environment, transport, labor, leisure, play and culture become so many commutable terms on the chessboard of the city, a homogenous space defined as a total environment."[6] These were the portentous sentences pronounced by two Europeans; even if both admitted certain examples of resistance—the copulating skyscrapers of Madelon Vriesendorp for Koolhaas, or the semionautical *graffitistes* for Baudrillard—the outlook was grim, and possibilities for intervention few.

This image of the city as machine dream and "total environment" presided over a still-existing urban order that had begun, in myriad ways, to fall apart. After a decade of budgetary shortfalls, in 1975 New York City experienced a fiscal crisis and very nearly declared bankruptcy; it was saved only by a last-minute investment in city bonds by the United Federation of Teachers, though not without wage freezes for city workers and serious cuts to city services.[7] The blackout of 1977, which was the occasion of mass looting, arson, vandalism, and civil disorder, had similarly left its mark on the city.[8] The atmosphere was one of radical decline—crime, economic precariousness, and spiraling abandonment—which nevertheless made room for the thriving underground culture Haring found so thrilling.

Bustling subculture, urban blight, and "total environment"—my point is not to argue that one of these was more true than the others, but instead to pose them as all true at once, a confounding trialectic of urban life in that moment. It was one that Haring registered in his work immediately on arriving in the city, perhaps most explicitly in his *Manhattan Penis Drawings for Ken Hicks* (fig. 36; see also pls. 37–53), which riffed gleefully and homoerotically on his new surroundings over the course of dozens of comical renderings. The twin towers of the World Trade Center become two erect penises, while other architectural details—awnings, water towers—similarly give up their phallic goods. Elsewhere in the series, the cocks become patterns (*Drawing Penises in Front of Tiffany's!*, he proudly declares) or chaotic fields of disembodied members. This was a city swollen with (male) sexual pleasure, even as that pleasure seems oddly curtailed, frozen at the moment of arousal; no orgasms await these rigid city-boners.

Still, it would be difficult to read this series as anything but joyful, a "delirious New York" that affirms and exceeds the plans of the Machine Age architects elaborated upon by Koolhaas (and already Haring's proliferating penises seem to understand this as a "city of signs," in Baudrillard's sense). A more ambiguous meditation on the urban is to be found elsewhere in Haring's 1978 notebooks and journals. It should be said that these notebooks are capacious documents, incorporating notes from his classes and readings; they show the young artist parsing, seemingly all at once, the history of modern art and theory, often recording critical notes and workings-through. In the process, the curator Raphaela Platow wrote, one can observe Haring "develop[ing] the shapes he used one by one, as if creating his own abstract alphabet."[9]

These drawings only sometimes render cityscapes proper: in one subtitled *Above the Trees* (fig. 37), for example, or in the fantasy architecture of *City with Underground Bomb Shelters* (fig. 38). Just as often they seem to discover, in the play of impressions of urban space, fragmented geometries and shapes that might be disassembled, simplified, reorganized, and—crucially—redeployed. In several cases, he assembles these "constructive elements" into a rectangular frame, as if sorting and considering them as a vocabulary; in one such drawing, he describes them as "abstracted force components." These codified fragments read city-space backward, from lived space to representation to the geometrical abstractness of the city's gridded plan. Yet read through "actual space," as well as in Haring's already fluent manual technique, these quasi-linguistic "force components" return not as a rational city grid, but as both uniquely individuated—drawn by hand, no two are quite the same—and loosened from their regimented urban structure (fig. 39). If, as Platow intuited, this was to be a vocabulary, there was as yet no sure sense of how its signs might articulate themselves into sentences or pictures—much less space as such.

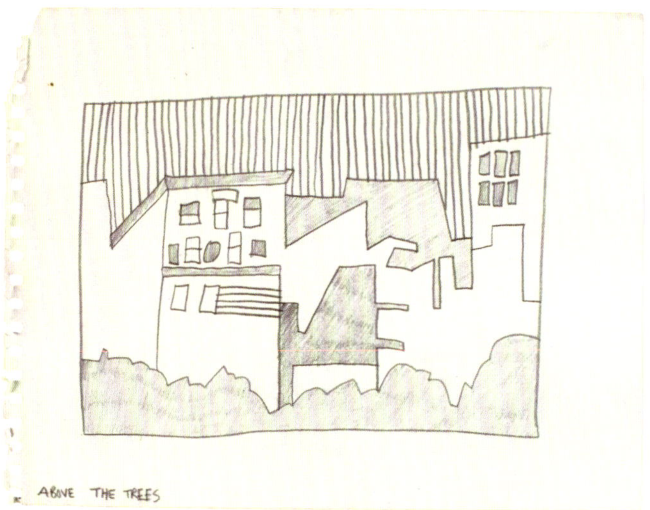

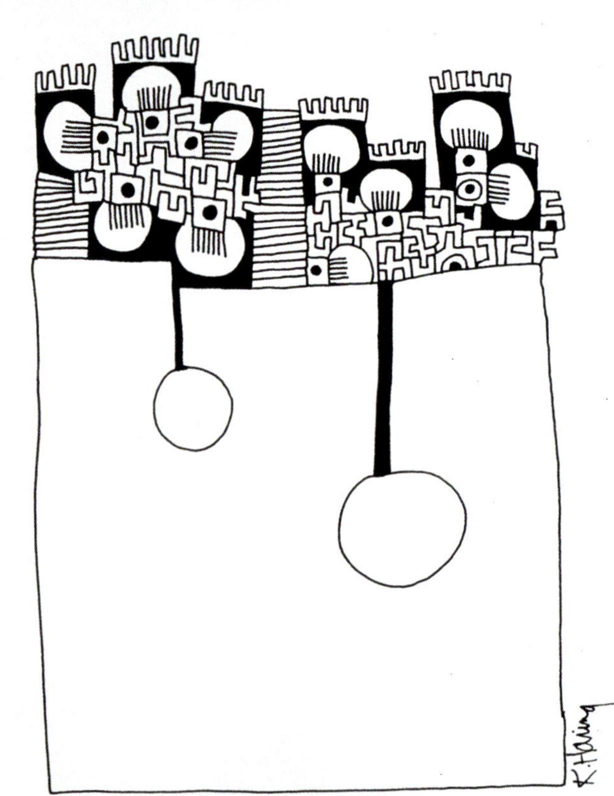

37 (above, top)

Keith Haring, untitled notebook page (*Above the Trees*), 1978. Graphite on paper, 8½ x 11 in. (21.6 x 27.9 cm). Collection of the Keith Haring Foundation

38 (above, bottom)

Keith Haring, *City with Underground Bomb Shelters*, 1978. Notebook page, ink on paper, 11 x 8½ in. (27.9 x 21.6 cm). Collection of the Keith Haring Foundation

39 (opposite)

Keith Haring, *Untitled Drawings* (*Variations*), 1978. Gouache on paper, various dimensions. Collection of the Keith Haring Foundation

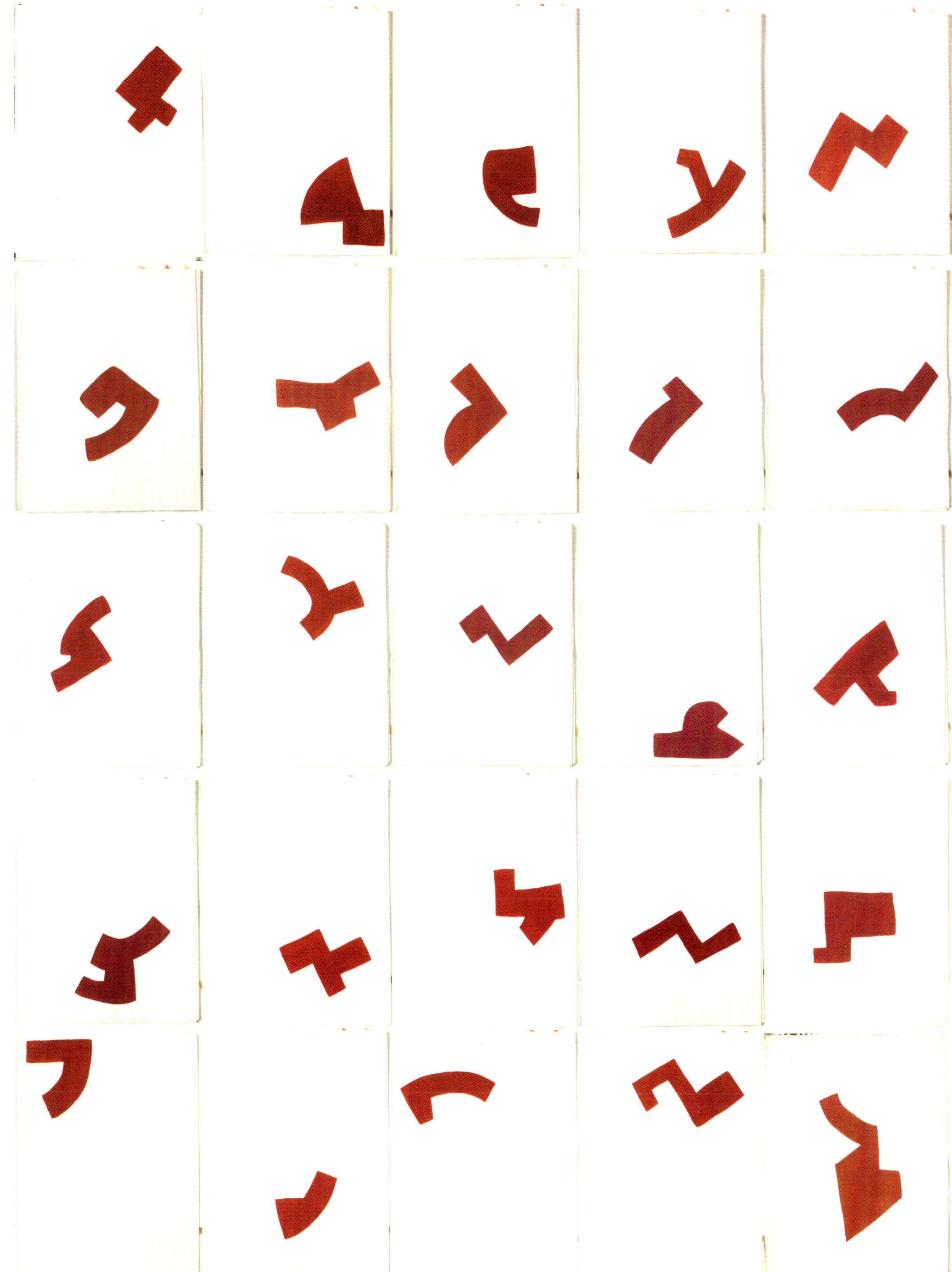

Dozens of drawings from this period show Haring agglomerating these utopian fragments back into something that looks like space. The results evoke many things—totem poles, landscapes, mounds of detritus—but frequently call up utopian or impossible cities: disjointed quasi-architectures on plateaus, pullulating aerial views of urban sprawl (see fig. 40). (These drawings also evoke an encounter with modernisms half-forgotten by the late 1970s: the spiritualism of Wassily Kandinsky, the introverted dream architectures of *Die Gläserne Kette*,[10] or the paned cityscapes of Paul Klee. A passage from Haring's journals records him reading Kandinsky's 1911 essay "Concerning the Spiritual in Art" and immediately afterward producing a series of abstract drawings and noting that "it is 'coincidences' like this that make me continue in the face of prevailing 'doubt.'")[11] Yet these pictures, for all their antic invention, evidently posed a sort of dead end for the artist, as would a 1979 video work shot at SVA that showed Haring composing an "environment" with his abstract shapes, pointedly titled *Painting Myself into a Corner* (see fig. 21). The video made the productive move from sketchbook to studio, and from represented to actual space, but the more radical move, into the city as such, and therefore into the perplexing trialectic set out above, was yet to come.

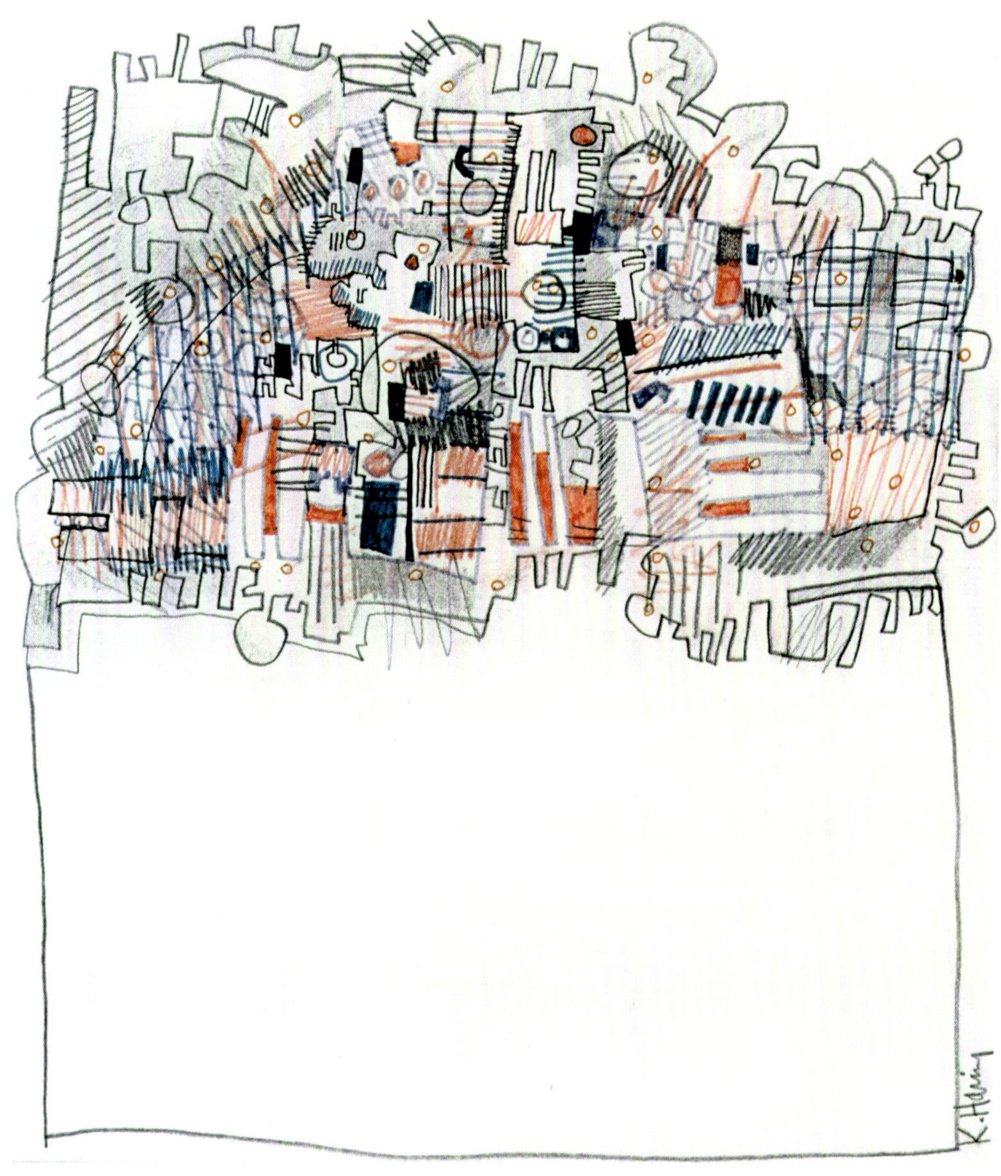

City-Seme

The "environments" of 1978–1979—alongside *Painting Myself into a Corner*, these included a first effort in the Student Gallery of the SVA, followed by two more in the basement of the Arts and Crafts Center at the Pittsburgh Center for the Arts—had engaged the form of a quasi-*Gesamtkunstwerk*. They entailed ripping preexisting paintings into pieces in order "to distribute the imagery more evenly," Haring related in his journal. "The most important idea involved in these three works is the freedom of will to rip, alter, obliterate images that I had created. . . . The only consideration while creating the environment is the environment itself."[12] Yet in these works the "environment" remained the interior, whereas the radical "obliteration" enacted on his works would succeed only if it were subsequently recomposed and reconciled into overall effect.

Haring's encounter with graffiti culture, by this point a ubiquitous visual feature of New York City, would impel him to shift both territory, from the gallery to public space, and formal/semiological strategy,[13] again privileging the fragment over

40 (above)

Keith Haring, *Untitled*, 1978. Marker and pencil on paper, 10 x 8 in. (25.4 x 20.3 cm). The Estate of Stephen and Diana Abtreu

41 (opposite, top)

Keith Haring, painting fragment, 1980. Collection of the Keith Haring Foundation

42 (opposite, bottom)

Keith Haring, painting fragment posted in New York City, 1980. Photograph by the artist. Collection of the Keith Haring Foundation

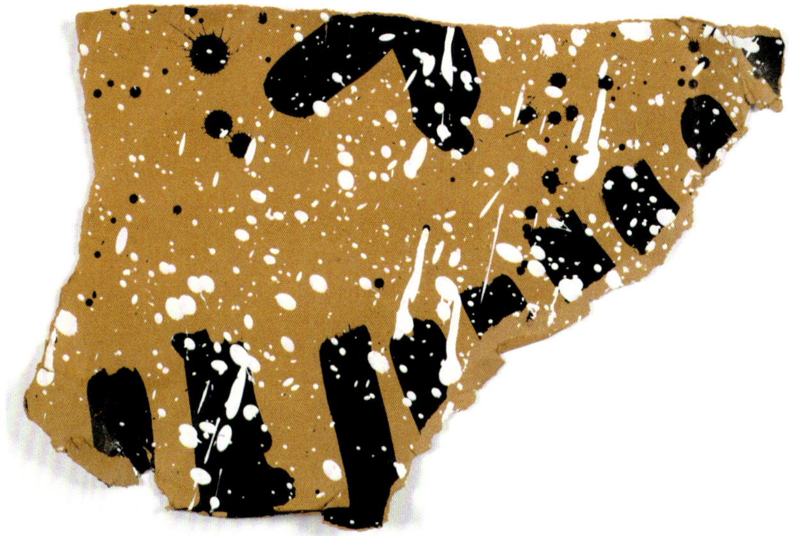

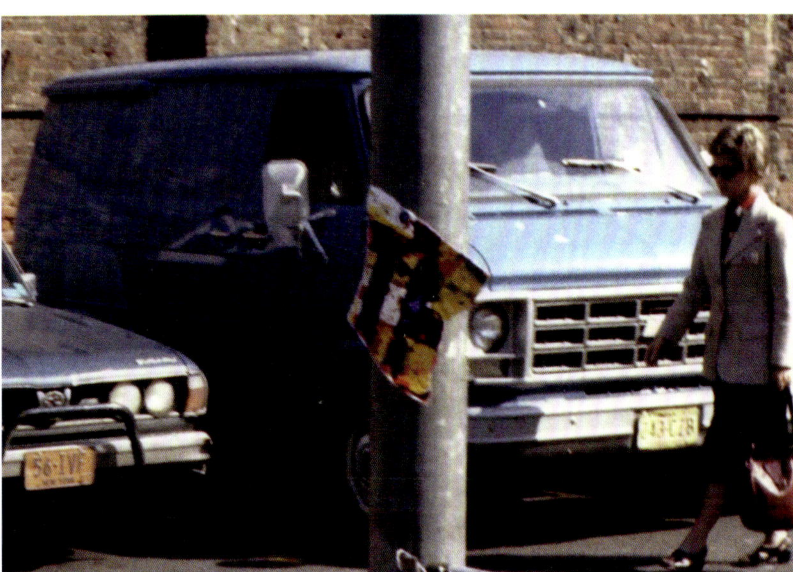

the whole. Rather than rearticulating his ripped canvases into an artwork at some higher order, he began placing isolated shards of gestural drip paintings (Jackson Pollock via New Wave) in public spaces, where they would now become part of a "total environment" of the city itself (figs. 41–42). Posted on a fence pole or attached to a door, awning, or trash can, these fragments of interrupted painterly flow were to be completed by the city's own activities and surfaces, as well as by the viewer who might (in whatever way) grasp them as aesthetic—even if not as "art," as legitimated by the institutions of his moment. The part-object of the painting fragment would be completed only in terms of its relationship to the city's crowded system of signs—as apprehended by city dwellers attuned to such patterns as a matter of everyday life.

Such work dreamed of reconciling modernist art (in the sign-form of the gestural drip) with the public (and public space) it had by 1980 largely left behind. Yet there is pathos to this dream in light of the works themselves; these painting-scraps appear oddly orphaned among their new surroundings, alienated both from their origins in the studio and their urban habitat. Emancipation, if it was to come, depended on the works being *recognized* as such (this Haring knew from the graffiti tags he adored); but such recognition was forestalled by the works' very abstraction, which rendered the artist's utopian fragments little more than another piece of visual noise in an already cacophonous city.[14] If he wanted his works to register in the "zone of signs"—to declare both the individual who made them and the collective style his work aimed to embody[15]—they would need to be more declarative and direct.

This demand, the consequences of which I will elaborate now, evinces a substantial distinction from the logic of the graffiti with which Haring's work is often associated. Baudrillard, for example, praised graffiti for its excess of "indeterminacy," "whose function is to derail the common system of significations";[16] in 1987, the critic and poet Susan Stewart would meditate on graffiti's "remoteness, abstraction, and simultaneity."[17] Even if inspired by the cut-up collages of William S. Burroughs and Brion Gysin—Haring had been deeply impressed by the *Nova Convention*, a retrospective of Burroughs's work organized by Columbia professor and *Semiotext(e)* editor Sylvère Lotringer in 1978—Haring's Xerox collages of 1980 are hardly as fragmented or arcane as the efforts of his heroes (see pls. 54–59). Posted in public spaces (see fig. 43), Haring's collages speak more directly and instrumentally: they imagine US president Ronald Reagan and Pope John Paul II as murdered (*Pope Killed for Freed Hostage*) and as murderers (*Ronald Reagan Accused of TV Star Sex Death: Killed & Ate Lover*). Bluntly offensive, they are insurrectionary and immature in equal measure. Fantastical they may be; what they are not is "indeterminate."

We turn back now to the photograph and moment with which my essay began, and to the style and practice for which the artist is still best known. Indeed, before the end of the 1980s, Haring would marvel at just how Pop-ubiquitous these vivid hieroglyphic figures had become—well beyond his own prolific productions (and self-branding) and on to bootleg key chains, T-shirts, music videos, and so on. More than that of any other artist, perhaps, his became a collective period style seen through the lens of the market. Even now, this style calls up a chain of reflexive, if inchoate or unsystematized, associations: Reagan, the pope, hip-hop, AIDS, commercialism, and so on.

Impossible as all this is to erase, it is worth trying, for a moment, to see the photograph afresh—and to discern there the important realization it represents for Haring's developing urban politics. Unlike the painting fragments and Xerox posters, this practice relied on neither modernist painting nor collage (each difficult to perform out of doors, or at the speed required by what was considered, let us not forget, a crime), but on *drawing*. Whereas previous works had required export from the studio, now Haring would work directly on the surfaces the city offered up, with the direct manual contact that drawing assumes. And he acted out this improvisation in real time, asserting, against increasing enclosure and privatization, his right and his profound desire to do so, for anyone who might see.

Which is to say that, despite its differences, Haring's work nevertheless enacted the radicalism native to all graffiti of the era (see fig. 44). As Susan Stewart argued, it represented "a violation of the careful system of delineation by which the culture articulates the proper spaces for artistic production and reproduction." [18] In the name of style, it attempted "a utopian and limited dissolution of the boundaries of property" [19]—a revolt, in its small and temporary way, as political as any occupation. Thus, if Haring's work still imagined the city he loved as both "total environment" and a "zone of signs," it was in a sense worth distinguishing from Koolhaas's delirium or Baudrillard's dystopia.

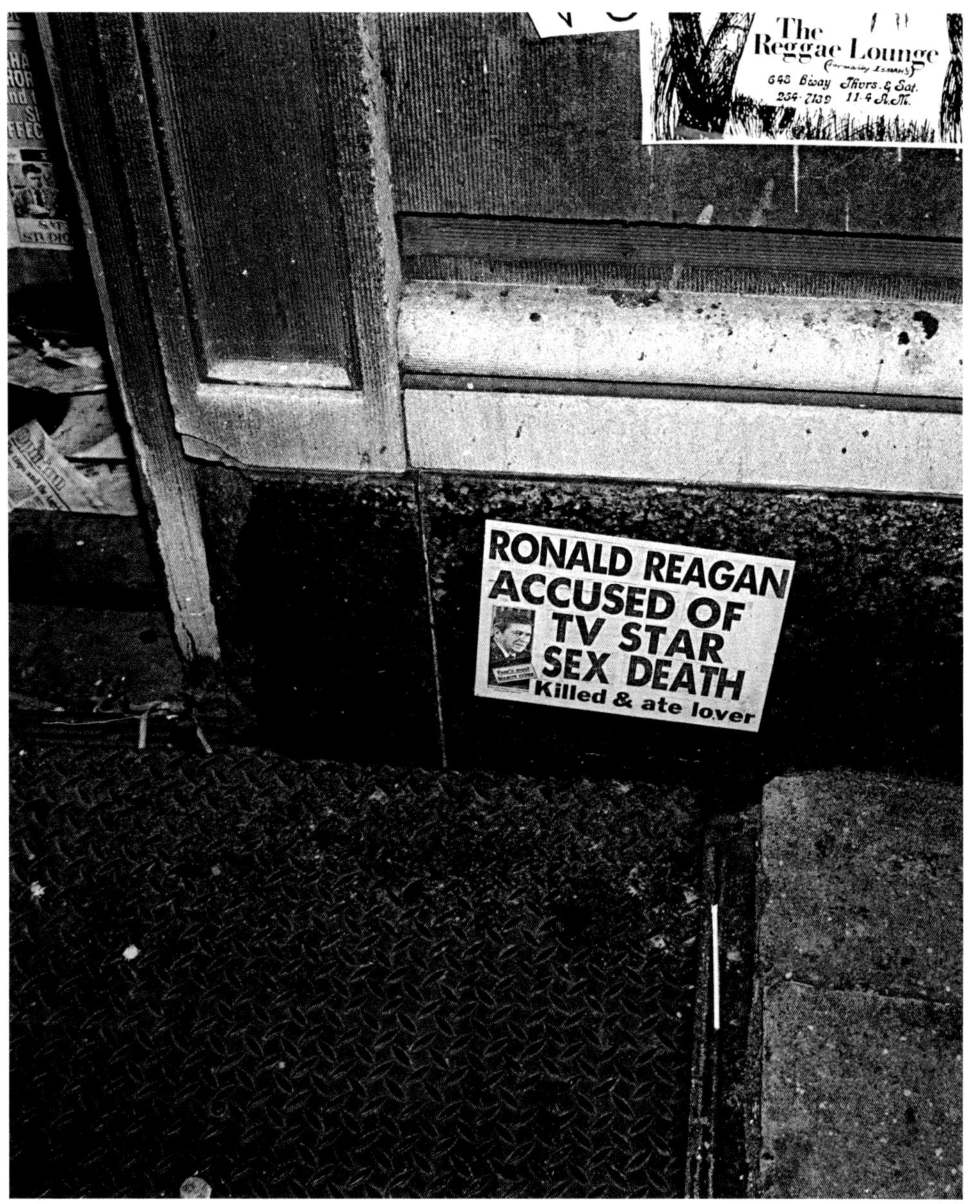

43

Keith Haring, *Ronald Reagan Accused of TV Star Sex Death*, posted in New York, 1980. Photograph by Joseph Szkodzinski

44

Keith Haring, New York City graffiti, 1981. Photograph by Klaus Wittmann

Notes

1. Haring would frequently bring photographers to witness his process of drawing in public, particularly in the years 1980–1982. Because the drawings would quickly be erased or covered over, and the artworks as such lost, it was important that such evidence be entered into the record. Most often he was accompanied and pictured by his close friend the artist Tseng Kwong Chi (see pp. 2–15), but others, such as Dalla Tana, Klaus Wittmann, and Joseph Szkodzinski, also captured him at work on subway drawings.
2. Keith Haring, *Keith Haring Journals* (New York: Viking-Penguin paperback ed., 1997), 15.
3. Rem Koolhaas, *Delirious New York* (New York: Monacelli Press, 1994 [1978]), 9–10.
4. Jean Baudrillard, "Kool Killer, or the Insurrection of Signs," in *Symbolic Exchange and Death*, trans. Iain Hamilton Grant (London: Sage Publications, 1993 [1976]), 78.
5. Ibid., 77.
6. Ibid.
7. See William Tabb, *The Long Default: New York City and the Urban Fiscal Crisis* (New York: Monthly Review Press, 1982).
8. Thousands of stores were looted or burned, causing "more than a billion dollars in damage that can be seen today on streets like still-battered Broadway in the Bushwick neighborhood in Brooklyn." Martin Gottlieb and James Glanz, *New York Times*, August 15, 2003, www.nytimes.com/2003/08/15/us/blackout-2003-past-blackouts-65-77-became-defining-moments-city-s-history.html?src=pm (accessed September 25, 2012).
9. Raphaela Platow, "Holding up a Frame," in Raphaela Platow, ed., *Keith Haring: 1978–1982*, exh. cat., Kunsthalle Vienna, May 28–September 19, 2010; Contemporary Arts Center, Lois and Richard Rosenthal Center for Contemporary Art, Cincinnati, Ohio, February 26–September 5, 2011; Brooklyn Museum of Art, New York, March 16–July 8, 2012 (Nuremberg, Germany: Moderne Kunst Nürnberg, 2011), 83.
10. *Die Gläserne Kette* (the Glass Chain) refers to a chain letter, initiated by Bruno Taut, sent among a group of German Expressionist architects from November 1919 to December 1920. Their "utopian correspondence" frequently took the shape of imagined and dreamlike buildings.
11. See Wassily Kandinsky, "Concerning the Spiritual in Art," excerpted in Charles Harrison and Paul Wood, eds., *Art in Theory, 1900–1990: An Anthology of Changing Ideas* (Oxford: Blackwell, 1993), 86–94; Haring, *Keith Haring Journals*, 38.
12. Haring, *Keith Haring Journals*, 23–26.
13. Haring's readings of semiology (Roland Barthes, *Mythologies* and *Elements of Semiology*) and information theory (Abraham Moles, *Information Theory and Esthetic Perception*) are registered in his journals. See references to Barthes in Haring's notebook pages reproduced in Platow, ed., *Keith Haring: 1978–1982*, 74–77, and to Moles in Haring, *Keith Haring Journals*, 57.
14. Haring's photographs of the painting fragments in situ realize his ambition more effectively than the works themselves would have in space, but they can do so only in retrospect, and in reproduction.
15. "Under these conditions, radical revolt effectively consists in saying, 'I exist, I am so and so, I live on such and such a street, I am alive here and now.'" Baudrillard, "Kool Killer," 78.
16. Ibid.
17. Susan Stewart, "*Ceci Tuera Cela:* Graffiti as Crime and Art," in Susan Stewart, *Crimes of Writing: Problems in the Containment of Representation* (New York: Oxford University Press, 1991 [1987]), 208.
18. Ibid., 227.
19. Ibid., 228.

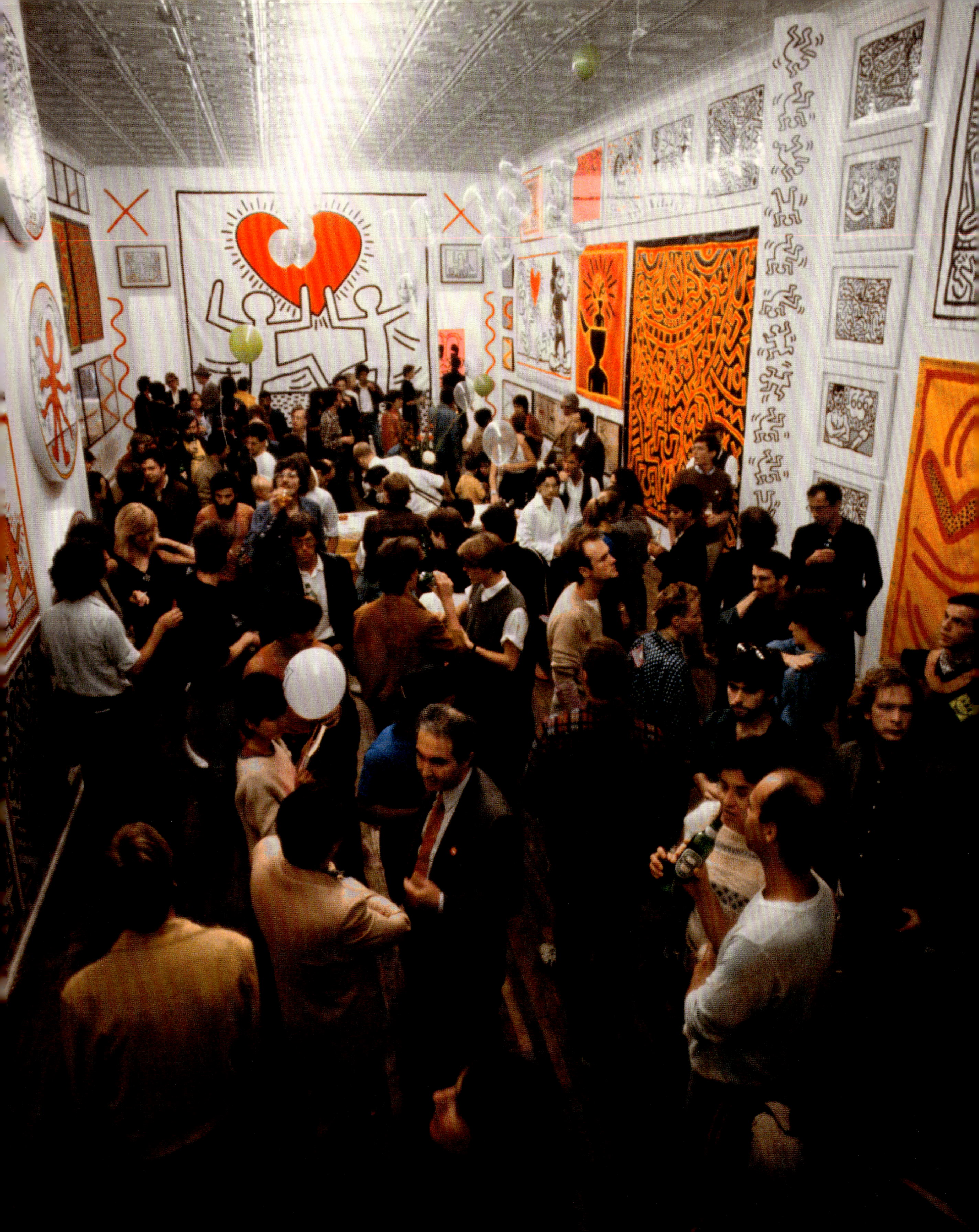

THE PERSISTENCE OF MEMORY AND THE FORTUNE OF HAVING BEEN THERE

Not so very long ago, before the art market engendered overly literal thinking and well-groomed businesspeople, art dealers tended to be as "out there" as the artists they were representing. Tony Shafrazi is just such an anachronism today. A philosopher, poet, artist, mischief-maker, bon vivant, iconoclast, and visionary, Shafrazi is daft, unorthodox, deeply committed to radical histories, and nonlinear, even baroque, in his thinking, in ways that make many artists seem merely eccentric. His idiosyncratic sensibilities and uncanny eye and his early championing, forceful advocacy, and enduring support of Keith Haring make him inseparable from the bigger story of Haring's life and work. It was a matter of chance that brought them together, yet it seems unfathomable now to think of any other gallerist who could have helped introduce this artist to the world at large.

This interview was conducted during a long bull session—amid some food and coffee—over a single afternoon in Tony Shafrazi's SoHo loft. And it has carried on in the many weeks since then as a kind of correspondence in which old reminiscences collide to remind each other of more details and clamber for some common footing that approximates "truth"—an obsessive process of re-vision that would seem inevitable to the manner in which Tony approaches life. It has, I hope, preserved much of his unmistakable voice, energy, and intensity, and, most important, it reveals how an anecdote means nothing unless it is part of a greater story that simultaneously goes back in time and suggests the future, because history, after all, is less about the particulars than about the bigger picture.

This final version remains, through the long process, as fresh to me as it was in the beginning. In it, I can still smell the food and see Tony amid the piles of books, the clutter of some perpetual epic renovation, the aesthetic trophies of a life well lived in the trenches of the art world—all speaking to a restless mind, an insatiable curiosity, and an eye unlike any in the art world today. When I first got there and commented on all this, Tony explained that he never invited people over to his loft, for, like many who are social in this town we live in, our apartments are our only sanctuaries. I'm as honored to have been there as I am to have had a chance to talk with him about this subject and this little piece of time about which we both care so much.

—Carlo McCormick

Keith Haring opening at the Tony Shafrazi Gallery, New York, October 1982. Photograph by Allan Tannenbaum

A CONVERSATION BETWEEN TONY SHAFRAZI AND CARLO McCORMICK

From the Prosaic to the Mudd Club

CARLO McCORMICK: Let's start with something prosaic, something really simple. Did you come across Keith through what he was doing with Club 57 and the Mudd Club, or was it through Fun Gallery? Or none of the above?

TONY SHAFRAZI: None of the above and *before all of that.*

CM: And you'd followed his work on the street?

TS: No, before that, too. I had opened a few spaces and presented exhibitions before, in London back in '68, and after a few years of helping put together a great collection for the Tehran Museum in the mid-'70s, I opened a gallery there in the fall of '78, which the so-called revolution came and blew away on opening day. Then, in early '79, I didn't have much money left, so I started a gallery where I was living on Lexington Avenue and East 27th Street. I was nervous, as it was a studio apartment on the fifteenth floor, far away from SoHo, 57th Street, and other galleries, but the light was good. At that time there were no alternative galleries, and my interest wasn't in money; looking back, the times were changing, and I suppose it was one of the first postmodern moves toward opening up the scene. I remember the bitterness that I had felt toward the bombastic, dictatorial rules and regulations of the art world of the late '60s and early '70s. After the euphoria of Pop art, various movements seemed to follow, at least one a year—Minimalism, Primary Structure, Systemic, Process, Conceptual, Anti-Form, Language, Land, Performance art, and whatever other movements I am leaving out—and seemed to operate in the oppressive climate of the last gasp of the modern movement, with its Hegelian, restrictive, and somewhat miserable regulations and conditions, with everyone starving and nothing colorful going on. None of those people could dance. It was time for change.

CM: A big shift that happens—and you're certainly a figure that is responsible for it—is that younger artists would go by and show their works to a gallery, and if a gallery was interested, they'd be like, "Oh, very interesting, come back next year and show us again." It seemed they wouldn't support a young artist; they were really looking for a more mature, mid-career artist. But with Keith and with what you were doing, there became this cult of youth around art, right?

TS: Yeah, I like that expression, "cult of youth." Youth was breaking out everywhere, if you remember, with the punk and radical music of the Ramones, the New York Dolls, Television, Talking Heads, and Debbie Harry and Blondie in New York, and the English sounds of David Bowie, the Sex Pistols, the Jam, and the Clash at small start-up underground clubs. A freedom of language with its own vocabulary came out of it, too. Other than the exhibition by Marcia Tucker in '78 called *Bad Painting*, at the New Museum, which was kind of a breakthrough for museums, there was nothing else happening. Even though a lot of that was clumpy . . .

CM: There were some pretty bad paintings . . .

TS: Yeah, I guess, but it introduced a few new voices. When I opened in '79, I showed quite a few really good exhibitions: Olivier Mosset, Sarah Charlesworth, Bill Beckley, Zadik Zadikian, and Bernd Naber . . . and of course the great show with Keith Sonnier. To answer your question about how I came across Keith Haring, one time Bill Beckley said, "Oh, if you need a couple of assistants to help out preparing for your exhibitions, I've got two of my students from Kutztown, Pennsylvania, who went to Carnegie; they're here at the School of Visual Arts [SVA]," which was only down the street. Well, I used to teach at the School of Visual Arts. When I moved from England in '69, Malcolm Morley helped me get a job lecturing there. Of course, back in those days, the late '60s and early '70s, all artists—famous or not—had to teach or do something to survive.

CM: Who was the other artist from Kutztown?

TS: He was somebody Keith went to school with. His childhood friend Kermit.

CM: Oh, Kermit! Kermit Oswald. I love Kermit. A beautiful man.

TS: How do *you* know him?

CM: Kermit and I did a lecture together in Pennsylvania. He told hilarious stories, like about Keith doing graffiti as a fifteen-year-old kid on a bridge. Kermit has great stories; I love him. So, they came in to help you, and how did that go?

TS: I was busy getting ready for the Keith Sonnier show, if I'm not mistaken, when they came to help. I remember them both, lanky and tall, but I remember Keith's movements were very unusual. It seemed like he could turn his head all the way around—talk about rubbernecking. His muscular mobility and flexibility were outstanding. I remember clearly being very impressed at how quickly he learned things. If I showed him something, he'd pick it up in a minute, practically, and then do it perfectly in an hour. His physical dexterity and grasp of things were so remarkable, they registered immediately with me.

CM: So that was innate for his street work? When you look at the body of work that he did in the subways, *muscular* is the adjective that comes to mind.

TS: Absolutely. He had a remarkable energy. There would never be a moment when he'd be sitting around, looking at me and waiting as if in need of help or assistance like everyone else, just . . .

CM: Self-motivated.

Running Wild

TS: [Keith was] always on the go, like running wild, [but] at the same time extremely respectful and attentive, checking you out and listening carefully, so if you pointed out something, it was taken seriously. I hadn't met anybody like that, then or since. When he first came to help me at the gallery painting the walls, I noticed that when he finished work, he would wash out and dry all the brushes, from tiny ones to the bigger ones, [as well as] his shoes, and lay them all out in a clean, orderly row.

CM: Not a messy painter!

TS: Exactly. There was much aesthetic in the spillover, what surrounded the work, so I knew he was very respectful of me, very respectful of the place and of the work he was doing, and the whole process involved in preparing an exhibition. During the opening, many of his friends came to help. Jean-Michel Basquiat (see fig. 47) would come by, I remember, in many different guises, with his Mohawk hair and his long overcoat splattered all the way to the floor in paint; or Drew, who acted as our barman when we had a show; Kenny Scharf, his young painter friend, crazy and fun and delightful, whom Keith found fascinating. How Keith and Kenny had met at the School of Visual Arts was very interesting. Do you know that story?

CM: Yeah, from Kenny, sure.

TS: They'd both heard of somebody doing amazing work, downstairs or upstairs, so one went looking for the other. Right away Keith found Kenny fascinating and funny, arriving at school pulling along a painted vacuum cleaner on a cord like a pet dog, and Keith had him "customize" and paint his forty to fifty pairs of eyeglasses. They ended up doing a lot of creative things together, including forming and opening the wonderful Club 57, which was a fantastic idea, with great announcement cards, Saturday science fiction movies, the Basquiat painting of a policeman behind the small bar, and a long list of wonderful young men and women who all became famous one way or another.

CM: I ended up working at Club 57 toward the end of the early '80s. Keith and Ann Magnuson and most of the originals had already moved on, but it was still wonderfully anarchic and silly. The club was in the basement of a Polish church on Saint Mark's Place and was supposed to be the youth center for the church, which was pretty ironic considering all the decadence that went on down there, like the radical

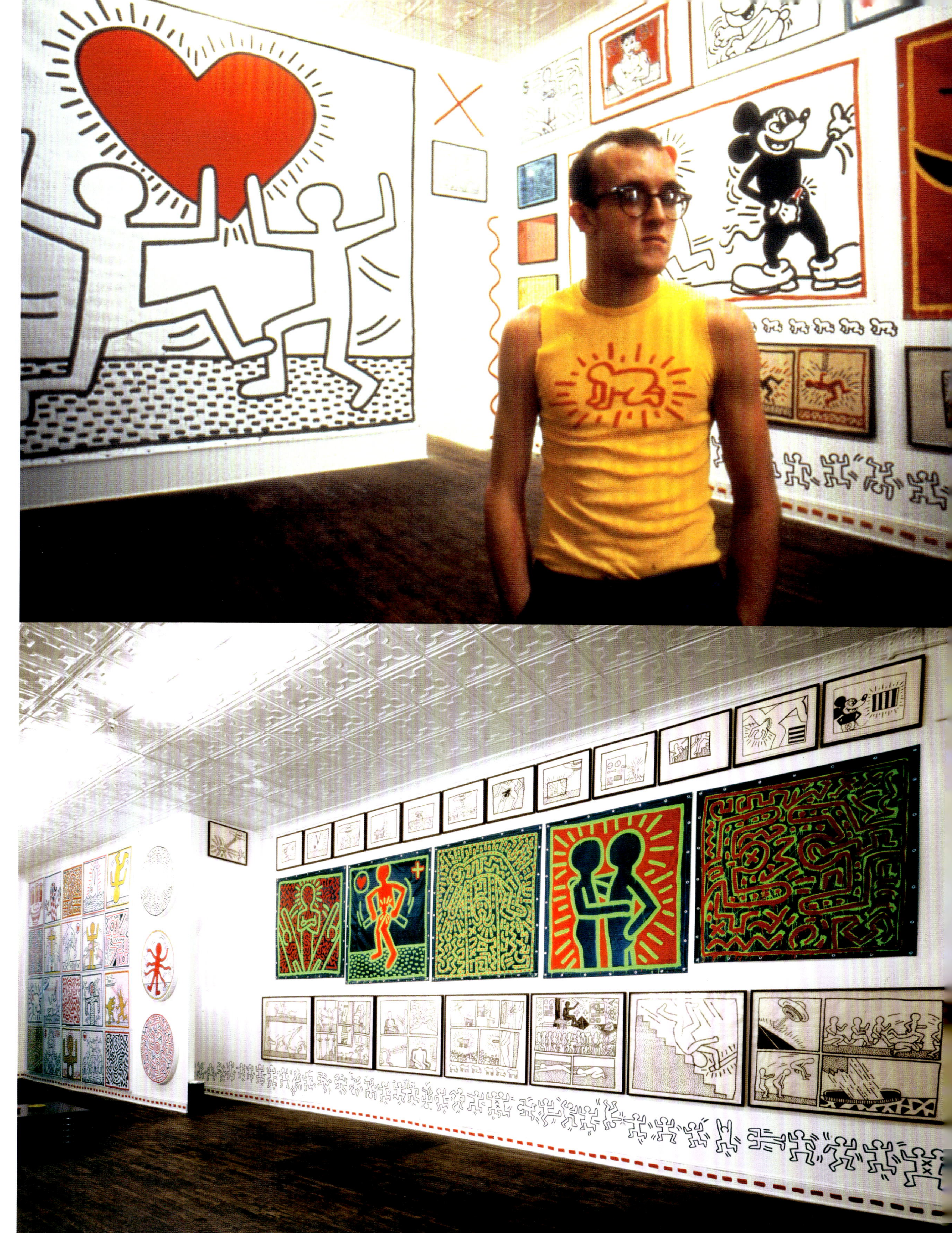

drag acts of John Sex, and the money that they made from the club went to the resistance movement in Soviet Poland. In fact, I was the last person out the door when it shut down, and I grabbed the paper towel dispenser from the bathroom that Keith and Kenny had customized. Unfortunately, I left it at my mom's apartment uptown, and she threw it out, thinking it was trash.

TS: Wow, what a pity. I'm sorry to hear that! All the time Keith was working in the gallery, I knew he was still a student, but there was never an occasion when he tried to show me his work. He never sat around as if waiting for advice or help or wanting to be given a chance. Nothing ever like that. I had to ask *him* what he was doing, you know. I remember saying, "When you finish your work someday, if you'd like to show me your work, I'd be happy to look at it." Rather than doing that, a few days later he handed me a crude announcement card, drawn and Xeroxed. It was an invitation to a show he had organized.

CM: So do you remember the card that Keith gave you?

TS: I remember two cards for two exhibitions—one was at P.S.122 and the other at Westbeth [an artist residence on the West Side Highway in Greenwich Village]—these were exhibitions of *his own* work that he had organized. The drawings were still pretty crude and raw, of all kinds of things in different sizes going all the way up the walls.

CM: Those were the single-line drawings he was doing at the time?

TS: Yes, the single-line drawings, mostly in ink and spray paints on paper, with babies, barking dogs, and flying saucers, stuff like that, but not thick lines yet.

CM: But it was already representational.

TS: Well, if you want to call it that, you can, but it was more like cartoon surrealist automatism. But, yeah, already the babies and stuff were crawling here and there . . .

CM: Because he starts pretty abstract and almost formalist, right?

TS: Well, that is one side of his work. His interest in cartoons as well as the allover patterns goes back to '76, '77, although [it's] not that clear; he was cartooning because he got the idea from his father, who liked cartoon drawings. When he was seventeen, eighteen, he was already doing the abstract allover paintings and drawings. At SVA, he did a painting that covered the floor and two walls to the ceiling, painting himself into the corner. Already there's something unique and outstanding about him.

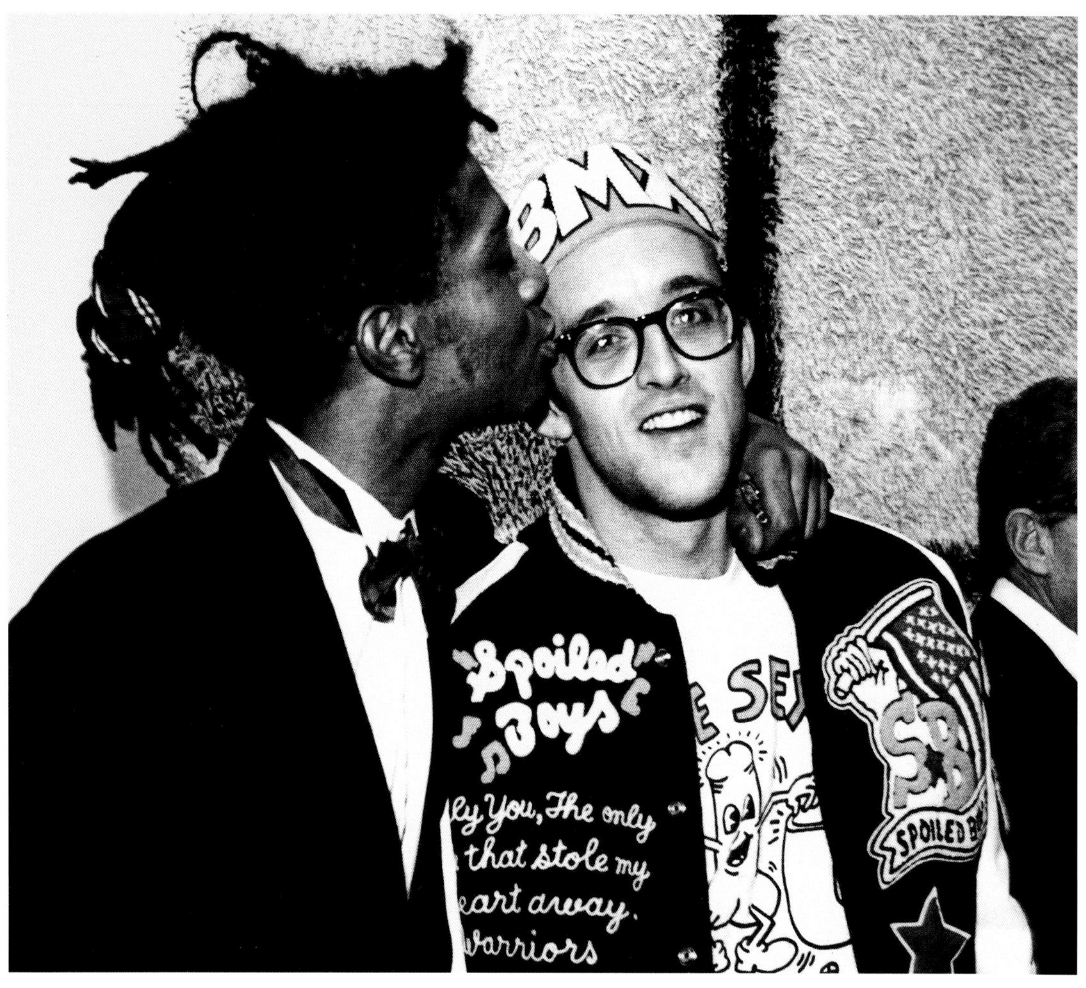

45 (previous page, top)

Keith Haring at the Tony Shafrazi Gallery, New York, 1982. Photograph by Allan Tannenbaum

46 (previous page, bottom)

Installation view of *Keith Haring* at the Tony Shafrazi Gallery, New York, October 1982. Photograph by Ivan Dalla Tana

47

Jean-Michel Basquiat and Keith Haring at the opening of the Julian Schnabel retrospective at the Whitney Museum of American Art, New York, 1987. Photograph by George Hirose

CM: Well, he had this innate sense of composition, right? That's one of the striking things to me: you could give him a page and he could start anywhere on it, or a canvas or a wall, and wherever he starts, it is without hesitation and it would fit perfectly.

TS: I'll give you the background of how that came along. What's important is that Keith came from Kutztown, Pennsylvania, from a German background, [he was] obviously highly animated as a figure, drawing at a young age, and having a relationship with his father around cartooning, etc. He went to school for a while in Pittsburgh and remembered an important show he had seen at the Carnegie when he was about fifteen or sixteen that had a lasting impression, which was the exhibition of the CoBrA school, with its most important artists, Karel Appel, Asger Jorn, Pierre Alechinsky, and so on. Keith liked that the moving snake was their symbol, and the allover patterns they sometimes used. I personally couldn't stand paintings by Karel Appel in the '60s because what I was doing at that time related to Pop and Minimalism. At that time, to me, their work looked grungy, but the origin of that work and the CoBrA movement in the early '40s was great; it came from the association with wildness, being poor, using any found material available in the streets, with an eye on the tropics and especially on the exotic faraway world.

CM: Like the Situationists; they were really radical.

TS: Yes, I agree. When Keith came to New York and started studying at SVA, he developed an interest in utilizing found, discarded things that caught his eye. Walking down the street was an adventure of discovery for him. Many of the ideas in the early work were developed on scraps and fragments, which he turned into his own vocabulary, sort of a perpetual state of the found object, painted and reinvigorated into a new sign. When we were in Paris in '84, Keith was twenty-five years old: I remember he went to visit Alechinsky, who was in his late fifties then. Alechinsky was very happy to meet him, and they exchanged artworks. Karel Appel used to come to every opening we had in the mid to late '80s; he fell in love with the gallery and we all became good friends. I remember he used to tell us with great excitement how much this generation reminded him of his early days in the '40s and the beginning of the CoBrA movement, when they were young, and they would use any old material they could find.

CM: I spoke at Karel's memorial. He was a really good friend.

TS: Really? How great. What a coincidence. I wish I'd been there. A very sweet man. It seems he felt he had a lot in common with Keith. Like all great artists, there is a huge emotional connection to the sensory experience. Just to give you an example—and one of the reasons that Keith stayed so faithful to me, as he wrote in his diaries, after having worked at the gallery for a while and helped prepare for the Keith Sonnier show in 1980—during the opening he had gone into the stairwell on the fifteenth floor at Lexington Avenue and sat on the cold step, crying his eyes out because he had been so moved by something. How an artist like me, for example, would put aside his own work to take care of other artists, and Keith Sonnier, as sweet as he was; at that time, all artwork was hard to sell because in 1980 there was hardly any market in the art world. Emotionally, it just flipped him out, the whole business of taking care of someone else's work, presenting it, believing in it, making an event around it. He saw the caring involved immediately, and so much so that it moved him, and he cried and wrote about it in his diaries. Aside from the orderliness of his tools and his "get up and go," that respectful openness to connecting and understanding something was a remarkable characteristic, because for him the true business of art was giving, caring, and being selfless. At one time, he had been an avid Dead Head [one who loves the music of the Grateful Dead and their continuously moving form of dance].

CM: Yes, he used to follow the Grateful Dead, but he also loved LSD and pot, which definitely triggered his imagination.

TS: You're talking about a seventeen-, eighteen-year-old, in '75, '76. It was unusual for a young kid like that to connect with an older-generation band.

CM: It was a tribal sort of thing where lots of kids would follow them around.

TS: When were you born?

CM: I was born in '61.

TS: So you're the same age as Keith—even three years younger. For me, it was unusual to see someone his age give that much serious dedication to being a Dead Head and not get burned by it, but literally utilize it, so rather like whirling dervish dancers, it gave him more mobility and balance. That is what I think helped instill in him this respectful connection to things and the spontaneous ability to start something with no fear of imbalance, mistake, failure, or abandonment.

CM: No preparatory sketches.

TS: None. Never. I've always tried to emphasize that, and to this day, I have never seen another artist work in so many sizes, starting without preliminary drawings or a plan.

CM: And on a huge scale. Never the need to sketch it out beforehand.

TS: Exactly. Whether it consisted of a single line, a simplified pattern or design, or a configuration of a multitude of little details, it required the same concentration, but there was never a mistake in his work—that's the weird thing. Later on, when he incorporated his drips and whatnot, it was all intentional; he utilized and caught it purposely. It's a way of proceeding that is remarkable.

CM: To me, Keith was kind of the ultimate "maximal" artist; he would fill up a page just like that, but he also had a real Minimalist sensibility. And you tell me he loved Keith Sonnier's work, which has that beautiful line as well?

TS: Yes, he loved Keith's work. I remember the remarkable respect that he had for Keith Sonnier. He was open to learning from everybody in an unusually *active* way. His capacity for respect or appreciation was so enormous and so distinct that when he talked with you, you could see him looking intensely, earnestly, paying attention to every detail, and taking it all in.

CM: Like a sponge.

TS: Incredible! Yeah, more like a vacuum cleaner! And immediately responding. Not in any neglectful or rude fashion.

On the Go

TS: He was always on the go, so *you* were always on your toes or else you'd miss something. You wanted him to say more, but he'd be gone already. And, of course, if you said something about it, he'd be humorous about it. Before I knew, the roles began to reverse. He was taller. So here I was, the active one, the famous one, the radical one, and he would put his arm around my shoulder and say, "Okay, let's go." It was like we were kids. Now—the other thing I wanted to say and bring attention to is the response when one *first* saw these works, especially when you saw what he presented and how he presented them at Westbeth and P.S. 122—these are all extremely crude drawings—very raw and full of shock. On the one hand, while a student at SVA he had already been doing all kinds of meticulous drawings, with tremendous skill, detail, precision, of incredibly elaborate patterns, and on the other hand, he had a deep interest in collages, images, cut-ups, words, and semiotics, but what he showed here was very crude, loosely drawn drawings with an enormous amount of sexuality presented in the most bizarre way.

CM: He liked penises.

TS: Yes, penises and patterns, figures and crowds, dogs and animals, buildings and flying saucers, drawn in sumi ink and spray paint on papers of different sizes [and] irregularities, pinned up all the way to the ceiling. Now, having come from a well-educated and trained background, having been an artist and qualified participant in the art world for more than twenty years, looking at this stuff was *insane*! But I remember the work having a distinct characteristic very early on. This is an important thing because very few people coming across something that is very new see it, come to accept it, and identify a sign of greatness in it. With everybody, it takes time, sometimes years. When looking at great art for the first time, the first reaction and pre-thought is shock and surprise, a double take; [it's] almost like an insult to one's intelligence. It is usually what turns people away; as generally stated, they feel as if they are being taken for a fool. After all, one thinks, "Anybody can do this." This raw experience should never fade. In great art, it continues into the future; whether it is in Picasso, Bacon, or Warhol, you have to be sharp and hip to catch it, dig it, and appreciate it.

CM: It was perhaps more casual than what you were used to.

TS: No, much more than that: more bizarre. But I realized if it does *that* to me—to make me go, "What?"—it is alive, it has a certain depth that I really dig, so I'm going to go with it. The immediate business of identification comes way before liking something. Art is not great because you like it; liking something [comes] when you've been familiar with it for some time, and you begin to see whether you like it or not. But it's before that, and it's what his work always generates; basically it makes you look and ponder (I hate to say "think") like an ape. This is true with Keith Haring as well as Jean-Michel Basquiat. So we became even closer friends, and I started looking at the work more intensely.

CM: I'm curious about the development of his voice, because you were catching him really before he had that down. New York did so much for him, but one of the most prominent things is what SVA gave him with regard to visual language. I see you have stacks of Deleuze and Guattari here; you have all the French and American philosophers piled around your loft, which are part of your background; I know that. I don't know how much of a reader Keith was, but semiotics got through to him at school, and by understanding language and, more important, how language and signs work with us, that's really where his communicative talents hold a touch of greatness. Did you talk about these ideas then?

TS: Well, yes; Keith was a super-intelligent, curious, very well-read, dynamic student and did all kinds of remarkable studies at SVA. He was an avid reader and very curious about philosophy and semiotics, it is

48

Keith Haring exhibition poster, Tony Shafrazi Gallery, 1983–1984

true, as well as language. He carried out many exciting experiments with word and image involving the idea of a pictographic type and sign.

CM: But it was kind of hieroglyphic-like markings.

TS: Yes, but Keith used to call it something else. We talked about it later, when I would point out certain pictographic elements or signs somewhat reminiscent of Paul Klee or Jackson Pollock, signs and markings that were becoming much bolder in Keith's later paintings on tarpaulin. He would find that interesting, and he was always open to intelligent discussion as he continued painting. The School of Visual Arts was a very exciting place to study, as many of the best artists were teaching there; it must have been a thrill for someone coming from Kutztown with notebooks full of organized drawings and cartoons and a head full of dreams.

CM: Will Eisner and Harvey Kurtzman were teaching there around that time. There were a lot of famous comic people at SVA. They always had all these great cartoonists.

TS: I wish I had known that at the time; I have a lot of admiration for cartoonists. I think the cartoons were already in his work, but possibly the desire to deal with pop culture and especially to communicate with the world was something he developed at SVA and in New York when he took the performative act of the cut-up collage and the act of drawing from the school out into the streets.

Out in the Streets

CM: When was the first time you noticed these kinds of things on the street? Did you walk around? Or did someone point them out?

TS: Coming back to New York after the tragic death of my friend Robert Smithson, who had been traveling with me in Amarillo, Texas, one of the first things I remember seeing, back in '73, was a small graffito that said, "FIGHT BACK." After many years of war and strife, the Vietnam War, Watergate, and all that shit gradually stopped by '76, '77, and the time was ripe for new beginnings in music, film, and art. Young artists like the filmmakers from the New Cinema took to the streets, partly inspired by the liberating spirit of Jack Smith, the Kuchar brothers, Andy Warhol, the underground cinema of the early '60s, and the New Wave cinema of Europe, as well as the brilliant camp Theater of the Ridiculous of Charles Ludlam. The streets of New York became ripe for expression. In these times, every once in a while when walking in the street, you would come across the first markings of Keith Haring and Jean-Michel Basquiat.

CM: But Keith's videos aren't that entertaining.

TS: I disagree because his videos were a little different. His videos already show a characteristic of breaking out of a mold. For example, even though I knew William Burroughs from '66, independently, Keith had picked up on Burroughs. As a student in the School of Visual Arts, he started experimenting with a variety of different kinds of painting, almost like allover painting on the floor, as well as collages and cut-ups with images and words. So he was aware of those things; as a young kid, [he] read Burroughs—the sexuality, the politics of liberation, and the adventure of science fiction fueled his imagination and drive to experiment and liberate both the nature of drawing and the word in such a way as to subversively topple the bombardment of media, images, and information that is thrown at us daily, and to be able to reprogram and talk back to the world. And by doing that, he unleashed the powers of individual freedom, and started doing his cut-up collages of *New York Post* and other headlines as well as paste-ups in the streets. The outside and city streets became his studio. Nobody had that get up and go, drive and bounce, to work in the street. The twenty-four-hour physicality, the energy, and the fearlessness involved are what no one is aware of. There was never a point of hesitation. [He would] look at something point blank, ten feet, twenty feet, forty feet, sixty feet in size, and in a few minutes decide what would be drawn. You could see his mind working, and then, moving like a cheetah, silently, he'd get the materials and start with no sketch, no preliminary doodle, nothing at all. All so-called respectable, well-known artists used the method of projecting, tracing, mapping, and planning; from Michelangelo to Picasso, Warhol, and all the European and American artists of the '80s, including all of the graffiti artists—all used sketches, drawings, and plans. Keith never needed to use any of that. So this element of the calligraphic line coming out of him was very important; it literally was a force that came out of his mind and body.

CM: You're working with another generation of artists with a more serious studio practice, but Keith was part of a whole group of people coming out of art schools who were looking at graffiti. Keith was the prototypical street artist. Did he try to run what he was thinking about graffiti by you? Did you ever have conversations about that?

TS: Oh, yeah. We were inseparable. At the time, I was exhibiting whatever I felt was interesting. The work that Richard Prince remembers, one of the first things he saw in New York back in '80—and to my surprise, he told me this on a beach some twenty-eight years later—was an incredible show by Sarah Charlesworth, the suicide pictures with people jumping out of windows, photographs torn from newspapers and blown up large—a wonderful show. And Bill Beckley's large photo-narrative constructions and Olivier Mosset's beautiful, colorful monochrome paintings. I could see [that] with Keith the energy was different—it was youthful, incredibly fun, and somewhat mischievous. He was very hip, very cool, really connected to everything and constantly moving around. Whereas most people tend to separate and compartmentalize things that are serious and things that are not, [and,] however great they might be as artists, rarely do they have any other remarkable characteristics, Keith was incredibly athletic; he was obsessed and surrounded by the latest music of every kind, his boyfriends being the best DJs. He shamelessly and fearlessly participated in everything; he lived out in public, he really cared for people, and the purpose [of] his energy was to communicate and touch as many people in as vast a territory as possible. He *was* the time. Just preparing his exhibition was a fantastic experience. We worked so well together. Rather like the way, in his complex allover pattern paintings, where everything fits together perfectly, in a completely original manner, we would frenetically install works of a wide variety of materials, sizes, and forms on all the walls up to the ceiling, and everything would find its "rightful" place. We went everywhere together: walking down the street, going to clubs, traveling around the world were thrilling experiences. He was attracted to everybody who was distinct and talented, and respectfully reached out to compliment them—in no time at all he became loved by all the great stars. Already when he started, all his friends were destined to become famous—I remember meeting Madonna when she was a lovely, shy, talented young girl and a serious dancer. Keith's friendships with Basquiat and Scharf were full of love and respect. The respect he had for their work was radically different and cool, and on a higher plane than everything I had witnessed before. You have to understand: we were witnessing the beginning of the beginning—no one had seen anything yet.

And Moving on to *Love's Body*

CM: I don't know how much you've kept track of the music scene, and I don't know if Keith tried to explain at any point how he could go from the Dead to disco, but the Grateful Dead is a particular strain of rock, very noodley and doodley; it has elements of what he would get into in house music, the ecstatic rapture in the trancelike qualities and disembodied vocals.

TS: It is true, Keith was very driven by music. At a young age, he very much loved and identified with the Grateful Dead. What was amazing about them was that their music, their concerts, their graphics, and their posters [were] all about sharing the joy with everyone. And, of course, we know that Jerry Garcia, coming from San Francisco, had great respect for the Beat generation, for Jack Kerouac, and the kind of mad wisdom, energy, and love that were Neal Cassady. That partly had to do with Keith's spirit, the responsibility of the artist to make art for the people, printing posters, making buttons, and constantly giving things away as well as doing all the Subway Drawings, which he never intended for sale. At the same time, traveling all the way from Harlem to Brooklyn, going dancing in all of the clubs, naturally he was exposed to disco as well as house music. He was one of the first [artists] to recognize, appreciate, and respect rap and the beginning of hip-hop and get to know and befriend groups like Run-D.M.C., Public Enemy, and many others. He did the album covers, murals, and playgrounds, and invited and introduced many of the best break dancers and scratch DJs, like Larry Levan from Paradise Garage, to perform at his openings and parties. In fact, when MTV started, all they had was white rock bands. It was partly through Keith's ability to recognize pioneers of new music and influence that rap was introduced to the MTV audience and ultimately gained acceptance, success, and recognition as the main music of our time.

Earlier, you mentioned the French and American philosophers I was reading and how they might have related to Keith. It seems that what he was lacking was what [Gilles] Deleuze and Nietzsche called "resentment," which comes from a quiet apprehension, fear, doubt, and separation. Like a fearless child, he ran to these situations, and when he listened to music, it went right through him. It was remarkable that he could *see* while listening to a beat, to music; right away he could feel it and he could go with it. He could dig what you were just beginning to hear together, and it was really limitless. It was somewhat reminiscent of Norman O. Brown's *Love's Body* [published in 1966]. It was this almost publicly sensual spirit of embracing everything in the world. That's why we could communicate so easily. As you were walking down the street, you encountered things; if you said something, he'd get it right away. It was a remarkable experience. It is such a rare thing you have with certain people, when you're in a great moment together, when you see something and you can just share, and you say it and the other person gets it, and it's so clear to both of you that you [will] never forget. That kind of a shorthand language of sign, well, he was extremely open to that. It came from an attitude of total acceptance.

CM: So that was basically the same openness he had to graffiti? He just picked up on the energy of things? Like, I think, a lot of artists.

TS: Because he was traveling in the subway. Most often he would make arrangements with [photographer Tseng] Kwong Chi to photograph what he did [see pp. 2–15]. By the time he made it to SVA, within a week or two, everybody was already with him, a whole gang around him.

CM: He would draw little maps for Kwong Chi showing where he'd gone so Kwong Chi could go back and document the work that [Haring] had done.

TS: He had an arrangement with Kwong Chi. I would go to Keith's loft as he was barely coming out of the shower in the morning, all wet, quickly putting on his jeans. . . . Keith Haring, Juan Dubose, Samantha McEwen used to share the space together, and Keith slept in a little tent set up in the middle of the apartment, and downstairs was a little studio. He'd get ready, put on his leather jacket, and say, "Kwong Chi is meeting us there." He'd grab a little box of white chalk, put it in his pocket, all ready to go; "See you later," and we'd be gone. We'd walk to the subway, meet Kwong Chi waiting there, and start the day by getting on a train. I'd ask him, "Where are we going?" He'd move his neck—this neck thing, rubbernecking, was so incredible; I've never seen anyone have that. It gave him more ability than everyone else—turning around, checking you out, and never forgetting you: "Wait, you'll see."

CM: Considering that some of that public work, and all of the Subway Drawings, wasn't legal, it probably kept him out of trouble a few times.

TS: Yes, probably this rubbernecking saved his neck once or twice. To be clear, this wasn't public property; these framed panels where the ads had run out were covered in perfect black paper. As we were riding, he was always looking, because he was tall and checking out his surroundings. As soon as he'd see one of those black panels they'd put up when no one had paid to put an ad in that spot, we'd jump out and he'd start drawing. Kwong Chi would take a picture. Often in silence, working quickly, drawing with speed and precision, rapidly filling the black panels with elaborate white markings, and the story would appear. Then back into the train and on to the next station.

CM: You'd ride a whole line?

TS: Yes, thirty, forty, fifty blocks sometimes or more. He did this all the time. All the way to Harlem and back to Brooklyn, so within a few weeks, there must have been hundreds of drawings—some would last for a few days, some a week or two, until they got to be covered with ads. Eventually people would steal them as collectibles. Within a few months, there must've been a few million people between the ages of five and eighty years old who traveled these lines to school or work, saw these drawings, and must have been amazed, wondering, "What's this shit going down?"

All the Subway Drawings were made with the commitment to the idea of a public dialogue—art for the people. He saw the world of people traveling underground as the real public in the *real* museum—after all, more people visited those stations and traveled those lines than all the museums put together. He was addressing all of Manhattan, Brooklyn, and greater New York, and everyone in it. Most probably, a majority of those people had never been to a museum, so he felt it was his duty as an artist to bring the museum and the business of art to them.

It was *incredible* that he was *gay*, rather active, masculine, and *white*, traveling at all hours in broad daylight and the dark of night, all the way from Brooklyn to the heart of Harlem, making all these stops to do his drawings, as well as the time it took to do so many murals in playgrounds, and just imagine in those years the streets riddled with danger and crime. He was getting to be known, highly respected, and, as they say in England, becoming "untouchable." He brought so much of the black and Hispanic culture that thrived in music, dance, and graffiti in the streets to the art world. A true believer in democratic ideals, he was instrumental in opening the art world so that it could be shared and used by everyone. Even the language he and Jean-Michel and friends would use together was cool: when they saw something they liked in each other's work, they'd say, "Oh, man, that's really fresh." What was fresh was cool. He brought a whole new crowd of people, a language, a vocabulary to the somewhat stodgy and dreary, mostly white and "square" art world.

CM: Everyone thinks that Warhol was so famous and beloved, and they don't realize that actually Andy's career was pretty much in the toilet in the '80s because he'd become incredibly irrelevant. It was Keith, Jean-Michel, and Kenny getting so hot and idolizing him as the master that reinvigorated him. They made him relevant again.

TS: Wait a minute; Warhol was a very intelligent, sensitive, and caring person. To put it in a nutshell, in the early '60s, Warhol lit up the art world with a meteoric flame, and [in] '68, at the same time as Robert Kennedy, he was shot and almost died. Then there was a time of recovery, and he came back, again painting vigorously, with some wonderful paintings in the '70s. It is true, by 1981, '82, he was moved and impressed and became rather envious of the innovative thrill and excitement that Keith Haring and his group of young friends had suddenly brought to the art world and the act of making art, so much so that for the first time since the early '60s, he became intimate friends with these guys, going to their studios and exhibitions and spending a lot of time with them. This might have inspired a new, liberated approach to the paintings he did in the '80s.

CM: Now. You're in charge of Keith's career, you're his gallerist, he always listened to you—and he actually listened to everyone—and you weren't the only smart person who'd been around the block a few times; there were a lot of people who talked to him at that time, because Keith was not shy about asking people, and people were giving him advice. The art market certainly understands

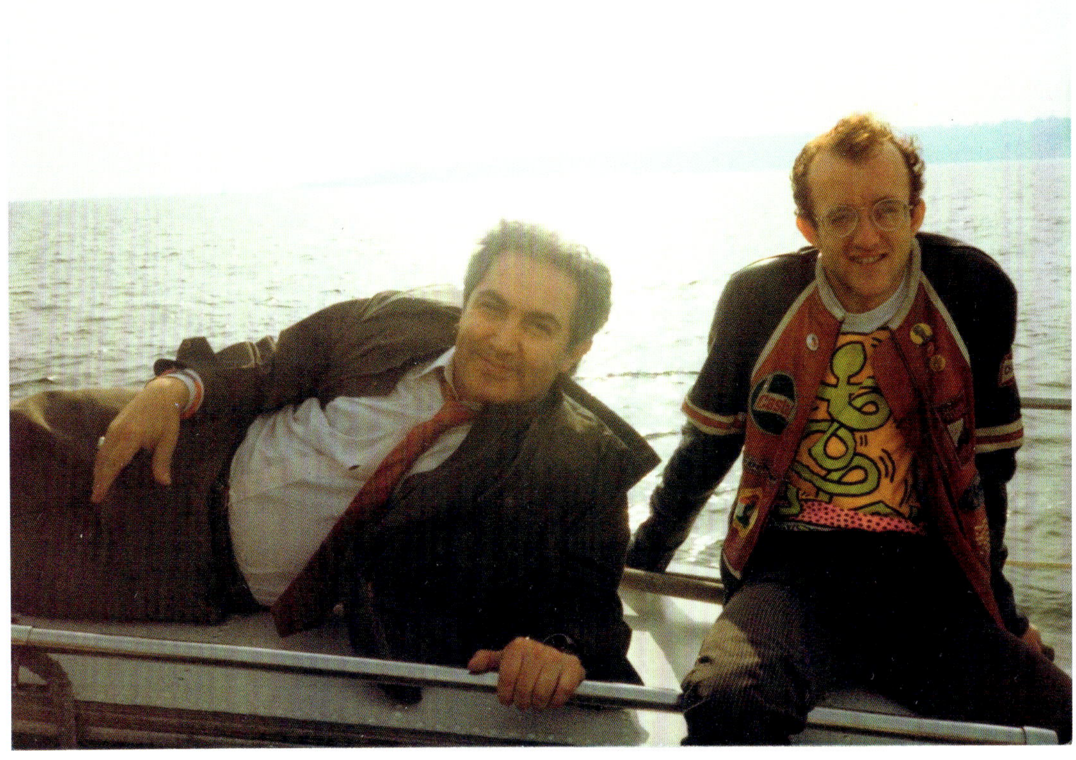

49

Tony Shafrazi and Keith Haring, Naples, Italy, 1983. Photograph by Lucio Amelio

supply-and-demand economics, and it can't be too keen on Keith signing every black book, doing drawings on people's clothes, basically giving his work away for free. Probably the best bet would have been to be choosier and less prolific, but instead he makes T-shirts, opens up a Pop Shop [in SoHo and, briefly, in Tokyo]. This is so radical.

TS: Well, you have to remember at that time, there wasn't much of a market. Besides that, Keith Haring and his friends weren't really interested in money or sales. In their mind, the purpose of art didn't have much to do with the art market or "supply and demand," as you call it. In fact, Keith, more than anyone, was absolutely moved by the tyrannies of capitalism, corruption, politics, war, religion, and the so-called Moral Majority. He was one of the few artists who addressed all of those things within his work. Here I would like to quote something that I remember having learned from Carl Andre at Max's Kansas City one night in 1970. He said, "Art is what we do and culture is what is done to us."

As for the Pop Shop—like you said—it's true he got a lot of flak for it, all [from] so-called serious older artists, especially critics, and certainly museum people criticized him endlessly and thought it was something ugly and commercial and that the artist was selling out, which was not true at all. Years later, we would find that the Pop Shop—the gift shop—is indispensible for all museums and Keith was well ahead of his time. It *was* incredible. Of course, he never made any money at it, but the idea was so remarkable: the idea that any individual can be an artist, any individual can be a producer of things, and your product is not necessarily about making money, but to bring joy, fun, the sense of freedom and play that one achieves through art to as many people as possible.

CM: So the T-shirts and the buttons, this was a whole different thing. The artist multiple had always been basically precious and handmade; Keith brought it to a level of mass manufacture.

TS: Because he was already doing his own announcements, this whole thing with the cards, this idea of completing it by doing the invitation, this business of giving little gifts, a token, as a commemorative thing; hence the posters, the T-shirts, especially the buttons were part of that. In the beginning it appeared innocent to me. I think it was, for him, a way of making an individual, personal history, the same way he'd overridden the restrictions and the rules of art-making of the previous generations—the industrial, the machine-made, and what was considered to be more "real." Instead of using the projector in order to have resemblance to "reality," his approach was to begin and point to a road to freedom, always to start a continuous line that never died, whether it was a line from one painting to another, or whether the line went somewhere else. But what matters is the continuity in a state of change, like in the philosophies of Nietzsche and Deleuze: the only time we are really alive is when we bring ourselves to that state of becoming. And the state of becoming, in their definition, is not going from one to the other; it's not turning into another. It's not becoming more complete, more successful; it's not that use of the word. It's being in a state of perpetual change. There is no state of completion. What Keith was doing, very clearly and fearlessly, was encountering states of freedom. There wasn't much of a clear distinction between the beginning and end of something; when something was finished, many other ones were started already, going on and on. I pointed this out to him early on, the nature of the continuity of his line and the line traveling from one surface to another, what would happen to the line if it traveled to something more substantial than paper. Right away he said he didn't want to do paintings on canvas like everyone else—he didn't want to be a studio painter. I said, "No, go out there, invent something." So he went out and he actually looked for it and came back all excited: it was tarpaulin. He'd seen it in the back of trucks—like Kerouac. In [Kerouac's] *Visions of Cody*, one of the greatest highlights is this image of a flapping tarp. So Keith went to the trouble of looking for it, had it made in special sizes with grommets, even went out of his way to find some industrial paint that would be the most suitable. That is how the paintings on tarpaulin were born. The point is that he was ready to learn and invent a whole new process.

In the same way, one day I took this little figurine that he'd painted on wood—a barking dog standing on two legs; I still have it here. I said, "Keith, check this out, close one eye." We were good friends and trusting enough to play around that way. "Can you imagine, with a landscape behind, how big that'll be? Visualize it. With one eye closed, it will help you fantasize. Can you imagine your drawing becoming something thick, even three-dimensional, whereby it could stand, it could be ten, fifteen, twenty feet tall? And it would be there forever, even after you die."

He said, "What? How can that be?" "You can make it out of steel." "I don't know how to make a sculpture."

I said, "The easiest would be to draw a line on a piece of cardboard, take scissors, cut out the thing; once you do that, you just hold it up, and you just need to stabilize it, so you find a way of making a leg. All you do is become aware and decide on the thickness." And he did that, and it resulted in these fantastic sculptures. I tell you, the people who made all of the sculptures at Lippincott, the famous fabricators who made all the sculptures for Ellsworth Kelly, Oldenburg, and all the sculptors, absolutely loved Keith and working with him. When it was done, it ended up being installed in [Dag] Hammarskjöld Plaza and was on the front page of the *New York Times*.

CM: He was interested in stretching the media that way.

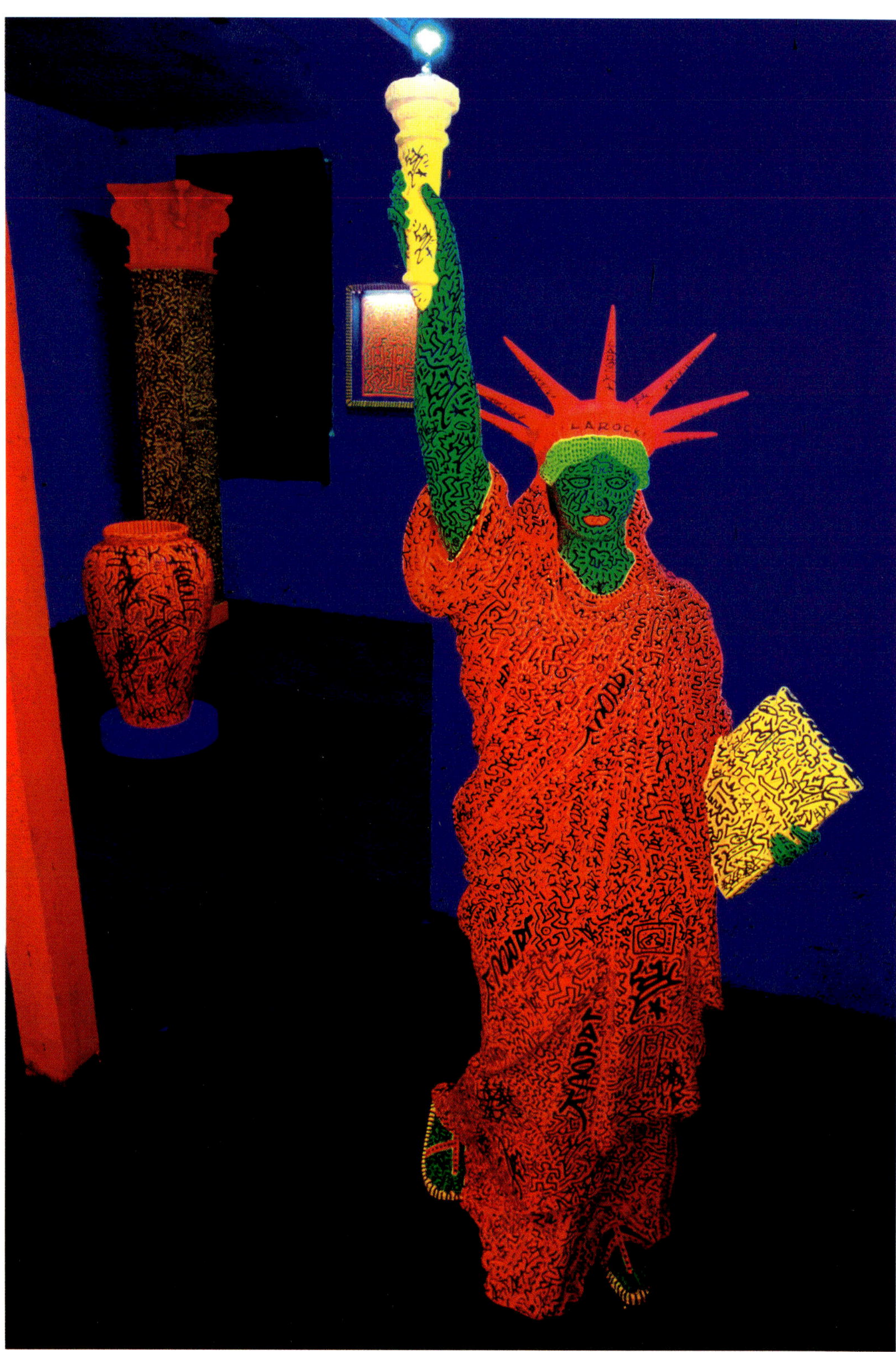

50

Black-light room installation view of *Keith Haring*, Tony Shafrazi Gallery, New York, October 1982. Photograph by Ivan Dalla Tana

(pp. 86–87)
Keith Haring painting *The Ten Commandments* at CAPC Musée d'Art Contemporain de Bordeaux, France, 1985. Photograph by Tseng Kwong Chi

TS: Yeah, any way he could speak to the world.

CM: And he moved to product culture. [Takashi] Murakami claims he learned it from Warhol, but he didn't; he learned it from Haring. When Keith goes to a shop and says, "I want fifteen thousand buttons with this image on it," that's different.

TS: Again, that came from this seventeen-year-old kid in the middle of a gigantic outdoor concert, spinning and spinning, wanting to communicate with everybody. Arriving at a point where he got to a Zen state of mind, where you focus, where you go beyond a mistake, so you never make a mistake, you keep going and everything fits together. He operated on that level. Wanting endless possibilities, there was no limit for him. His need to communicate was completely unselfish. One of the things I remember, just before our exhibition in '82, was a big antinuclear rally in Central Park for which Keith drew and printed out some twenty thousand posters, rolling them up. He and a couple of his friends had the tireless ability to give them all out! Can you imagine having the strength and patience to hand out tens of thousands of posters? Each one, to the last person; it was a gift to that individual. No one did that before.

On the one hand, you had this young artist who wanted to make his own things into an industry, but that industry was about giving it away to everybody; it wasn't about profit. On the other hand, the vocabulary of drawing that he was introducing, through cartoon-like figuration, always had some elements of science fiction incorporated into it, had language, had some resemblance and association to primitive languages and Maya hieroglyphs, but was absolutely based in politics—politics of sexuality, politics of imagination, of freedom of will, and antiwar values. He was one of the few artists who brought that critical vocabulary of protest and liberation from slavery to his paintings and the polemical dialogue of art. He became so conscientious about everything, so much more mature. It was fascinating for me to watch. So, yes, he moved to product culture, but it was about communication, not profit. It took him no time at all to design the store, to paint it, and the painting that he did was genius. He got nothing but flak for it, year in, year out.

CM: That's the thing: he came across as a sellout, but the much more corrupt and careerist artists would actually cut back on their work, play the market. But if the Pop Shop is brilliant, a lot of the big public art sculptures, made posthumously seem to me kind of lame.

TS: No, the big sculptures I am talking about were made in '84 and exhibited at Castelli in '85, and they're great. He introduced a wonderful sense of color and vitality to sculpture that hadn't existed since Léger, Calder, Oldenburg, and, later, Lichtenstein. I think that Keith made some of the most celebrative forms, translating movements from capoeira dancers in Brazil [and] the unusual motions of break dancing, as well as the idea of mother and child; sadly, he did not have time to make that many. I think that the work he was doing would have continued on to become even more remarkable. The spirit that it came from was all about this balanced animation. The show at Castelli Gallery was a knockout. Keith not only installed all the sculptures there, but he did a drawing all along the walls of [Castelli's] Greene Street gallery. Castelli had enormous respect for him. Having discovered and introduced so many artists since 1957, when he'd first opened his gallery [on East 77th Street]—Rauschenberg, Johns, Twombly, Chamberlain, Warhol, Oldenburg, Lichtenstein (who loved Keith's work and his sculptures), and many others—having done all of that, he was speechless and spoke openly of Keith's originality in historic terms.

Groovin' to the Music

CM: Your gallery on Mercer Street was originally just the ground floor, and the basement was opened for Keith's second show, right?

TS: No, the basement in Mercer Street, as wet and damp as it was when we first started, is where Keith made his first tarp paintings in '81. After a few group exhibitions, as we got ready to have Keith's first one-man show in the fall of '82, Keith transformed the basement into a black-light jungle of tropical delights, with all kinds of drawings, cut-ups, and sculptures, as well as the *Statue of Liberty*. Even the walls and columns were all painted in fluorescent lines and colors lit and glowing in black light. It was amazing. The night of the opening, the basement was full; upstairs, where there were paintings and drawings, was chock-a-block full, with the crowd spilling into the street, blocking traffic. As the opening proceeded, break dancers started while DJs mixed and scratched. The party went on until 6, 6:30 in the morning, way beyond the limit of anyone's patience.

Haring kept a constant vigil, picking up bottles, burning cigarettes, and trash all night; as I was going down the stairs, I saw a young man who had fallen, smashed his head, blood everywhere. It turned out no one knew him—someone who had crashed the party. Still, I had to call a cab or an ambulance, I can't remember, to take him to Bellevue Hospital emergency room, as drunk as he was. It wasn't until 8:30 in the morning that they got to see him, give him a few stitches. Exhausted and relieved that he was okay, I left to go home in the chill of the morning, thankful that nothing serious had happened to this young man no one knew.

CM: When Steven Rubell and Ian Schrager first opened the Palladium, they had [Francesco] Clemente and Jean-Michel do something, and did Keith do something for them as well?

TS: Yes, well, he was the main guy. I had known Steve since the '70s, during Studio 54, [and] when he and Schrager first started to plan the opening of the Palladium, in early '83. They contacted me through Anne Livet because she was organizing fundraisers and nonprofit benefits and art events. Steve said, "The stars of the '70s had been movie celebrities and sports figures, well represented in Andy Warhol's portraits, [but] now the scene is downtown, and stars of the '80s are the artists. So, Tony, I want your help in doing something great." Jean-Michel did a long painting for behind the bar, in a way reenacting what he had done in Club 57 only a few years before, as well as a great painting for the Michael Todd Room. Kenny Scharf did all the telephones, telephone booths, and the lounges downstairs; Clemente did a small circular fresco above the staircase. Keith did an enormous, twenty-five-foot-tall multicolored painting that would be in the center of the dance floor. Later, the Party of Life, a party Keith organized [in 1985], was so popular it broke all attendance records.

The Persistence of Memory and the Fortune of Having Been There

Tony Shafrazi was always adamant that my voice be more evident in the conversation we had. This not only runs contrary to my notion of an interview and the values of journalists, who know exactly when to shut up and listen, but also, in truth, when Tony gets going with a story, the only thing harder than stopping him is imagining any reason to stop him. He may not often take the most direct route, but it is always the most scenic route possible, nearly every unlikely turn revealing some view that can change the way you see things. Looking back on this interview now, with some hindsight, I might add only that for all memory may lack in terms of certainty, it proffers abundant wisdom. No doubt there are many scholars out there who could correct us on dates, places, and people, for reminiscence is more poetic than exact, and is ultimately directed by the narrative of how these things profoundly changed our lives. Memory is never about actually being there in the past, but about simply the link that those who were there share through time. Shafrazi understands this truly. It is why he would consider this a conversation rather than an interview. To have witnessed Keith Haring become one of the greatest communicators of his day and with such speed that you could see it in real time, and to have all around at that time in New York so many people who were just as phenomenal in their own ways, was an experience. At the time, Keith Haring seemed so of the moment, but with the passing of that moment into history, what might be most remarkable of all is just how timeless that briefest of instances turned out to be.

—Carlo McCormick

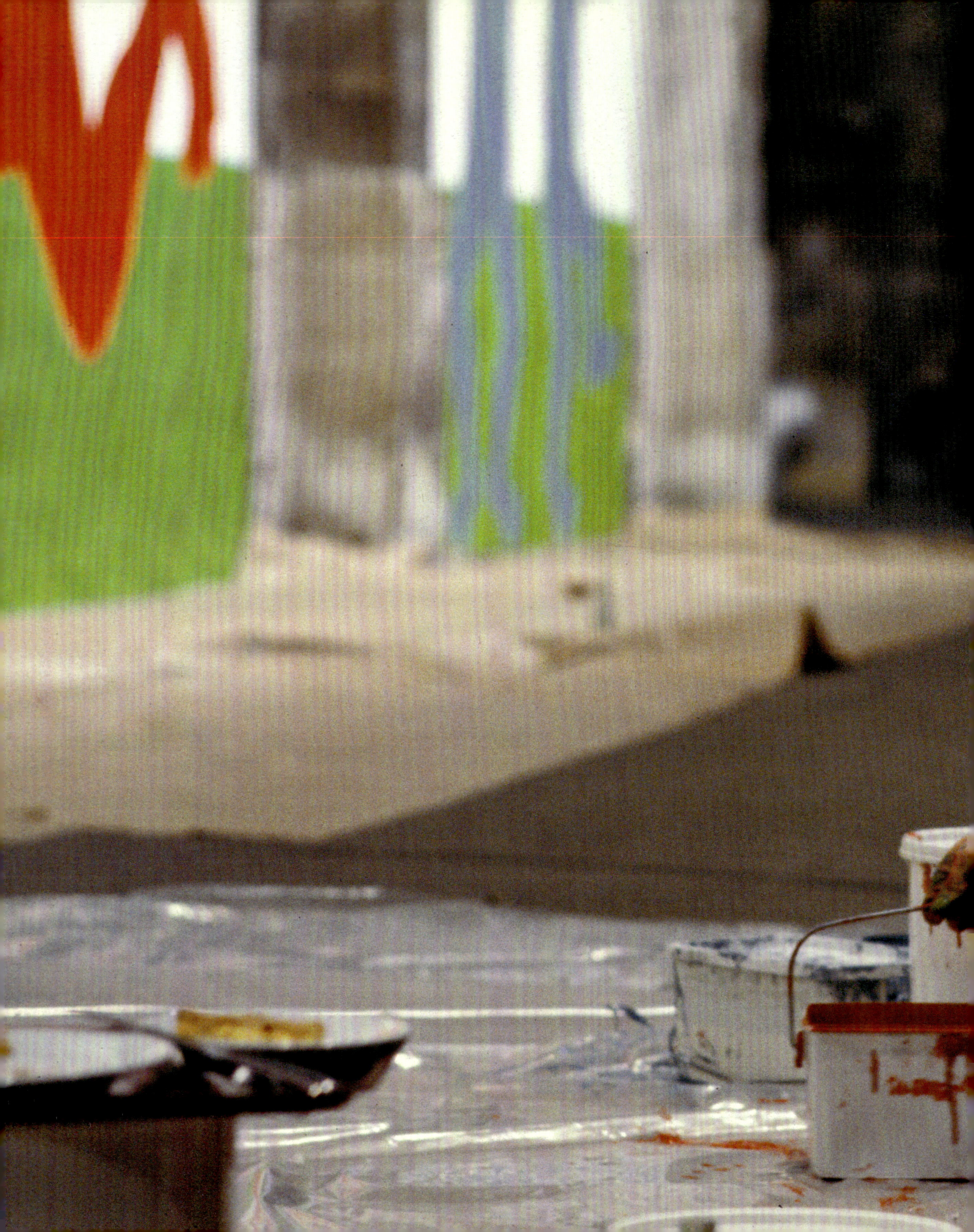

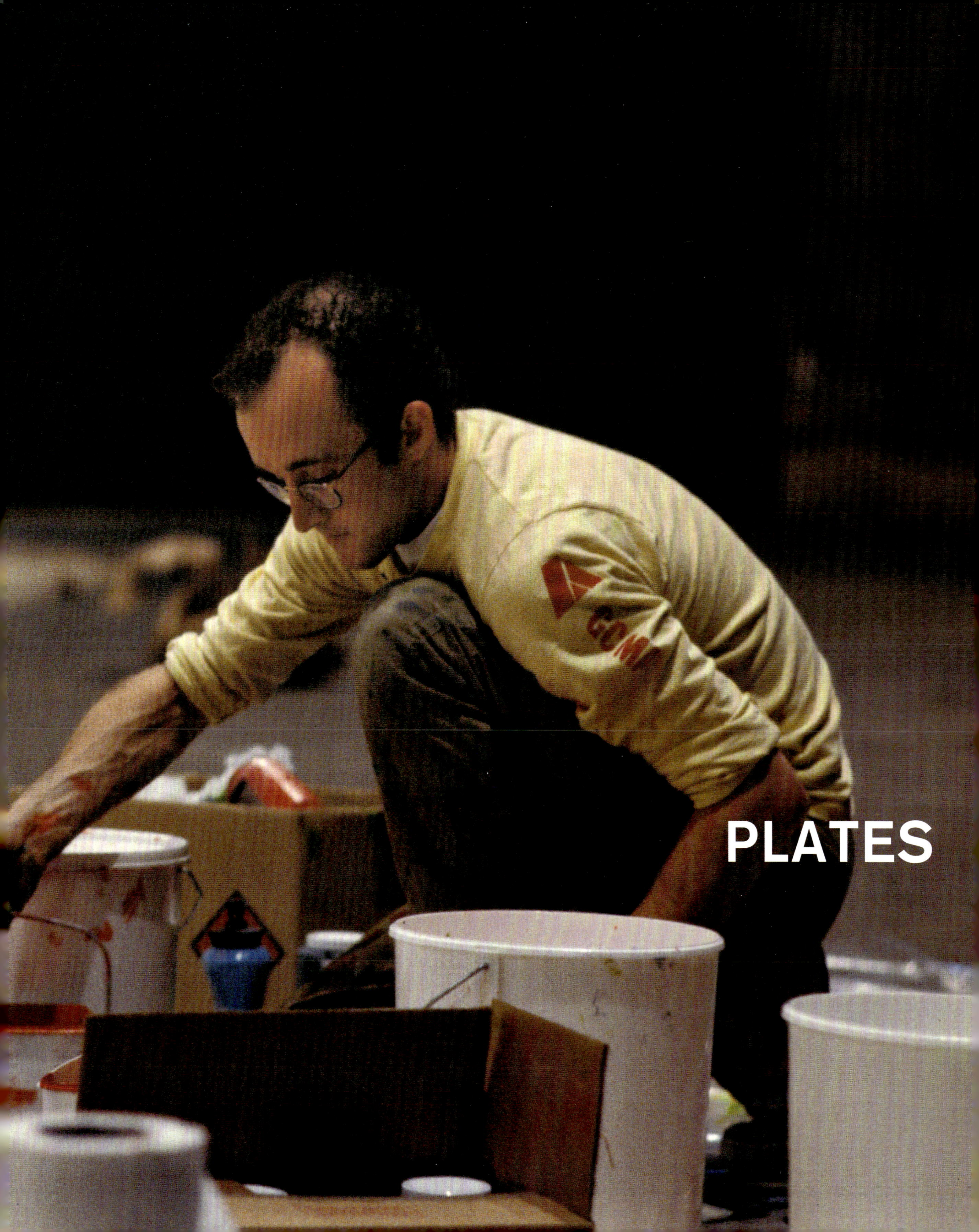

PLATES

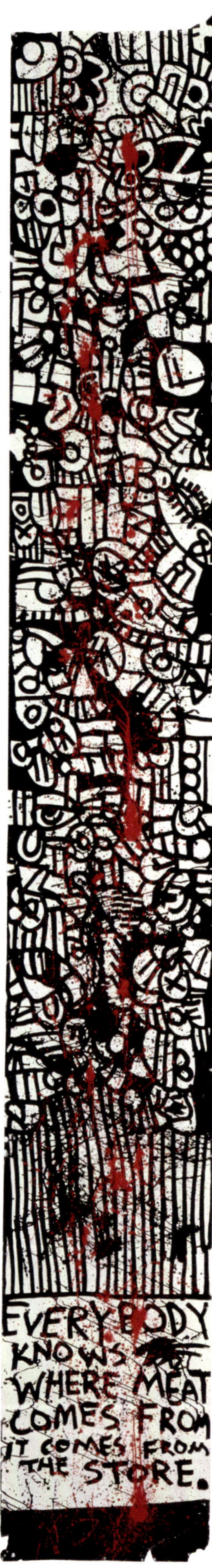

1

Everybody Knows Where Meat Comes from, It Comes from the Store, June 4, 1978. Sumi ink and tempera on paper, 250 x 35½ in. (635 x 90.2 cm)
Collection Tony Shafrazi, New York

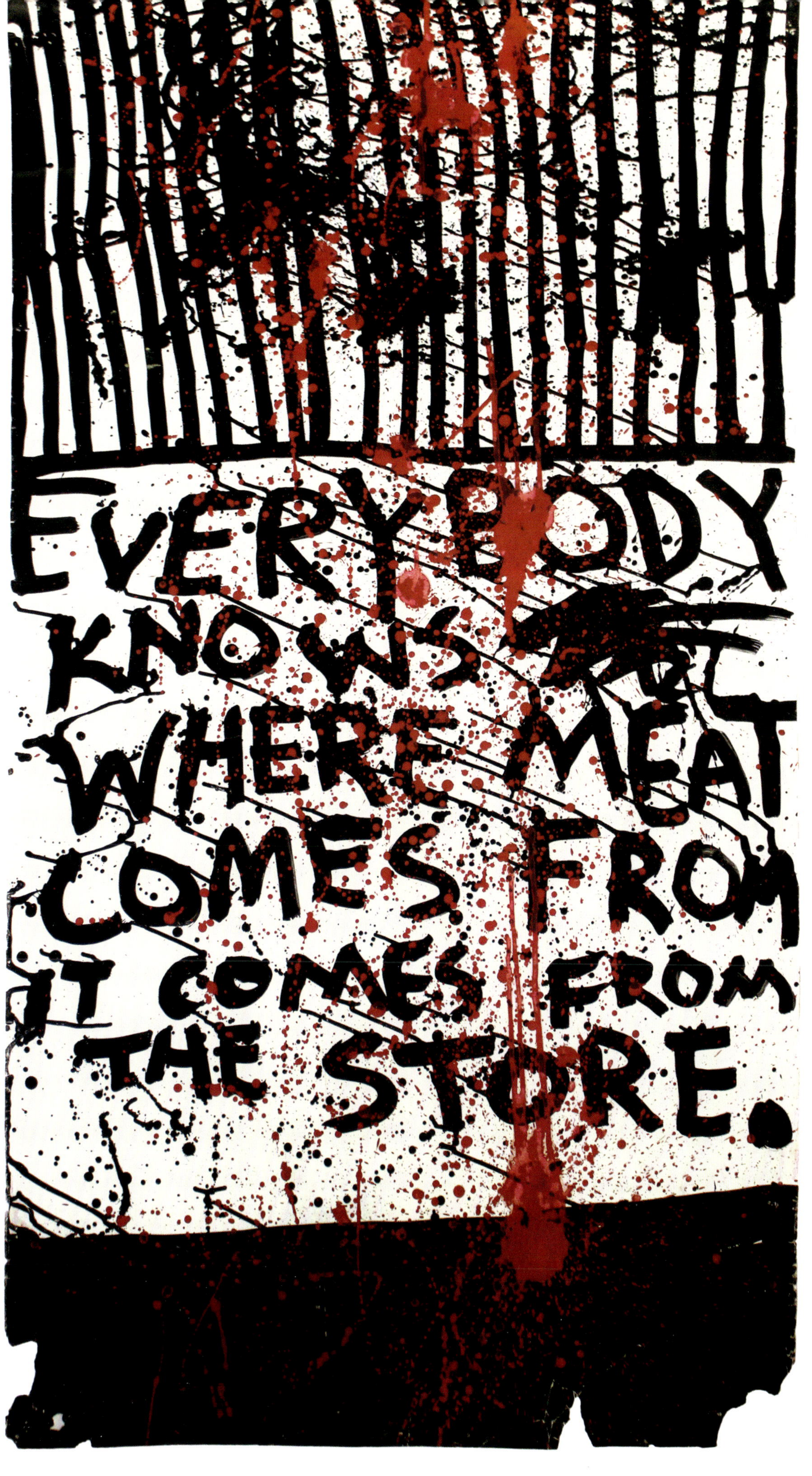

EVERYBODY
KNOWS
WHERE MEAT
COMES FROM
IT COMES FROM
THE STORE.

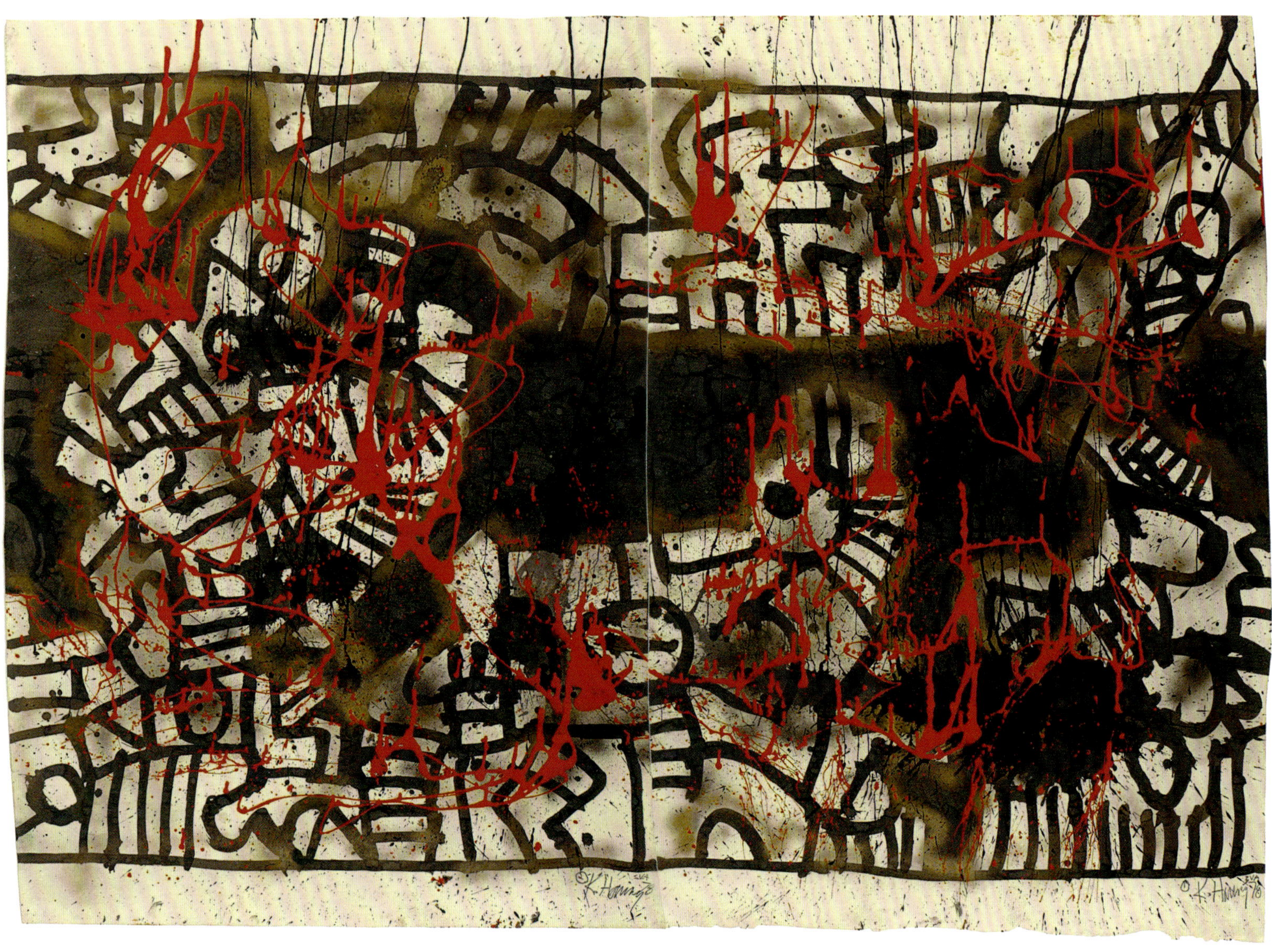

2

Untitled, 1978. Sumi ink, acrylic, and spray enamel on paper, 49 5/8 x 75 1/4 in. (125.9 x 191.1 cm)
Private collection, courtesy Tony Shafrazi Gallery

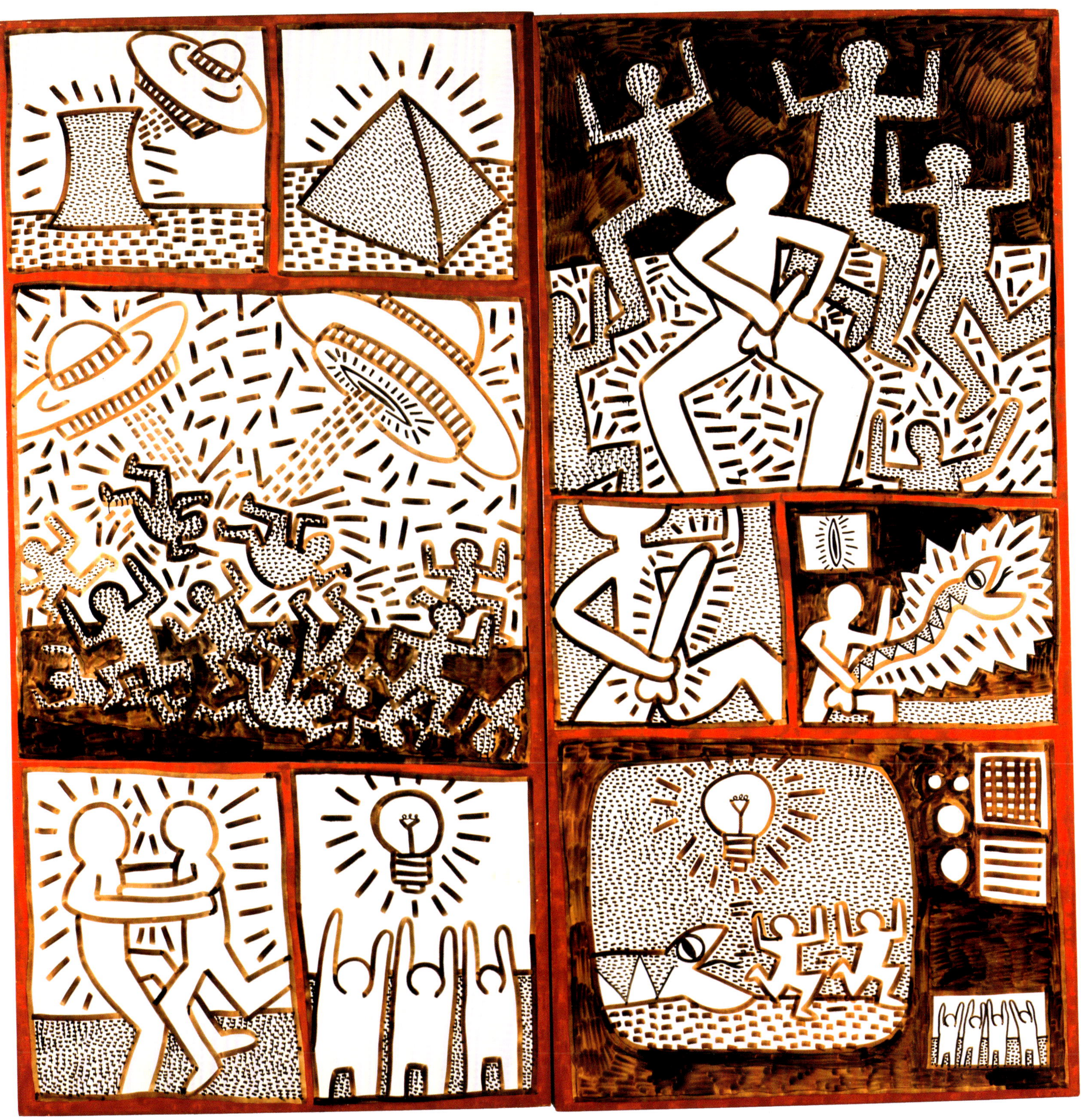

3

Untitled, 1981. Diptych: acrylic and enamel on fiberboard, 96 x 96 x 3/4 in. (243.8 x 243.8 x 1.9 cm)
Rubell Family Collection

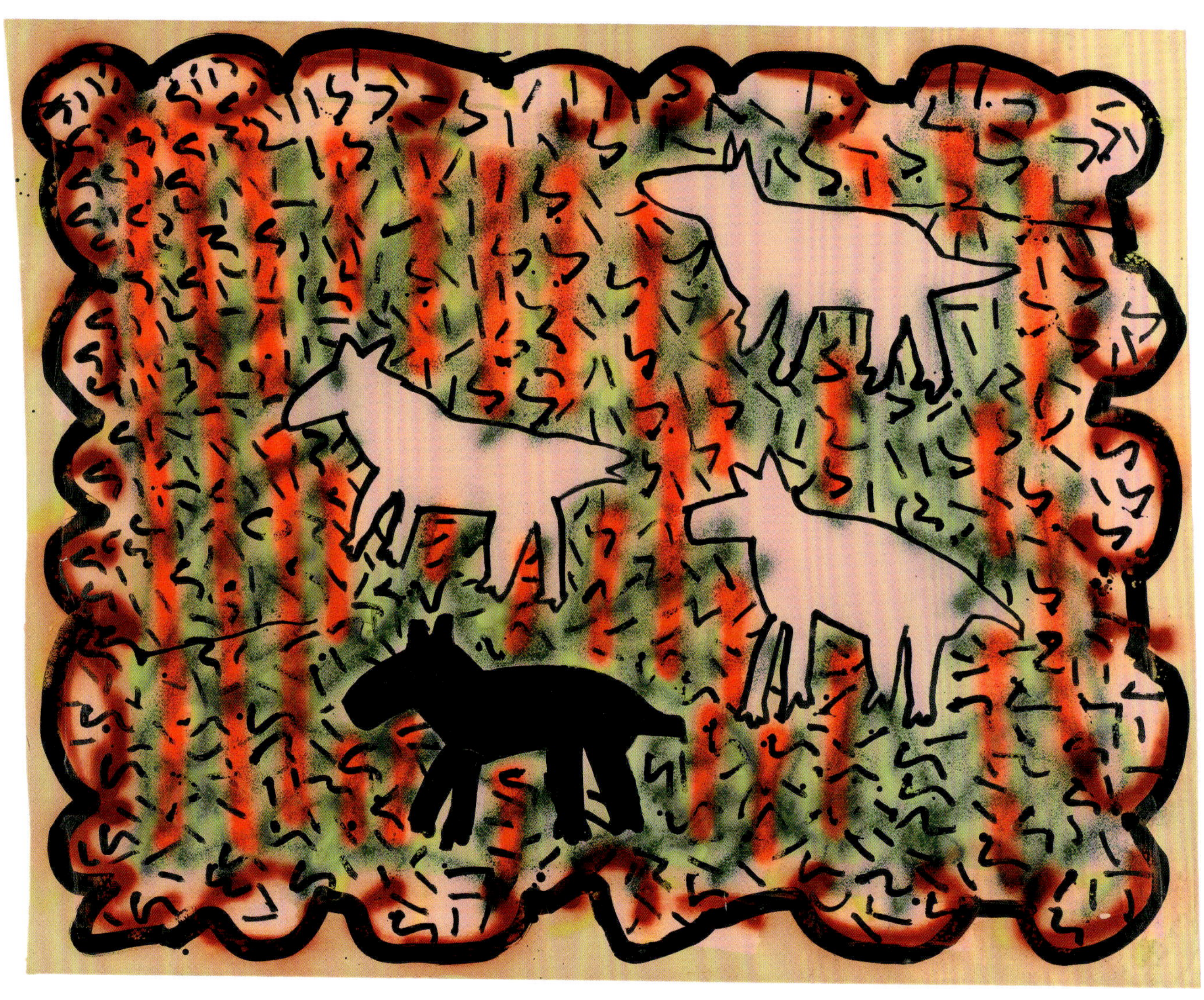

4

Animals, 1980. Acrylic, spray enamel, and ink on paper, 48½ x 61 in. (123.2 x 154.9 cm)
Collection of Larry Warsh

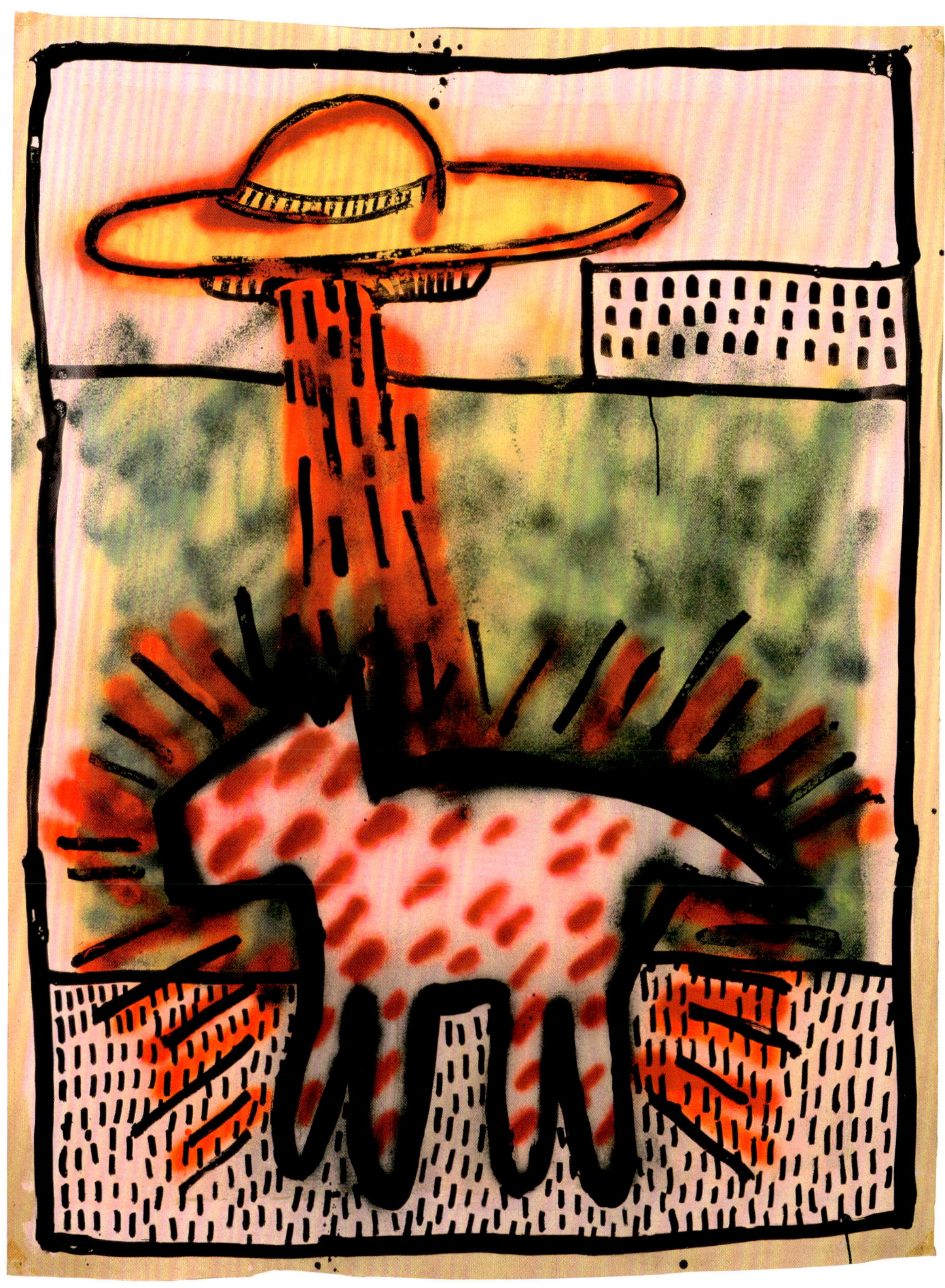

5

Untitled, 1980. Acrylic, spray enamel, and ink on paper, 63¾ x 48 in. (161.9 x 121.9 cm)
Collection of Roy Liebenthal and Fabienne Terwinghe, New York

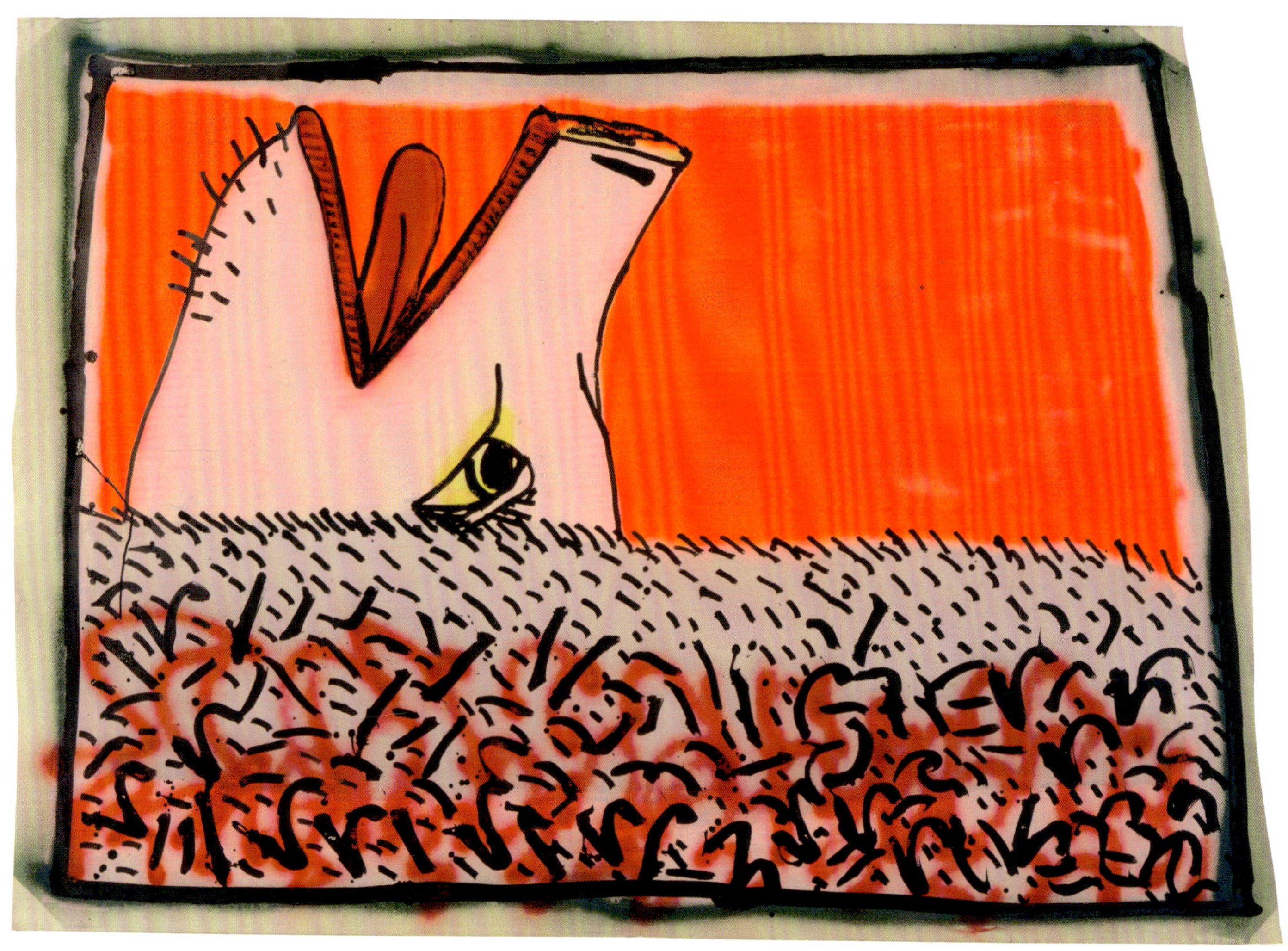

6

Untitled, September 2, 1980. Acrylic, spray enamel, and ink on paper, 31 ¼ x 48 in. (79.4 x 121.9 cm)
Collection of the Keith Haring Foundation

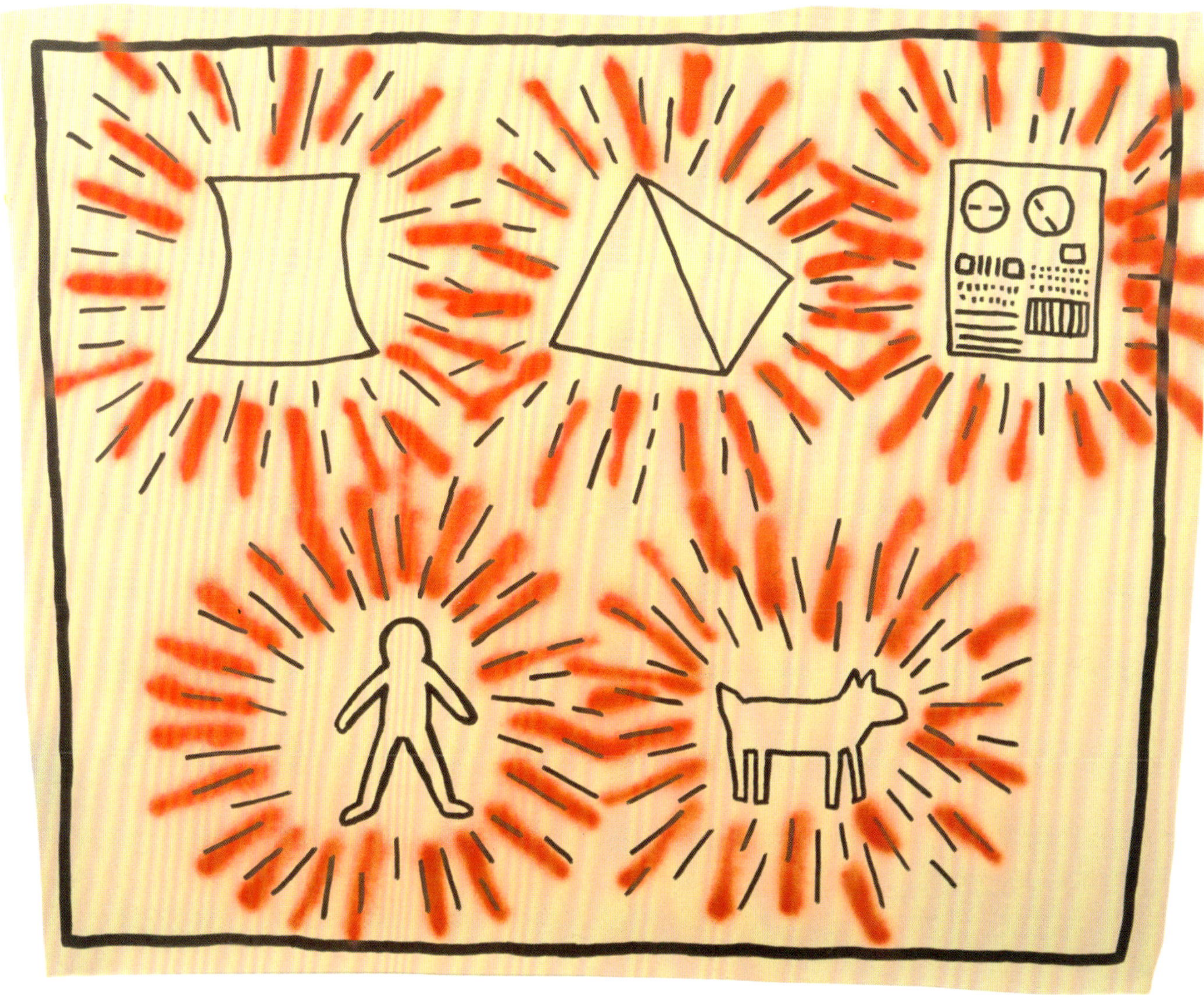

7

Untitled, September 2, 1980. Spray enamel and ink on paper, 44 1/2 x 54 1/2 in. (113 x 138.4 cm)
Collection of the Keith Haring Foundation

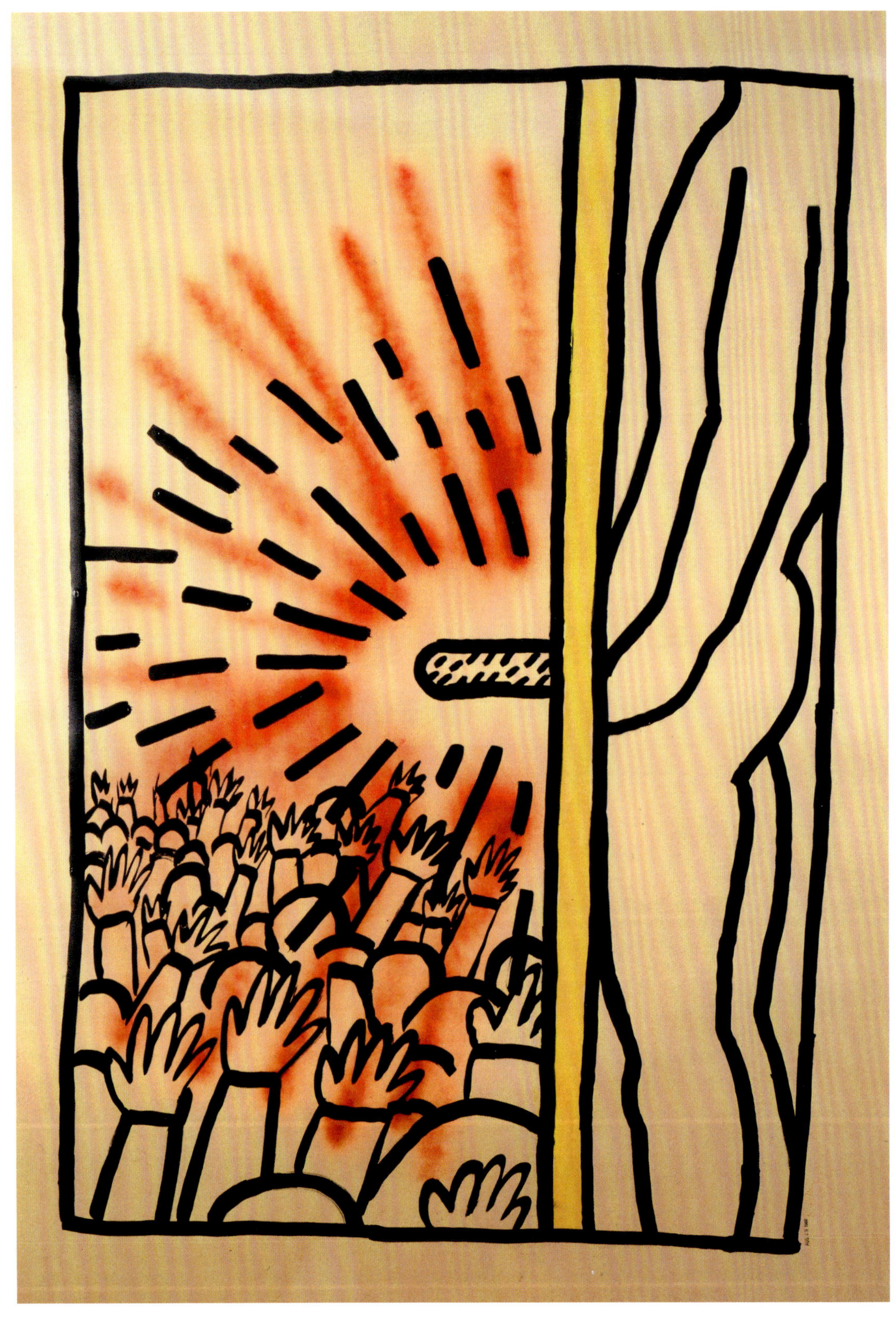

8

Glory Hole, 1980. Acrylic, spray enamel, and ink on paper, 48 x 35½ in. (121.9 x 90.2 cm)
Collection of Muna Tseng

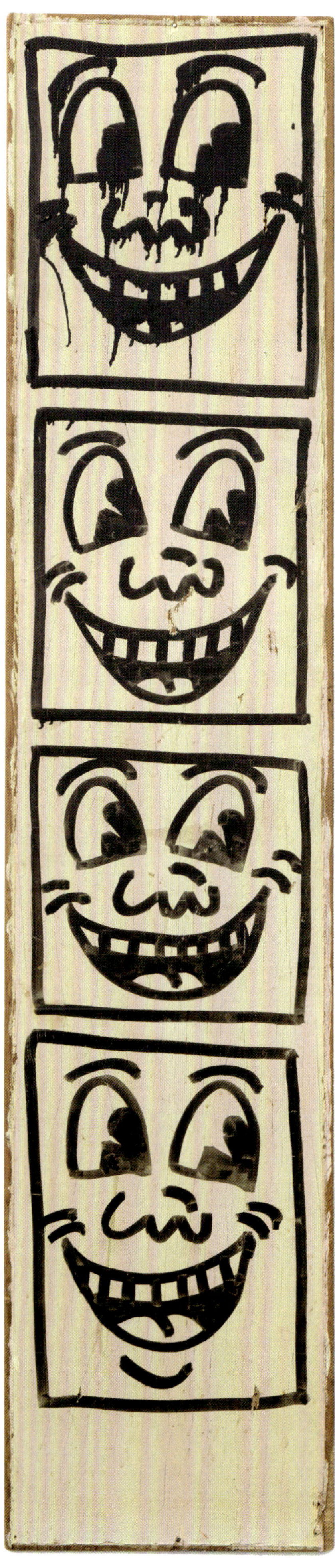

9

Untitled, 1981–1982. Acrylic on wood, 71 x 15 3/4 in. (180.3 x 40 cm)
Collection of Jose Martos

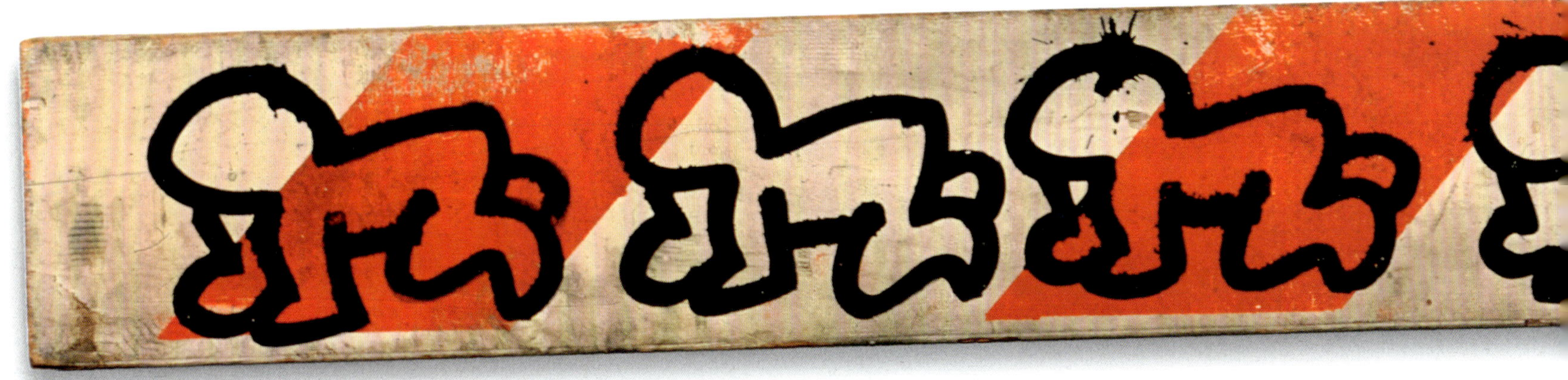

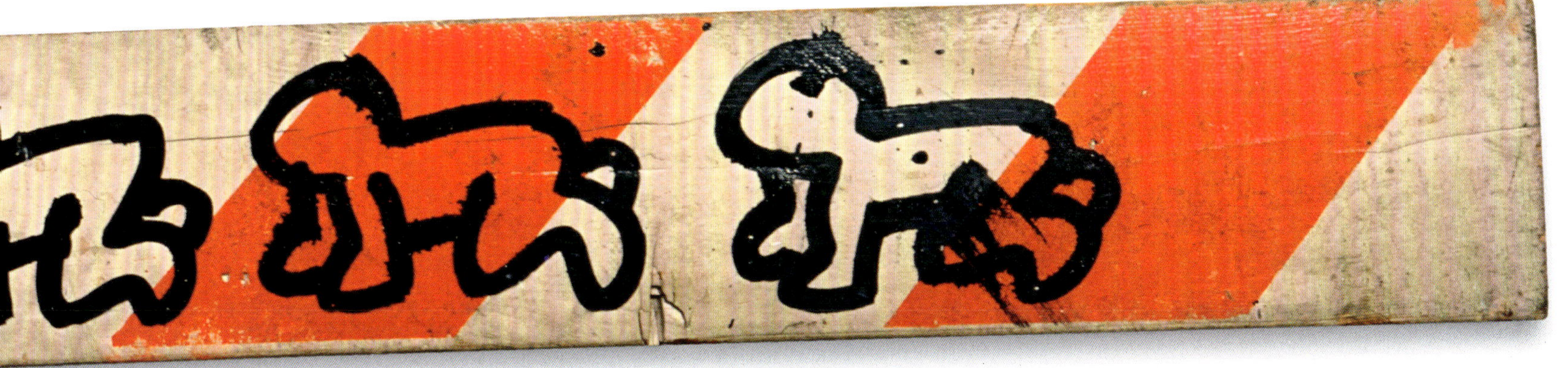

10

Untitled, 1981. Felt-tip pen on wooden police barricade, 7¼ x 72 x 1¾ in. (18.4 x 182.9 x 4.5 cm)
Private collection

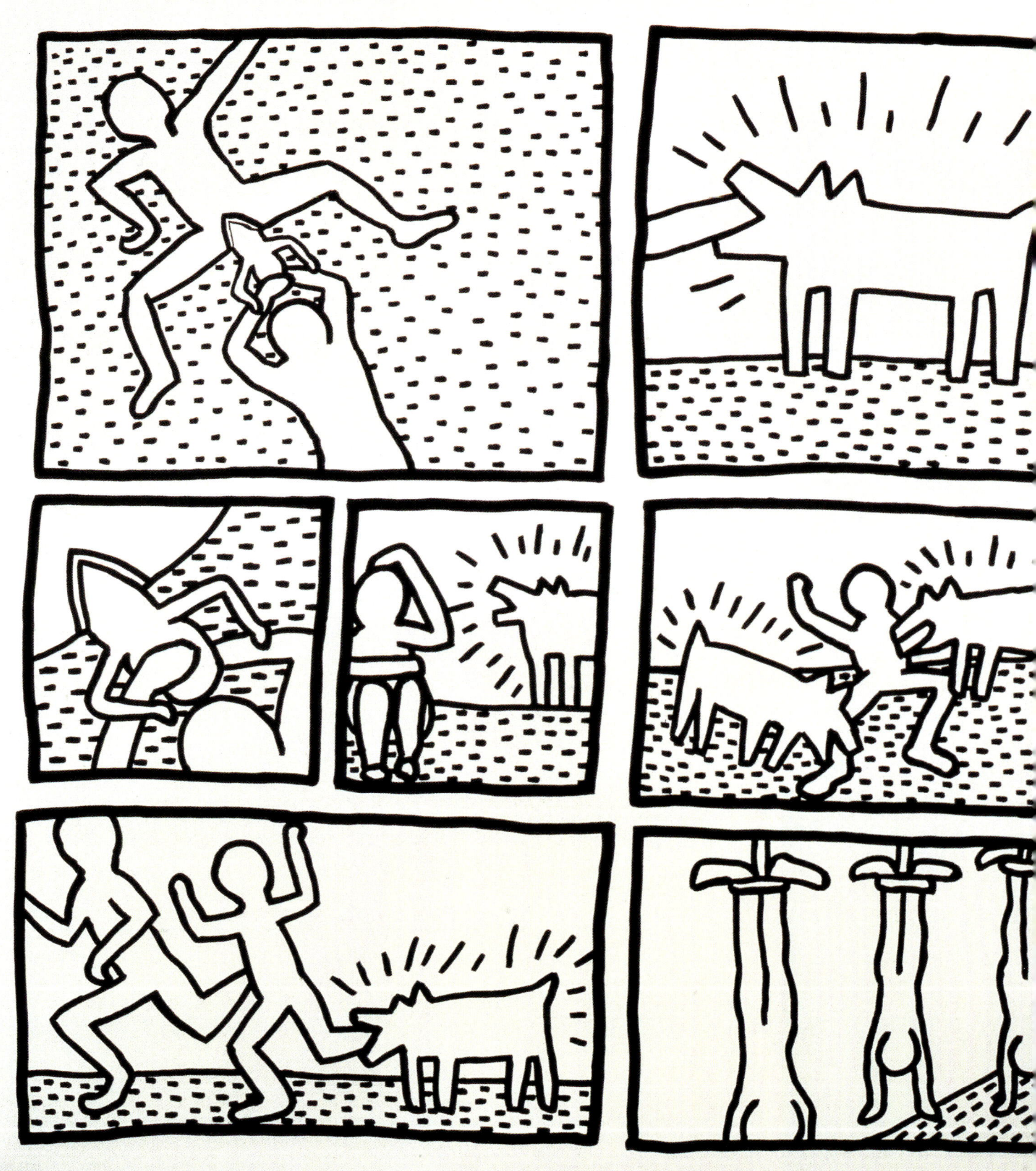

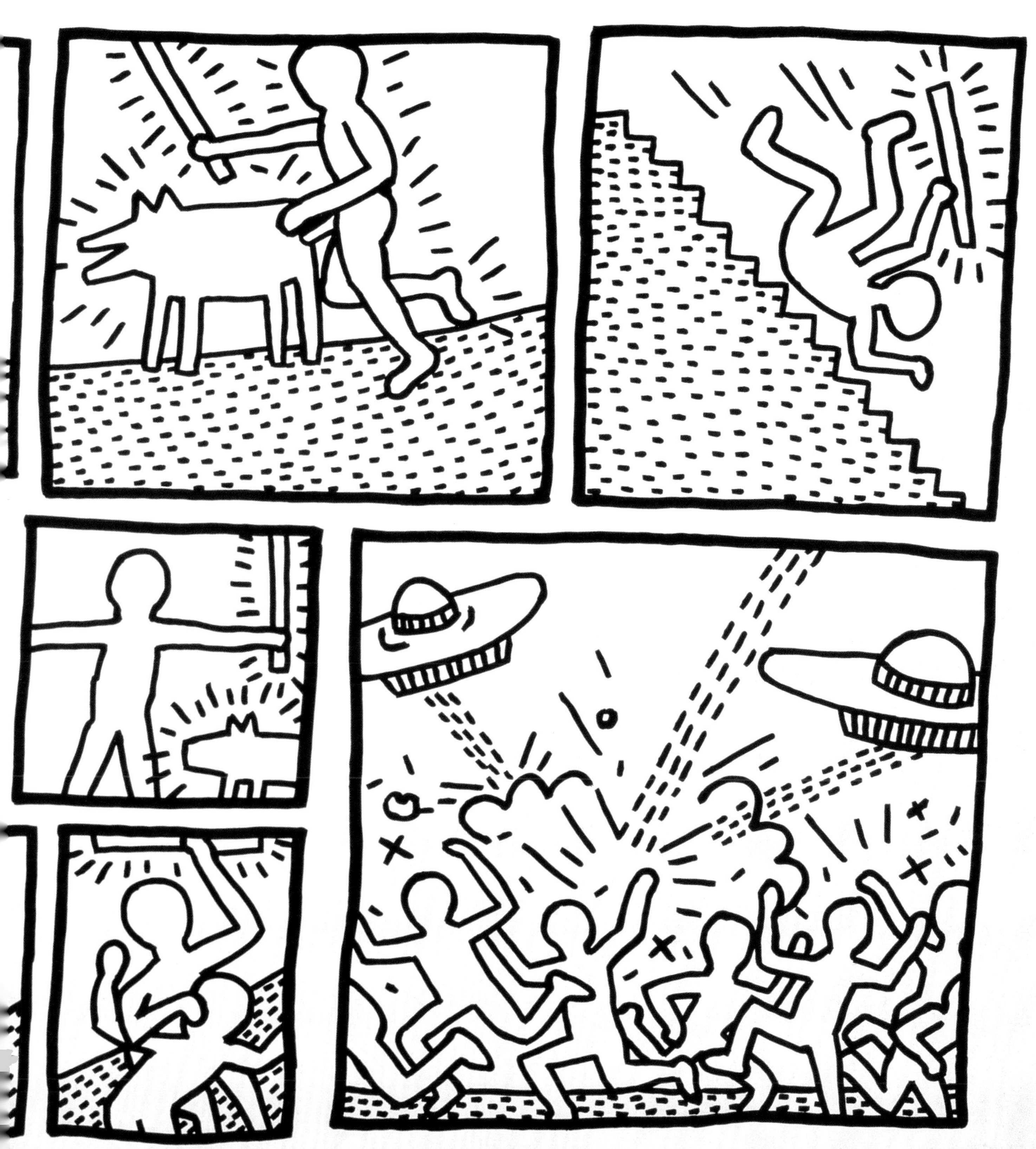

11

Untitled, 1981. Sumi ink on paper, 41 3/4 x 81 1/4 in. (106 x 206.4 cm)
Mugrabi Collection

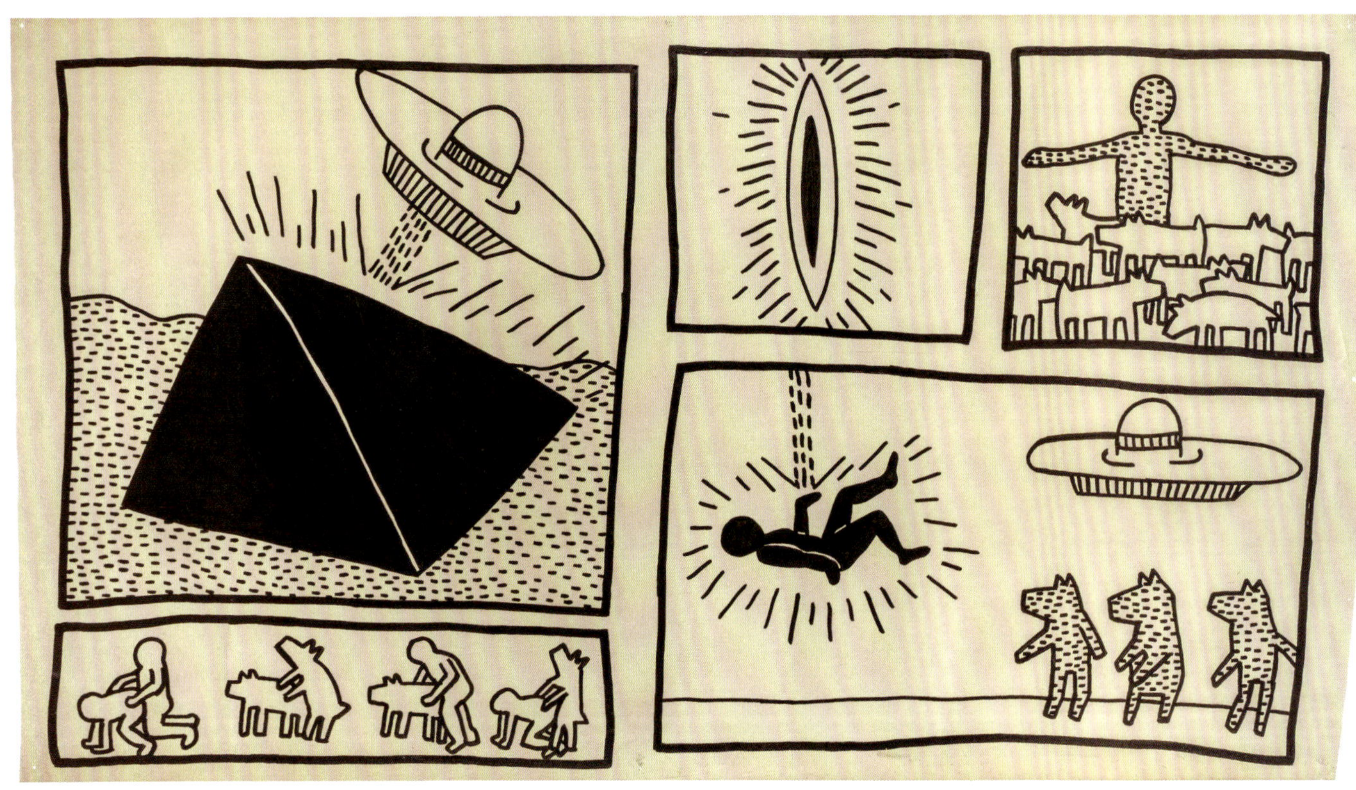

12

Untitled, 1980. Ink on posterboard, 48 x 89¾ in. (122 x 228 cm)
Collection of Alona Kagan

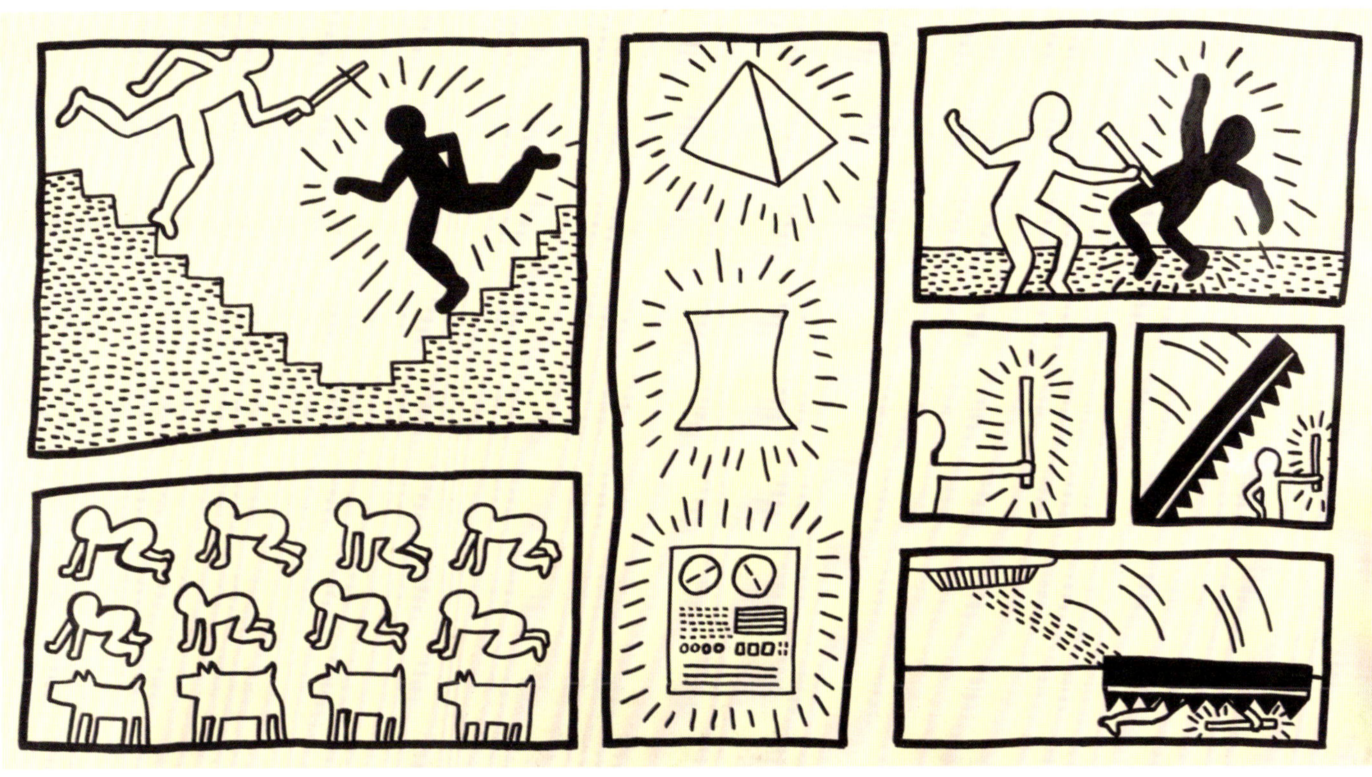

13

Untitled, 1980. Ink on posterboard, 48 x 90⅝ in. (121.9 x 230.2 cm)
Collection of the Keith Haring Foundation

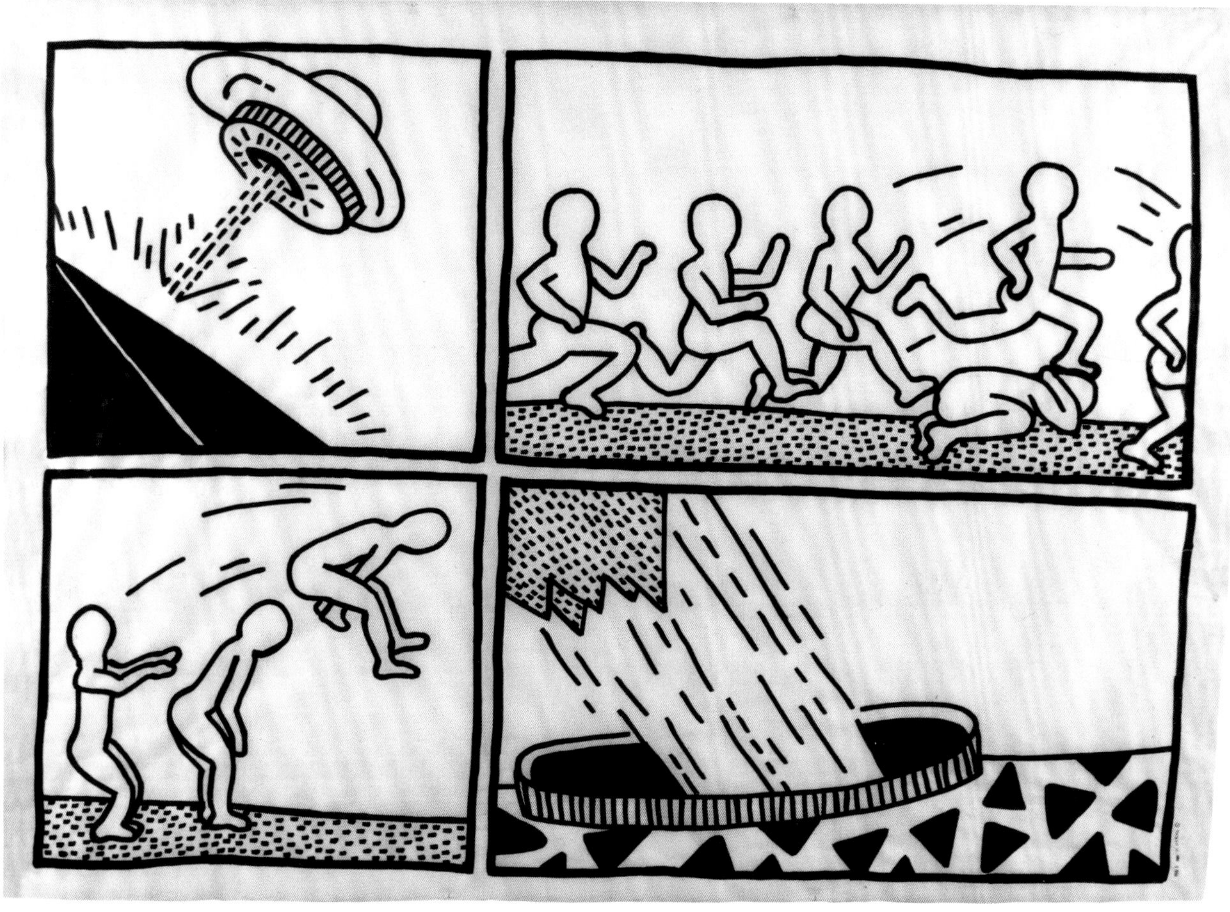

14

Untitled, February 3, 1981. Sumi ink on vellum, 41 ½ x 58 in. (105.4 x 147.3 cm)
Glenstone

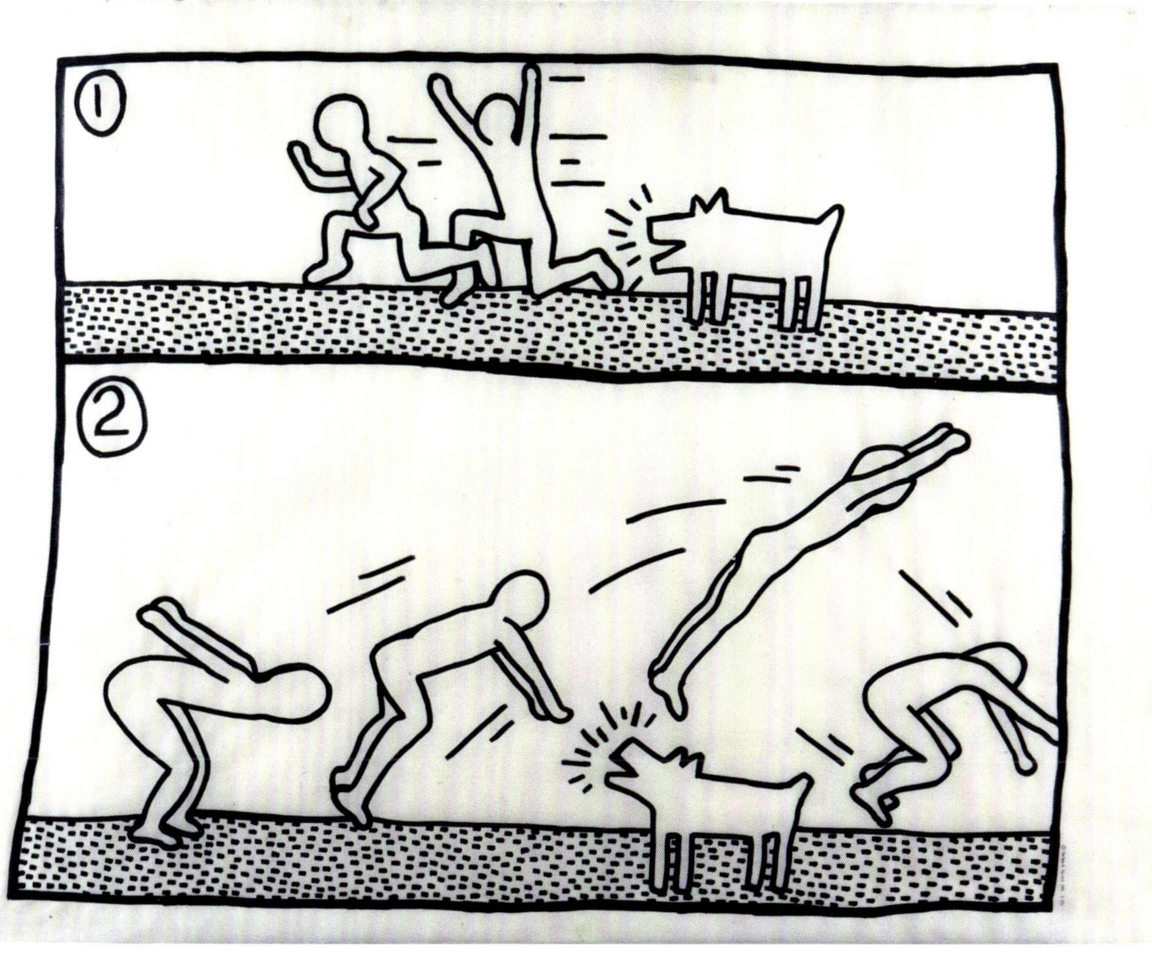

15

Untitled, February 3, 1981. Sumi ink on vellum, 42¼ x 52¾ in. (107.2 x 134.1 cm)
Glenstone

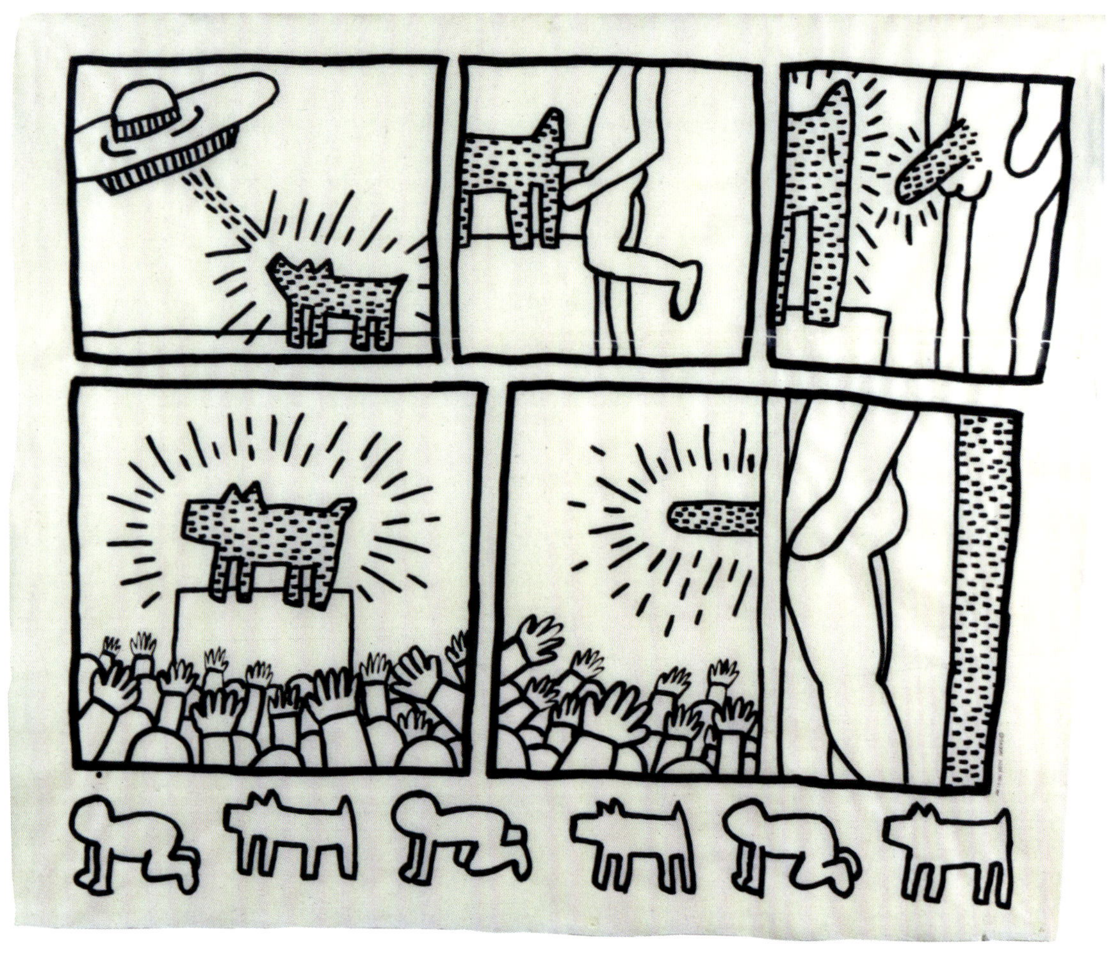

16

Untitled, January 16, 1981. Sumi ink on vellum, 41½ x 50½ in. (105.4 x 128.3 cm)
Skarstedt, New York

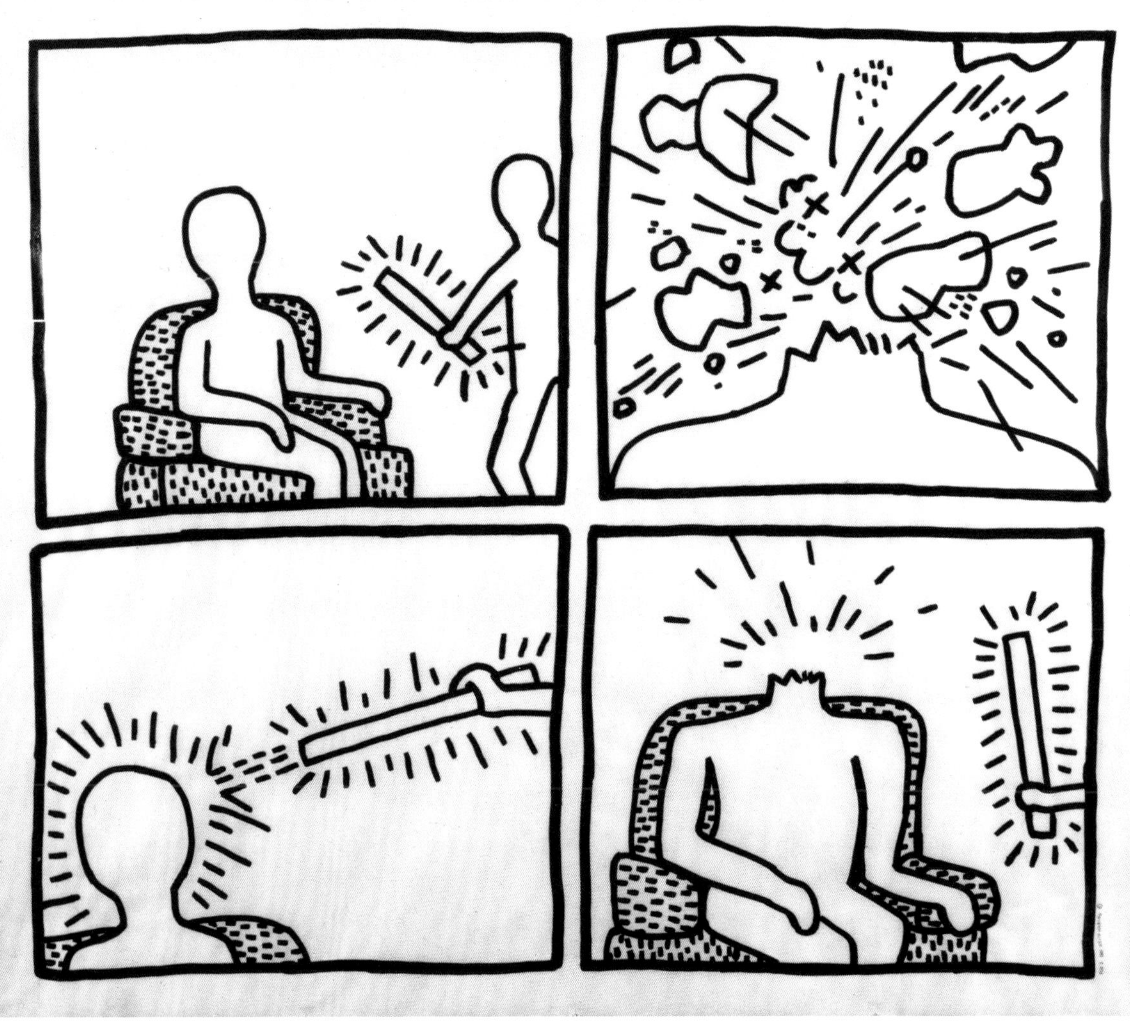

17

Untitled, 1981. Sumi ink on vellum, 43 x 49 in. (109.2 x 124.5 cm)
Private collection

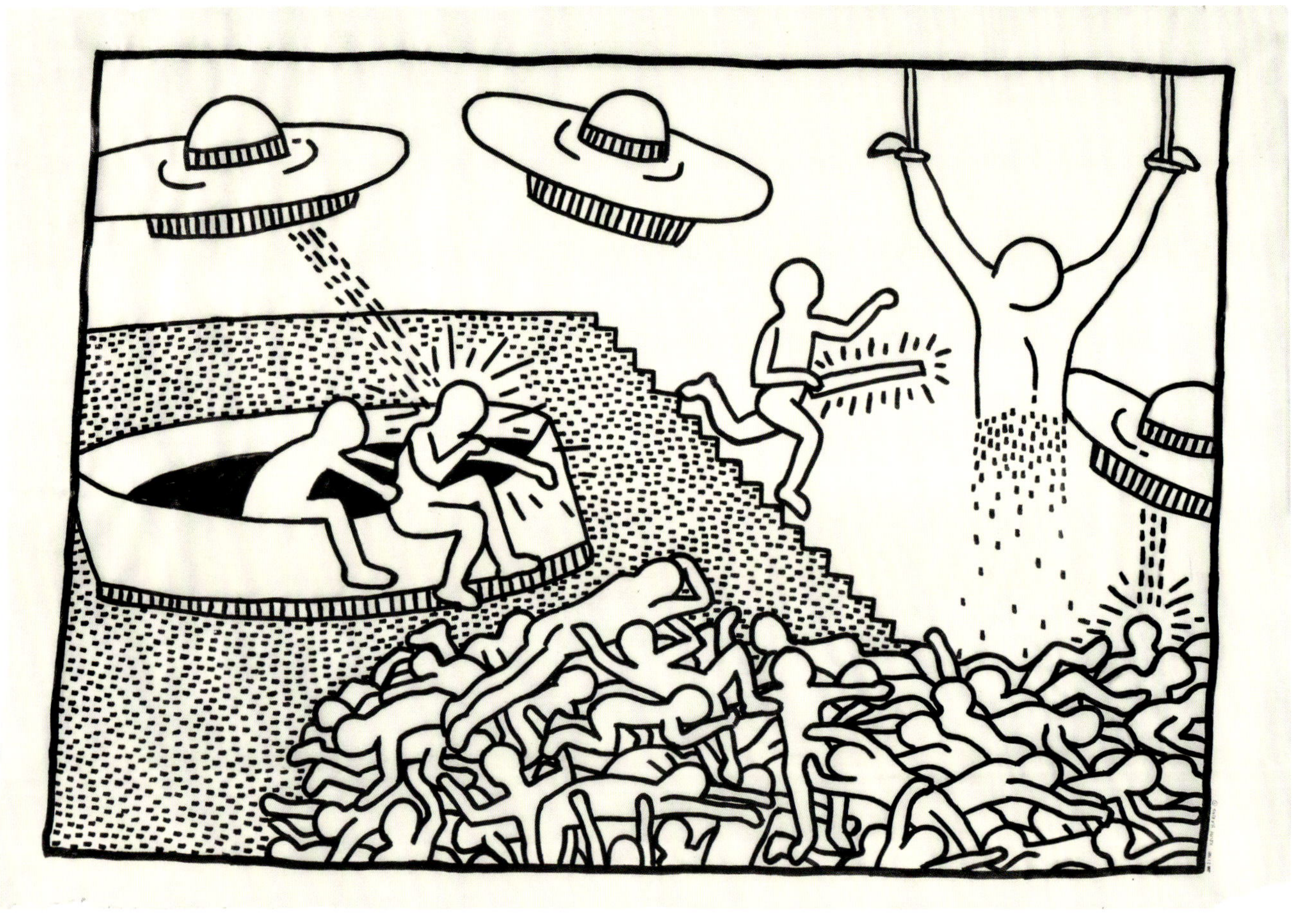

18

Untitled, 1981. Sumi ink on vellum, 41½ x 61½ in. (105.4 x 156.2 cm)
Collection of Alona Kagan

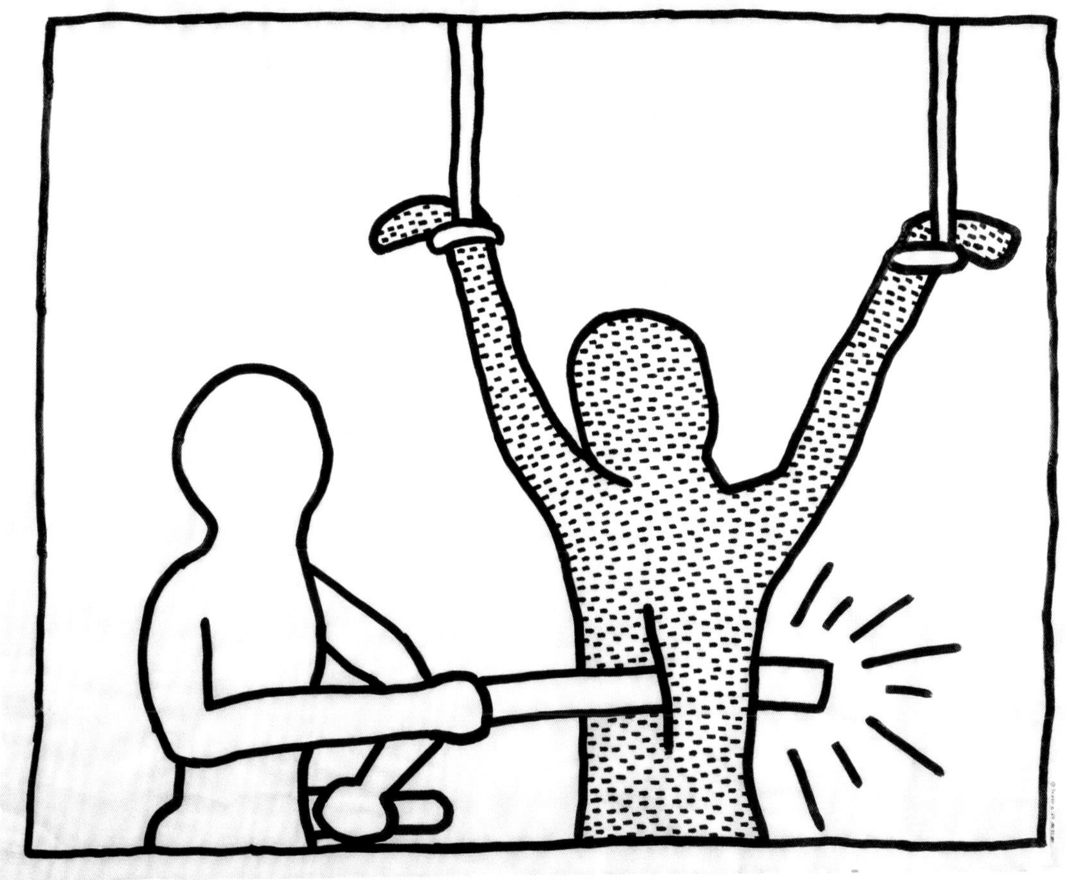

19

Untitled, January 26, 1981. Sumi ink on vellum, 41½ x 52 in. (105.4 x 132.1 cm)
Collection of Alona Kagan

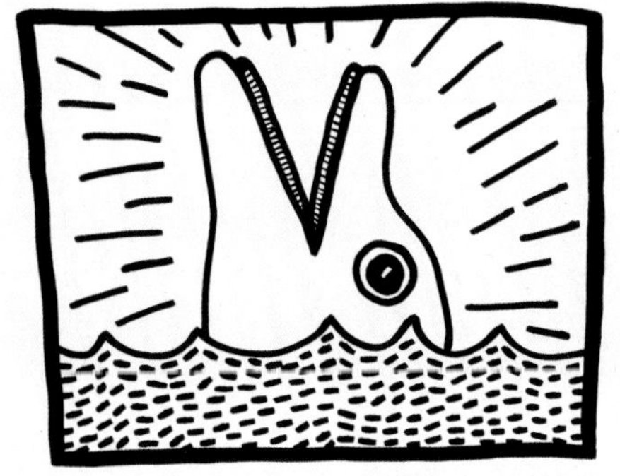
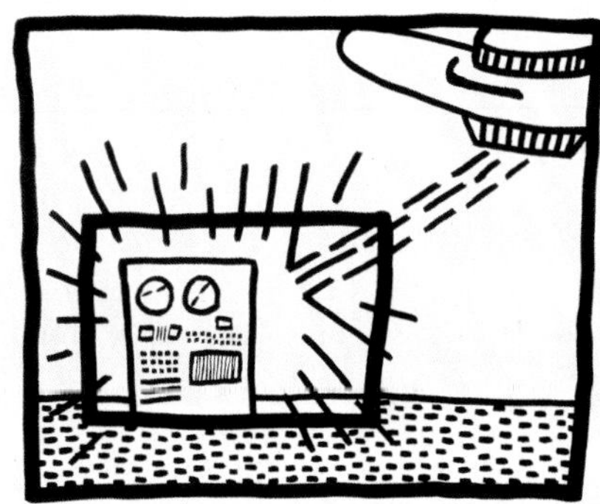
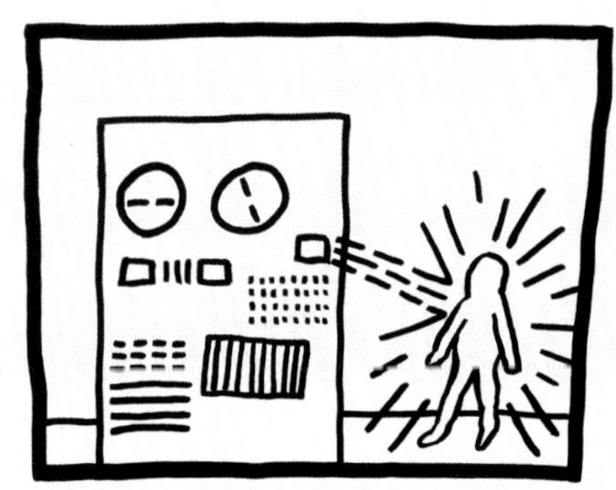
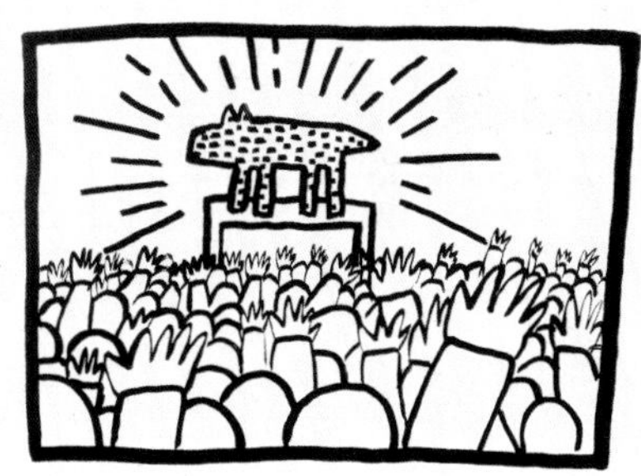
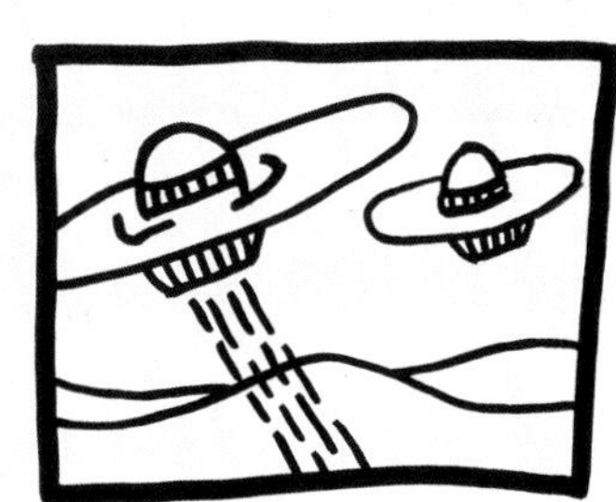
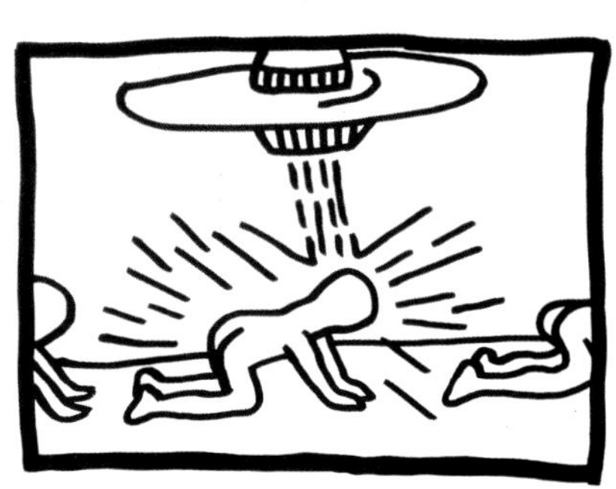
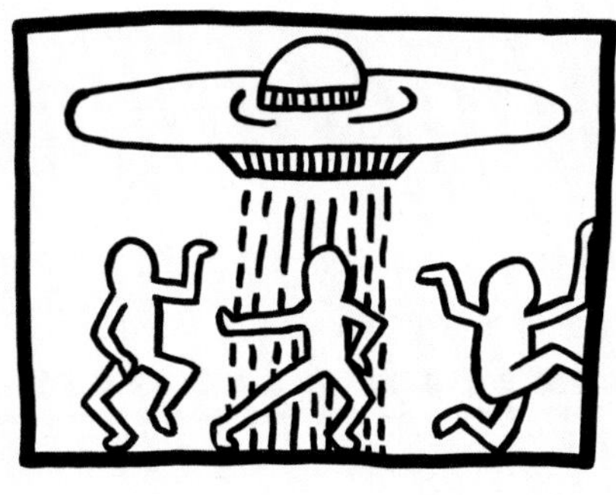
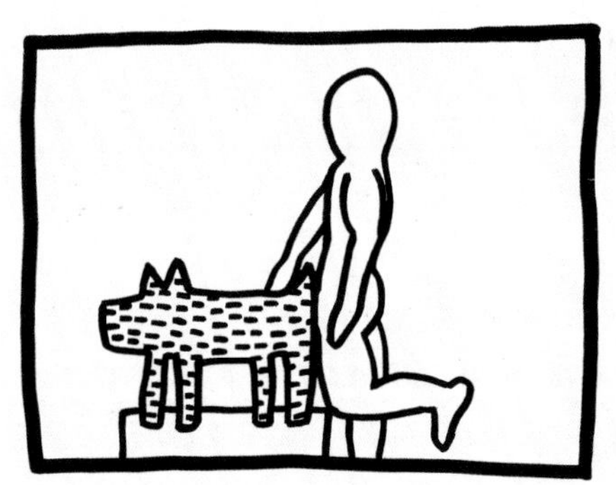
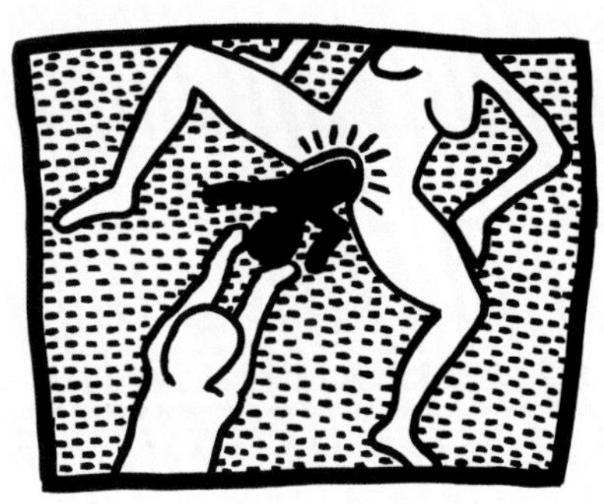
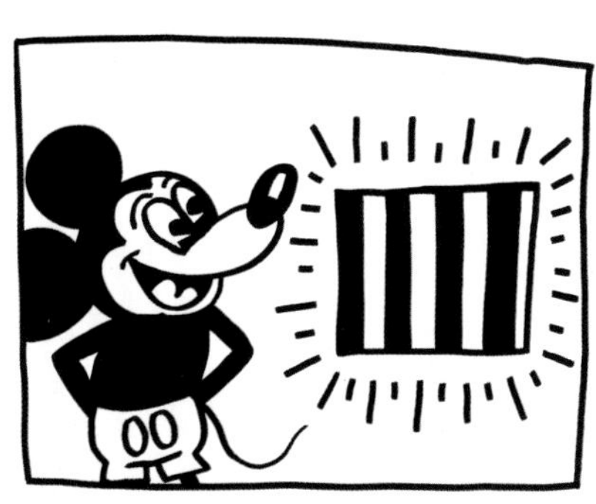
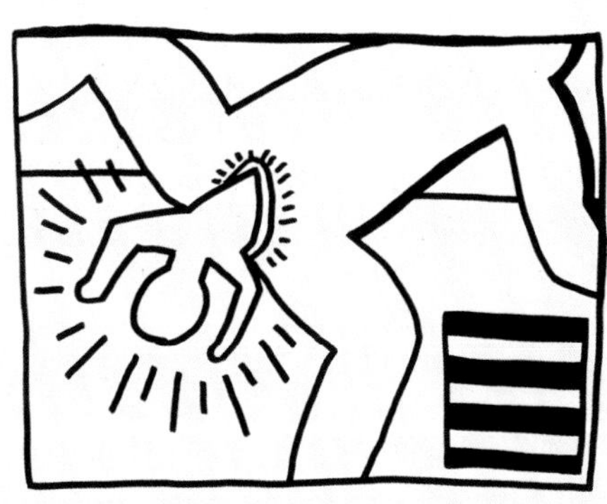

20–30

Left to right, top to bottom:
Untitled, September 22, 1980. *Untitled*, September 8–9, 1980. *Untitled*, September 8–9, 1980
Untitled, 1980. *Untitled*, September 8–9, 1980. *Untitled*, September 8–9, 1980
Untitled, September 8–9, 1980. *Untitled*, September 8–9, 1980. *Untitled*, September 8–9, 1980
Untitled, September 8–9, 1980. *Untitled*, September 8–9, 1980
Ink on Bristol board, each 20 1/8 x 26 in. (51 x 66 cm)
Collection of the Keith Haring Foundation

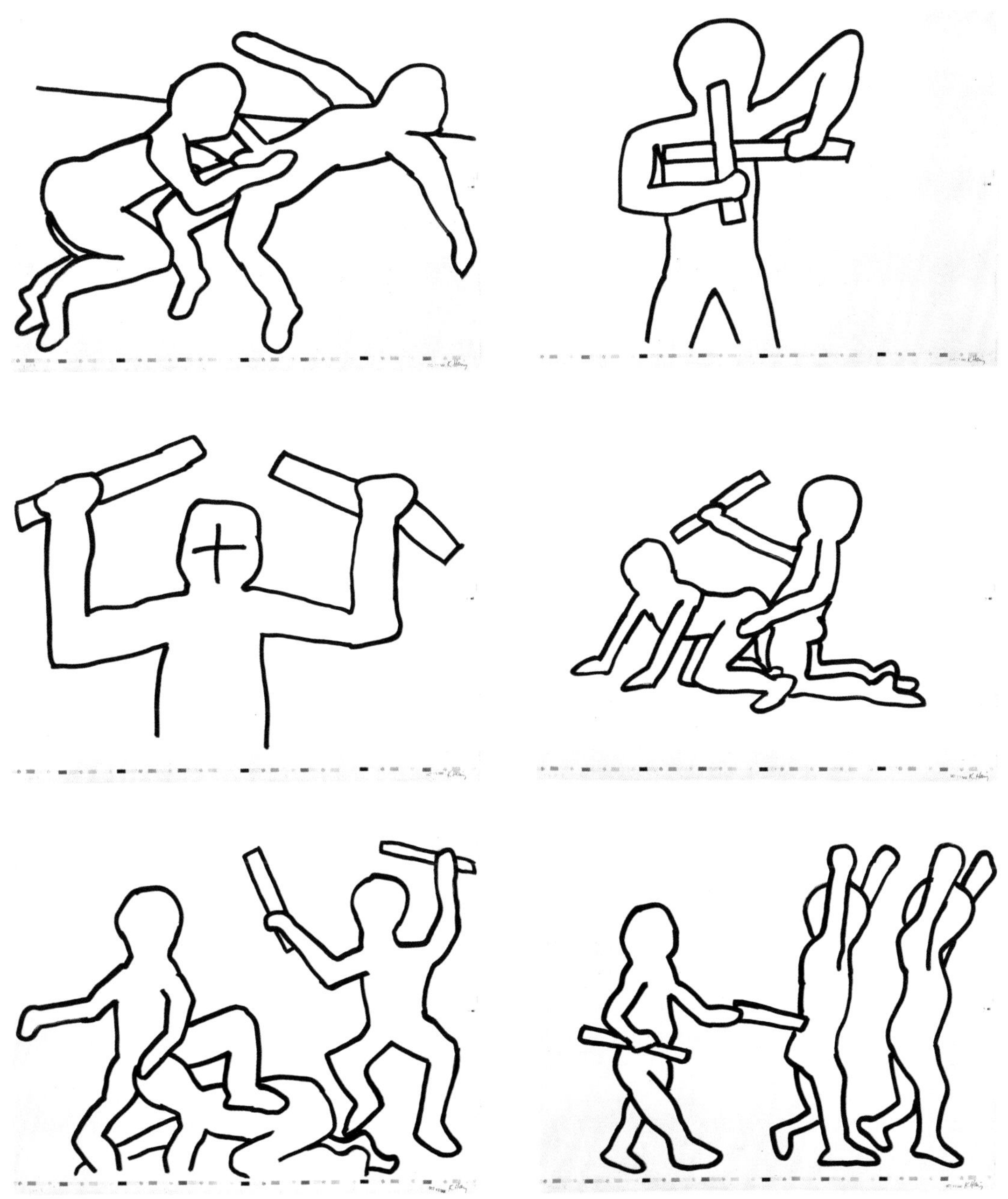

31–36

Untitled, October 12, 1980. Sumi ink on paper, 6 drawings (from a series of 8), each 20 x 27 in. (50.8 x 68.6 cm)
Collection of the Keith Haring Foundation

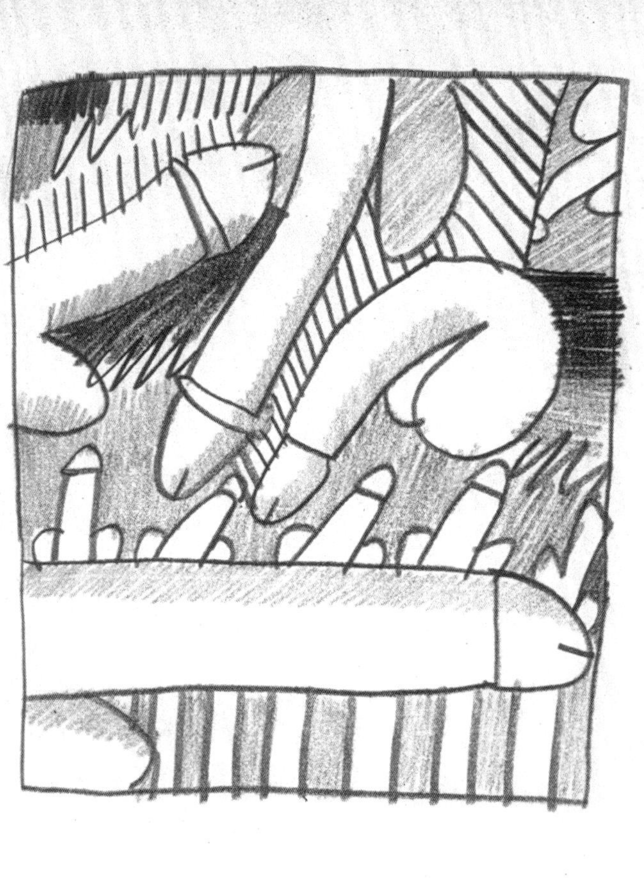

37–53

Manhattan Penis Drawings for Ken Hicks, 1978. Graphite on paper, 17 drawings (from a series of 88), each 8 ½ x 5 ½ in. (21.6 x 14 cm)
Collection of the Keith Haring Foundation

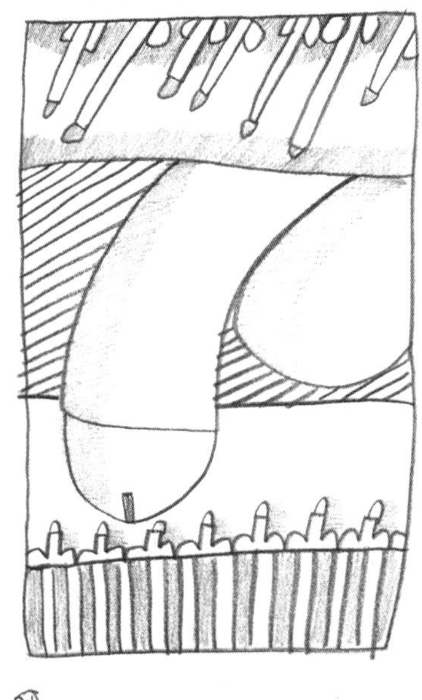

24

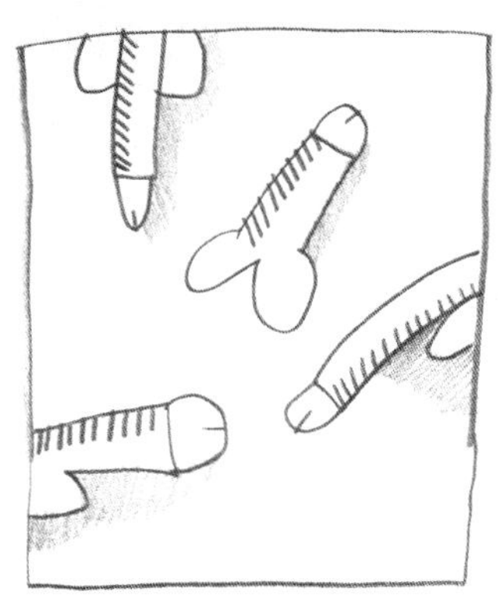

DRAWING PENISES IN
FRONT OF TIFFANY'S

25

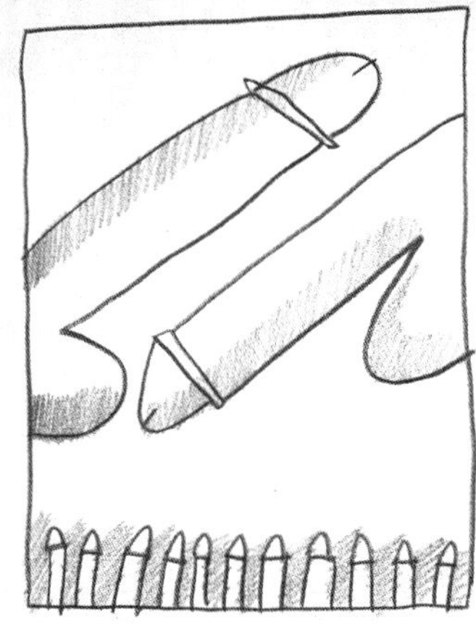

DRAWING PENISES
IN FRONT OF
~~THE~~ TIFFANYS'

26

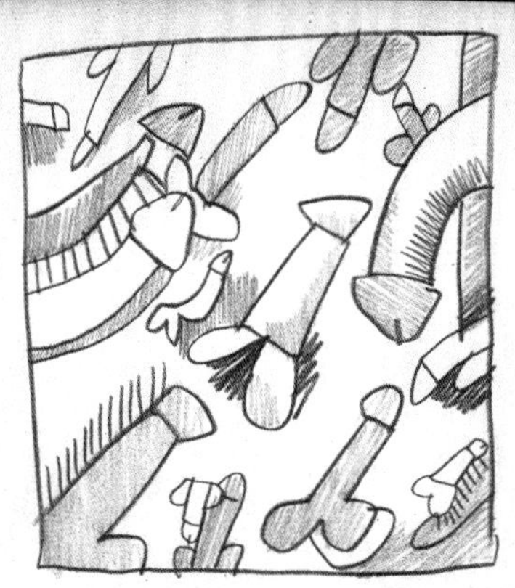

DRAWING PENISES
IN FRONT OF TIFFANYS'

27

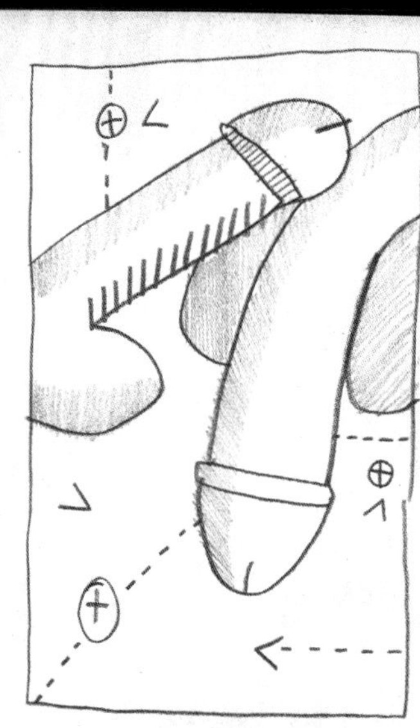

DRAWING PENISES IN
FRONT OF TIFFANYS'

28

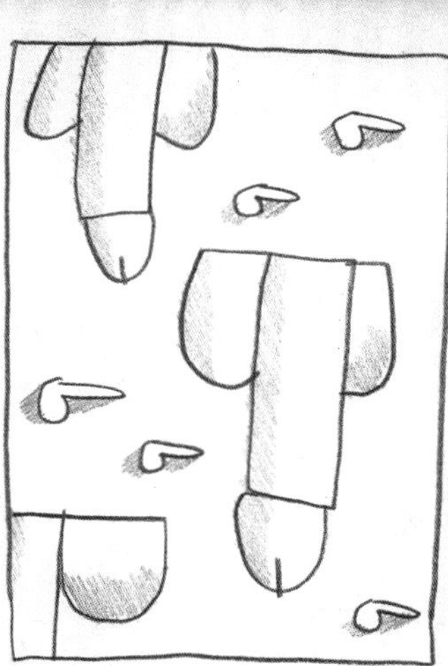

DRAWING PENISES IN
FRONT OF TIFFANYS'

29

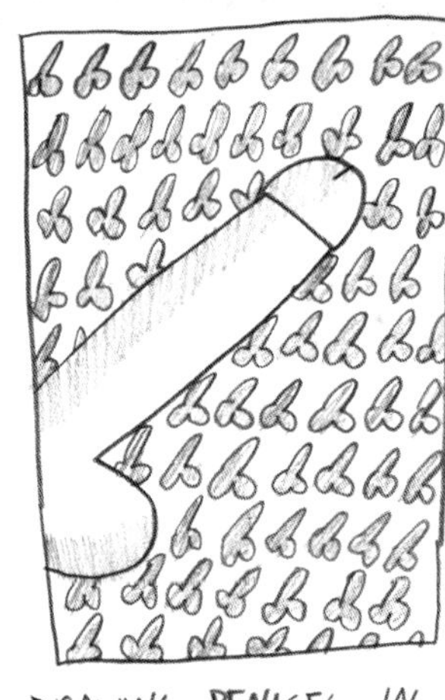

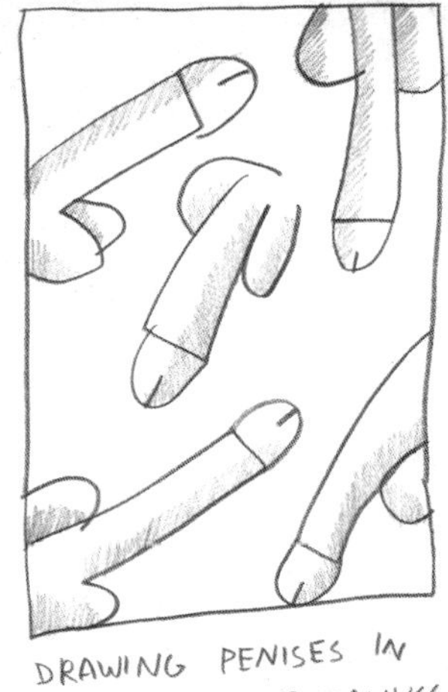

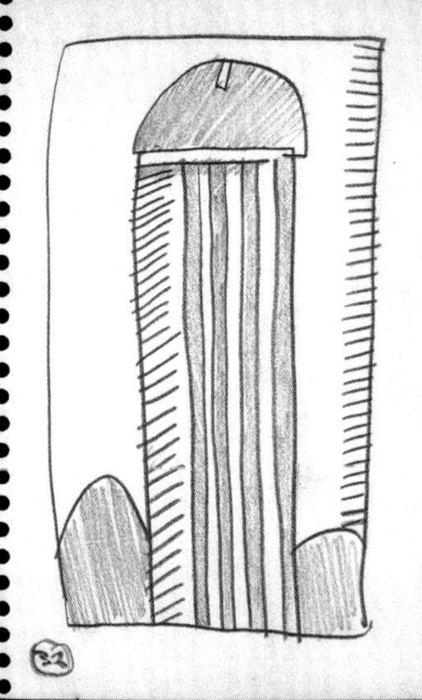

33

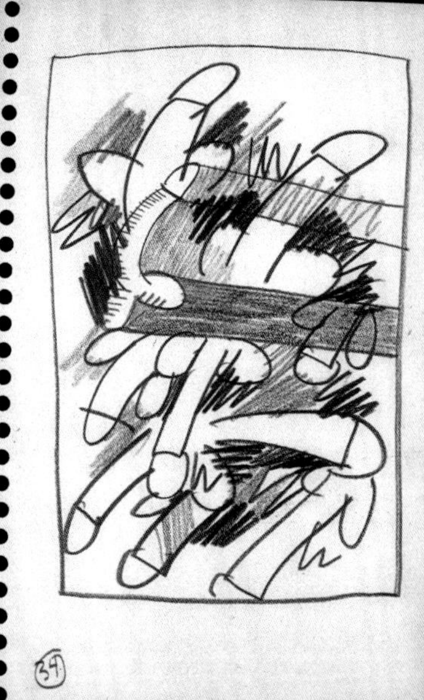

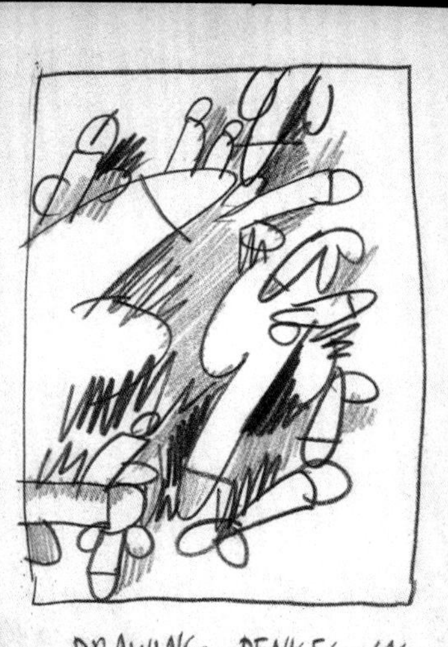

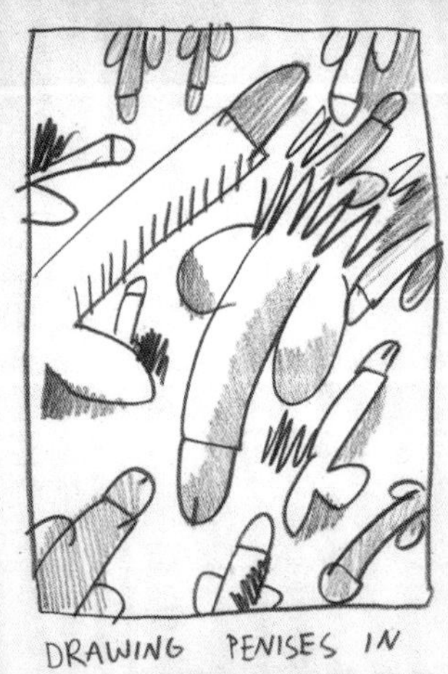

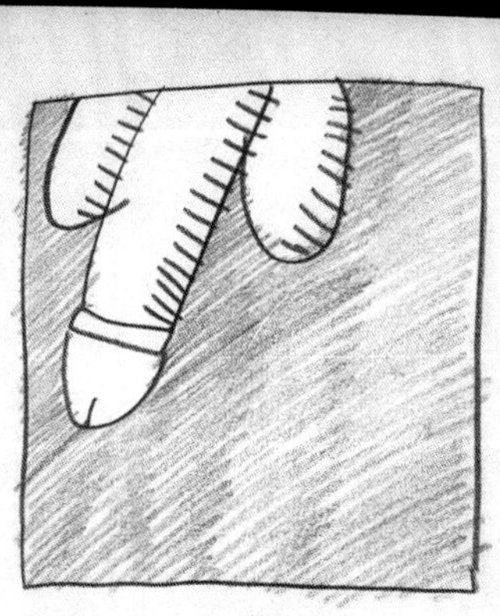

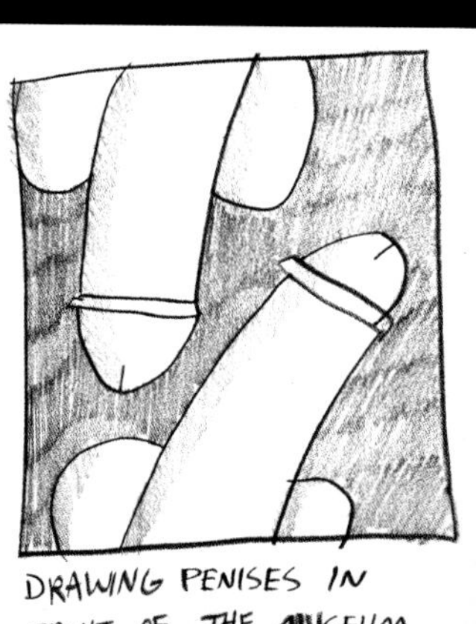

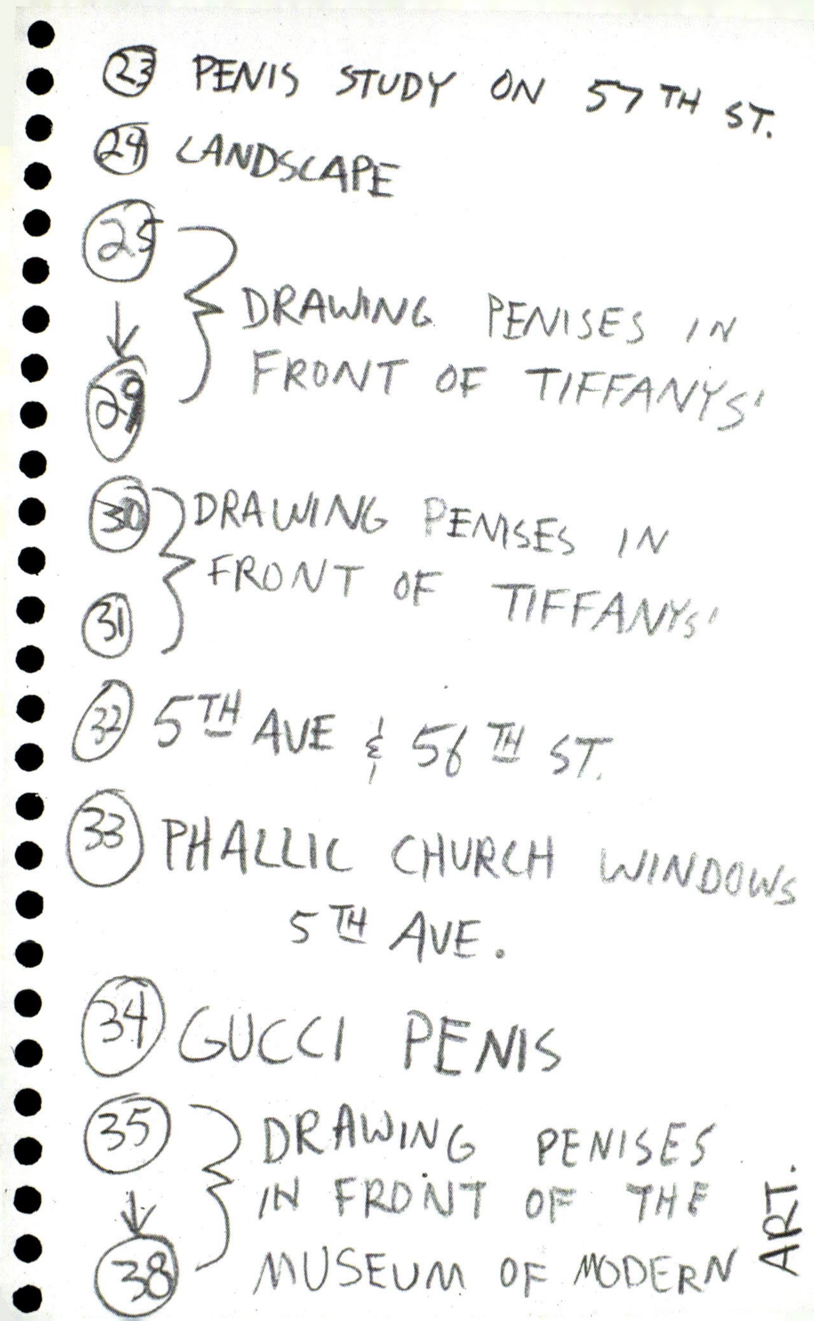
23 PENIS STUDY ON 57TH ST.
24 LANDSCAPE
25 → 29 DRAWING PENISES IN FRONT OF TIFFANYS'
30 31 DRAWING PENISES IN FRONT OF TIFFANYS'
32 5TH AVE & 56TH ST.
33 PHALLIC CHURCH WINDOWS 5TH AVE.
34 GUCCI PENIS
35 → 38 DRAWING PENISES IN FRONT OF THE MUSEUM OF MODERN ART.

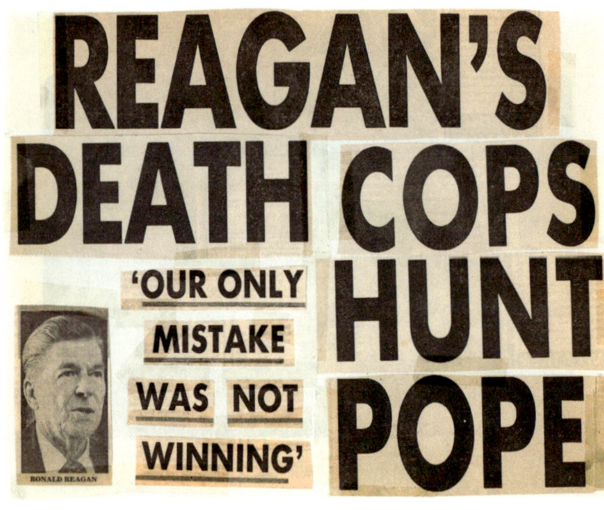

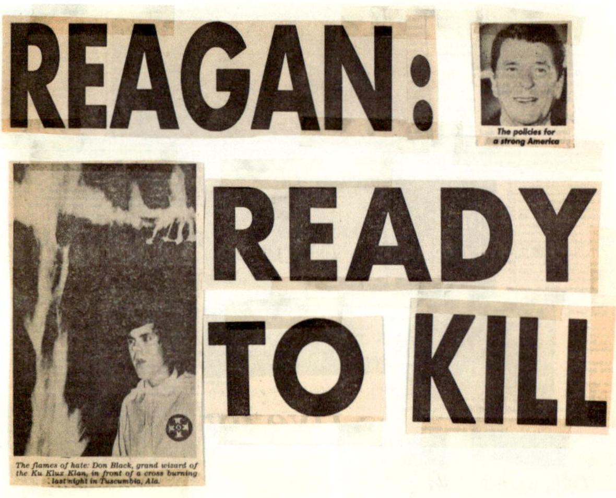

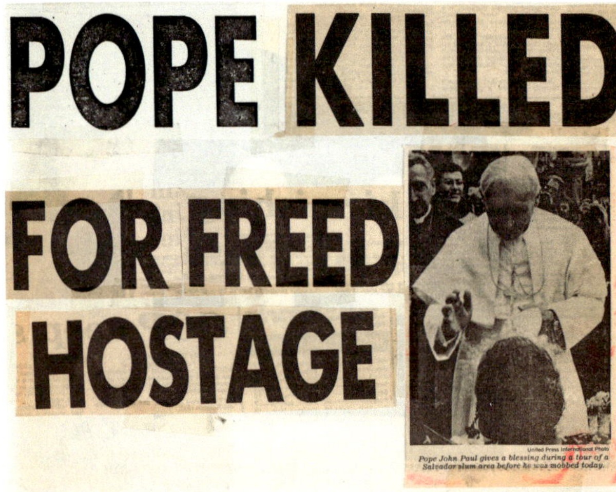

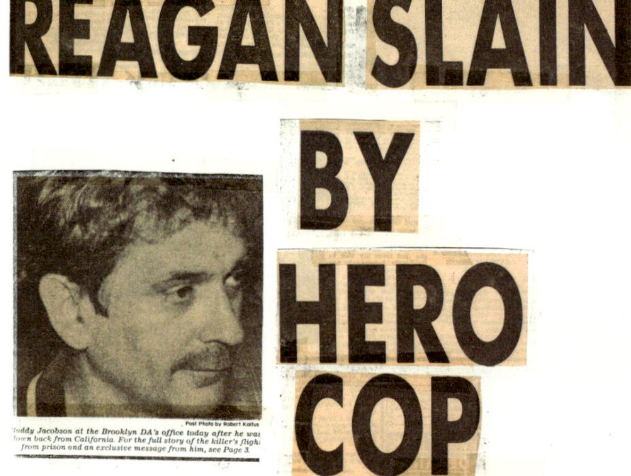

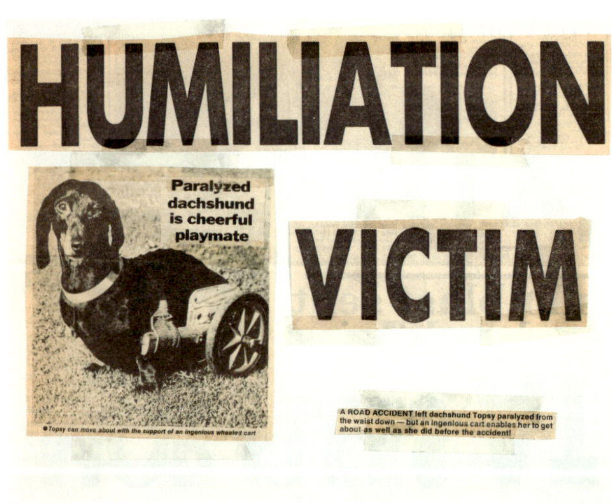

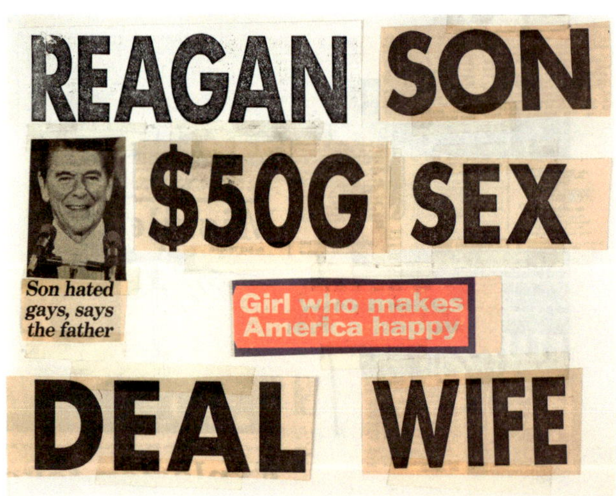

54–59

Reagan's Death Cops Hunt Pope, *Reagan: Ready to Kill*,
Pope Killed for Freed Hostage, *Reagan Slain by Hero Cop*,
Humiliation Victim, and *Reagan Son $50G Sex Deal Wife*,
1980. 6 newspaper fragments and tape on paper (from a series of 8), each 8 1/2 x 11 in. (21.6 x 27.9 cm)
Collection of the Keith Haring Foundation

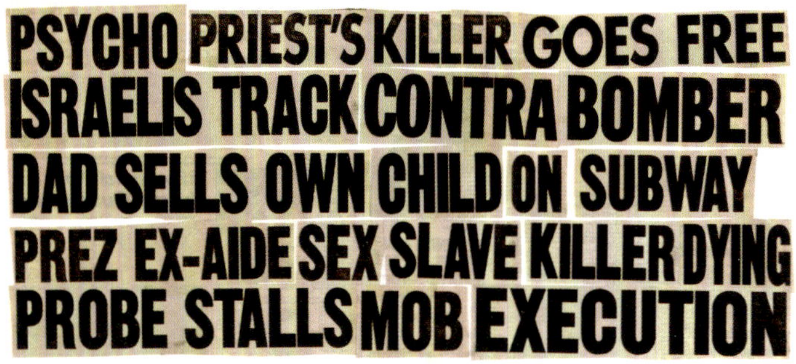

PSYCHO PRIEST'S KILLER GOES FREE
ISRAELIS TRACK CONTRA BOMBER
DAD SELLS OWN CHILD ON SUBWAY
PREZ EX-AIDE SEX SLAVE KILLER DYING
PROBE STALLS MOB EXECUTION

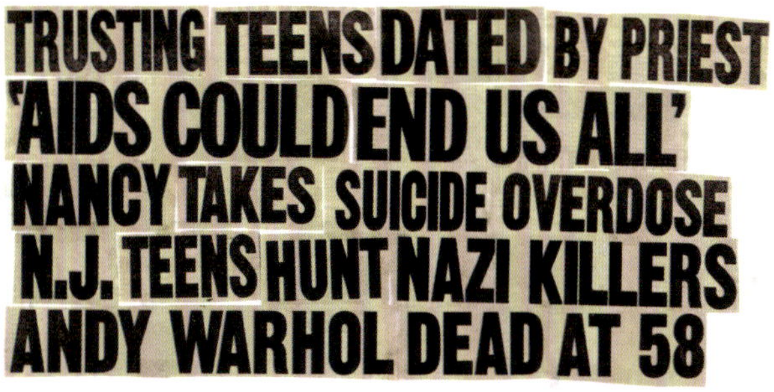

TRUSTING TEENS DATED BY PRIEST
'AIDS COULD END US ALL'
NANCY TAKES SUICIDE OVERDOSE
N.J. TEENS HUNT NAZI KILLERS
ANDY WARHOL DEAD AT 58

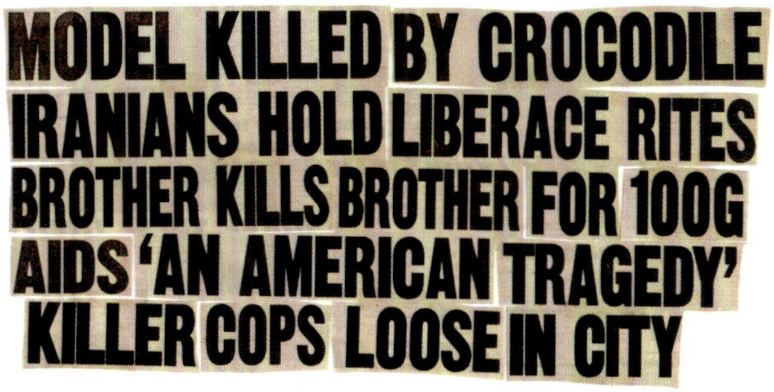

MODEL KILLED BY CROCODILE
IRANIANS HOLD LIBERACE RITES
BROTHER KILLS BROTHER FOR 100G
AIDS 'AN AMERICAN TRAGEDY'
KILLER COPS LOOSE IN CITY

60–62

Costume design elements for *Interrupted River*, choreography by Jennifer Muller and music by Yoko Ono, 1987
Newspaper and tape on paper, each 19 ½ x 25 ½ in. (49.5 x 64.8 cm)
Collection of the Keith Haring Foundation

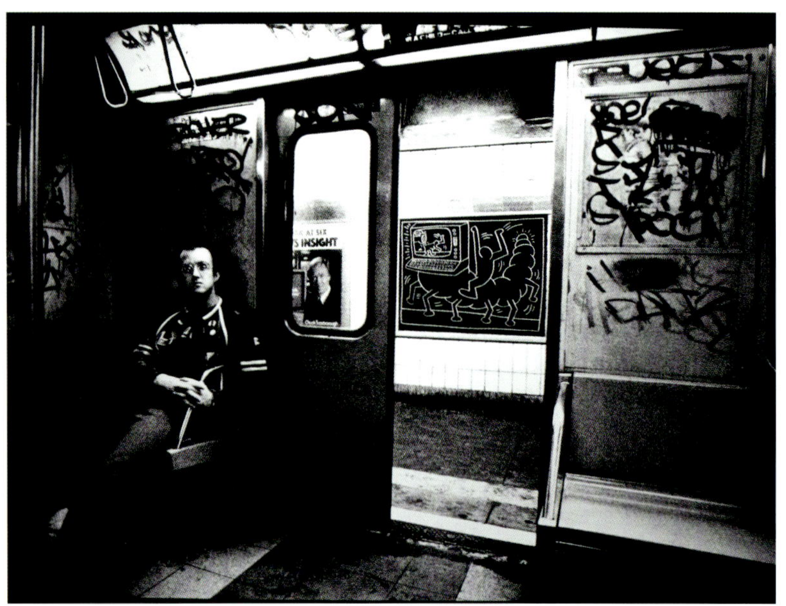

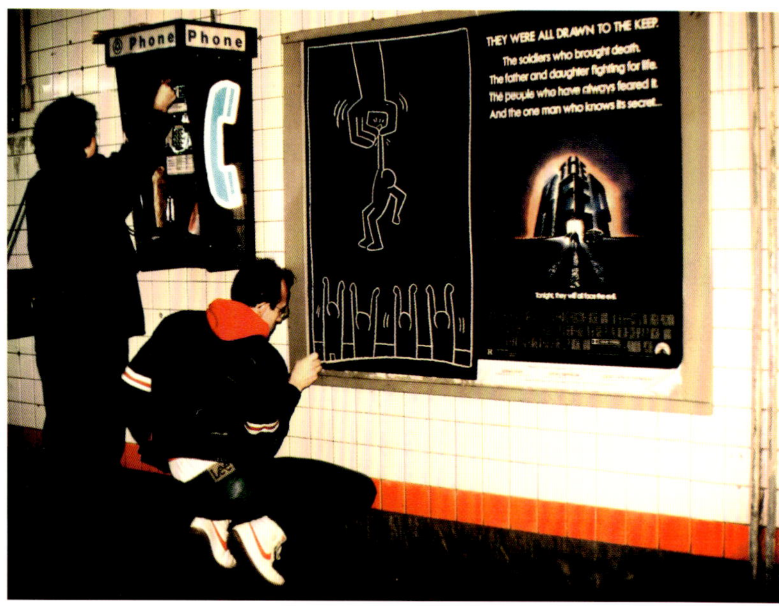

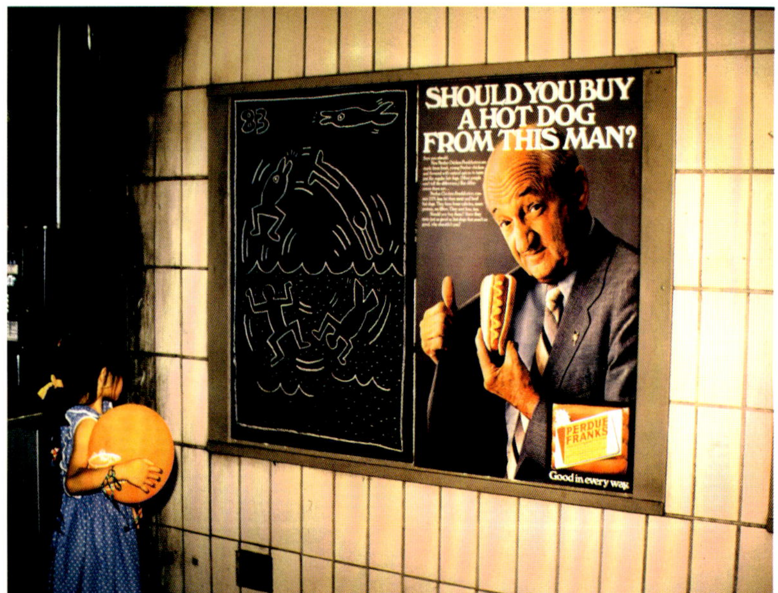

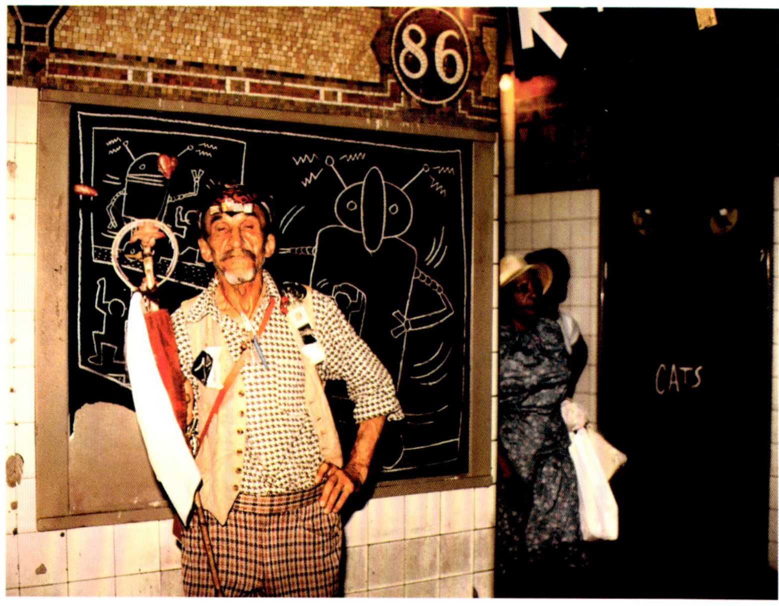

63–70

Tseng Kwong Chi, *Slide Light Boxes with Photos*, 1982–1984. 8 slide boxes with Ektachrome photographs (from a series of 10), each 10 1/4 x 19 3/4 x 25 5/8 in. (26 x 50 x 65 cm)
Collection of Muna Tseng

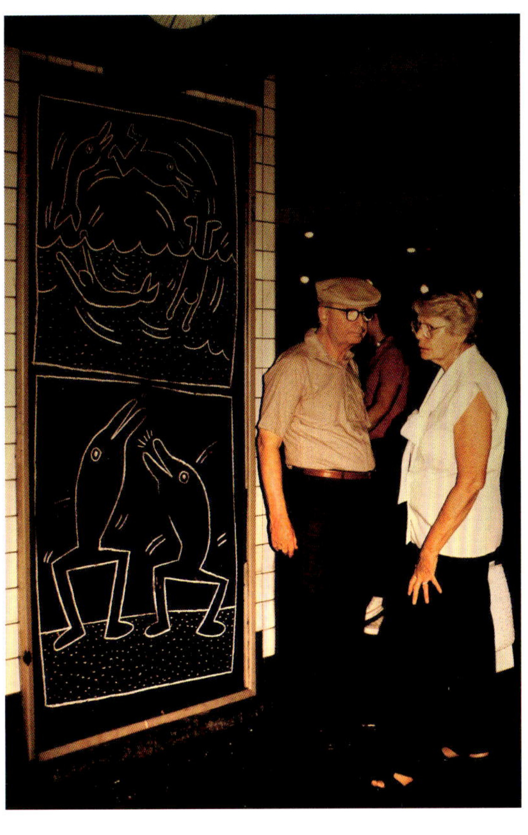

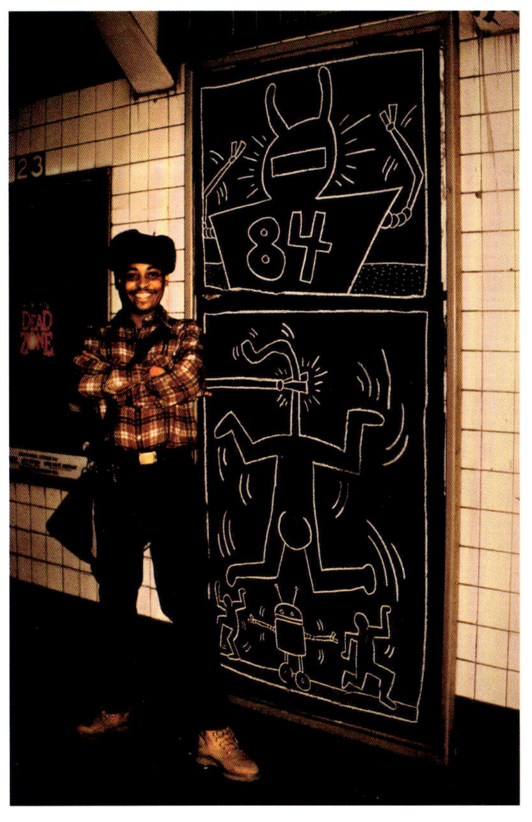

84

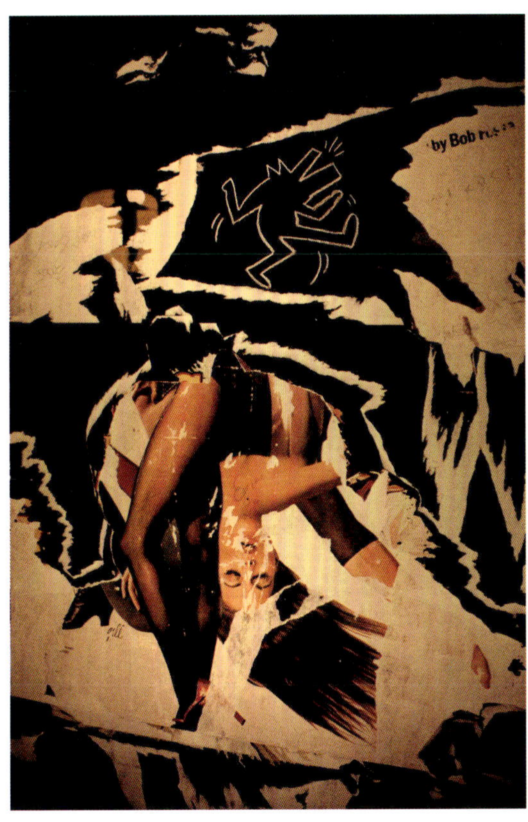

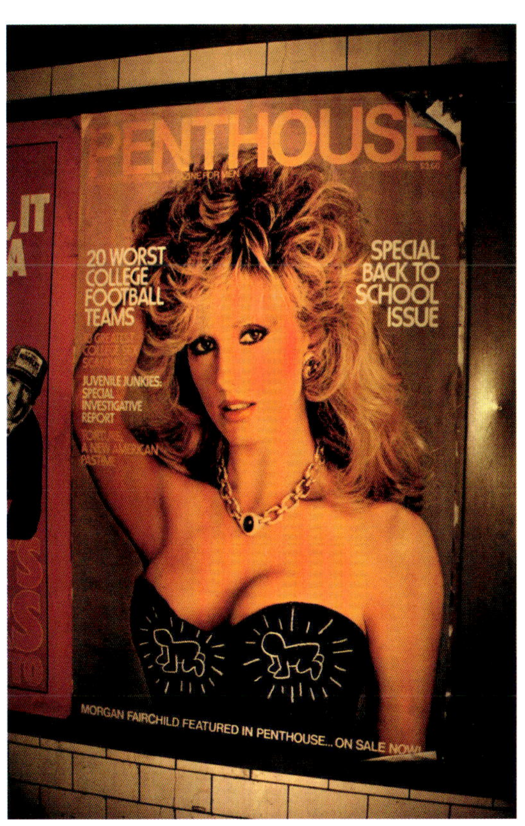

PENTHOUSE
20 WORST COLLEGE FOOTBALL TEAMS
SPECIAL BACK TO SCHOOL ISSUE
JUVENILE JUNKIES: SPECIAL INVESTIGATIVE REPORT
MORGAN FAIRCHILD FEATURED IN PENTHOUSE... ON SALE NOW

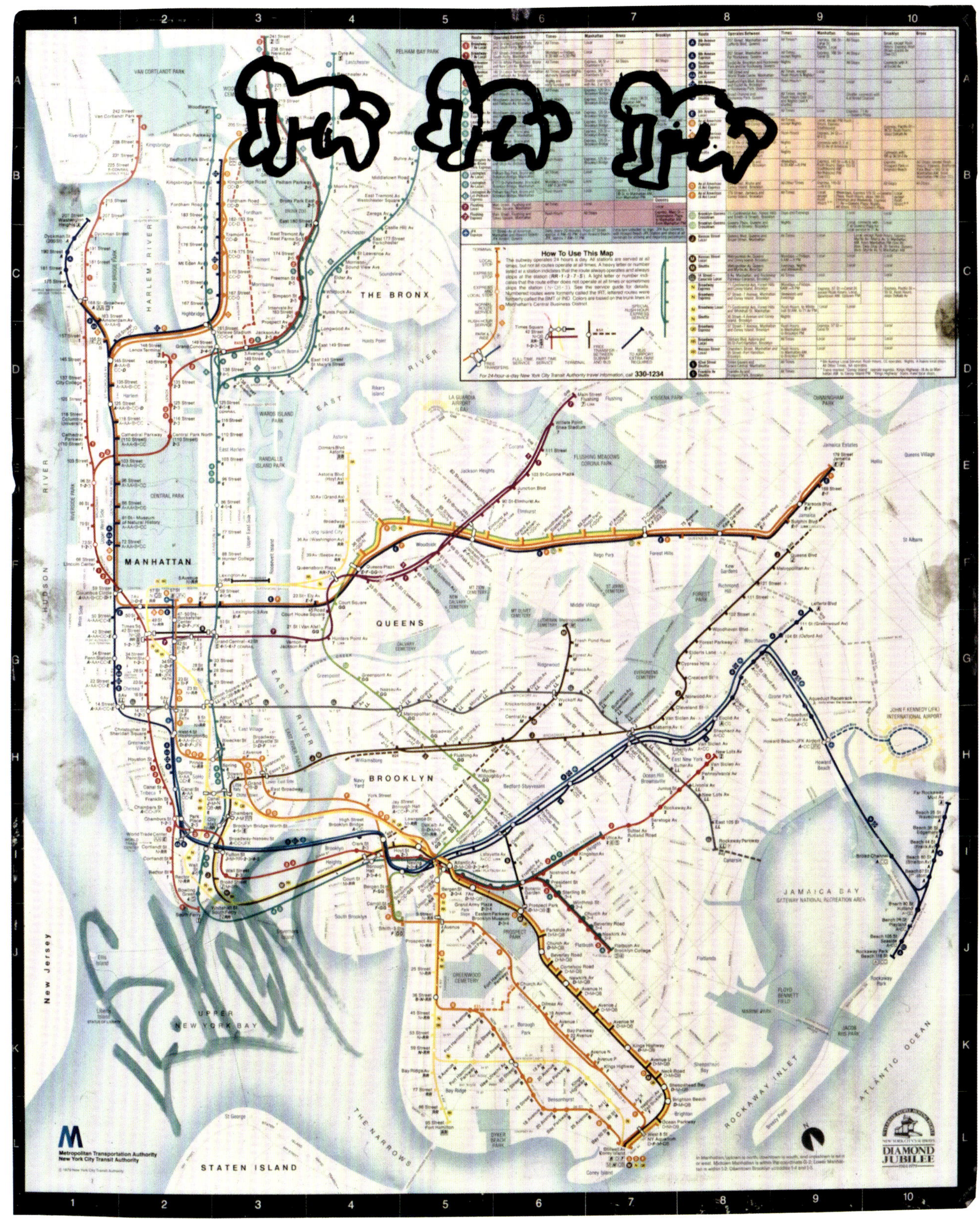

71

Drawing on New York subway map, 1983. Sumi ink on map in original frame, 28 3/8 x 22 7/8 in. (72 x 58 cm)
Collection of Muna Tseng

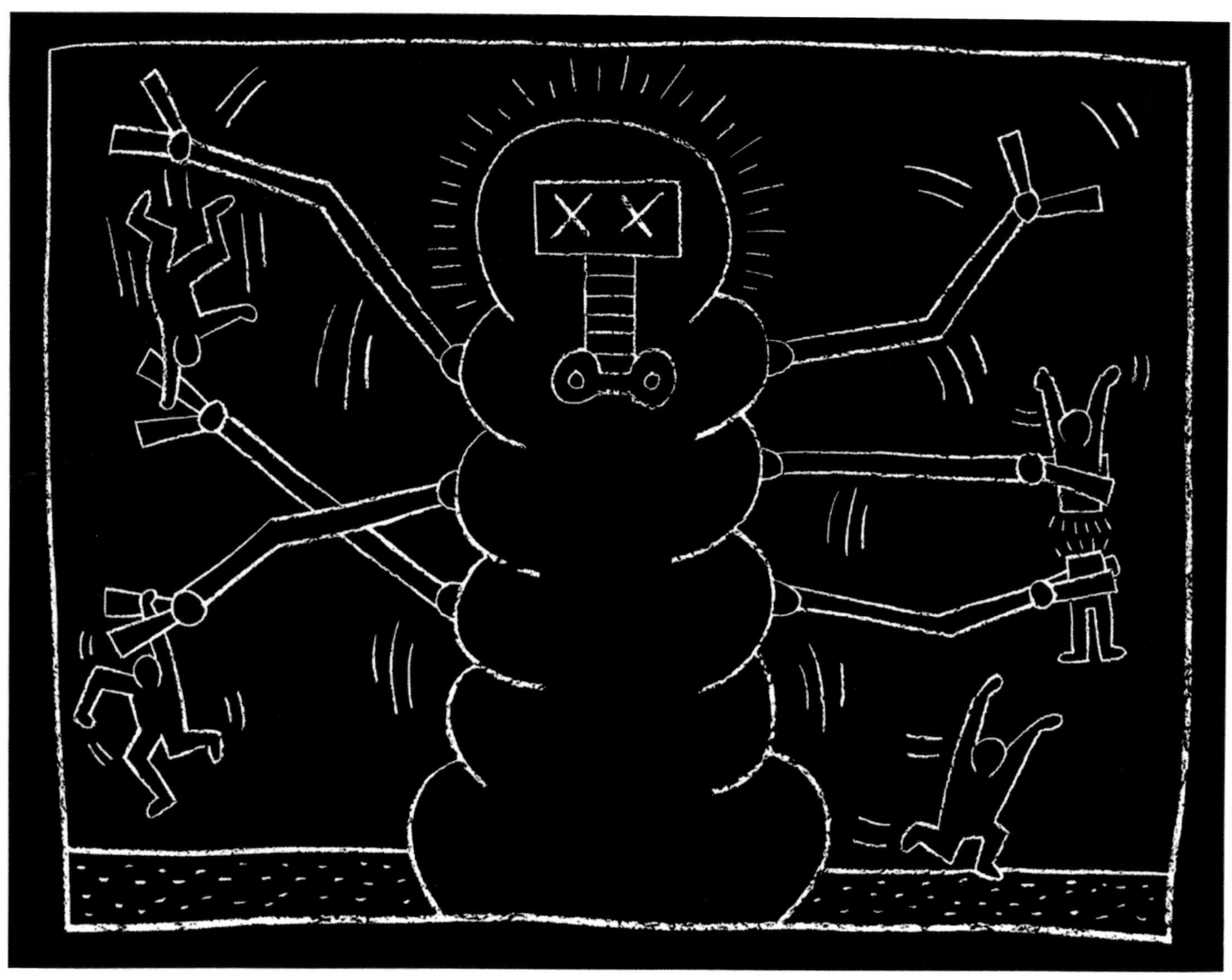

72

Untitled (*Subway Drawing*), 1981. Chalk on paper, 49 1/4 x 68 1/8 in. (125 x 173 cm)
Erika and Joseph Ades, courtesy of 99 Cents Fine Art, New York

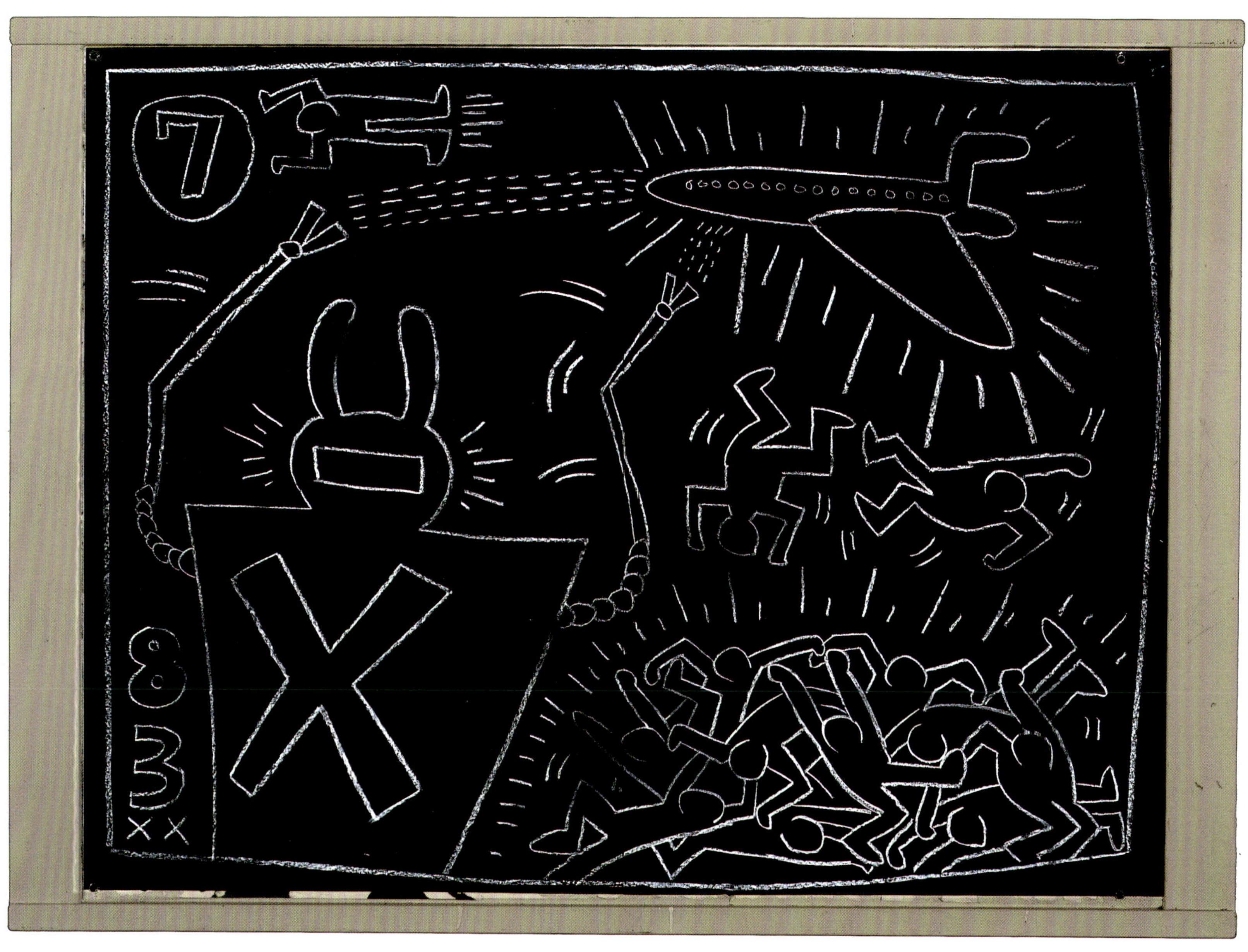

73

Untitled, 1983. Chalk on paper, 49 x 68 in. (124.5 x 172.7 cm)
Private collection

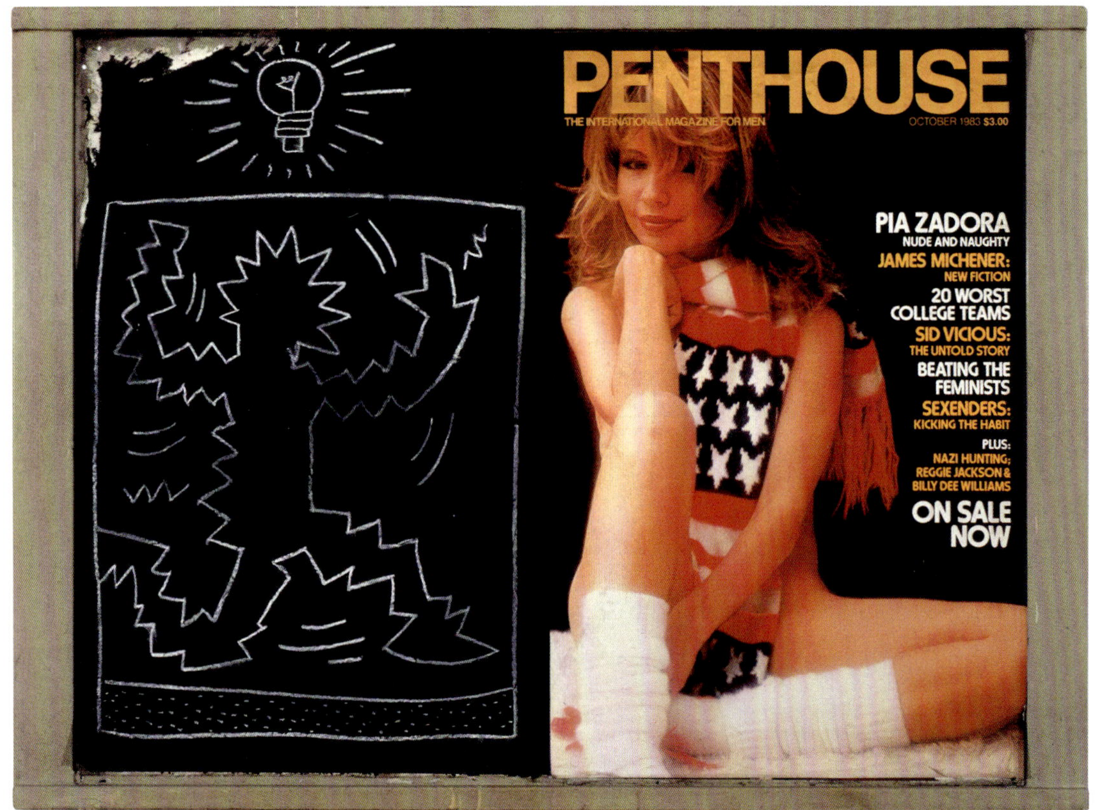

74

Untitled (*Subway Drawing*), 1983. Chalk on paper, 49 x 68 in. (124.5 x 172.7 cm)
Mugrabi Collection

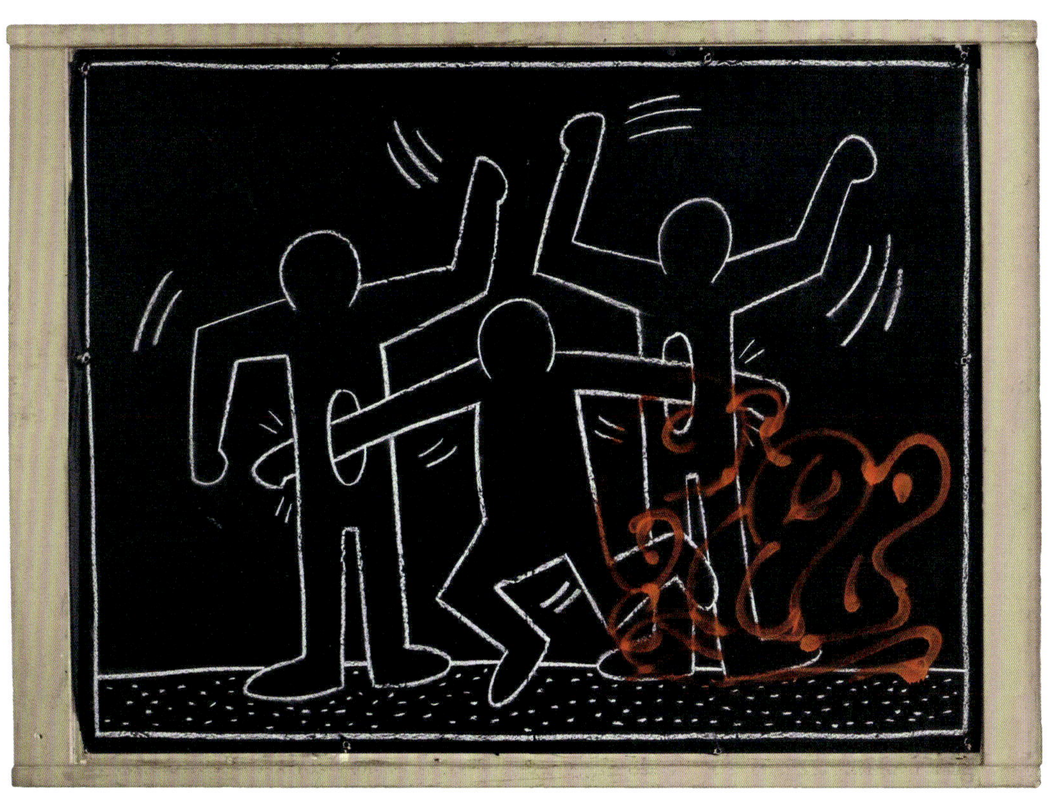

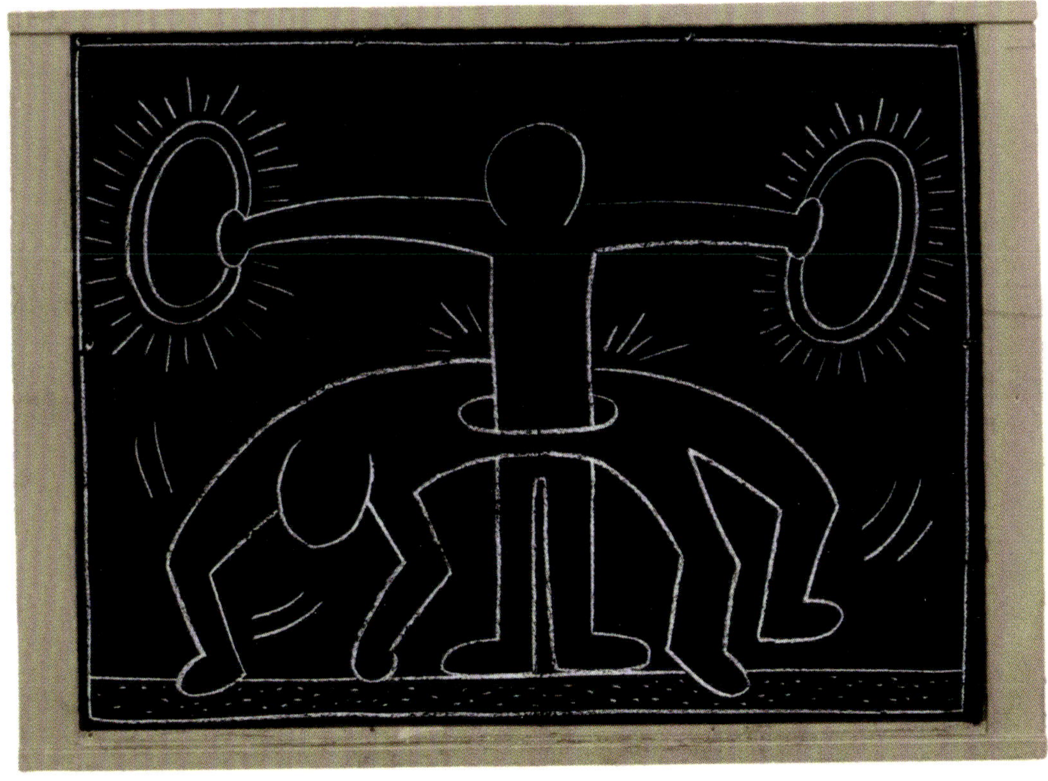

75–76

Untitled (*Subway Drawing*), 1982–1984. Chalk on paper, 45 1/4 x 59 7/8 in. (115 x 152 cm)
99 Cents Fine Art, New York, and private collection

Untitled (*Subway Drawing*), 1982–1984. Chalk on paper, 45 1/4 x 59 7/8 in. (115 x 152 cm)
99 Cents Fine Art, New York, and private collection

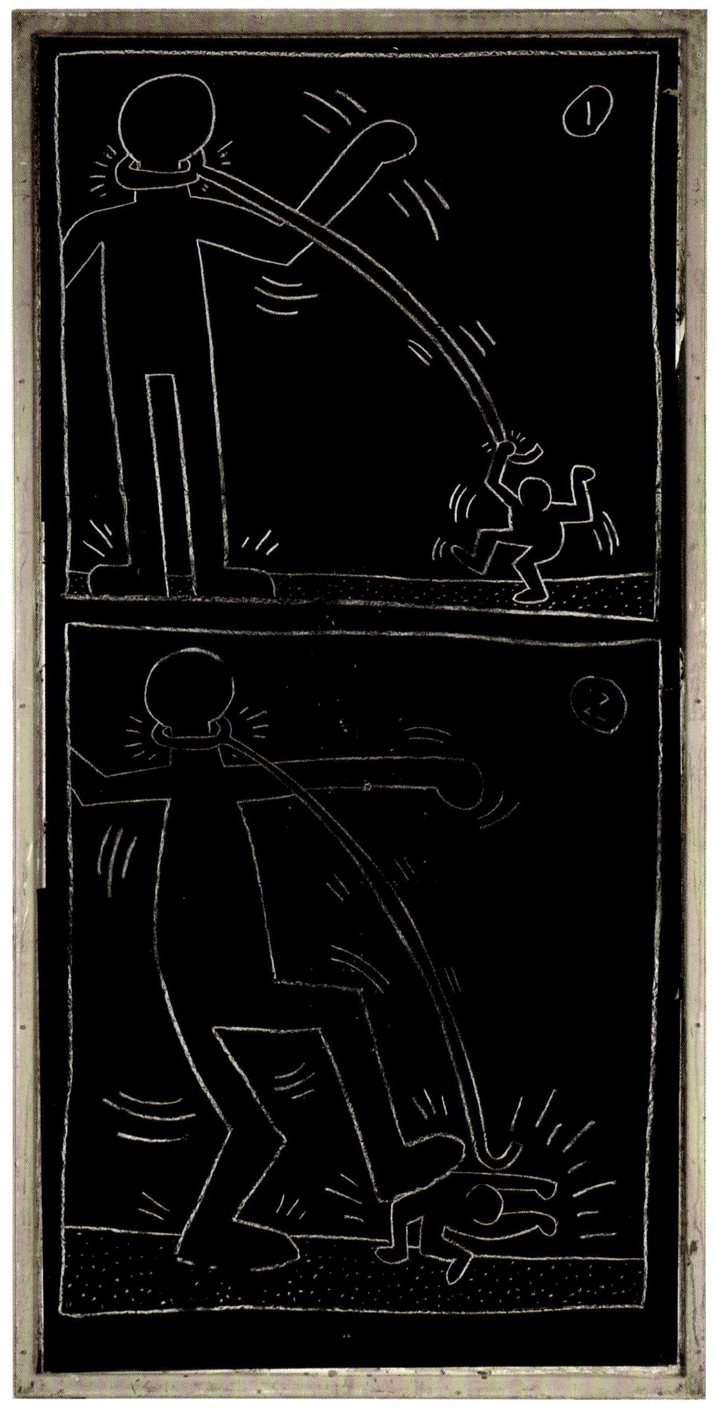

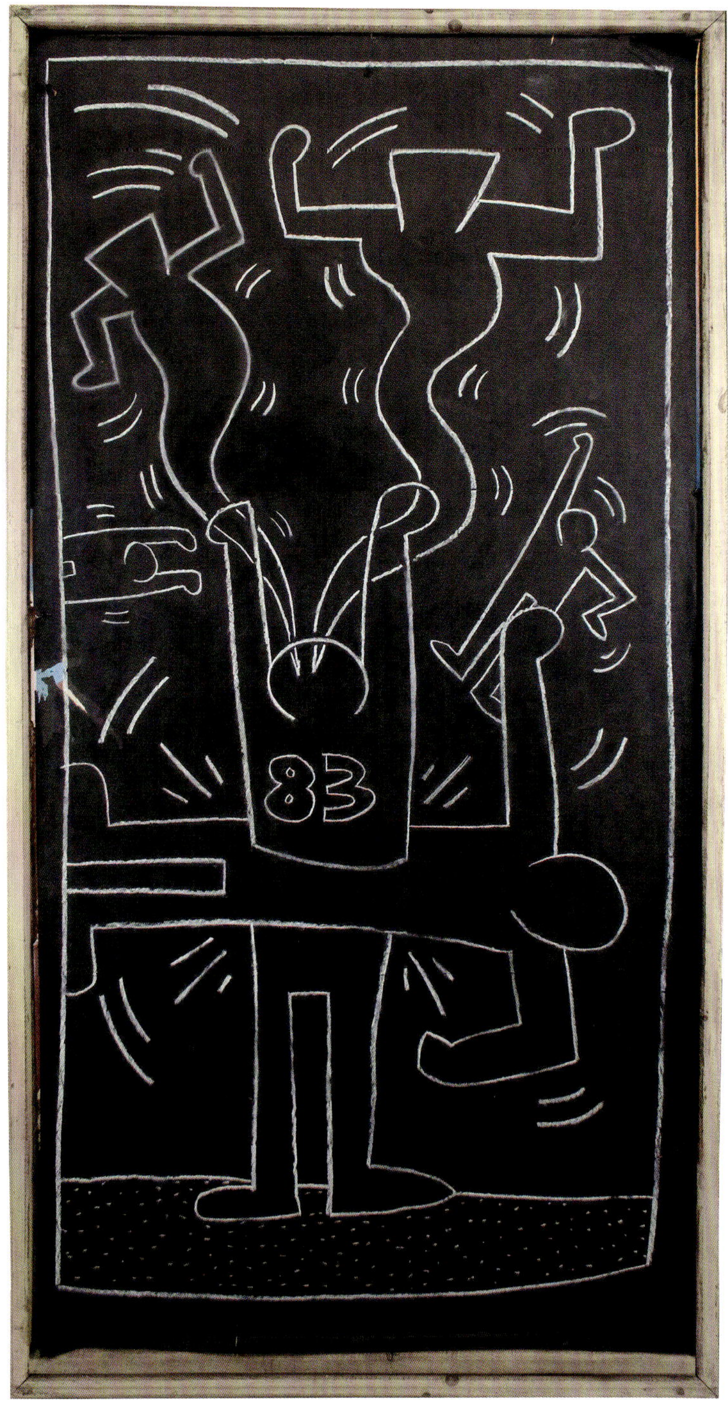

77–78

Untitled (*Subway Drawing*), 1982. Chalk on paper, 86 5/8 x 44 7/8 in. (220 x 114 cm)
Collection of Justin Warsh

Untitled (*Subway Drawing*), 1983. Chalk on paper, 86 5/8 x 44 7/8 in. (220 x 114 cm)
Collection Tony Shafrazi Gallery, New York

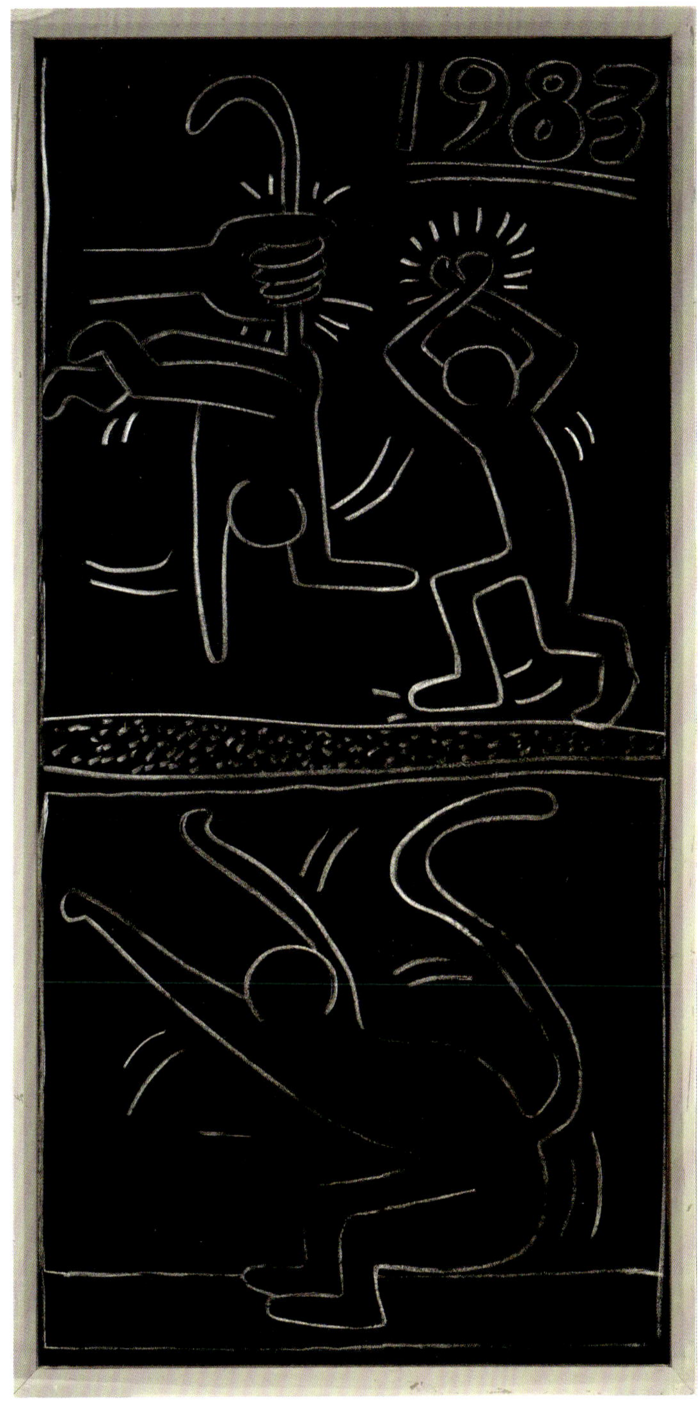

79–80

Untitled (*Subway Drawing*), 1983. Chalk on paper, 86 5/8 x 44 7/8 in. (220 x 114 cm)
Collection of Larry Warsh

Untitled (*Subway Drawing*), 1985. Chalk on paper, 86 5/8 x 44 7/8 in. (220 x 114 cm)
Collection of Larry Warsh

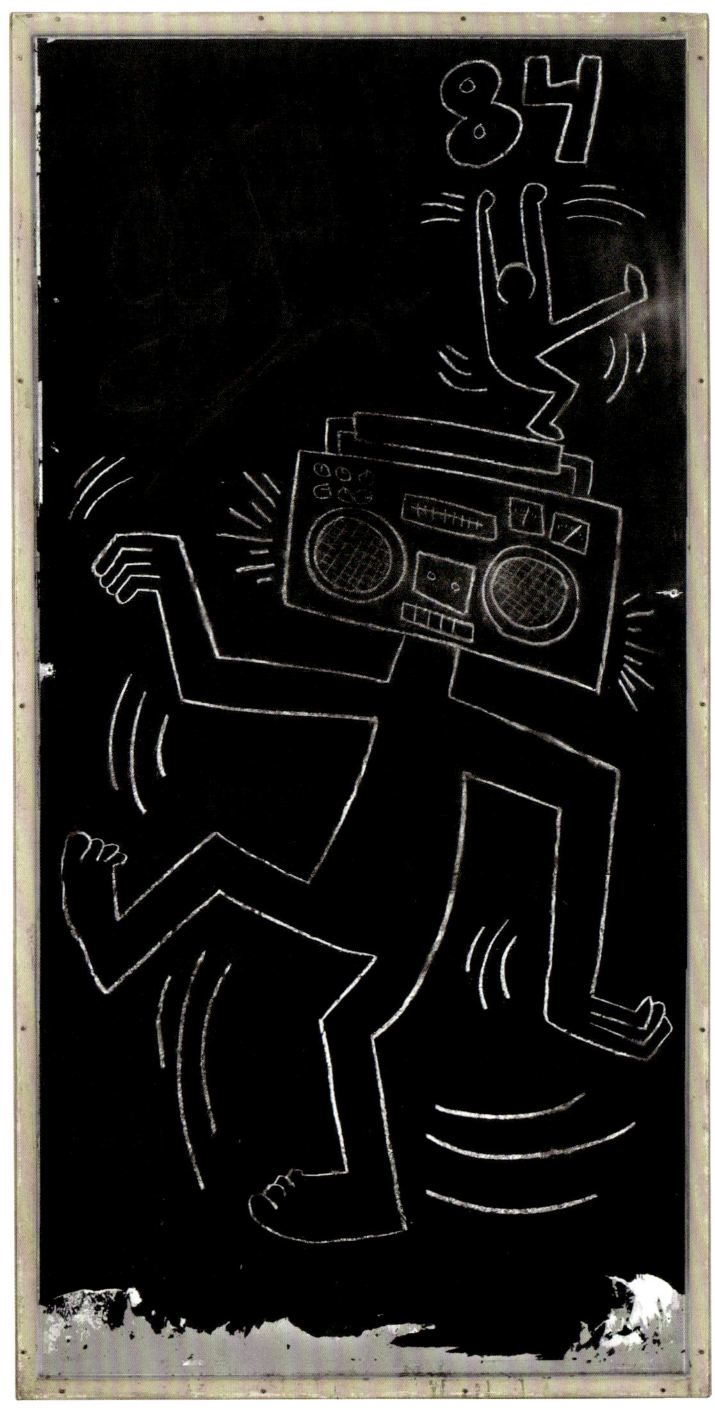

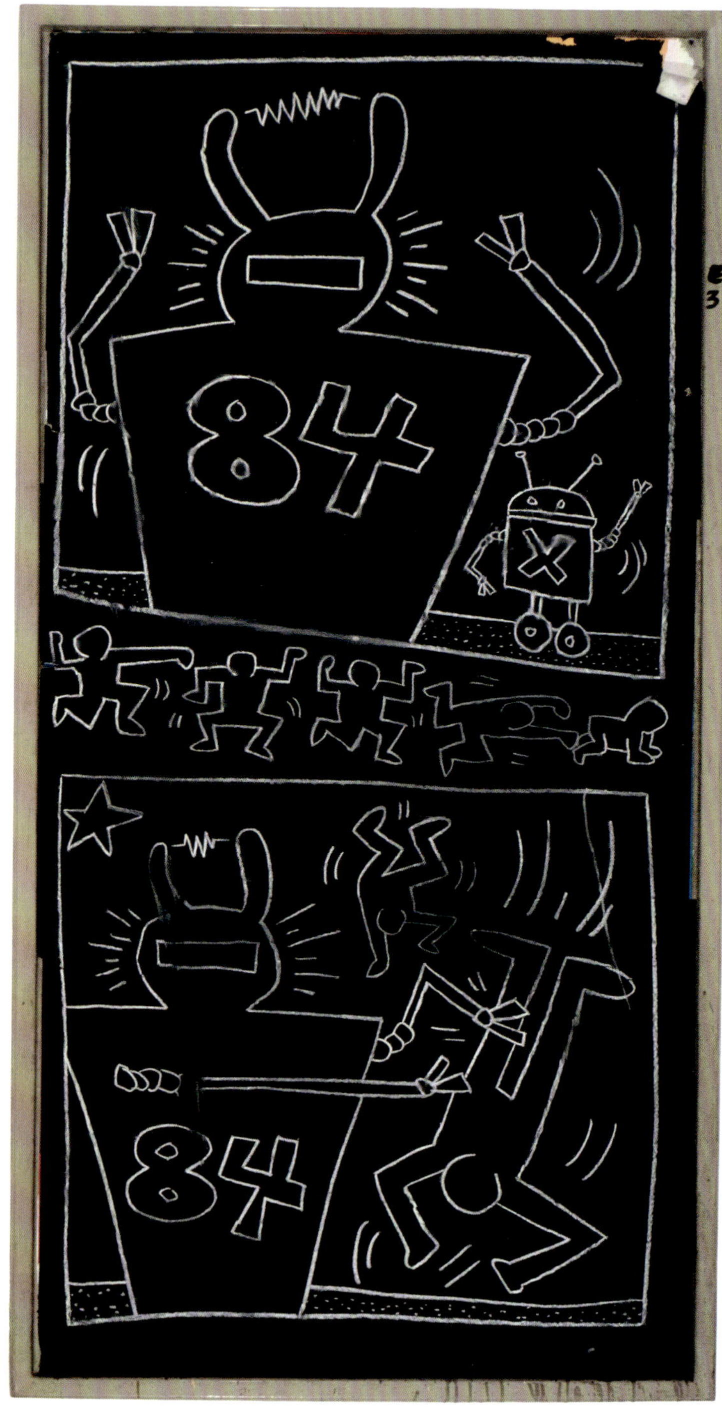

81–82

Untitled (*Subway Drawing*), 1984. Chalk on paper, 86 5/8 x 44 7/8 in. (220 x 114 cm)
Collection of Justin Warsh

Untitled (*Subway Drawing*), 1984. Chalk on paper, 87 3/8 x 45 1/4 in. (222 x 115 cm)
Collection Tony Shafrazi Gallery, New York

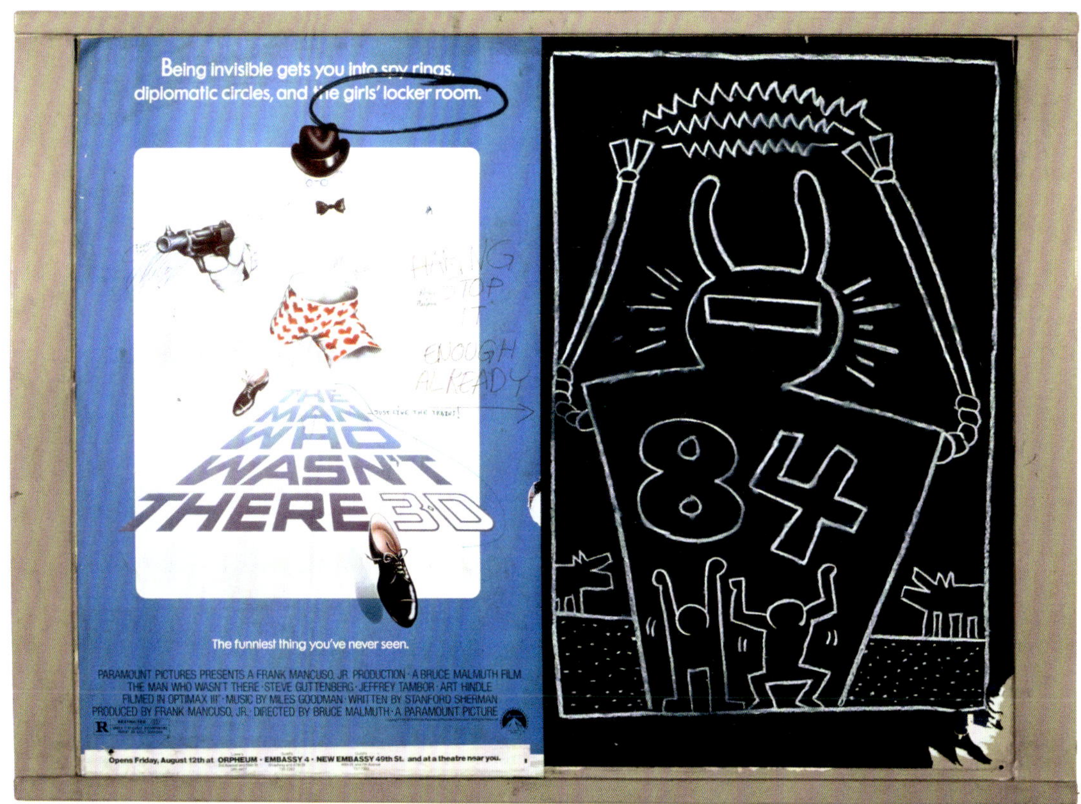

83

Untitled (*Subway Drawing*), 1984. Chalk on paper, 49 x 68 in. (124.5 x 172.7 cm)
Private collection

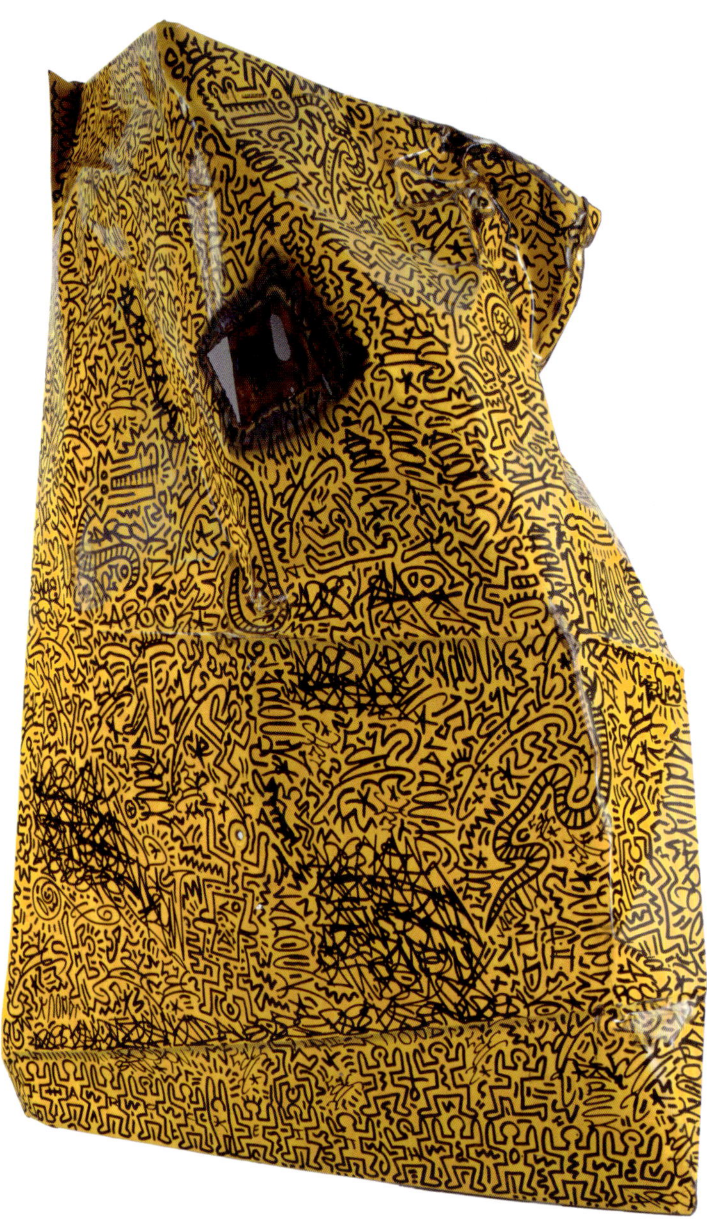

84

With LA II (Angel Ortiz), *Untitled*, 1982. Marker on taxi hood, 63 x 51 x 29 in. (160 x 129.5 x 73.6 cm)
Collection of Justin Warsh

85

With LA II (Angel Ortiz), *Statue of Liberty*, 1982. Acrylic and fluorescent enamel on fiberglass with black light, 95 x 35 x 14 in. (241.3 x 88.9 x 35.6 cm)
Rubell Family Collection

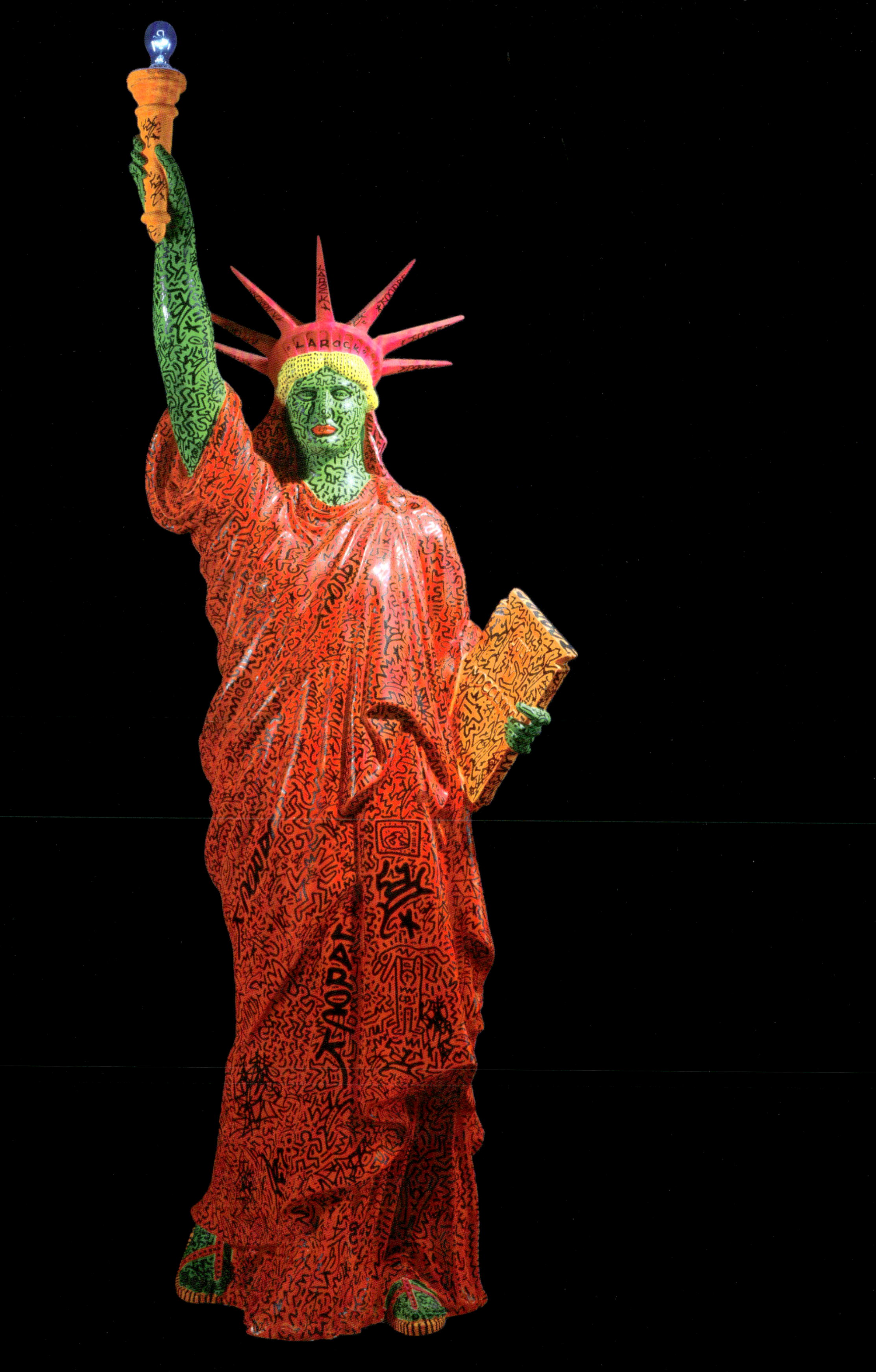

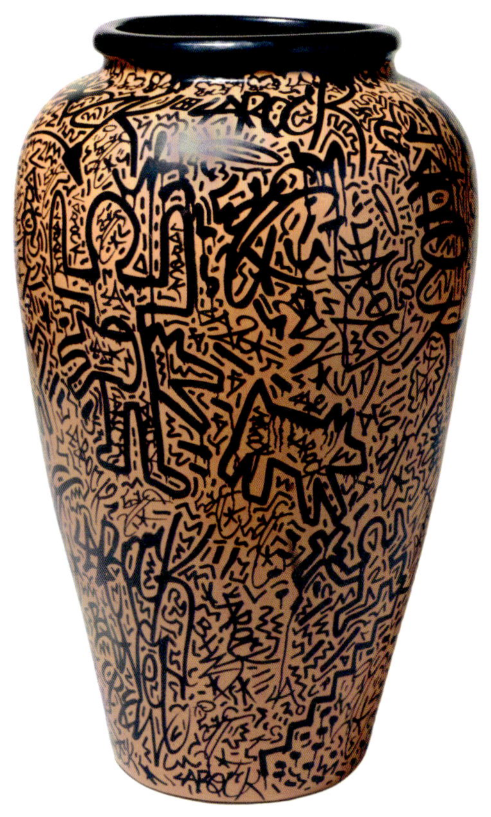

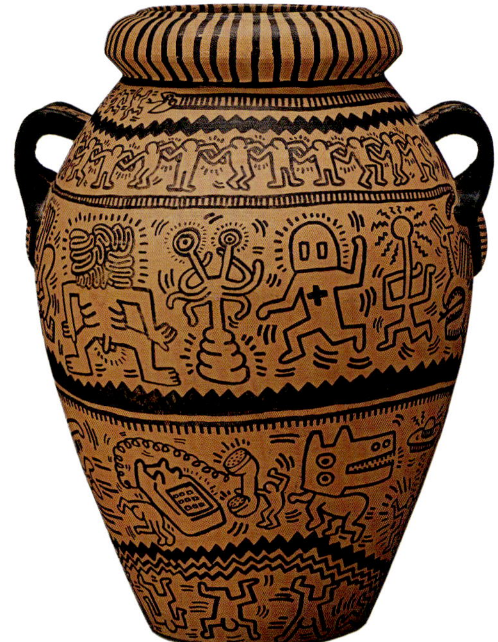

86–87

With LA II (Angel Ortiz), *Untitled*, January 18, 1982. Ink on fiberglass vase, 40 1/2 x 27 x 27 in. (102.9 x 68.6 x 68.6 cm)
Skarstedt, New York

Untitled, 1984. Ink on terracotta vase, 21 1/2 x 17 1/2 x 17 1/2 in. (54.6 x 44.5 x 44.5 cm)
Collection of Larry Warsh

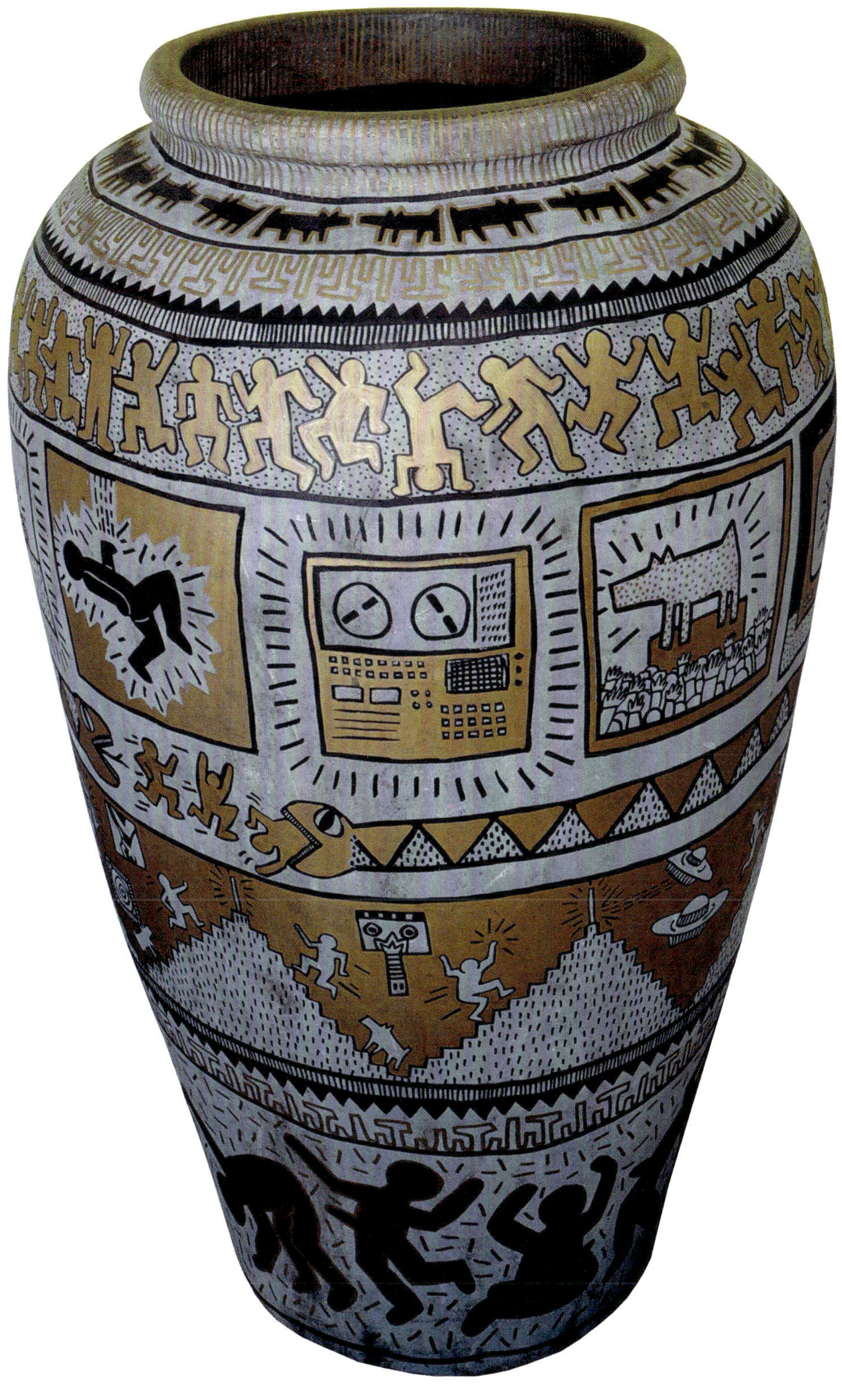

88

Untitled (*Gold Vase*), 1981. Enamel and marker on fiberglass vase, 40 x 25 x 25 in. (101.6 x 63.5 x 63.5 cm)
Collection of Justin Warsh

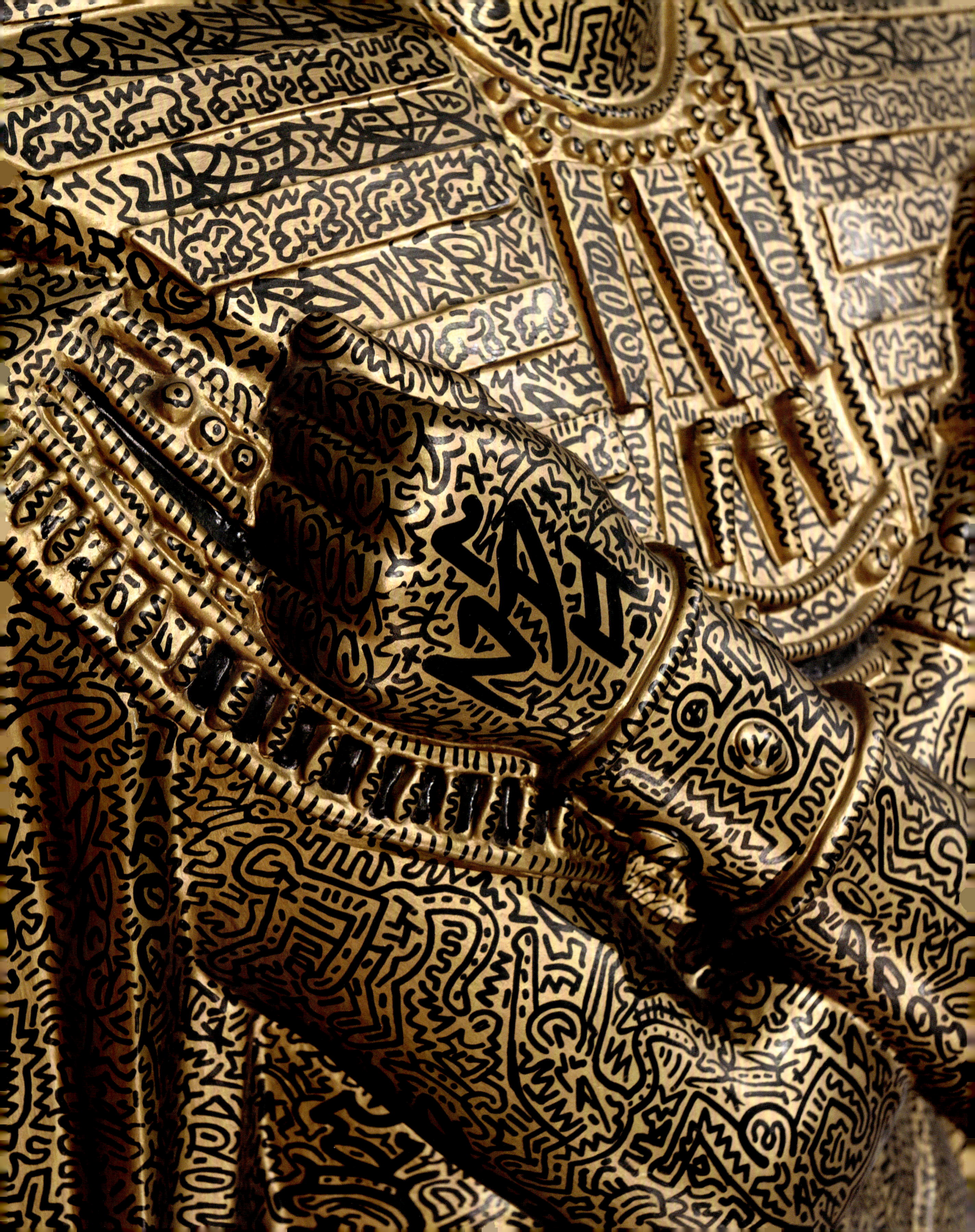

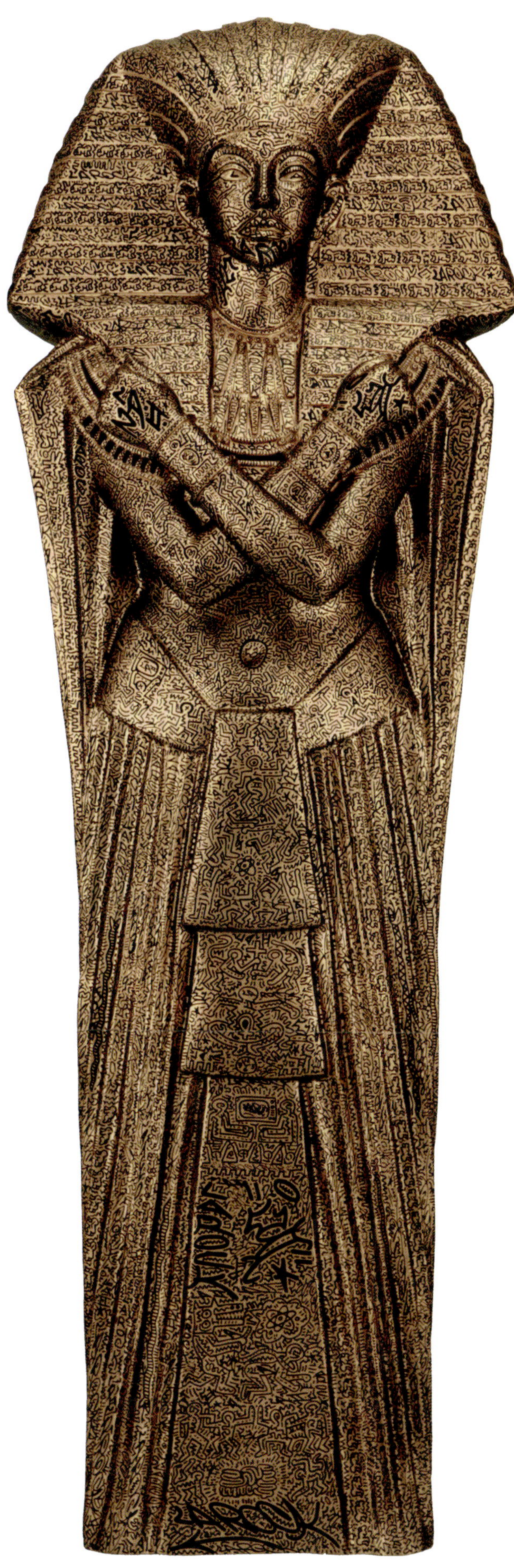

89

With LA II (Angel Ortiz), *Sarcophagus*, 1983. Acrylic and marker on fiberglass, 98 x 34 x 22 in. (248.9 x 86.4 x 55.9 cm)
Holzer Family Collection

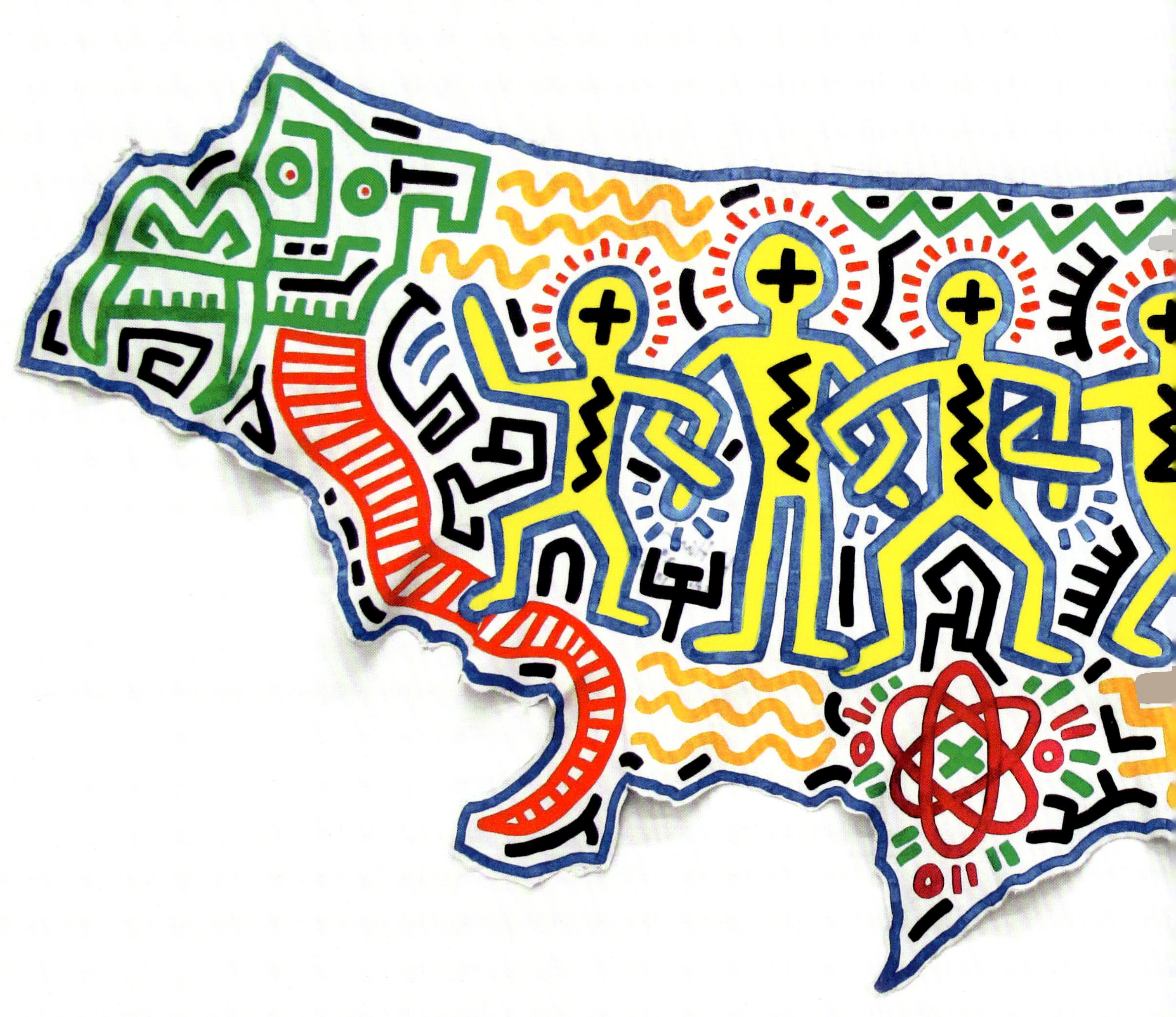

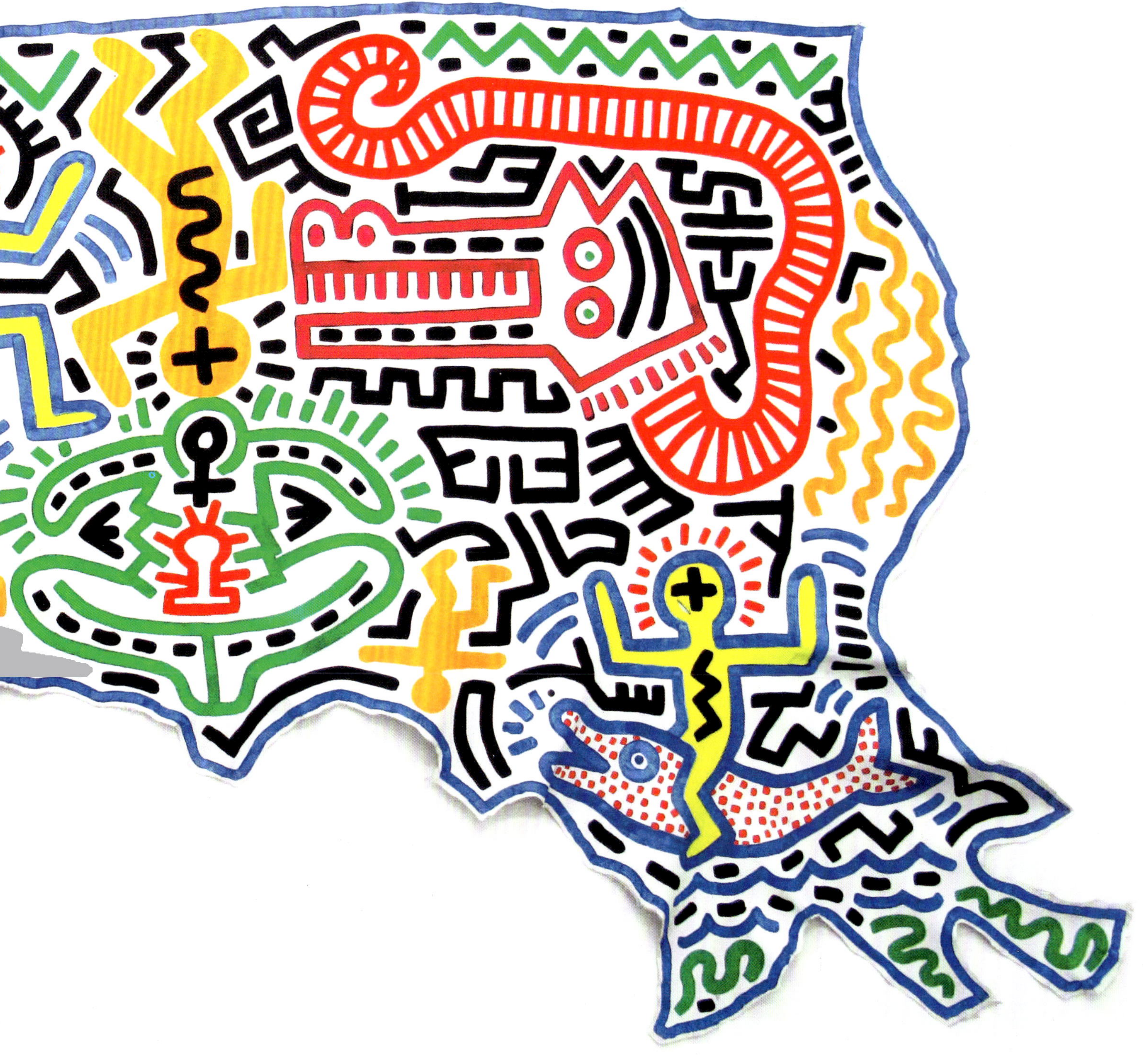

Untitled, 1983. Acrylic on leather, 53 x 116 in. (134.6 x 294.6 cm)
Collection of Jose Martos

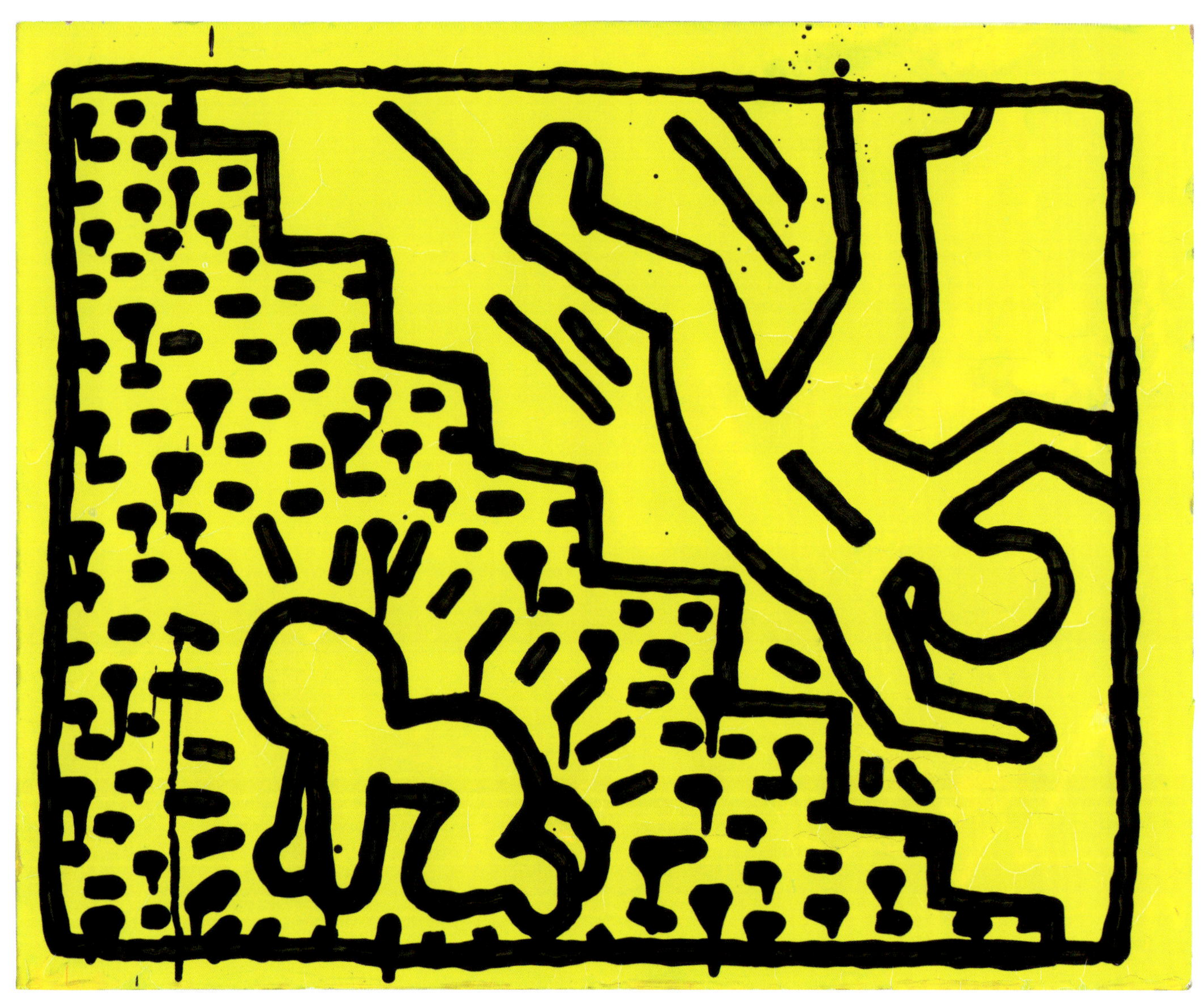

91

Untitled, 1982. Acrylic on wood, 16 x 20⅛ in. (40.6 x 51.1 cm)
Collection of Larry Warsh

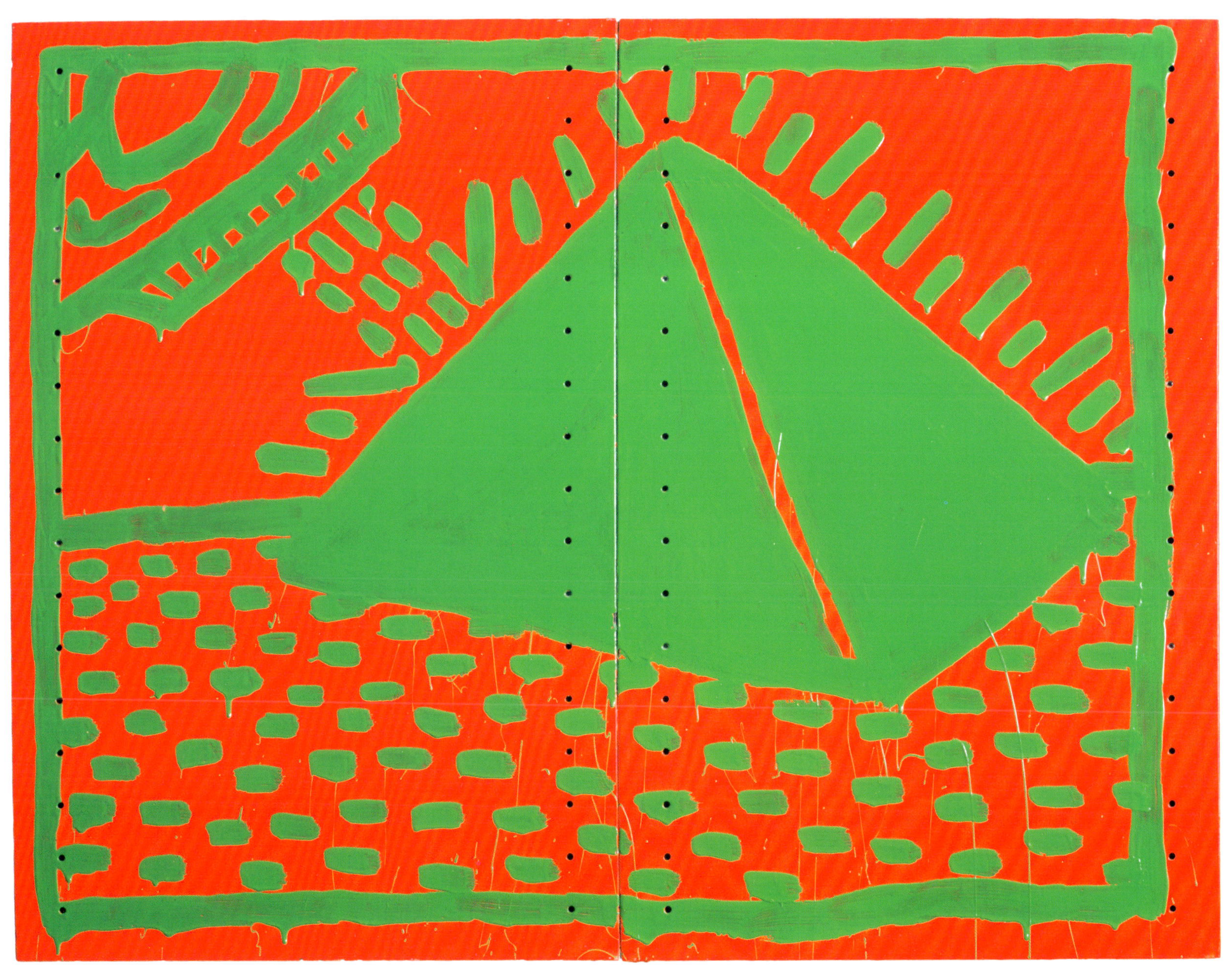

92

Untitled, March 1982. Day-Glo enamel paint on metal, 36 x 48 in. (91.4 x 121.9 cm)
Collection of Kemal Has Cingillioglu

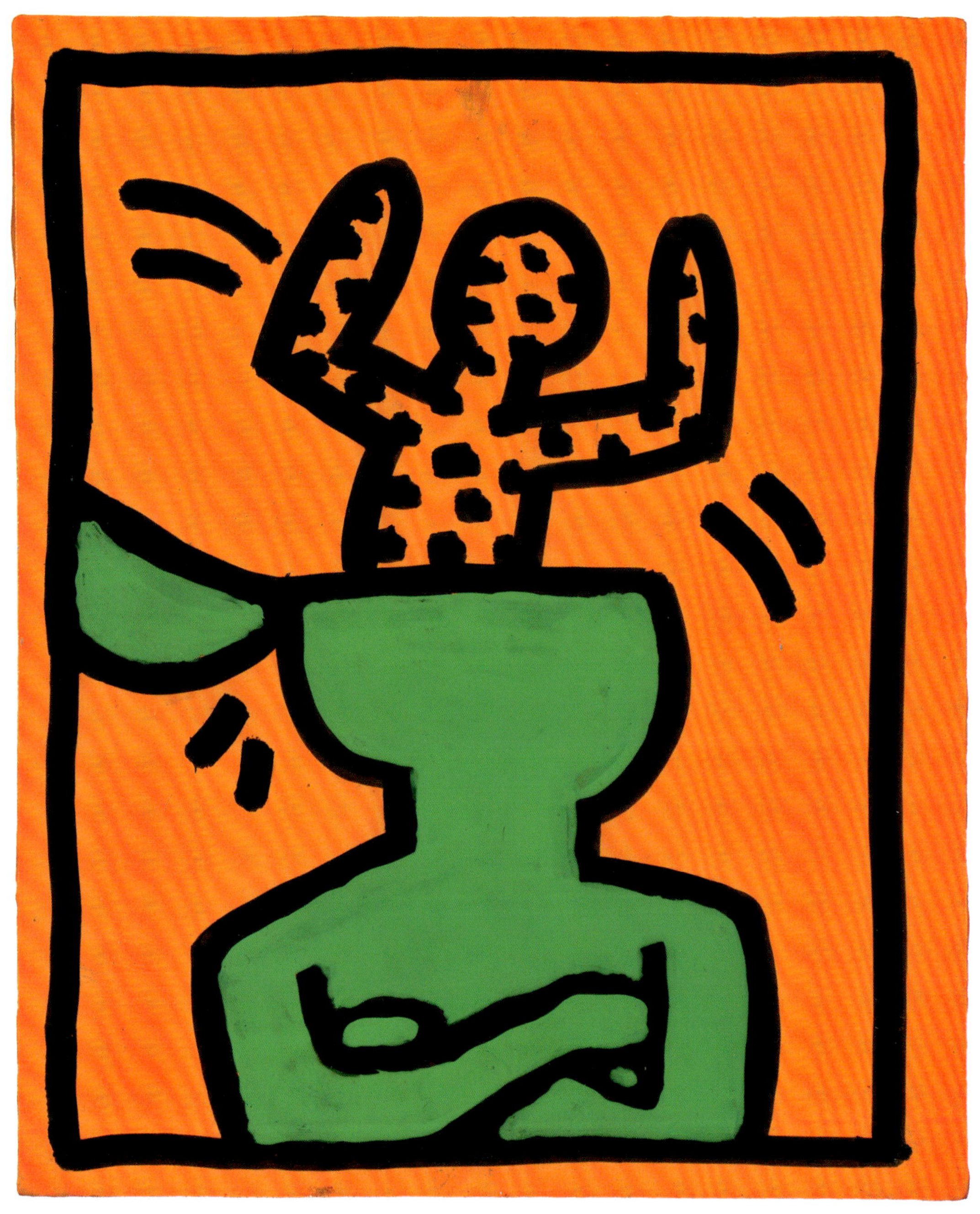

93

Untitled, 1982. Mixed media and acrylic on particle board, 8 x 6 in (20.3 x 15.2 cm)
Collection of Larry Warsh

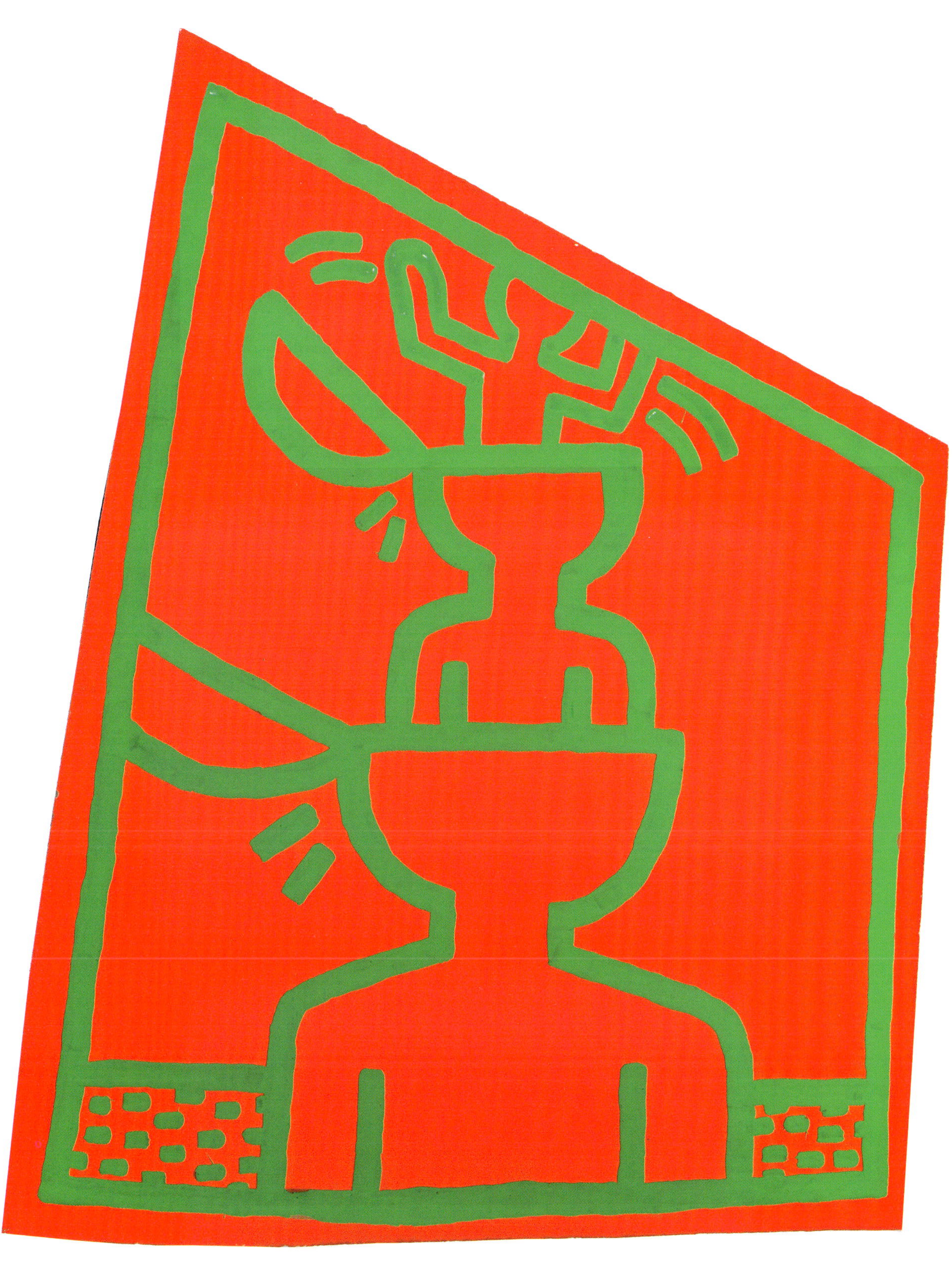

94

Untitled, March 1982. Day-Glo paint on wood, 8½ x 4½ in. (21.5 x 11.4 cm)
Collection of Larry Warsh

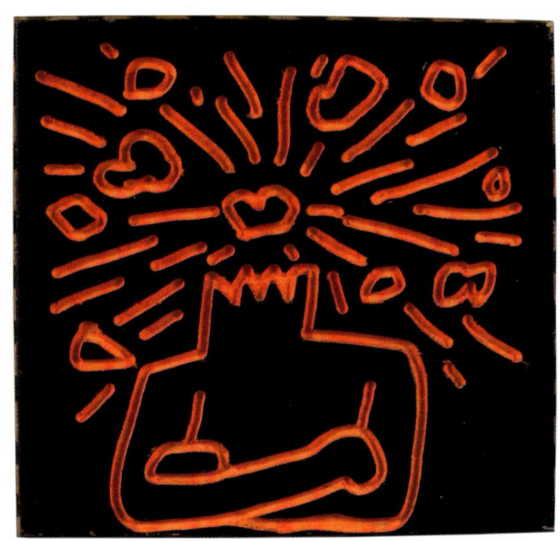

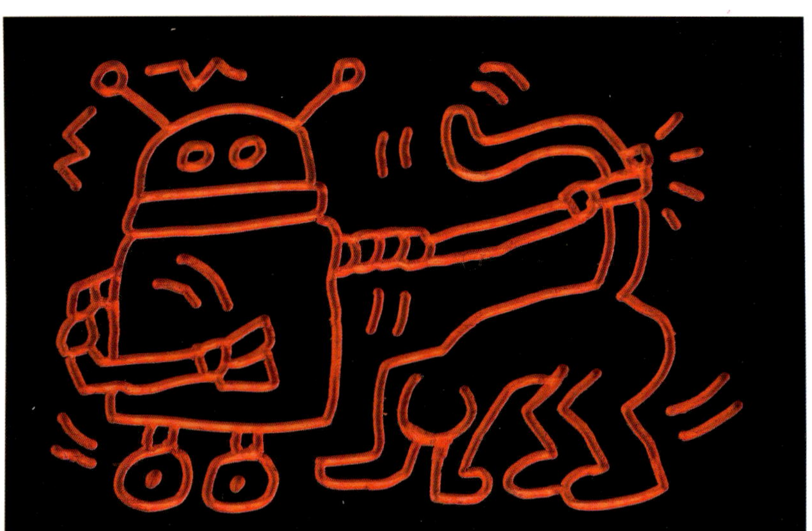

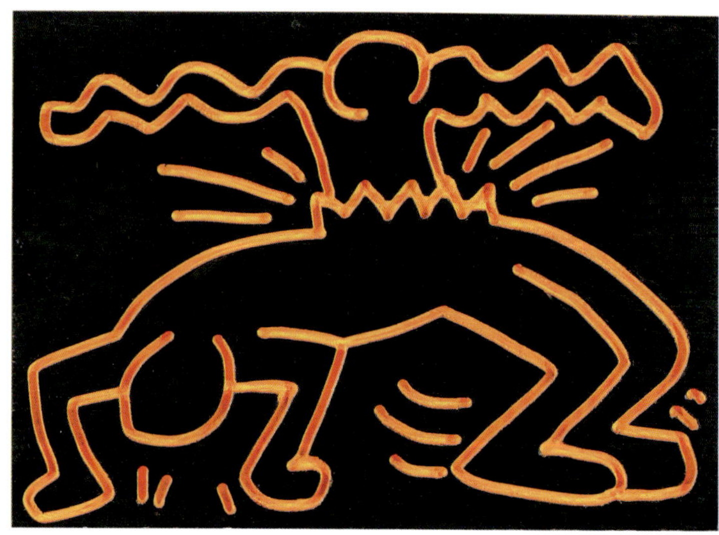

95–97

With Kermit Oswald, *Untitled*, 1983. Enamel on incised wood, 11 x 12½ in. (27.9 x 31.8 cm)
Collection of Justin Warsh

With Kermit Oswald, *Untitled*, 1983. Enamel on incised wood, 10 x 22 in. (25.4 x 55.9 cm)
Collection of Justin Warsh

With Kermit Oswald, *Untitled*, 1983. Enamel on incised wood, 20½ x 21 in. (52.1 x 53.3 cm)
Collection of Justin Warsh

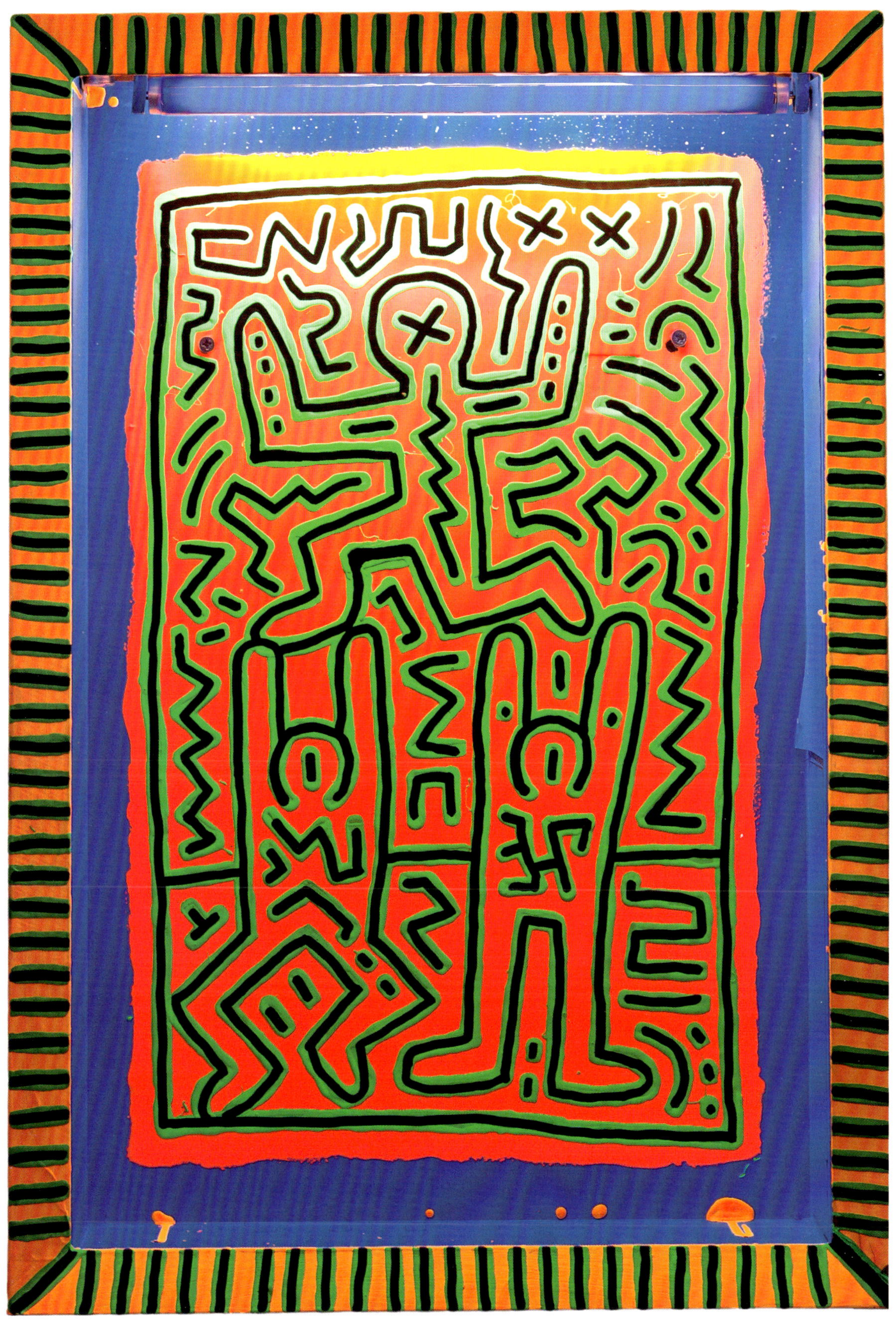

98

Untitled, August 11, 1982. Day-Glo paint on found metal object, 32 x 22 ½ x 5 ½ in. (81.3 x 57.1 x 13.9 cm)
Private collection, courtesy Tony Shafrazi Gallery, New York

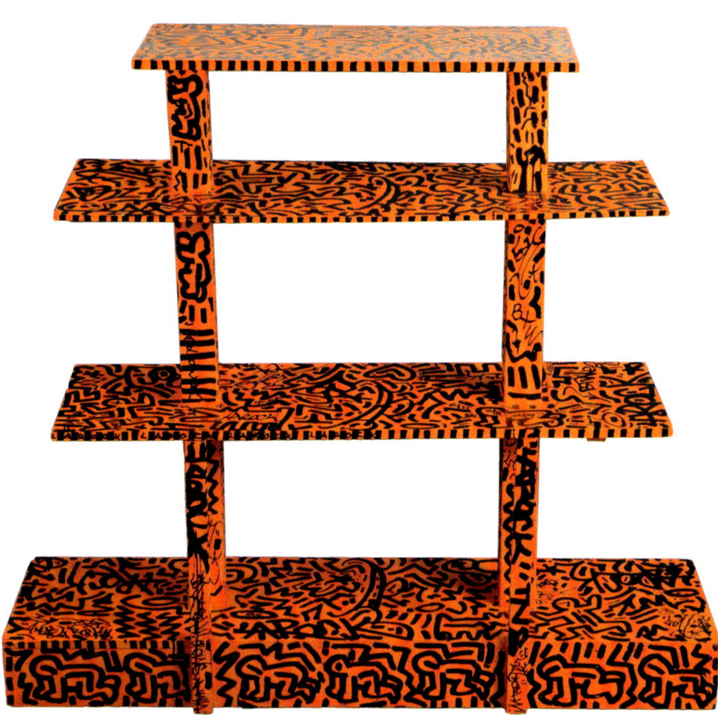

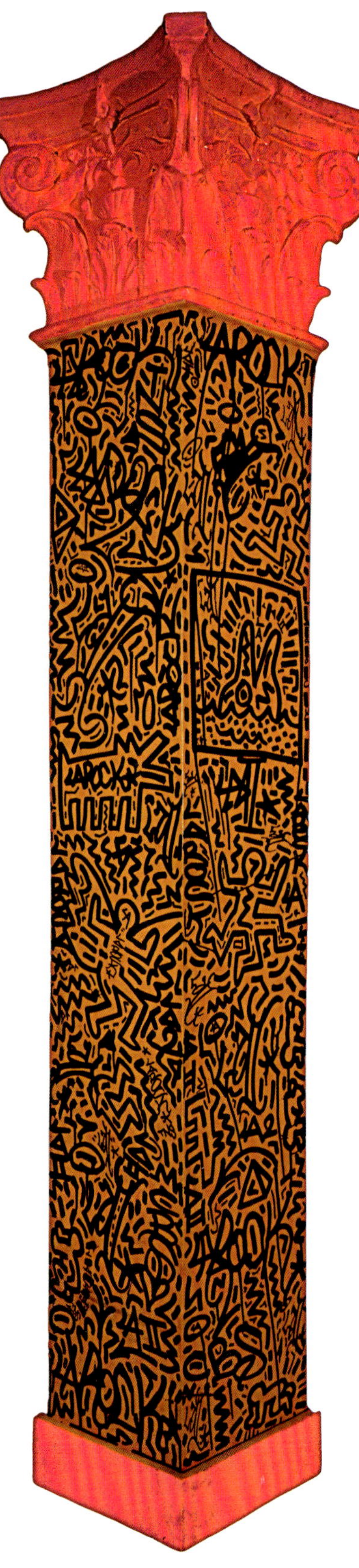

99–100

With LA II (Angel Ortiz), *Shelf*, 1982. Day-Glo paint and ink on wood, 55 x 60¾ x 15¼ in. (139.7 x 154.4 x 38.7 cm)
Collection of Justin Warsh

With LA II (Angel Ortiz), *Column*, 1981. Day-Glo paint and ink on wood, 118⅛ x 20 x 20 in. (300 x 50.8 x 50.8 cm)
Collection of the Keith Haring Foundation

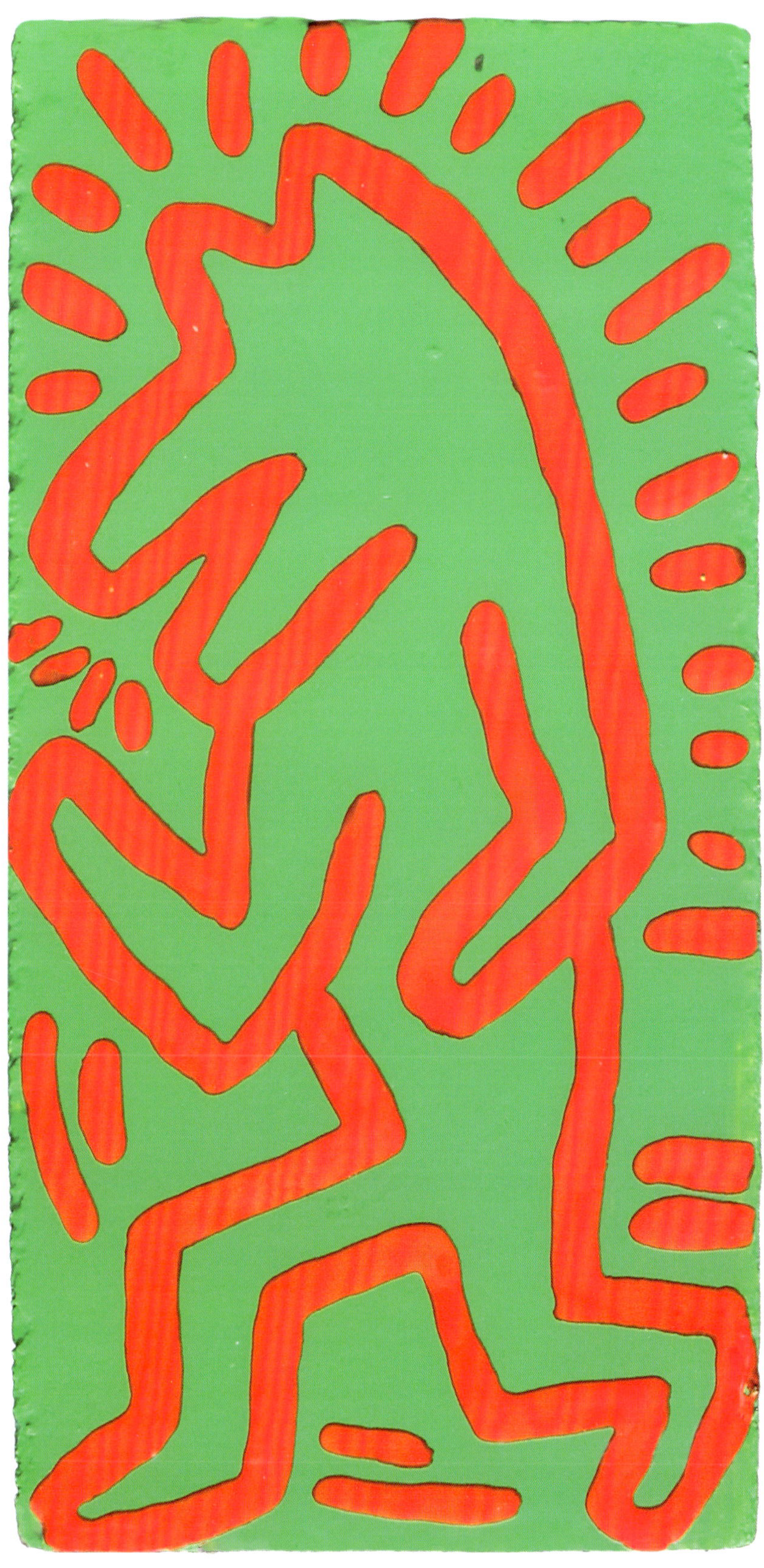

101

Untitled, March 1982. Day-Glo paint on wood, 8 ½ x 4 ½ in. (21.5 x 11.4 cm)
Collection Tony Shafrazi Gallery, New York

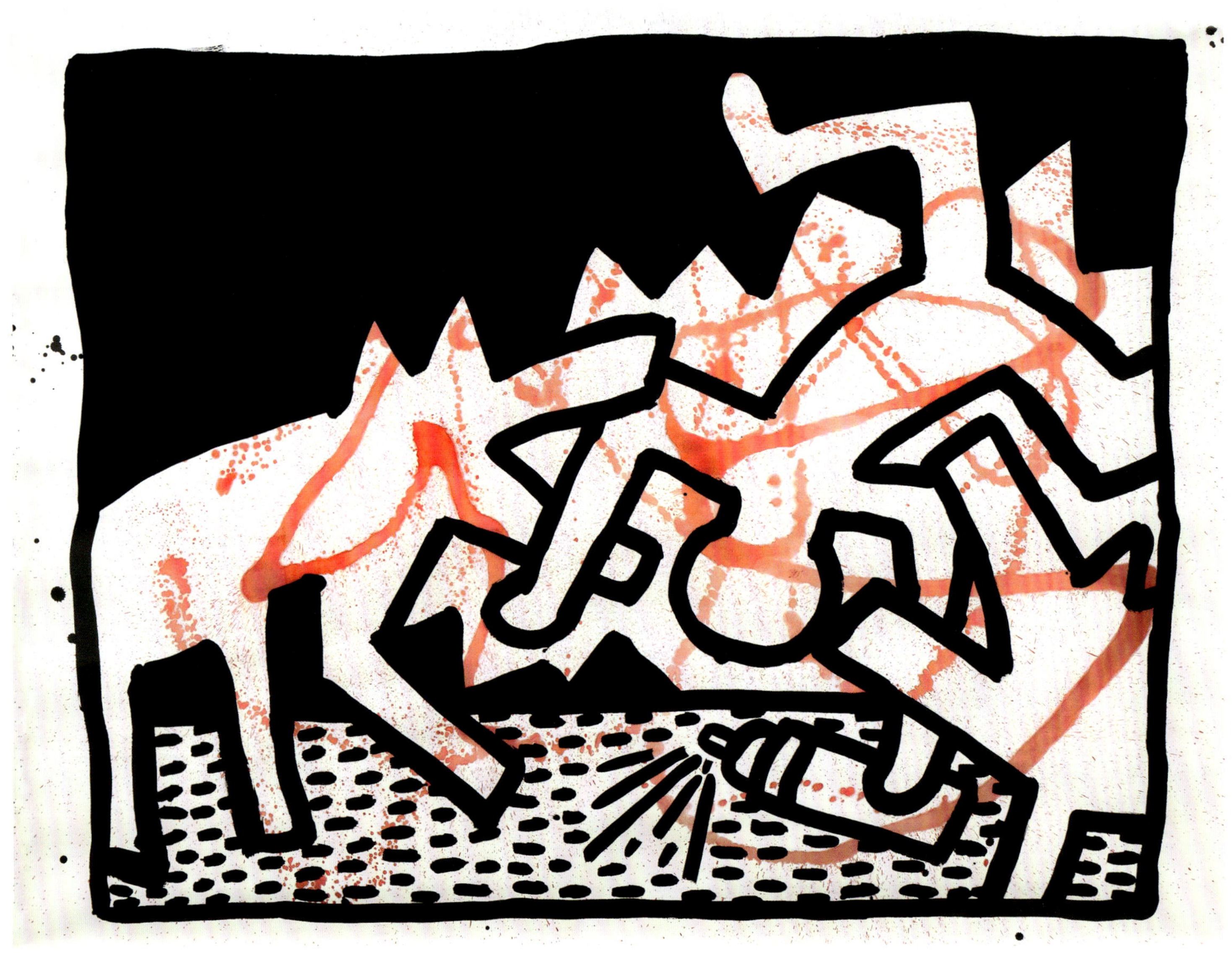

102

Untitled, 1981. Sumi ink and spray paint on paper, 38 x 50 in. (96.5 x 127 cm)
Collection of Viktor Van de Weghe

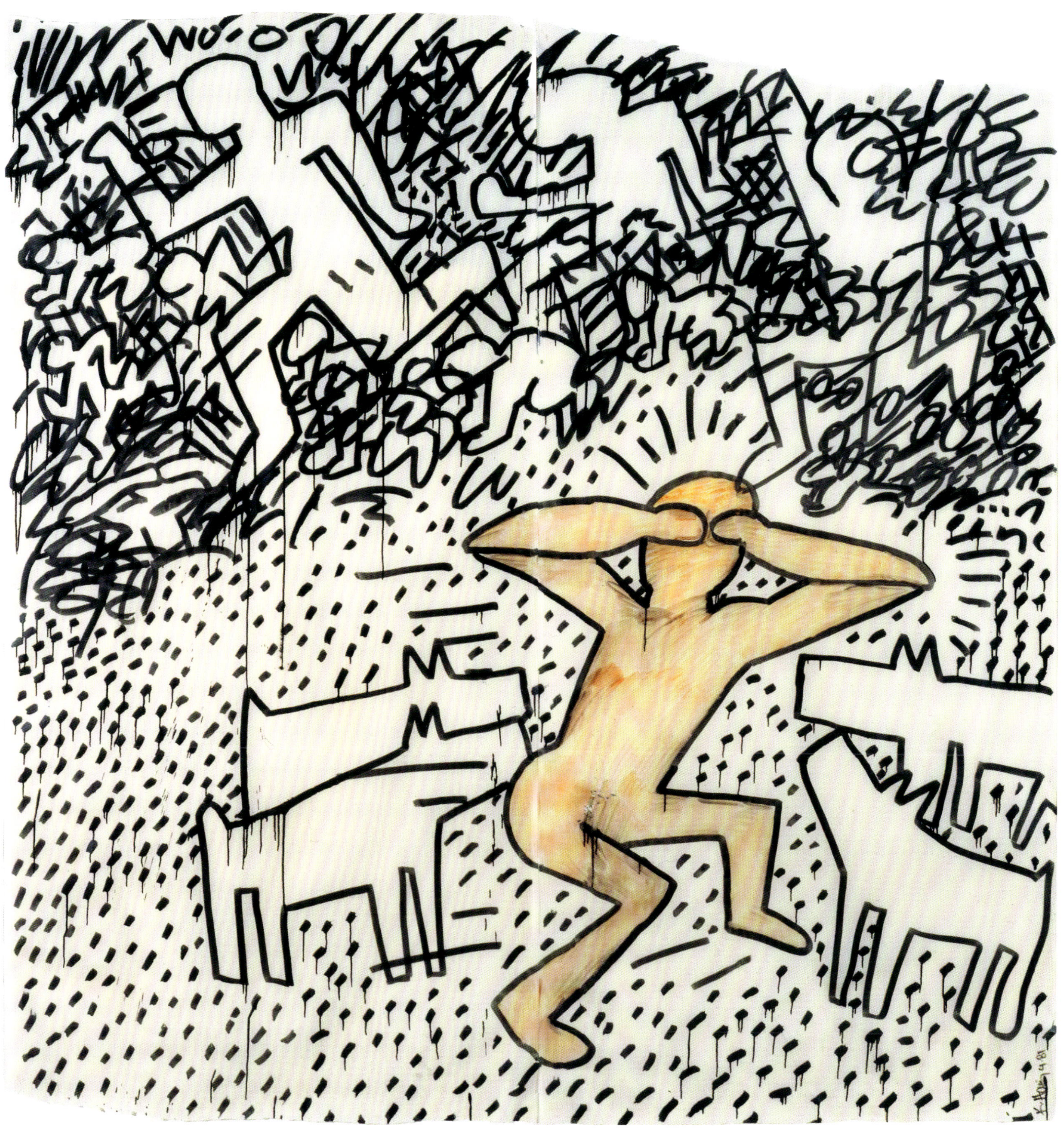

103

Untitled, 1981. Ink on vellum, $85^{1}/_{2}$ x 84 in. (217.2 x 213.4 cm)
Rubell Family Collection

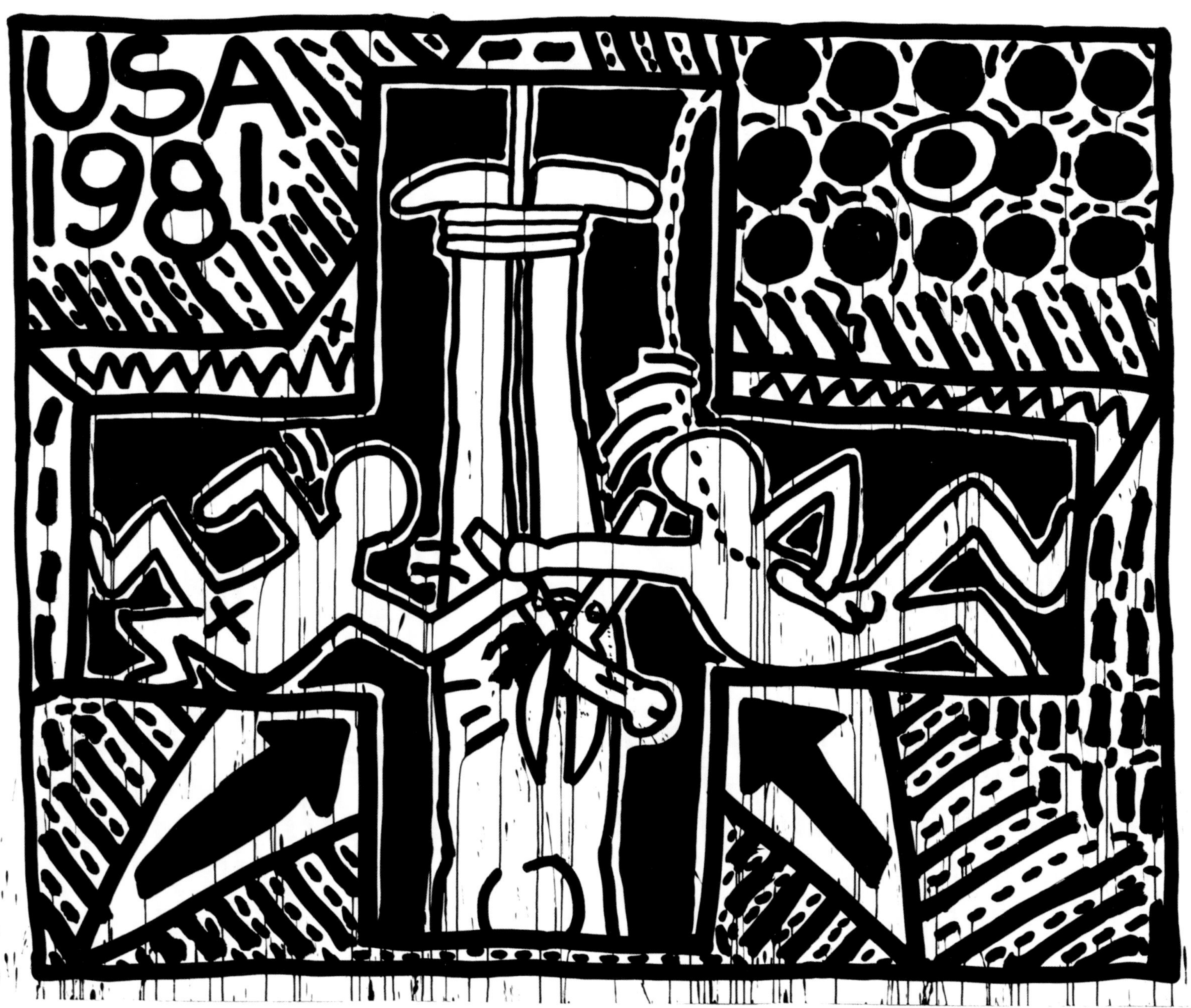

104

USA 1981, 1981. Gouache and ink on paper, 72 x 91 in. (182.9 x 231.1 cm)
Collection of the Keith Haring Foundation

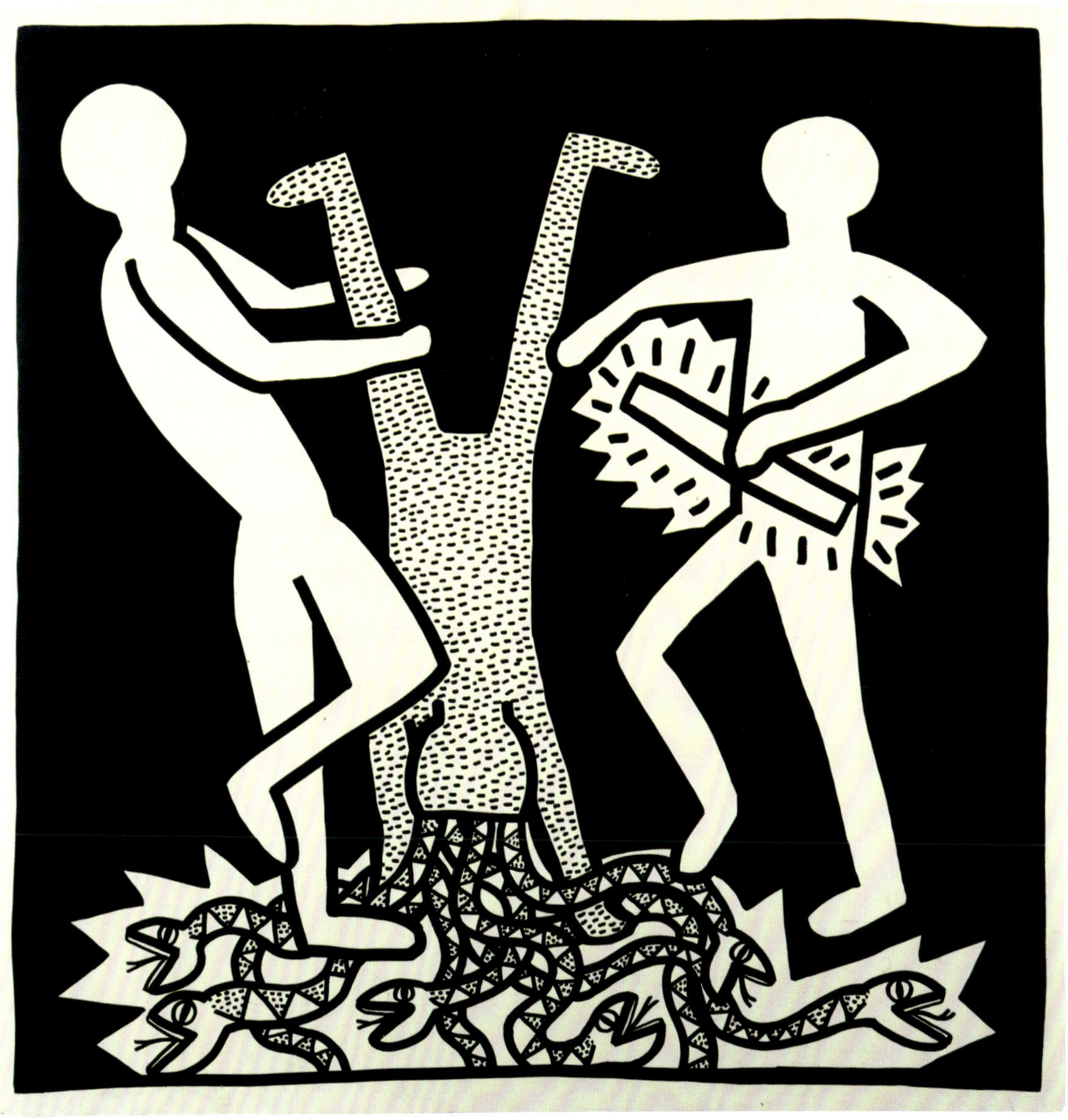

105

Untitled, August 22, 1981. Acrylic on board, 47 1/4 x 46 3/4 in. (120 x 118.8 cm)
Collection of Sir Elton John and David Furnish

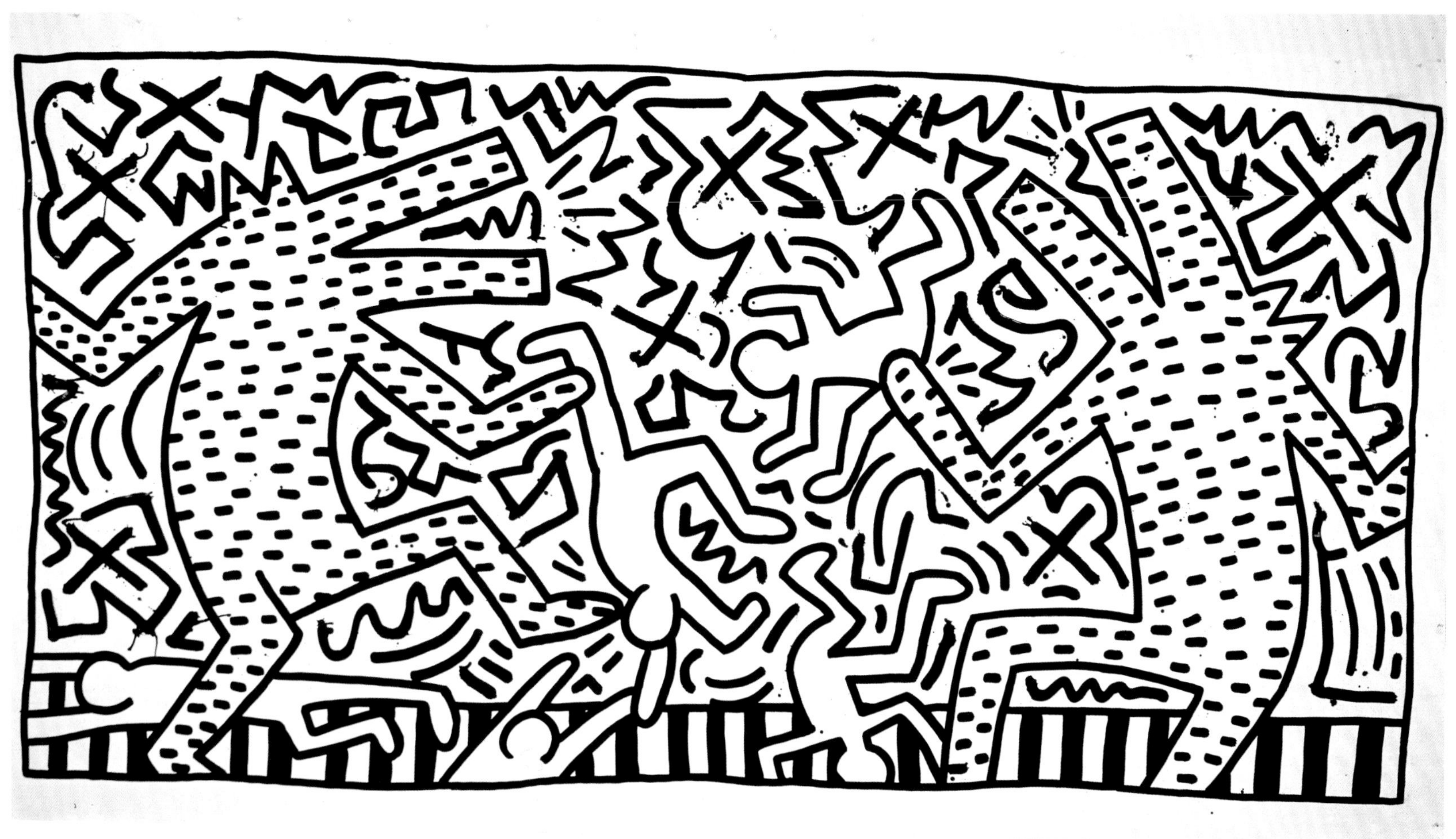

106

Untitled, 1982. Sumi ink on paper, 107 7/8 x 210 in. (274 x 533.4)
Private collection

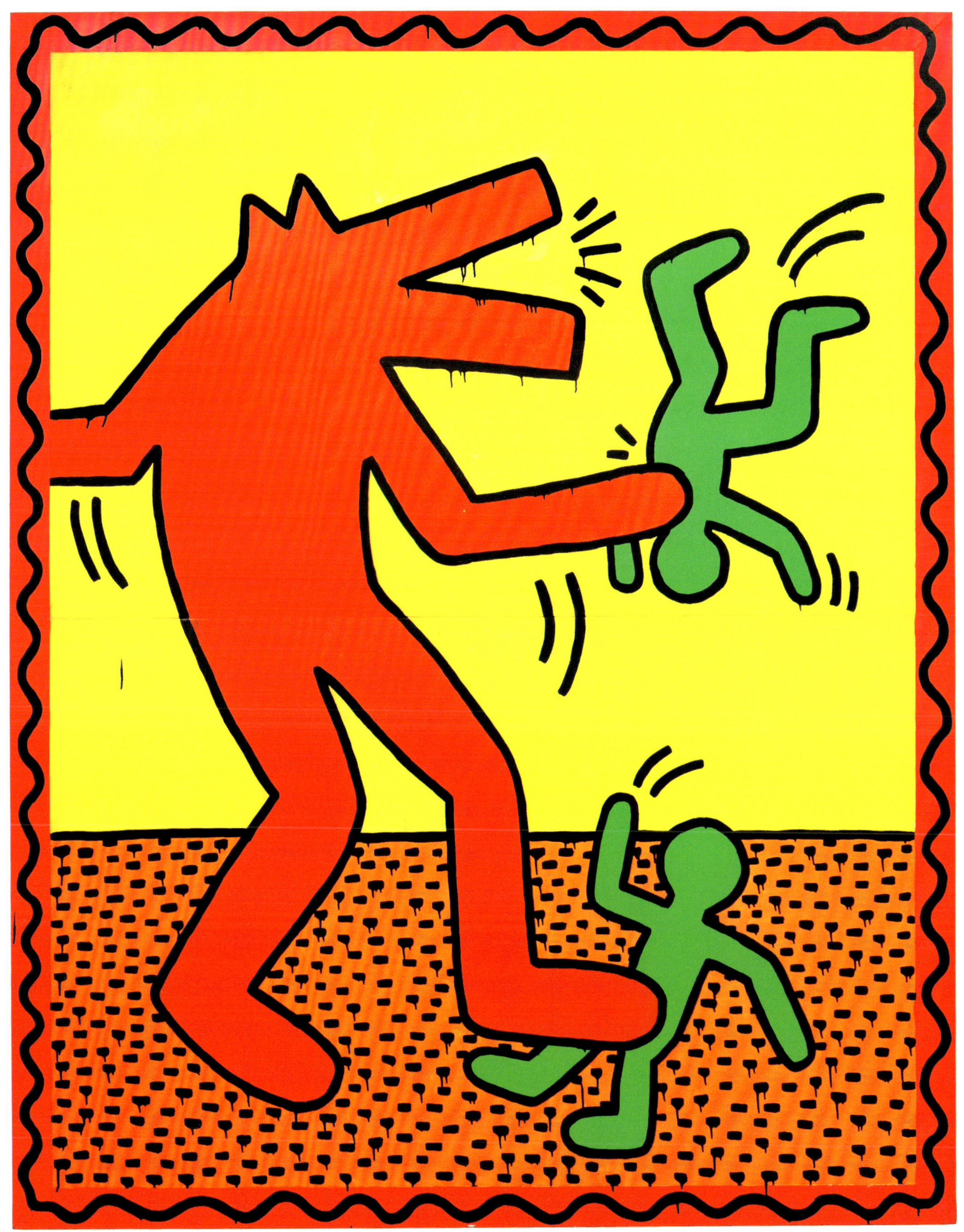

107

Untitled, October 1982. Enamel and Day-Glo paint on metal, 90 1/2 x 72 3/8 in. (229.8 x 183.8 cm)
Collection of the Keith Haring Foundation

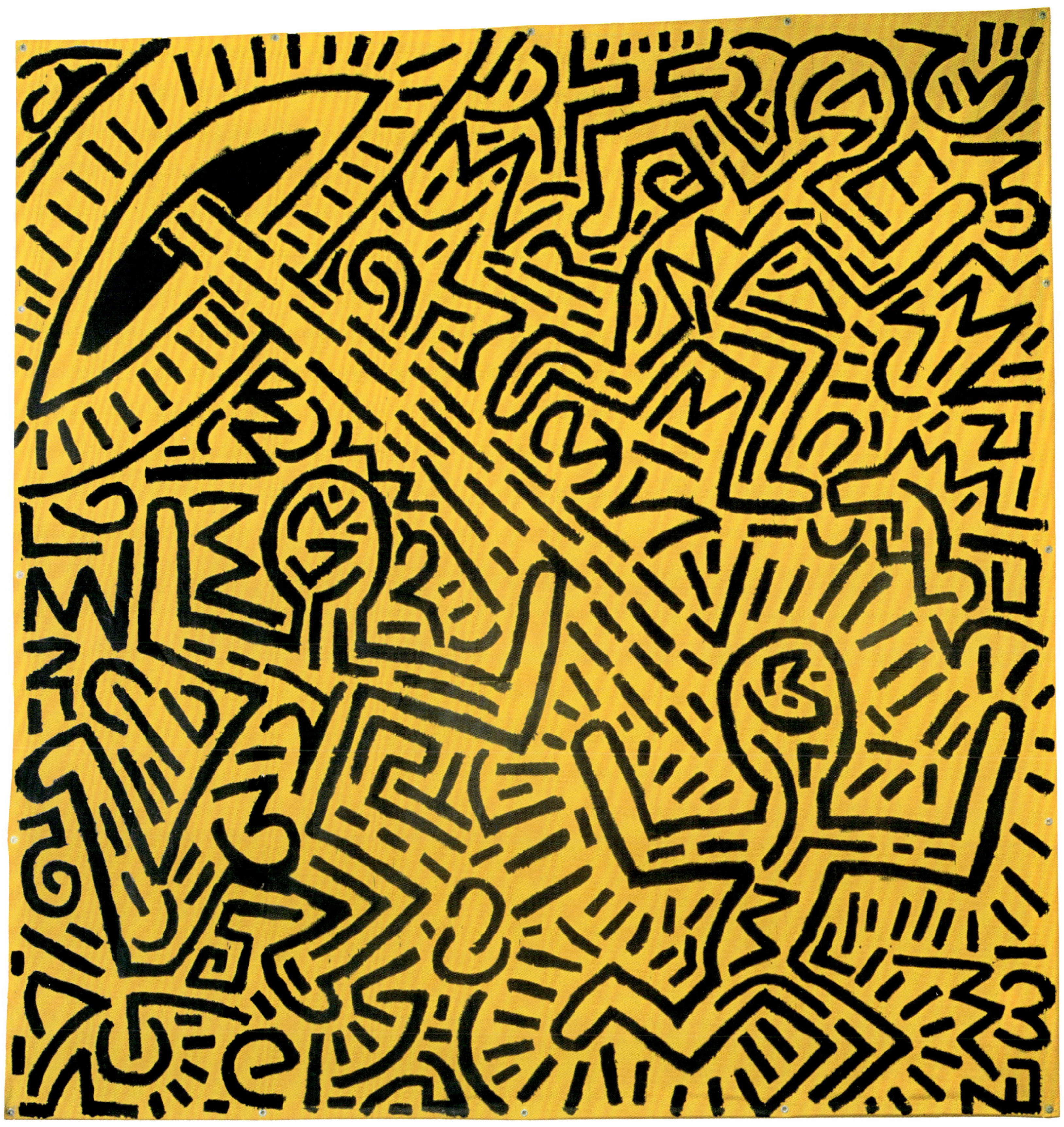

108

Untitled, 1981. Vinyl paint on vinyl tarpaulin, 144 x 144 in. (365.8 x 365.8 cm)
Carnegie Museum of Art, Pittsburgh, Pennsylvania, gift of the Lannan Foundation

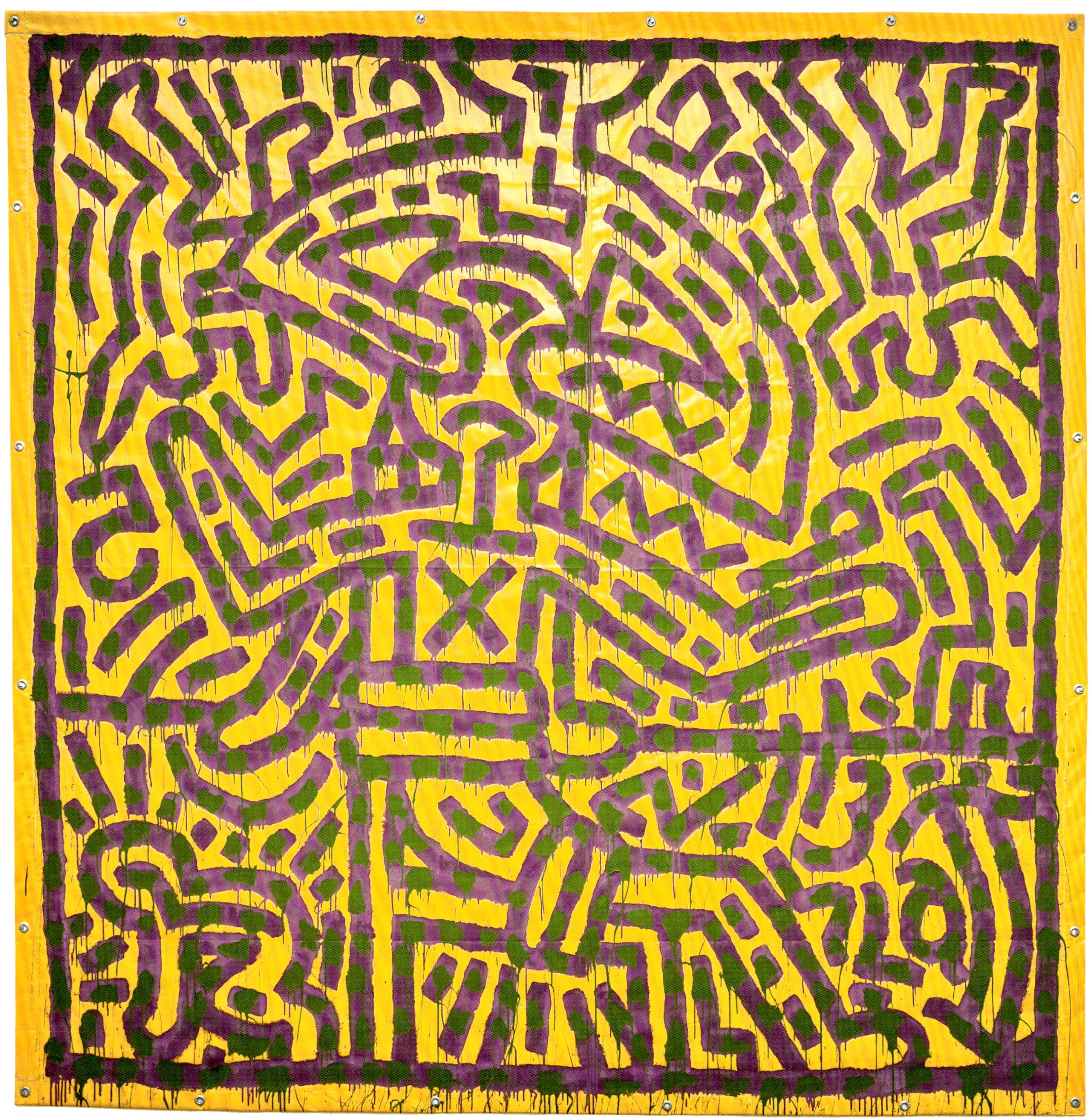

109

Untitled, January 16, 1982. Acrylic on vinyl tarpaulin, 108 x 109 ⅛ in. (274.3 x 277.2 cm)
Private collection

110

Untitled, 1981. Acrylic on canvas, 50 x 50 in. (127 x 127 cm)
Private collection

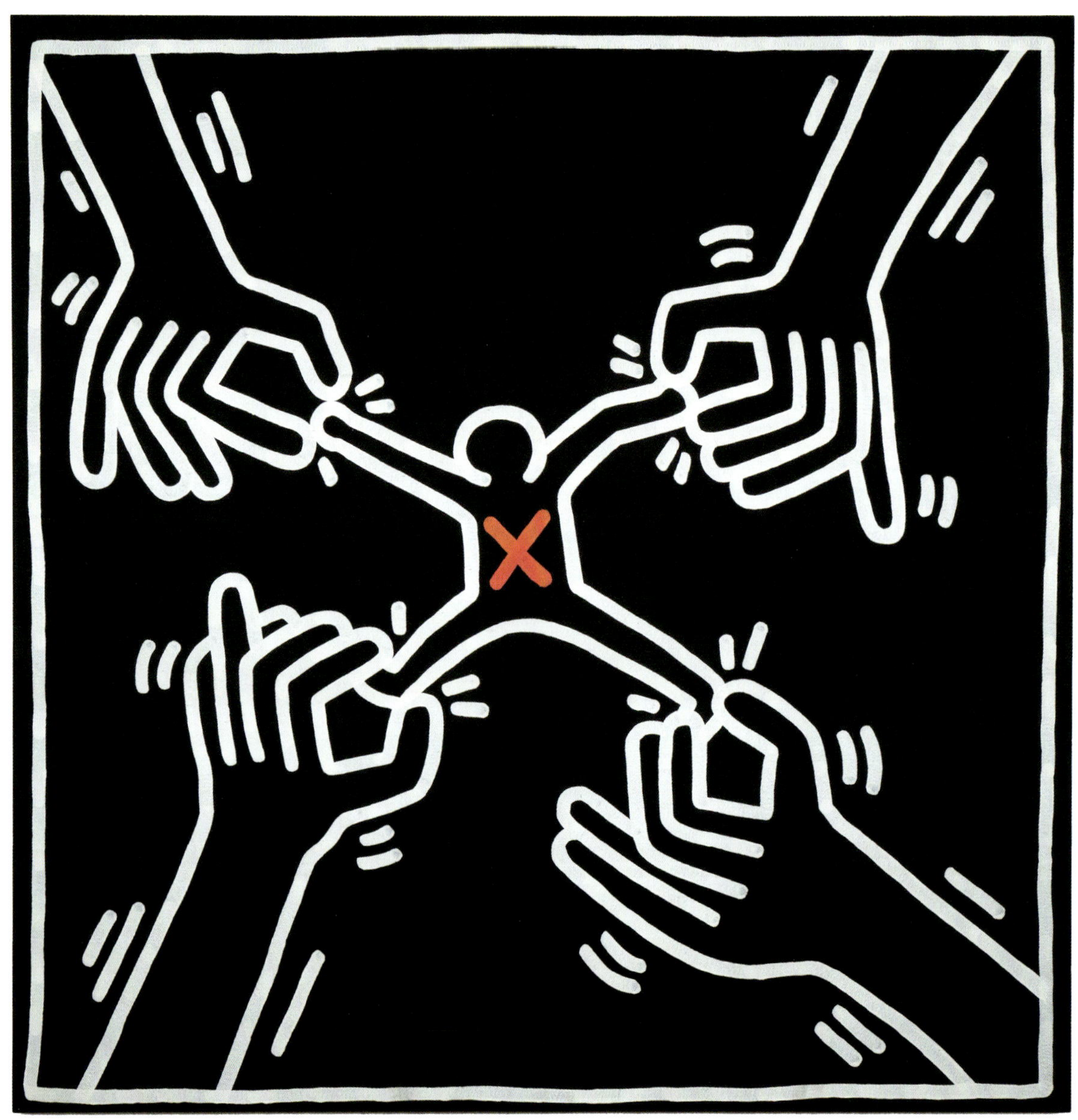

111

Untitled, 1985. Acrylic on canvas, 59 x 59 in. (150 x 150 cm)
Collection of Alona Kagan

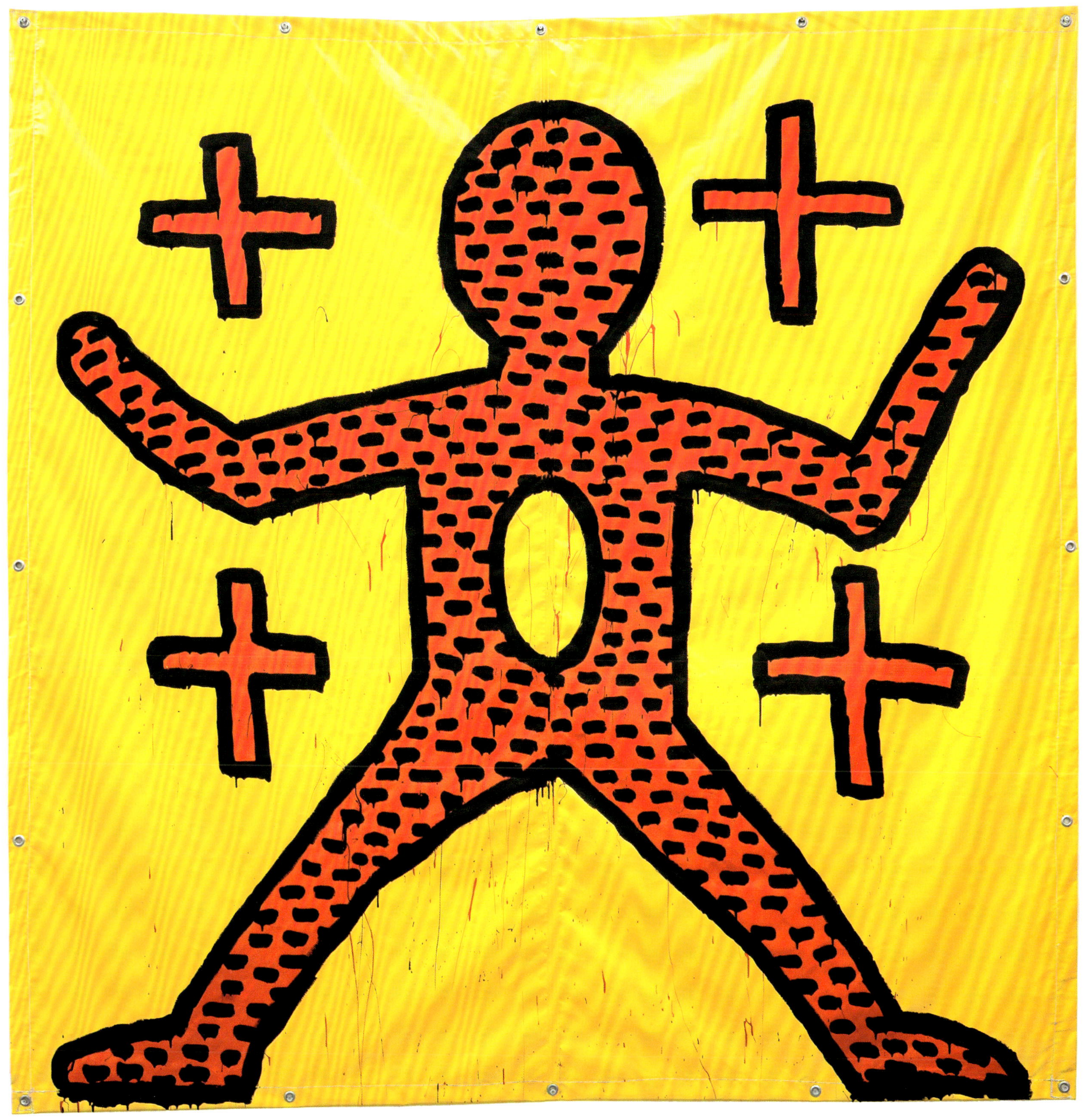

112

Untitled, 1981. Vinyl paint on vinyl tarpaulin, 96 x 96 in. (244 x 244 cm)
Private collection, courtesy of Museum der Moderne Salzburg

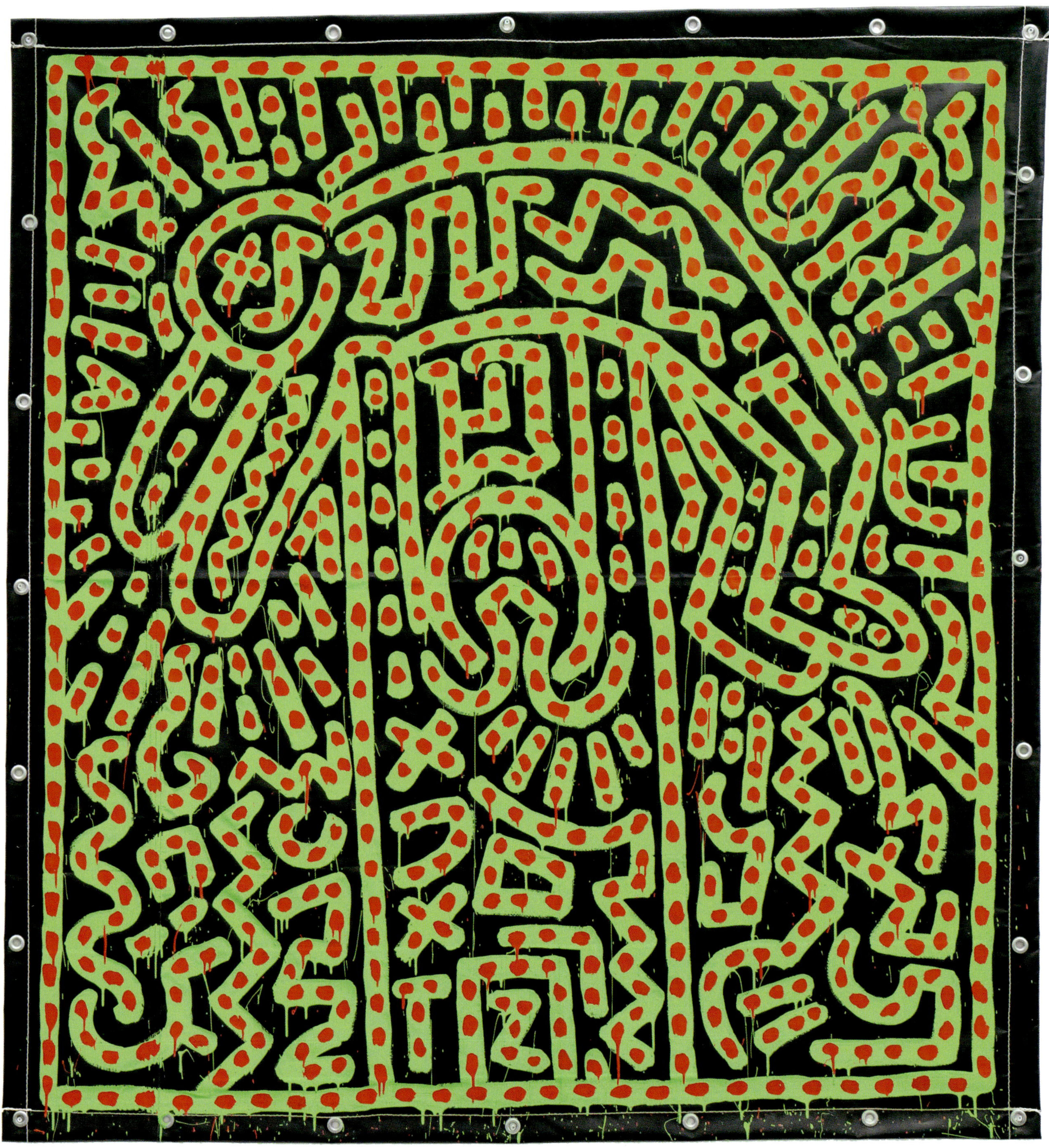

113

Untitled, October 1982. Vinyl paint on vinyl tarpaulin, 73 x 69 in. (185.4 x 175.2 cm)
Private collection, Bologna, Italy

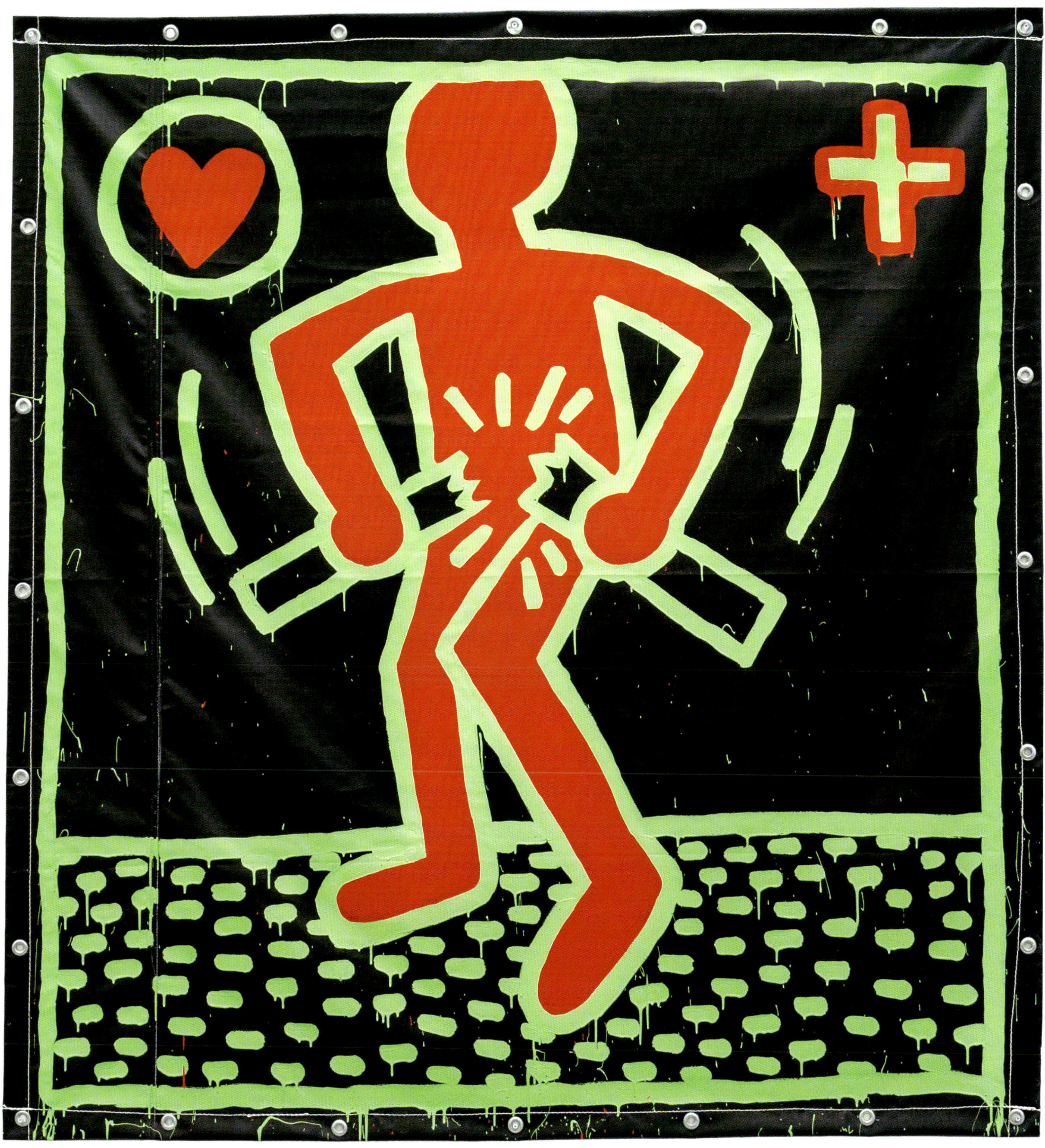

114

Untitled, 1982. Vinyl paint on vinyl tarpaulin, 72 x 72 in. (182.9 x 182.9 cm)
Collection of Sloan and Roger Barnett

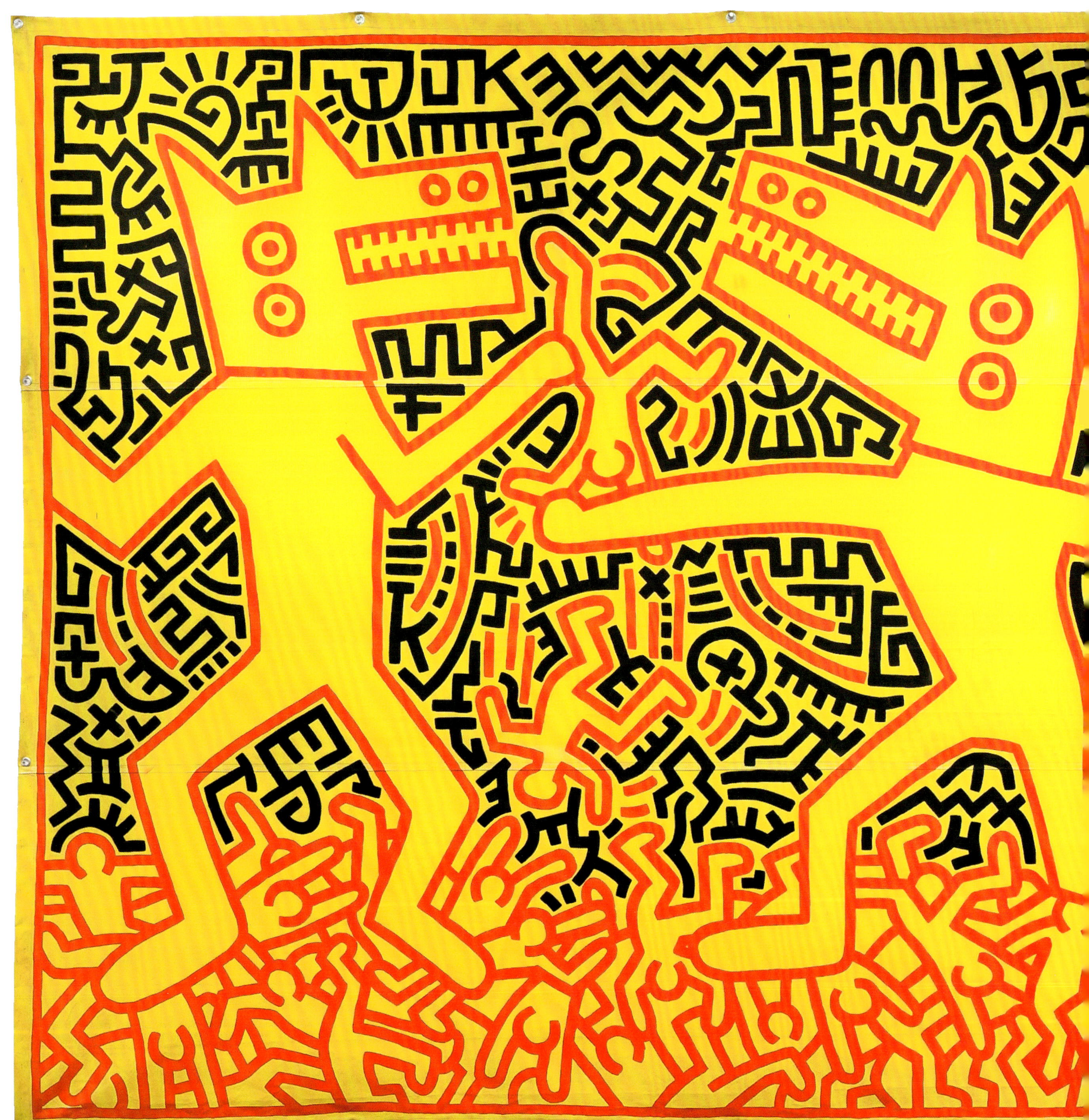

115

Untitled, 1983. Acrylic on vinyl tarpaulin, 114 1/8 x 232 1/4 in. (290 x 590 cm)
Collection of Terrae Motus, Palazzo Reale, Caserta, Italy

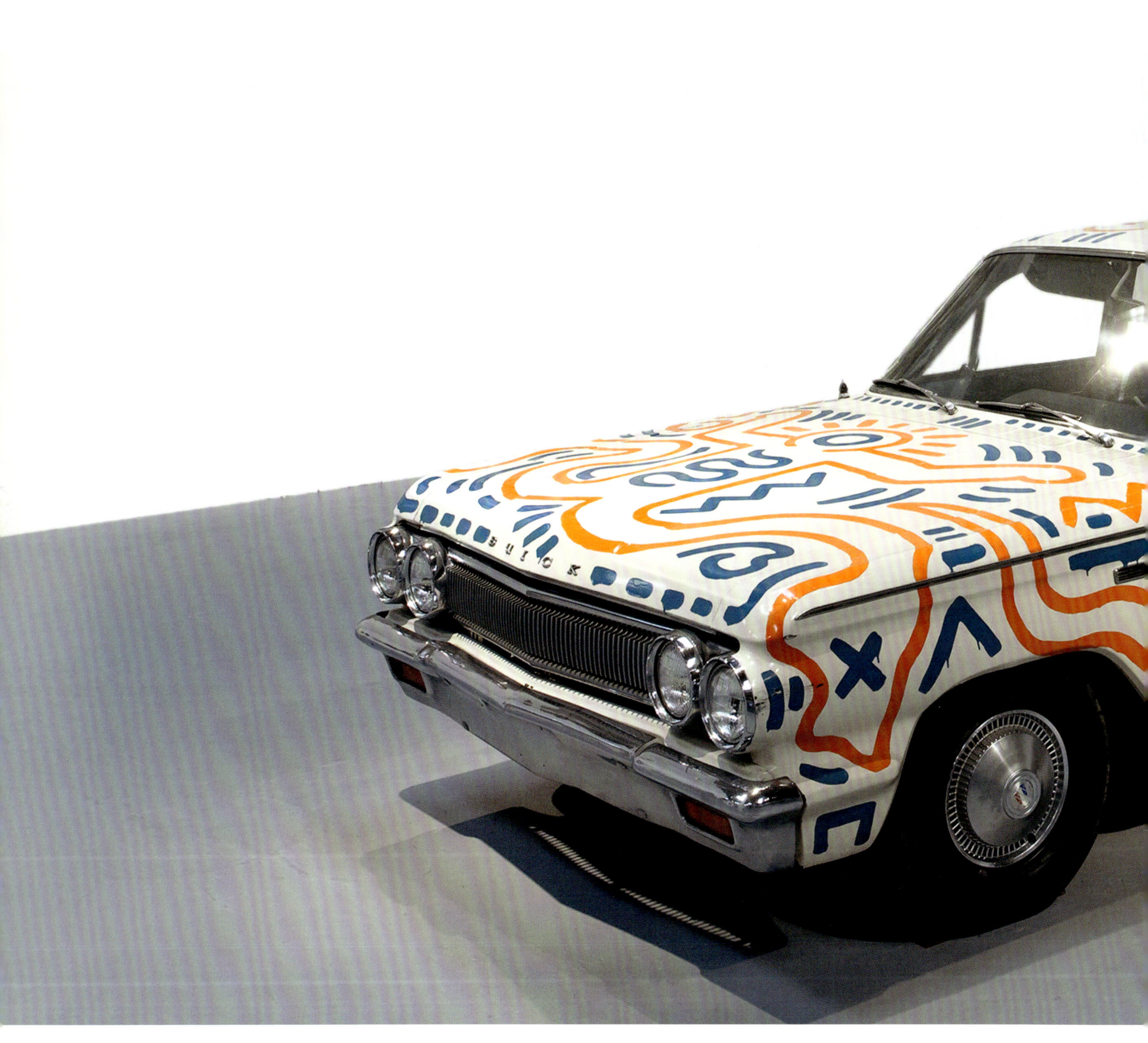

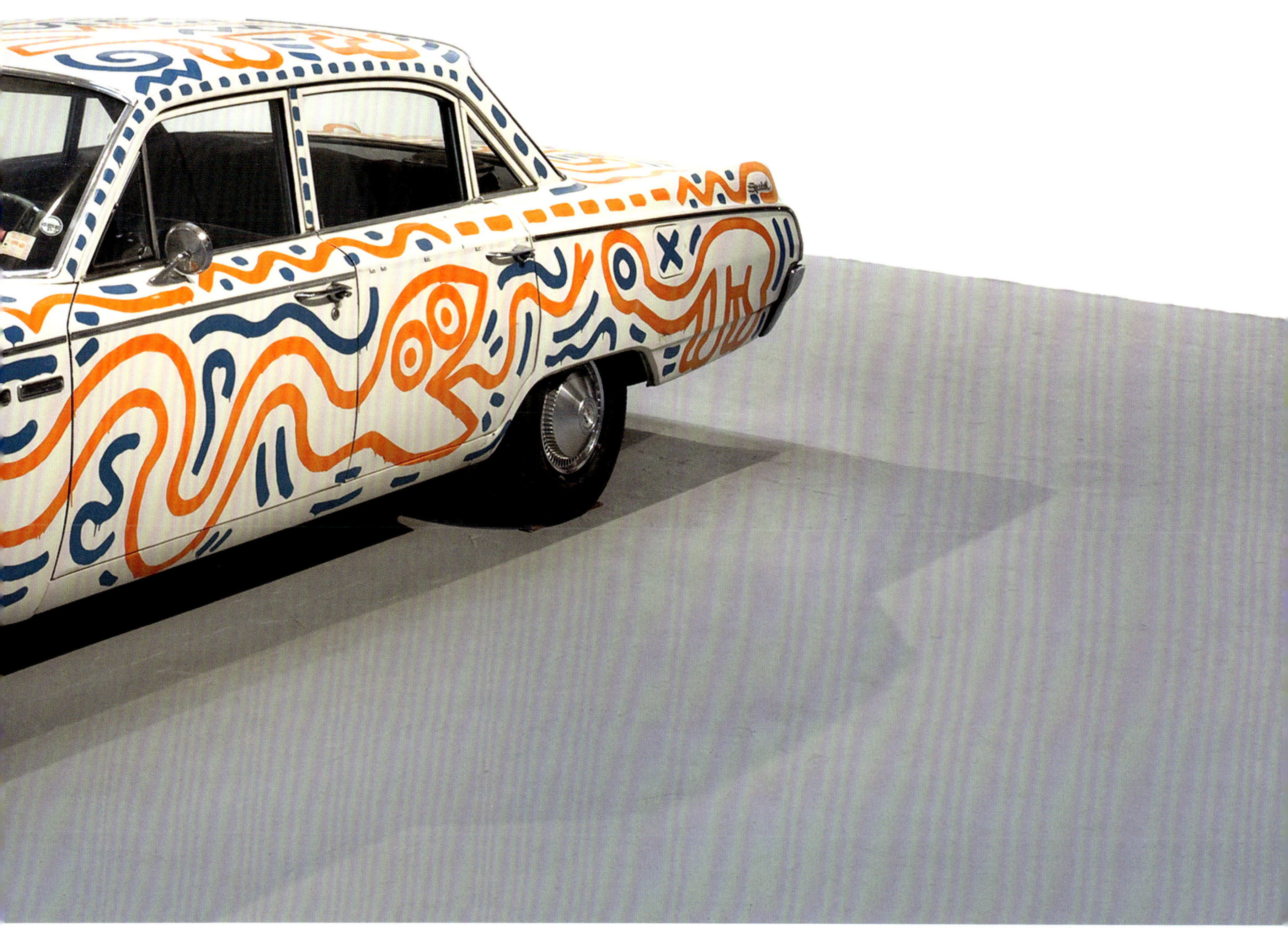

116

Untitled (*Car*), 1986. Enamel on 1963 Buick Special, 54 x 70 ⅞ x 189 in. (137 x 180 x 480 cm)
Collection of Justin Warsh

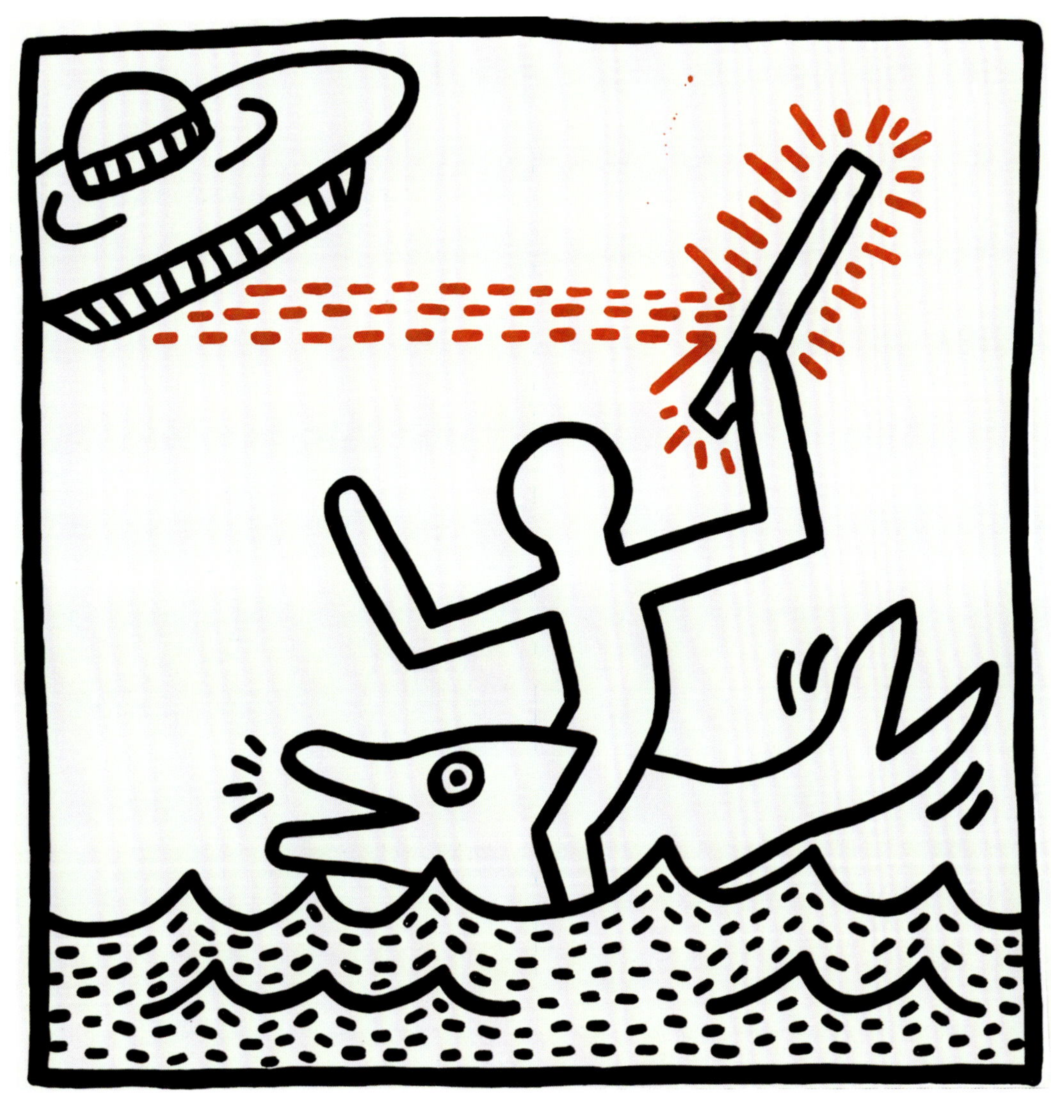

117

Untitled, 1982. Baked enamel on steel, 43 x 43 in. (109.2 x 109.2 cm)
Collection of Larry Warsh

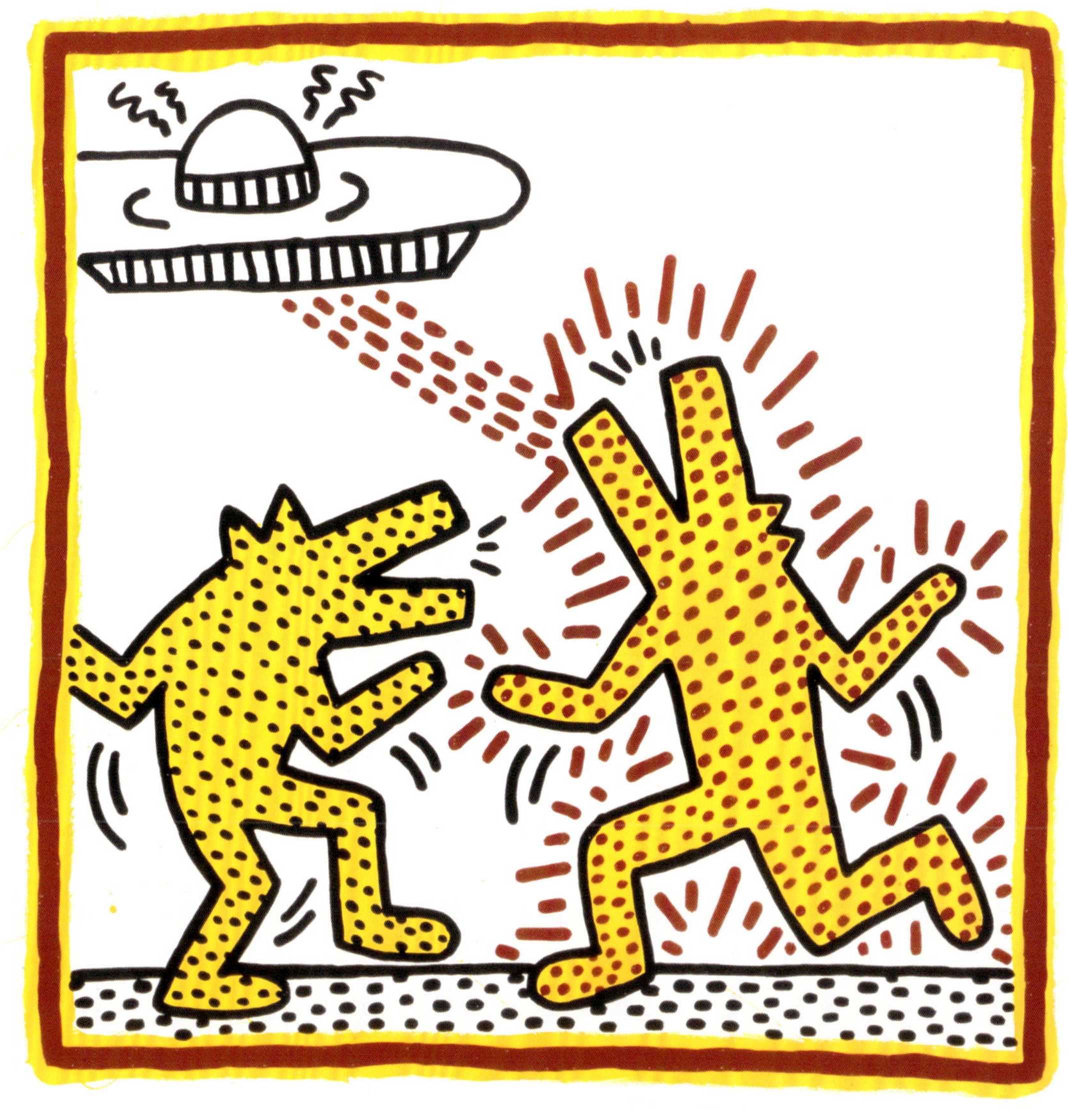

118

Untitled, 1982. Baked enamel on steel, 43 x 43 in. (109.2 x 109.2 cm)
The Eli and Edythe L. Broad Collection, Los Angeles

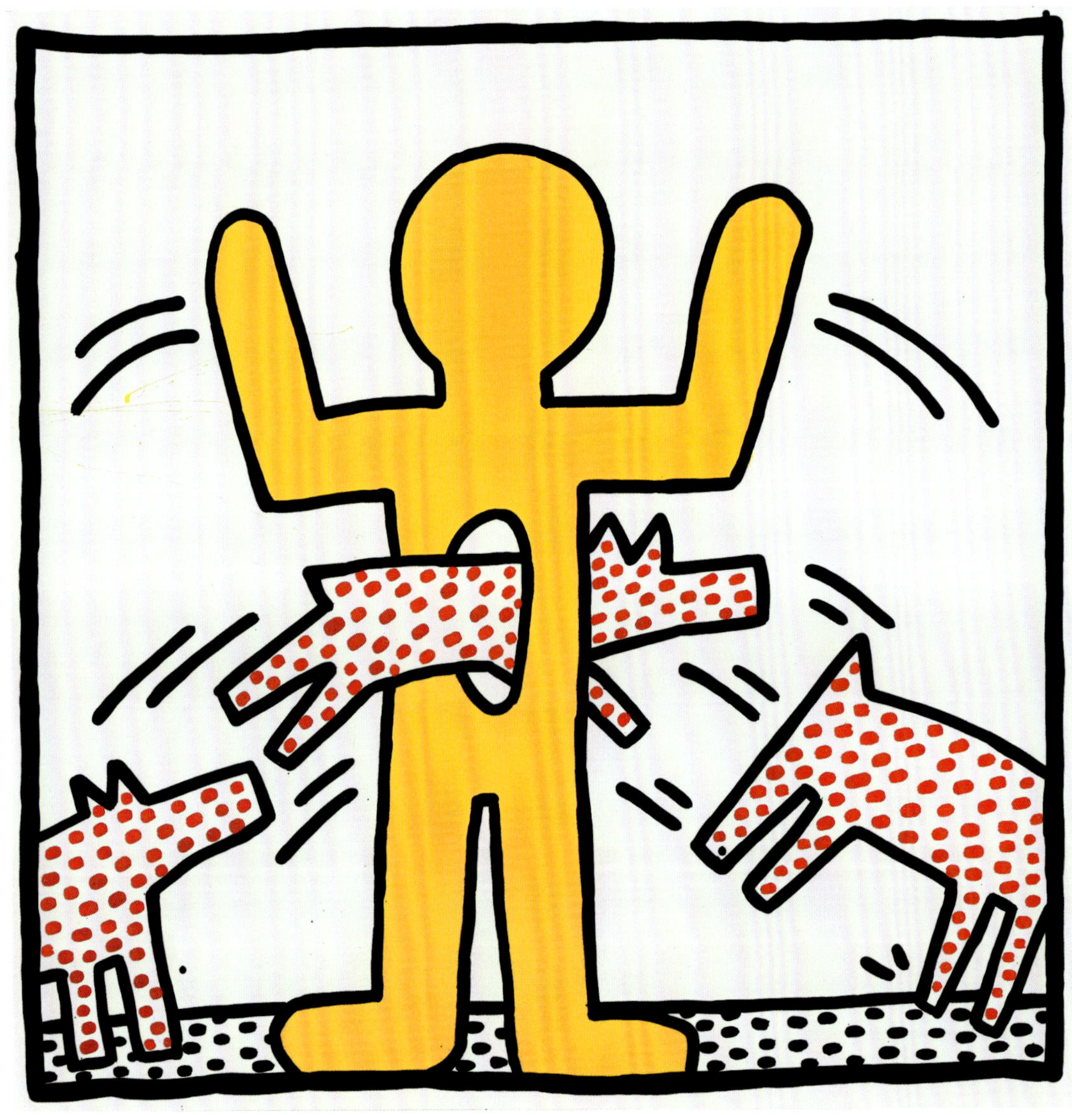

119

Untitled, 1982. Baked enamel on steel, 43 x 43 in. (109.2 x 109.2 cm)
Collection of Larry Warsh

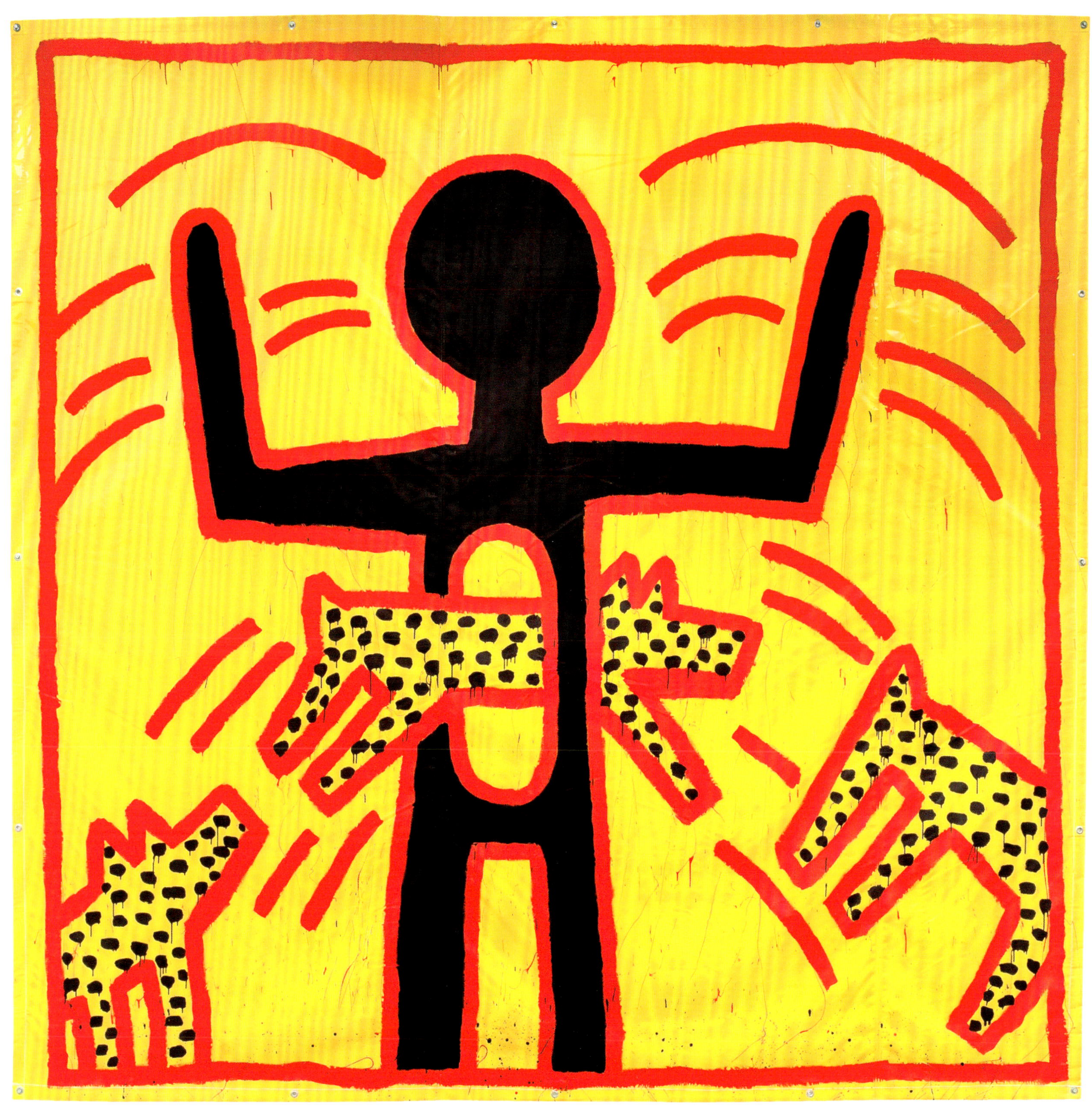

120

Untitled, 1982. Vinyl paint on vinyl tarpaulin, 144 x 148 in. (365.7 x 375.9 cm)
Collection of Her Highness Sheikha Salama bint Hamdan Al Nahyan

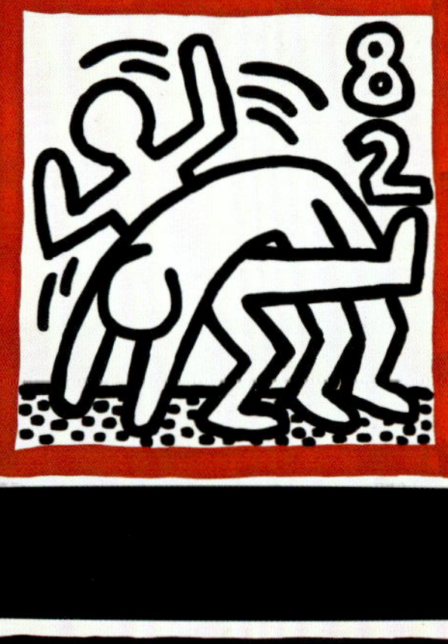
82
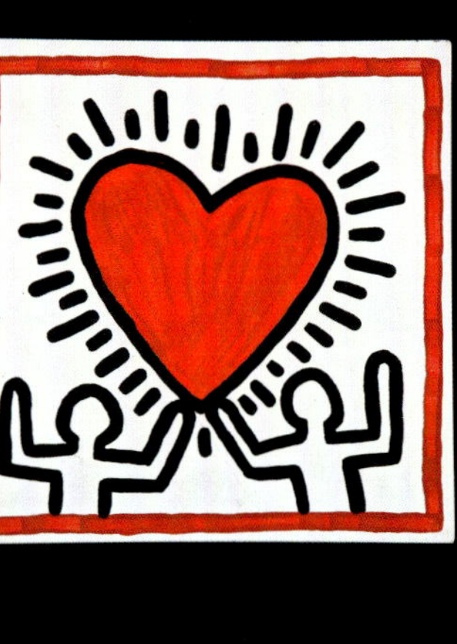
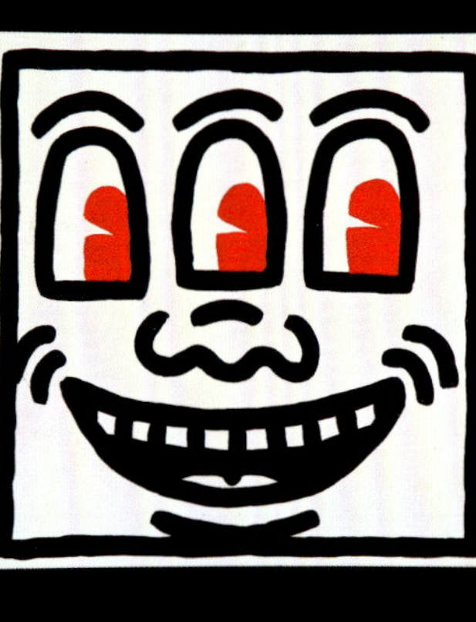
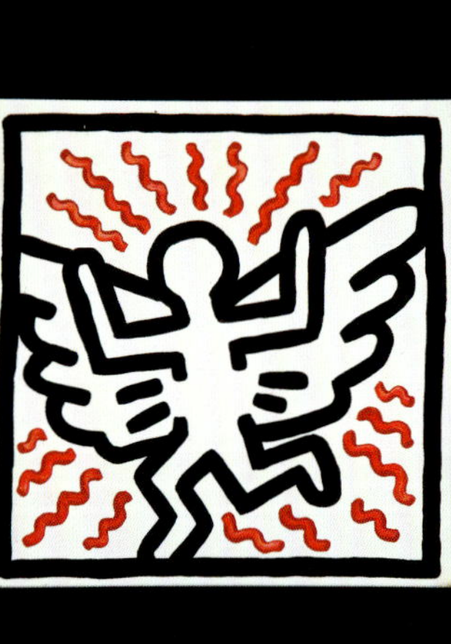

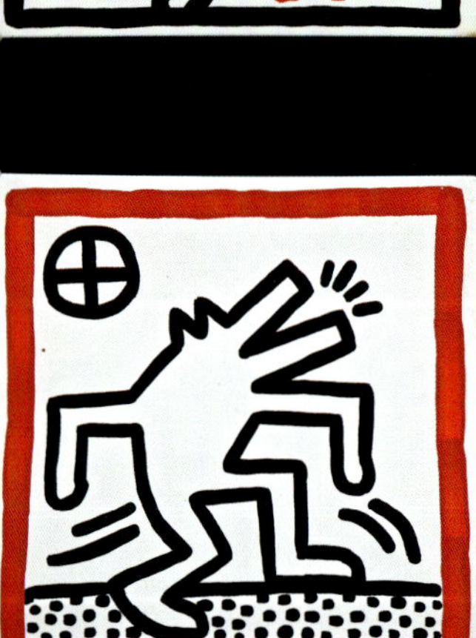
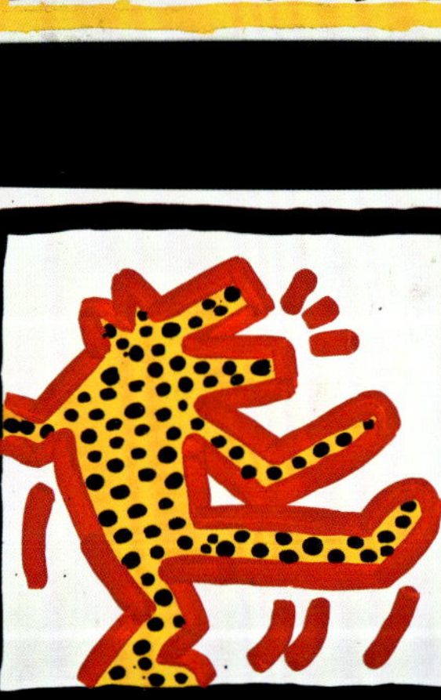

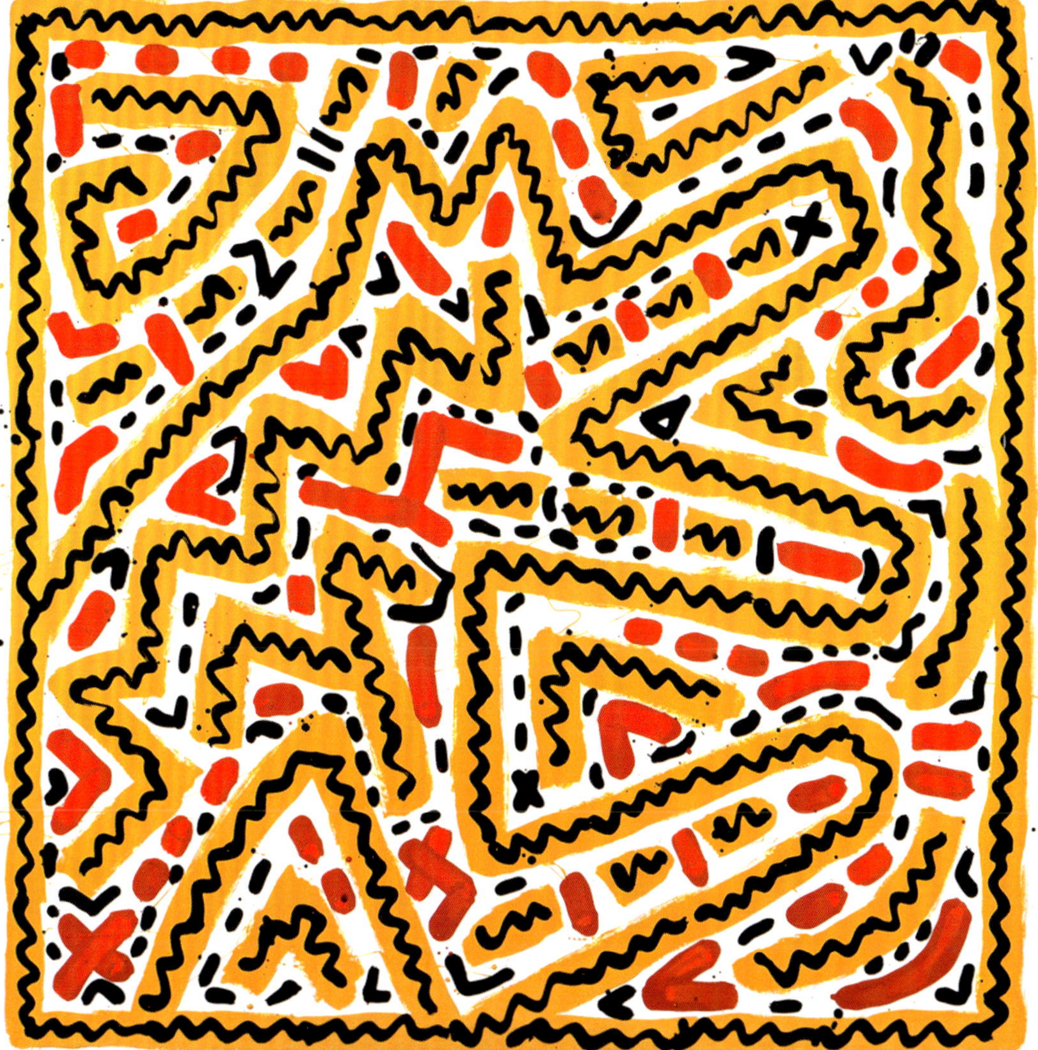

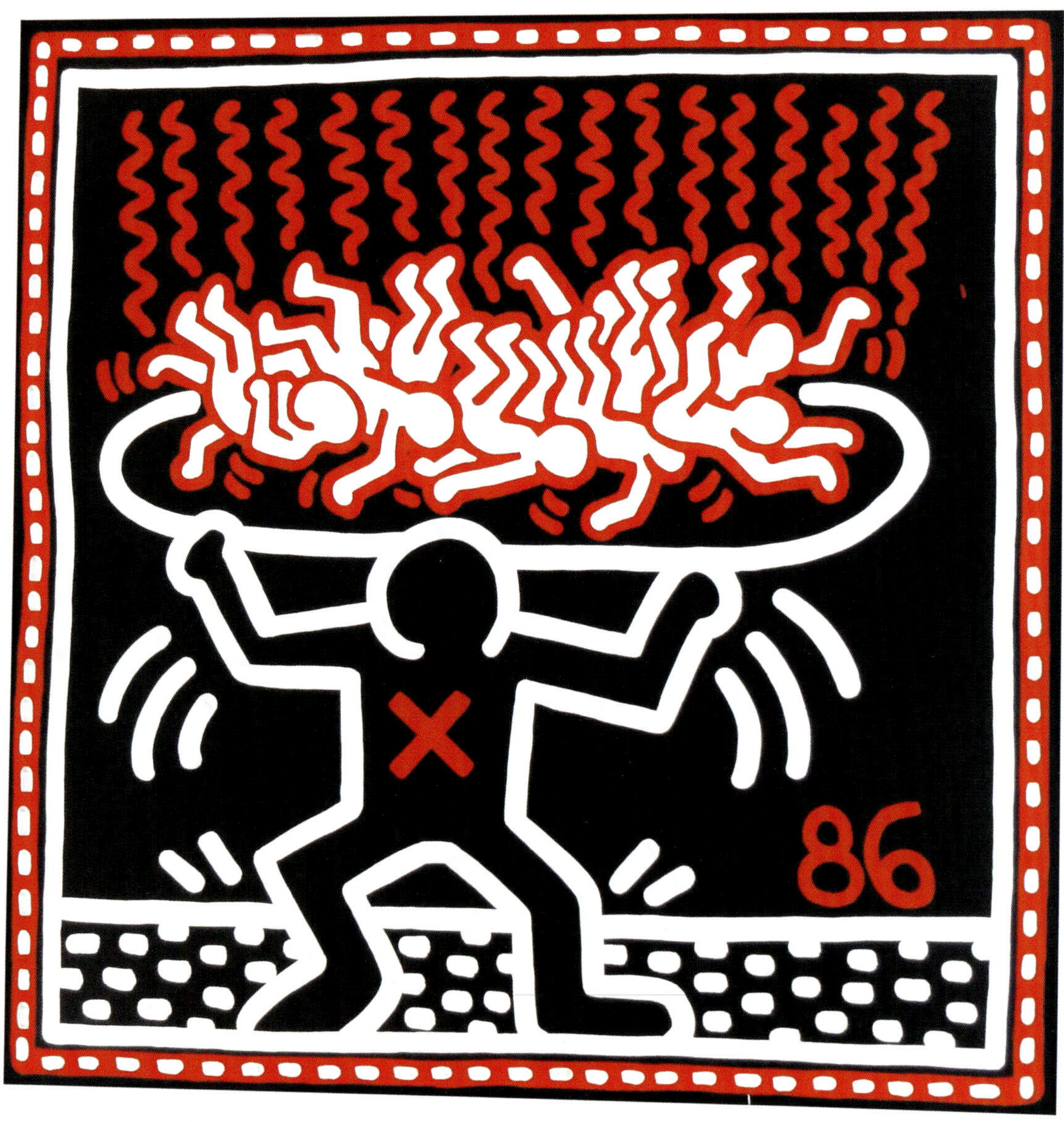

130

Untitled, 1986. Acrylic on canvas, 60 x 60 in. (152.4 x 152.4 cm)
Collection of Jose Martos

131

Untitled, 1982. Vinyl paint on vinyl tarpaulin, 120 x 120 in. (304.8 x 304.8 cm)
Private collection

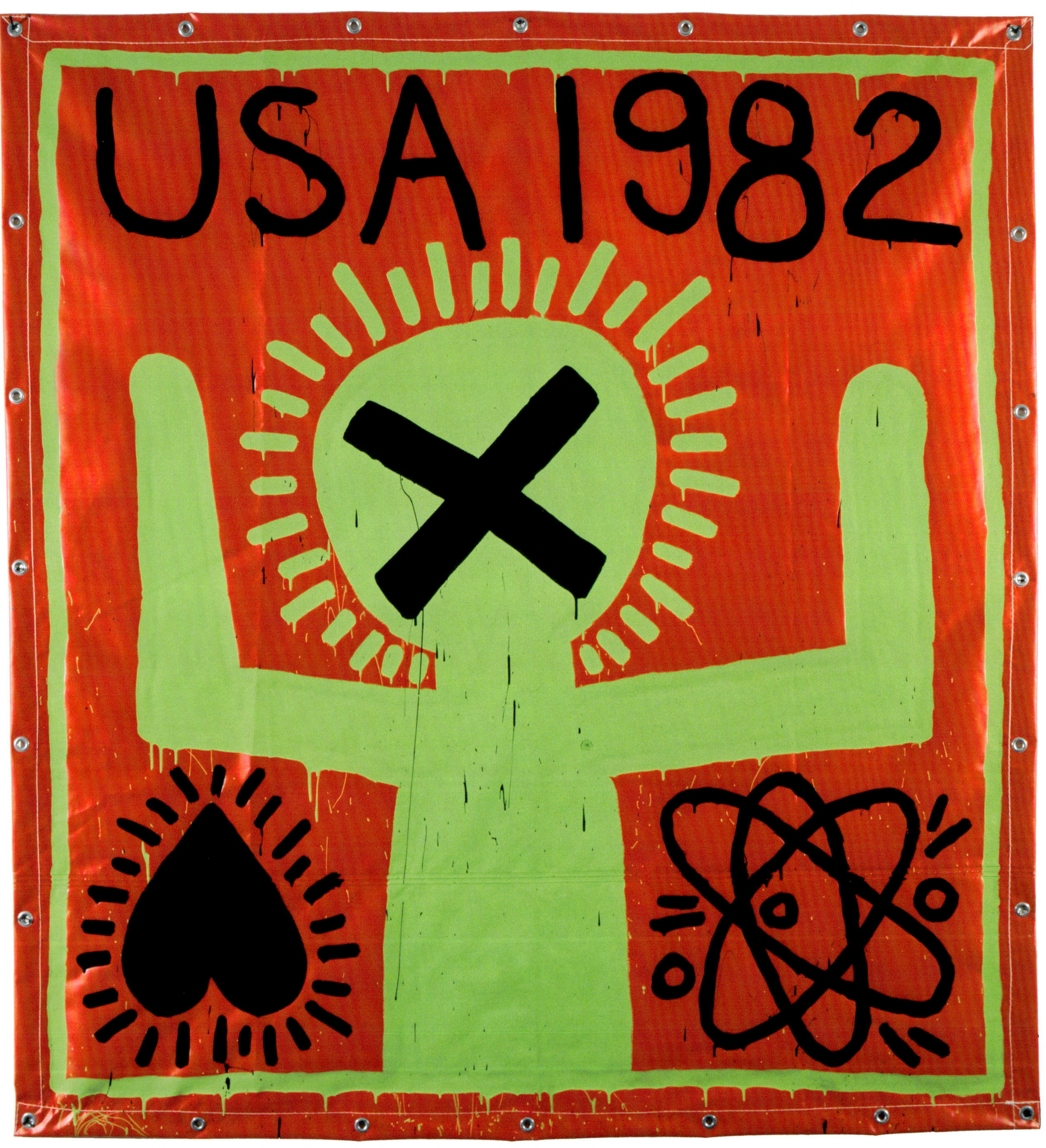

132

Untitled, June 11, 1982. Vinyl paint on vinyl tarpaulin, 77 1/2 x 73 in. (196.8 x 185.4 cm)
Private collection

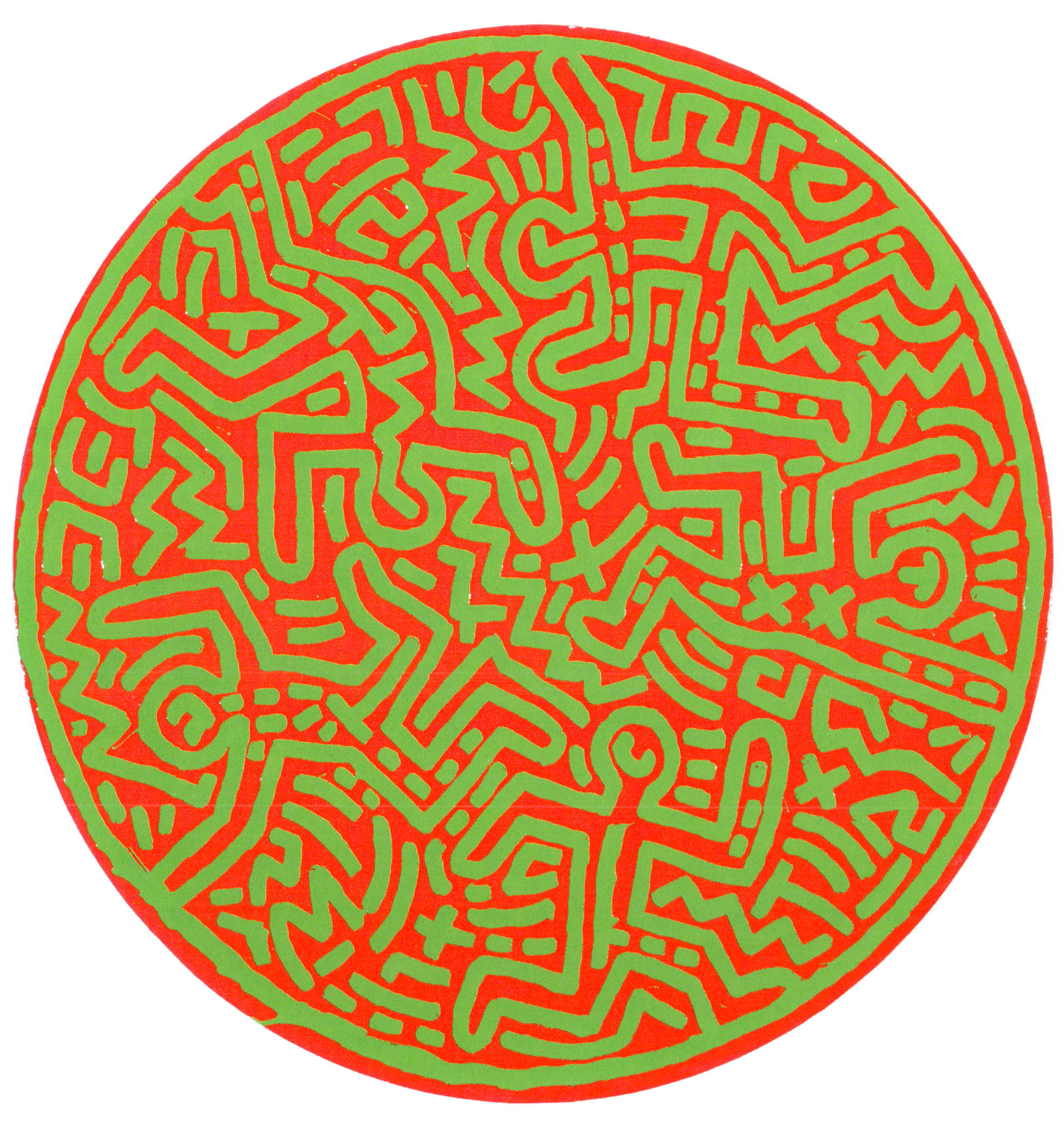

133

Untitled, March 1982. Enamel on wood, 48 in. diam. (121.9 cm diam.)
Private collection, courtesy Tony Shafrazi Gallery, New York

134

Untitled, 1982. Acrylic and ink on paper, 36 ¾ x 48 ¾ in. (93.3 x 123.8 cm)
Private collection

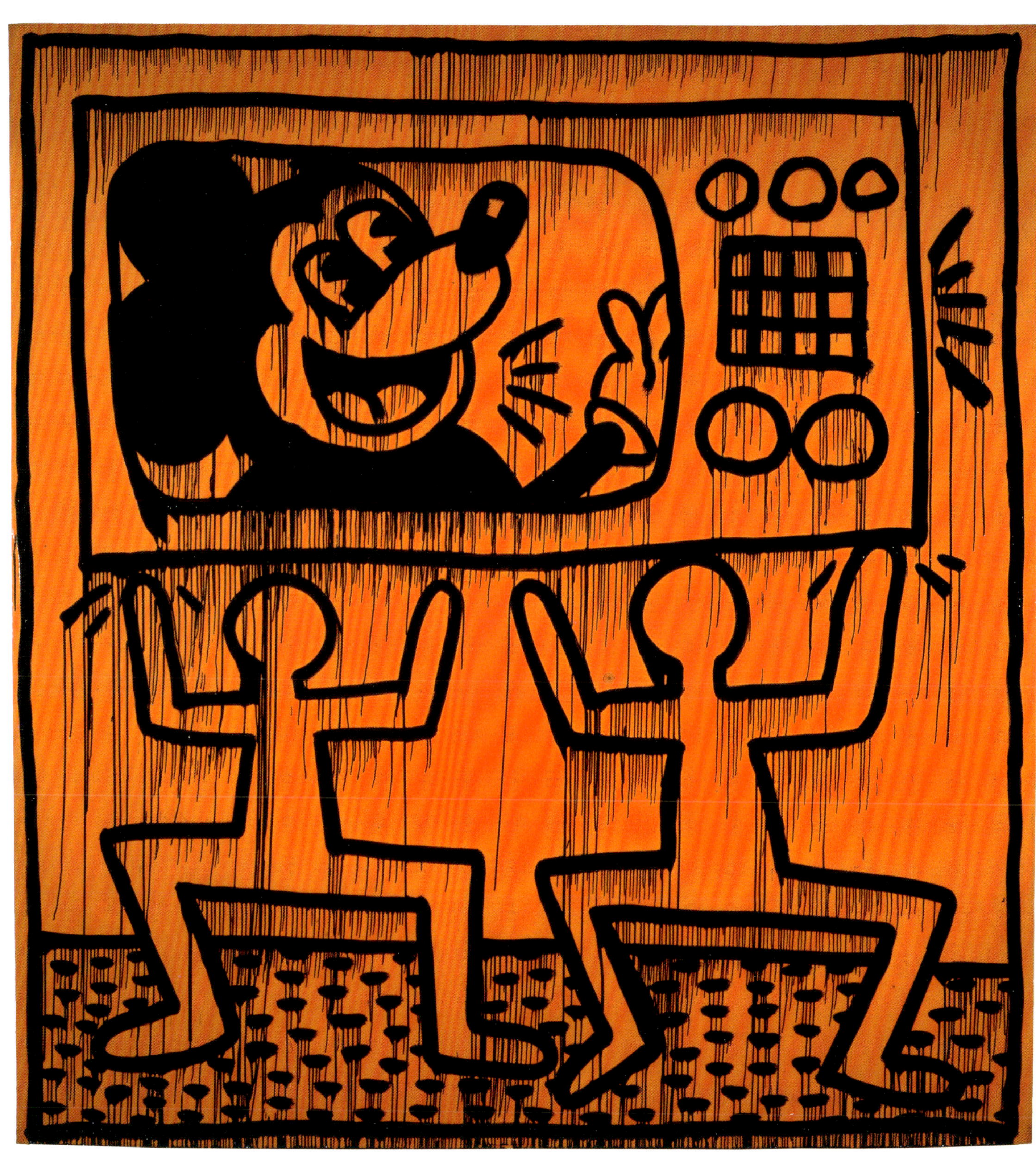

135

Untitled, 1982. Liquid marker ink and acrylic on found canvas, 86 x 86 in. (218.4 x 218.4 cm)
Lustgarten Collection

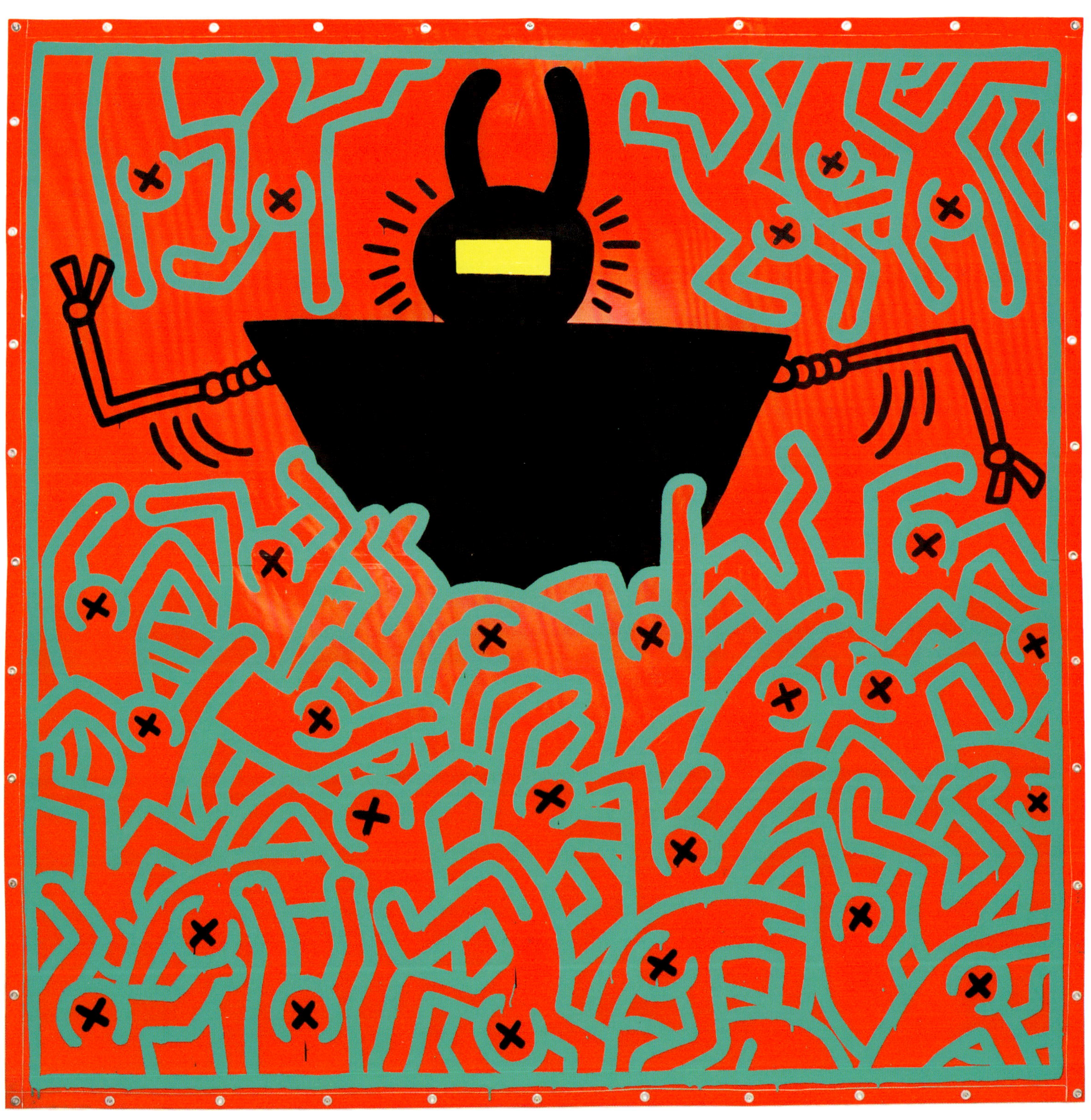

136

Untitled, 1983. Vinyl paint on vinyl tarpaulin, 120 x 120 in. (304.8 x 304.8 cm)
Staatliche Museen zu Berlin, Nationalgalerie, Sammlung Marx, Berlin

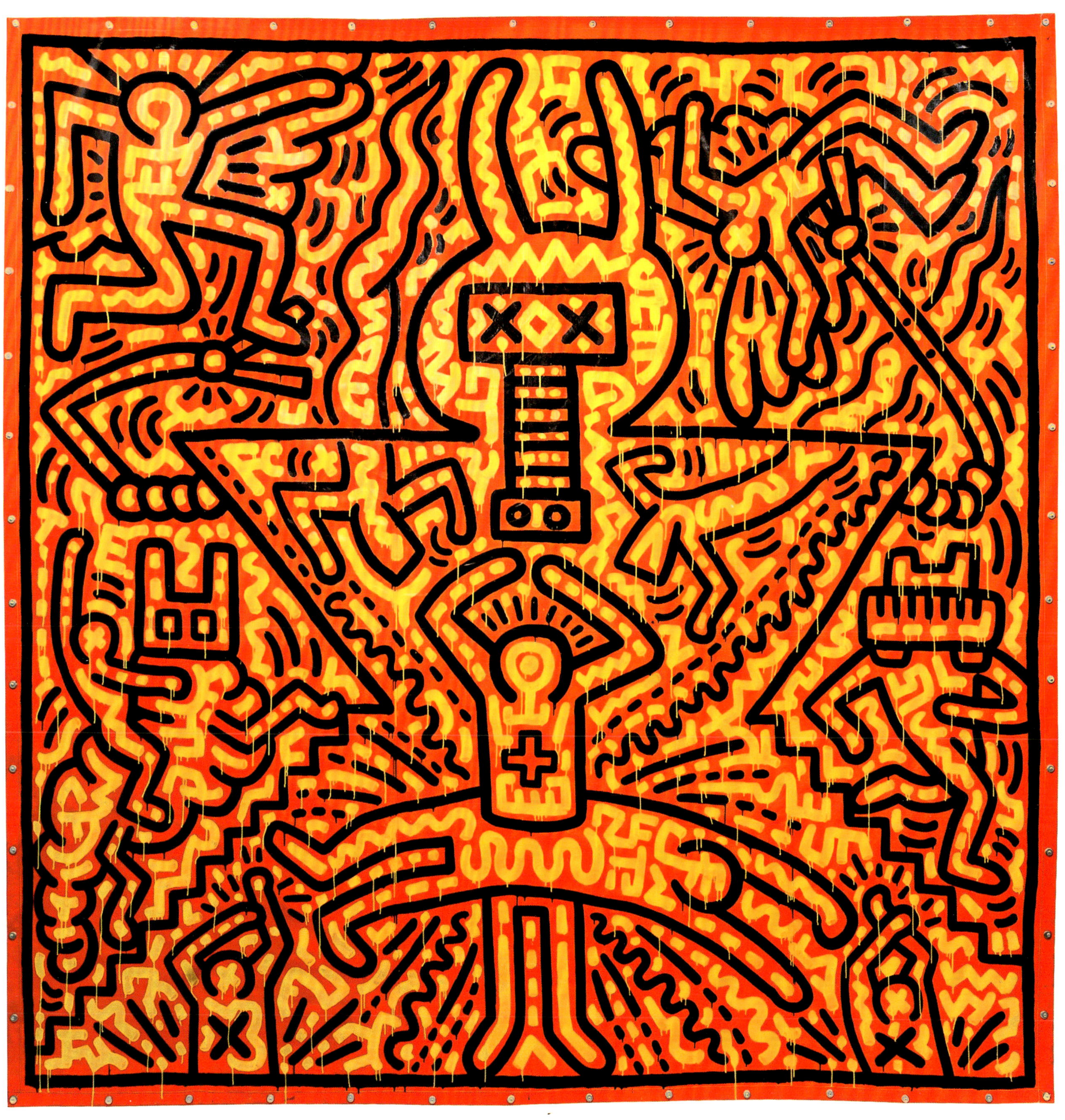

137

Untitled, 1983. Acrylic on tarpaulin, 156 x 156 in. (396.2 x 396.2 cm)
Glenstone

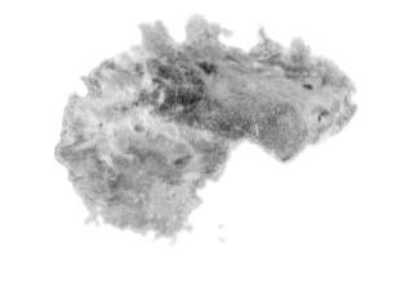

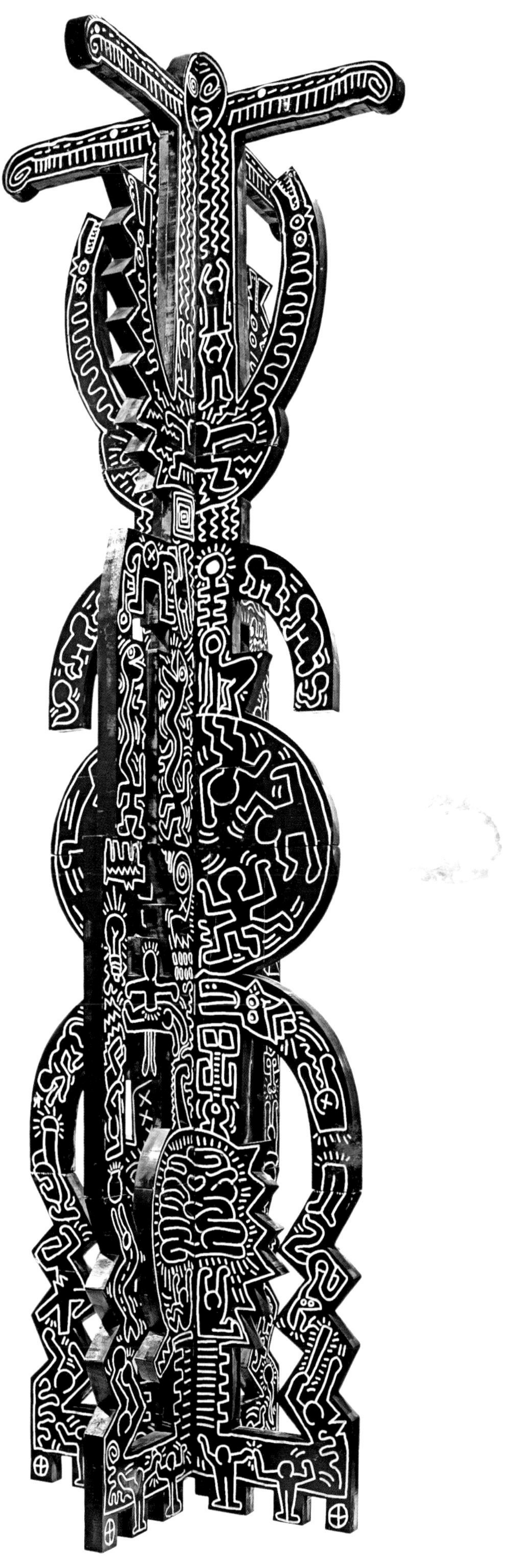

138

With Kermit Oswald, *Untitled* (*TOTEM*), 1983. Enamel on incised wood, 156 x 35 3/8 x 35 3/8 in. (396.2 x 90 x 90 cm)
Courtesy of Mike de Paola, New York

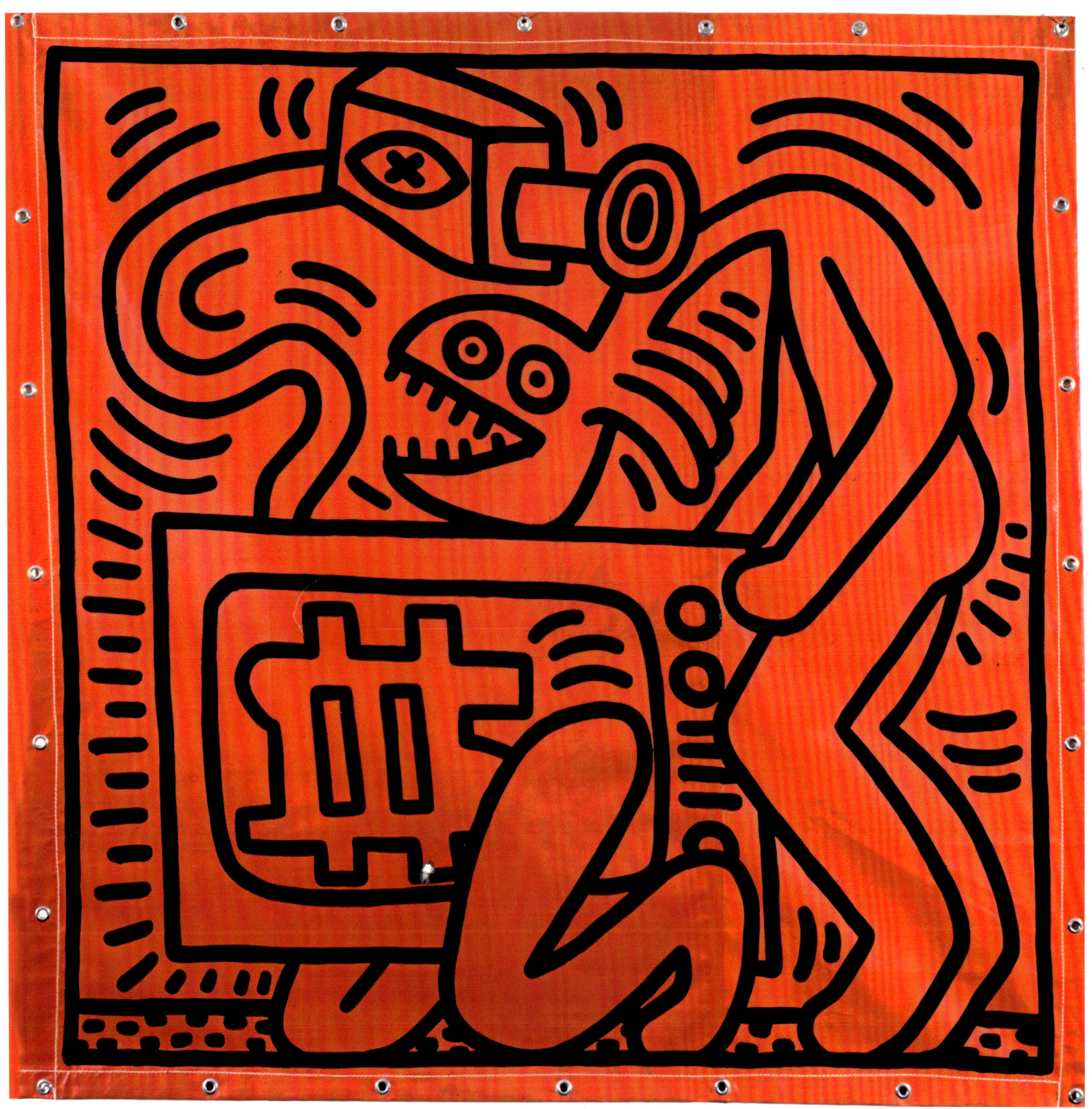

139

Untitled, 1984. Vinyl paint on vinyl tarpaulin, 72 x 72 in. (182.9 x 182.9 cm)
Private collection, courtesy of Gladstone Gallery

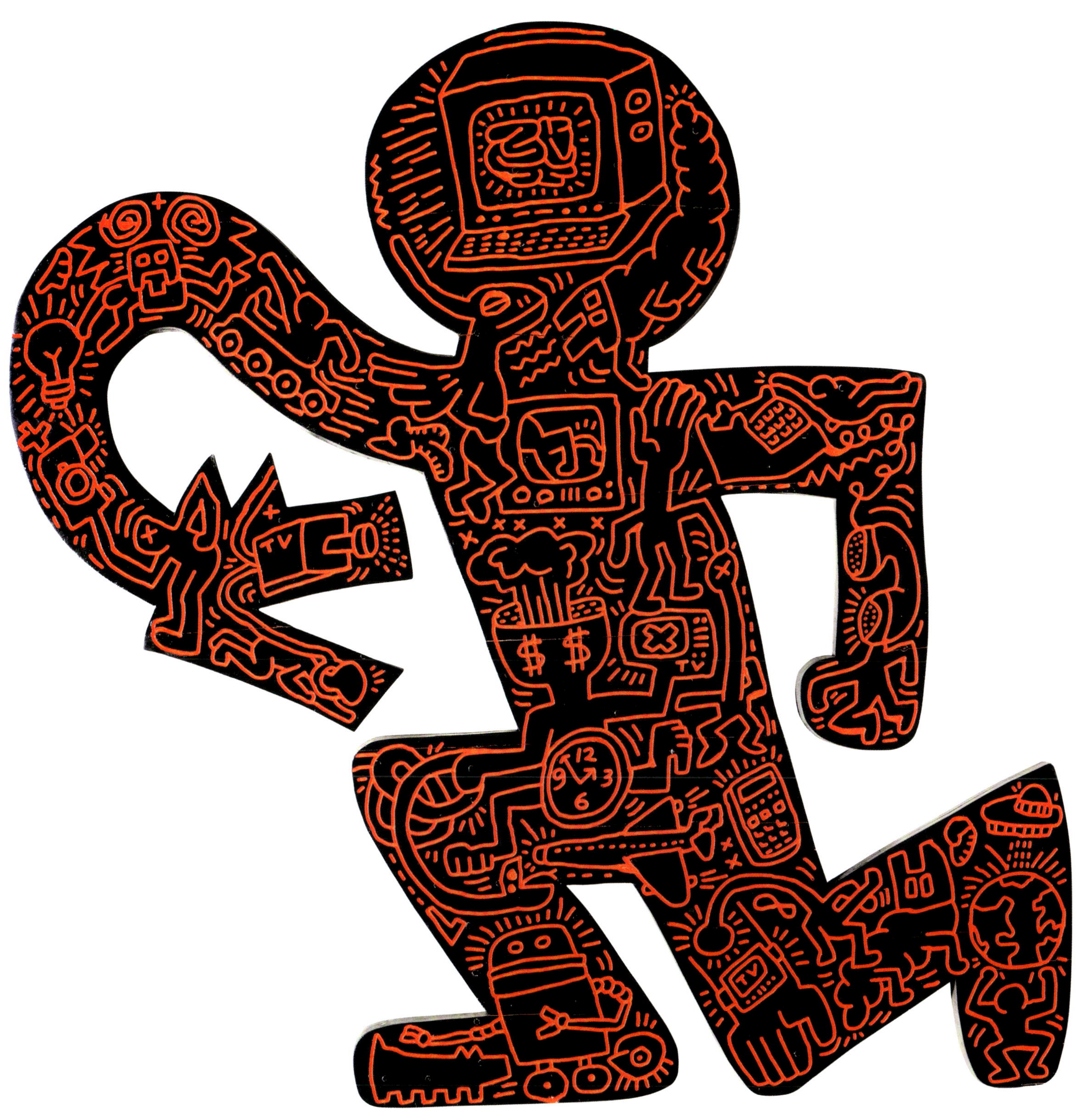

140

With Kermit Oswald, *Untitled*, 1983. Enamel on incised wood, 72 x 72 x 3 in. (182.9 x 182.9 x 7.6 cm)
Collection of Justin Warsh

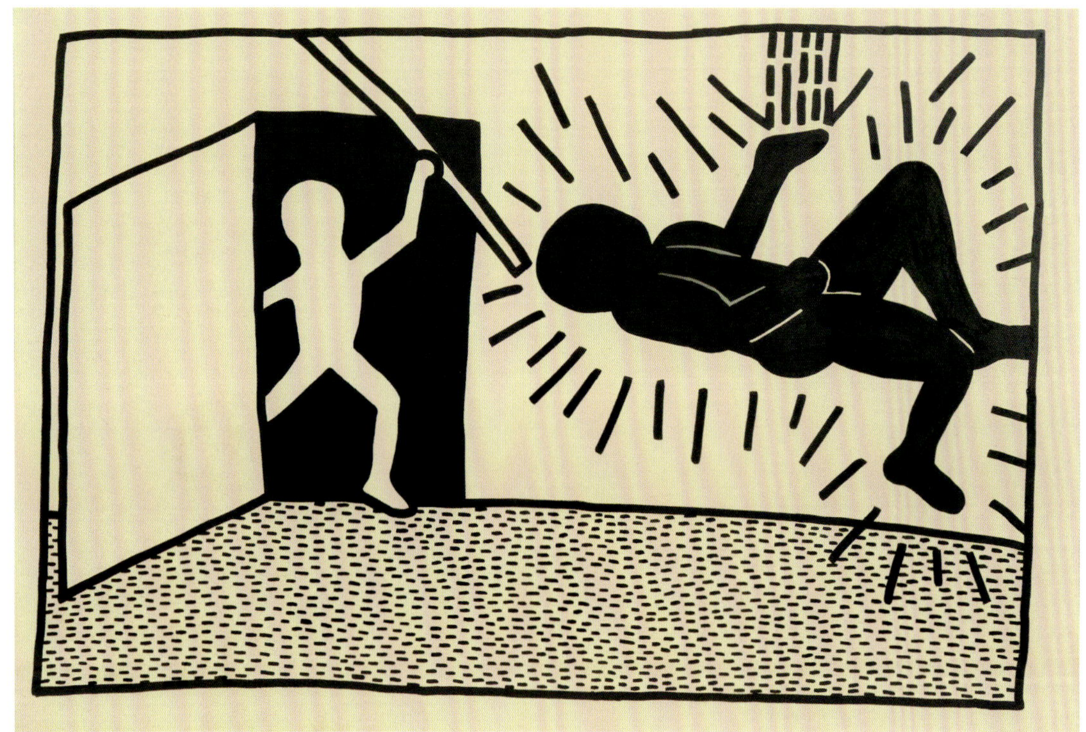

141

Untitled, 1980. Ink on posterboard, 47¼ x 71½ in. (119.9 x 181.6 cm)
Collection of Jose Martos

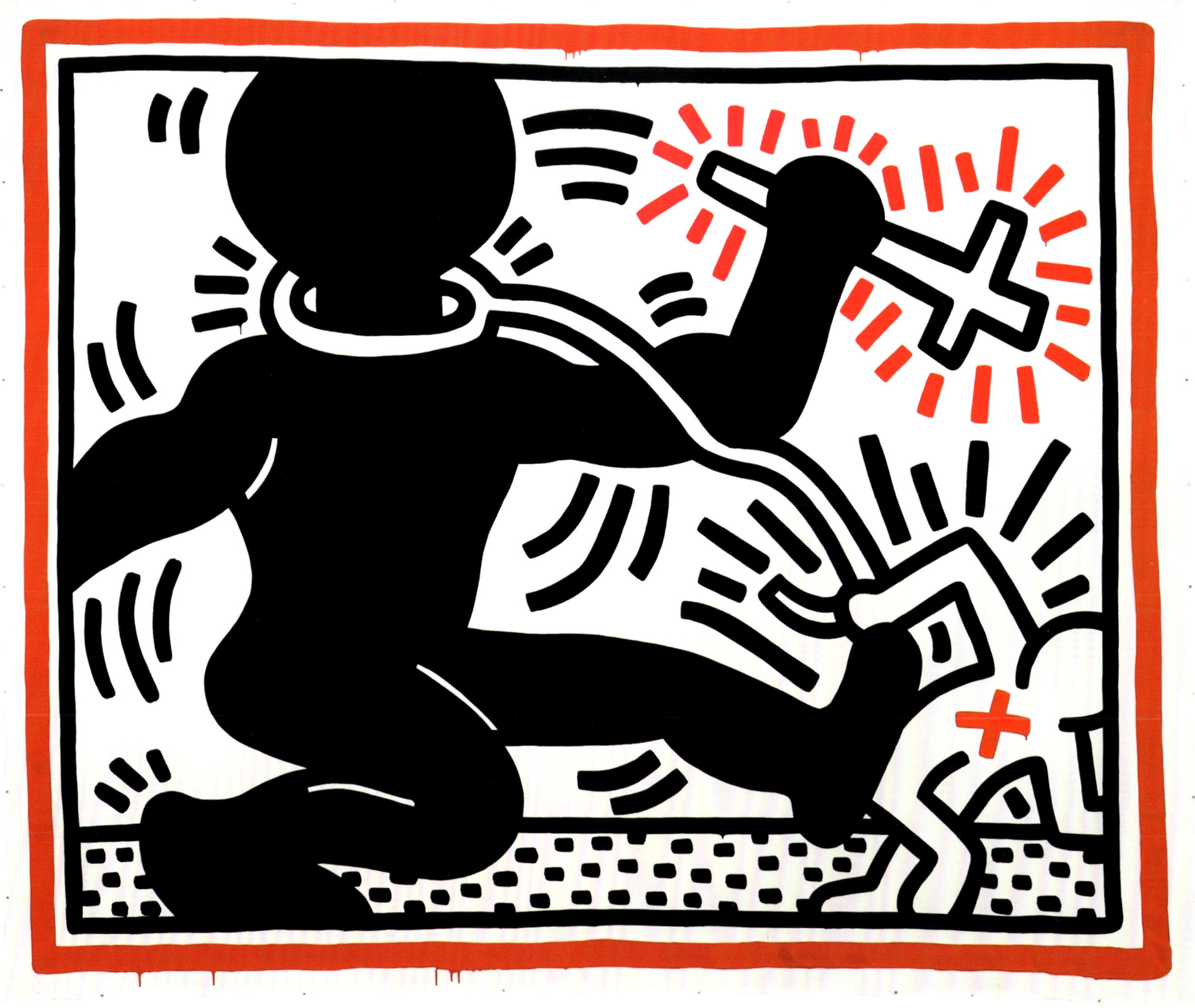

142

Untitled (*Apartheid*), 1984. Acrylic on canvas, 117 3/8 x 143 3/4 in. (298 x 365 cm)
Stedelijk Museum, Amsterdam

143

The Great White Way, November 27, 1988. Acrylic on canvas, 168 x 45 x 4½ in. (426.7 x 114.3 x 11.4 cm)
Collection of the Keith Haring Foundation

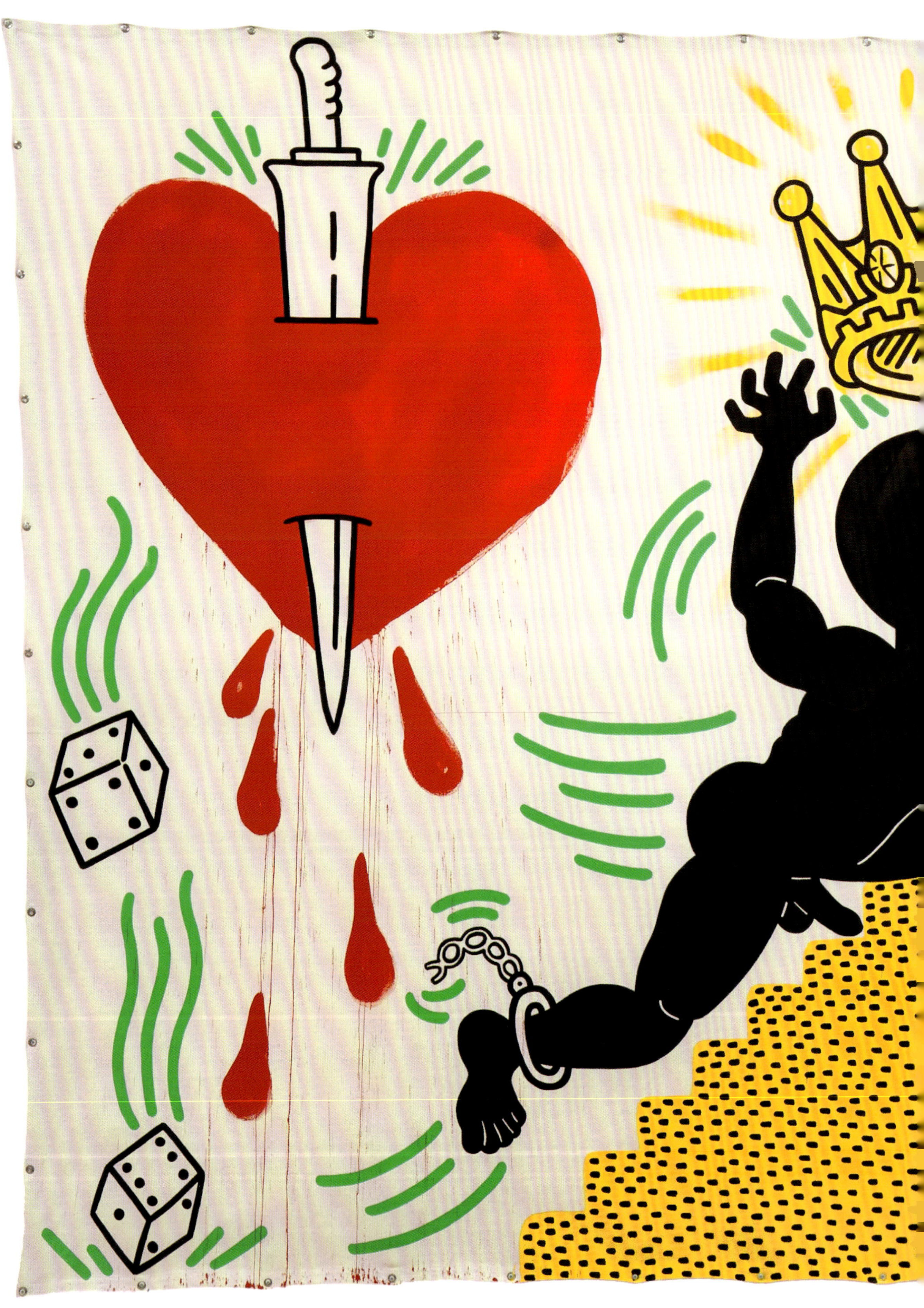

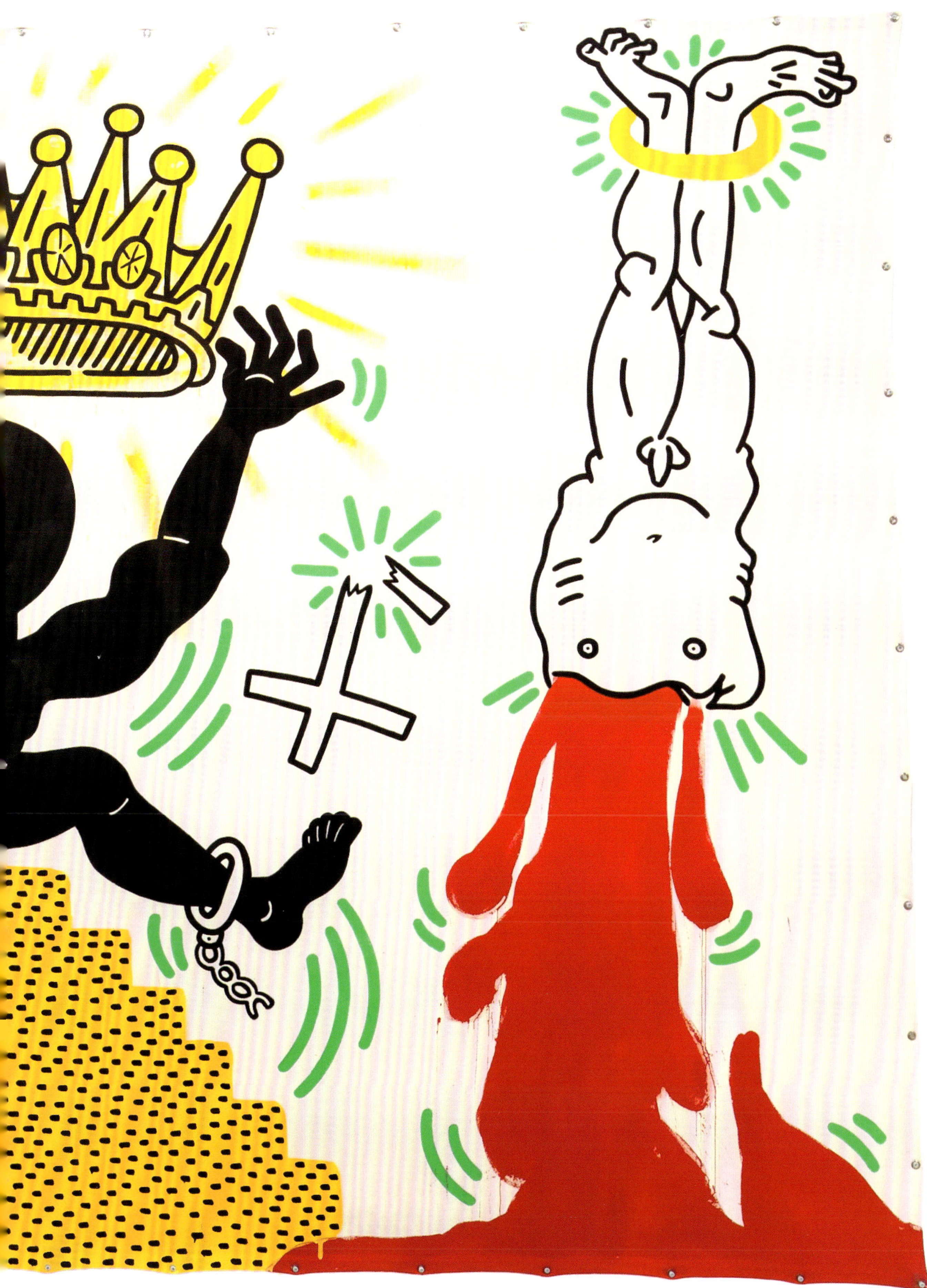

144

Prophets of Rage, 1988. Acrylic on canvas, 120 x 180 in. (304.8 x 457.2 cm)
Collection of the Keith Haring Foundation

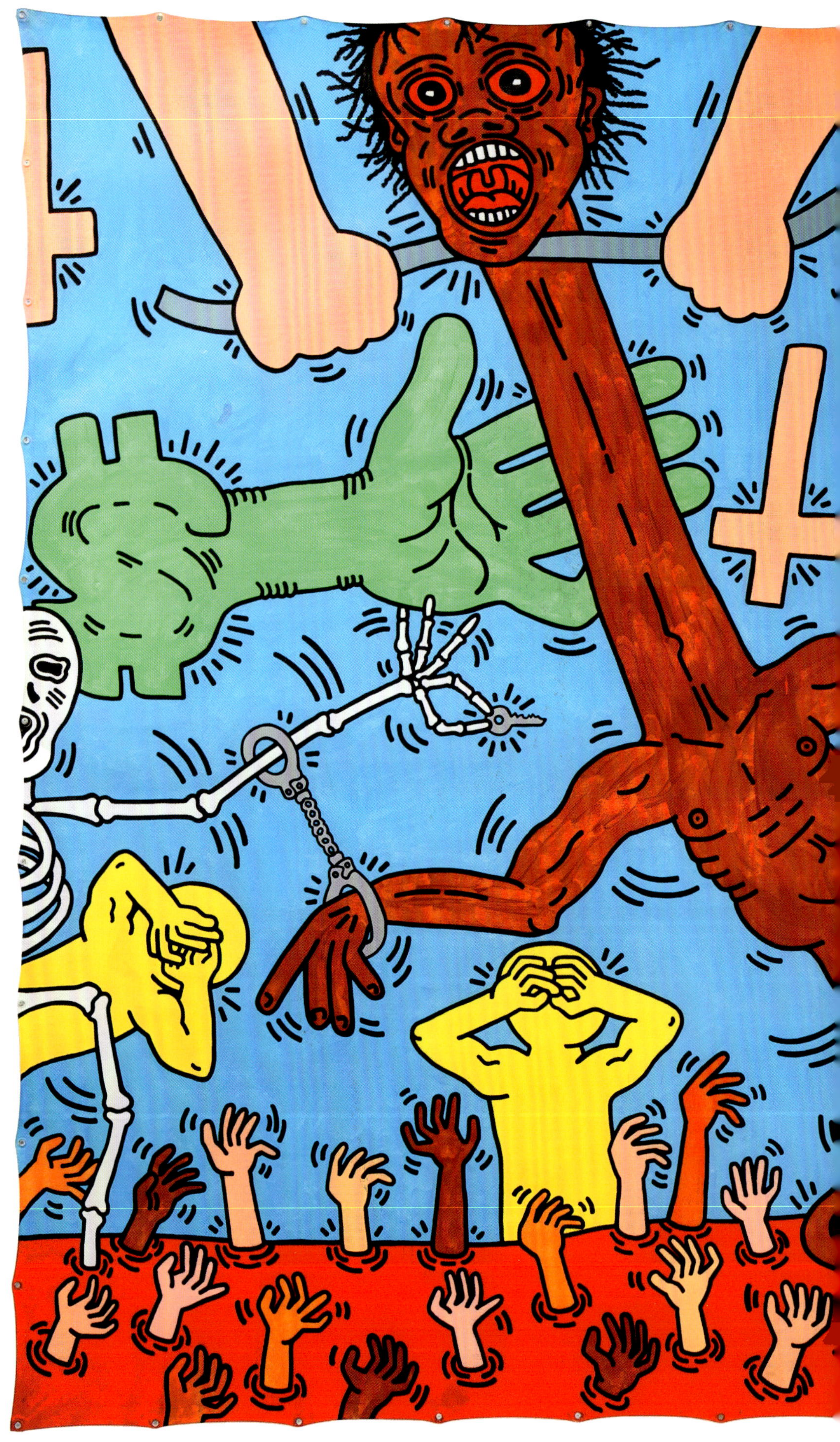

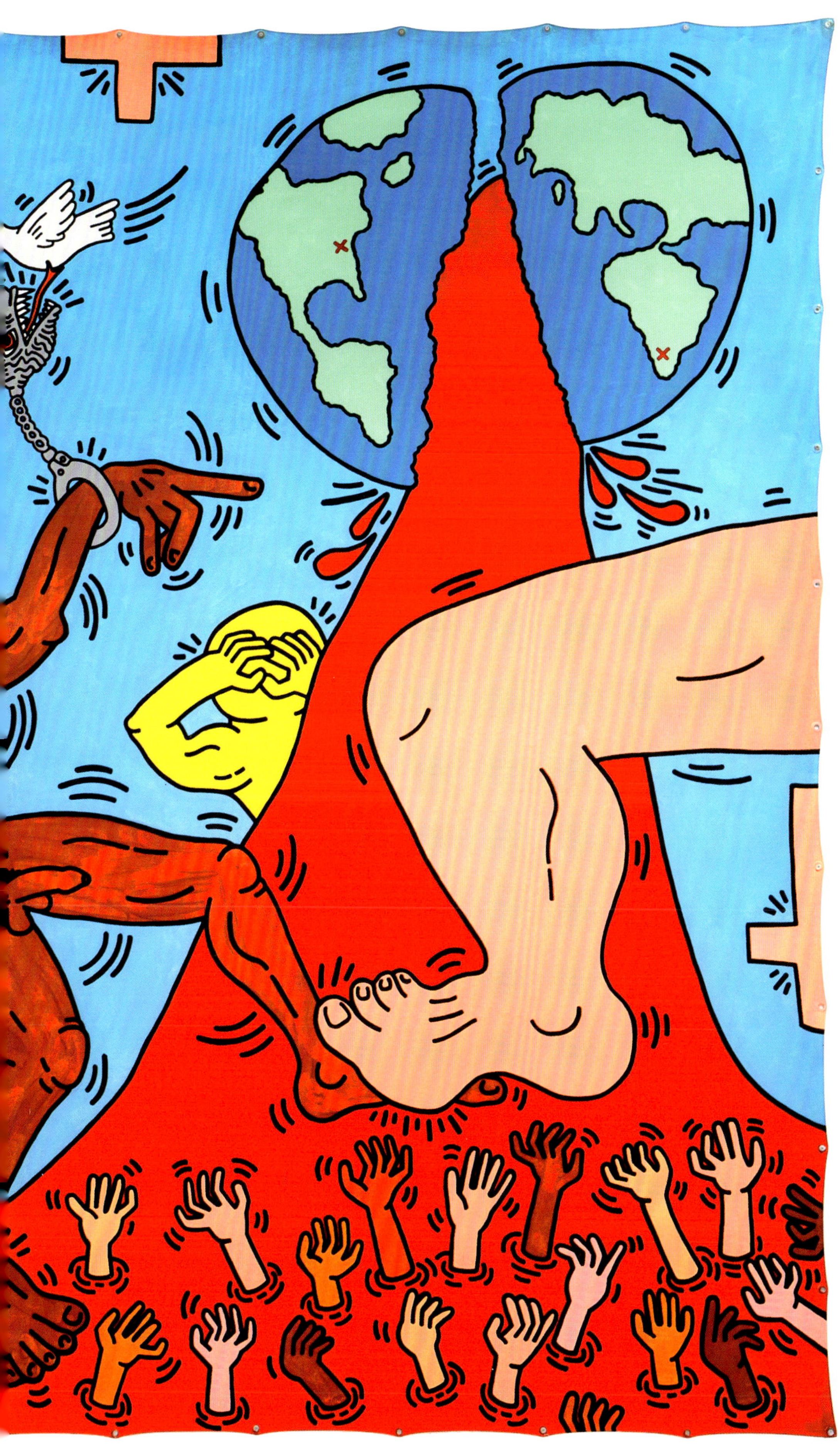

145

Michael Stewart—USA for Africa, 1985. Acrylic and oil on canvas, 116 1/8 x 144 1/2 in. (295 x 367 cm)
Collection Lindemann, Miami Beach

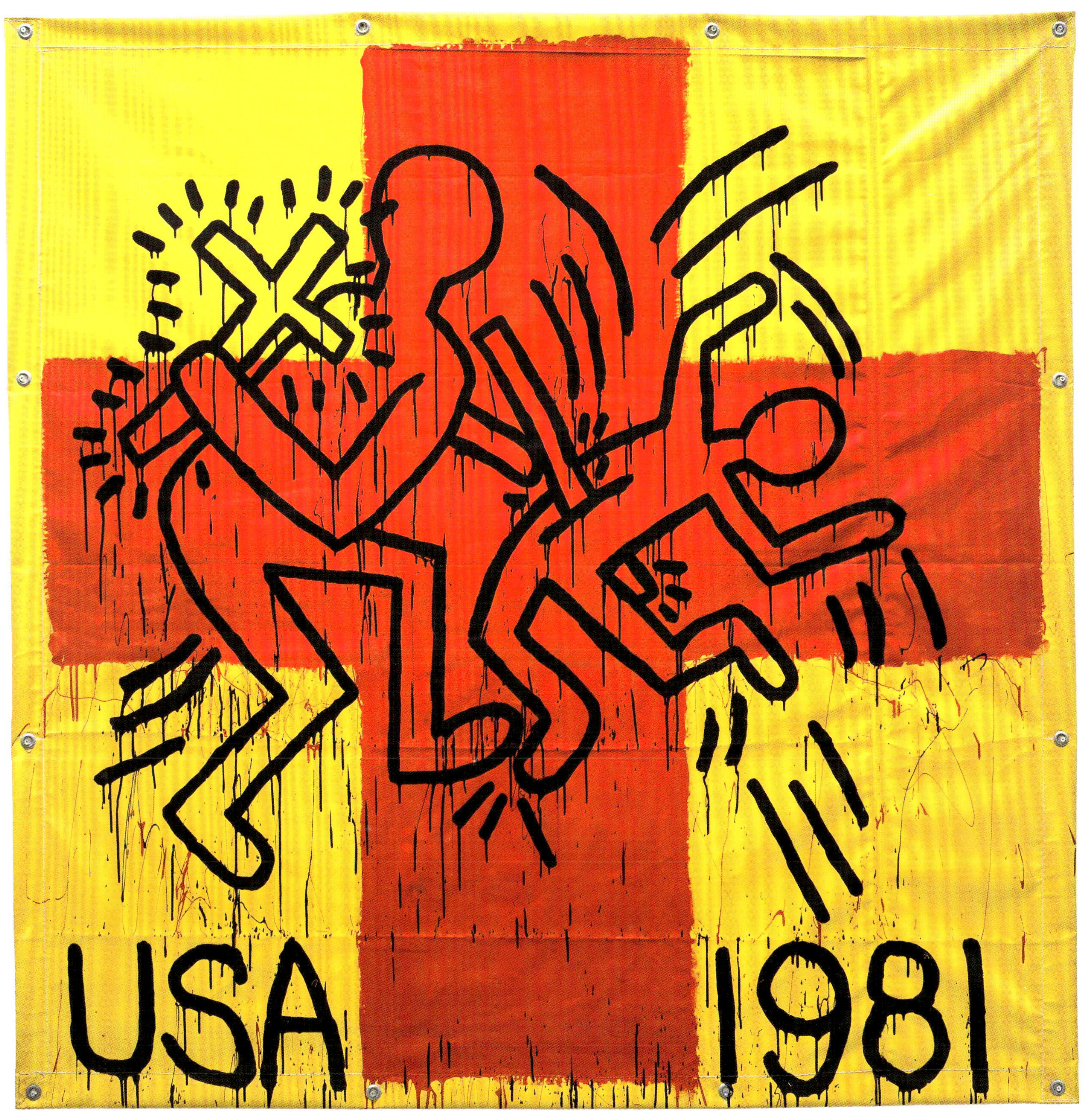

146

Untitled, 1981. Vinyl paint on vinyl tarpaulin, 72 x 72 in. (182.9 x 182.9 cm)
Private collection

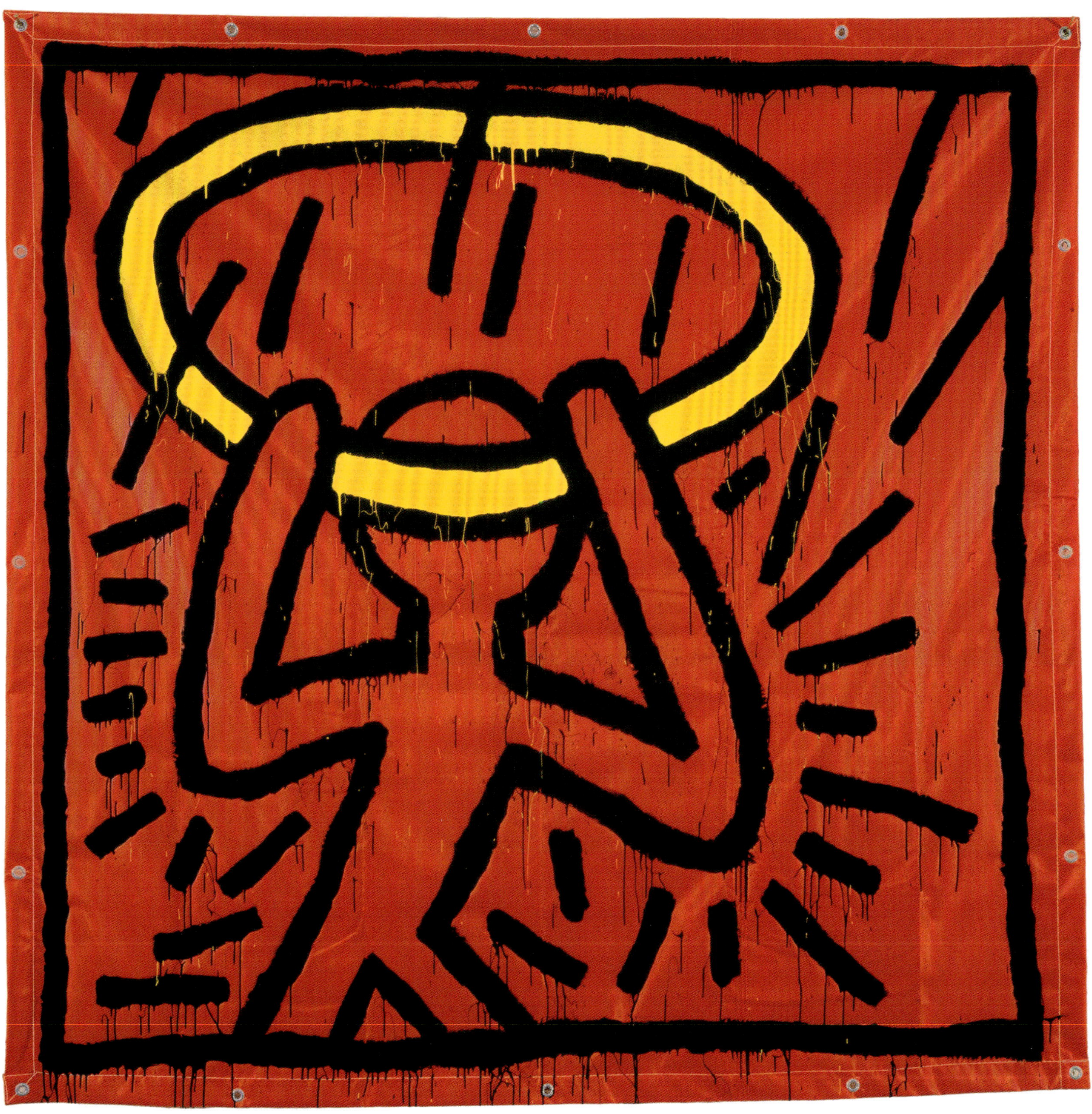

147

Untitled, January 1982. Vinyl paint on vinyl tarpaulin, 84 x 84 in. (213.4 x 213.4 cm)
Private collection

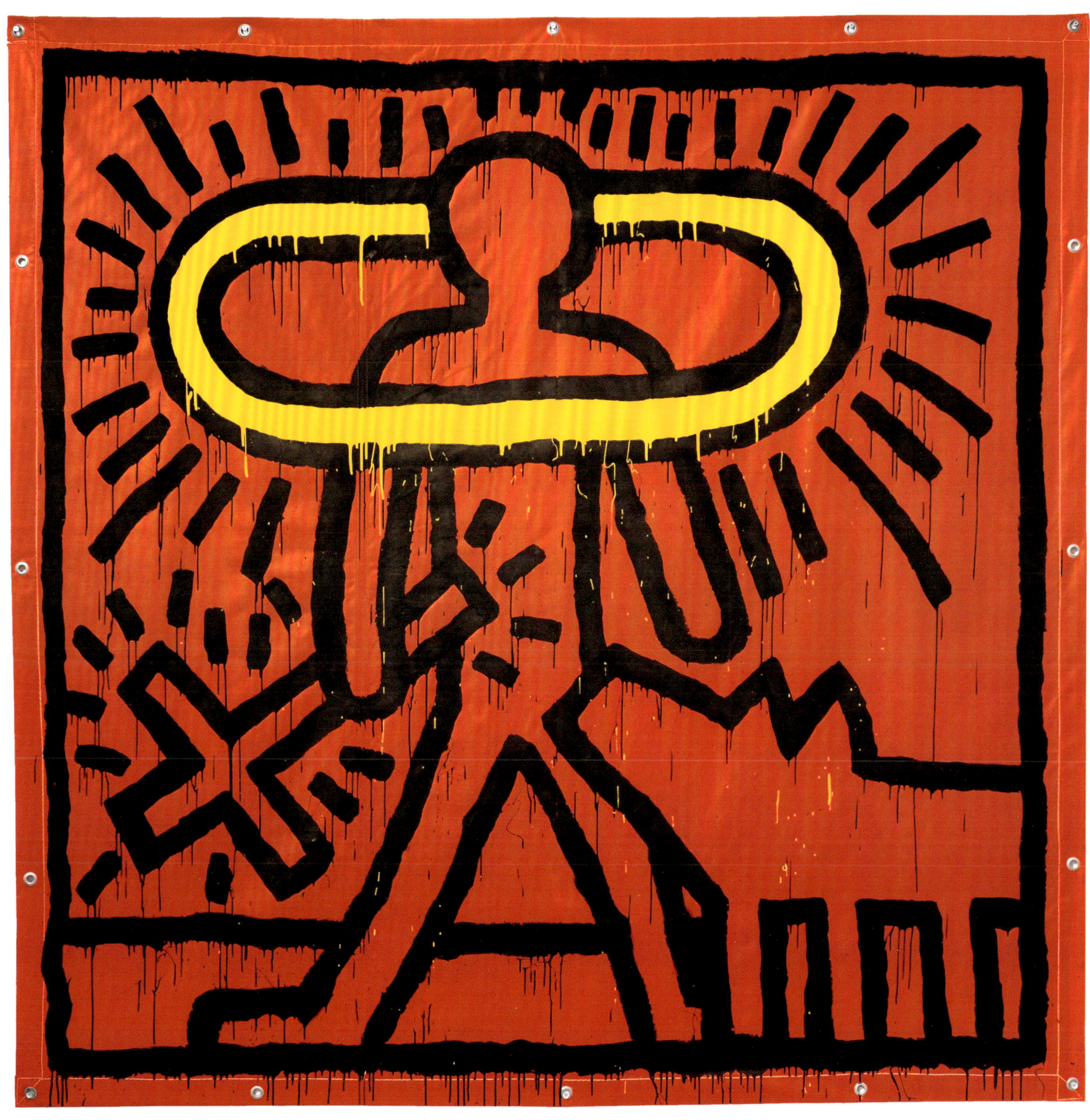

148

Untitled, 1982. Vinyl paint on vinyl tarpaulin, 84 x 84 in. (213.4 x 213.4 cm)
Private collection

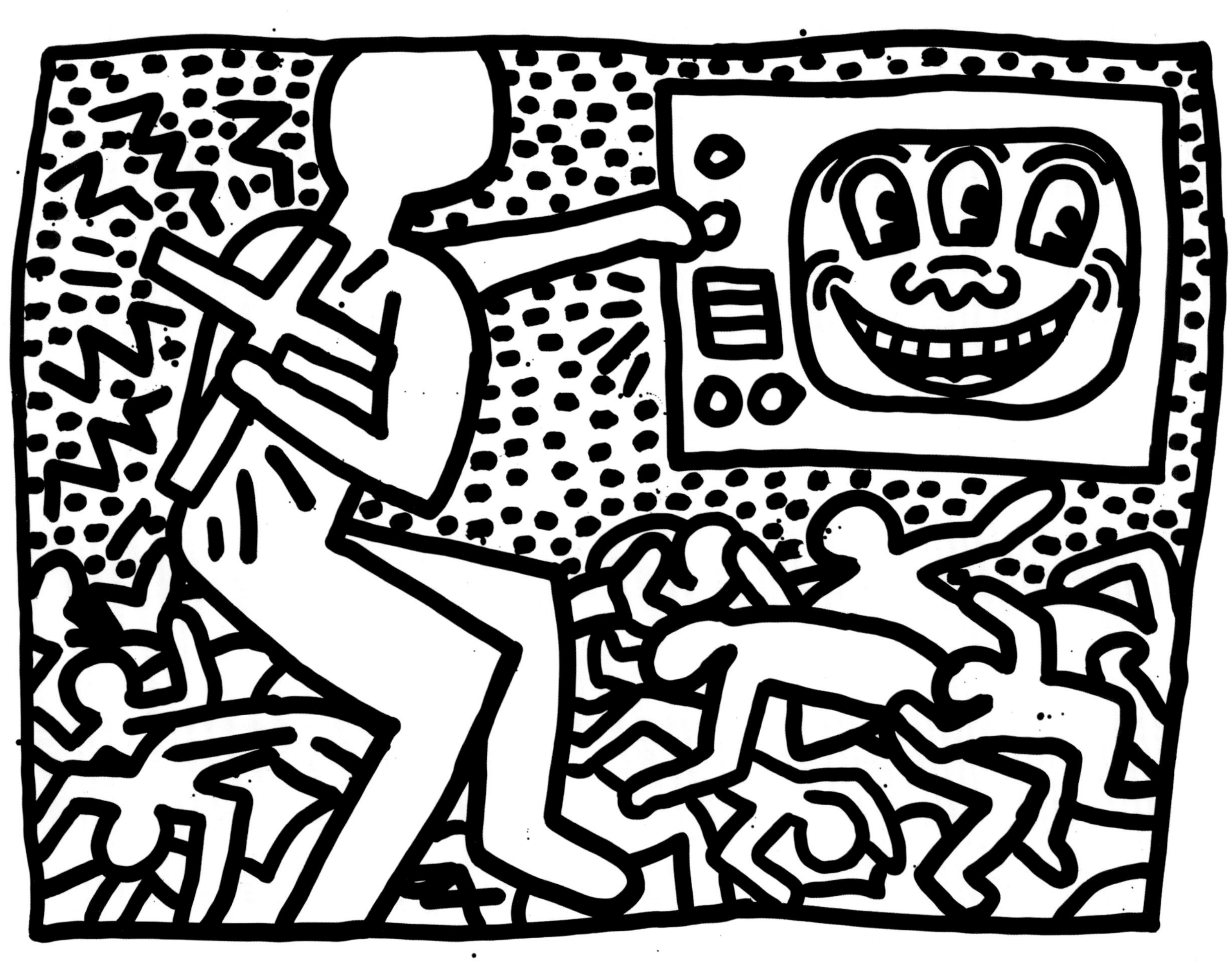

149

Untitled, 1981. Sumi ink on paper, 72 x 96 in. (182.9 x 243.8 cm)
Private collection

150

Three Men Die in Rescue Attempt Six Months after John Lennon's Death, June 15, 1981. Sumi ink and acrylic on paper, 38 1/4 x 50 in. (97 x 127 cm)
Private collection, courtesy Tony Shafrazi Gallery, New York

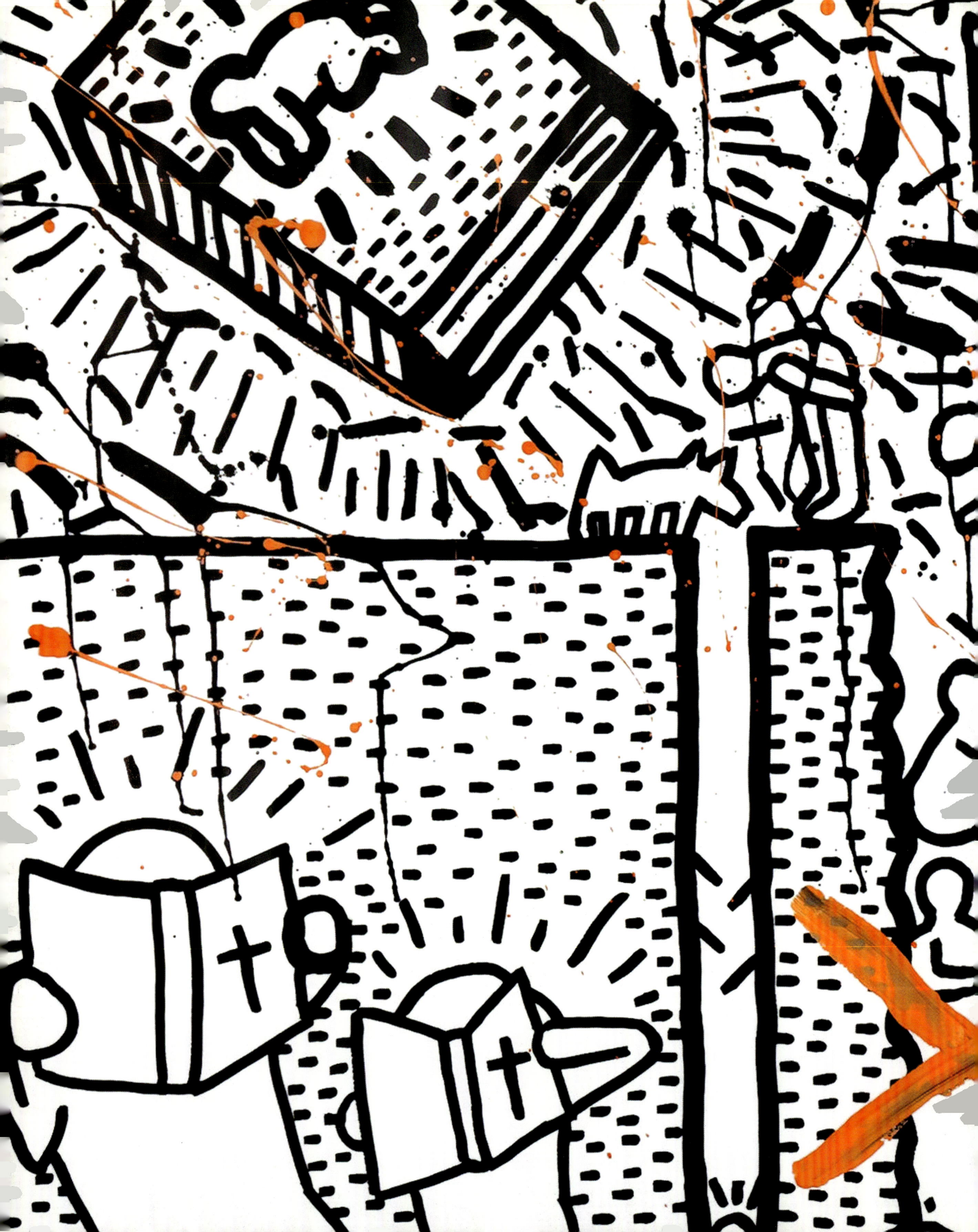

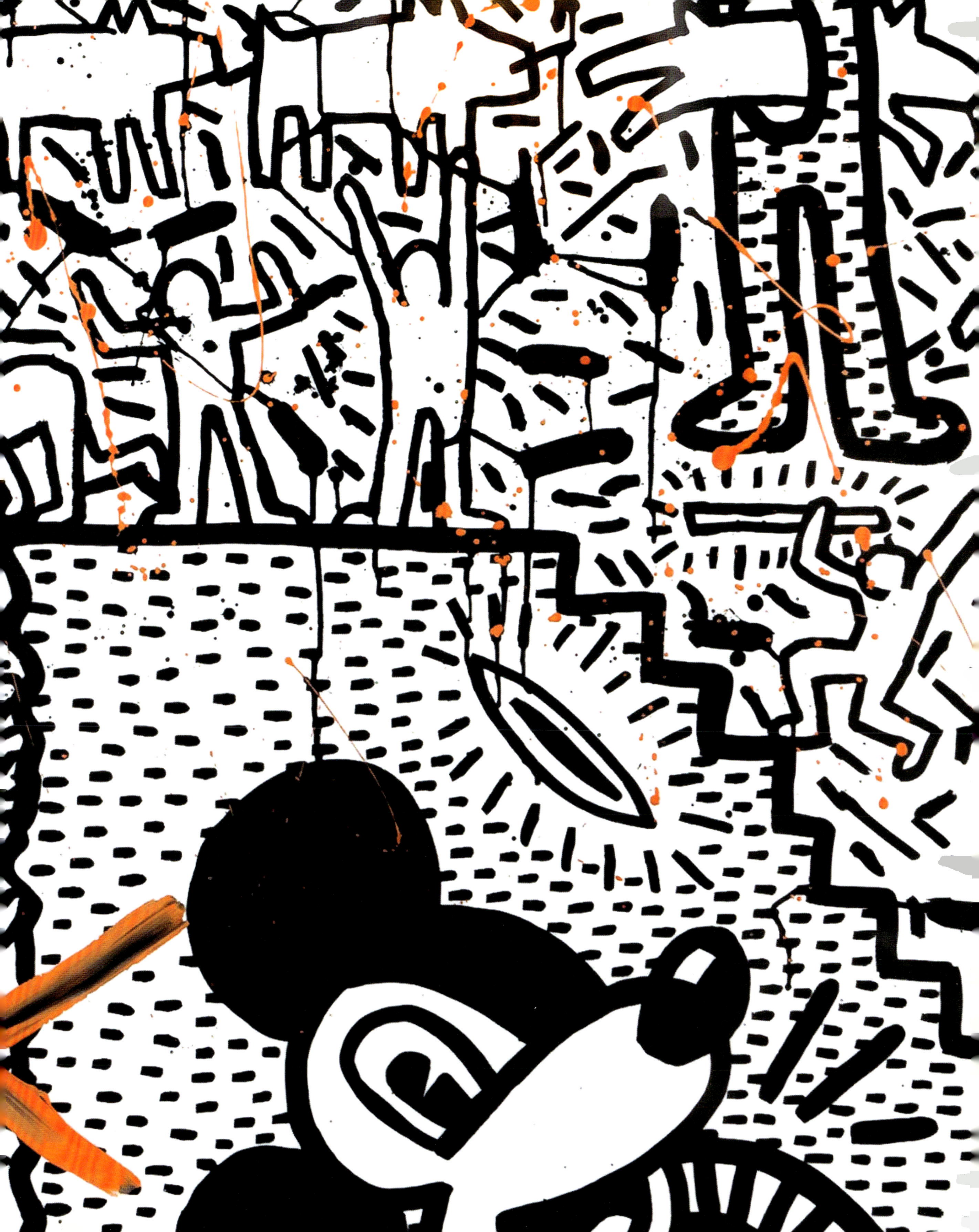

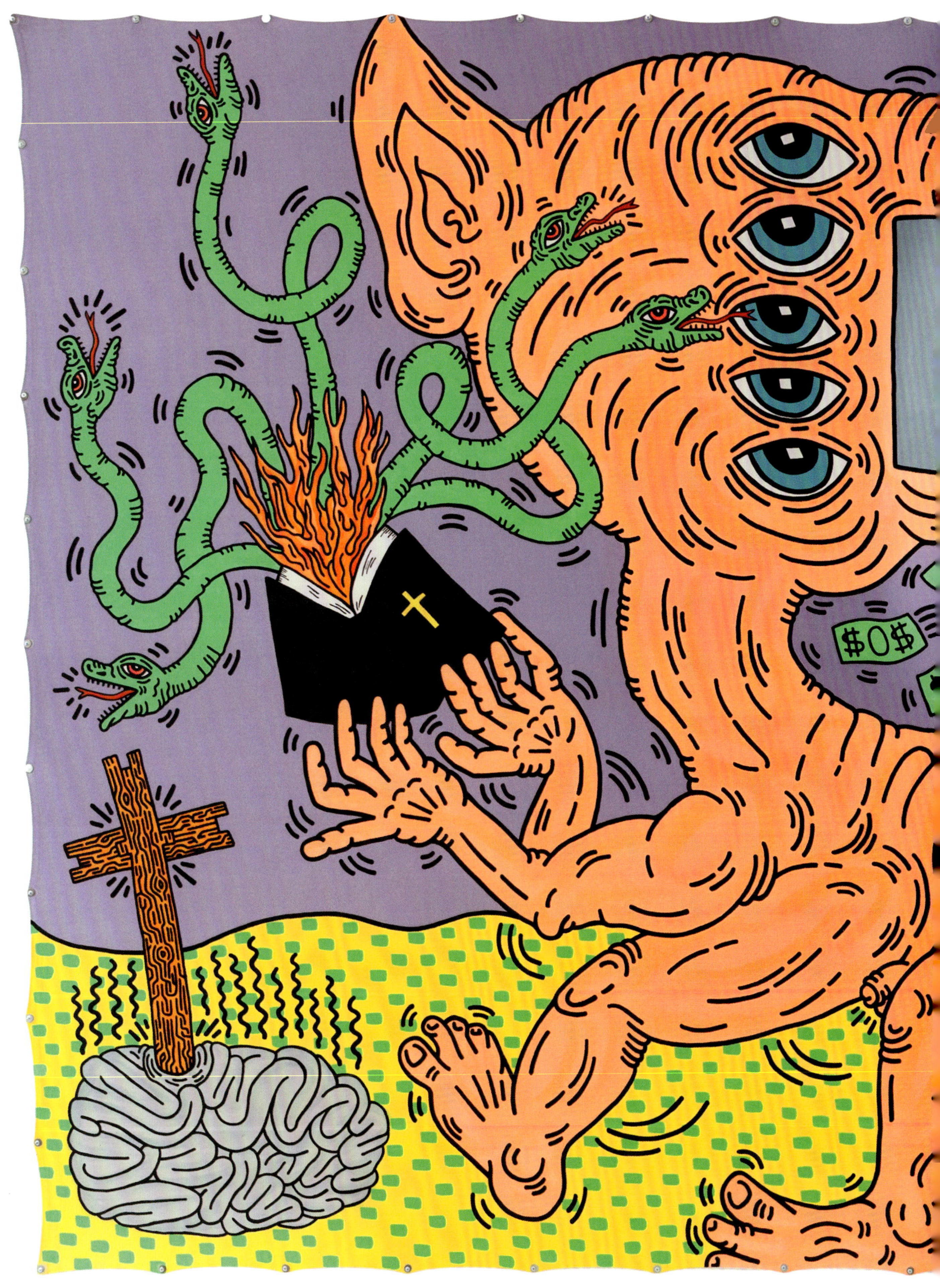
0

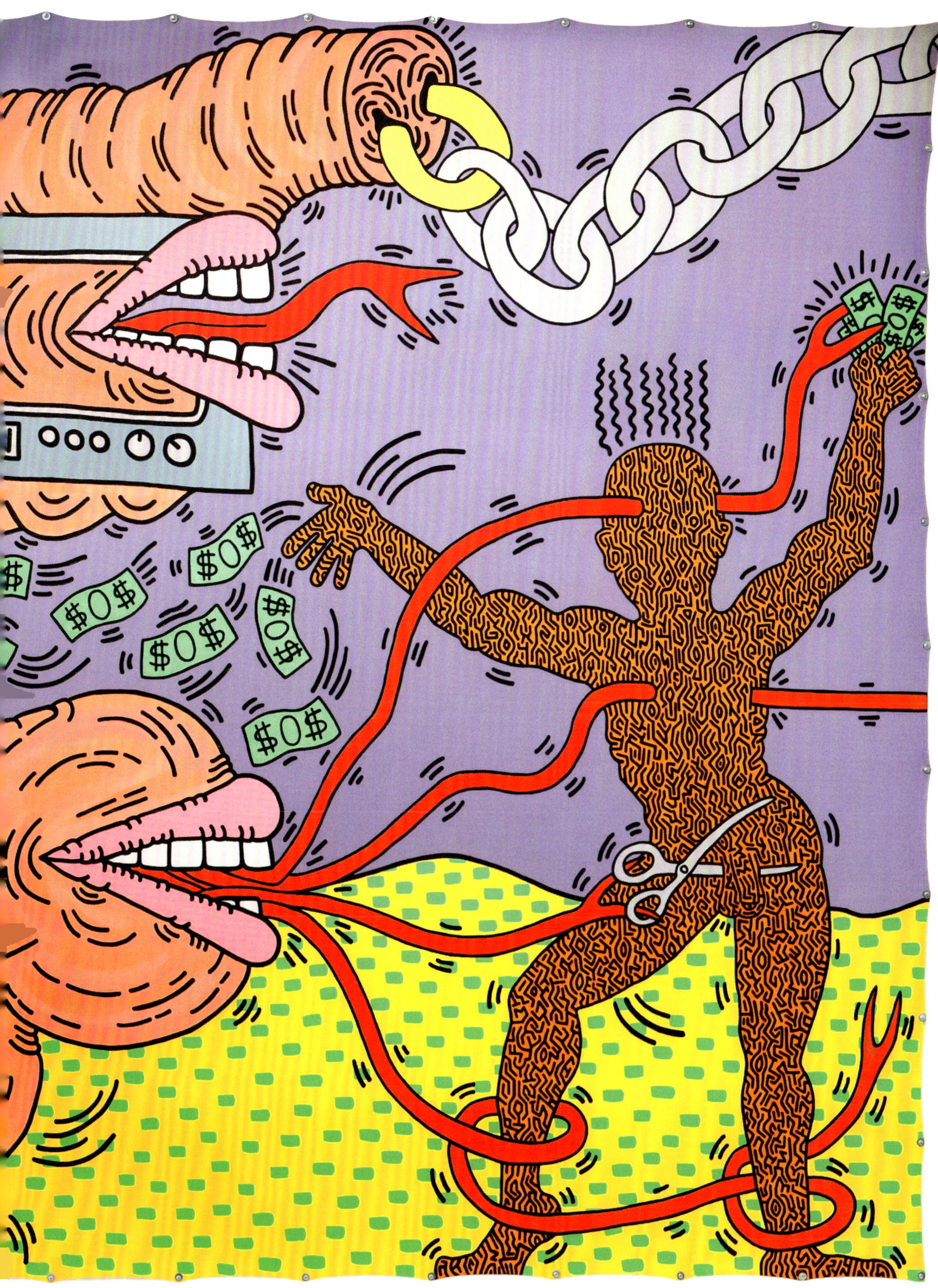

151

Untitled, September 25, 1985. Acrylic and enamel on canvas, 120 x 180 in. (304.8 x 457.2 cm)
Glenstone

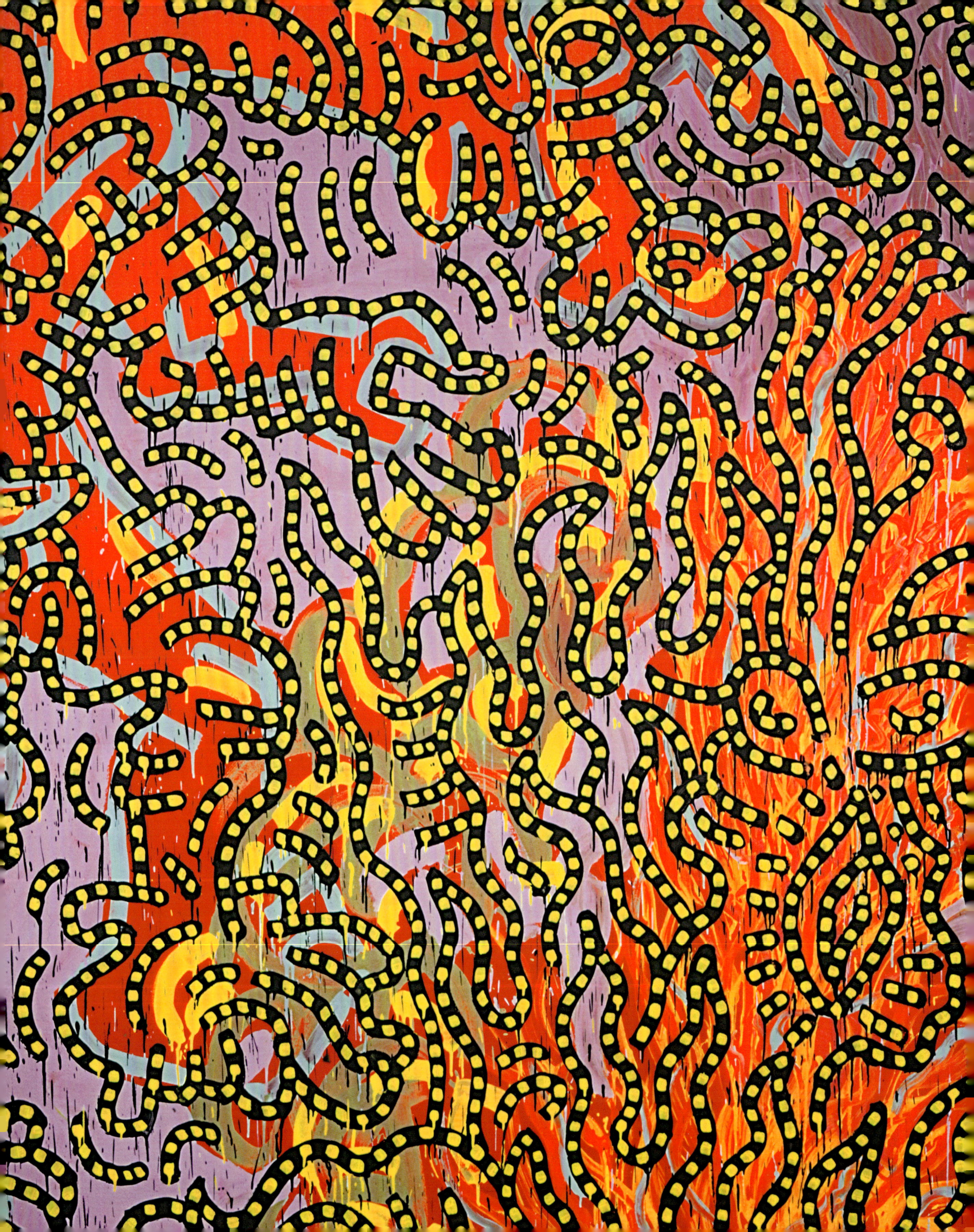

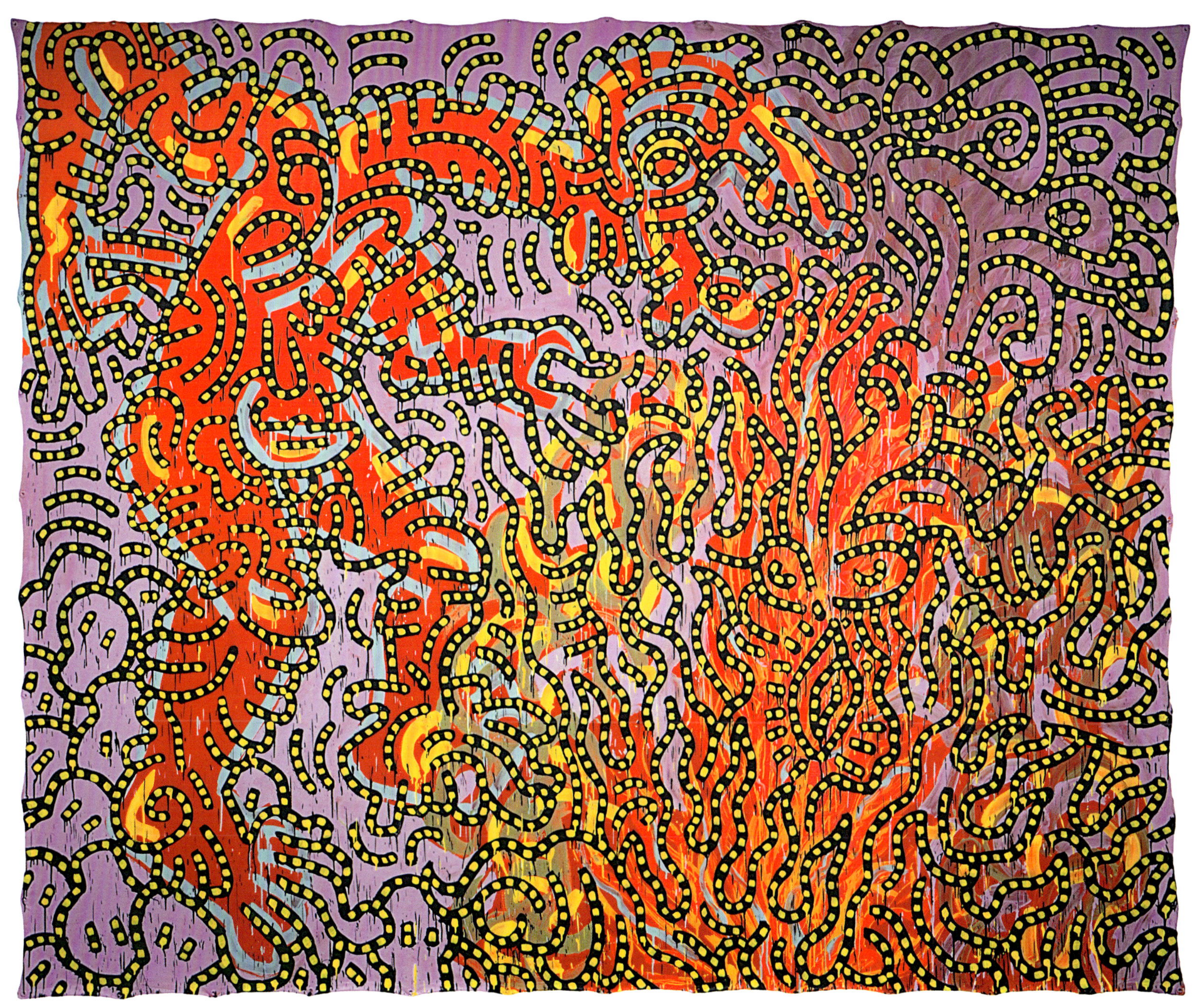

152

Moses and the Burning Bush, 1985. Acrylic and oil on canvas, 120 x 144 in. (304.8 x 365.8 cm)
Courtesy of Gladstone Gallery

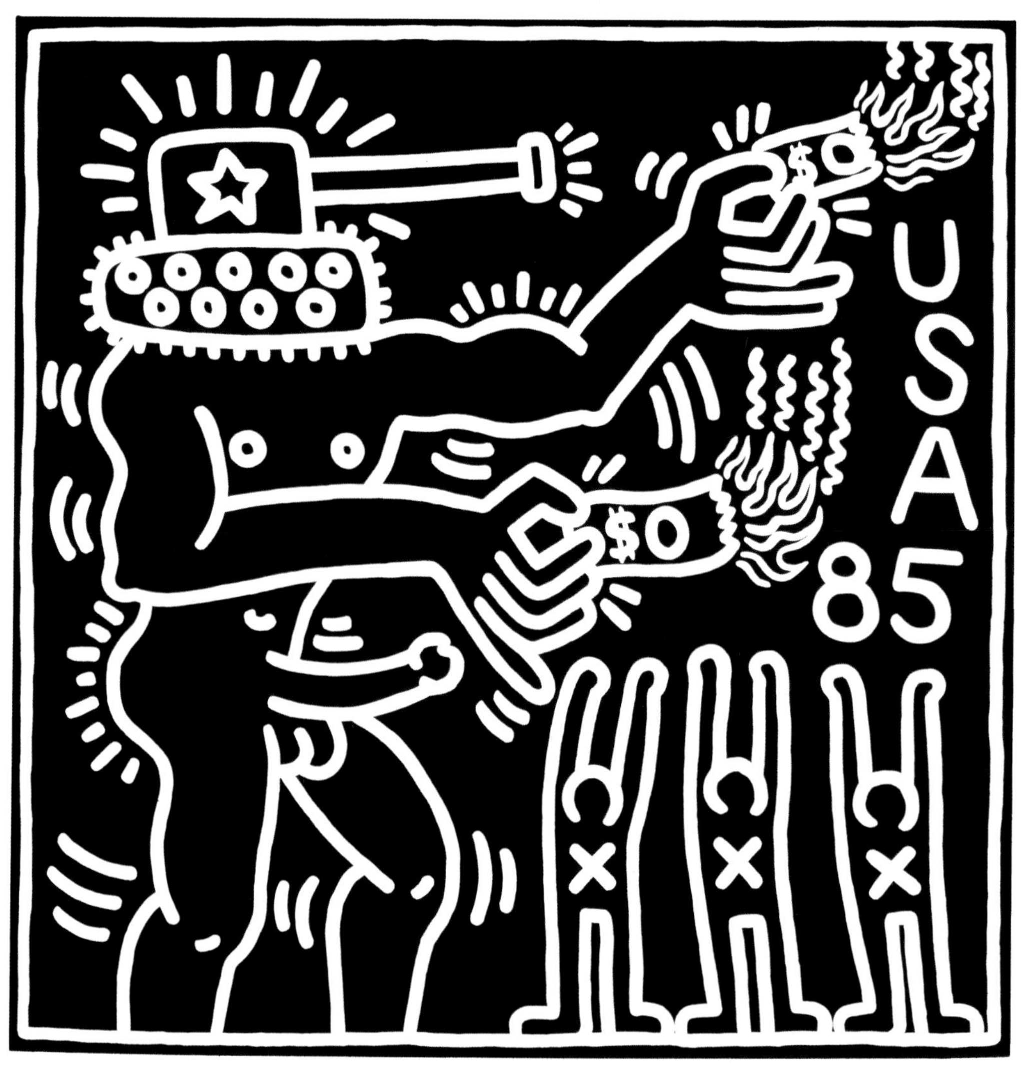

153

Untitled, 1985. Acrylic on canvas, 60 x 60 in. (152.4 x 152.4 cm)
Private collection, courtesy of Gladstone Gallery

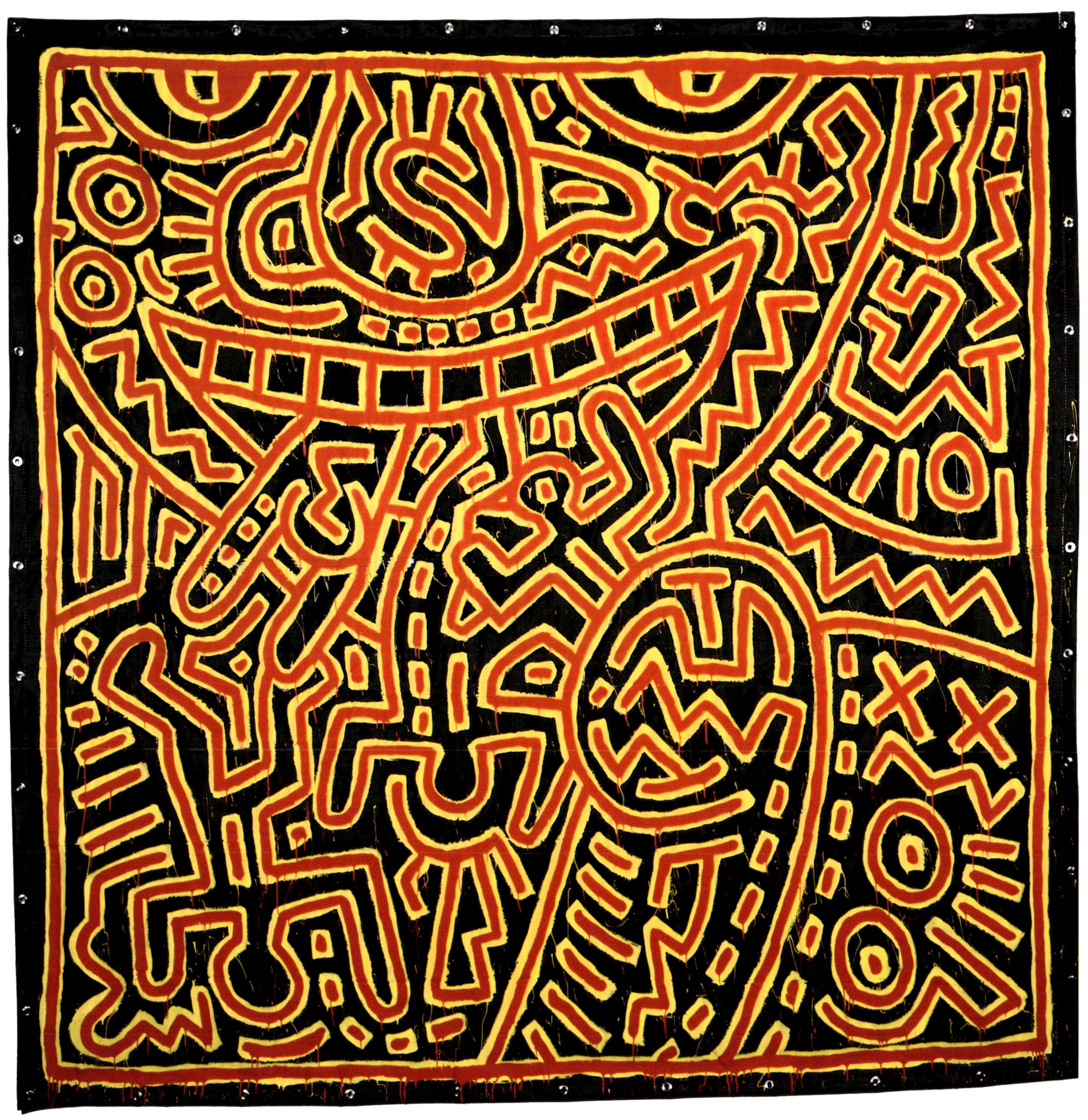

154

Untitled, 1982. Vinyl paint on vinyl tarpaulin, 120 x 120 in. (304.8 x 304.8 cm)
Private collection, courtesy Tony Shafrazi Gallery, New York

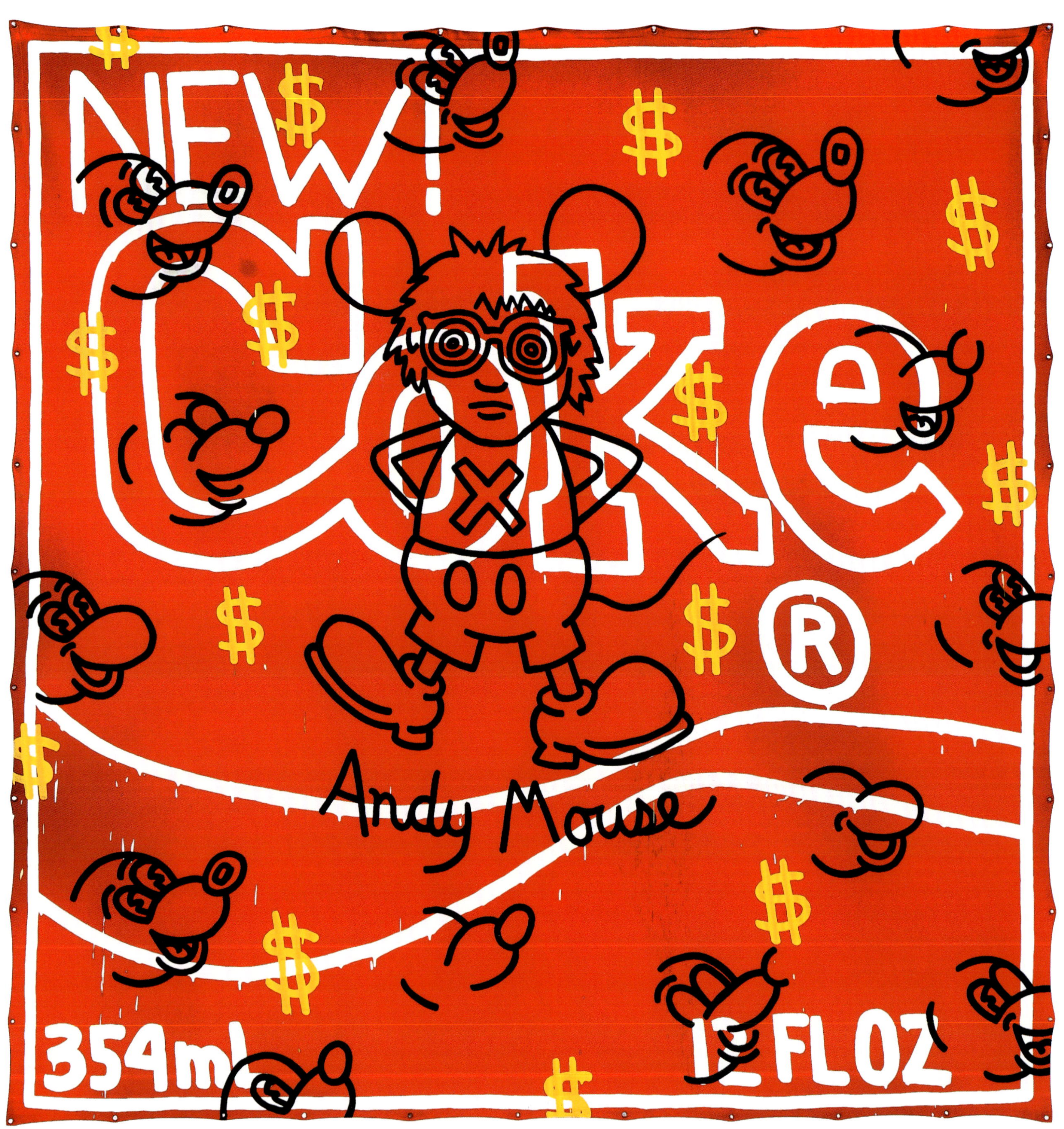

155

Andy Mouse—New Coke, 1985. Acrylic on canvas, 119 1/2 x 116 3/4 in. (303.5 x 296.5 cm)
Private collection, courtesy of Galerie Gmurzynska, Zurich

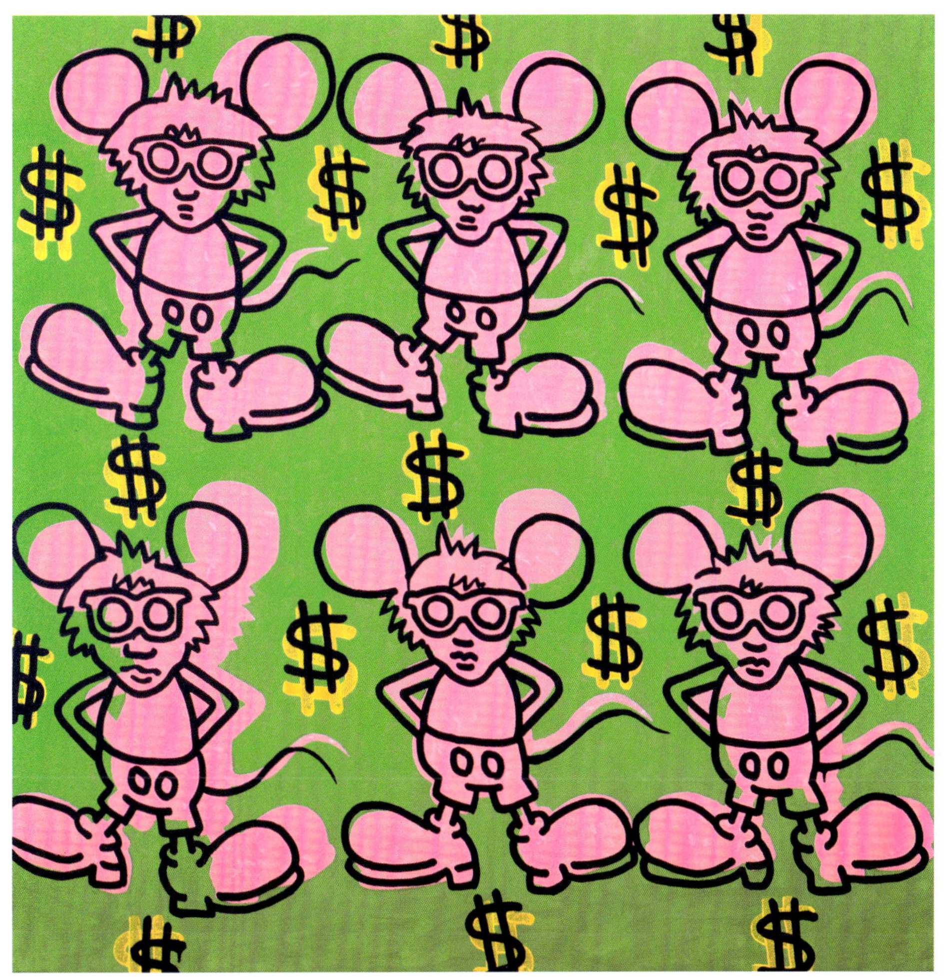

156

Andy Mouse, 1985. Acrylic and oil on canvas, 60 x 60 in. (152.4 x 152.4 cm)
Private collection

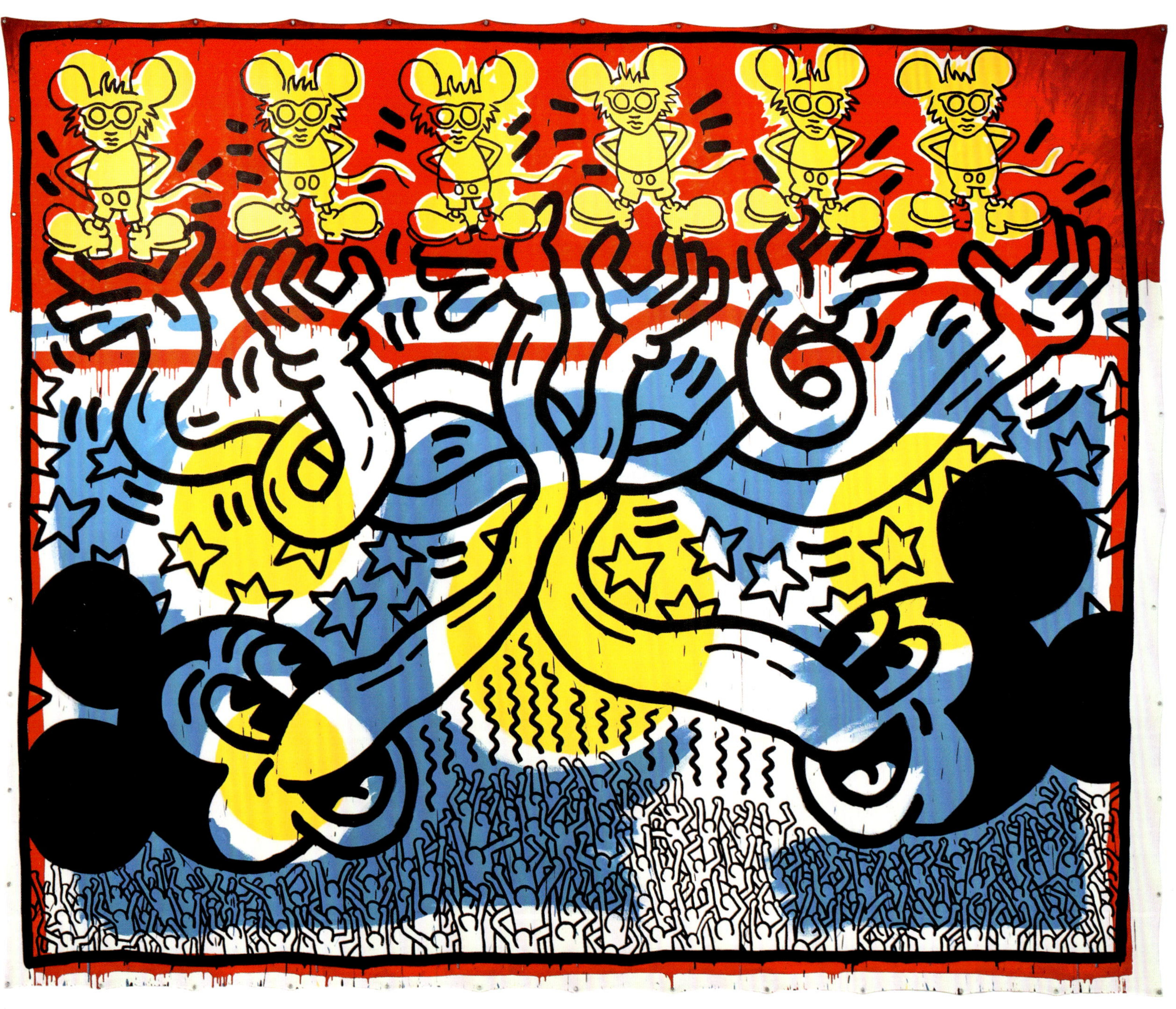

157

Untitled, 1985. Acrylic and oil on canvas, 120 x 144 in. (304.8 x 365.8 cm)
Private collection

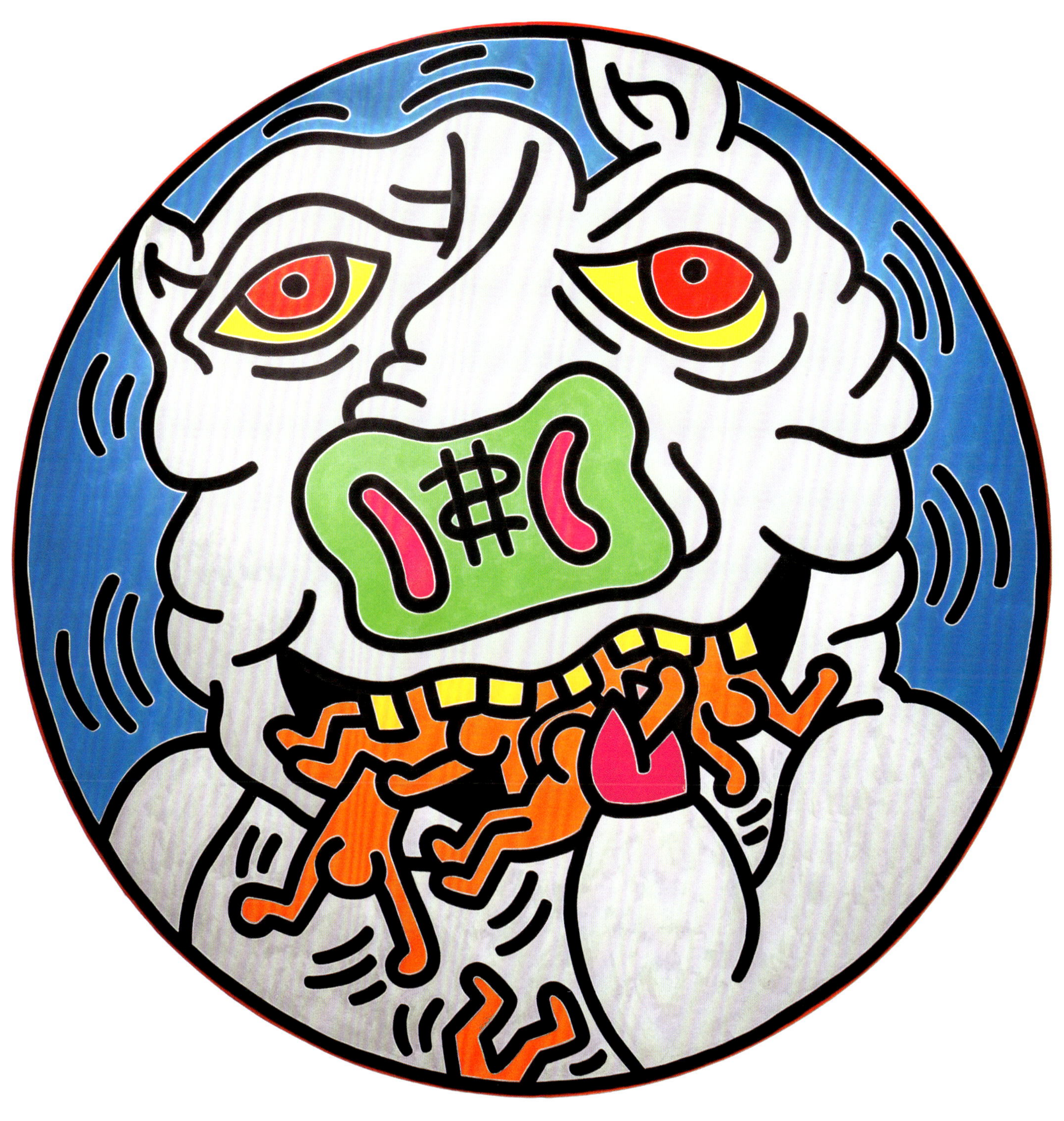

158

Untitled, 1988. Acrylic on canvas, 120 in. diam. (304.8 cm diam.)
Collection of the Keith Haring Foundation

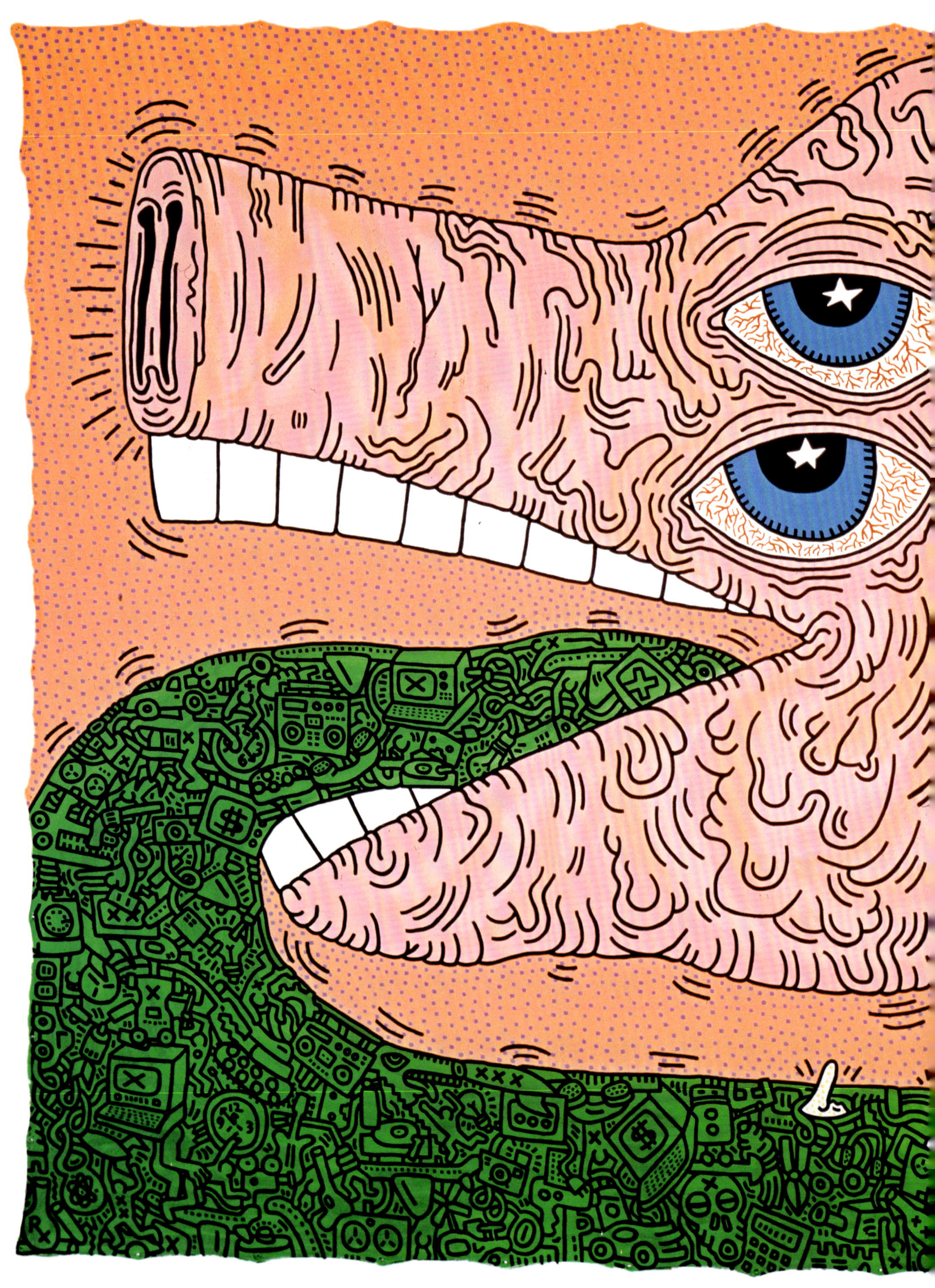

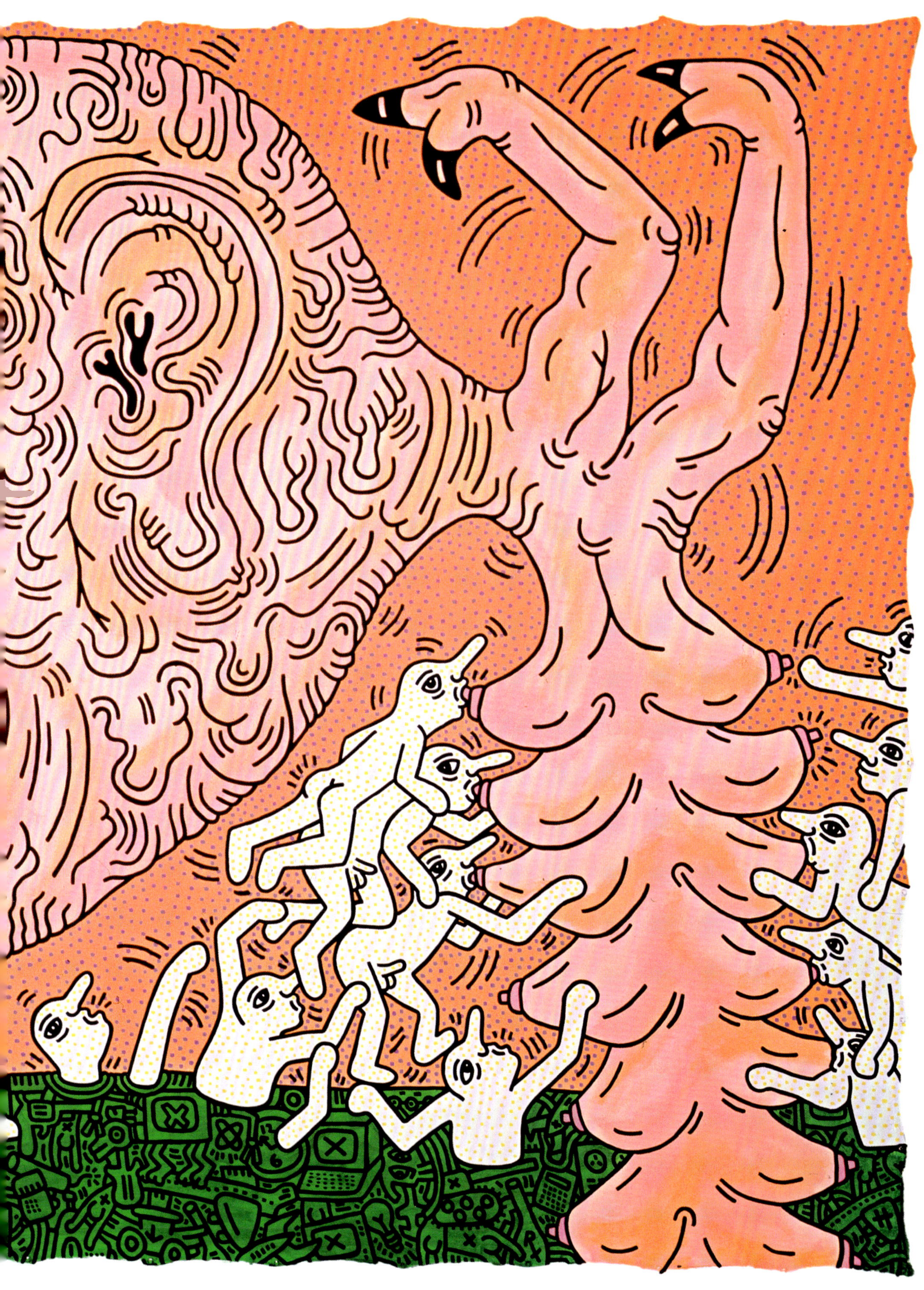

159

Untitled, 1984. Acrylic and enamel on canvas, 120 x 180 in. (304.8 x 457.2 cm)
The Broad Art Foundation, Santa Monica

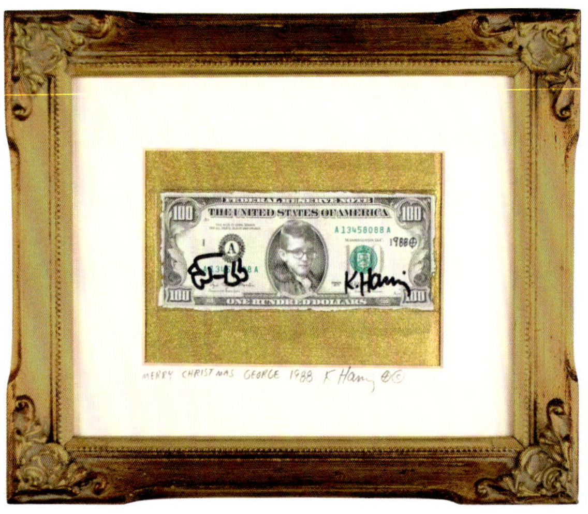

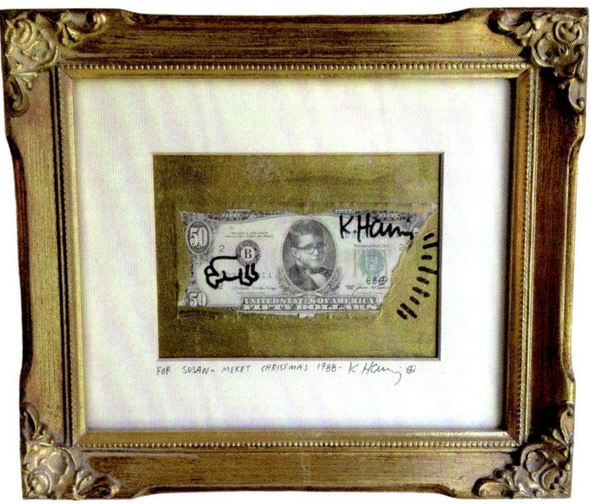

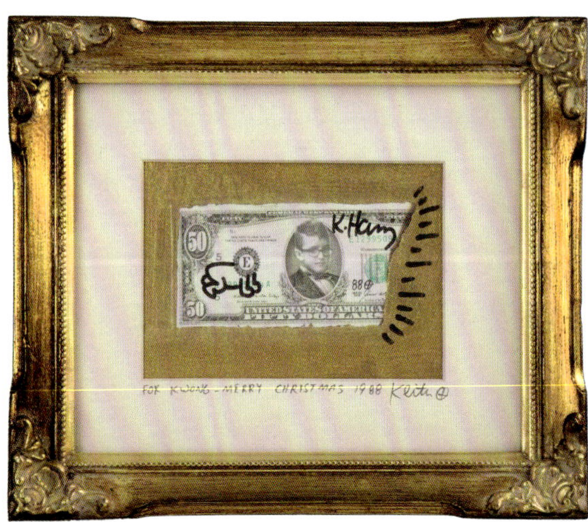

160–162

Untitled, 1988. Marker and paper collage on framed $100 bill, 10 3/8 x 12 5/8 in. (26.5 x 32 cm)
Private collection, courtesy Tony Shafrazi Gallery, New York

Untitled, 1988. Marker and paper collage on framed $50 bill, 10 3/8 x 12 5/8 in. (26.5 x 32 cm)
Private collection, courtesy Tony Shafrazi Gallery, New York

Untitled, 1988. Marker and paper collage on framed $50 bill, 10 3/8 x 12 5/8 in. (26.5 x 32 cm)
Private collection

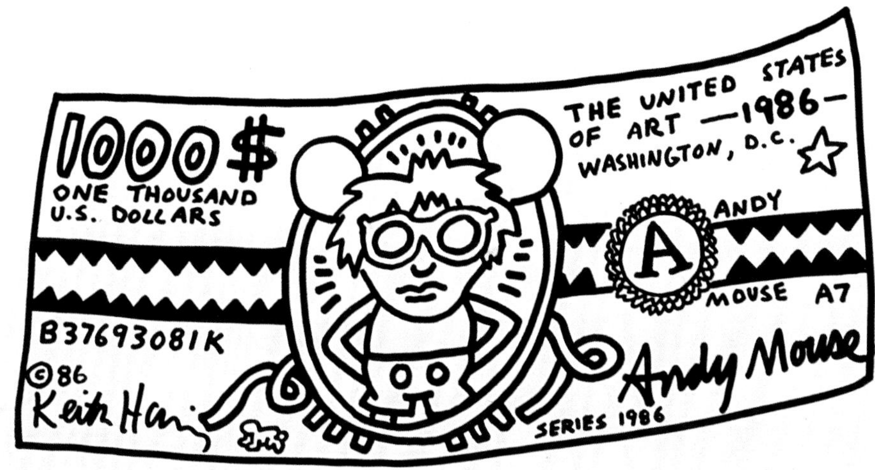

163

Money Magazine Andy Mouse Bill, September 15, 1986. Felt-tip pen on paper, 11 x 14 in. (28 x 35.6 cm)
Collection of the Keith Haring Foundation

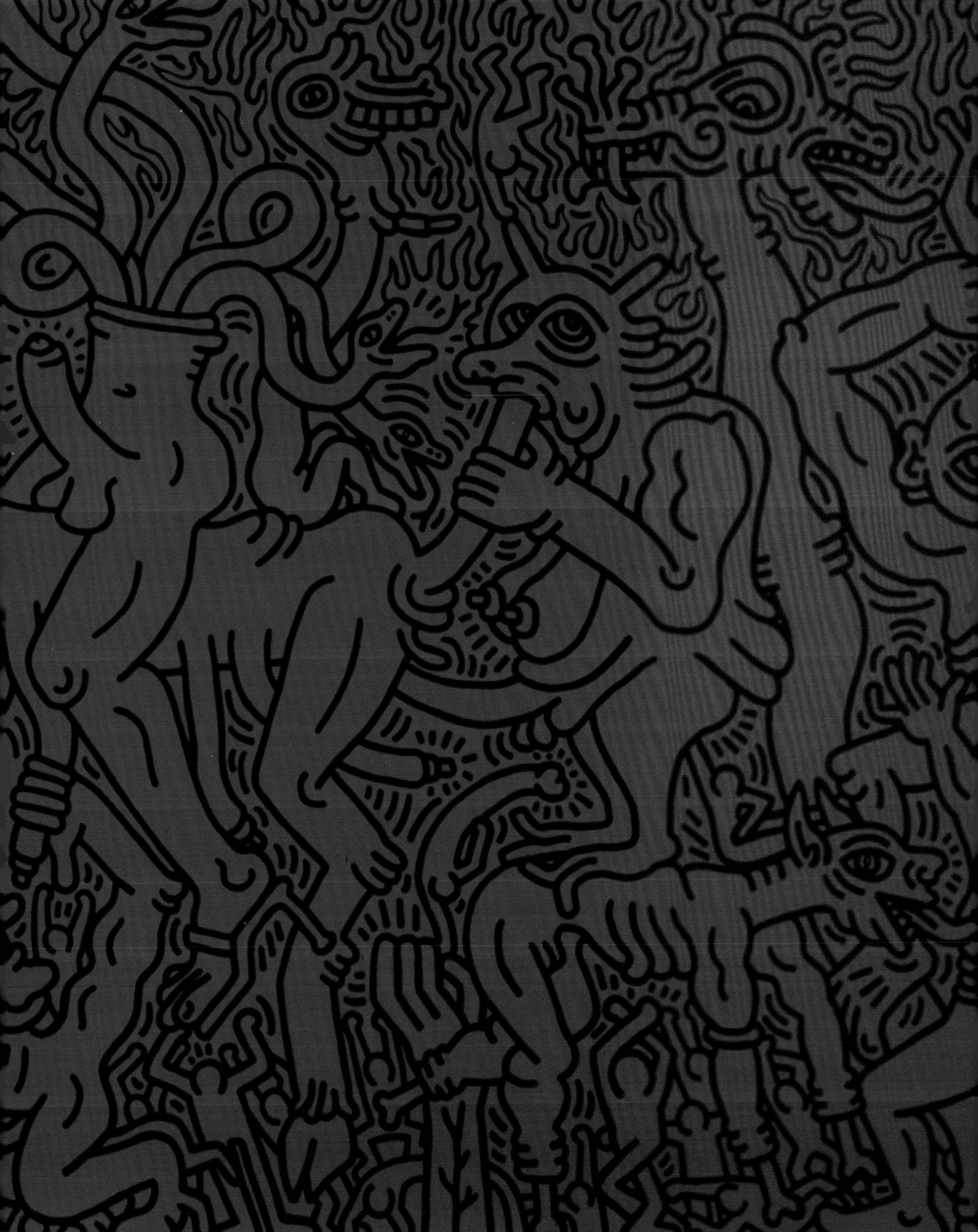

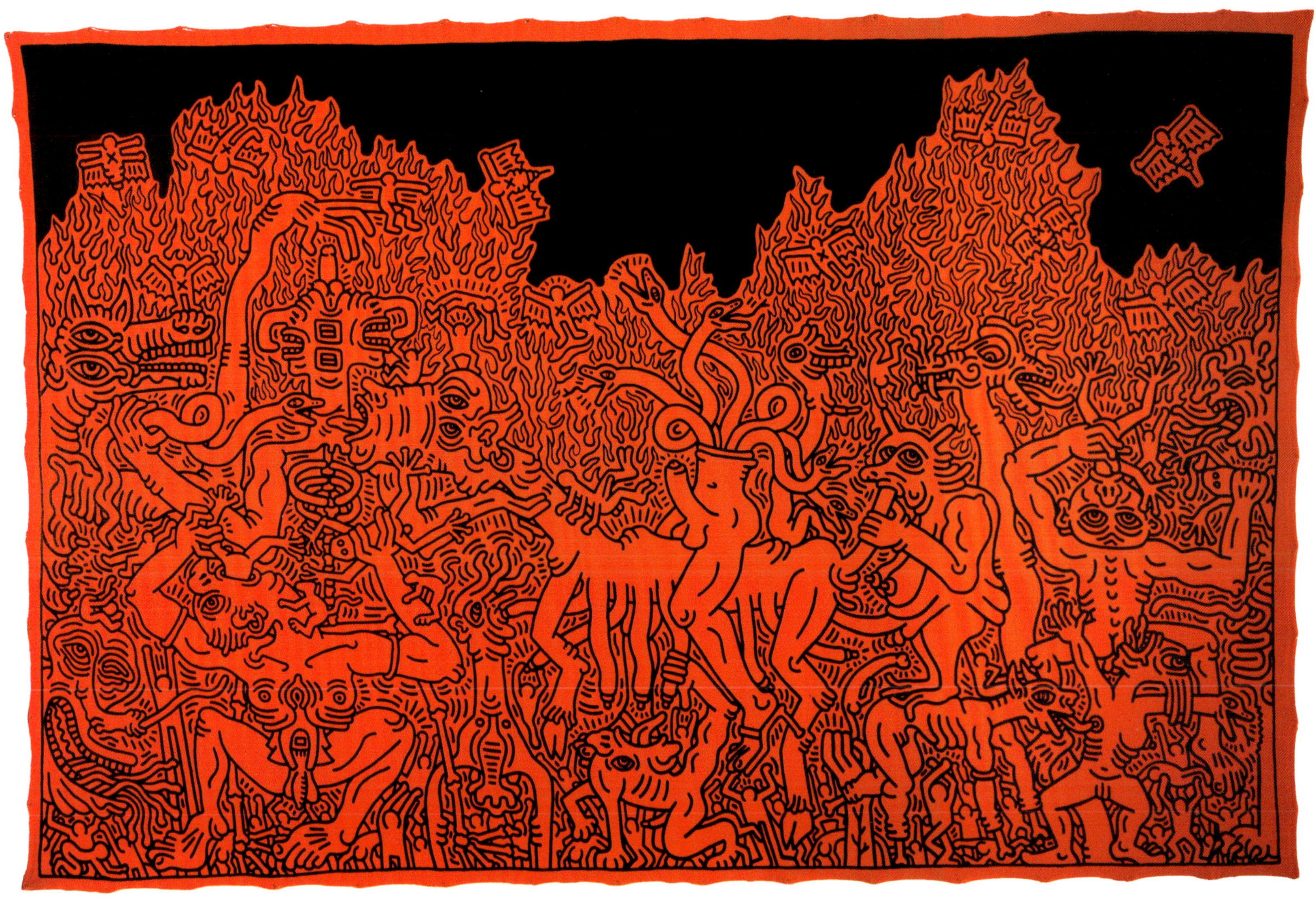

164

Untitled, 1985. Acrylic and oil on canvas, 120 x 180 in. (304.8 x 457.2 cm)
Sender Collection

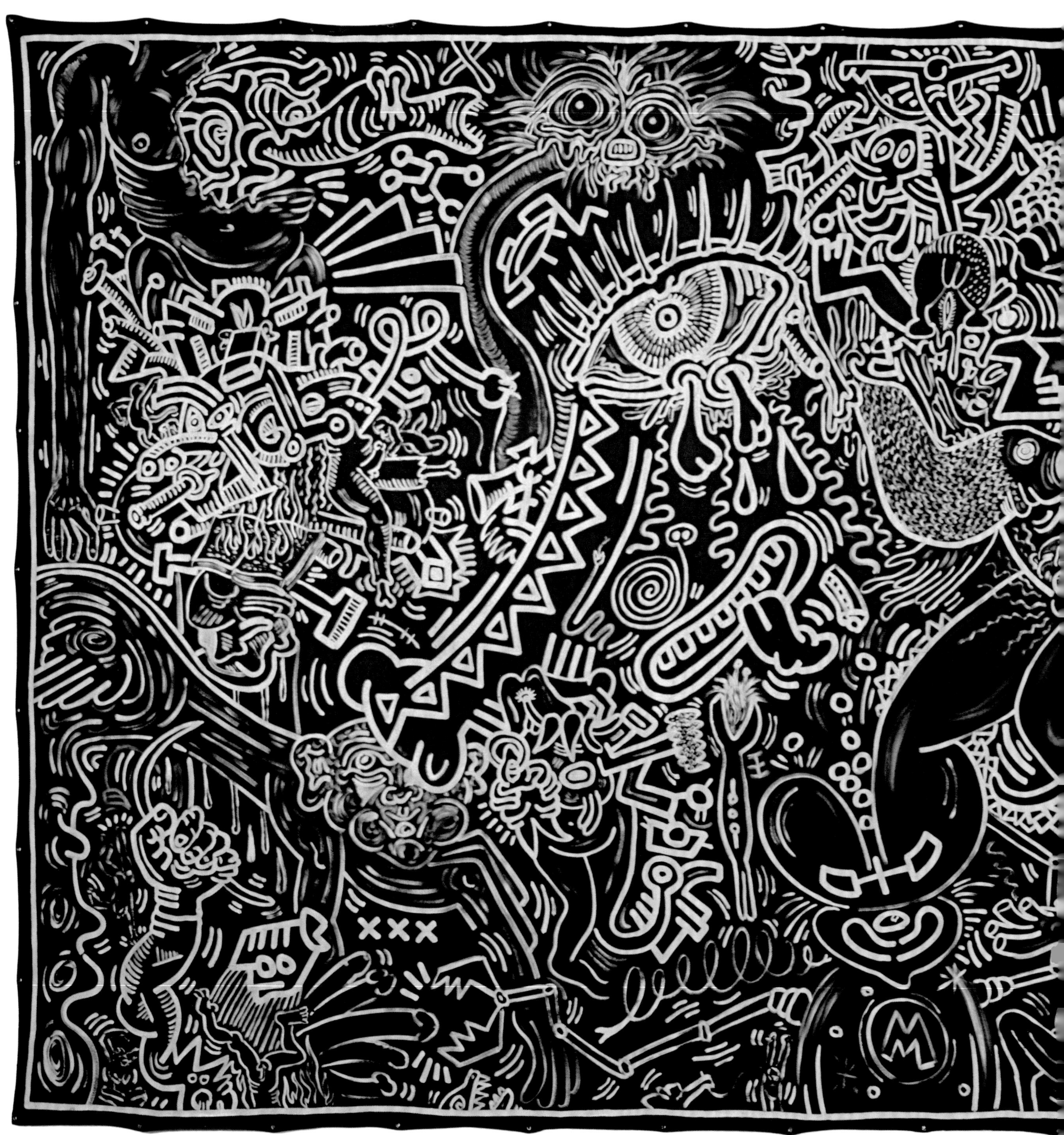

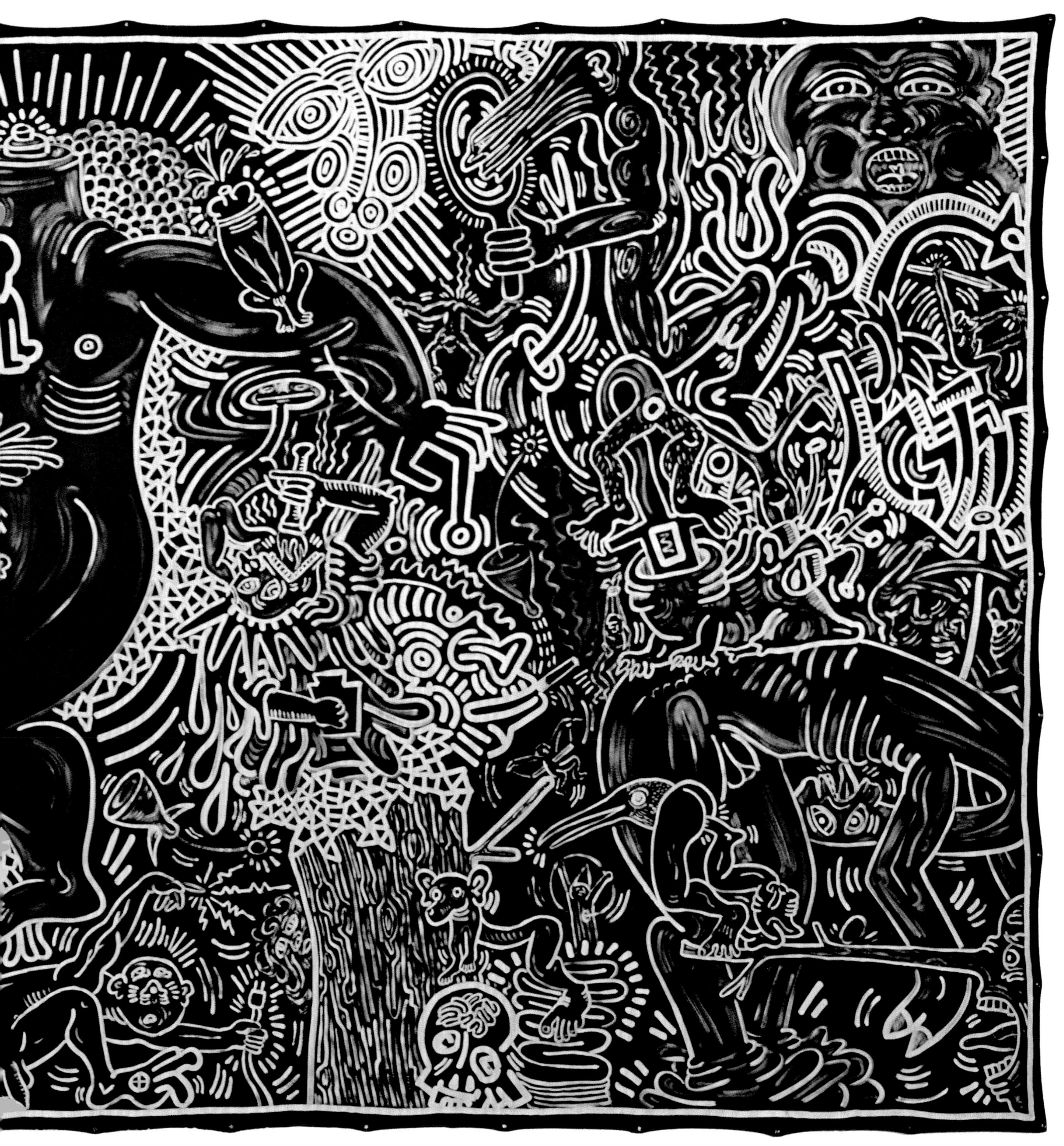

165

Untitled, September 14, 1986. Acrylic and enamel on canvas, 94¾ x 189½ in. (240.7 x 481.3 cm)
Collection of Sloan and Roger Barnett

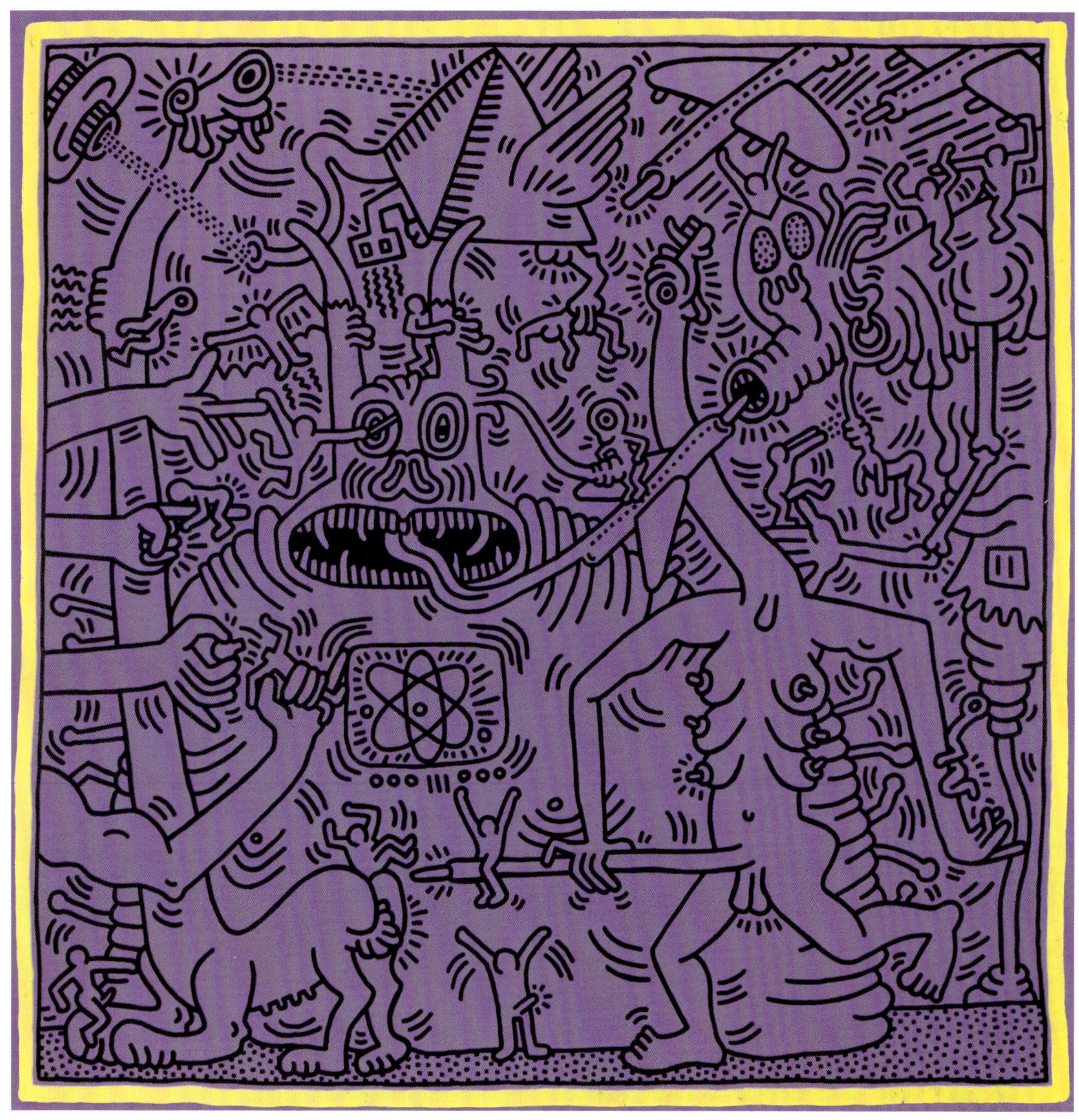

166

Untitled, May 29, 1984. Acrylic on canvas, 94 x 94 in. (238.8 x 238.8 cm)
Skarstedt, New York

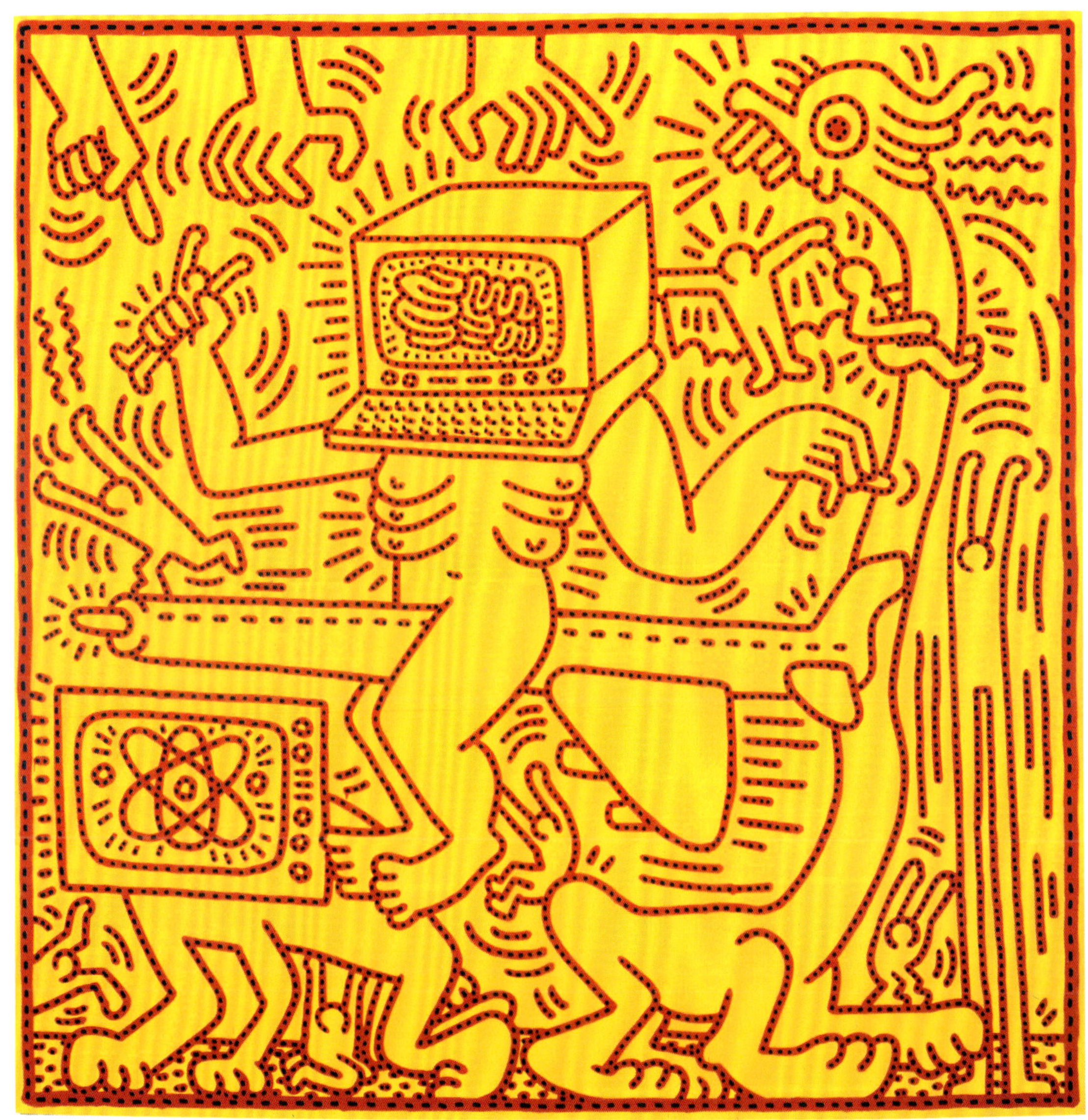

167

Untitled, May 31, 1984. Acrylic on canvas, 94 x 94 in. (238.8 x 238.8 cm)
Private collection, courtesy of the Heller Group

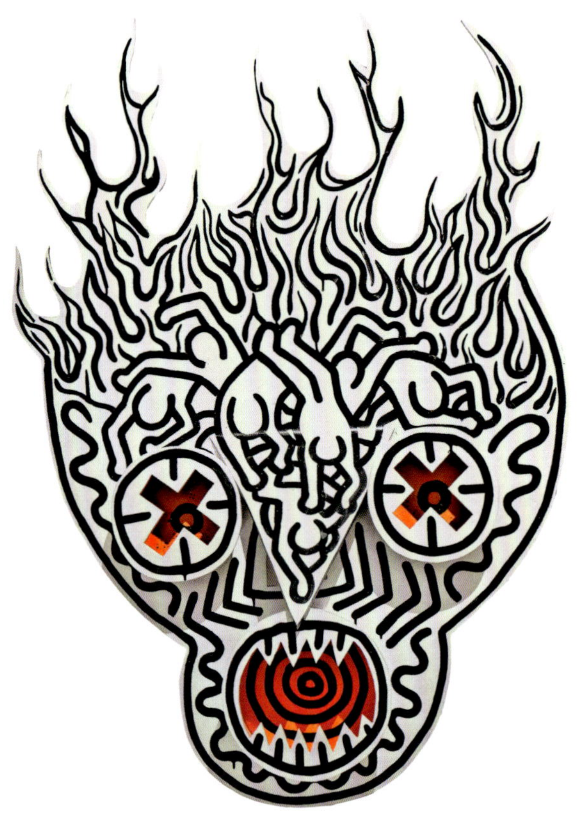

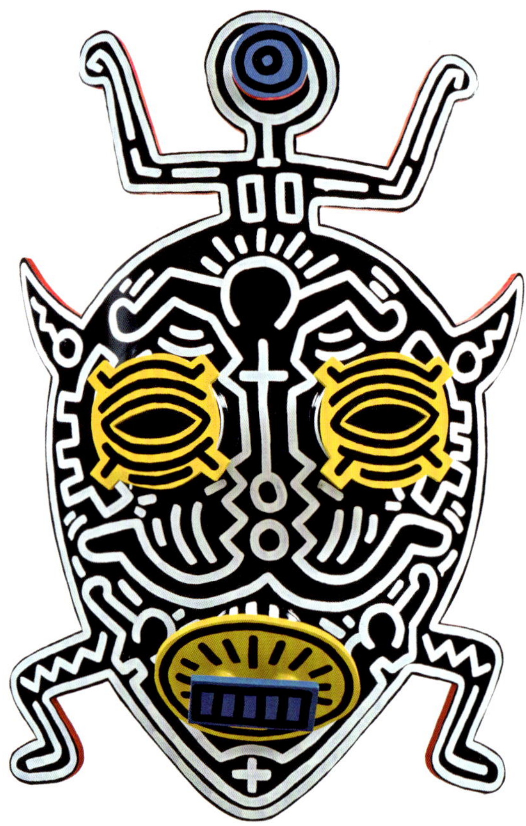

168–169

Untitled (*Burning Skull*), 1987. Enamel on aluminum, 44 1/8 x 31 x 9 in. (112 x 78.7 x 23 cm)
Mugrabi Collection

Untitled (*Hollywood African Mask*), 1987. Enamel on aluminum, 48 x 36 x 10 in. (121.9 x 91.4 x 25.4 cm)
Private collection, courtesy of the Heller Group

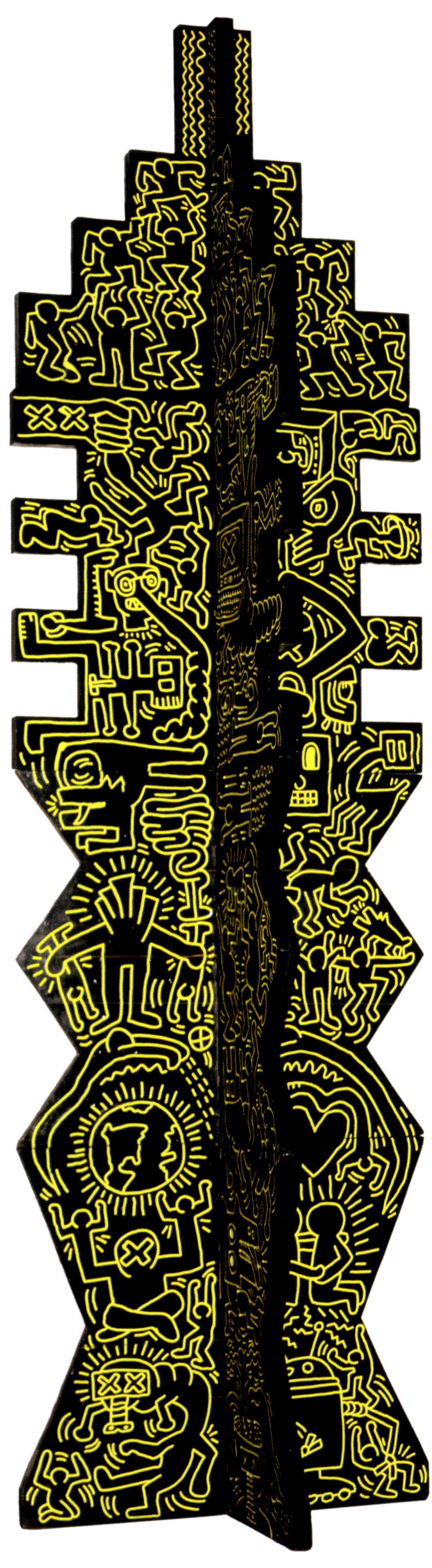

170

With Kermit Oswald, *Untitled* (*TOTEM*), 1983. Enamel on incised wood, 168⅛ x 50 x 50 in. (426.9 x 127 x 127 cm)
Collection Tony Shafrazi, New York

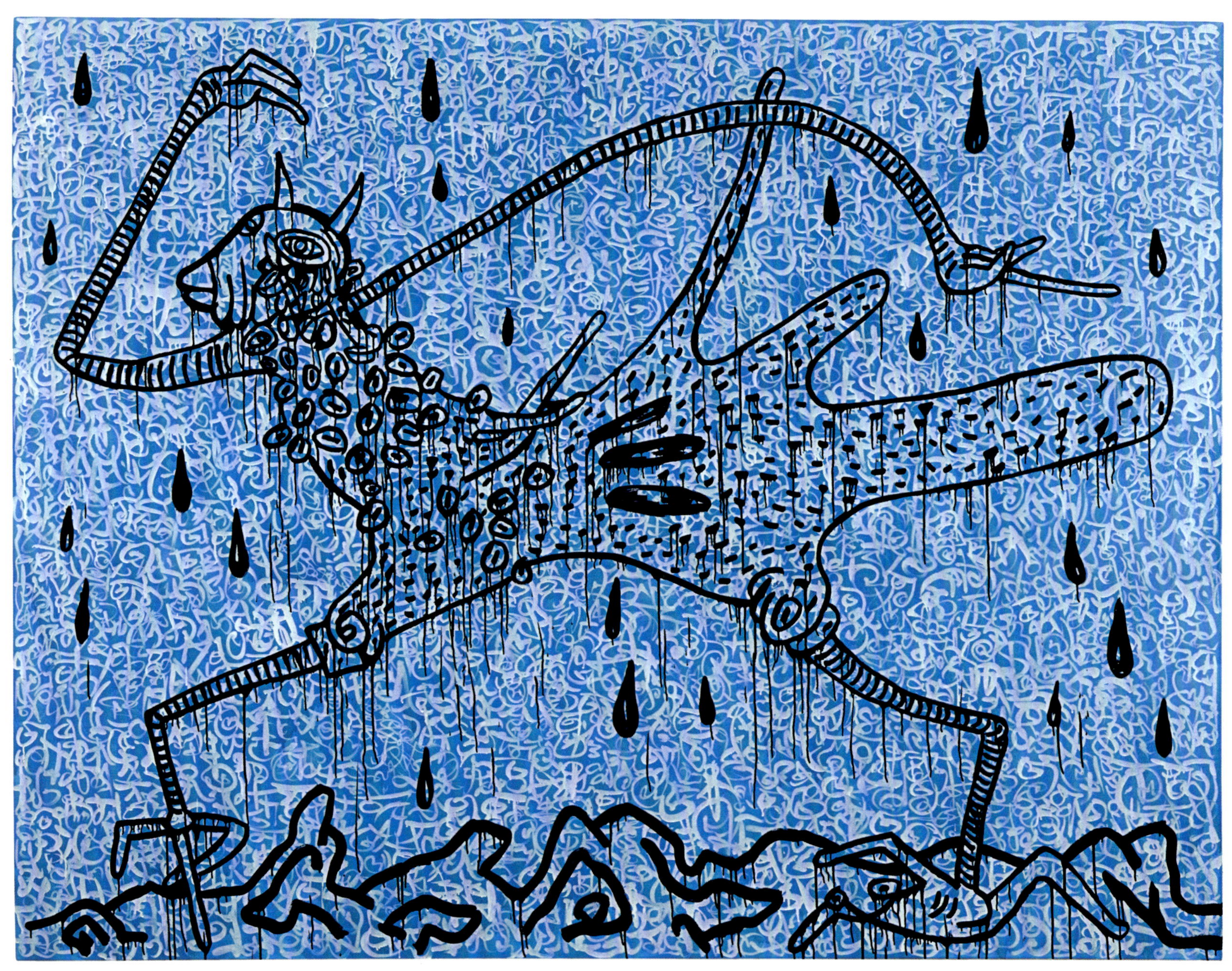

171

Walking in the Rain, 1989. Acrylic and enamel on canvas, 72 x 96⅛ in. (182.9 x 244.1 cm)
Collection of the Keith Haring Foundation

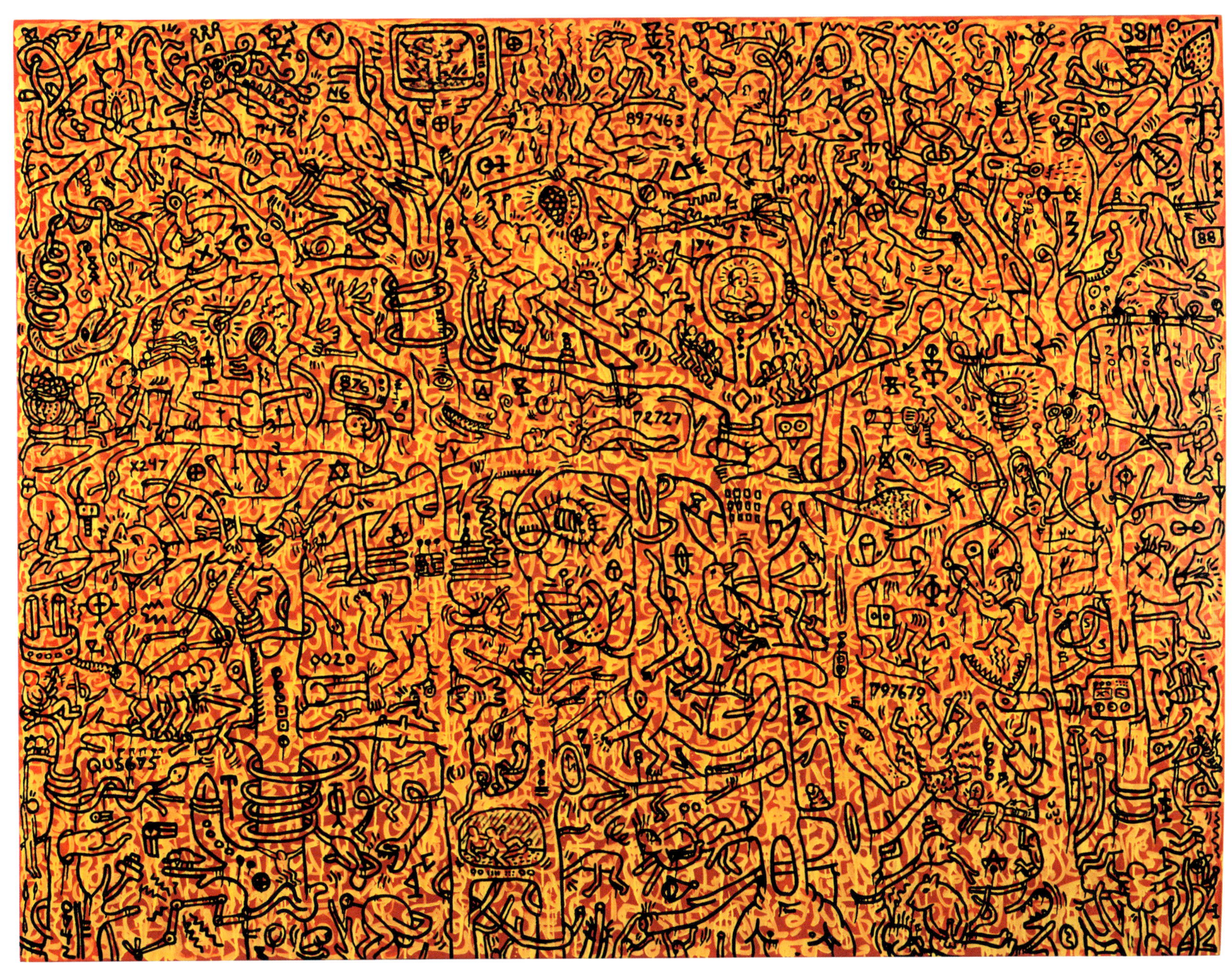

172

The Last Rainforest, 1989. Acrylic and enamel on canvas, 72 x 96 in. (182.9 x 243.8 cm)
Private collection

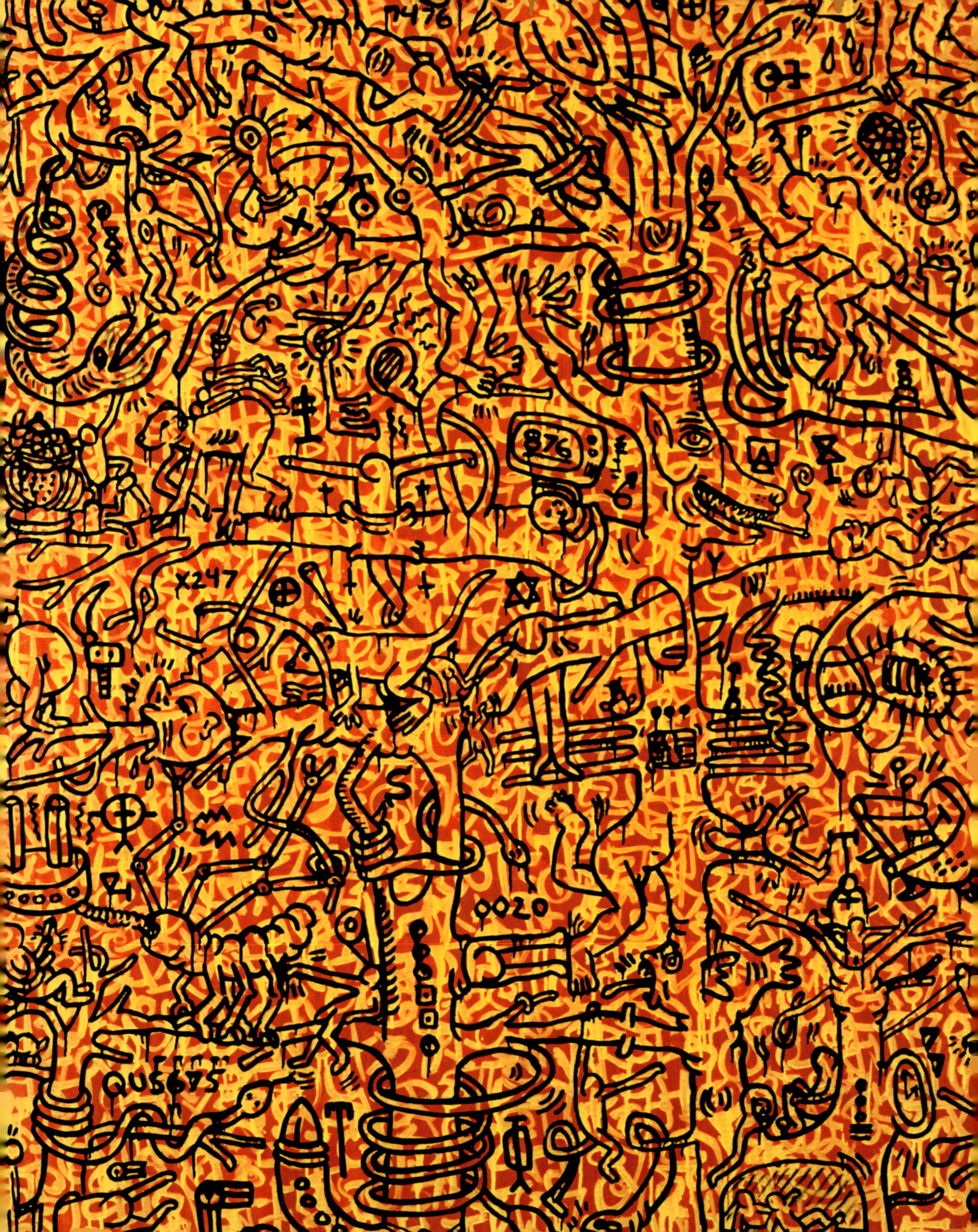
876
X247
0020

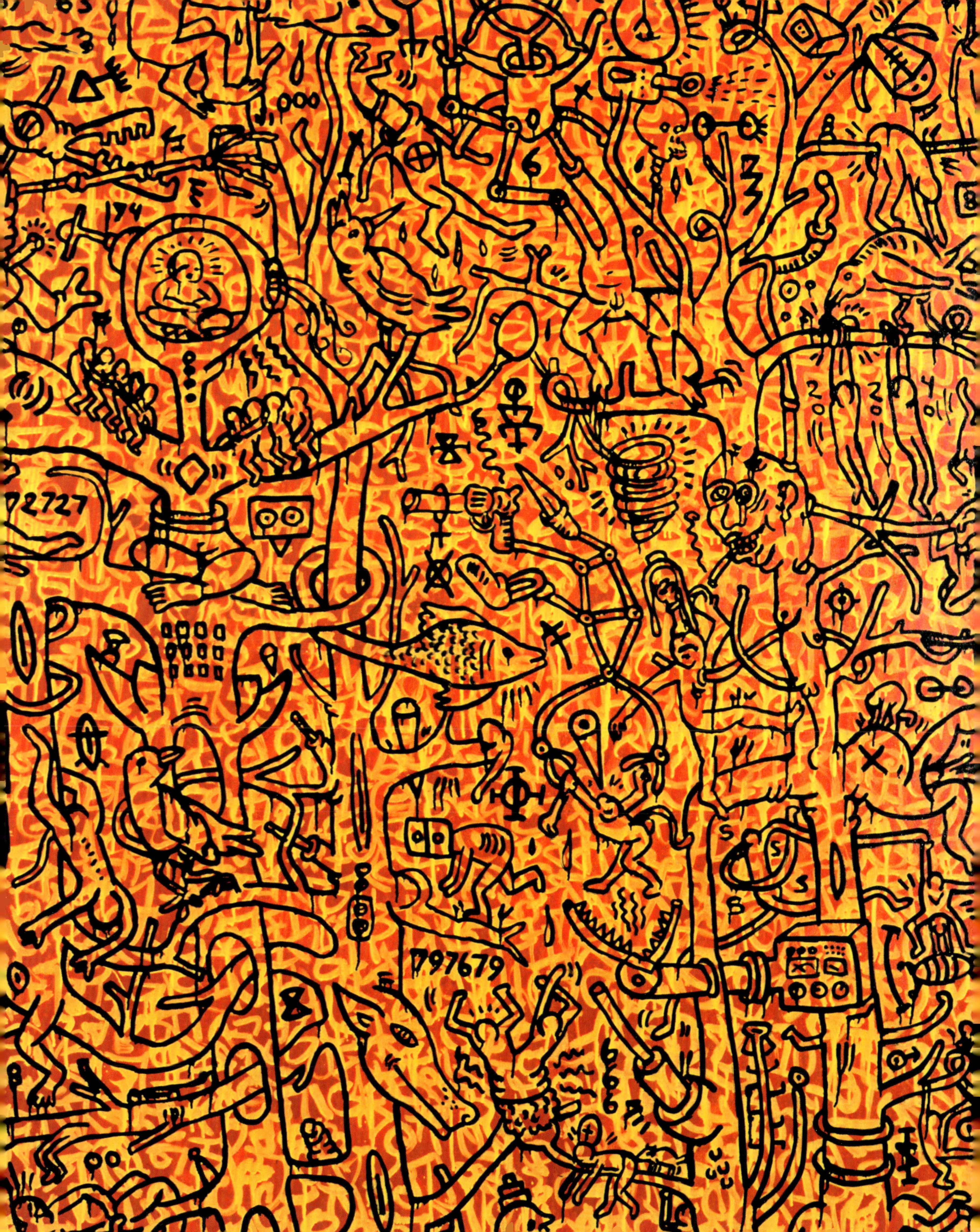
72727
797679

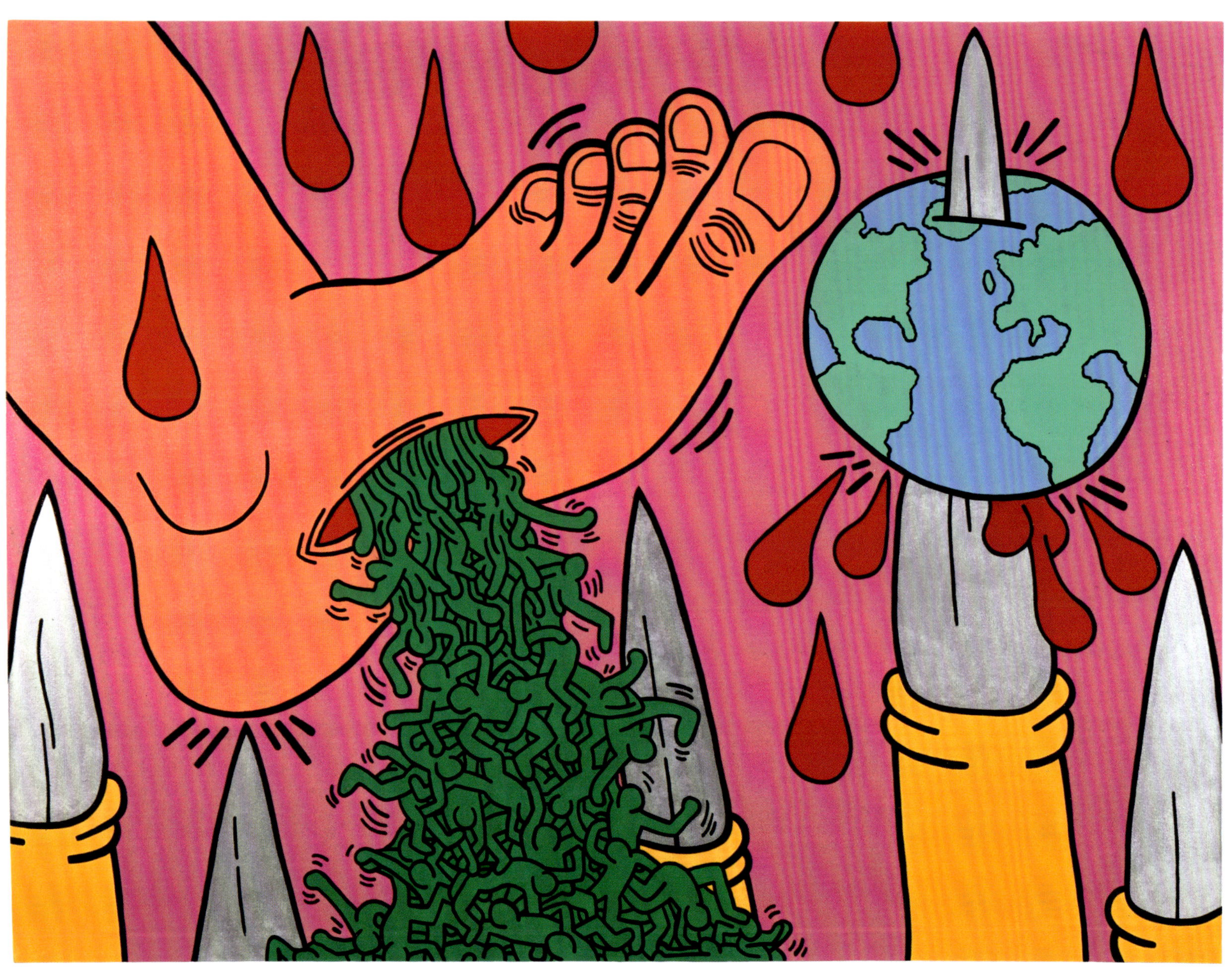

173

Untitled, 1989. Acrylic and enamel on canvas, 72 x 96 in. (182.9 x 243.8 cm)
Collection of the Keith Haring Foundation

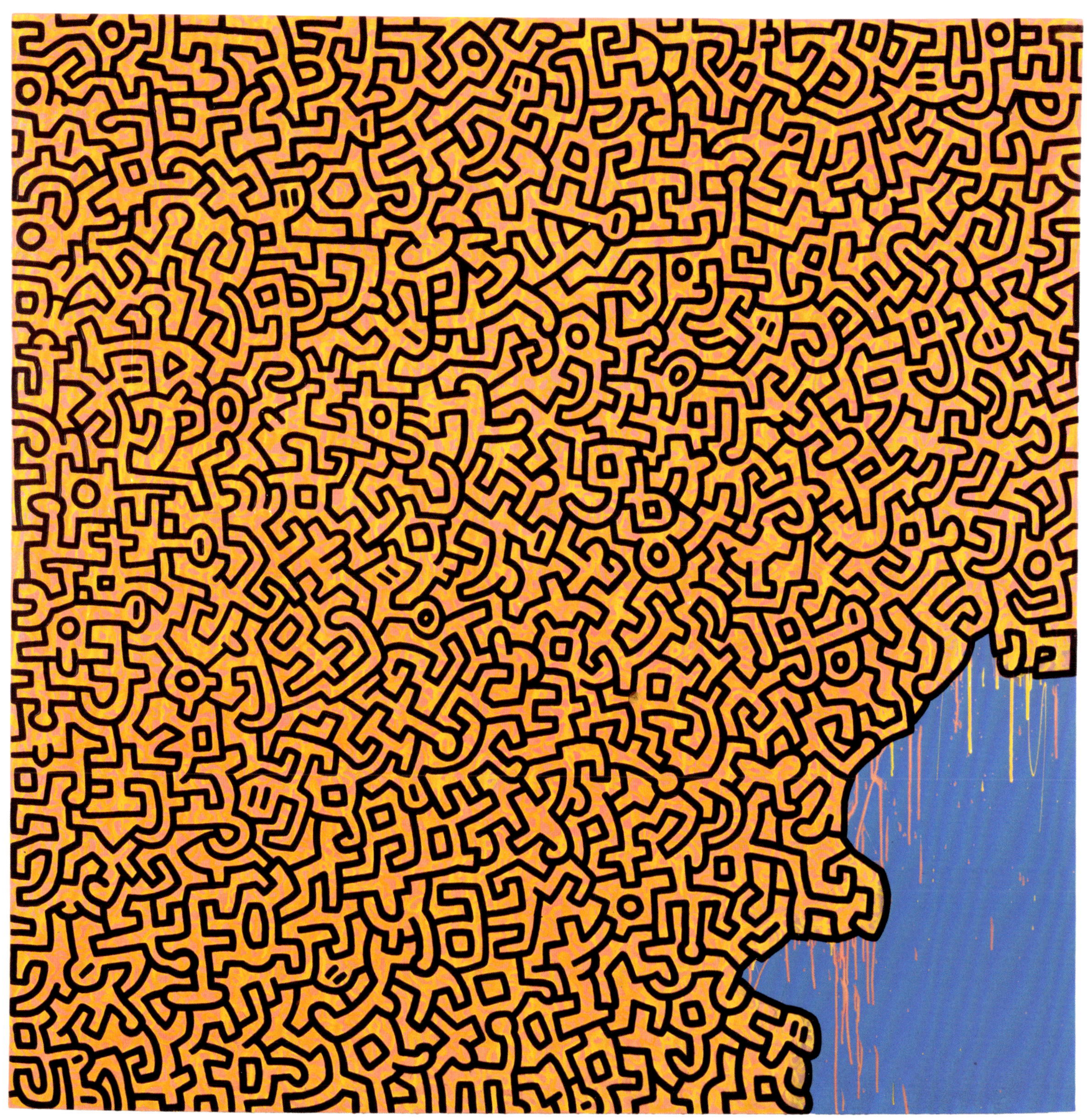

174

Brazil, 1989. Acrylic and enamel on canvas, 72 x 72 in. (182.9 x 182.9 cm)
Glenstone

20 DRAWINGS
OCT. 3, 1989

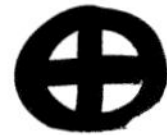

20 DRAWINGS
OCT. 3, 1989 K. Haring
⊕

BÉBERT, ROTTERDAM

This book is dedicated to the memory of Steve Rubell - not because of the content, but because these drawings were created with the same energy and intensity with which he lived his life.

20 DRAWINGS
OCT. 3, 1989

These drawings were created one afternoon in October in my studio in New York City. As usual, they were created instantaneously, without a pre-determined plan or concept. The materials were very simple - handmade Dutch linen paper, brush, and Sumi inks which I got in Japan.

All the drawings generate from what happens in the first drawing. I just "let" it happen. Each drawing builds on the previous drawings and advances the "story". It's very difficult (and against the basic principal of their existence) to explain the "meaning" of my drawings. In this case, however, there may be a clue. During the first 2 hours or so I was listening to Marvin Gaye's classic album "What's Going On?" over and over. In it, pessimistly he questions the future of the planet. The remaining time was spent listening to Bob Marley's songs of oppresion and peoples' struggle for freedom. Sometimes music is a "backround" for drawing, but sometimes it becomes an essential part of the creation of the work.

These drawings are about the Earth we inherited and the dismal task of trying to save it - against all odds.

K. Haring JAN. 27 - 1990 N.Y.C.

20 DRAWINGS - OCT. 3 1989 WAS PUBLISHED WITH THE COLLABORATION OF MERA AND DONALD RUBELL BY BÉBERT PUBLISHING HOUSE IN SPRING 1990.

THE EDITION CONSISTS OF 2500 HARD COVER COPIES OF WHICH 500 ARE NUMBERED (1/500 - 500/500) AND SIGNED BY THE ARTIST.

THE EDITION WAS PRINTED ON ACID-FREE RIVOLI PAPER BY NIEUWE GRAFISCHE IN ROTTERDAM AND BOUND BY STOKKINK B.V. IN AMSTERDAM.

ISBN: 90.5245.011.0 THIS IS NUMBER

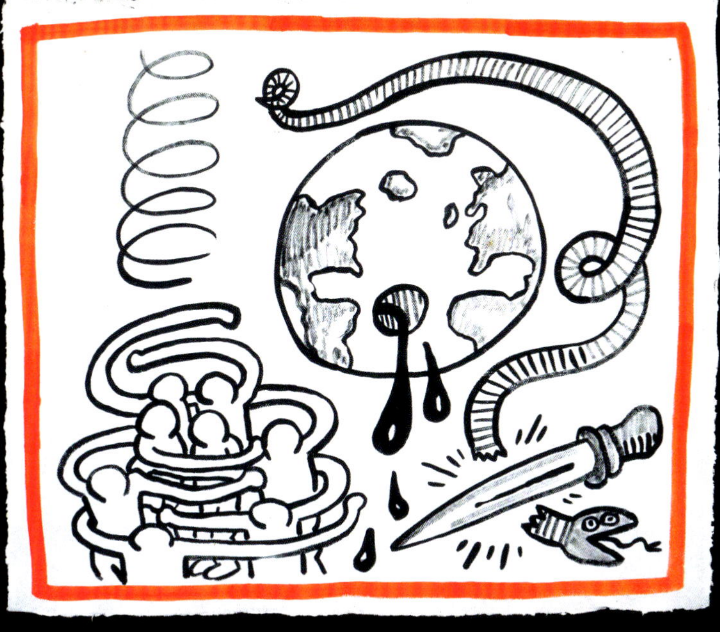
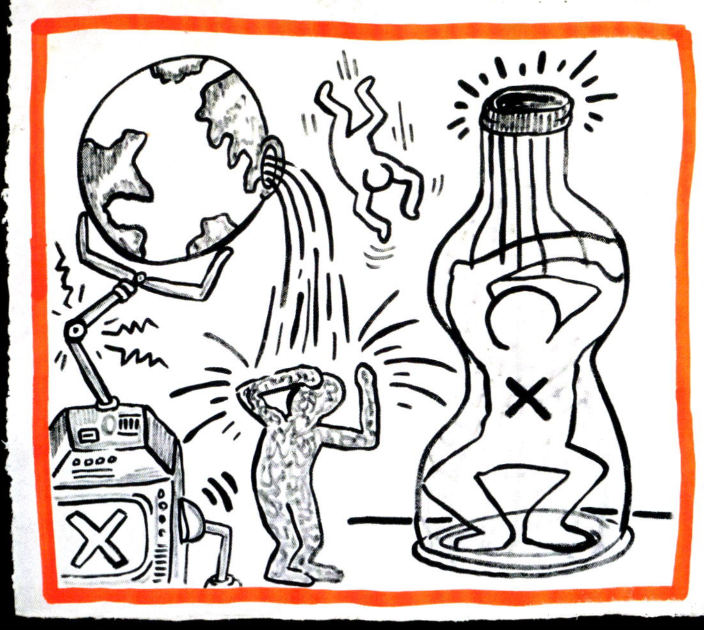
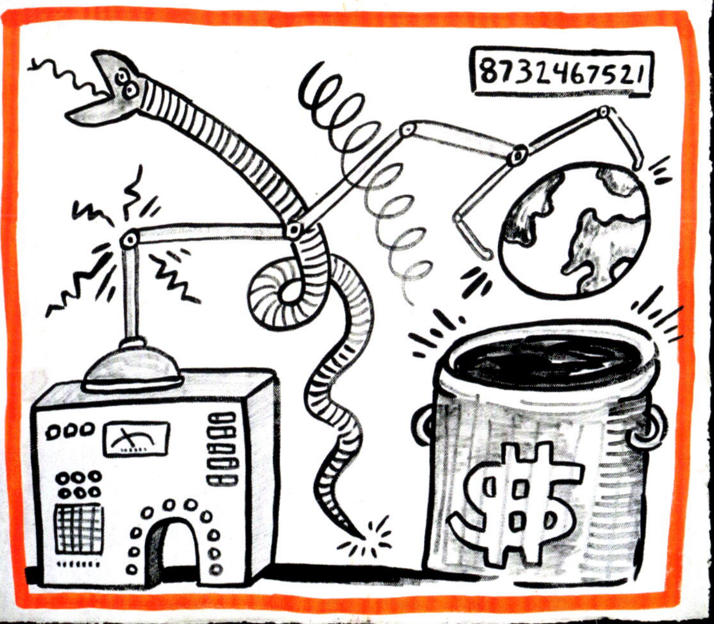
8732467521
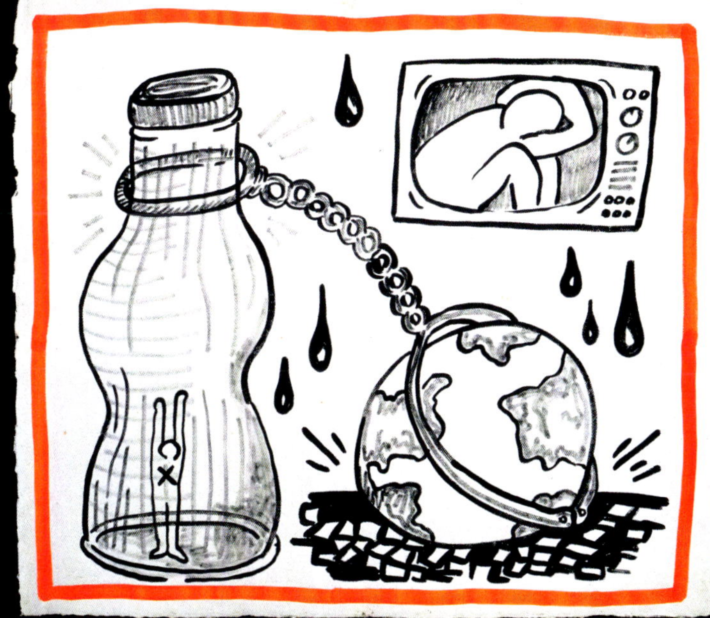

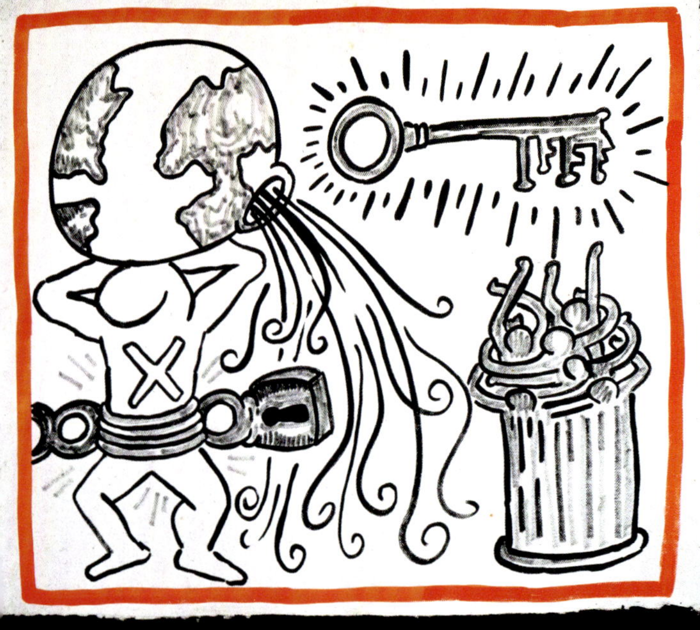

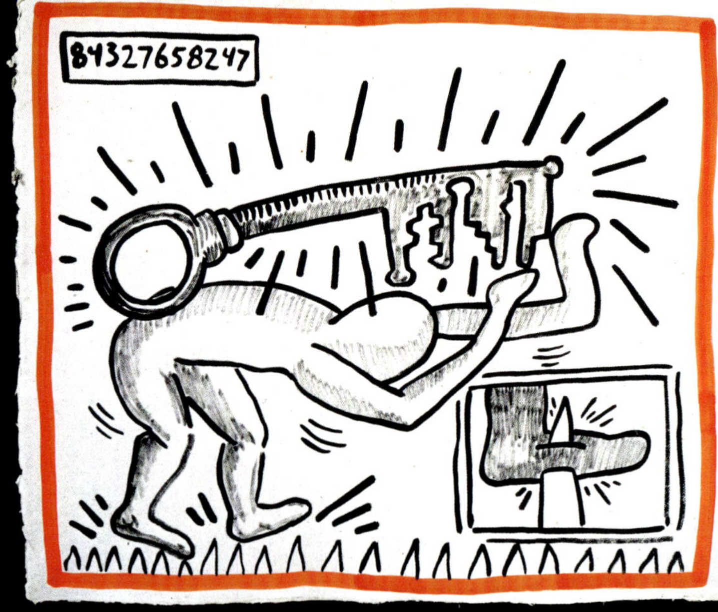
84327658247

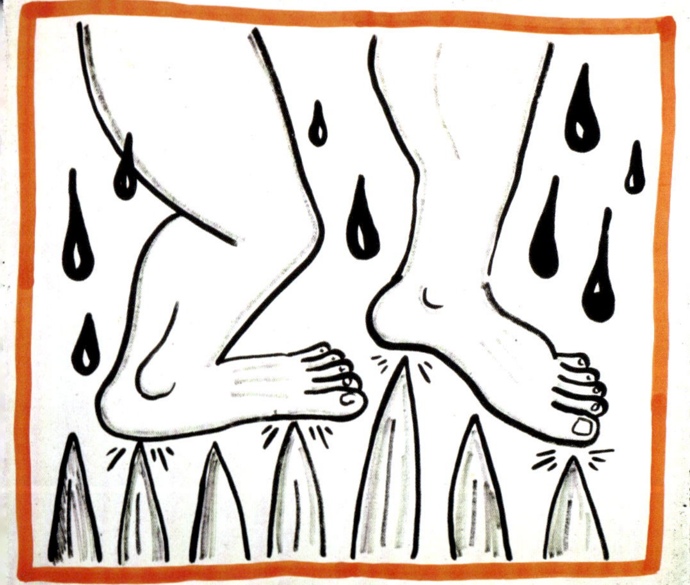

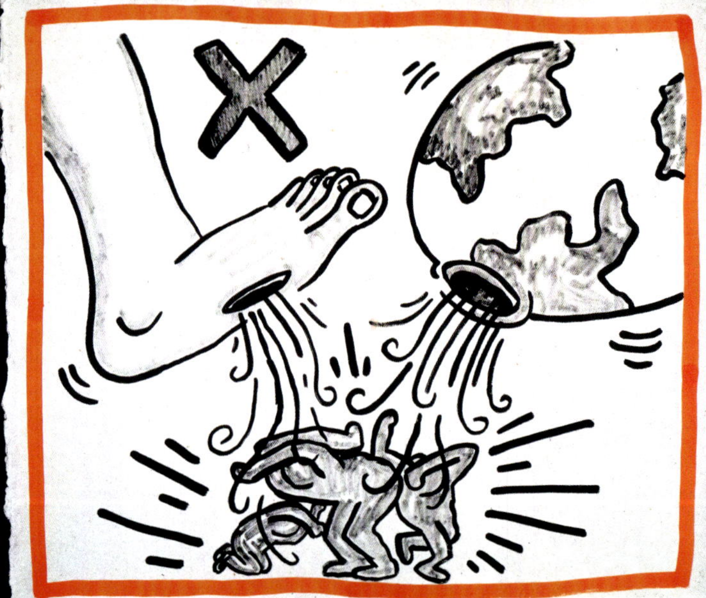

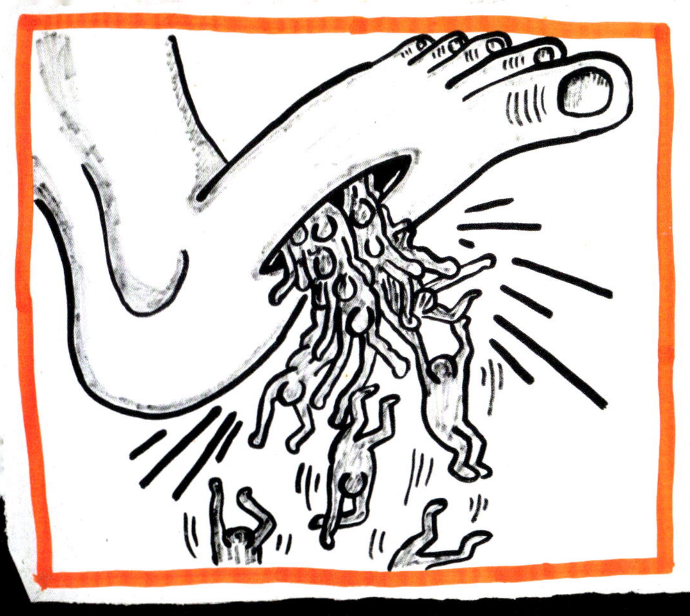

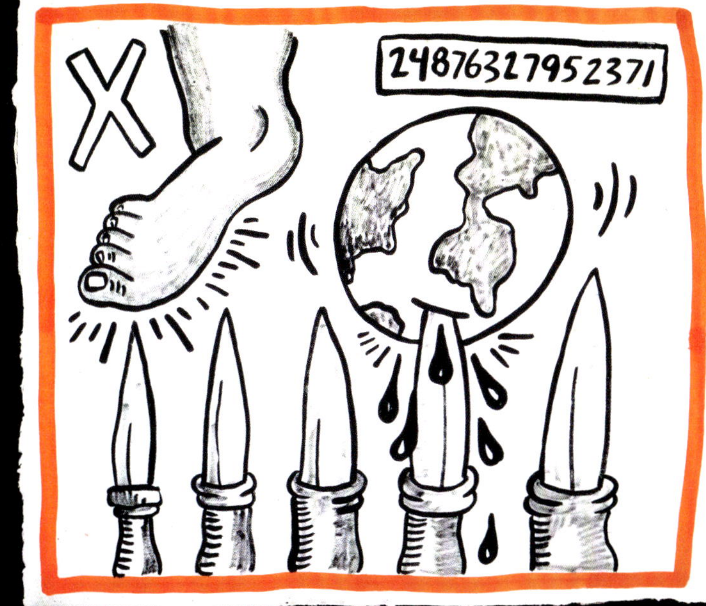
24876327952371

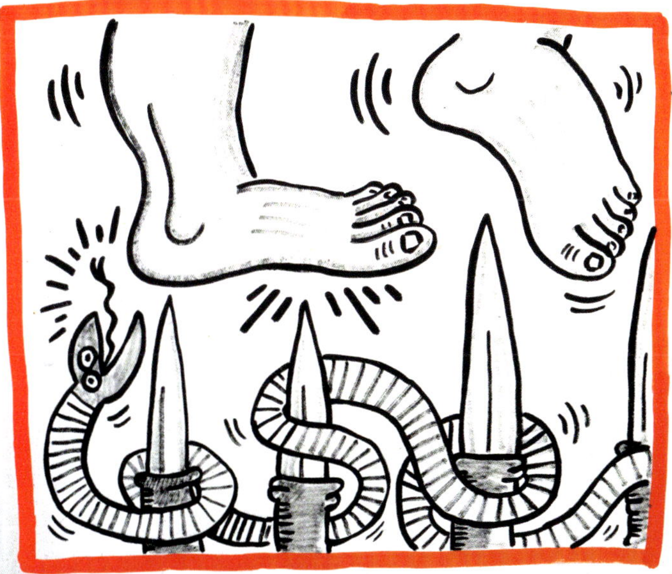

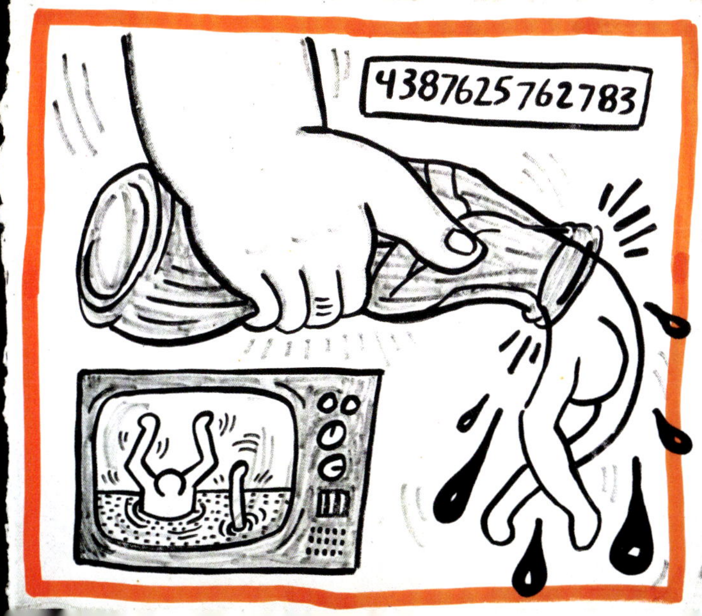
4387625762783

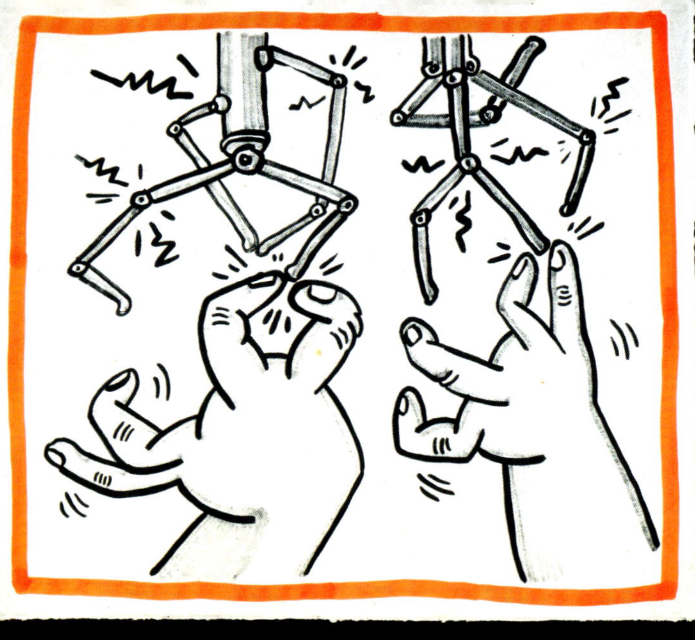

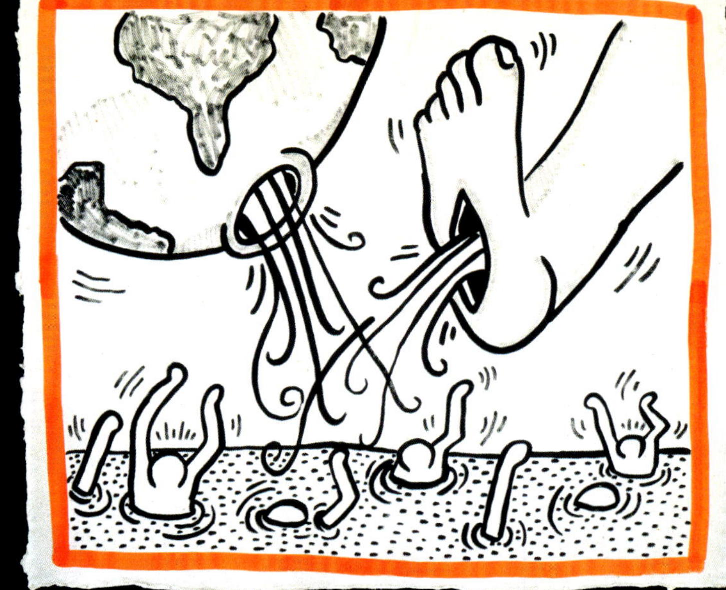

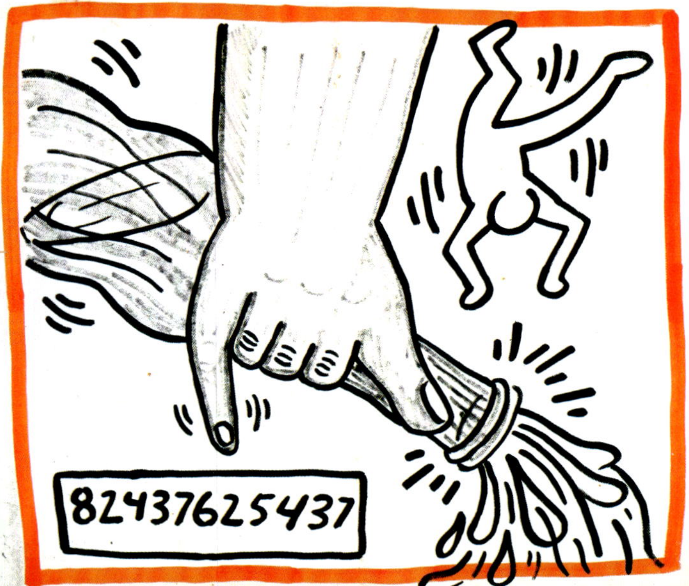
82437625437

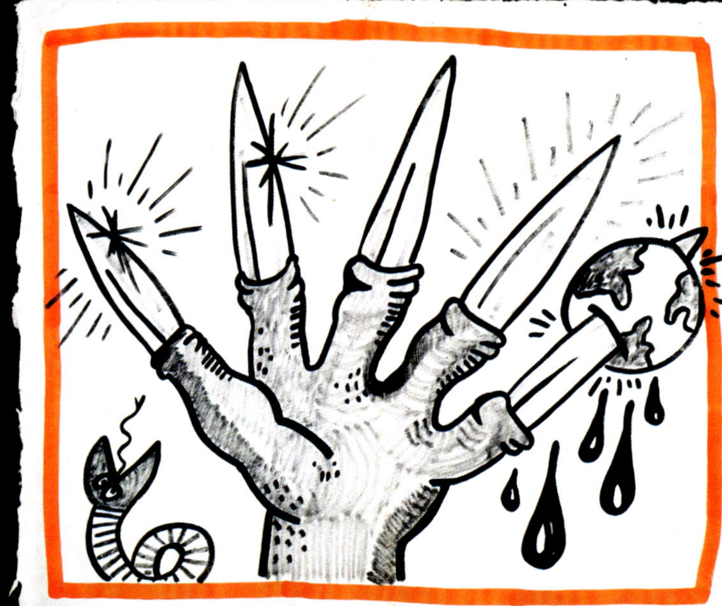

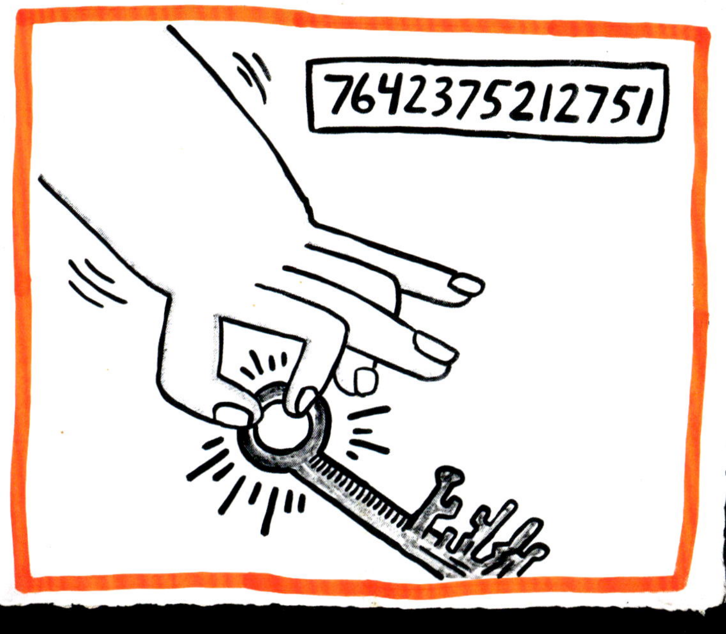
76423752127 51

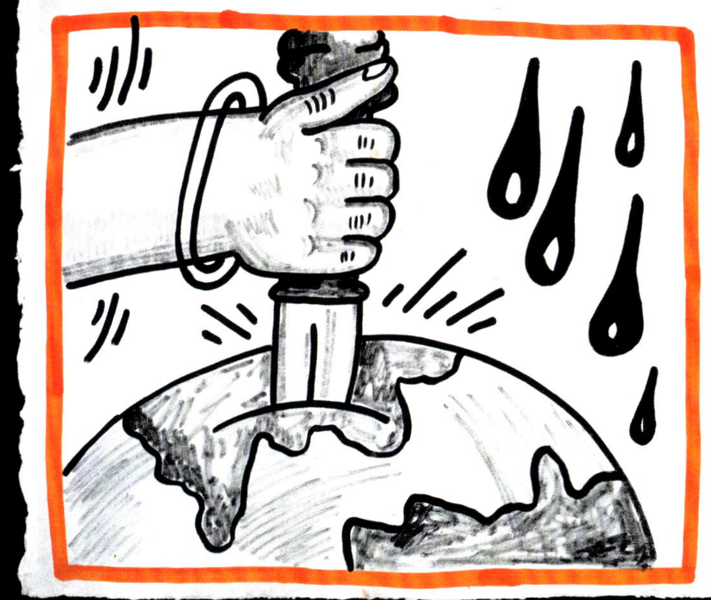

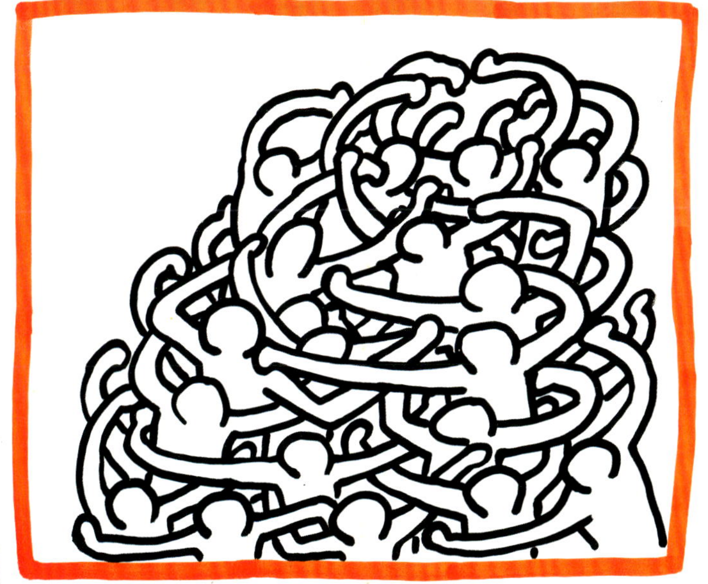

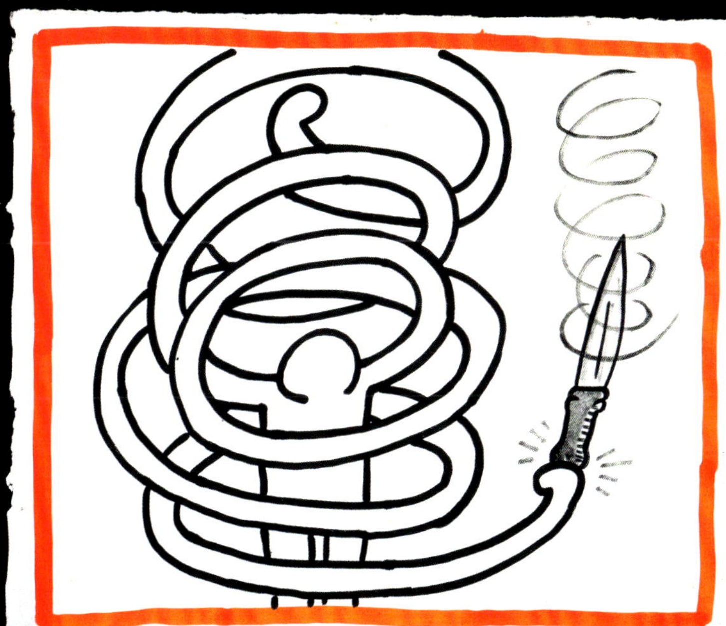

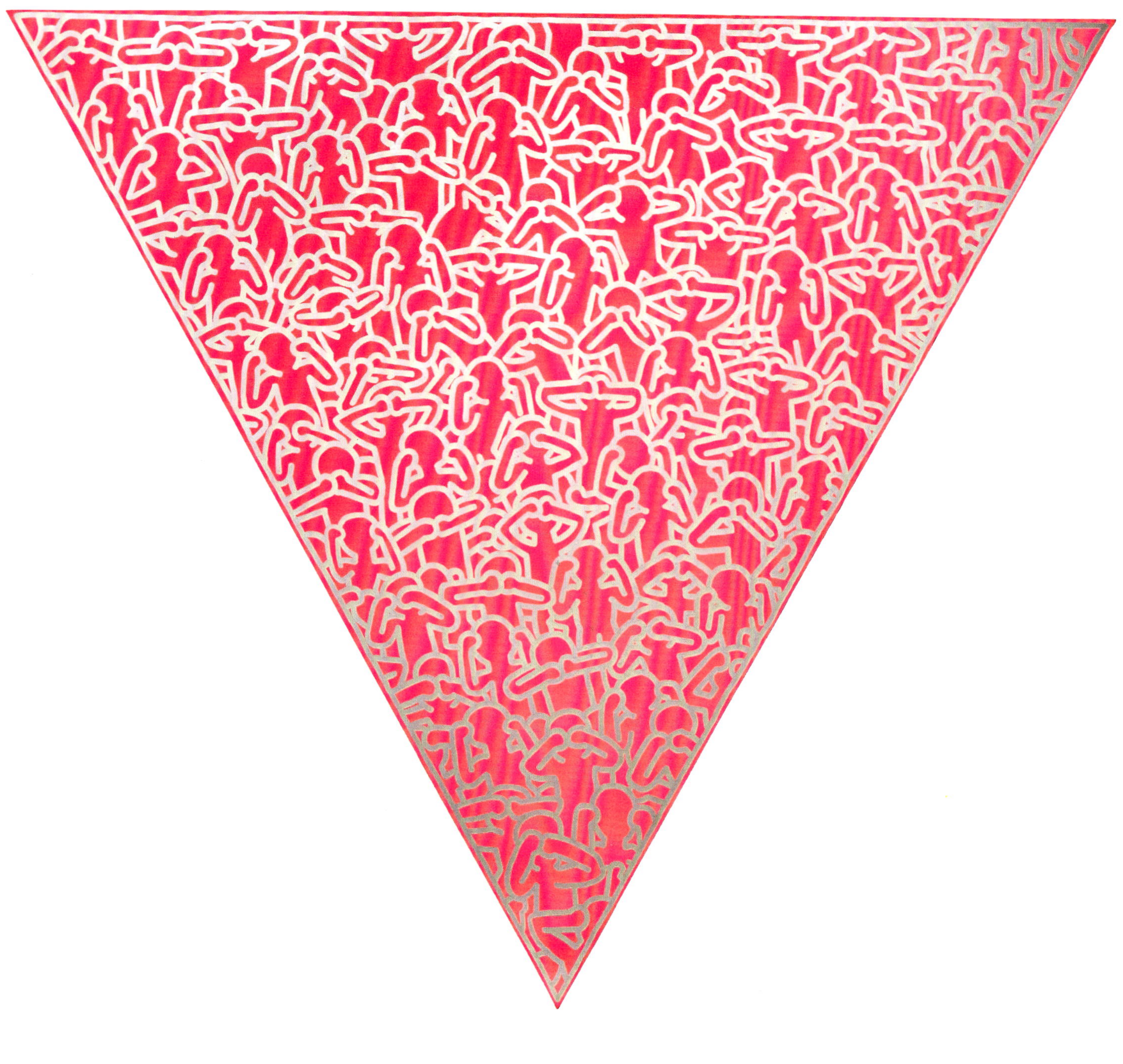

195

Silence=Death, 1988. Acrylic on canvas, 108 x 120 x 108 in. (274.3 x 304.8 x 274.3 cm)
Private collection

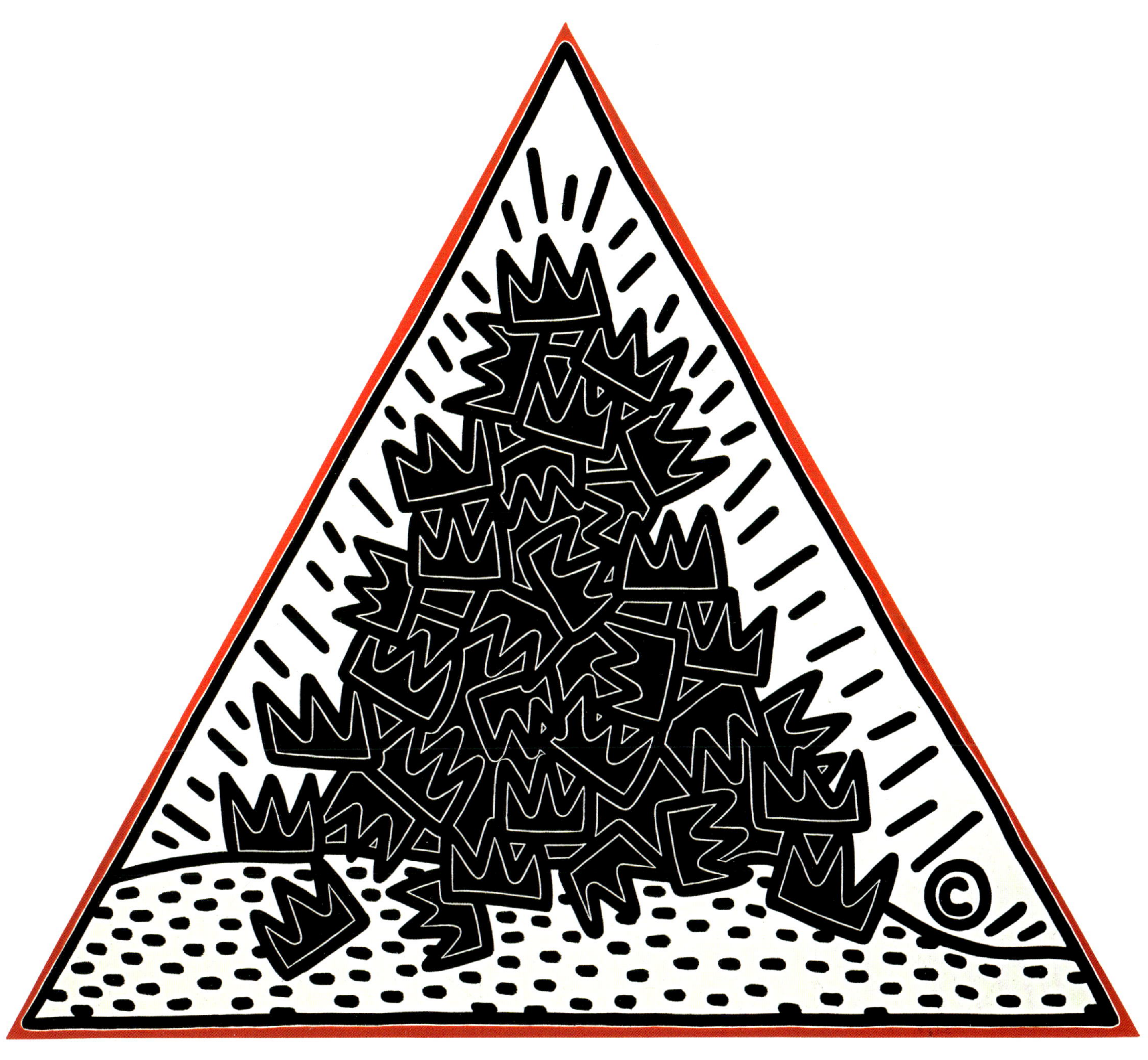

196

A Pile of Crowns for Jean-Michel Basquiat, 1988. Acrylic on canvas, 120 x 120 x 120 in. (304.8 x 304.8 x 304.8 cm)
Collection of the Keith Haring Foundation

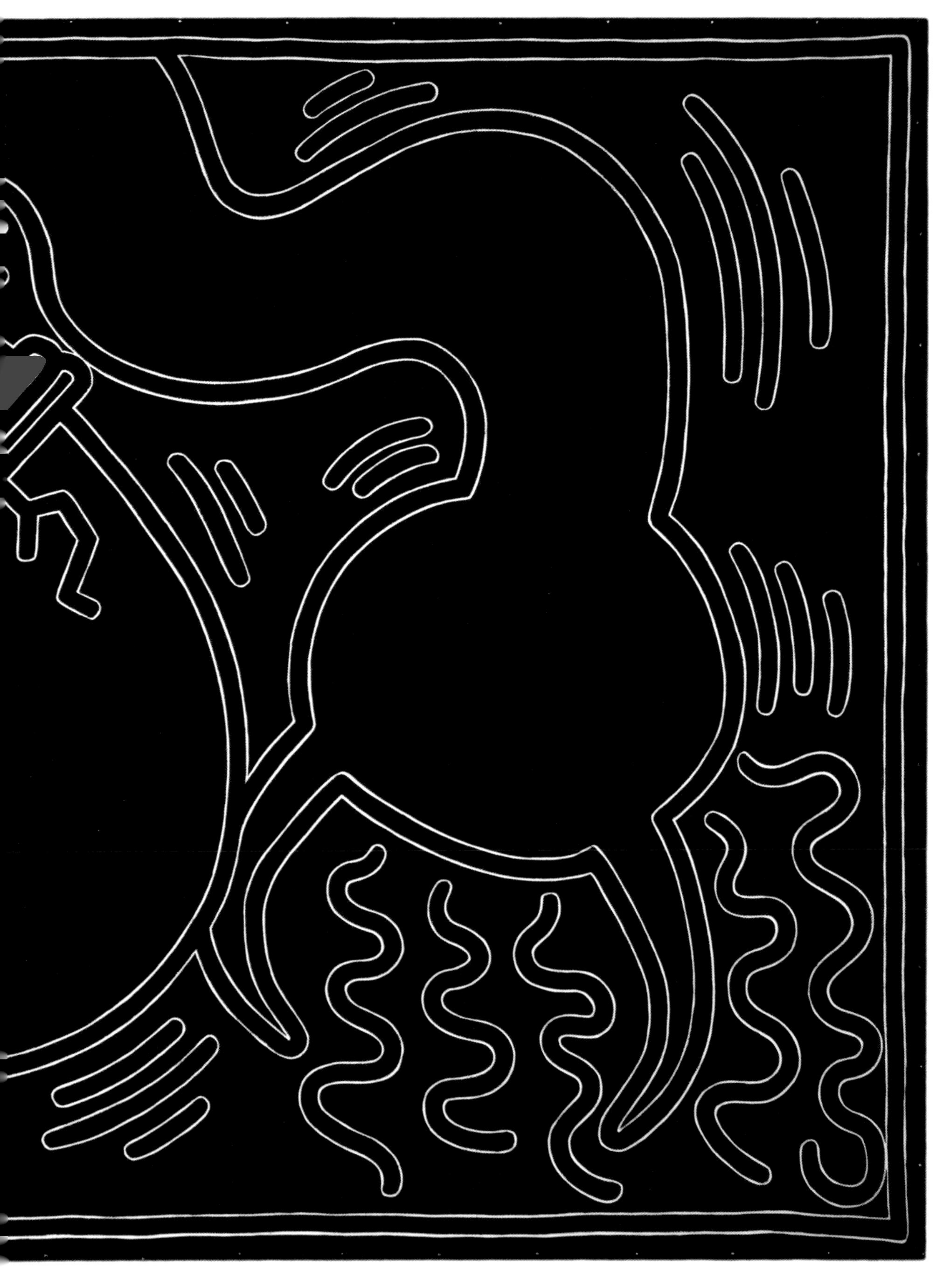

197

Untitled, May 7, 1988. Acrylic on canvas, 137 x 216 ⅛ in. (348 x 549 cm)
Private collection

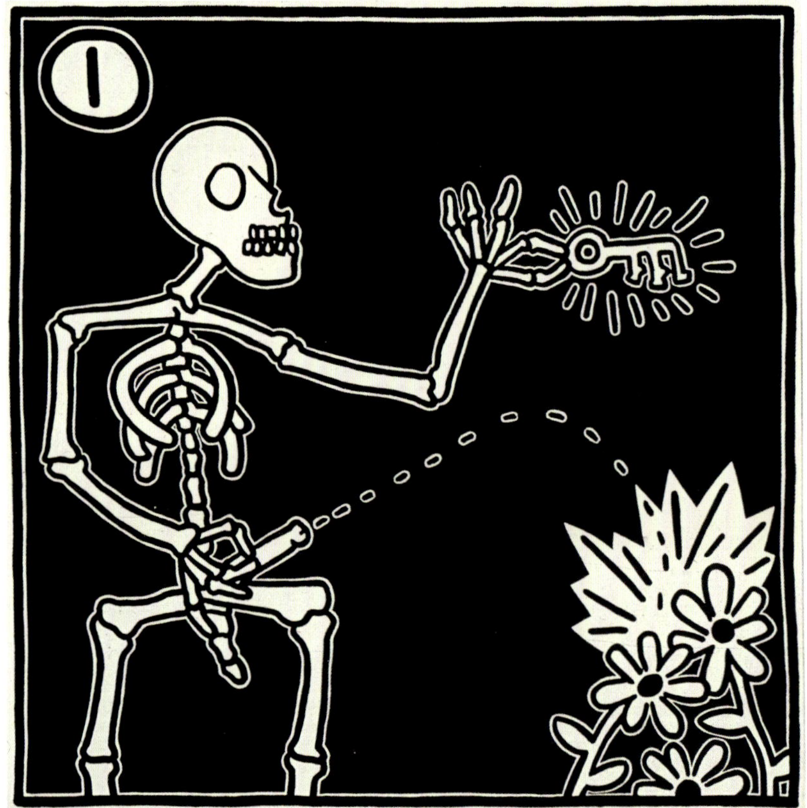

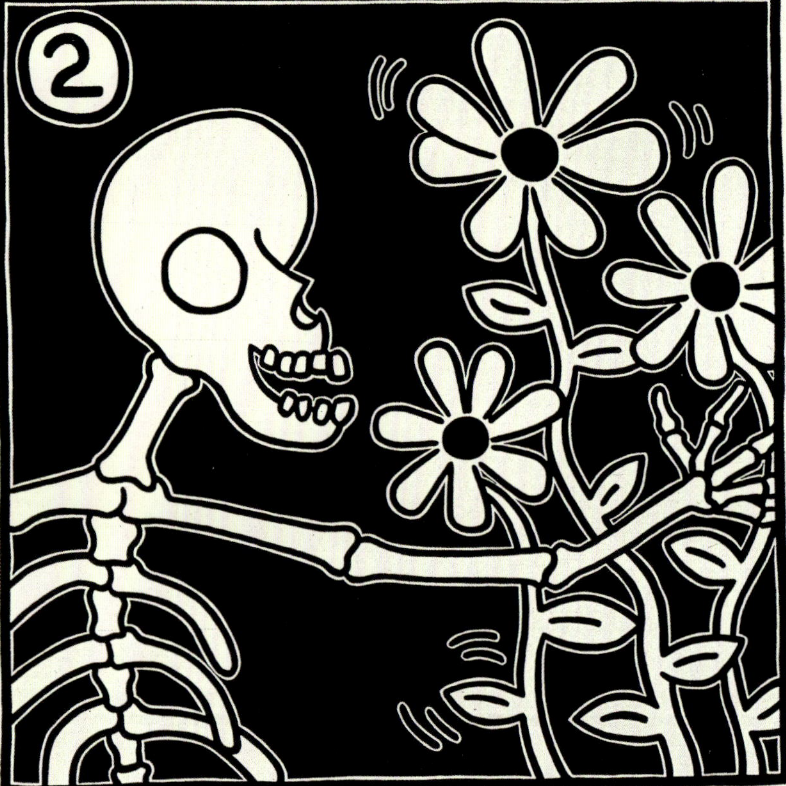

198

Untitled (*for James Ensor*), May 5, 1989. Diptych: acrylic on canvas, each $39\frac{3}{8}$ x $39\frac{3}{8}$ in. (100 x 100 cm)
Courtesy of Arario Gallery, Korea

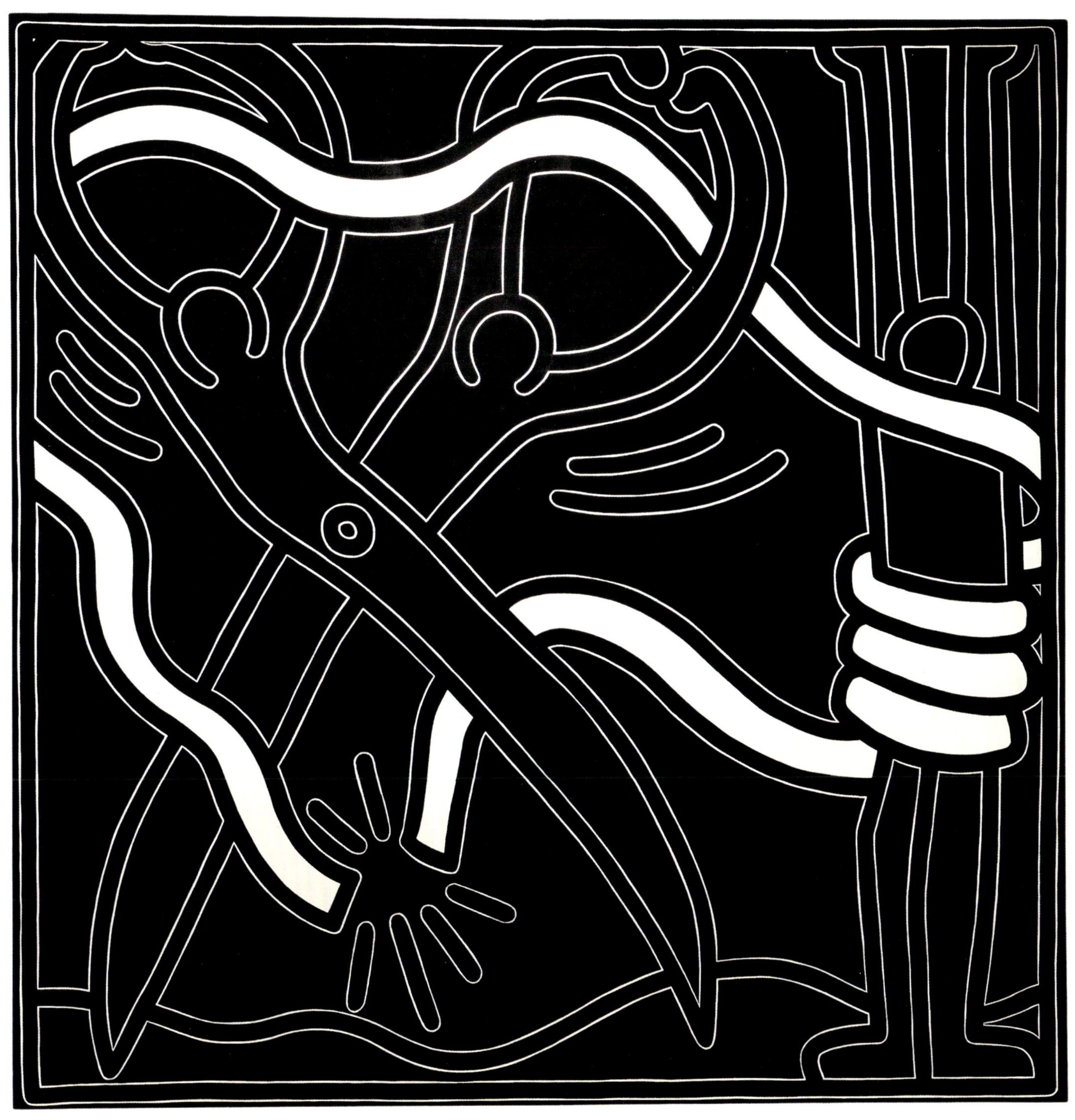

199

Untitled, November 8, 1988. Acrylic on canvas, 120 ⅛ x 120 ⅛ in. (305 x 305 cm)
Private collection

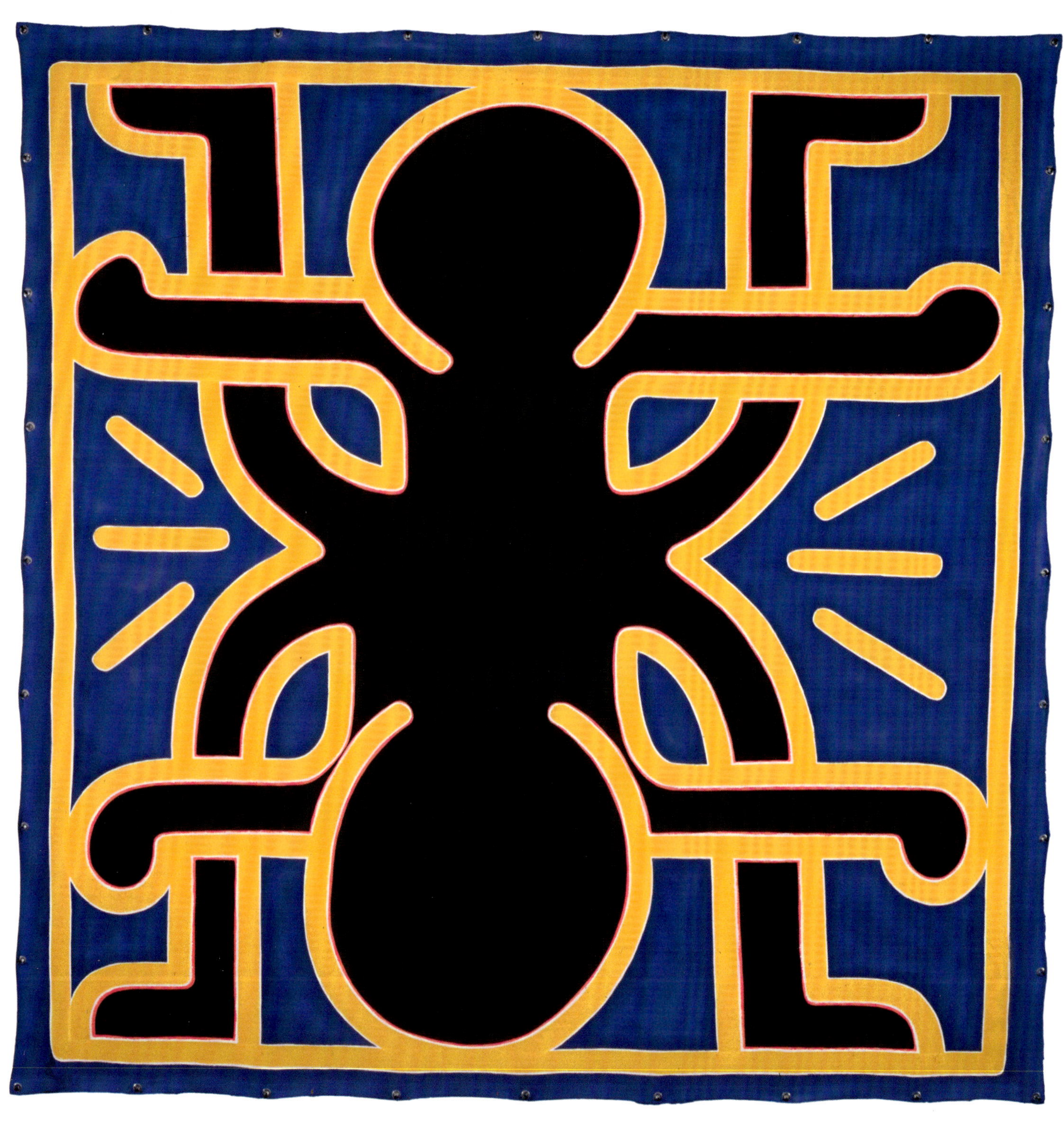

200

Untitled, 1988. Acrylic on canvas, 96 x 96 in. (243.8 x 243.8 cm)
Private collection

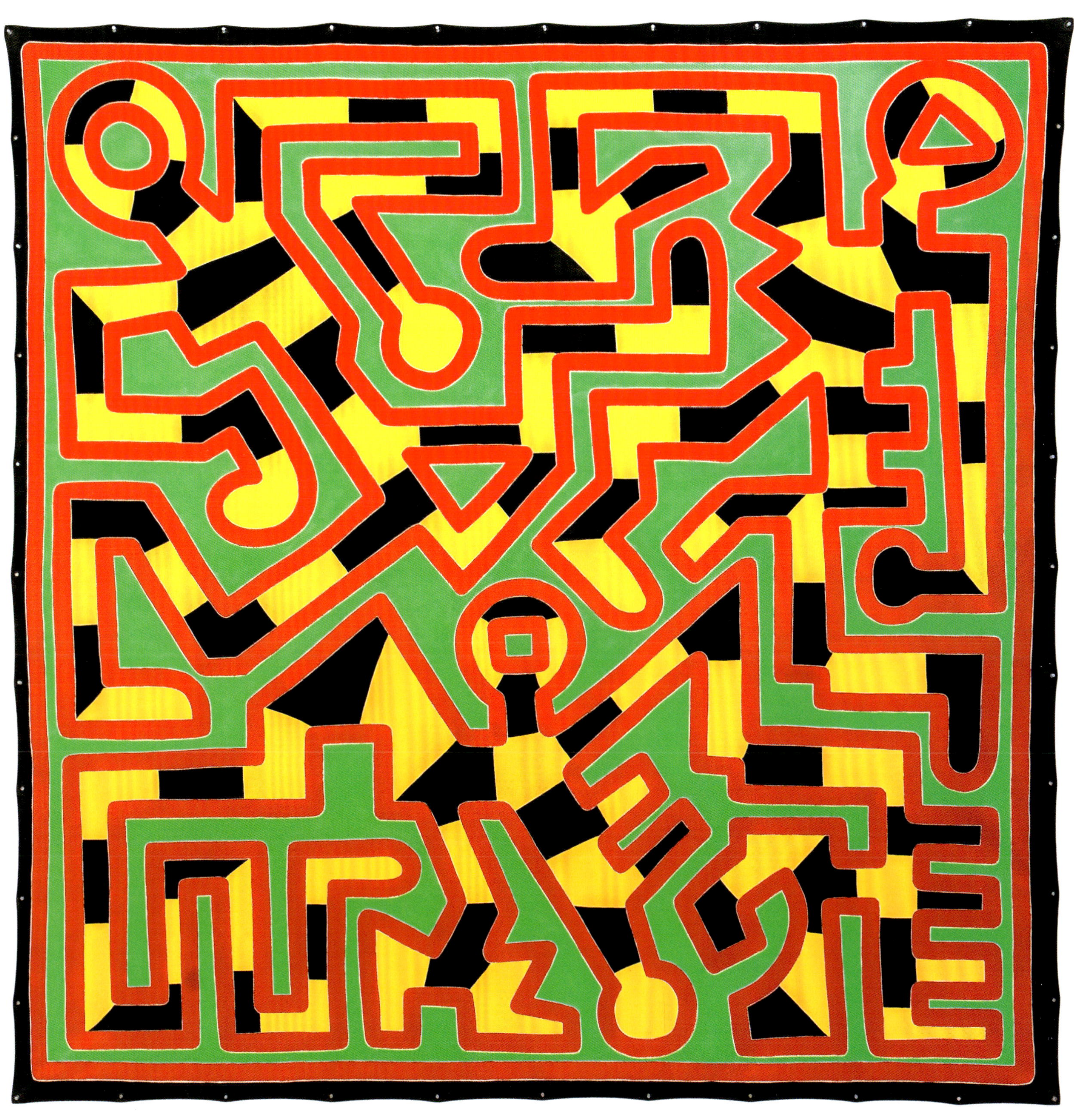

201

Untitled, June 10, 1988. Acrylic on canvas, 118 1/8 x 120 1/8 in. (300 x 305 cm)
Private collection, courtesy Tony Shafrazi Gallery, New York

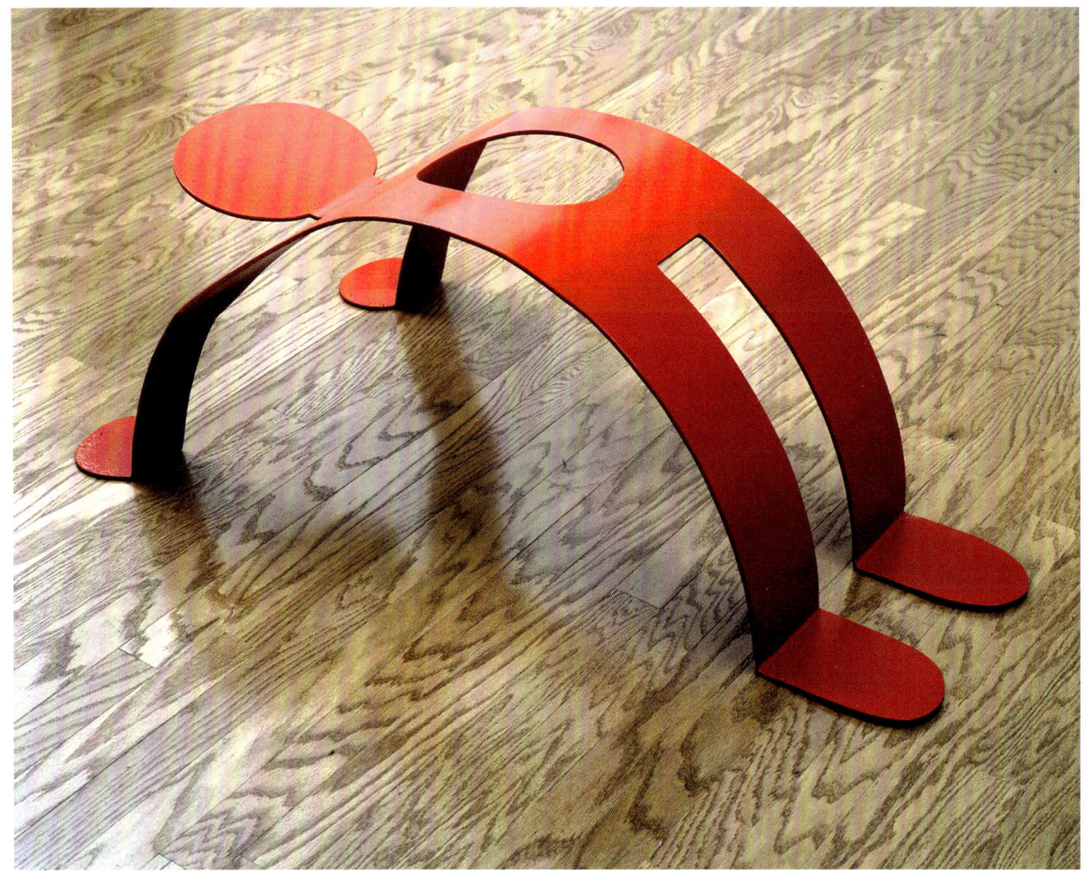

202

Untitled (*Red Arching Figure*), 1985. Enamel on steel, 50 x 30 x 38 in. (127 x 76.2 x 96.5 cm)
Collection of Jose Martos

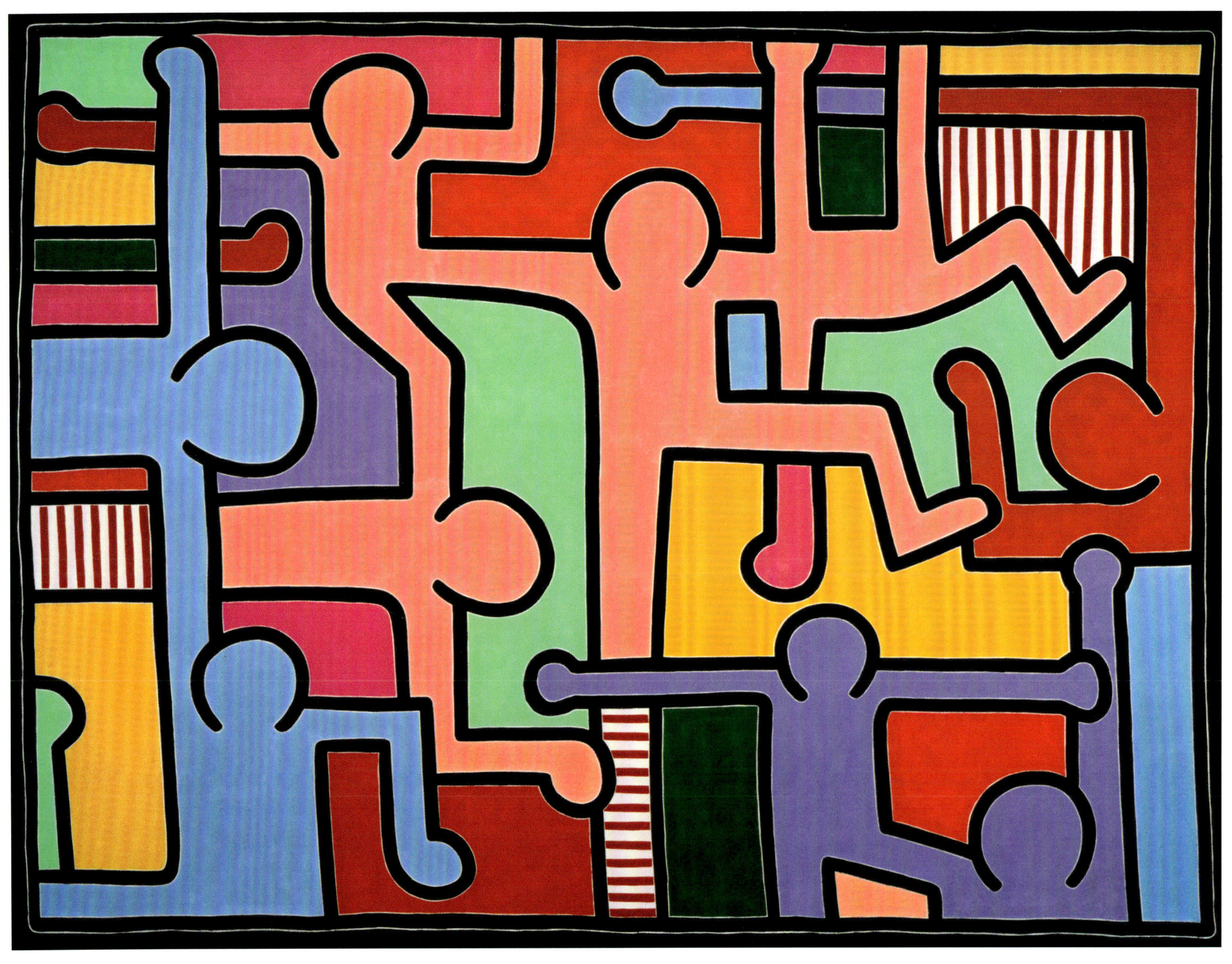

203

Untitled, 1988. Acrylic on linen, 108 x 144 in. (274.3 x 365.8 cm)
Private collection

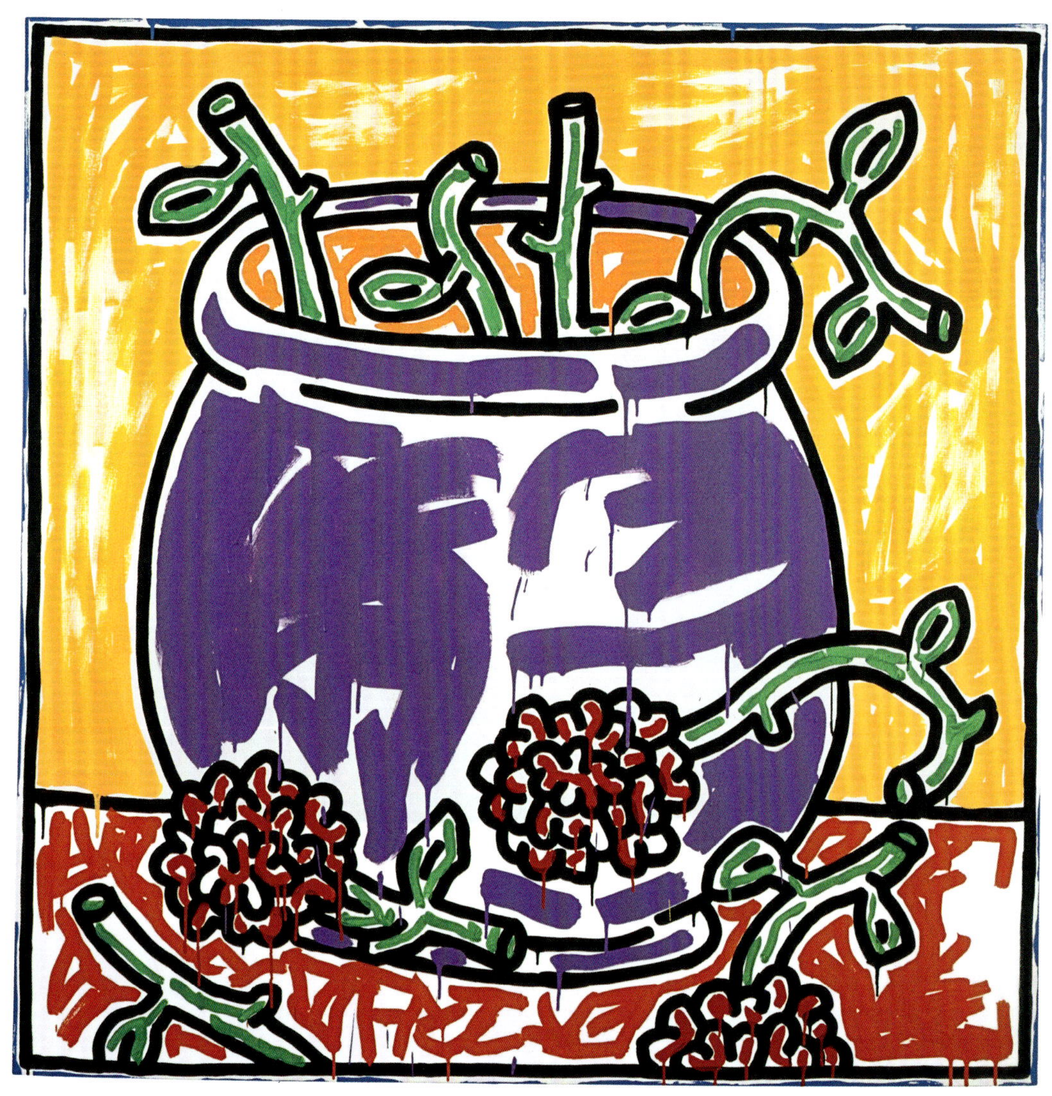

204

Untitled, February 4, 1989. Acrylic on canvas, 60 x 60 in. (152.4 x 152.4 cm)
Elliot K. Wolk 2012 Family Trust

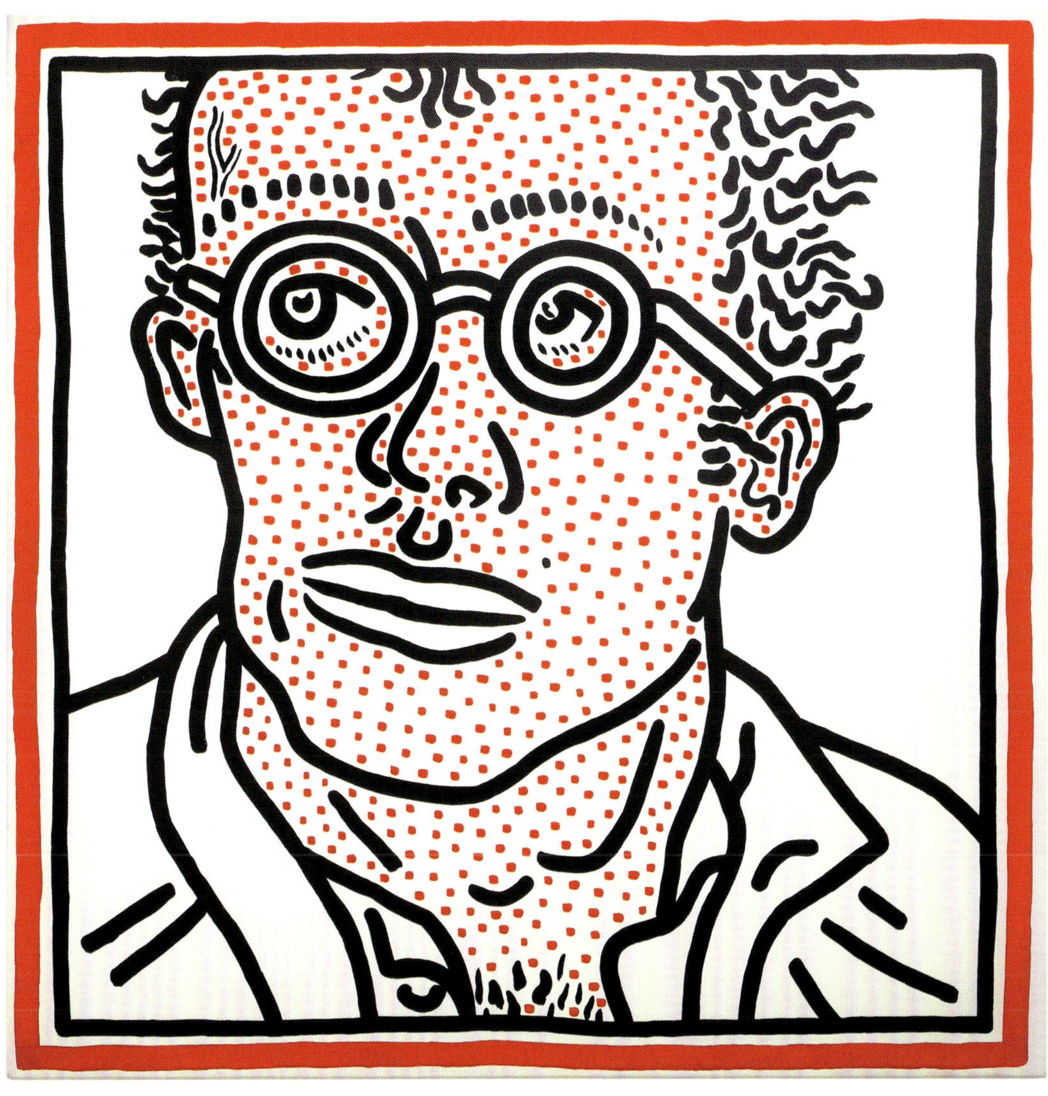

205

Untitled (*Self-Portrait*), February 2, 1985. Acrylic on canvas, 48 x 48 in. (121.9 x 121.9 cm)
Private collection

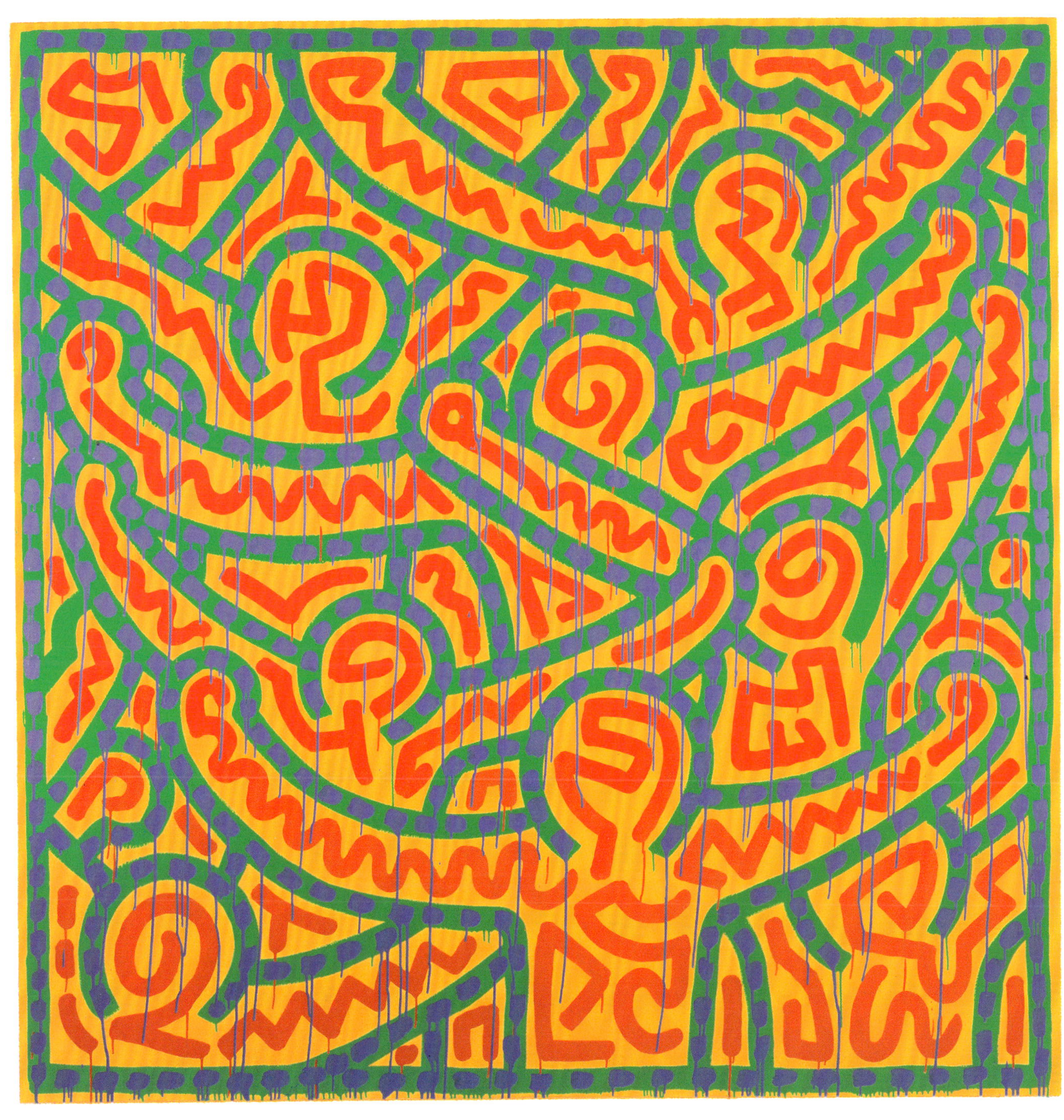

206

Untitled, 1989. Acrylic and enamel on canvas, 72 x 72 in. (183 x 183 cm)
Collection of the Keith Haring Foundation

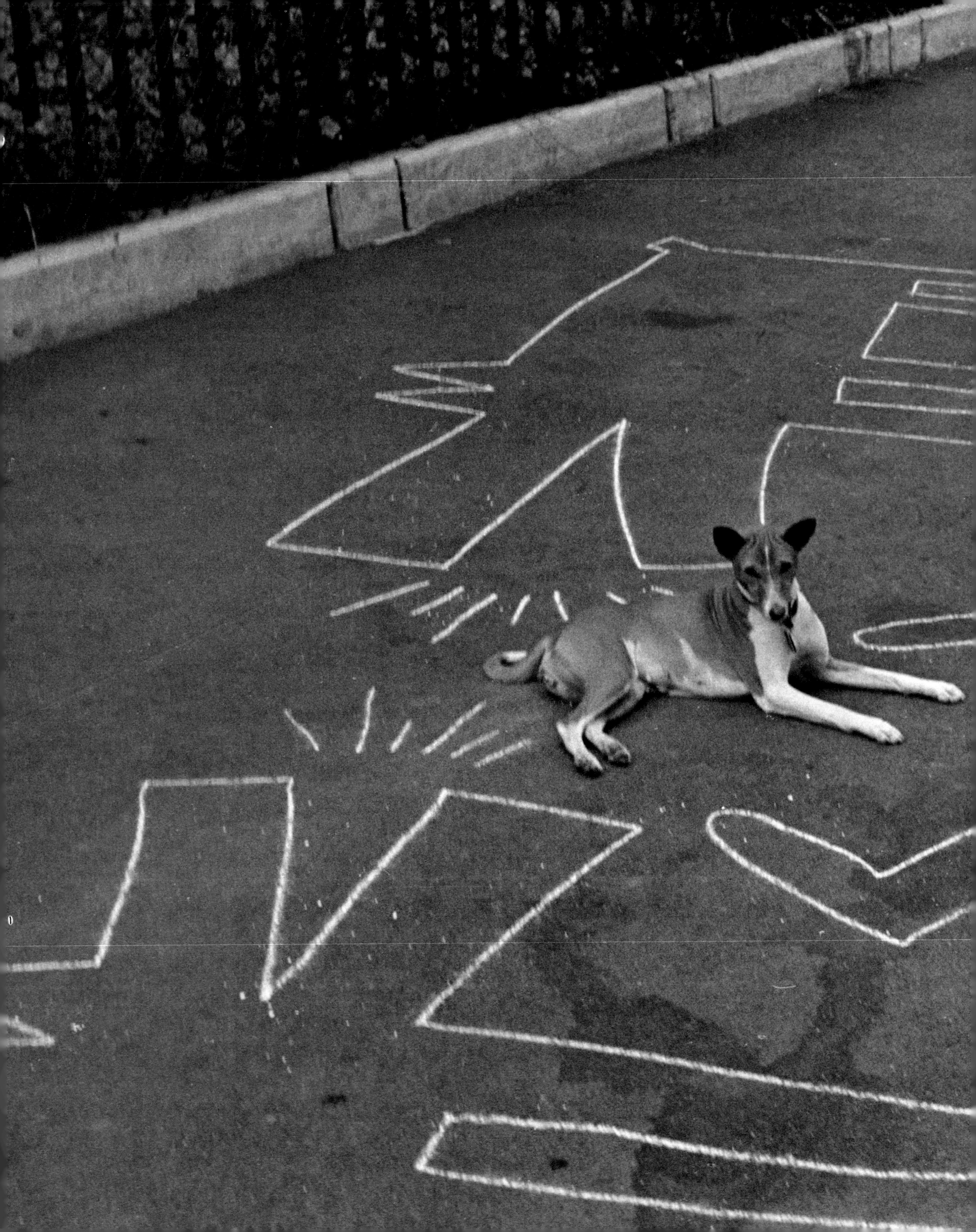

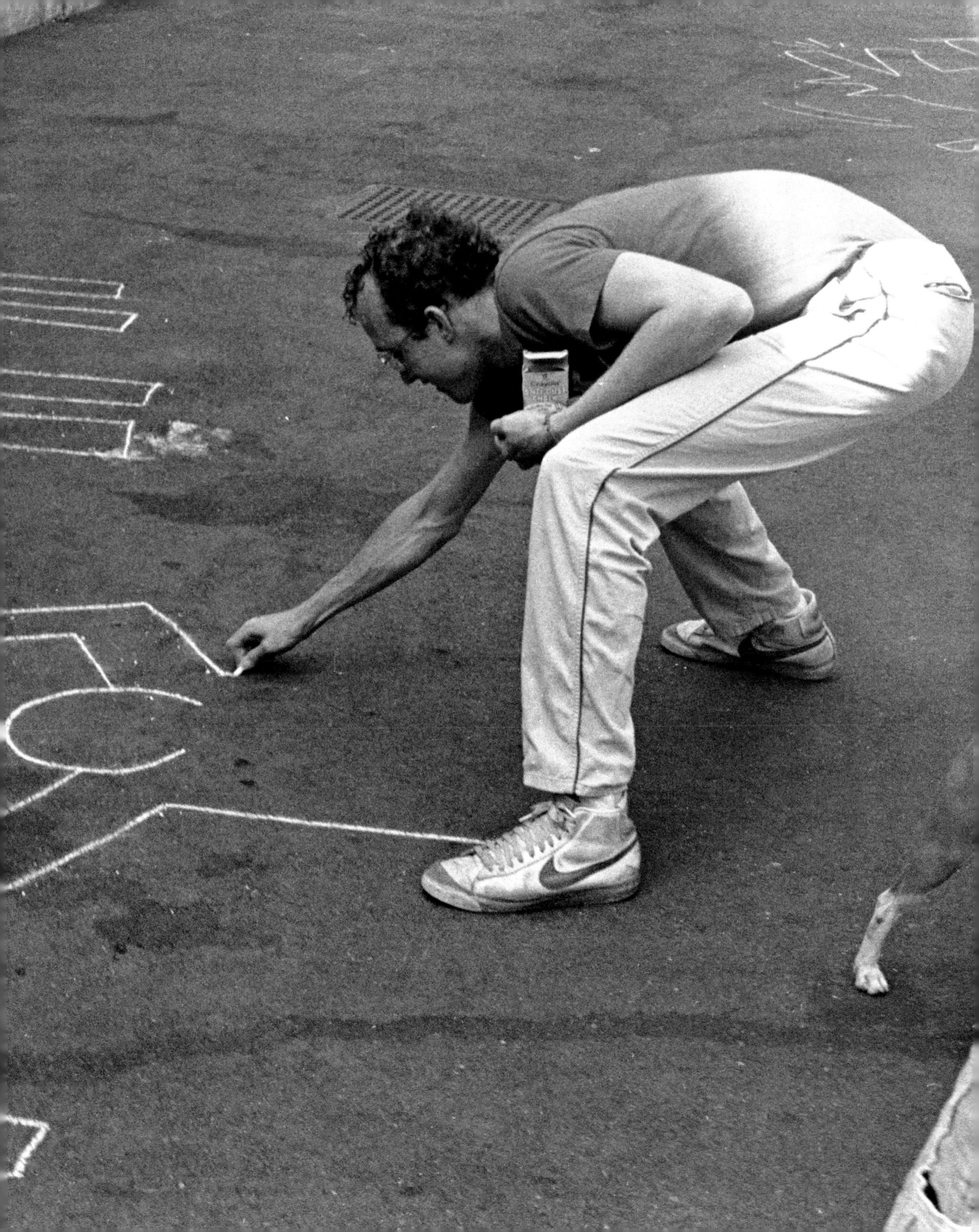

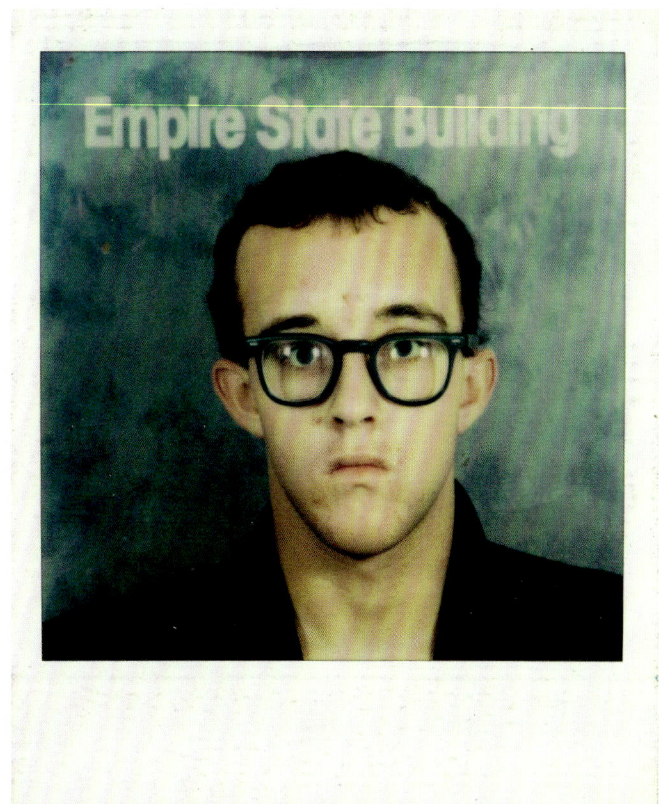
Empire State Building

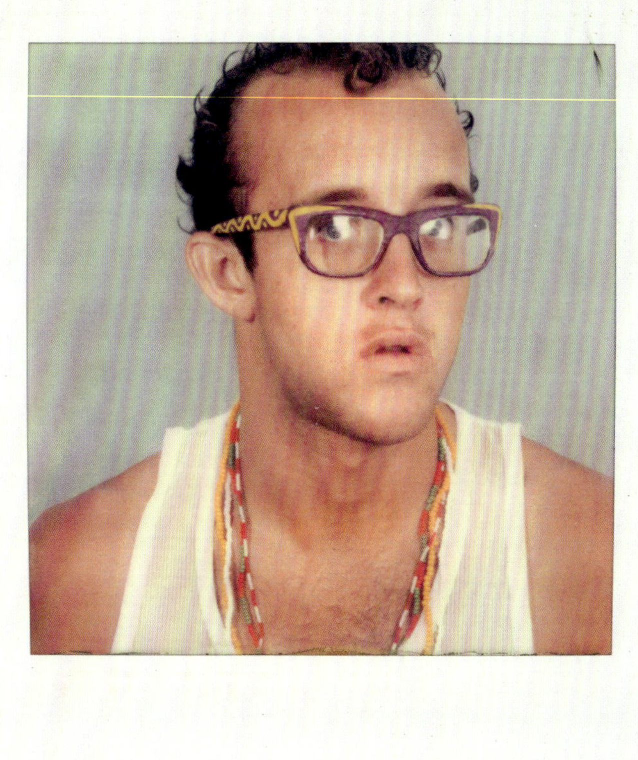

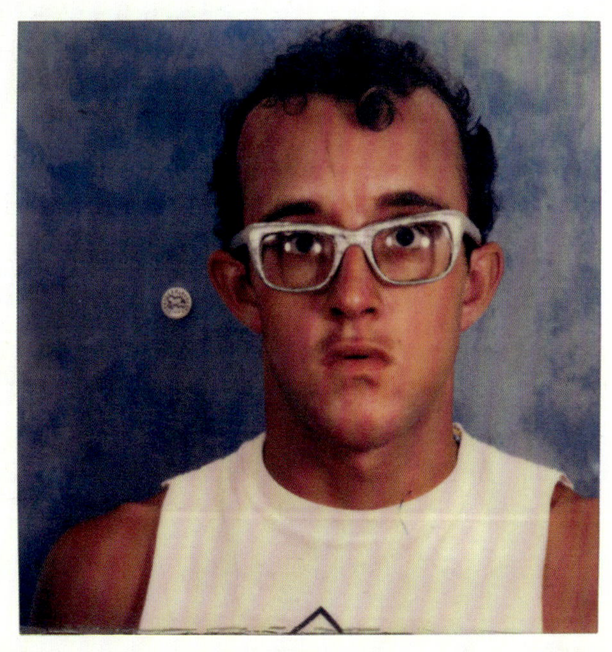

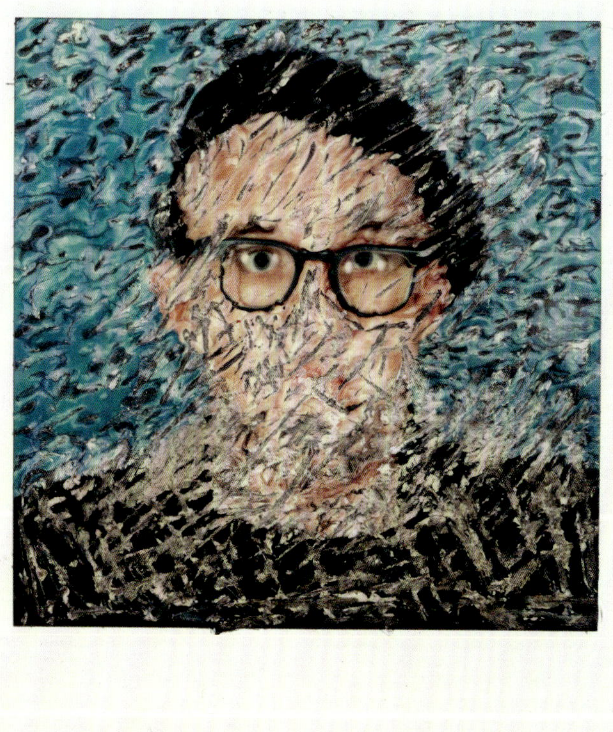

KEITH HARING'S PLACES AND NON-PLACES: A CHRONOLOGY

Early Years: Childhood and Moving to New York City

Keith Haring is born in Reading, Pennsylvania, on May 4, 1958, and grows up in nearby Kutztown. He is the first-born child of four, and the only son. In 1976, at his parents' recommendation, he enrolls in the Ivy School of Professional Art in Pittsburgh, but drops out after one year to pursue independent studies in visual art. He studies the works of Paul Klee, Jean Dubuffet, Mark Tobey, Jackson Pollock, and Pierre Alechinsky. In 1978, he enrolls in the School of Visual Arts in New York, where his professors include Simone Forti, Keith Sonnier, and Joseph Kosuth. There, he creates performance pieces, videos, and large-scale painted environments (see p. 46 and fig. 21).

GIORGIO VERZOTTI
WITH CONTRIBUTIONS BY
DIETER BUCHHART AND JULIA GRUEN

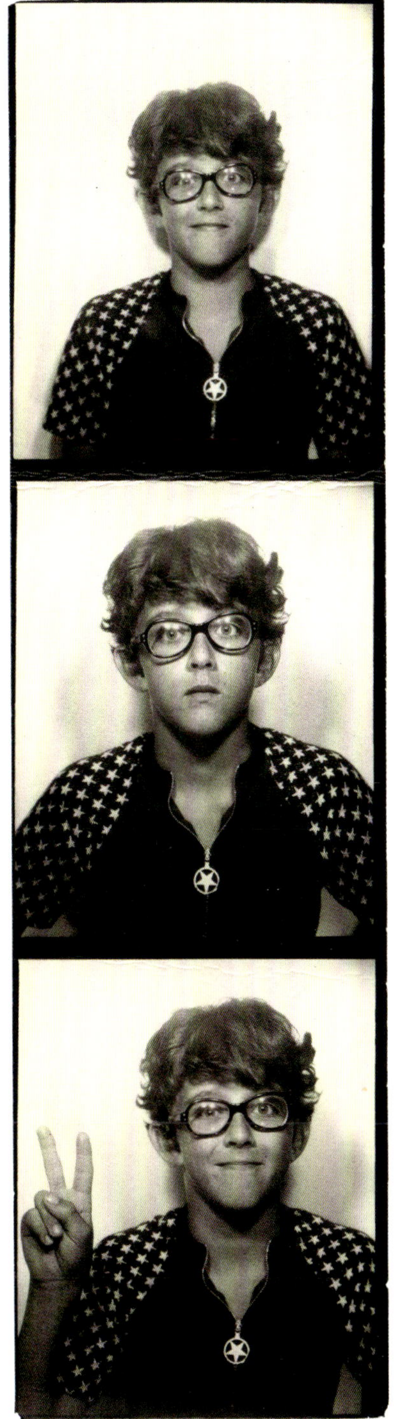

(pp. 246–247)
Keith Haring drawing with chalk on pavement at the dog run at Mercer and Houston Streets, New York, n.d. Photograph by Tseng Kwong Chi

51–54 (opposite)

Keith Haring, self-portraits, 1980–1981. Four Polaroids. Collection of the Keith Haring Foundation

55 (above)

Photo-booth portraits of Keith Haring, c. 1970–1972. Collection of Mr. and Mrs. Allen Haring

1979–1981: Political Messaging in Public Spaces and Tagging on the Street

After leaving the School of Visual Arts, Haring devotes himself to various forms of street art in New York. In public places, he posts photocopies of collaged newspaper headlines directed against authority figures such as Ronald Reagan and Pope John Paul II (1980) (see pls. 54–59); he also promotes events and organizes exhibitions at such trendy venues as Club 57, P.S. 122, and the Mudd Club. These activities are a crucible for developing his personal artistic vocabulary. In the winter of 1980, he makes drawings on various public surfaces, including advertising billboards, scaffolds of construction sites, and the pavement. He creates signature images (or "tags") to identify himself within the graffiti world; these include a crawling baby and a barking dog, drawn with very simple outlines and easily replicated. An interesting aspect of his street art is its rhythmic visual iteration determined by the serial disposition of the images. This repetitive narrative distinguishes the works of the artist from those of more conventional graffiti artists. The latter treat any surface as a single flat plane or picture space for their colorful inscriptions, whereas Haring demonstrates an interest in the narrative sequencing of comic strips.

In June 1980, Haring is among approximately one hundred artists included in the month-long *Times Square Show*, held in an abandoned building at 201 West 41st Street and organized by the artists' collective Colab.

In December 1980, in New York subway stations, he creates his first white-chalk drawings on sheets of black paper used to cover expired advertisements. Haring uses the brief interludes of these advertising voids to convey his own messages and to intervene directly in existing social communications, adopting an illegal act of appropriation similar to that of European *affichistes* (Raymond Hains, Domenico "Mimmo" Rotella, Jacques Villeglé, and others). In 1981, he shares a space on Broome Street with fellow artists Kenny Scharf and Samantha McEwen and his lover DJ Juan Dubose. Until this time, paper has been Haring's preferred medium, but from 1981 onward, he paints on a variety of materials: found objects, leather, metal, and especially vinyl tarpaulins, which will become an iconic surface for his art.

In August 1981, he receives his first public commission when the high school P.S. 22, at Columbia and East Houston Streets on the Lower East Side, one of the most desolate neighborhoods in the city, invites Haring and other artists (including Lady Pink, Futura 2000, and Crash) to create a mural on the outside of the building. While the other artists paint their images and colored words on the mezzanine wall, Haring's contribution is limited to the lower border of the first floor, where he creates a long frieze with a continuous line of small figures, including a baby and dog, two-headed snakes, phones, and computers.

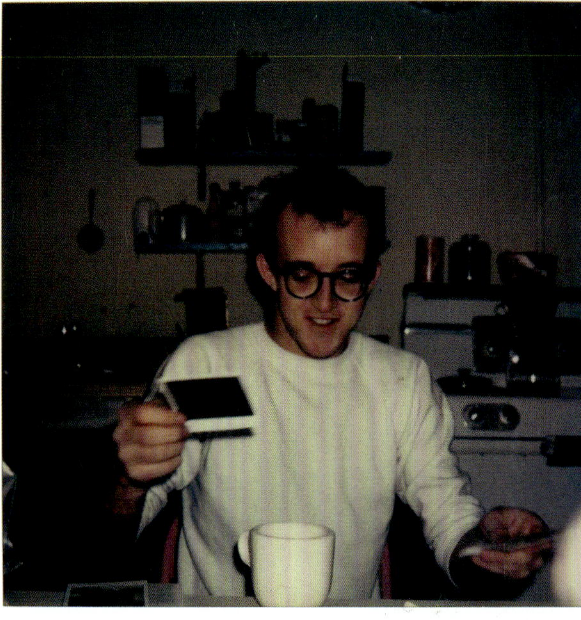

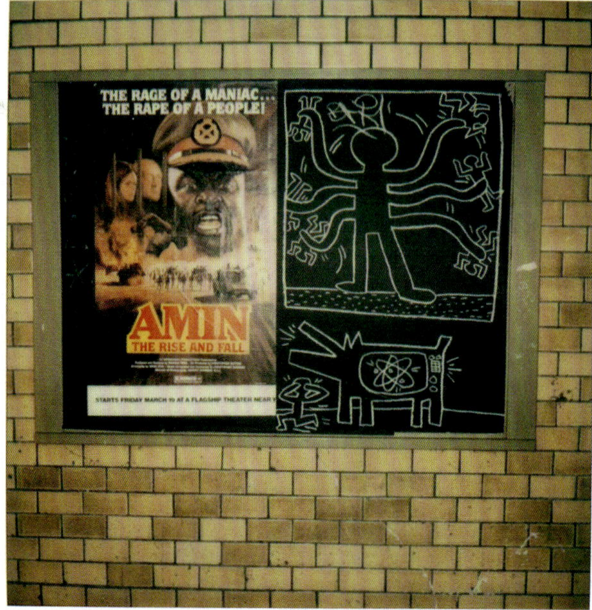

56

Unknown photographer, Keith Haring, 1981. Polaroid.
Collection of the Keith Haring Foundation

57

Unknown photographer, Subway Drawing by Keith Haring with poster for *Amin: The Rise and Fall*, April 17, 1982. Polaroid.
Collection of the Keith Haring Foundation

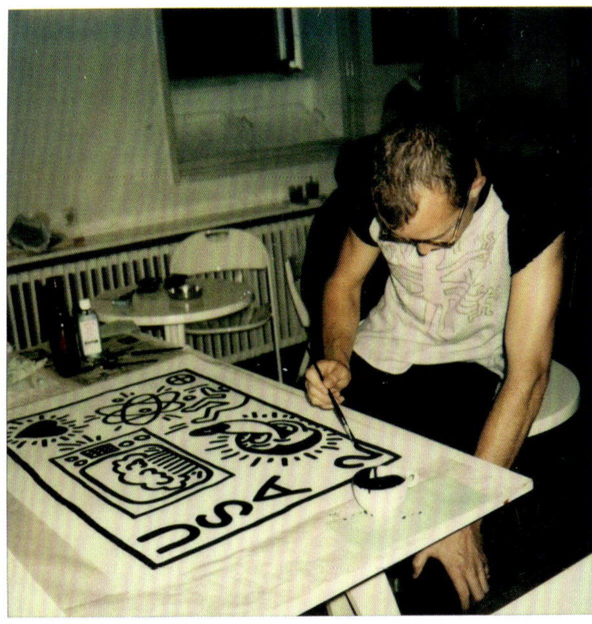

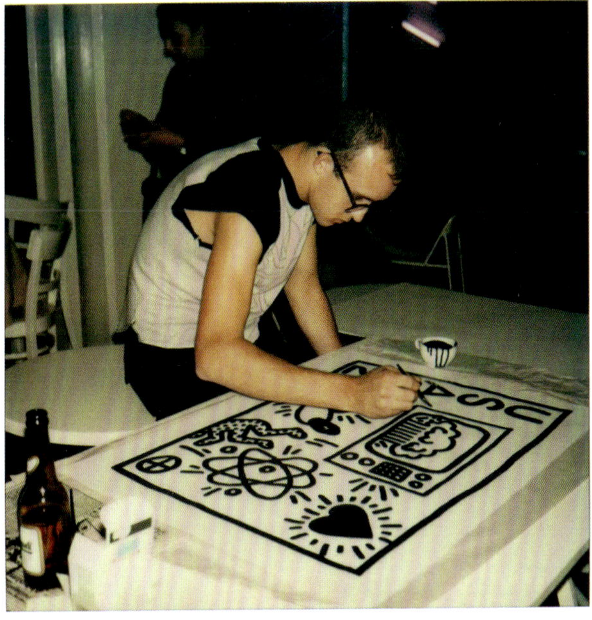

1982:
Antinuclear Rally, Houston Street Mural, and International Recognition

The New York Public Art Fund invites Haring and eleven other artists to create work to be animated for display on the electronic Spectacolor billboard in Times Square (January 15–December 31). Haring's animation is thirty seconds long and is shown once every twenty minutes for a month (see figs. 10–12). It shows a man with a cross; a man stabbing another man with a stick; several dogs jumping through the wounded man; and a baby, a lightbulb, and a motionless but radiating dog.

Haring's sociopolitical awareness is manifested very early in his art. Among the Subway Drawings are antiwar subjects aimed explicitly at US foreign policies, and the dollar sign is employed in association with images of weapons and war machinery. On June 12, during a rally for nuclear disarmament in Central Park, he distributes twenty thousand posters he printed in support of the event (see fig. 5).

In July, he creates a large painting on a wall in front of a building at Houston Street and the Bowery (see pp. 14–15). He divides the space into two sections: on the top, between two large, square, three-eyed fuchsia faces, four big pale-green figures dance upside down. In the lower section, two rows of figures run toward each other from opposite ends and meet in the center. Along the edges, inside yellow squares, are atomic signs, each with three nuclei. The colors are fluorescent. The images of dancing figures, so numerous in Haring's artistic production, explicitly refer to the rhythmic, almost mechanical movements of break dancing. With his paintings and his street performances, the artist responds to the energy emanating from hip-hop culture, which includes rap music as well as break dancing, a counterculture from the streets that will soon become a part of the new mass culture.

In October, Haring receives his first important solo gallery exhibition, at the Tony Shafrazi Gallery in SoHo. He fills almost every inch of the space with drawings, paintings, and decorated sculptures. He also creates a black-light installation and, together with graffiti artist LA II (a.k.a. Angel Ortiz), he paints on the surfaces of various three-dimensional objects. Haring is also invited to Documenta 7, one of the most important contemporary exhibitions in the world. It is the first of many international events he will be invited to participate in, including the Whitney Biennial (1983), the Venice Biennale (1984), and the Sculpture Project in Münster (1987).

Haring's activities on the subway arouse the interest of the public, and people often stop to watch him draw. The police also become interested, and he is arrested more than once. Haring decides to produce two metal pins, one featuring his radiant baby and one his barking dog, to distribute to his fans. In the subway, for the 1982 Christmas season, he draws nativity scenes and New Year's greetings that include words and phrases.

58–59

Unknown photographer, Keith Haring, 1982. Two Polaroids. Collection of the Keith Haring Foundation

1983:
Collaboration with LA II

Haring moves his public interventions beyond the New York subway system. In February, he is invited by Marquette University in Milwaukee, Wisconsin, to draw on both sides of a long white wooden construction fence built in anticipation of the groundbreaking for the college's new Haggerty Museum of Art. On one side, in orange, he creates a sequence of babies over a sequence of dogs; on the other side, he renders large men, dogs, angels, televisions, and a large square face with three eyes (the latter image appears with increasing frequency from this point onward, becoming another of Haring's signature icons, like the baby and the dog).

Also in February, on the occasion of Haring's solo show at the Galerie Watari in Tokyo, he paints (in collaboration with LA II) a large mural on the front of a building across from the gallery. The event is covered live on Japanese national television. Haring also creates chalk drawings on the streets and organizes a birthday party for Juan Dubose, his lover, at the club Tamatsubaki, where the owner asks Haring and LA II to paint the walls, delivering spray cans of paint to the artists on a tray.

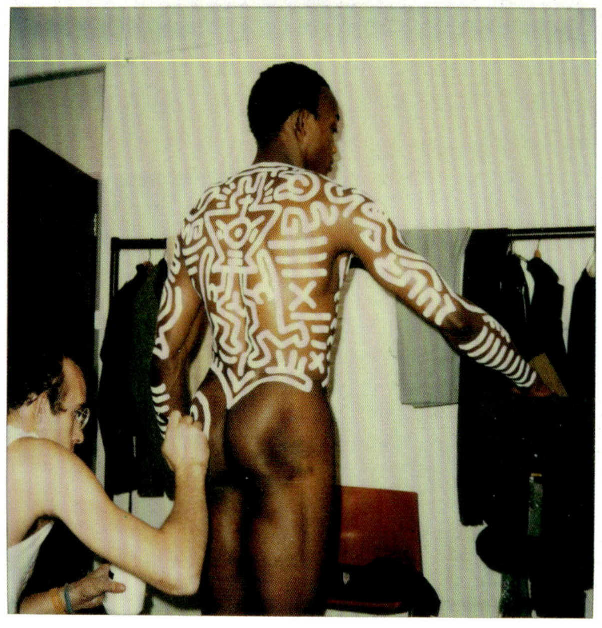

In May, the artist works in Naples, Italy. A few days before the opening of his exhibition at the Galleria Lucio Amelio, he paints the naked body of a young man for a photograph that appears in the magazine *Frigidaire*. At the opening, the artist paints on the chest of another young man. Both bodies are covered by abstract black symbols strongly reminiscent of tribal decorations. While still in Naples, he draws with white chalk on the pavement in the gardens of Villa Comunale, paints with black paint on the window of a shop in the city center, and decorates a car.

In July, Haring joins a group of artists to create a mural on a wall of a building on Avenue D in Manhattan's East Village. He draws a large robot-DJ spinning records with his four arms. The surface of the painting is densely covered by the colorful tags of the artists.

Official (though unpaid) commissions become more numerous for Haring. He designs the poster for the seventeenth Montreux Jazz Festival, held in July. The poster features a twirling figure reproduced in three versions in various colors. In Montreux, he also paints the Jeep he uses there; covers the fence of a local construction site with a set of large figures (some with tails, others twirling) in red, blue, and green on a yellow background; and paints on roadside billboards. He draws on large sheets of paper during several concerts and dedicates the drawings to the bands, using specific iconographic clues to indicate each one. (For the 1986 edition of the same festival, he will again create the poster, this time collaborating with his friend Andy Warhol.)

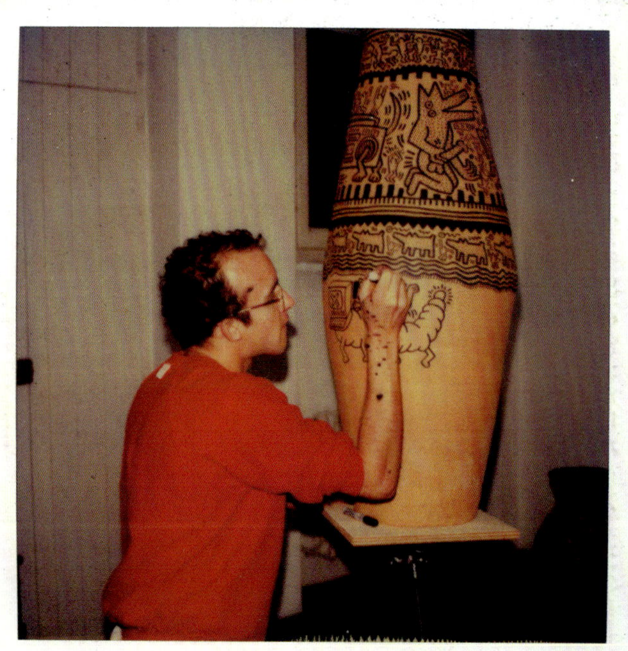

In October, he visits Milan at the invitation of the designer Elio Fiorucci. There, with LA II, he paints the walls, desk, and dressing rooms of the Fiorucci boutique behind the Piazza del Duomo. With fast strokes of fluorescent paint, he outlines his trademark figures, which LA II then fills in with dynamic lines and tags, blurring their iconic recognizability in the intermixing of colored and energetic signs. Haring's process is often based on a repetition of lines that, collectively, achieve a type of hyper-decoration, creating the appearance, as in this case, of an abstracted form.

In London, during the run of another solo show at the Robert Fraser Gallery (October 19–November 12), the artist uses white acrylic on the naked body of his friend the dancer Bill T. Jones (see fig. 60), with whom he collaborated in 1982 on the dance sequence *Long Distance*, performed between September 30 and October 3 at The Kitchen in New York. Tseng Kwong Chi's 1983 photographs of the painted dancer will be exhibited at Haring's second solo exhibition at Tony Shafrazi Gallery in New York in January 1984. (Further paintings on the bodies of models will be realized during Haring's show at Galerie Paul Maenz in Cologne in May 1984.)

1984:
Popularity and Criticism

In February, the National Gallery of Victoria, Melbourne, invites Haring to create several murals, which leads to the first controversy surrounding the content of Haring's public art. He works on the Waterwall near the entrance to the museum (see p. 20). In the middle of the glass, in white paint, he renders a large totem, its head composed of red concentric circles, surrounded by men or robots who have either snake heads or extremely long spiral necks. The event is recorded by the students of the Australian Film School. Upon completion of the work, the local press accuses Haring of appropriating styles belonging to traditional Aboriginal cultures. The controversy highlights a characteristic of Haring's style: its so-called primitive and pictorial language, in which his iconic signs can be seen as words using an ideogrammatic alphabet. Haring's archaism, reconsidered as a reference to childhood through comic strips, also reflects the lack of visual perspective in his flattened compositions, which are always built upon pure contiguity of figures on a single plane. After the National Gallery mural, the artist is given an unpaid commission for a permanent mural at the Collingwood Technical School in the same city. On a wall of the school building, he paints a long millipede with a computer-shaped head, ridden by two blue men, on a yellow background.

Also in February, at the invitation of the National Gallery of New South Wales, Sydney, he creates a huge black-on-white mural on the upper half of a wall close to the museum entrance; some of the large figures are typical of his work, and others, such as the kangaroo, are inspired by the location.

Back in the United States, Haring holds one of his many series of activities with students in various schools; a drawing workshop is held at the Ernest Horn Elementary School in Iowa City on March 27–28.

In May, he organizes a birthday party—the First Annual Party of Life—at the Paradise Garage, his favorite club. His friend Madonna wears a leather suit designed by the artist as she debuts songs from her album *Like a Virgin*. With LA II's help, Haring decorates the venue with fluorescent banners and flags. The invitation is a cotton handkerchief printed with the title, venue, and date.

In July, he decorates the interior of George's Candy Store on Avenue D in Manhattan, a shop that is also a meeting spot for neighborhood kids. On the blue walls, the artist paints large, vaguely monstrous red-orange figures; big faces with wide-open mouths on small, misshapen bodies; three-legged figures; black skeletons; and a red atomic mushroom cloud. Haring uses the monstrous or deformed features of his typical figures to vary his visual repertoire and enrich it with new iconographic implications.

The New York City Department of Sanitation organizes an antilitter campaign and commissions Haring to create a logo for posters, stickers, pins, and television advertisements. The subject is a cartoon pig inside a prohibition sign. At the campaign's summertime launch, Haring is publicly thanked by the mayor of New York, Ed Koch; the artist presents the mayor with his book *Art in Transit*, which includes photographs of Haring's Subway Drawings. Ironically, Koch has been a leading advocate of the city's campaign against graffiti.

In October, on FDR Drive, he creates a new image of a large man trampling a much smaller man on a leash (see pl. 142). This image will also be used for the 1985 "Free South Africa" antiapartheid campaign (see fig. 18). (He will protest racism closer to home with a 1985 painting that references the 1983 death of graffiti tagger Michael Stewart during an arrest by New York City police officers [pl. 145].)

In November, Haring designs sets and costumes for *Secret Pastures*, a production choreographed and performed by Bill T. Jones and Arnie Zane, with music by Peter Gordon. Included is a tent decorated with Haring's schematically outlined human figures. Two scrims framing the stage are covered with motifs reminiscent of eroticized Matisse flowers, with various abstract and linear elements. The tent is moved around on the stage and rotated as the dancers perform in and around it.

In December, Haring visits Paris for the group show *5/5, Figuration libre, France/USA,* held at the Musée d'Art Moderne de la Ville de Paris. While there, he draws on advertising spaces at the Alma-Marceau and Dupleix metro stations. In the first station, he fills the metro's wall with figures outlined with a black brush; in the latter, he draws a large man with a dangling head and a large penis, outlined in red with orange dots on a blue background.

After Paris, he travels to Marseille, where he creates the backdrop for the ballet *Le mariage du ciel et de l'enfer*, based on the poem by William Blake and choreographed by Roland Petit for the Ballet National de Marseille. Using black pigment on a white background, Haring paints two long arms whose hands span the canvas vertically and meet in the center. The upper hand places a ring on a finger of the lower hand. Numerous angels, representing the heavens, float in the upper half, and the bottom half—hell—is littered with corpses. It is the largest painting ever realized by the artist and arguably among the most powerful.

60

Unknown photographer, Keith Haring painting Bill T. Jones, October 1983. Polaroid. Collection of the Keith Haring Foundation

61

Unknown photographer, Keith Haring painting a terracotta vase, Milan, Italy, 1984. Polaroid. Collection of the Keith Haring Foundation

1985:
Painting and Hip-Hop

In February, Haring curates an exhibition titled *Rain Dance*, benefiting the United States African Emergency Relief Fund for UNICEF, for which he designs a poster in collaboration with Jean-Michel Basquiat, Andy Warhol, Yoko Ono, and Roy Lichtenstein. The exhibition is held in a newly leased space on Lafayette Street that, one year later, will become Haring's Pop Shop. He also organizes a benefit party at the Paradise Garage in New York (January 30).

Also in February, for the Brooklyn Academy of Music, he creates the set design for the ballet *Sweet Saturday Night*, choreographed by Lenwood Sloan, Arthur Hall, and Mama Lu Parks. The backdrop features figures decorated with abstract signs; from the white space at lower center (which represents a door) emerges a man with a radiant spiral-shaped body who creates white anthropomorphic shapes for the dancers to hold up during the performance.

In March, he designs the cover of *Scholastic News*, a publication distributed to almost three million American students. For Keith Haring Day at the Children's Village, a residential school for underserved children in Dobbs Ferry, New York, he draws a logo with a clown's face and hands out T-shirts and balloons. (In August, at P.S. 97 in New York, on the school's handball court, he will create a mural depicting an enormous boombox surrounded by flying monsters and his more typical dancing figures.)

In the spring, Haring moves from theaters to clubs, creating a permanent installation inside the Palladium: a large backdrop on canvas in fluorescent colors reminiscent of a large puzzle, whose colored pieces interact with the club lights.

Love of music motivates the artist to realize further real-time performances during concerts, including Live Aid, held on July 13 at the John F. Kennedy Stadium in Philadelphia to raise funds for African famine relief; the musicians include, among others, Tina Turner, Michael Jackson, and Mick Jagger. Haring's large drawing, depicting two large hands holding a big red heart with planet Earth at its center, is created during the concert and is eventually auctioned, with proceeds benefiting African famine relief.

A meeting with Grace Jones leads to "Her Grace at Paradise," a concert held on October 1 at the Paradise Garage in which the pop star performs with her body painted with Haring's tribal symbols (see fig. 22). Otherwise dressed only in chains, metal headgear, and a metal bra, all designed by David Spada, Jones starts the show chained to two decorated columns. She next appears riding a bass drum and wearing a skirt made of black and white threads and a headdress constructed out of Haring's figures. Both the headgear and the costume were produced when Warhol asked Haring to paint Jones's body for a Robert Mapplethorpe photo shoot the previous year (see fig. 8).

October 26 marks the opening of concurrent shows at the Tony Shafrazi and Leo Castelli galleries. Haring considers the latter space "sacred," which pushes him to become irreverent. He shows his new sculptures there, but also fills the walls with a frieze of cartoon characters based on drawings he made when he was ten years old.

December 15 marks the opening of Haring's first solo museum exhibition, at the CAPC Musée d'Art Contemporain de Bordeaux, France (see p. 24 and pp. 86–87). Featured are paintings, sculptures, and numerous drawings; the centerpiece is a monumental work titled *The Ten Commandments*, consisting of ten arched canvas panels placed back to back within the towering arches of the salon on the ground floor. The iconography, which is both fantastic and aggressive, does not follow the biblical canon, and, unsurprisingly, it provokes religious fundamentalists. (The show will travel to the Stedelijk Museum in Amsterdam in March 1986, where Haring will work with spray paint on the large scrim placed under the central skylight to protect artworks from direct light.)

In December, Haring works with children in an afterschool program at the Saint Patrick's Day Care Center in San Francisco. In black on white, he paints a frieze of children and animals on the wall of the center's gymnasium (fig. 3), using a style he had previously tested at his exhibition at the Leo Castelli Gallery, among other venues.

1986:
Engagement against Drugs and the Cold War, Art for Everybody

Haring and Grace Jones collaborate again in connection with her music video "I'm Not Perfect (But I'm Perfect for You)." Haring creates an enormous white skirt covered with an abstract pattern, and David Spada contributes a bodice and a red and yellow hat. The video features a time-lapse recording of the artist painting the skirt on the floor of a studio in Paris. The clip ends with the audience running under the skirt, which Jones is now wearing, while she appears to levitate. Also in 1986, Haring decorates a fiberglass cast of the bodybuilder Mr. Universe with black symbols for a scene in the movie *Vamp*, in which Jones plays one of the main characters.

In April, Haring opens the Pop Shop on Lafayette Street in Manhattan, where he sells merchandise, clothes, and other items emblazoned with his own imagery, as well as a few select items by other artists. He decorates the white-walled interior with an allover pattern that creates a continuous maze of abstract forms reminiscent of the artist's ambient paintings, made when he was a student.

In May, he is invited to Vienna for the 1986 Wiener Festwochen, where he collaborates with Jenny Holzer to create a large mural (fig. 63). Below the red writing "Schütz mich vor dem was Ich will" (Holzer's famous statement "Protect Me from What I Want"), Haring paints a long frieze of figures overshadowed by a TV set and three standing figures with Xs on their chests, posed to illustrate the concept "see no evil, hear no evil, speak no evil." The two artists also design posters that are displayed at bus stops. The image of the three figures will often return in Haring's sociopolitical works, especially those intended to raise awareness of the AIDS epidemic.

In June, he creates various works on the theme of "Crack Is Wack" (see fig. 4): on Harlem River Drive at East 128th Street, he decorates a handball wall in a small park overlooking the highway (see pp. 10–11). The slogan, painted in black on fluorescent orange, is centered on the wall and surrounded by flying skulls; on the right is a man with bound feet who is about to be devoured by some sort of sea monster. The mural is created without city permission and Haring is fined; he paints over the mural, as required by law.

In July, he collaborates with the youth organization CityKids for the celebrations surrounding the centenary of the Statue of Liberty. With the help of nearly one thousand young people, he paints an image of the monument on an enormous yellow banner (fifteen stories high) (fig. 67; see also pp. 6–7), which is then hoisted onto the side of a building. The collective work remains in place for ten days as a backdrop to concerts and performances by Philip Glass and Herbie Hancock, among others.

In August, in the lobby of Brooklyn's Woodhull Hospital, Haring realizes a mural on two levels. In the lower section he paints a series of small dancing figures, and in the upper section he creates figures and dogs. The latter figures are outlined in black on a background that includes red, blue, and yellow spots floating against the white of the wall. The choice to separate the color from the images, an elegant stylistic variation, adds a new dynamism to Haring's compositions.

In October, Haring returns to Harlem River Drive to realize a new *Crack Is Wack* mural (see pp. 22–23), this time with permission from the city, and uses both sides of the handball wall. Again using fluorescent orange and black paint, on one side he paints a large horizontal skeleton looming over a spread of corpses; on the other he draws a snake chasing a running figure, and below he adds dancing figures with Xs on their chests. On the wall of a playground at P.S. 97, he sketches a large cloud containing the phrase "Life Is Fresh, Crack Is Wack."

Also in October, Haring is invited to Berlin by the Checkpoint Charlie Museum to create a mural on the Berlin Wall (see pp. 8–9). Haring takes over more than 328 feet (100 meters) of the wall, painting a long human chain in red and black on a yellow background, the colors of the German flag. The very schematized horizontal figures hold each other by their hands and legs, conveying a message of unity and equality that contrasts with the division represented by the wall itself. This artistic intervention stimulates the creativity of many other visitors to the wall, who add to Haring's painting. Among the many journalists covering the phenomenon are representatives from the *New York Times*, the *Herald Tribune*, *Time*, and *People*.

Later in October, the artist also dedicates time to working with and on behalf of young people. In coordination with CityKids New York, he accompanies American schoolchildren to Milan, Italy, where his *CityKids Speak on Liberty* banner (see fig. 67 and pp. 6–7) tarpaulin is displayed in the Rotonda della Besana; and he designs a poster for Channel 13's Ninth Students' Art Festival in New York, encouraging students to "draw me a story." In Paris, he decorates a wall inside the toy store Jouets & Cie.

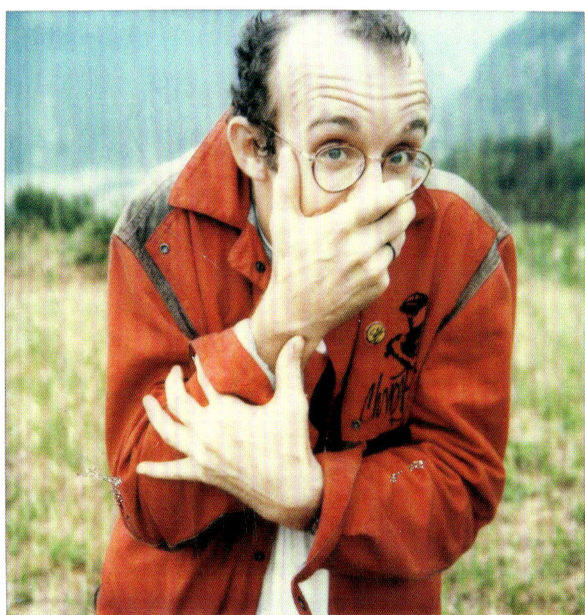

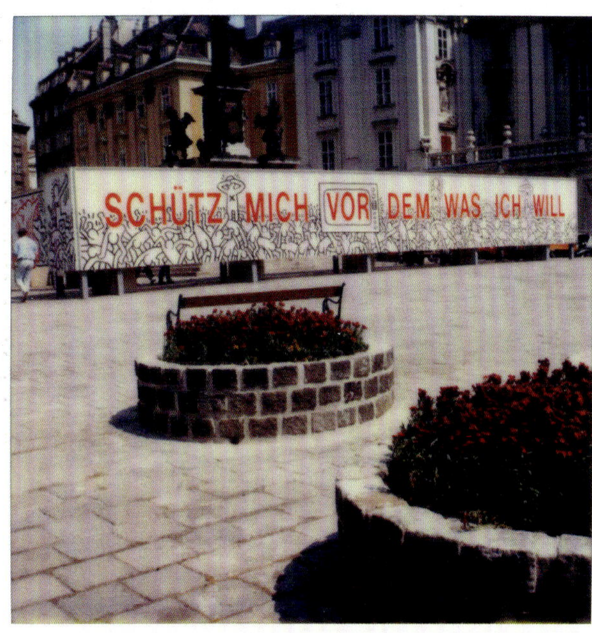

62

Unknown photographer, Keith Haring, Montreux, Switzerland, 1986. Polaroid. Collection of the Keith Haring Foundation

63

Unknown photographer, Keith Haring's collaboration with Jenny Holzer for the Wiener Festwochen, Vienna, Austria, 1986. Polaroid. Collection of the Keith Haring Foundation

1987:
For Youth and the Future

Haring continues to collaborate with young people from CityKids in New York and Philadelphia, creating a large mural with dancing figures titled *We the Youth* (fig. 66).

On February 22, Andy Warhol dies from complications following gallbladder surgery.

In April, Haring designs the set design for *Interrupted River*, a dance piece choreographed by Jennifer Muller with music by Yoko Ono, performed at the Joyce Theater in New York (see figs. 74–75 and pls. 60–62).

Also in April, in Paris, on the concrete tower containing the fire stairs of a building at the pediatric Necker—Enfants Malades Hospital, he paints large spots of color and large figures that seem to be climbing. The casual relationship between color and shape lends dynamism to the scene, underlined by long and harmonious wavy lines.

In May, he designs two murals and a carousel to be installed in Hamburg for Luna Luna, an amusement park that also incorporates the work of artists such as Jean-Michel Basquiat, Joseph Beuys, Salvador Dalí, David Hockney, Roy Lichtenstein, Kenny Scharf, and Jean Tinguely. On the carousel's partitions, Haring draws his black-on-yellow cartoon figures and a purple frieze of small men; the seats of the carousel are shaped like the monumental metal sculptures that he is also producing at this time. One of these large sculptures is installed in New York outside Schneider Children's Hospital, which is Haring's first official sculpture commission. The work is made of steel and depicts three figures in a delicate balancing act. The largest of them, in blue, stands on its head and holds two smaller figures on its feet, one red and one yellow. (In September, the same hospital commissions a permanent Haring mural inside its walls.)

Shortly afterward, Haring works at the Carmine Street swimming pool, creating a frieze on the upper part of one wall (fig. 68). He draws colored patches on the concrete and adds aquatic figures. Some motifs, such as the dolphin and the merman, have been seen in his previous works, but a human swimmer with fins, a salamander, and a fish eating a man are presented for the first time.

In June, in Antwerp, in the cafeteria of the Museum van Hedendaagse Kunst, he creates a mural on a white background dotted with yellow spots. Its figures have an anthropo-mechanomorphic appearance, especially in their facial features, that is reminiscent of Picasso's works. This style, which Haring also explores in his paintings, results in a new pictorial theme: the mask portrait.

In September, he paints figures reading, as well as boxers, swimmers, volleyball players, and weight lifters, on one massive wall of the gymnasium of the Boys Club of New York (see fig. 65), located on Pitt Street on the Lower East Side. The figures are outlined characteristically in black on a white background, under which colored patches have been painted.

In September, for the Cranbrook Academy of Art in Bloomfield Hills, Michigan, he introduces a new style in a mural covering all four walls of one gallery in the museum. The surface is treated with large irregular blotches of color and also incorporates intentional drips. Between the anthropo-mechanomorphic figures appear other forms, made of lighter, more fluid lines. New subjects are introduced: jesters, misshapen human bodies, fetuses, masks, men hung by their feet, skulls, Buddhas, and naked popes. The work exhibits clear references to Hieronymus Bosch and Dalí, as well as Basquiat and Francesco Clemente.

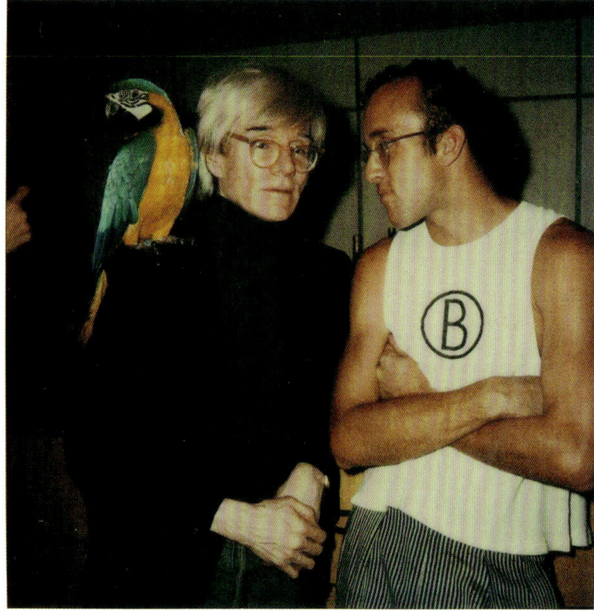

64 (above)

Unknown photographer, Andy Warhol and Keith Haring, c. 1983–1984. Polaroid. Collection of the Keith Haring Foundation

65 (opposite, top left)

Unknown photographer, Keith Haring and children during the painting of the mural for the Boys Club of New York, September 1987. Polaroid. Collection of the Keith Haring Foundation

66 (opposite, top right)

Unknown photographer, *We the Youth* mural by Keith Haring in collaboration with CityKids, Philadelphia, 1987. Polaroid. Collection of the Keith Haring Foundation

67 (opposite, bottom left)

Unknown photographer, *CityKids Speak on Liberty* banner by Keith Haring in collaboration with nearly one thousand public schoolchildren, New York, 1986. Polaroid. Collection of the Keith Haring Foundation

68 (opposite, bottom right)

Unknown photographer, Carmine Street pool mural by Keith Haring, New York, 1987. Polaroid. Collection of the Keith Haring Foundation

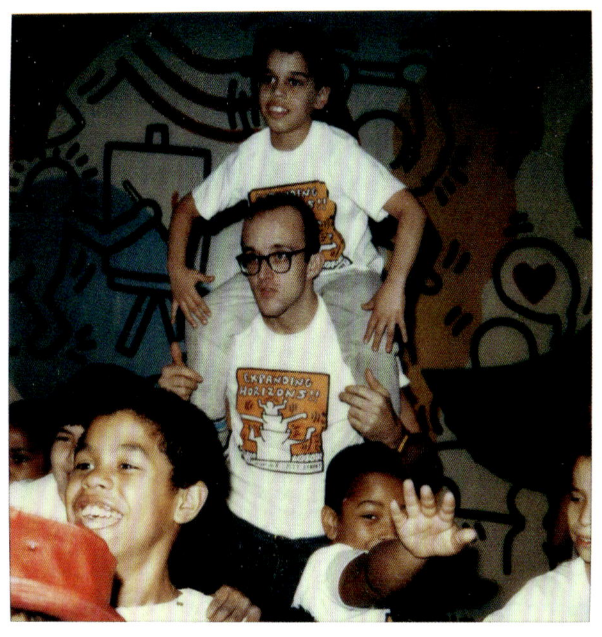
EXPANDING
HORIZONS

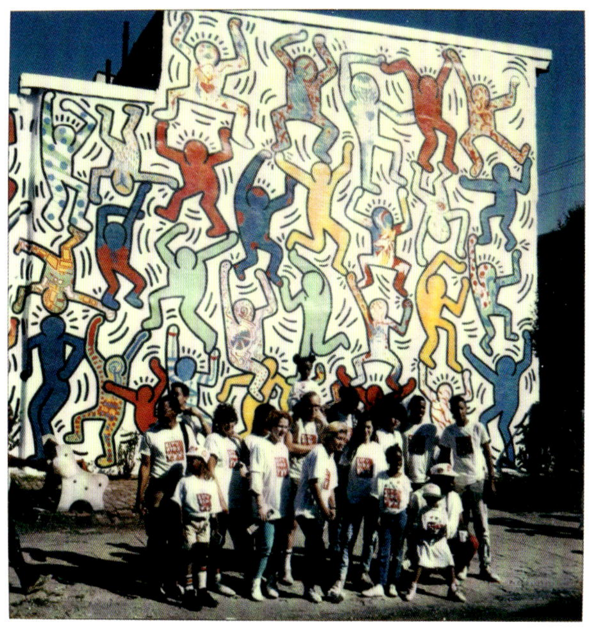

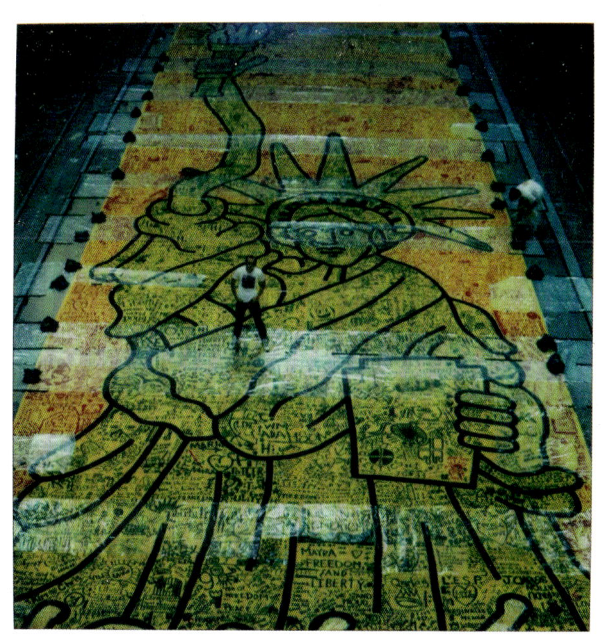

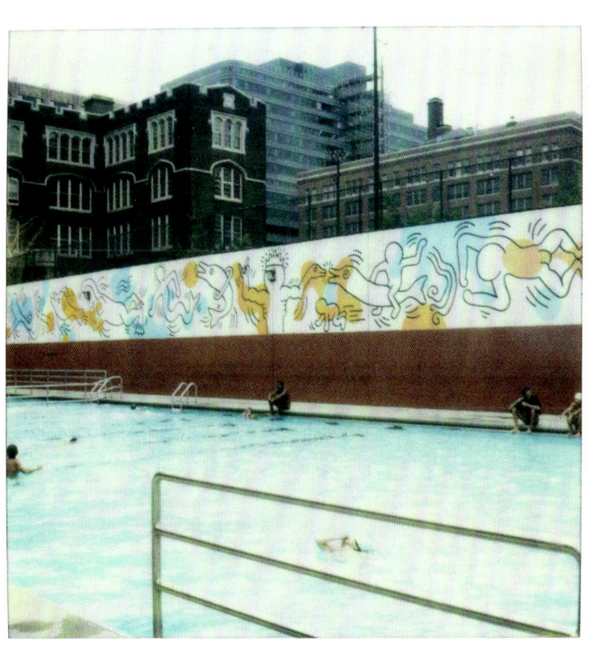

1988:
The Fight against AIDS

Haring is diagnosed with AIDS.

Early in 1988, Haring opens a Pop Shop in Tokyo. The store consists of two large shipping containers, painted white on all sides, with enormous figures painted in black on their roofs. Like that of its New York counterpart, the shop's interior is completely painted. The design is complemented by a series of videos that show several of Haring's public performances. Behind the counter he hangs a large red tondo decorated with figures. The shop closes within a year due to the uncontrollable proliferation of counterfeit Haring merchandise.

At the 1988 Body and Soul dance festival, presented at the Deutsches Theater in Munich beginning March 11, Haring creates the costumes and the stage design for the ballet *Tribal Dance*, choreographed by George Faison, with music by Zazou-Bikaye and RAM034. The white-on-black backdrop includes a central stylized totem surrounded by snakes and dancing figures.

The Public Library Association of New York, with the support of Fox Broadcasting's Channel 5, commissions Haring to design a poster for its literacy campaign. Haring's "Fill Your Head with Fun! Start Reading" design features a smiling face seen in profile, its head filled with a menagerie. The artist also appears in a related televised public-service announcement in which another poster can be seen; it contains the slogan "Drop Everything and Read." (In September 1985, Haring had created a poster for the New York Book Fair.)

In April, for Easter at the White House, Haring installs an outdoor "Creative Keith Haring Fun Center" with the participation of youth. He makes a painting on a white panel in front of an audience, adopting the familiar combination of colored spots and superimposed figures. The panel is later installed at Children's National Medical Center in Washington, DC. Grady Hospital in Atlanta, Georgia, also gets a work by Haring: a mural in the pediatric-emergency waiting room with figures of children and animals in various bright colors. As is customary for Haring, these projects are undertaken pro bono.

In May, in Phoenix, Arizona, Haring creates a mural between Washington and Adams Streets with the collaboration of students who color in his large figure outlines.

In July, at P.S. 97 in New York, Haring creates a new mural (fig. 70) incorporating the phrases "Don't Believe the Hype," "Safe Sex or No Sex," "Respect Yourself," and "Knowledge," alternated with complex symbols: from right to left appear a green staircase being climbed by a man seemingly drawn to a large radiant key floating in midair. At the top, a yellow crown is paired with a pierced heart, and below is a torso of a naked man with extended arms, his left hand in the shape of a dog and his right hand dropping gold coins. On the far left, five flying dollar bills drip blood that pools at the bottom, submerging three figures with raised arms, one of whom has been struck by a syringe.

On August 12, Jean-Michel Basquiat dies of a heroin overdose.

In October, Haring designs the poster for National Coming Out Day.

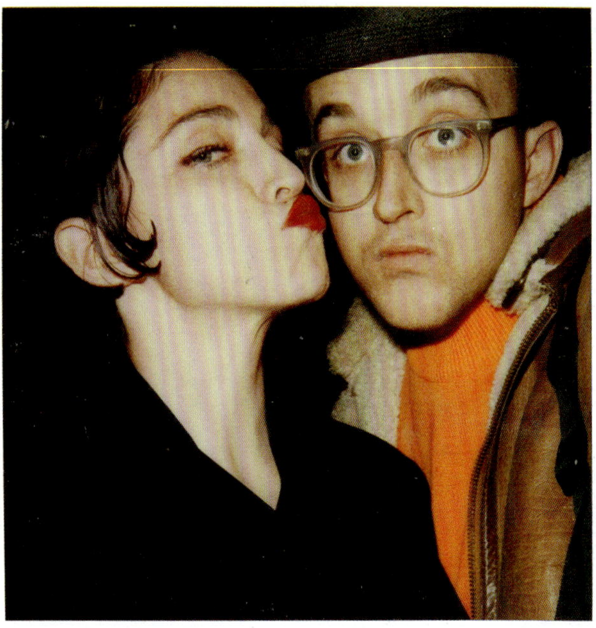

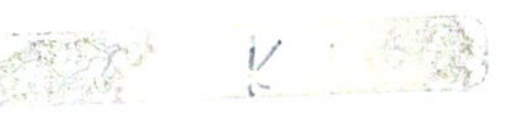

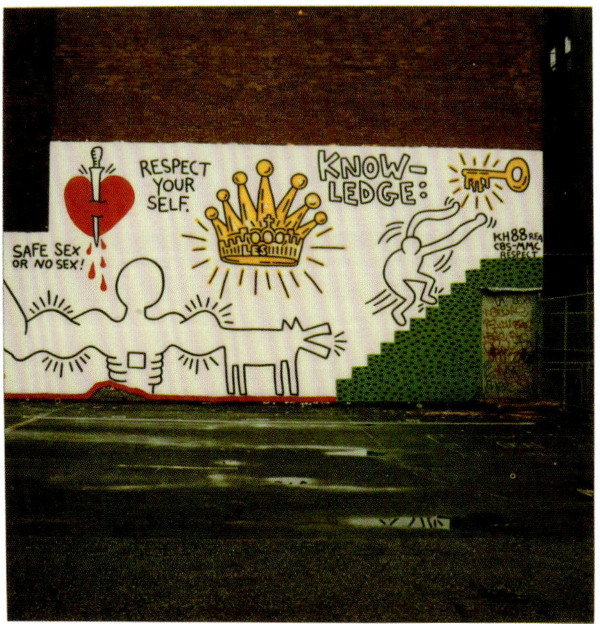

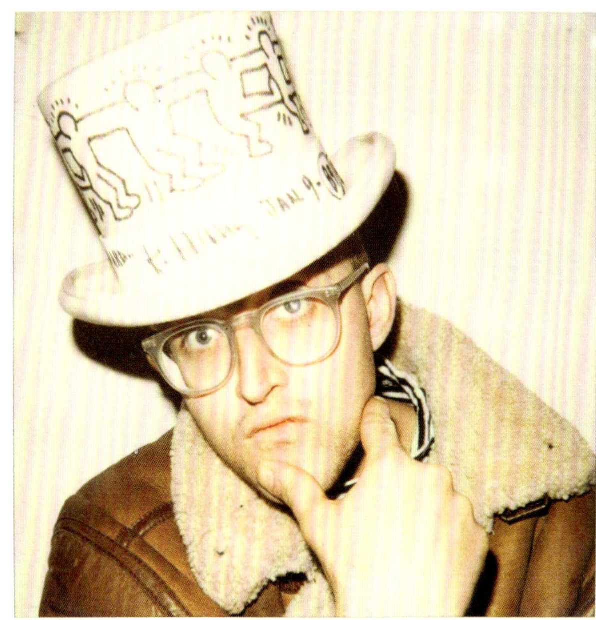

69 (opposite, top)

Unknown photographer, Keith Haring and Madonna after her performance in *Speed the Plow*, New York, 1989. Polaroid. Collection of the Keith Haring Foundation

70 (opposite, bottom)

Unknown photographer, *Don't Believe the Hype* mural by Keith Haring, P.S. 97, New York, 1988. Polaroid. Collection of the Keith Haring Foundation

71 (above)

Unknown photographer, Keith Haring, 1989. Polaroid. Collection of the Keith Haring Foundation

1989:
Murals for the People, Life and Last Works against All Odds

In February, Haring paints a mural on the wall of a building in the Barrio Chino in Barcelona, Spain, then one of the most underserved areas of the city. On the right, the phrase "Todos juntos podemos parar al SIDA" ("Together We Can Stop AIDS") towers over a chain of small radiant figures holding hands. On the left is a long snake, the incarnation of the disease, with a radiant condom on its tail. The widemouthed snake chases four figures, one of whom carries a child; a large pair of scissors cuts the beast in half. Although perhaps less visually dramatic than the P.S. 97 mural, the chromatically plain Barcelona mural contains symbolic transparency that conveys an alarming message.

For ACT UP (AIDS Coalition to Unleash Power), the AIDS advocacy group, he creates a poster that includes his now-familiar three "see no evil, speak no evil, hear no evil" figures with crosses on their chests as symbols of indifference and ignorance. Above and below the figures, written on blue banners, appear the phrases "Ignorance=Fear" and "Silence=Death. Fight AIDS. Act Up."

In May, for the Chicago Museum of Contemporary Art and the Chicago public schools, with the assistance of the city's students, Haring adorns 492 feet (150 meters) of a fence with a complicated maze of black paint strokes. Local television station WTTW-TV broadcasts a short documentary on the project, titled *Off the Wall with Keith and Kids* and narrated by Dennis Hopper. During this week in Chicago, declared Keith Haring Week by Mayor Richard M. Daley, the artist also creates murals at Wells High School and at Rush–Presbyterian/St. Luke's Medical Center, where he paints a large red-dotted heart with a vertical cut in the middle and a man passing through it, surrounded by dancing figures.

Also in May, he creates a mural at the LGBT Community Center in New York's Greenwich Village commemorating the twentieth anniversary of the Stonewall riots. He chooses to paint his mural in the men's restroom, where he depicts sexual organs and acts, using black paint on the white walls. Incorporated in this homoerotic work is its title, *Once upon a Time. . . .* The style is reminiscent of Jean Cocteau's drawings and Pablo Picasso's erotic sketches. The images are happily polymorphic and perverse and harken back to the sexual freedoms of the pre-AIDS era, which is touching in light of the fact that Haring is HIV positive.

In June, Haring is invited by the city of Pisa to paint a mural on the exterior wall of the church of Saint Anthony, near the Piazza Vittorio Emanuele II and the train station. He outlines large figures, more complex than usual, covering the entire surface. The numerous spectators are then invited to color in the figures, using a palette of particularly subtle hues chosen by Haring to echo the city's overall color tonalities. Haring also designs the poster and the banners advertising the event, referred to as "Keith Haring Progetto Italia." It is useful to recall that Haring never prepares preliminary sketches for his monumental works, but instead works directly on the surfaces.

Also in June, the city of Paris requests that Haring and Russian artist Erik Bulatov create two large canvases to be placed on the sides of a zeppelin intended to fly above the city in celebration of the bicentenary of the French Revolution; for technical reasons, it flies only from London, where it was built, to Calais. Haring's contribution is a large red figure strangled by a black snake, which is in turn cut in half by a pair of scissors.

In July, the New York City Department of Health invites the artist to design a poster promoting the city's AIDS hotline; the resulting image features three blue figures holding a red telephone against a yellow background.

In August, at the invitation of Caroline, Princess of Monaco, Haring paints a mural on a wall of the maternity ward of the Princess Grace Hospital in Monte Carlo. In it, the central figure of a radiant pregnant woman is surrounded by a jumble of abstract curvilinear or spiral-shaped images and signs, concentric circles, and colored surfaces. The warm color tones range from yellow and ocher to blue, and the figures seem to float on the white space of the wall. In appreciation of this contribution, Princess Caroline awards Haring the honorary title of Chevalier de l'Ordre du Mérite Culturel at a ceremony at the Palais du Prince in Monaco. At the age of thirty-one, he is the first American and the youngest recipient of this honor.

In November, Haring establishes a charitable foundation in his name to ensure the continuation of his philanthropic work after his death. He appoints as its director his longtime studio manager, Julia Gruen. Haring himself crafts the mission and goals of the Keith Haring Foundation: to make grants to not-for-profit groups engaged in charitable and educational activities, concentrating its giving in support of organizations that provide educational opportunities to underprivileged children and/or engage in AIDS and HIV education, prevention, and care.

Haring additionally charges his foundation with continuing, promoting, and protecting his artistic legacy. The foundation maintains a collection of art along with archives that facilitate historical research about the artist. The foundation also supports arts and educational institutions by funding exhibitions, educational programs, acquisitions, and publications that contextualize and illuminate the artist's work and philosophy.

In December, Haring creates a mural at the Pasadena Art Center College of Design on the occasion of the World Health Organization's first Day Without Art, commemorating World AIDS Day, an event observed at more than six hundred art institutions in the United States.

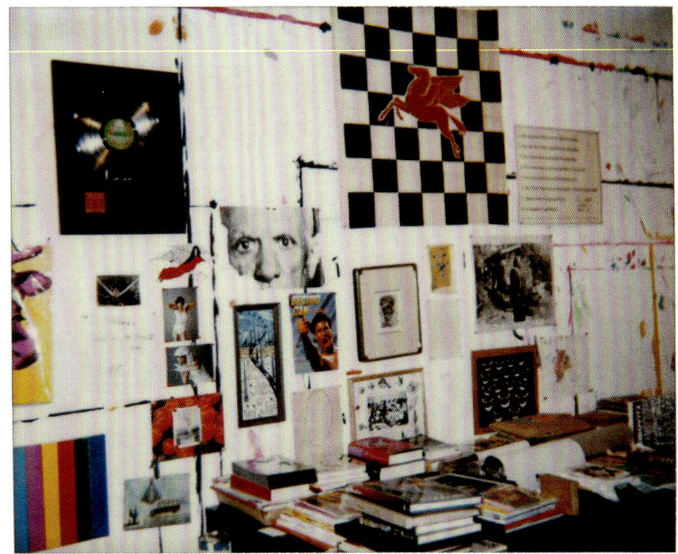

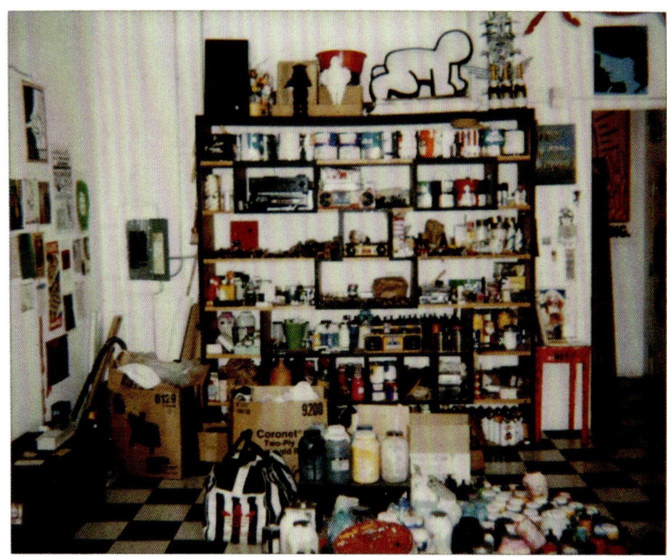

72–73

Unknown photographer, Keith Haring's studio, New York, 1990.
Two Polaroids. Collection of the Keith Haring Foundation

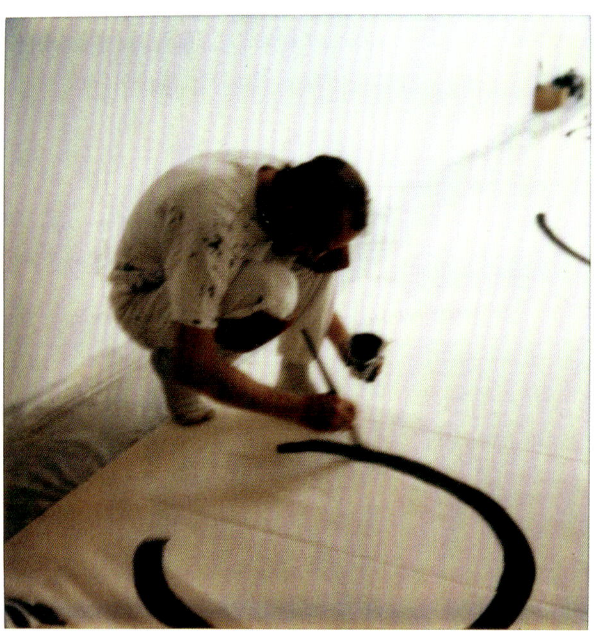

1990: Death, Memorial, and Legacy

On February 16, at age thirty-one, Haring dies of AIDS-related complications.

On March 16, his final work is unveiled. Commissioned by the World Federation of United Nations Associations, it is a cachet for the envelope accompanying the issuing of a stamp calling attention to the group's efforts in the fight against AIDS worldwide. It depicts a man bending forward, carrying a pile of radiant dead bodies on his back.

On May 4 (which would have been his thirty-second birthday), a memorial service for Haring is held at the Cathedral of Saint John the Divine in upper Manhattan, with more than one thousand people in attendance. On the same date, Tony Shafrazi opens *Keith Haring: A Memorial Exhibition: Early Works.*

In September, *Future Primeval*, the first touring retrospective of Haring's art, premieres at the Queens Museum before traveling to two other museums in the United States.

74–75

Unknown photographer, Keith Haring painting the set design for *Interrupted River*, New York, 1987. Two Polaroids. Collection of the Keith Haring Foundation

SELECTED BIBLIOGRAPHY OF BOOKS AND CATALOGUES

1982

Cortez, Diego. *The Pressure to Paint.* Exh. cat. New York: Marlborough Gallery.

Flood, Richard. *Keith Haring.* Exh. cat. Rotterdam, the Netherlands: Rotterdam Arts Council.

Fuchs, R. H., Coosje van Bruggen, Germano Celant, Johannes Gachnang, et al. *Documenta 7.* Exh. cat. Kassel, Germany: Documenta.

Haring, Keith. *Drawings: Keith Haring.* New York: Appearances Press.

Pincus-Witten, Robert, Jeffrey Deitch, and David Shapiro. *Keith Haring.* Exh. cat. New York: Tony Shafrazi Gallery.

1983

Giménez, Carmen. *Tendencias en Nueva York.* Exh. cat. Madrid: Palacio de Velázquez.

Honnef, Klaus. *Back to the U.S.A.: Pattern and Decoration, New Image, New Wave, New Expressionism.* Exh. cat. Bonn, Germany: Rheinisches Landesmuseum and Rheinland-Verlag.

Shafrazi, Tony. *Champions.* Exh. cat. New York: Tony Shafrazi Gallery.

1984

Freeman, Phyllis, Eric Himmel, Edith Pavese, and Anne Yarowsky, eds. *New Art.* New York: Harry N. Abrams.

Hagenberg, Roland. *Untitled '84: The Art World in the Eighties.* Introduction by Robert Pincus-Witten and photographs by the author. New York: Pelham Press.

Haring, Keith. *Art in Transit: Subway Drawings.* Introduction by Henry Geldzahler and photographs by Tseng Kwong Chi. New York: Harmony Books; Tokyo: Kawade Shobo Shinsha [1986].

Hopkins, Henry. *The Human Condition.* Exh. cat. San Francisco: San Francisco Museum of Modern Art; Washington, DC: Smithsonian Institution Press.

Lee, Marshall, et al. *Art at Work: The Chase Manhattan Collection.* Exh. cat. New York: E. P. Dutton and International Archive of Art.

Marquez, Fidel. *New Attitudes: Paris/New York.* Photographs by Tseng Kwong Chi. Exh. cat. Pittsburgh: Pittsburgh Center for the Arts.

Rubin, William, ed. *"Primitivism" in 20th-Century Art: Affinity of the Tribal and the Modern.* Exh. cat. New York: The Museum of Modern Art.

1985

Belsito, Peter, ed. *Notes from the Pop Underground.* Berkeley, CA: Last Gasp of San Francisco.

Gorgoni, Gianfranco. *Beyond the Canvas: Artists of the Seventies and Eighties.* Introduction by Leo Castelli and photographs by the author. New York: Rizzoli.

Pailhas, Roger, Jean-Louis Marcos, and Marcelin Pleynet. *New York 85.* Exh. cat. Marseille: ARCA Centre d'art contemporain.

Sanchez, Marc, Sylvie Couderc, Jean-Louis Froment, et al. *Keith Haring: Peintures, sculptures et dessins.* Exh. cat. Bordeaux: Musée d'art contemporain de Bordeaux.

1986

Deitch, Jeffrey. *Keith Haring: Paintings, Drawings and a Vellum.* Exh. cat. Amsterdam: Stedelijk Museum.

Dickhoff, Wilfried, ed. *What It Is.* Exh. cat. New York: Tony Shafrazi Gallery.

Hager, Steven. *Art after Midnight: The East Village Scene.* New York: St. Martin's Press.

Hunter, Sam, ed. *An American Renaissance: Painting and Sculpture since 1940.* Exh. cat. New York: Abbeville Press.

Time-Life Books, ed. *Input/Output.* Alexandria, VA: Time-Life Books.

COMPILED BY DIETER BUCHHART

1987

Blistène, Bernard. *L'Époque, la mode, la morale, la passion. Aspects de l'art d'aujourd'hui, 1977–1987.* Exh. cat. Paris: Centre Georges Pompidou.

Bussmann, Klaus, and Kasper König. *Skulptur Projekte Münster 1987.* Exh. cat. Cologne, Germany: Dumont Buchverlag.

Fehlemann, Sabine, and Raimund Thomas. *Kunst aus den achtziger Jahren.* Exh. cat. Munich, Germany: A11 Artforum.

Fox, Howard N. *Avant-Garde in the Eighties.* Exh. cat. Los Angeles: Los Angeles County Museum of Art.

Goodman, Cynthia. *Digital Visions: Computers and Art.* Exh. cat. New York: Harry N. Abrams; Syracuse, NY: Everson Museum of Art.

Spiel, Hilde, and André Heller. *Luna Luna.* Exh. cat. Munich, Germany: Wilhelm Heyne Verlag.

Wagstaff, Sheena, ed. *Comic Iconoclasm.* Exh. cat. London: Institute of Contemporary Arts.

1988

Als, Hilton. *Andy Warhol, Jean-Michel Basquiat: Collaborations.* Introduction by Keith Haring. Exh. cat. London: Mayor Rowan Gallery.

Cameron, Dan. *Keith Haring 1988.* Introduction by Martin Blinder. Exh. cat. Van Nuys, CA: Martin Lawrence Limited Editions.

Rosenblum, Robert. *The Dog in Art: From Rococo to Post-Modernism.* New York: Harry N. Abrams.

1989

Haring, Keith. *Eight Ball: Keith Haring.* Tokyo: Kyoto Shoin.

1990

Blinderman, Barry, et al. *Future Primeval.* Exh. cat. Normal, IL: University Galleries, Illinois State University. Republished New York: Abbeville Press, 1992.

Coetzee, Mark. *Against All Odds: Keith Haring in the Rubell Family Collection.* Text and drawings by Keith Haring. Rotterdam, the Netherlands: Bébert Publishing House; New York: Mr. and Mrs. Donald Rubell. Republished Palm Springs, CA: Palm Springs Art Museum; Miami: Rubell Family Collection; New York: Distributed Art Publishers, 2008.

Haring, Keith. *Against All Odds, 20 Drawings—Oct. 3, 1989.* Rotterdam, the Netherlands: Bébert Publishing House.

Keith Haring: A Memorial Exhibition. Exh. cat. Introduction by Tony Shafrazi. New York: Tony Shafrazi Gallery.

The Last Decade: American Artists of the 80's. Exh. cat. New York: Tony Shafrazi Gallery.

Subway Drawings. Exh. cat. Introduction by Nikolaus Sonne and Christian Holzfuss. Berlin: Galerie Sonne and Edition Achenbach.

1991

Armstrong, Richard, ed. *1991 Biennial Exhibition.* Exh. cat. New York: Whitney Museum of American Art and W. W. Norton.

Compassion and Protest: Recent Social and Political Art from the Eli Broad Family Foundation Collection. Exh. cat. San Jose, CA: San Jose Museum of Art; New York: Cross River Press.

Gruen, John. *Keith Haring: The Authorized Biography.* New York: Prentice Hall.

Rubin, David S. *Cruciformed: Images of the Cross since 1980.* Exh. cat. Cleveland: Cleveland Center for Contemporary Art.

Storr, Robert. *Devil on the Stairs: Looking Back at the 80s.* Exh. cat. Philadelphia: Institute of Contemporary Art.

1992

Atkins, Robert, and Thomas W. Sokolowski. *From Media to Metaphor: Art about AIDS.* Exh. cat. New York: Independent Curators International.

Celant, Germano, ed. *Keith Haring.* Munich, Germany: Prestel Verlag.

Coming from the Subway: New York Graffiti Art. Exh. cat. Groningen, the Netherlands: Groninger Museum.

Hollevoet, Cristel, Karen Jones, and Timothy Nye. *The Power of the City/The City of Power.* Exh. cat. New York: Whitney Museum of American Art.

Kurtz, Bruce D., ed. *Keith Haring, Andy Warhol, and Walt Disney.* Exh. cat. Phoenix: Phoenix Museum of Art; Munich, Germany, and New York: Prestel.

1993

Celant, Germano. *Keith Haring: A Retrospective.* Exh. cat. Tokyo: Mitsukoshi Museum of Art.

Haring, Keith, and William S. Burroughs. *Apocalypse.* Paris: Le Dernier Terrain Vague.

Littmann, Klaus, Julia Gruen, and Jehle Werner. *Keith Haring: Complete Editions on Paper, 1982–1990.* Ostfildern, Germany: Hatje Cantz Publishing.

1994

Celant, Germano. *Keith Haring.* Exh. cat. Turin, Italy: Castello di Rivoli; Sydney: Museum of Contemporary Art.

Haring, Keith. *Nina's Book of Little Things!* Munich, Germany, and New York: Prestel.

1995

Anderson-Spivy, Alexandra. *Keith Haring: Works on Paper 1989.* Exh. cat. New York: André Emmerich Gallery and Estate of Keith Haring.

Blake, Nayland, Lawrence Rinder, and Amy Scholder. *In a Different Light: Visual Culture, Sexual Identity, Queer Practice.* San Francisco: City Lights Books.

Hatfield, John, Laura Trippi, Marcia Tucker, et al. *Temporarily Possessed: The Semi-Permanent Collection.* Exh. cat. New York: New Museum of Contemporary Art.

1996

Haring, Keith. *Keith Haring Journals.* Preface by David Hockney and introduction by Robert Farris Thompson. New York: Viking-Penguin paperback edition, 1997; Penguin Classics deluxe edition, 2010. Italian edition: Milan: Mondadori Editore, 2001; Spanish edition: Barcelona: Galaxia Gutenberg, 2001; British edition: London: Penguin, 2012.

———. *Keith Haring: The Ten Commandments.* Exh. cat. Introduction by Tilman Osterwold. Kassel, Germany: Kunsthalle Fridericianum.

1997

American Graffiti. Exh. cat. Naples, Italy: Electa Napoli.

Galloway, David. *Keith Haring: On Park Avenue.* Exh. cat. Introduction by Tom Eccles and Susan Freedman. New York: André Emmerich Gallery.

Haring, Keith, Désirée la Valette, and Gerdt Fehrle. *Keith Haring: I Wish I Didn't Have to Sleep!* Munich: Prestel Verlag; English edition: New York: Prestel.

Marshall, Richard. *In Your Face: Keith Haring, Jean-Michel Basquiat, Kenny Scharf.* Exh. cat. New York: Lio Malca.

Sussman, Elisabeth, David Frankel, Jeffrey Deitch, Ann Magnuson, et al. *Keith Haring.* Exh. cat. New York: Whitney Museum of American Art; Boston: Bulfinch/Little, Brown. Dutch edition: Hedel: Librero, 1998; French edition: Cologne: Evergreen, 1998; German edition: Cologne: Evergreen; Taschen, 1998; Italian edition: Cologne: Benedikt, 1998.

1998

Art Performs Life: Merce Cunningham, Meredith Monk, Bill T. Jones. Exh. cat. Minneapolis: Walker Art Center.

Haring, Keith. *Big.* New York: Hyperion Books for Children.

———. *Ten.* New York: Hyperion Books for Children.

Weiermair, Peter. *Ideal and Reality.* Exh. cat. Salzburg, Austria: Rupertinum; Zurich, Switzerland: Edition Stemmle.

1999

Fairbrother, Trevor J., and Bagley Wright. *The Virginia and Bagley Wright Collection.* Exh. cat. Seattle: Seattle Art Museum.

Fuku, Noriko, Amelia Arenas, and Takayuki Nasu. *Keith Haring.* Exh. cat. Tokyo: Art Life, Ltd.

Galloway, David. *Keith Haring—12 Sculptures.* Exh. cat. Paris: Galerie Jérôme de Noirmont.

Hahn, Otto. *Souvenir of Keith Haring.* Exh. cat. Knokke-le-Zoute, Belgium: Casino Knokke.

Haring, Keith. *Dance.* New York: Bulfinch/Little, Brown.

———. *Love.* New York: Bulfinch/Little, Brown.

Keith Haring. Exh. cat. London: Peter Gwyther Gallery.

Mercurio, Gianni, Wolfgang Becker, Enrico Pedrini, Achille Bonito Oliva, et al. *Keith Haring.* Exh. cat. Pisa: Palazzo Lanfranchi; Milan: Electa.

Noirmont, Jérôme de, Bernard Lorquin, François Boisrond, George Condo, et al. *Keith Haring: Made in France.* Exh. cat. Paris: Musée Maillol.

2000

Barilli, Renato. *Keith Haring, art e dossier.* Florence, Italy: Giunti.

Cochrane, Gail, et al. *Dire AIDS: Arte nell'epoca dell'AIDS* [*Art in the Age of AIDS*]. Exh. cat. Turin, Italy: Castello di Rivoli; Milan, Italy: Charta Milano.

Hague Sculpture 2000: Man in Motion. Exh. cat. The Hague, the Netherlands: The Hague Sculpture 2000.

Haring, Keith. *Babies.* New York: Bulfinch/Little, Brown.

———. *Dogs.* New York: Bulfinch/Little, Brown.

Keith Haring. Exh. cat. Aachen, Germany: Ludwig Forum. Italian edition: Milan: Electa Milano.

Keith Haring. Exh. cat. Helsinki, Finland: Amos Anderson Art Museum.

Keith Haring. Exh. cat. Rome: Chiostro del Bramante; Milan: Electa Milano.

Keith Haring. Exh. cat. Tokyo: Isetan Museum.

Keith Haring: The SVA Years, 1978–1980. Exh. cat. New York: School of Visual Arts.

2001

Barron, Stephanie, Lynn Zelevansky, Thomas E. Crow, and Eli Broad Family Foundation. *Jasper Johns to Jeff Koons: Four Decades of Art from the Broad Collections.* Exh. cat. Los Angeles: Los Angeles County Museum of Art; New York: Harry N. Abrams.

Decter, Joshua. *Tele(visions).* Exh. cat. Vienna, Austria: Kunsthalle Wien.

Yee, Lydia, Franklin Sirmans, and Greg Tate. *One Planet under a Groove: Hip Hop and Contemporary Art.* Exh. cat. New York: Bronx Museum of the Arts.

2002

Adriani, Götz, ed. *Keith Haring: Heaven and Hell.* Exh. cat. Karlsruhe, Germany: Museum für Neue Kunst, ZKM Karlsruhe; Ostfildern, Germany: Hatje Cantz Verlag.

Davvetas, Demosthenes, Glenn O'Brien, and Tama Janowitz. *New York Expression.* Exh. cat. Bergen, Norway: Bergen Kunstmuseum.

Gundel, Marc. *Keith Haring: Short Messages. Posters 1982–1990.* Munich: Prestel Verlag.

Made in USA. Exh. cat. Oberhausen, Germany: Ludwig Galerie; Schloss.

The New York Scene: Selections from the Whitney Museum of American Art at City Hall. Exh. cat. New York: Whitney Museum of American Art.

2003

Calabrese, Omar, Roberta Cecchi, and Piergiorgio Castellani. *Tuttomondo: Chronicle of a Mural.* Photographs by Antonio Bardelli. Pisa, Italy: Edizioni ETS.

The DaimlerChrysler Collection. Exh. cat. Karlsruhe, Germany: Museum für Neue Kunst; Ostfildern, Germany: Hatje Cantz Verlag.

2004

Cameron, Dan, et al. *East Village USA.* Exh. cat. New York: New Museum of Contemporary Art.

Coetzee, Mark. *Not Afraid: Rubell Family Collection.* London: Phaidon.

Happy Birthday! Exh. cat. Paris: Galerie Jérôme de Noirmont.

Kolossa, Alexandra. *Keith Haring.* Cologne, Germany: Taschen Basic Art Series. 25th anniversary special ed., 2009.

2005

Dance of the Avant-Garde: Paintings, Sets, and Costumes from Degas and Picasso to Matisse and Keith Haring. Exh. cat. Milan: Skira.

The Downtown Book: The New York Art Scene 1974–1984. Exh. cat. New York: Grey Art Gallery, New York University; Princeton, NJ: Princeton University Press.

Drawing from the Modern, 1975–2005. Exh. cat. New York: The Museum of Modern Art.

Galloway, David. *Keith Haring Sculptures.* Exh. cat. New York: Deitch Projects; Paris: Galerie Jérôme de Noirmont.

La Valette, Désirée. *Keith Haring: Et l'art descend dans la rue!* Paris: Palette.

Mercurio, Gianni, ed. *The Keith Haring Show.* Exh. cat. Milan: Skira, 2005. Republished Paris: Skira-Flammarion, 2009.

Perfect Painting: 40 Years, Galerie Hans Mayer. Exh. cat. Düsseldorf, Germany: Langen Foundation.

2006

Faster! Bigger! Better! Exh. cat. Karlsruhe, Germany: Museum für Neue Kunst; ZKM Karlsruhe.

2007

Carter, Curtis L., and Enrico Mascelloni. *Keith Haring: Il murale di Milwaukee.* Milan: Skira.

Haring, Keith. *Il grande libro delle piccole cose.* Milan: Mondadori.

Keith Haring. Exh. cat. Luxembourg: Fondation l'Indépendance; Paris: JGM Galerie–Monumental Art Project; Galerie Enrico Navarra.

Kuhn, Jonathan. *The Outdoor Gallery: 40 Years of Public Art in New York City Parks.* New York: New York City Department of Parks and Recreation.

Panic Attack! Art in the Punk Years. Exh. cat. London: Barbican Art Gallery.

2008

Deitch, Jeffrey, Suzanne Geiss, and Julia Gruen. *Keith Haring.* New York: Rizzoli.

Haring, Keith. *Keith Haring: Houston and Bowery Mural.* Photographs by Tseng Kwong Chi. New York: Deitch Projects and Goldman Properties.

Mercurio, Gianni. *Keith Haring.* Exh. cat. Lyon: Musée d'art contemporain de Lyon; Milan: Skira.

2009

Apocalypse Wow! Pop Surrealism, Neo Pop, Urban Art. Exh. cat. Rome: Museo d'arte contemporanea.

Keith Haring. Exh. cat. Ulm, Germany: Kunsthalle Weishaupt.

Re-View: New Perspectives on the Stedelijk Museum Collection. Exh. cat. Amsterdam: Stedelijk Museum.

2010

The 80s Revisited. Collection Bischofberger. Exh. cat. Bielefeld, Germany: Kunsthalle Bielefeld.

Thompson, Mimi. *Keith Haring: Selected Works, LitMedia.* Exh. cat. Rio de Janeiro and São Paulo, Brazil: Caixa Cultural.

——. *Pop: Art Superstar Keith Haring.* Exh. cat. Seoul, Korea: Soma Museum of Art.

2011

Art in the Streets. Exh. cat. Los Angeles: Museum of Contemporary Art.

Keith Haring, Sketchbooks. Exh. cat. New York: Gladstone Gallery.

Platow, Raphaela, ed. *Keith Haring: 1978–1982.* Exh. cat. Nuremberg, Germany: Moderne Kunst Nürnberg.

2012

Cooper, Shawna, and Karli Wurzelbacher. *Times Square Show: Revisited.* Exh. cat. New York: Hunter College.

Lemoine, Stephanie. *L'art urbain: Du graffiti au street art.* Paris: Gallimard.

The Naked Man. Exh. cat. Linz, Austria: Lentos Kunstmuseum Linz.

2013

Buchhart, Dieter, Odile Burluraux, Robert Farris Thompson, Julian Myers-Szupinska, et al. *Keith Haring: The Political Line.* Exh. cat. Paris: Musée d'Art Moderne de la Ville de Paris.

Kalb, Peter R. *Art since 1980: Charting the Contemporary.* Boston: Pearson.

Once upon a Time: The Keith Haring Mural at the Lesbian, Gay, Bisexual & Transgender Community Center. Photographs by Travis Dubreuil. New York: The Lesbian, Gay, Bisexual & Transgender Community Center.

Op+Pop: Experimente Amerikanischer Künstler AB 1960. Exh. cat. Stuttgart, Germany: Staatsgalerie Stuttgart.

Palmer-Smith, Glenn. *Murals of New York City: The Best of New York's Public Paintings from Bemelmans to Parrish.* New York: Rizzoli.

INDEX

Illustrations without a figure or plate number are indicated by an italicized page number(s).

ACKNOWLEDGMENTS

This exhibition and publication would not have been possible without the generous support and enthusiasm of the Keith Haring Foundation, New York. We thank Julia Gruen, Annelise Ream, Elen Woods, and Julie Joseph for their many helpful and judicious contributions. We further offer our gratitude to the trustees of the Keith Haring Foundation and the Haring family. Our thanks also are extended to independent art historian and guest curator Dieter Buchhart, who conceptualized this project and brought it to fruition, first at the Musée d'Art Moderne de la Ville de Paris and now at the Fine Arts Museums of San Francisco, where it was shepherded by our founding curator of photography and chief administrative curator, Julian Cox. Julia, Dieter, and Julian shared their insights in the pages of this catalogue, alongside those of Carlo McCormick, Julian Myers-Szupinska, Glenn O'Brien, Tony Shafrazi, Robert Farris Thompson, and Giorgio Verzotti. We are appreciative of the scholarship and stories that they have offered to foster Keith Haring's legacy.

At the Fine Arts Museums, we extend our gratitude to Diane B. Wilsey, president of the Board of Trustees, and Colin B. Bailey, director of museums, for their support of this endeavor. Richard Benefield, deputy director, is thanked heartily for his savoir-faire in bringing this project to the de Young after he viewed it in Paris. We also thank Michele Gutierrez-Canepa, chief financial officer and foundation fiscal officer, for her assistance in making this presentation viable; Suzy Peterson, executive assistant in the art division, who marshaled so many of the finer details; and Stuart Hata, director of retail operations, and Tim Niedert, book and media manager, for their insight and advisement.

In Vienna, alongside Dieter, we thank his curatorial assistants, Anna Karina Hofbauer and Dzenana Mujadzic. We are also grateful to Fabrice Hergott for originally realizing the project at the Musée d'Art Moderne de la Ville de Paris.

Further thanks are given to the Museums' exhibitions team: Krista Brugnara, director of exhibitions; Sarah Hammond, senior exhibitions coordinator; Therese Chen, director of collections management; Steven Correll, collections manager; Kimberley Montgomery, assistant registrar; Craig Harris, manager of installation and preparation; and Daniel Meza, graphic design director. We are grateful also to Sheila Pressley, director of education; Renee Baldocchi, director of public programs; Maureen Keefe, director of marketing and communications; Erin Garcia, assistant director of communications; and Clara Hatcher, communications associate.

This catalogue was managed by Leslie Dutcher, director of publications, who seamlessly wove together its many intricate parts, with assistance from Laura Harger and Danica Michels Hodge, editors, and Diana K. Murphy, editorial assistant. We thank Harriet Whelchel for her graceful edits; Todd Foreman, Tessa Lee, and Nick Navarro at Public for their vibrant design; Roberto Conti, Marta Conti, Laura Cuccoli, Ann Faughender, Pietro Petruzzi, Alfredo Zanellato, and their colleagues at Conti Tipocolor for the beautiful printing of this book; and Mary DelMonico, Karen Farquhar, and their colleagues at DelMonico Books • Prestel for their publishing counsel and esteemed partnership. We also wish to thank Hélène Studievic and Aurélie Foure at the Musée d'Art Moderne de la Ville de Paris; John Czaplicki, George Horner, and Hiroko Onoda at the Tony Shafrazi Gallery, New York; and Muna Tseng and Cindy Lee at the Estate of Tseng Kwong Chi for their kind help with our book. This catalogue is published with the assistance of the Andrew W. Mellon Foundation Endowment for Publications.

Our patrons make our projects viable. For this presentation, we thank Penny and James George Coulter, Sloan and Roger Barnett, the Ray and Dagmar Dolby Family Fund, the Shimmon Family, the Buena Vista Fund of the Horizons Foundation, the Keith Haring Foundation, and Richard and Peggy Greenfield. We also are deeply grateful to our many lenders, whose generosity and passion for the work of Keith Haring have enabled us to share it with our audiences.

Published by the Fine Arts Museums of San Francisco and DelMonico Books • Prestel on the occasion of the exhibition *Keith Haring: The Political Line*, de Young, San Francisco, November 8, 2014–February 16, 2015

This exhibition is organized by the Fine Arts Museums of San Francisco.

Director's Circle
Penny and James George Coulter

Curator's Circle
Sloan and Roger Barnett
Ray and Dagmar Dolby Family Fund
The Shimmon Family

Conservator's Circle
The Buena Vista Fund of Horizons Foundation

Patron's Circle
The Keith Haring Foundation

Supporter's Circle
Richard and Peggy Greenfield

This catalogue is published with the assistance of the Andrew W. Mellon Foundation Endowment for Publications.

This catalogue is adapted from the original French edition of *Keith Haring: The Political Line* © 2013, Paris, Musées, les musées de la Ville de Paris, ISBN: 978-2-75960216-2.

Library of Congress Cataloging-in-Publication Data

Keith Haring (Fine Arts Museums of San Francisco)
Keith Haring: The Political Line / by Dieter Buchhart, Julian Cox, Robert Farris Thompson, Julia Gruen, Glenn O'Brien, Julian Myers-Szupinska, Tony Shafrazi, Carlo McCormick, and Giorgio Verzotti. — First English language edition.
pages cm
Includes bibliographical references and index.
ISBN 978-3-7913-5410-1 (hardback)—ISBN 978-3-7913-6573-2 (paperback)

1. Haring, Keith—Exhibitions. 2. Art—Political aspects—United States—Exhibitions. I. Buchhart, Dieter. Endless political line. II. Haring, Keith. Works. Selections. III. M.H. de Young Memorial Museum. IV. Title.
N6537.H348A4 2014
709.2—dc23

2014019147

Fine Arts Museums of San Francisco
Golden Gate Park
50 Hagiwara Tea Garden Drive
San Francisco, CA 94118–4502
www.famsf.org

Leslie Dutcher, Director of Publications
Laura Harger, Editor
Danica Michels Hodge, Editor
Diana K. Murphy, Editorial Assistant

Translations by Chris De Angelis
Edited by Harriet Whelchel
Proofread by Laura Harger and Susan Richmond
Index by Jane Friedman
Designed and typeset by Tessa Lee and Nick Navarro, Public, San Francisco
Production management by Karen Farquhar
Separations, printing, and binding by Conti Tipocolor, Italy

DelMonico Books is an imprint of Prestel, a member of Verlagsgruppe Random House GmbH

Prestel Verlag
Neumarkter Strasse 28
81673 Munich
Germany
Tel: 49 89 4136 0
Fax: 49 89 4136 2335
www.prestel.de

Prestel Publishing Ltd.
14–17 Wells Street
London W1T 3PD
United Kingdom
Tel: 44 20 7323 5004
Fax: 44 20 7323 0271

Prestel Publishing
900 Broadway, suite 603
New York, NY 10003
Tel: 212 995 2720
Fax: 212 995 2733
Email: sales@prestel-usa.com
www.prestel.com

Photography credits

Unless otherwise noted, all photographs are courtesy of the Keith Haring Foundation.

pp. 2–15, 20, 22–24, 32, 46, 86–87, 246–247; figs. 18, 22; pls. 63–70: photographs by Tseng Kwong Chi, © Muna Tseng Dance Projects, Inc., New York, www.tsengkwongchi.com. p. 19 and fig. 44: Klaus Wittmann. p. 58: Baptiste Lignel/Otra Vista. p. 64; figs. 46 and 50; back cover: Ivan Dalla Tana, © Maggie Dalla Tana. p. 75; figs. 45, 50: Allan Tannenbaum. p. 89: courtesy Tony Shafrazi Gallery, New York; photograph by John Czaplicki. fig. 2: © 2014 The Andy Warhol Foundation for the Visual Arts, Inc. / Artists Rights Society (ARS), New York; courtesy of the J. Paul Getty Museum, Los Angeles. figs. 5, 17, 43: Joseph Szkodzinski, www.thefoundimage.com. fig. 10: John Marchael, courtesy Public Art Fund, New York. fig. 13; pl. 116: Adam Reich. fig. 16; pls. 102, 109, 112–115, 120, 136–138, 142–146, 148, 150–151, 155, 157–158, 168, 174, 195, 199, 201, 205; front cover: Photos Pierre Antoine. figs. 23–24: Martha Cooper. fig. 29: Ian Churchill; courtesy of Robert Farris Thompson. fig. 33: © 2014 The Andy Warhol Foundation for the Visual Arts, Inc. / Artists Rights Society (ARS), New York. fig. 35: courtesy of the New-York Historical Society, The Raymond Hood Photograph Collection. fig. 47: George Hirose. fig. 48; pls. 2, 78, 82, 88, 92, 98, 101, 117, 133, 154, 160, 162, 170, 204: courtesy of Tony Shafrazi Gallery, New York. fig. 49: Lucio Amelio; courtesy of Tony Shafrazi Gallery, New York. fig. 55: courtesy of Mr. and Mrs. Allen Haring. pls. 4, 77, 79–81, 87, 91, 93–97, 99, 119, 121–128, 140: courtesy of Larry Warsh. pls. 9, 90, 130, 141, 202: courtesy of Martos Gallery. pls. 12, 18–19, 111: courtesy of Alona Kagan; photography by Florian Kleinefenn. pl. 75: © Charles Benton. pl. 118: courtesy of The Broad Art Collection, Santa Monica; photography by Douglas M. Parker Studio, Los Angeles. pl. 129: courtesy of Edward Tyler Nahem Fine Art, LLC. pl. 134: © Christie's Images Limited 1992. pl. 161: Susan Hawes Yanosick.